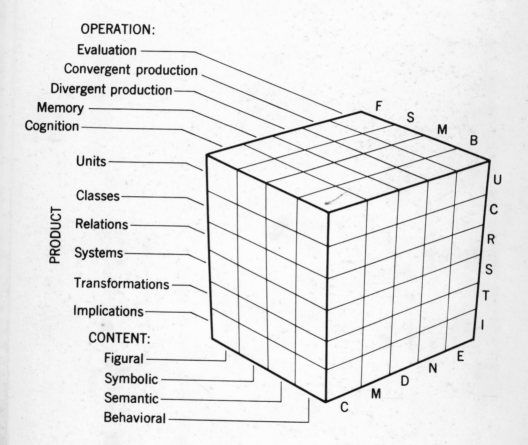

The nature of human intelligence

McGraw-Hill Series in Psychology

Consulting Editors
Norman Garmezy   Harry F. Harlow   Lyle V. Jones   Harold W. Stevenson

John F. Dashiell was Consulting Editor of this series from its inception in 1931 until January 1, 1950. Clifford T. Morgan was Consulting Editor of this series from January 1, 1950 until January 1, 1959. Harry F. Harlow assumed the duties of Consulting Editor from 1959 to 1965. In 1965 a Board of Consulting Editors was established according to areas of interest. The board members are Harry F. Harlow (physiological, experimental psychology), Norman Garmezy (abnormal, clinical), Harold W. Stevenson (child, adolescent, human development), and Lyle V. Jones (statistical, quantitative).

The Nature of
Human Intelligence

J. P. Guilford
Professor of Psychology
University of Southern California

McGraw-Hill Book Company
New York   St. Louis   San Francisco   Toronto   London   Sydney

The nature of human intelligence

Preface

The major aim of this volume is to give to the concept of "intelligence" a firm, comprehensive, and systematic theoretical foundation. From the very beginning of the era of mental testing, such a theory has been lacking. A firm foundation must be empirically based. A comprehensive theory should include all aspects of intelligence, many of which have been seriously neglected in traditional intelligence testing. Any good theory should be systematic, embracing perhaps numerous phenomena within a logically ordered structure. The only serious earlier attempts to achieve a general theory took their beginnings from the right kind of source, namely, findings from factor analysis, but they proved to be abortive, for lack of sufficient information and because of persistent adherence to the belief in Spearman's g.

A second major aim, not far behind in importance, is to put intelligence within the mainstream of general psychological theory. Alfred Binet, one of the very few who were concerned about a theoretical-psychological basis for testing, was a respected experimental psychologist of his day, and he leaned upon findings from the psychological laboratory as a source of test material and as a basis for selection of tests. It is hoped that an important outcome of this volume will be a better two-way communication between testers and experimenters, if not a wedding or even a merging of the two. Special effort will be given to pointing out how theory derived from individual differences in intellectual abilities can serve useful purposes of general psychological theory.

The author's structure-of-intellect theory, which has been under development and under experimental examination during the past twelve years, grew out of experimental applications of the multivariate method of multiple-factor analysis. Although it might seem premature to write this book when the theory has not been tested in all its aspects, enough appears to be known to lend support to the expectation that in large part the theory is sound and that research in the future will continue to provide empirical support for it. Implications from the theory and its concepts have led to many new interpretations of already-known facts of general significance in psychology. Thus it appears timely to let the linkages between a psychometrically based theory and general psychological theory be brought out for more general consideration.

Quite apart from the psychometric approach with psychological tests, Jean Piaget has developed over the years a rather different type of theory. His methods have been largely direct-observational, with emphasis upon intellectual development. By virtue of great quantities of observations and rare insights, Piaget has arrived at a theory that some psychologists regard as a theory of knowledge and its development rather than of intelligence. Because the theory proposed in this volume finds an important role for information as well as for operations, it is possible to find many links with Piaget's views, links that will be pointed out.

Three chapters provide an introduction. The first presents a short history of tests and discusses the leading historical conception that intelligence is the ability to learn. The second chapter compares three major approaches to the investigation of intelligence and makes a case for the need of a taxonomic approach that tells us *what* variables prevail in human intelligence and hence in human behavior. A brief introduction to the theory and operations of multiple-factor analysis is followed by presentation of the outlines of hierarchical models for the intellectual factors, as developed by Cyril Burt and Philip E. Vernon. An outline of the structure-of-intellect (SI) theory is then presented, with considerations of Louis Guttman's facet theory and Benjamin Bloom's educational taxonomy.

Five chapters lay the empirical foundation for the SI theory, presenting the known factors within the five operation categories and their definitive tests. Consideration is given to the age levels of populations within which analyses have shown some of the factors. Two chapters, one on operations and one on information, delve more deeply into the meaning and significance of the SI categories and their concepts, pointing out similarities and connections with concepts coming from other sources.

Four chapters then attempt to see how an operational-informational type of psychology, to which SI theory leads, can account for some of the phenomena encountered in the areas of perception, learning, retention, recall, problem solving, and creative production. Models are suggested for perception, for psychomotor activity, and for problem solving.

Further ramifications and apparent applications for the SI concepts are considered in two chapters on the determination of intellectual status. One chapter considers the physical bases, including heredity and the brain and its functions. Another considers environmental determiners of status on intellectual abilities.

A chapter treats development, with special attention to SI abilities, where there is available information. A chapter on decline of abilities completes the picture of relations of abilities to age. A final chapter attempts to encapsulate the preceding ones and to point out some of the more obvious implications for testing and for education.

Acknowledgments for assistance from various sources must be numerous. First, without the initiation and development of factor-analytic methods, this book could not have been written at all. To Charles Spearman, Cyril Burt, L. L. Thurstone, and others, we all owe great debts. Next, I should mention the University of Nebraska for appointing me director of the Bureau of Instructional Research, in connection with which I was able to initiate a research program on aptitudes of college freshmen.

World War II brought an invitation from John C. Flanagan to take part in his Army Air Forces Aviation Psychology Research Program. I am indebted for assignment to direct the research unit whose primary responsibility was intellectual aptitudes. It was fortunate that officers assigned to that unit were partial to the factor-analytic approach, among them being Lloyd G. Humphreys, John I. Lacey, and Merrill Roff. In the immediate postwar period, collaborators in factor-analytic studies were Benjamin Fruchter, William B. Michael, and Wayne S. Zimmerman.

Since 1949 investigations of intellectual abilities have been continued in the Aptitudes Research Project at the University of Southern California. This research has been supported continuously by the Office of Naval Research, Personnel and Training Branch, with occasional support from the U.S. Office of Education, Department of Health, Education, and Welfare, and the National Science Foundation Psychobiological Program. For considerable computer service the project has been indebted to the Western Data Processing Center at the University of California at Los Angeles and the Health Sciences Computing Facility, also at UCLA. Through it all, the University of Southern California and its department of psychology have generously provided working space and moral support. Of the many graduate students who have participated in the project, I can take space here to mention only three who have served successively in the capacity of assistant director: Paul R. Christensen, Philip R. Merrifield, and Ralph Hoepfner. Others will be mentioned in many references.

I am indebted to many authors and publishers who have granted permission to use illustrations and other material. Appropriate acknowledgments will be made as those materials appear.

For critical reading of the manuscript and for offering suggestions, I am indebted to James E. Birren, who read Chapter 18; to Herman Harvey, who read Chapter 15; and to William B. Michael, who read the entire manuscript. None is responsible for any shortcomings that still remain.

J. P. Guilford

Contents

III   Implications for psychological theory

V   Reflections

I Introduction

1 Historical background

Although this book is about the nature of intelligence rather than about intelligence tests, it will be necessary to give considerable attention to tests for two reasons. One reason is that, throughout the years, development of tests has generally far outrun the development of the understanding of that which tests have measured. This historical introduction will accordingly have much to say about tests. The other reason is this volume's persistent concern that, wherever possible, only empirically grounded concepts shall be utilized. Quite frequently the referents will be in the form of particular tests or categories of tests and deal with the behavior that is required to do well with those tests.

After a brief sketch of the highlights of test development, this chapter will be concerned with what various people have thought about the nature of intelligence, with special attention to the most popular conception that intelligence is equivalent to learning ability.

Development of mental tests

The account of how intellectual-aptitude tests in general came about can be treated in the beginning along national lines—British, German, French, and the United States American. Tests have been of some concern longest in Great Britain, because that nation was the site of Darwinism and its implications for individual differences. The British interest was first in the use of tests as a means to an end, the scientific study of individual differences in connection with heredity. Later, with Charles Spearman, Cyril Burt, Godfrey Thomson, and others, interest turned, with curiosity aroused as to the fundamental nature of intelligence.

German interest was largely prompted by the desire for instruments to be used in experimental studies of psychopathology and other psychological and educational problems, with little concern about theory. French concern with tests was mostly practical from the beginning, with only Binet showing much curiosity about the nature of intelligence. Had Binet lived longer, he might well have made some important contributions in this respect. In the United States, the most extensive use has been made of tests, in research and in practical affairs, with only rare pockets of concern about the nature of human abilities, on the part of such investigators and thinkers as E. L. Thorndike, Herbert Woodrow, and L. L. Thurstone.

Galton and his early tests   As early as 1870, Galton (1869) remarked on the extensiveness of individual differences, even within the range of mathematics students at the university level. Inspired by the idea of evolution and its principle of variation, he set about comparing members of families and family strains. In order to do this, it was necessary to have quantitative descriptions of individuals in various characteristics.

In approaching the problem of what mental characteristics to measure, Galton was influenced by the traditional associationism of philosophical origin and by the physiological psychology of Alexander Bain. From the former theoretical foundation he derived the principle that all we know has come through the avenues of our senses; therefore, good senses, good intellect. He was confirmed in this theory by his observation that idiots have very poor sensory functioning. From the latter source he apparently accepted the principle that even moral and intellectual features of men are dependent upon physical ones. The former source of theory led to an emphasis upon measurement of sensory functions, and the latter led to an emphasis upon measurement of motor qualities.

When Galton set up his famous anthropometric testing laboratory in the South Kensington Museum in 1882, his tests included measures of sensory thresholds, both absolute and differential, and simple psychomotor tests, such as strength of handgrip and reaction time.

Early German tests   In the context of psychopathology, where it can be supposed that he had liberal opportunity to observe different varieties of mental defect, Kraepelin initiated about 1889 the experimental use of different tests, which appeared obviously to be more "mental" than those of Galton. His student Oehrn (1895) administered tests of counting letters on a page, cancellation of a certain letter, finding errors during the act of proofreading, memorizing digits and nonsense syllables, association, addition, writing from dictation, reading rapidly, and motor functions. It is reported that Oehrn determined intercorrelations of the tests, perhaps being the first to do so (Peterson, 1925). Kraepelin later proposed a list of traits that it would be well to measure in both normal and abnormal people: gain with practice, retention (general memory), specific memory abilities, fatigability; recovery from fatigue, depth of sleep, concentration of attention against distractions, and ability to adapt to a task. A test was developed for each trait, in some cases by adapting the task of addition in various ways.

Other early German originators of tests may be mentioned. Hugo Münsterberg (1891) described tests given to children, without reporting results. These tests included reading aloud rapidly; naming colors of named objects; naming plants, minerals, and animals and also giving the class name of each; naming geometric forms and colors; adding; demonstrating memory spans for letters and digits; bisecting a visual interval; locating a sound; and constructing an equilateral triangle or a square, given a line for the base. Time scores were used for the speed tests. The list is interesting for the variety exhibited, and the tests are interesting as precursors of those to come later.

Hermann Ebbinghaus (1897), the father of experimental psychology of learning, was called upon to make a study of fatigue in schoolchildren, in connection with which he used three tests: computation, memory span, and sentence completion. The sentence-completion test was to find use later, particularly in Thorndike's battery of tests for college aptitude. Support for such use was given by Ebbinghaus, who found this test to be the only one of his three that correlated with school grades.

The French—Binet   Although Alfred Binet was a pinnacle among mental testers, in the world as well as in France, a few Frenchmen preceded him in the use of tests. J. E. D. Esquirol, a distinguished psychiatrist, had made a distinction between the insane and the feebleminded, the former not always being mentally defective and the latter always so from an early age. He also recognized degrees or levels of feeblemindedness and found that language tests served best in distinguishing among individuals in those levels. Another medical man, E. Seguin (1907), was pioneering in the training of feebleminded individuals by exercising their sensory and motor functions. His form board, which has been a part of some modern test batteries and of which many variations were later devised, was designed as one of those instruments of sensory exercise. Another who was concerned with the mentally deficient was the Italian S. de Sanctis, who published a series of six tests designed to identify the feebleminded in years seven to sixteen. The tests included memory for colors, recognition of forms, sustained attention, reasoning involving relations, following instructions, and thinking. These tests lost out in later competition with the Binet tests.

It is well known that Binet was first of all an experimental psychologist and that before he undertook to construct mental tests he had engaged in studies of mental functions. He quite readily carried over into his research on tests, conducted with Henri, things he had learned in the psychological laboratory. Binet and Henri (1896) criticized tests of the Galton type as being too sensory and too simple. Even the memory tests were regarded as inadequate, for they thought varieties of memory, such as memory for letters, colors, paired associates, and so on, needed to be taken into account. One must specify which memory is being measured, and a variety of memory tests should be used. They expressed a strong preference for the more complex tests and proposed that 10 functions be explored by means of tests: memory, imagery, imagination, attention, comprehension, suggestibility, aesthetic appreciation, moral sentiment, muscular force and force of will and motor skill, and judgment of visual space. Nor does it appear that they regarded these 10 to be unitary traits, for they suggested varieties of tests for each one. The 10 were thus regarded as categories of traits.

Meanwhile, Binet continued his famous research on thinking processes, using his daughters Marguerite and Armande as subjects. Types of functions that he investigated included abstraction, ideation, imagination, imagery, imageless thoughts, attention, reaction time, and memory. The listing of Binet's categories and the emphasis upon them here are to point out that in his view of intelligence he was very comprehensive and that his later introduction of a single score for measurement of intelligence was in obvious contradiction to his own convictions.

Binet's 1905 scale   Many readers know that Binet and Théodore Simon, a medical doctor, were commissioned in 1904 to find a procedure for determining how to segregate the slow learners in the Paris schools; Simon, because mental deficiency had by tradition been regarded as a province of the domain of medicine, and Binet, because of his known readiness to contribute the needed technical skills. The objective of the first Binet scale was then a discrimination between normal and mentally deficient children by a more direct method, to supplement or to replace the less certain physical, social, and educational signs of retardation (Binet & Simon, 1905).

The practical aim was in the direction of a graded scale of tests varying in difficulty, with age norms, by which the tester could decide just how much advanced or retarded a child is intellectually. With his comprehensive view of mental ability, Binet sought to include a great variety of tests, with emphasis on certain categories that he had already recognized: judgment, common sense, initiative, and ability to adapt. The list of 30 tests that composed the 1905 scale is given here, both to show how they reflected findings regarding earlier tests and how they set the pattern for many tests that still remain in service in revised Binet scales. The 30 tests were:

1. Visual coordination.
2. Prehension on contact (grasping a cube after touching it).
3. Prehension on sight.
4. Recognize food (choice between wood and chocolate).
5. Seek food (in response to chocolate wrapped in paper).
6. Follow simple orders or repeat gestures.
7. Point to objects (head, nose, etc.).
8. Recognize objects in picture.
9. Name objects in picture.

10. Discriminate two lines for length.
11. Repeat three digits.
12. Discriminate two weights.
13. Resist suggestions.
14. Define simple words.
15. Repeat sentence of 15 words.
16. Give differences between pairs of objects.
17. Visual memory.
18. Draw forms from memory.
19. Memory span for digits.
20. State similarities between objects.
21. Discriminate lines rapidly.
22. Order five weights.
23. Identify missing weight (of the five weights in test 22).
24. Give rhyming words.
25. Complete sentences.
26. Construct sentence containing three given words.
27. Answer questions, e.g., "What should you do when sleepy?"
28. Give time after hands of a clock have been interchanged.
29. Folding and cutting paper.
30. Distinguish between abstract terms, e.g., *sad* and *bored*.

In commenting on this list, something might be said about the general composition of the collection that formed the 1905 scale, in view of much emphasis later in this volume on types of tests. The first 3 in the list are tests of motor development, and the 27 following may be generally accepted as being "mental." Of the 27, 18, or two-thirds, appear to be tests of cognitive abilities, i.e., tests of comprehension or of "decoding of information," to use computer technology. Five are well-known types of memory tests (numbers 11, 15, 17, 18, 19), and true to his belief, Binet introduced some variety among them. Three tests (24, 25, and 26) are of types that measure what the writer has called "divergent-production" abilities, abilities that involve productive thinking, in that the child's reactions must supply information from his memory storage to fulfill a specified need.

Binet's 1908 scale By 1908, the emphasis was said to have shifted from merely discriminating the mentally defective from the normal children to differentiating among normal children (Peterson, 1925). Several general principles, growing out of experiences with the 1905 scale, had been recognized. One principle is that mental development is lawful and therefore should be subject matter for scientific investigation. Another principle is that the child's intellect is not just a miniature of the adult intellect. But quite in disharmony with the practice of using a single score, Binet's impression was that intelligence is much more complex than had previously been conceived.

In the 1908 revision, still with an interest in knowing how much a child might be advanced or retarded, for convenience the tests were grouped in age levels, from age three to age thirteen. The age level for a test was chosen as that at which 75 percent could pass the test, for at that percentage the great middle 50 percent pass the test. Approximations had to be tolerated, of course. There was some checking on the adequacy of the scaling of tests as a group, by noting that equal numbers of children were accelerated as were advanced. A very rough validation was carried out, by noting that a small number of children who were retarded in school also tested below age and some accelerated children tested above age. Binet did not regard intelligence and scholastic ability as being the same thing, for the latter depends also upon other traits.

Binet's 1911 scale   The 1911 revision involved minor changes in scaling of tests composing the scale, some being moved up and some down, in view of further experience with them. Of more significance was the decision to see that there were the same number of tests at each age level (five, except at age four) and to adopt the principle that each additional test passed should add two-tenths of a year to the child's mental age. The mental-age concept thus became more firmly established.

Tests in the United States   The early mental testing in America had much of its focus on the person of James McKeen Cattell. As a student in the 1880s, Cattell had become imbued with the Darwinian spirit of the times and, like Galton, had seen the significance of individual differences (Boring, 1950). Studying under Wilhelm Wundt at Leipzig, he broke faith with the introspective psychology of that locale and initiated studies of individual differences in reaction time.

His later personal contacts with Galton gave Cattell acquaintance with the latter's tests. He forthwith adopted the simple, Galton type of tests in preference to the complex, Binet type of tests, and thereby hangs a tale. It was said (Peterson, 1925) that Cattell's logical defense of this choice was that the complex functions that Binet was testing would sometime be found to reduce by analysis to the simpler functions such as Galton had been testing. Returning to the United States, he initiated research on tests of the Galton type at the University of Pennsylvania. In describing these tests in an article (1890), Cattell used for the first time in print the expression "mental test."

Validation of the Cattell tests   Following Cattell's move to Columbia University, a large battery of his tests was given to entering freshmen each year. The test battery included tests of perception of size (lines and angles), size of head, strength of hand, fatigue, visual acuity, color vision, hearing acuity, reproduction of pitch, perception of weight, two-point discrimination, pain sensitivity, color preference, reaction time, cancellation of *A*s, dotting accuracy, reproduction of rhythm and rate, word association, imagery, digit span, memory for meaningful content, and incidental memory for line length. From today's perspective, the list seems overwhelmingly unpromising; but this is hindsight.

The major responsibility for validation of the test battery for prediction of grades in college fell to the anthropologist-psychologist Clark Wissler (1901). Wissler thought it imperative to find out what the tests actually measured, and he thought the best approach was through application of the relatively new correlation method of Galton and Karl Pearson. If the tests all measure the same ability, they should correlate positively with one another; if any two tests correlate zero, they measure totally different abilities. If the tests measure mental ability that is important for success in college, they should correlate positively with course grades.

The sad story was that the intercorrelations among the tests were very low. Even outstanding exceptions are not at all impressive; they include a correlation of .38 between tests of drawing and of bisecting a line, correlations of .29 and .39 between auditory and visual digit spans, and of .21 between naming colors and marking *A*s. Grades in college courses correlated substantially with one another, typically in the range .50 to .75, but they correlated near zero with the tests. The average grade correlated .19 with the test of substance memory and .16 with digit span. The grade in Latin correlated .22 with the score on substance memory.

The Sharp study   Wissler's findings dealt quite a blow to a budding young test movement that had hardly gotten off the ground. Matters were not helped at all by the outcome of another study by Sharp (1898–99) at Cornell University. In the Cornell Psychological Laboratory, a faithful offshoot of Wundt's Leipzig laboratory, one should not have expected a very sympathetic response to the idea of mental tests. Sharp's aims were to find out whether this new test method held any promise for the experimental psychologist whose concern is the discovery of facts about the basic, general nature of the human mind and, more incidentally, to determine whether there should be any preference for complex versus simple tests.

She used only seven graduate students as subjects, in a laboratory where such small numbers were typical in psychological experiments. She administered tests of the Binet-Henri type to the same subjects in retests several times at weekly intervals. She did not apply correlation procedures, but she noted that the rank orders of the subjects were very inconsistent from test to test and from time to time in the same test. Not being sophisticated with respect to statistical theory of tests, she did not realize that with graduate students there would possibly be little variance to begin with and that with practice in repeated testing they would all be likely to approach the ceilings of the tests, thus further reducing variances and lowering accuracy of measurement and chances for intercorrelations.

It may be true that Sharp's conclusion that the tests were measuring different functions was correct, but without information about reliability of the scores one cannot tell whether that conclusion is justified. She was struck by the fact that experimental control of what the examinee does is often poor, a circumstance that has not bothered testers as much as it should, and that tests offered little promise for use by the experimental psychologist. She seemed unaware of the fact that, with Ebbinghaus's first experiments on memory, psychological tests had already been introduced into experimental psychology. Since Ebbinghaus, the most widely utilized device of the experimental psychologist has been various forms of psychological tests. Wherever he measures performance, he is using a psychological test.

Terman and the Stanford-Binet scales   As Cattell was fading out of the mental-test scene, Lewis M. Terman was fading in. About the time of Binet's first edition, Terman was doing some studies with tests at Clark University (Terman, 1906). He selected the 7 brightest and the 7 most stupid boys from 500 in the local schools to see how differently they would perform on a number of tests. Even at that time, he showed a preferential interest in tests of the more complex type, including what he supposed to be measures of inventive and creative imagination, logical processes, mathematical ability, mastery of language, insight (interpretation of fables), learning ability (e.g., in playing chess), memory abilities, and motor ability, including the learning of motor skills.

It should have been almost a foregone conclusion that, with so vast a gulf between his extreme groups, all except the motor tests, at least, should show correlations with his criterion; and they did. The only exception was a small difference in the measure of inventive and creative imagination, and there was a negative relationship for the motor tests. It may have been the small relationship for the test of creative performance that accounts for Terman's later ignoring of that important quality. It is more certain that the similar relationships of all other mental tests to his criterion of intelligence led him to conclude that intelligence does not develop along special lines and that the measurement of a single trait—intelligence—is feasible.

This conclusion was based upon very questionable evidence. It is not known just how much correlation there was among the tests. Even though all tests correlated with the criterion, the correlations between tests could have been small, if not zero. It was not even known how much correlation there was between the tests and judgments of brightness versus dullness, had all 500 cases been taken into consideration. Thus, an ill-supported decision made subsequent psychological history.

Terman's apparent success with tests of the Binet type led him to become Binet's champion in America. He added a few tests, such as those on interpretation of fables and the ball-and-field test, and came out with the standardized Stanford-Binet Scale in 1916. Two new forms, L and M, based upon the 1916 revision, were published in 1937 (Terman & Merrill, 1937) and a new combined L-M form in recent years (Terman & Merrill, 1960). The most significant changes involved in the development of these successive forms included the use of the IQ or intelligence-quotient index, the idea for which has been attributed to William Stern; the extension of the scale to the superior-adult level; and the institution of national norms.

Over the years, there was little evident concern on the part of Terman regarding the nature of human intelligence. He defined that concept as the ability to perform abstract thinking, without defining "abstract thinking" satisfactorily. It is obvious that the tests of his scale do not serve well as referents for a single concept, owing to their great heterogeneity. Many of them would fail to satisfy most observers' conception of what abstract thinking entails. But Terman did not show concern for psychological theory.

The Wechsler scales   The statement that the Stanford-Binet scales dominated the testing world for many years cannot be challenged. They were not only the models for other scales but also the standards against which others have been evaluated. H. H. Goddard had translated Binet's 1908 revision for use at the Vineland Training School, but his form quickly lost out in competition with Terman's scale. Only within the past twenty years has the Stanford-Binet Scale had a substantial competitor, in the form of the Wechsler scales. Those scales are of interest here because of some new principles of testing and some new kinds of uses that they have served.

One shortcoming of the Terman scales to which Wechsler was reacting was the fact that the tests composing the various year categories differed from year to year. Only such tests as vocabulary and memory span appear with any degree of frequency, but even then without regularity. Terman could afford not to be disturbed by this fact because he regarded all tests as measures of the same variable of intelligence anyway. Wechsler had serious reservations on this point and wanted to measure the same abilities at all ages. This he hoped to achieve by using the same tests at different ages. He realized that this step presents some problems, for example, in the fact that certain kinds of tests are more natural and more acceptable to individuals at different ages. To this we may add the caution that one cannot be sure that the same test, even if it can be adapted to all ages, will everywhere necessarily measure the same ability. The principle of presenting the same tests or the same kinds of tests at different age levels had been applied earlier in the Yerkes-Bridges Point Scale (Yerkes, Bridges, & Hardwick, 1915) as an alternative to mental-age scales composed of shifting test composition, but that scale was never popular.

Wechsler's initial scale, known as the Wechsler-Bellevue Intelligence Scale (WBIS), was composed of tests in two categories, verbal and performance; and a verbal and a performance score are obtained as well as a total score, the two scores being in recognition of the generally lower correlations between tests of the two kinds. This step was in line with accepted practice in college-aptitude testing, in which a verbal score and a quantitative or mathematical score were in vogue and had been for a number of years; a practice that has continued to the present time. The composition of Wechsler's two categories of tests is worth noting:

Verbal tests:

Information
Comprehension (intended to measure judgment or common sense)
Arithmetic
Digits Forward and Backward
Similarities (state how two given things are alike)
Vocabulary

Performance tests:

Picture Completion (state what is missing in each picture)
Picture Arrangement (put four pictures from a comic strip in correct temporal order)
Object Assembly (jigsaw puzzles)
Block Design (construct color-pattern designs in duplication of given patterns)
Digit Symbol (code substitution, each of nine simple symbols to be substituted for its digit mate)

The WBIS was designed to give more room at the top for adults and thus to overcome another weakness in the earlier Stanford-Binet scales. A deviation IQ equivalent was derived to meet the popular demand for such an index. A similar scale known as the Wechsler Intelligence Scale for Children (WISC) was developed later and the WBIS now bears the title "Wechsler Adult Intelligence Scale" or WAIS (Wechsler, 1958).

The principle of differential scoring of the Wechsler scales has gone beyond the two main scores, verbal and performance. Test users have sometimes given attention to profiles of single-test scores and to differences among the scores. Total scatter of part scores has sometimes been taken as indication of psychopathology. Attempts have been made to interpret the meaning of particular high and low points and particular differences between scores. No details of all this will be given here, and no attempt will be made to evaluate these practices.

The point of interest here is the recognition of multiple aspect of this thing called "intelligence." Wechsler has been rather ambivalent on this point, however. On the one hand, he has recognized from the far-from-perfect correlations among tests the clearly indicated fact that something other than a monolithic unit is involved and that it pays to give attention to the added information that a more analytical scoring provides. On the other hand, when he selected tests for his battery, he favored tests that correlated better with the composite score, for such tests were regarded as better measures of *intelligence*. The psychometric facts of life, however, are such that if one wanted to emphasize differential information, one would aim at tests that correlate as *low* as possible with one another, which would mean that they would also correlate lower with the sum of all the scores. Here is a case in which one cannot have one's cake and eat it too. Perhaps Wechsler was all too cognizant of the deeply rooted conception of a unitary intelligence that had been forged by the success of the Stanford-Binet scales.

Group intelligence tests

Army Alpha and Beta examinations With the growing success of individual testing and the increasing demands for their use, it was inevitable that the mass-production principle of the United States American economy should be invoked in the testing field. Mass testing became a necessity, for example, when the United States entered World War I in 1917. Alert to the possible contributions that tests could make to the armed forces, the American Psychological Association appointed a committee on tests, of which Robert M. Yerkes was chairman. Arthur S. Otis had already been experimenting with group testing, and the committee drew upon his experiences in planning a test battery for military purposes. The result was the Army Alpha Examination, which was to be administered to more than 1.5 million servicemen (Yerkes, 1921). The scores were used in rejecting small numbers of recruits, in selecting men for officer training, and in making work assignments. The Army Alpha was composed of eight parts, mostly involving verbal and number content, but a single total score was used. For the illiterate and for those who did not have the normal use of the English language, the Army Beta Examination, a set of performance or nonverbal tests, was designed. More than anything else the Army Alpha and Army Beta examinations called widespread attention to tests, and an almost immediate consequence was the development of college-aptitude tests and many other group tests, for use with children as well as with adults.

Multiple-aptitude tests It was soon realized that although intelligence tests made useful predictions of academic achievement, as Binet had designed his tests to do originally, they often failed to predict success in special, less verbal, less academic endeavors, as for mechanics, clerical work, art, and music. Hence, other types of tests were tried for the assessment of aptitude for those activities as well as for others. The usually unspoken implication was that the abilities thus involved are outside the realm of intelligence, a conclusion that findings in recent years have proved false where "intelligence" is interpreted with appropriate comprehensiveness.

Even within the sphere of intelligence testing, events led to what some call "differential-aptitude" testing, a practice that goes well beyond the simple differentiation of verbal and nonverbal scoring. This trend is obviously attributable to L. L. Thurstone's multiple-factor theory and to factor-analysis findings from utilization of his multiple-factor methods. Although his first classical investigation of primary mental abilities made something of an impact when it was published in 1938, the scientific and practical consequences have been slow to follow. In tangible form, there was the publication of the Thurstones' Primary Mental Abilities test batteries at three age levels, each including about a half-dozen tests and each test being designed to measure a separate ability that had been segregated by factor analysis.

Other test batteries have shown the same kind of influence. The United States Employment Service, with Thurstone as guiding consultant, developed the General Aptitude Test Battery, with about a dozen parts (Dvorak, 1947). Based upon factor-analytic experiences during World War II in the Army Air Forces, the Guilford-Zimmerman Aptitude Survey, a battery of seven tests, was constructed (1948). The Army Air Forces' eminently successful Aircrew Classification battery had been constructed very much along factorial lines (Guilford & Lacey, 1947) and had been administered to more than half a million young men during the war. Since that time, a number of commercially available test batteries, not always constructed along factorial lines, have become available. As test users learn how to employ them effectively, their unique values are becoming known and appreciated.

Infant and preschool tests Very early in the use of the Binet tests their limitation at the lower end of the age scale was quite apparent. It was desired to know something about the child's mental potentialities, even in the cradle, in connection with decisions about adoption into foster homes and other dispositions that might be under consideration. The first scale designed for such young children was F. Kuhlmann's revision of the Binet (Kuhlmann, 1912). His later revisions extended the Binet scale down to the four-month level (Kuhlmann, 1939).

Over the years, Arnold Gesell and his coworkers at Yale studied intensively the development of infants at regular intervals and in the course of time constructed an age scale called the Gesell Developmental Schedules (Gesell and staff, 1949). Four areas of behavior were included:

Motor behavior (bodily control)
Adaptive behavior (reactions to objects)
Language behavior (bodily expressions, vocalizations, and speech)
Personal-social behavior (cultural habits and interpersonal relations)

Items were standardized by age levels covering the range from four weeks to thirty-six months.

Other infant and preschool scales drew upon the Gesell list of tests as well as the Binet tests, among them being the Cattell Infant Intelligence Scale (P. Cattell, 1940), developed by Psyche Cattell, a daughter of J. McK. Cattell; the California First-Year Mental Scale, designed for use in a longitudinal study of mental development at the University of California at Berkeley (Bayley, 1933); and the Merrill-Palmer Scale of Mental Tests (Stutsman, 1931). Only the better-known scales are mentioned here.

It is to be noted that Gesell did not claim that his scale measures intelligence but that others used many of his items and other items like them in scales that they regarded as measures of *intelligence,* only to be sadly disappointed, as we shall see later. It is sufficient to say here that the abilities measured by the infant and preschool scales are radically different from those measured by the Stanford-Binet and Wechsler scales, a circumstance that has come to be recognized, at least by some test users.

Perhaps it was the overemphasis upon the criterion of correlation of intelligence with age that was misleading, giving rise to the conclusion that any test that has a greater probability of being passed as age increases is therefore a measure of intelligence. Human attributes other than intelligence also increase with age; hence the correlation of a test item with age is no sure criterion of its being a measure of mental ability.

Conceptions of Intelligence

While we are in the context of history, it is well to consider in an organized manner the threads of thinking concerning the nature of intelligence. A consideration of definitions, as such, can be very dull, and there is little to be gained by a mere parade of them. Since we are concerned with present-day issues, however, the latter are better understood by seeing how they grew out of the past.

Origin of the concept   According to Cyril Burt (1955), the term *intelligence* goes back to *intelligentia,* a term introduced by Cicero. Spearman (1927) reported that the "monarchic" view of a unitary thing called intelligence was popular back as far as the fifteenth century. Both writers credit the bringing of the term into psychology to Herbert Spencer (1895), who had earlier emphasized its role in biology. Having defined life as "the continuous adjustment of internal relations to external relations," Spencer believed that adjustment is achieved by virtue of intelligence in man and by virtue of instincts in lower animals. Defining intelligence as the "power of combining many separate impressions" (1895, p. 403), Spencer also tied the concept to the doctrine of evolution in a way that was to set the pattern for psychologists for many years to come.

Attempts at logical definitions   After tests had been invented to measure intelligence, quite a number of thinkers felt the urge to define it. Symposia were held on the problem, and numerous voices were heard. The outcomes were far from agreement. As Spearman (1927) put it, intelligence became a "mere vocal sound, a word with so many meanings that finally it had none." He further quoted J. S. Mill in a statement that described the situation well and that should serve as a warning: "The tendency has always been strong to believe that whatever receives a name must be an entity of being, having an independent existence of its own. And if no real entity answering to the name could be found, men did not for that reason suppose that none existed, but imagined that it was something peculiarly abstruse and mysterious" (1927, p. 14).

Binet's conception   According to Peterson (1925), Binet never stated in published form a formal definition of intelligence. He did have views, however. We have already seen that he rejected the British emphasis upon sensory and motor functions, ruling them out of his concept. In his earlier thinking, Binet placed some stress on memory and imagery, although he rejected the association principle. A second emphasis was upon voluntary attention, which he regarded as a high form of adaptability to a task. A third was on judgment or common sense. For a time he tied to this conception the trait of resistance to suggestibility, until he recognized that the low-grade feebleminded are not at all suggestible.

Binet's emphasis later turned to thinking or problem-solving operations, in which he recognized three steps: direction, adaptation, and autocriticism. Direction is equivalent to the more recent concept of "mental set," in which goal-seeking activity is an important aspect. Adaptation involves finding means to reach ends, the invention of methods and the choice of methods. Autocriticism is self-evaluation. Still later, Binet (1909) added a fourth step, comprehension. With the four steps of direction, comprehension, invention, and criticism, Binet's description of thinking or problem solving is quite congruent with recent thinking (see Chapter 14).

A view of Binet's, which was evident in connection with his choice of tests for measuring intelligence, as related earlier in this chapter, and which is pertinent to the next chapters, had to do with the rejection of the monarchic nature of intelligence, as Spearman called it. Preferring complex tests and often remarking on the great complexity of intelligence, Binet (1909) also stated that ". . . the mental faculties of each subject are independent and unequal; with little memory there may be associated much judgment. . . . Our mental tests, always special in their scope, are each appropriate to the analysis of a single faculty."

By the use of the term *faculty,* Binet was not committing himself to the philosophical tradition of faculty psychology. His *general* conception of the nature of the human mind might have been the same, but the faculties of Binet were very different. In adopting a single score for his scale, Binet appeared to be inconsistent; Spearman (1927, p. 24) described it as "inconceivably illogical." It is obvious that Binet did not carry his conception of independent faculties to the logical conclusion in terms of measurement. In the practical situation in which he found himself, all he needed was a means by which to reach a single administrative decision about each child. A single score was a natural means to that end.

Approaches to operational definitions   A serious weakness of most definitions of intelligence is that they contain undefined (and often undefinable) terms. A definition that satisfies the needs of univocal communication must contain referents in the real world or must point unambiguously to something that points to referents in the real world. Wechsler gives what he proposes as an operational definition when he says that ". . . intelligence, operationally defined, is the aggregate or global capacity of the individual to act purposefully, to think rationally, and to deal effectively with his environment" (1958, p. 7). He makes some comments about "aggregate," "global," "purposefully," and "rationally," but he does not supply empirical referents for them.

E. G. Boring (1923) gave an essentially operational definition when he stated that ". . . intelligence as a measurable capacity must at the start be defined as the capacity to do well in an intelligence test." In other words, Boring was saying that intelligence is whatever intelligence tests test. We are thus thrown completely on the tests for a definition of intelligence, and without proof that one intelligence test measures the same thing or things as another we have as many definitions of intelligence as there are different intelligence tests. In terms of accurate application of terms and for unambiguous communication with others, we should need to speak of Stanford-Binet, Form L, intelligence, WAIS intelligence, or Raven Progressive Matrices intelligence; otherwise we are using the same label to mean different things. One who wanted a more precise operational use of the term *intelligence* might demand not only the name of the test but also statements about other conditions: the circumstances under which the test was administered and even by whom.

But in this direction of extreme empiricism lies chaos. There might be no end to the meticulous specification of conditions and operations that could well be demanded, and a resulting multitude of concepts would be highly uneconomical and bewildering. In such a test world, there would be little information of general significance or usefulness. Certain steps toward a unitary referent for the term *intelligence* could be in the form of conventional agreement as to the composition of a test and as to the operations of testing. Such agreement could be achieved on a purely conventional basis as by popular vote or by the imposition of a constant test battery by some bureau of standards. A far better way of achieving unanimity of reference would be to find a foundation in psychological theory to which by experimental demonstrations those who construct tests would feel persuaded to assent.

Fortunately, there is such a way. To some readers, Boring's statement may seem facetious or even cynical, but actually he was calling attention, in the proper direction, to a careful study of the tests themselves. What is it that they actually measure? Boring gave the proper cue when he went on to say that we should be able to gain insight into the nature of intelligence tests through the method of correlation. Much earlier, Wissler (1901) made a similar suggestion when he faced the prospect of intercorrelating the Cattell tests at Columbia. He pointed out that it was imperative to find out what the tests actually measure and that the best approach is through correlations.

Such information regarding tests is now known technically as *construct validity*. If we say that a test measures ability K, we need to show that it correlates at least substantially with other tests that are also purported to measure ability K. If two tests that are believed to measure K correlate low with one another when both have high reliability, either one or the other is lacking in construct validity for measuring K or both are invalid for that purpose; they may well have construct validity for measuring some other abilities M and Q.

Finding the intercorrelations among a set of tests is only a step in the direction of a factor analysis which is well designed, with proper use, to lead to conclusions regarding underlying variables (abilities or other traits), each measured in common by a subgroup of tests. When such underlying variables are verified repeatedly in connection with the same tests, confidence develops in a constant of some kind, which can well be given a name. A number of writers who themselves are not known as factor analysts have pointed out such a solution to the definition problem and to other problems of intelligence (Bayley,

1955; Freeman, 1940; Spiker & McCandless, 1954; Wechsler, 1958). Much more will be said concerning factor analysis and its role in the investigation of the nature of intelligence in the chapters to come.

Intelligence as learning ability

Learning ability as achievement status   Appearing very commonly in definitions of intelligence is the statement that it is learning ability or *the* ability to learn. The same statement is often glibly made in many connections; hence while we are on the subject of definitions, it is important that we give some attention to the idea. There are some very important issues involved anad some misconceptions that need to be cleared away.

The common relating of intelligence to "adaptation to new situations" in some definitions suggests the relevance of learning, for adapting to new situations does imply learning. It has been obvious, from Binet on, that individuals who score higher on the tests are likely to be accelerated in school and those who score lower are likely to be retarded. The accelerated individuals have learned more rapidly; the retarded ones, more slowly. The common inference is that the child is advanced *because* he is more intelligent and the retardate is behind *because* he is less intelligent. But it could be argued the other way round: a child scores higher on the test because he has learned more, and another child scores lower because he has learned less.

The fact of correlation, by itself, does not tell us which is cause and which is effect. Measures of achievement and of aptitude for achievement are commonly found by factor analysis to be measuring the same factors by different kinds of instruments. If it is pointed out that the measure of aptitude given at the early age of six predicts with some accuracy the individual's relative status after six, ten, or even more years and that this surely shows that his status at six prepared him to perform in similar rank position years later, it could be just as easily said that an appropriate achievement test given at six could predict as well (if we assume that such a test could be devised). Or the aptitude test at six indeed indicates general mental *achievement* to that time, and relative achievement of the future is likely to be consistent with relative amount of achievement today.

Intercorrelations of learning scores   Husband (1939) took *learning ability* to mean performance in learning tasks and instituted an investigation involving the intercorrelations of scores from a variety of tests, each of which involved relatively rapid gains in performance. Examples to show the variety among his 17 tests are:

Memorizing of names associated with faces
Spool packing
Mirror tracing
Cancellation
Memory for prose (visual and auditory)
Pursuit (on a pursuit rotor)

With 100 college students as subjects, the intercorrelations proved to be very low. Only 8 out of 91 coefficients were .30 or larger. With some evidence that the higher *r*s were among subsets of similar tests, Husband concluded that learning ability is not unitary but that there are a number of relatively independent learning abilities, depending upon the kind of task.

In a subsequent experiment, in which the subjects practiced on six of the same tests, each four times as long as before in order to ensure higher reliability of the scores, the intercorrelations ranged from −.32 to +.30, with a median of +.20, compared with the earlier median of .13 (Husband, 1941a). In order to determine whether larger correlations would be found in a population with greater range of ability, Husband (1941b) repeated the experiment with six tests in a sample of 60 children in grades 7 and 8. The rs ranged from −.27 to +.37, with a median of +.10. No change in conclusion was necessitated by either of the two later experiments.

Learning ability as rate of change   But learning ability is often interpreted as something determining *rate* of learning, not status after learning or status in tasks obviously involving learning. To indicate rate of learning, some index is needed of how far the individual progresses from an initial score to a final score, given a standard amount of practice time and holding motivation and other variables constant. A simple difference between final and initial scores in a task or some function of that difference has been used as an index of rate of learning with which to test the hypothesis that learning ability is a unitary trait and the hypothesis that it is identical with intelligence. These are two different hypotheses, one of which could be true and the other false, or both could be true or both false. There are certain knotty problems with regard to the fact that different subjects begin at different positions on their learning curves for a task, but we shall have to ignore those problems; they have commonly been ignored by investigators of the problem from this approach. We shall see at least one way of meeting some of the difficulties.

Intercorrelations of gain scores   One of the simpler, more straightforward experiments on intercorrelations of gain scores was done by Heese (1942). His 50 subjects practiced two times a week for five weeks in six different tasks: Addition, Mirror Drawing, Maze Running, Sorting, Tapping or Marking, and a Double Hand Test (something like a two-hand coordination test). The intercorrelations of the six difference scores [derived from standard scores z, where $z = (X − M_x)/\sigma_x$, to make units of measurement more comparable] ranged from .05 to .57, most of them being very small. A factor analysis indicated the presence of three factors, which were not interpreted. The hypothesis of a single learning ability calls for only one common factor among rate-of-learning scores.

An explanatory note is important in connection with this approach through intercorrelating difference scores. Difference scores derived from the same test are often notoriously of low reliability; hence they cannot correlate so very high with other difference scores. If the initial and final scores for a test are denoted by X_i and X_f, respectively, the gain score X_g is the difference $X_f − X_i$. We can estimate the reliability of a difference, knowing the reliabilities of the two terminal scores X_f and X_i and their intercorrelations r_{fi} by using the following formula (Guilford, 1954, p. 394):

$$r_{gg} = \frac{r_{ff} + r_{ii} − 2r_{fi}}{2(1 + r_{fi})} \tag{1.1}$$

where the constants have already been defined.

From equation (1.1) we can deduce the conclusion that r_{gg} cannot be high unless r_{ff} and r_{ii} are very high and r_{fi} is low. It is experimentally possible to achieve high reliabilities for the two terminal scores, but r_{fi} is not likely to be low unless there is a long practice period between initial and final trials from which X_i and X_f are derived, for r_{fi} is actually a retest reliability coefficient.

Let us take a realistic example. Assume that the two terminal scores both have reliability coefficients of .8 and an intercorrelation of .4. Applying the equation, we find that

$$r_{gg} = \frac{.8 + .8 − 2(.4)}{2(1 + .4)} = \frac{.8}{2.8} = .29$$

As r_{fi} approaches the mean of r_{ff} and r_{ii}, r_{gg} approaches zero. Thus, intercorrelations among gain scores should be expected to be on the low side, except where r_{fi} is quite small and the terminal reliabilities are high.

Factors in gain scores   Woodrow performed a number of very informative experiments on the intercorrelations of gain scores and factor analysis of those intercorrelations. Fortunately, variables that are factor-analyzed need not have high reliabilities. Experience shows that fairly satisfactory factor-analytic solutions can be obtained even when some variables have reliabilities as low as .4.

In one study, 56 students had practice in seven different tasks extending over a period of thirty-nine days (Woodrow, 1938). The factor analysis involved not only the seven gain scores but also nine marker tests, selected for inclusion because Woodrow suspected that they might measure the same factors that should be represented in the gain scores. The initial and final scores from the seven practice tests were also included. Three of the nine marker tests were administered both before and after the practice days and the other six either before or after, but not both.

Nine factors were found, with the usual information regarding the factor loadings (correlations between each test and the factors).[1] It is to be noted, first, that the intercorrelations of the gain scores were very low, as usual, and that they did not show a single rate-of-learning factor in common to them and to them alone, as the unitary-learning-rate hypothesis would demand.

Changes in factor structure with learning   Other findings are of interest here, since they have relevance for the relation of learning to aptitude factors. There is evidently no unitary learning ability, but there are relationships between intellectual abilities and learning. One might better say "learnings" in the plural here, because the indications are that, as for intelligence, there is no simple referent for learning when a factor-analytic inspection of learning data is made.

One result of Woodrow's study was that the loadings for some of the factors were different for the initial and final scores of a task. In fact, a similar, systematic effect was found for certain factors. An example is the factor of verbal comprehension. The loadings on verbal comprehension decreased in going from the initial to the final trials. In none of Woodrow's seven practice tasks was the verbal-comprehension loading higher at the end of practice. Evidently the subjects' verbal comprehension of the tasks had something to do with whether or not they performed well during early trials but not so much with their performance during final trials. Since such changes did not occur in the three marker tests that were administered before and after the practice interval but were not practiced in the meantime, Woodrow was able to conclude that the change in factor loadings was attributable to practice.

Gain factors and terminal scores   Further discussions of the relation of factors to learning will be found in Chapter 12. One additional point should be mentioned here, however, because of its relevance to the factorial nature of gains in performance. In another place, Woodrow (1939c) gave mathematical proof that the common factors in gain scores must be the same as those in initial and final scores, one or both.

An intuitive reason is that a gain score is derived from those two scores, i.e., $X_g = X_f - X_i$. The proof goes as follows. The gain score may be regarded as a weighted

---

[1] True of factor loadings only where factors are orthogonal (uncorrelated). For some technical information on factor analysis, see Chapter 3.

sum of two scores, where the weights are $+1$ and -1, respectively. We could write the sum as follows: $(+1)X_f + (-1)X_i$. If we know the factor loading for a certain factor A for each of these two components (where factor loadings are correlations of tests with the factor) and their standard deviations, we can compute the loading on the same factor for a weighted sum of the two components. The formula, adapted to this particular application, reads (Guilford, 1965a, p. 427):

$$r_{ag} = \frac{\sigma_f r_{af} - \sigma_i r_{ai}}{\sigma_g} = \frac{\sigma_f r_{af} - \sigma_i r_{ai}}{\sqrt{\sigma_f^2 + \sigma_i^2 - 2r_{fi}\sigma_f\sigma_i}} \tag{1.2}$$

where

σ_f = standard deviation of final score
σ_i = standard deviation of initial score
r_{af} = loading for factor A in final score
r_{ai} = loading for factor A in initial score
σ_g = standard deviation of gain scores

From this line of proof, it can be seen that there can be no common factor represented in a gain score that is not represented in one or both of the two terminal scores. When r_{af} and r_{ai} both equal zero, the numerator equals zero, also r_{ag}.

In the same article, Woodrow reported another learning experiment. There were four learning tasks: Horizontal Adding, Code Test (letter-digit), Two-Digit Cancellation, and Four-Digit Cancellation. Practice was continued for 66 trials in each task. In addition to the eight initial and final scores, 21 marker-test variables were included in the factor analysis. Six factors were found and interpreted psychologically, their natures not being relevant here. No completely general factor could be expected among the gain scores, for their intercorrelations were very low and some were even negative. Factor loadings were computed for the gain scores by using equation (1.2), and it was learned that each gain score, nevertheless, was related moderately to two or more of the group factors found more heavily represented in the marker-test-score variables and the terminal-score variables.

Intercorrelations of learning parameters Woodrow (1939a) properly expressed doubts about the use of the crude difference scores for the purposes of finding intercorrelations of gains. The problems of lack of control of starting positions and of the "ceiling" for scoring have been mentioned previously. Woodrow suggested that some kind of score based upon the learning curve for each individual might be a better index of learning rate, which would be unaffected by these uncontrolled features.

Such an approach was taken by the writer in an unpublished study carried out with others [1] during World War II. The objective was to find a learning-rate score for each individual on each of five psychomotor tests—Complex Coordination, Two-Hand Coordination, Rotary Pursuit, Discrimination Reaction Time, and Finger Dexterity—derived from a learning curve for each individual in each test. The practice on each test was continued until there were enough trial scores to determine at least part of a learning curve in each test. Two tests, Two-Hand Coordination and Rotary Pursuit, had a ceiling of 100 percent accuracy (keeping a contact on a moving button 100 percent of the time for a trial). The other tests had no mechanical limit, but of course there were limits determined by the subject's own speed of performance. The latter limits did vary somewhat from person to person. The subjects were 180 aviation students, and the tests were part of an extensive classification battery. Having taken the battery, the subjects came back a day or two later for the learning sessions in the five tests.

[1] The principal coinvestigator in this experiment was Neil D. Warren.

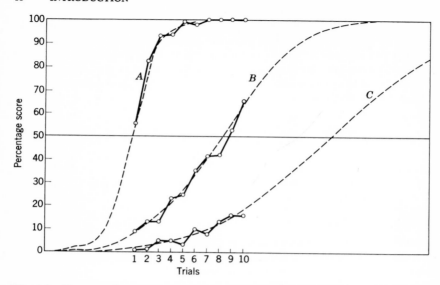

Fig. 1.1   Ten practice scores on a psychomotor task, obtained by each of three individuals, with fitted ogives (dotted lines) used as theoretical, complete learning curves.

Figure 1.1 shows the kind of graphic display made for the scores, trial by trial, for each subject. Let us say that three individuals, A, B, and C, are represented with respect to one task, with the 10 trials on the abscissa and the percentage score on the ordinate. The solid lines indicate the actual changes in score from trial to trial, as in an ordinary learning curve. For a rate-of-learning score, we need a number that represents slope in each learning curve. Where should this slope be taken, to be fair to every man?

It was decided to apply a rational theory in order to solve this problem. It was assumed that if each man's learning curve were complete, extending from something very close to zero to something very close to perfect, it would be in the form of an S-shaped trend; that from the very beginning there would be a positively accelerated trend, which would make a transition to a negatively accelerated trend on reaching the 50 percent level. Hardly any subject showed such a complete curve, but there were clearly many segments of such curves.

A curve that fulfills the requirements is the cumulative normal distribution curve, which L. L. Thurstone (1930) once proposed as the standard pattern of learning curve for certain types of tasks. Applying that curve in this experiment made possible the achieving of slope scores. From the segment of points given by each S's data on a test, it was possible to construct his entire hypothetical learning curve, represented by the dotted lines in Figure 1.1.

The slope index used for a rate score is essentially the reciprocal of the standard deviation of the cumulative distribution. Subject C's curve has the largest standard deviation and lowest slope or rate score; A has the smallest standard deviation and hence the largest rate score, with B intermediate. One thing to be noted is that such a score should be much more reliable statistically than a crude gain score, since it is based upon all the trial scores whereas the gain score is based on only two, i.e., the terminal points. Another thing to be noted is that the order of the slope-rate scores for these three subjects is not the same as for the gain scores, for A and B exchange rank positions. A's gain is 45 percentage points, limited by the score ceiling, and B's gain is 55 percentage points. On the whole, however, it can be seen that there should be some correlation between rate scores and gain scores in the same test. There is also a tendency for rate scores to be correlated with the initial scores and with the final scores. This is the basis for the factors found in common for gain scores on the one hand and terminal scores on the other. This is especially true where the same two limits apply to all Ss; in other tests where the limits also can vary, such correlations could be smaller. All such restraints or lack thereof should be taken into account in experiments on learning-rate scores.

To come back to the psychological findings, the intercorrelations of the slope scores from different tests were all close to zero, with a mean of about .07. Thus even when presumably better rate-of-learning scores are used, there is still no sign of a general learning-rate factor. Of incidental interest is an effort also made in the experiment to predict whether or not the aviation students would pass or fail in learning to fly an airplane in primary flying school. One reason for doing the learning experiment was the hypothesis that learning to fly an airplane in a limited time of nine weeks was largely a matter of learning rate; most students could probably have mastered the task if given enough time. Therefore, it was reasoned, a predictor score that emphasized rate of learning rather than initial status on a test would be a better predictor. It was known that the initial scores from all five tests had some correlation with the flying-training criterion of pass-fail in the range of .2 to .4, statistically significant because of the very large samples used.

The outcome was rather decisive; the validity coefficients for the rate scores were near zero. This result does not necessarily go against the conclusion of Woodrow, that the learning-rate scores have in them the same factors as the terminal scores; they *may* have such factors but need not have them. One thing lacking in the way of information in this case is the validity coefficients for the final scores; they could have been very small and probably were lower than for the initial scores because of the restriction of range. From equation (1.2) we can see that even if factor A is involved in both initial and final scores, the difference between the two numerator terms could reduce to zero with certain combinations of standard-deviation and factor-loading values.

Relation of learning scores to measures of intelligence

There have been some studies that bear on the other hypothesis, to the effect that intelligence, as usually measured by recognized intelligence tests, is related to gains in achievement. G. G. Thompson and S. L. Witryol (1946) correlated scores from the Otis test with three learning scores in a blindfold–maze-learning task. Although scores for the number of trials needed to reach a standard, scores for time, and scores for errors intercorrelated .73 to .84 $(N = 40)$, they correlated with Otis scores .03 (for trials), .16 (for errors), and .28 (for time). Even the correlation of .28 falls short of statistical significance.

In the academic-learning setting, the rate of acquiring knowledge in beginning psychology was correlated with an intelligence-test score by Carlson, Fischer, and Young (1945). The same achievement examination was administered at the beginning of the term and again at the end. The Otis-test score correlated .56 with the initial score and .43 with the final score. Use of equation (1.2) gave a correlation of −.04 with gain. Thus, the Otis score predicts amount of knowledge both before and after taking the course but not the amount of gain, where gain was measured by a certain kind of achievement examination. This result was probably largely attributable to the ceiling effect in the final examination and the fact that the more intelligent (testwise) knew more of the facts represented in the examination at the beginning of the course.

Another study attempted to avoid the ceiling effect (Tilton, 1949) by using test items that very few subjects could answer correctly in the initial test. The subjects were 134 in a seventh-grade social-studies course and 156 in a twelfth-grade course in American history. In the first case, items were selected so that none was passed by more than 25 percent in the initial administration. In the second case, no item in the initial testing was passed by more than 45 percent. The time intervals between testings were eleven weeks in the first case and a full year in the second. In both cases, the correlation of intelligence score (Otis score in the seventh grade and Terman Group score in the twelfth) with gain was .49. This is a more reasonable finding than that of Carlson et al. because of the very probable involvement of the verbal-comprehension factor in both the intelligence-test scores and the achievement scores. Since equation (1.2) indicates that we may not expect any factor in the gain scores that is not represented in either or both of the terminal scores, it would be important to see that the "intelligence" score represents the appropriate factors if we are to expect significant correlations with gain.

Summary

We have seen something of the history of the development of mental tests, most of which have been regarded as being in the intellectual area, from which we gain some information on changing conceptions of the nature of intelligence, the chief concern of this volume.

The early Galton tests were invented and assembled for the purpose of studying human heredity, based upon the associationist doctrine that development of intelligence depends upon the senses. Most other developments of tests were initiated for practical reasons in connection with psychopathology in Germany and mental deficiency in France. Experimental psychology provided the source for a great variety of tests.

Over the many years, we have seen a march from single scoring, which was initiated by Binet in direct contradiction to his convictions about a unitary intelligence, to multiple scoring, which has been indicated by factor-analytic theory and investigation.

The very popular conception that intelligence is learning ability and that it is a universal ability, regardless of the thing being learned, has definitely been exploded by a number of experiments. Relations of intellectual abilities to learning will be a subject of major interest in Chapter 12. It can be said here that both "learning ability" and intelligence involve many different component abilities and that they share the same components, depending upon the nature of the learning task and intelligence test.

2 The investigation of intelligence

We are not particularly concerned in this chapter with techniques of investigation of intelligence. But since we are concerned with the nature of intelligence and since the scientific findings with regard to any phenomenon are in part functions of the methods of investigation used, it is desirable, for further purposes of orientation, to see what kinds of information the various methods have had to offer and also what needs for information they expose. Three major types of method or approach will be treated: experimental, genetic, and multivariate, plus a number of more incidental approaches, including psychopathology, mental deficiency, neurology, and psychopharmacology.

Intelligence in experimental psychology

The "experimental psychology" intended in this discussion is of the traditional type. It is the area of the investigator who is interested in basic psychological problems, his subjects are likely to be human, and his research is conducted in the psychological laboratory.

On occasion, such a psychologist would not hesitate to use an intelligence test as a means of matching experimental and control groups, and he may even occasionally use intelligence-test scores for one of his independent or dependent variables, but usually not. He would probably be surprised to be told that his research makes contributions to the understanding of the nature of intelligence, however, for he is likely to think of intelligence only in the context of individual differences, a kind of variable that he tries to avoid. Individual differences have traditionally been a bother and a disturbance to the typical experimental psychologist. Concerned with seeking laws that have general application, he finds individual deviations upsetting, and he usually arranges for them to be restricted to his "error term" in statistical treatment of his results. He probably also suspects intelligence measurements of being less precise than those he ordinarily tries to obtain. This point is debatable.

Intellectual factors and laboratory research   But let us not belabor the general point, that the experimental psychologist avoids commerce with individual differences, which is sometimes called to our attention, for example, by Noble (1961). The present concern is to suggest how numerous experimental psychologists are actually investigating aspects of intelligence in their own ways and are adding information about its nature. Binet was primarily an experimental psychologist, and he fully recognized that what he was doing in the laboratory had important relevance for understanding intelligence. Many of his tests and others were devised directly from tasks that had come out of the psychological laboratories of Germany and elsewhere. It would have been well if later test developers had kept closer connections with the psychological laboratories and their findings.

In order to make this point more forcefully, it is perhaps necessary to remind both those in the laboratory and those testing in the field of the many points of contact that at least potentially exist. To do this, let us consider the 140 single tests composing the latest revision of the Stanford-Binet Scale (Terman & Merrill, 1960) to see how some of them tie up with laboratory problems. Very recently, Bonsall and Meeker (1964) have hypothesized for each of the 140 tests which of the intellectual-aptitude factors represented in the writer's structure-of-intellect model are most prominently represented (Guilford, 1959b). It is through this link that the connections with laboratory problems can be more clearly seen.

A number of the tests are of different aspects of memory. The memory-span tests are in the category of rote, serial learning, still so commonly investigated in the laboratory. Tests of memory for associations remind us of the numerous experiments using paired associates. Tests of memory for ideas are parallel to laboratory studies of meaningful or logical memory. And, of course, memory for visual forms comes into both contexts.

A second major category of tests comes under the heading of cognition or comprehension. Those involving the cognition of figures and visual objects in general have their counterpart in laboratory studies of visual perception. Tests involving comprehension of words and the awareness of classes suggest the many studies of concept formation. The tests of comprehension of patterns or systems, the seeing of relationships and implications, have their parallels in various combinations in studies of problem solving. Tests of orientation and spatial visualization suggest problems in space perception.

Problem-solving investigations in the laboratory also have relevant connections with tests in two other major categories: productive thinking and evaluation. Tests of productive thinking are illustrated by those calling for completion of analogies, elaborations upon given information, and the production of arrangements, deductions, and changes. Tests of evaluative abilities call for matching of items of information, seeing incongruities, and judging interpretations, relations, or logical conclusions. When the components of intelligence are viewed in terms of structure-of-intellect factors, a great many new types of laboratory problems are generated. In other words, the path between the laboratory and the psychological test is no longer very much a one-way street; there is much information about conceptions of intelligence that could pass in the opposite direction.

Genetic approach

A search among the studies of development of intelligence shows two major sources of information. One kind of study pertains to measured increases in performance as a function of age, with the use both of intelligence-test scores and of scores from numerous special tests in the intellectual area. The other kind relates to Jean Piaget, who has dominated the picture from a long-time devotion to study of the ways in which young children develop.

Our major interest in this chapter is in what might be called the taxonomy of intelligence. Superficially, a taxonomy in biology has to do with the classification of plants and animals. Superficially it deals with phenotypes. But class ideas are abstractions or genotypes, or they readily suggest genotypes, the underlying, basic concepts that make a science. Decisions about genotypes establish answers to the question of *what* exists in an area of investigation. In the progress of a science it is essential that we have good answers to the question of *what* before we attempt to answer the questions of *how* and *why*. In the present context, in which the basic conviction has been no secret, the primary interest is in the multiple-aptitude concepts that are needed for a thorough understanding of intelligence.

This being the case, in this chapter we shall look to the studies from the genetic approach mainly to see what they have to offer in the way of taxonomic, genotypal concepts. On the one hand, the studies of mental growth by psychometric procedures have given us almost no information about basic concepts. They have, however, often emphasized the need for a multiple-aptitude view of intelligence, as will be pointed out later. Although Piaget's work, as well as other investigations along the same line, is richer in terms of information regarding the way in which *particular* knowledge develops, it does have many suggestions to make regarding general concepts. His numerous contributions to the picture of mental development will receive considerable attention in Chapter 17. Here we shall consider only some of his more general concepts and theory.

Piaget's conceptions of intelligence   In understanding Piaget's view on psychological theory, which centers in intelligence, it is helpful to know that he began his scientific career as a biologist and carried over into psychology some of the biological concepts of his time and milieu. He was also a student of philosophy and gave particular attention to modern logic and epistemology. His view is that understanding how human individuals acquire and use knowledge is the key to understanding intelligence and the operations of the human mind. The relation of logic to psychology is a double one. On the one hand, Piaget's view is that it will be possible to construct psychological theory in general in terms of modern logic, that modern logic is to psychology what (nonfinite) mathematics has been to theoretical physics. On the other hand, development of the individual's intellectual functioning goes increasingly in the direction of formal logic, some individuals going much farther than others (Inhelder & Piaget, 1964; Piaget, 1953). The virtues and faults in such conceptions will not be discussed here. There will be occasion to return to them in later chapters.

Before we proceed to present some of his major concepts, a word should be said concerning Piaget's methods of research. He calls his method "clinical," for want of a more precise term. His observations are usually made in an informal manner, with little experimental control, on a more or less opportunistic basis. That is, he often watched an infant or child in a natural situation, at home as well as in the laboratory. Older children are given simple problems to solve, depending upon their degrees of readiness. They are encouraged to talk, and they are asked questions. Piaget's data are commonly in the form of written protocols, sometimes with numerical information but without the kind of statistical treatment to which experimenters are accustomed. In spite of this informality of method, his observations have been numerous and his insights have been fertile. The outcomes, however, are in the form of only partially tested hypotheses, to say the least. Fortunately, other investigators are replicating his less informal studies. Sometimes his conclusions are supported, sometimes not.

Functions of intelligence   With respect to general views of intelligence, Piaget distinguishes three aspects: content, function, and structure.[1] *Content* involves the observable aspects of behavior, the source of information with which the psychologist goes to work. *Function* pertains to broad principles of intellectual activity, principles that apply quite generally regardless of the age or state of development of the individual. One might say that function is constituted of the concepts and "laws" that the scientist infers from the observed content. *Structure* is essentially equivalent to knowledge. This aspect changes with age and with experience. It develops through activity. It is structure with which most of the writings of Piaget are concerned because of his genetic interests.

Let us see, first, what there may be in some of Piaget's functional concepts that might be considered in relation to the multiple aptitudes of the psychometric psychologist. Ap-

[1] For excellent summaries of Piaget's views in English, see J. McV. Hunt (1961) and Flavell (1963).

parently, Piaget had little interest in what either psychometric or experimental psychologists had to offer in terms of concepts or findings. His lexicon had little use for the concept of "ability" and for the traditional concepts of the experimental psychologist as well. We find him introducing his own terminology, with little attempt to equate it to that of historical consensus. But let us see whether we can derive anything that implies multiple abilities from his concepts on function.

Piaget's general theory is in the category of cognitive psychology, but he pays so much attention to sensorimotor activity, at least in the young child, that he almost qualifies as a behaviorist. In Piaget's conception of cognitive development, the infant begins life in the external environment with bodily structures that have built into them from hereditary sources only a few reflexes, such as sucking, kicking, arm waving, grasping, and looking. It is on the bases of these innate *schemas* that all knowledge is built through functioning. A schema is an organized sensorimotor action sequence. The individual's knowledge (cognitive structure) is generated from functioning of these few hereditary schemas, which readily change by modification to become largely acquired schemas.

There are two important ways of functioning (schema building in the young child), two ways of adapting: assimilation and accommodation. Here Piaget's biology shows. *Assimilation* is by way of analogy to incorporating food into bodily structures. Psychological assimilation is a matter of taking input from sensory inlets and incorporating new elements into the existing structure of knowledge. As with food intake, the new informational stuff must be worked over to make it a part of the existing structure. *Accommodation,* on the other hand, means self-adjustment on the part of the individual, modifying an already-existing structure to make it better adapted to the new additions.

Also in connection with function, Piaget makes considerably more of two other concepts, perhaps because they have more relevance for different stages in development. Assimilation and accommodation the individual has with him always; two other operations are featured in the child with a relative transition from the one to the other. These two kinds of operation are concrete and formal. *Concrete* operations are more characteristic of the typical child under eight. The mental structure in the way of knowledge that he develops stays very close to its sensorimotor origin. Like perception in general, concrete operations are time-bound; they are restricted to a certain natural time order. There is little abstraction in the sense that ideas are formed with separation from objects and events in the "real" world.

Formal operations are more characteristic of adolescents and adults, although no one ever outgrows concrete operations. Piaget makes a great deal of "reversibility" in connection with formal operations. Knowledge of the formal-operation type is not time-bound; it is free to be treated with liberties, even well detached from sensorimotor sequences. To such operations the rules of formal logic apply more freely and more completely. Although formal operations are freed from a sensorimotor context, they develop out of the schemas of childhood. In Piaget's conception, it can be said that thought is internalized action. Even logic shows the consequences of origins of thinking in sensorimotor action. Thus, Piaget's psychological thinking has a very strong motor bias.

Piaget's concern with structure   There is little in the two pairs of Piaget's concepts of assimilation and accommodation and concrete and formal operations to suggest hypotheses in the form of unique or unitary abilities. We shall see later, however, how his concrete and formal operations have by implication some interesting relationships with a number of recognized intellectual abilities in two major categories. They would not be so readily related to test concepts in either the Binet or the Terman lists.

Many of the structural concepts of Piaget have much clearer implied relationships to intellectual abilities. Pointing out such relationships will also have to wait, but we can consider the types of structures of knowledge to which he has given most attention. His studies have been focused upon the development of particular concepts but concepts having some degree of generality. Some of the concepts that have come in for investigation are classes, relations, quantity, number, conservation of quantity, and space. In each case, Piaget asks what the typical child of each age already knows about the concept, how he develops it, and in what order conceptions naturally come. We shall see later that a number of intellectual abilities found by factor analysis have to do with space; others have to do with classes, or with relations, or with numbers. Very few can be found in a clear one-to-one or many-to-one relation with quantity or the conservation of quantity. Some of Piaget's studies have also dealt with more complex mental structures such as hierarchies and lattices, which can be regarded as systems. Quite a number of intellectual factors pertain to abilities for dealing with systems. Thus, from independent sources and methods, some similar conceptions of intellectual functioning have been derived.

Multivariate approach

In considering the multivariate type of approach, we shall give attention first to some of the general characteristics of multivariate experimental methods, in contrast to the more traditional bivariate experimental methods. The major type of outcome from this direction is in the form of factors or, in the context of intelligence, of differentiated, basic, intellectual abilities; consequently some space will be given to the needs for such information as indicated by investigations by other methods and to some criticisms of the factor approach.

Features of multivariate methods   The multivariate methods most pertinent in this discussion are intercorrelation and factor analysis, the needs for which in the search for different basic abilities measured by tests were pointed out in Chapter 1. The usual application is to samples, each of N individuals, each of whom has taken n tests. The empirical data are in the form of a score matrix composed of N rows and n columns of numbers. Within such a matrix of numbers, we look for an underlying order or system, some lawfulness that should represent something psychologically meaningful regarding the individual differences in scores on the tests. In this general statement lie several differences from the traditional type of psychological experiment.

The capitalizing upon individual differences as the source of variance in the data is the most obvious feature. In the traditional bivariate type of experiment, the experimenter applies "treatments" in the form of varying stimulus conditions, or time conditions, or number of exposures, and so on. As is often pointed out, he is interested in S-R dependencies (response R as some function of stimulus S), whereas the factor analyst deals with R-R dependencies, in which scores from different tests are regarded as response variables. One crucial difference that works to the advantage of the multivariate approach is the fact that the investigator can take his individual subjects very much as they come, within a specified population, with relatively less concern regarding how they got that way.

The correlation method is such that it makes little difference what the means and standard deviations of the measurements are in the different variables. In the bivariate experiment, the meat of the findings is in the means and variances. These are affected by numerous conditions prior to the experiment, which means that the experimenter should be aware of the past histories of his subjects if he is to proceed with assurance that only his treatments produce his result. Noble (1961) also emphasizes this point. Only in the case of controlled animal colonies is this ideal, of substantial knowledge of the individual's past, approached.

Conditions for good factor analyses   This is not to say that the multivariate experimentalist can afford to be oblivious of certain experimental conditions. Unfortunately, some who factor-analyze proceed as if no experimental controls were necessary. Unfortunately, it is possible to apply factor analysis to any correlation matrix that comes along. Thurstone repeatedly warned against this practice, as have other writers, with apparently little effect. The journals abound with analyses the outcomes of which have little meaning and are often actually misleading.

A good factor analysis does give attention to two important sources of determination of the results: the selection of the sample of individuals and the selection of experimental variables. It is important that the sample of individuals, for a study of basic traits of personality, which includes intelligence, be fairly uniform in such characteristics as common culture, age, education, sex, and other demographic variables that may influence the correlation coefficients. Such variables should not be disregarded unless it is shown that they have no appreciable influence on intercorrelations.

Where age during childhood is allowed to vary in the sample, for example, since most abilities increase with age and scores are therefore correlated with age, intercorrelations are boosted all along the line. The effect is the appearance of a g factor of the Spearman type. Many a study that seems to support the g hypothesis may have done so because age, education, and sex have not been controlled, as Truman Kelley (1928) pointed out.

The effects of sex may be a little different. Suppose that in one subset of tests boys excel appreciably and in another subset girls excel, while in other tests there is no sex difference. There would be a tendency to generate two factors attributable to sex or one bipolar factor. Not knowing of the confounding with sex, the experimenter might attempt to give psychological interpretation to these extra factors.

On the question of the selection of test variables for a battery, the author has written at length (Guilford & Zimmerman, 1963). The pitfalls of variable sampling were discussed, as were their consequences with regard to analytic versus graphic rotations and orthogonal versus oblique rotations. Here it is important to stress the less technical matter of how to ensure the finding of psychologically significant factors. One of the most serious shortcomings is the failure to include enough tests in the test battery to ensure the separation of all the common factors represented there, as the writer has pointed out before (Guilford, 1952).

An example of this, since there apparently must be a striking illustration to give weight to the point, is an analysis by Corter (1952); there are others. Corter's test battery included 5 tests from Thurstone's PMA battery and 16 other tests, some of which were from a Wechsler scale. The nature of these 21 tests suggests that as many as 15 intellectual-aptitude factors (such as appear in the writer's structure of intellect) are represented. Only 3 factors are represented by 3 tests each, whereas for overdetermination of each factor a minimum of 3 tests is commonly advocated. Another 2 factors were represented by 2 tests each, and the remaining 10 factors by only 1 test each. There could be some excuse for not recognizing that some of the less well-known factors were not adequately represented; there could be no excuse for not representing each of Thurstone's well-known factors by a bare minimum of 2 tests. The same kind of mistake is made again and again by other investigators, using Thurstone's PMA tests singly in a factor-analyzed battery. A consequence in Corter's results was that no single factor could be interpreted in line with previously reported factors. Even the factor that he interpreted as "space" did not have the PMA Space test loaded significantly on it.

Why factors are needed   It would not be necessary to devote any space to the subject of why we need factors in the understanding of intelligence were it not for the fact that some psychologists and others, even a few with influential voices, support the doctrine of one monolithic *intelligence*. Even the followers of Spearman in the belief in a universal *g* factor usually recognize a multivariate view of intelligence. It is not necessary to assemble all the available evidence; even a small sampling should be sufficient, taken together with what is to follow in other chapters. The evidence comes from many directions: the obvious intraindividual differences, the unevenness that appears in normal populations as well as in the mentally deficient, in the highly gifted, and in pathological populations; the differing patterns of differential growth and decline; the low intercorrelations of many tests with IQ-test scores and with one another; the inadequate predictions often found for IQ tests and the differential predictive validities for factor tests; the differential intellectual symptoms found associated with brain injuries and brain insults of other origins; and the need for analytical examination of educational processes when diagnostic steps are required in connection with failure.

Unevenness of ability within persons   Without benefit of high-speed computers and even without correlating scores, Binet and Henri (1896) observed that children were unequally capable, even within the limited area of memory tests. Allowing for score reliabilities that were possibly not high, these observed intraindividual differences were apparently sufficient to lead those investigators to formulate hypotheses concerning five relatively independent memory abilities: visual memory, memory for sentences, memory for musical tones, memory for colors, and memory for digits. With the exception of "memory for musical tones," the hypothesized abilities apparently resemble abilities differentiated by factor analysis (Christal, 1958).

The finding of differentiated factors of intellectual abilities in itself, of course, implies intraindividual differences, with the possibility of describing each person in terms of a profile rather than a single score. Unevenness in profiles is found throughout the range of general intellectual level, from the mentally deficient to the near-genius level. After reviewing numerous studies on subnormality, Sarason and Gladwin (1958) often stressed the point that individuals who test as mentally deficient frequently make surprisingly good social and economic adjustments. They conclude that this may be attributed to the fact that intelligence tests miss abilities that are responsible. One might suggest that some of these missed abilities are in the area of social intelligence, which involves understanding of other individuals and skills in coping with them. That mentally deficient populations at mental ages of two, four, and six show essentially the same differentiation of some abilities as do nondeficient children of the same mental ages has been demonstrated by Meyers, Dingman, Orpet, Sitkei, and Watts (1964).

There are notable examples of unevenness among the highly gifted, as seen in the one-sided geniuses of historical importance. Sándor (1932) studied striking examples of one-sided giftedness, one of whom was the Polish Dr. Finkelstein, who exhibited unusual feats in numerical memory and numerical computation. He could memorize a matrix of numbers 5 × 5 in very short order and a list of 35 digits in one minute, and yet he was only average in his ability to memorize visual figures. Among four such individuals, there was a difference in preferred mode of presentation of numbers for memorizing; some preferred visual presentation, and some auditory.

In an ordinary kind of population, Bloom (1963) found that if we were to define as "gifted" a child who is in the highest 10 percent on any one of Thurstone's PMA tests, as many as 60 percent could be regarded as gifted. If the number of tests were increased to extend the range of intellectual factors involved, the percentage might approach 100, reminding us that where abilities differ in kind and the number is large, almost any child can be "gifted" in something.

Dramatic instances of uneven abilities are also to be seen in the so-called idiot savants. Scheerer, Rothmann, and Goldstein (1945) cite an eleven-year-old boy who stood very high in certain respects and very low in others. He had good musical aptitude, played by ear, and had absolute pitch. He had remarkable memory for words and unusual numerical skills. On the other hand, he had little general information, was lacking in social awareness, and was generally low in verbal tests, with an IQ of 50.

Another instance was reported by Anastasi and Levee (1959), of a young man with an IQ of about 70 on either the Stanford-Binet or the Wechsler-Bellevue scale. He became an accomplished pianist and composer and was a good sight reader of music. He could recite 2½ pages of prose after reading it once, but he could not report ideas from the passage. He did well in reciting lists of digits backward and remembered dates very well. He was especially poor in visual memory and in tests of induction and made a zero score on the Picture Arrangement test. His verbal IQ was 92, but his performance IQ was 52 on the Wechsler scale.

A certain small class of individuals, not recognized as idiot savants, is the autistic group, members of which are notoriously deficient in certain respects but exhibit islands of even superior performance (Rimland, 1964). There is often especially good memory in some respects: for visual objects and for their arrangements in space, for example. One child could reproduce an aria sung in a foreign language on hearing it once. There may be unusually good musical talent, and the child may become an expert at reading aloud, without comprehending anything read. Speech is acquired only in a parrotlike manner, not used as a means of communication. Almost all these drastic hiatuses in special abilities can be logically accounted for in terms of groups of primary mental abilities or factors.

Group differences also appear along factorial lines. In a study of sex differences by means of seven of Thurstone's PMA tests, Hobson (1947) found in large samples from eighth and ninth grades that boys as a group were significantly higher in a test of space cognition, whereas girls were significantly higher in tests of word fluency, reasoning, and memory, with no significant differences in tests of verbal and number abilities. When sex differences in composite scores are sometimes in favor of boys and sometimes in favor of girls or when there is no significant difference, the reason may be a function of the factorial composition of the composite. Comparisons of composite scores often cover genuine sex differences. Using total scores thus loses information.

Unevenness in mental growth and decline   Growth curves commonly presented for intelligence are usually faulty for two reasons. When composite scores are used, the fact that different component abilities grow at different rates is obscured. And when scores from different individuals are averaged, individual differences in rate of growth at different age levels are obscured, whether either a composite or a special-ability score is used. L. L. Thurstone (1955), after applying his absolute scaling procedures to scores from his PMA tests, in order to ensure comparability of scaling for different abilities, plotted a growth curve from age five through age nineteen for each ability. The shapes of the curves were different (see Chapter 17), and the age at which each ability reached maturity appeared to be different in each case.

At the other end of the age scale it is also found that there are differential rates of decline. It is well known among those who have used the Wechsler scales that means in certain tests hold up better with increasing age beyond the ages of forty-five to fifty and that other tests show more rapid declines in normal aging. Trembly (1964b) has reported both growth and decline curves for five of the Johnson O'Connor tests, which, although not offered as factor tests, have relatively low intercorrelations, indicating much factorial independence. The curves, which were based upon very large samples, were distinctly different in shape.

Other studies of mental decline in old age have used tests whose factor content is better known. Bilash and Zubek (1960) used seven tests of the King Factored Aptitude Series with subjects aged sixteen to eighty-nine and found definite indications of differential rates of decline. Schaie, Rosenthal, and Perlman (1953) used the Thurstone PMA tests with subjects aged fifty-three to seventy-eight and found differences in decline curves. Intercorrelations among the tests were very low, ranging from .06 to .31, a condition that gives much room for differential rates of decline. From results such as these, it can be seen that the use of a single, composite score in a decline curves loses a great deal of information. The extension of investigation of decline curves well beyond the limitations of the PMA list of factors would undoubtedly show even more variety in rates and forms of decline.

Correlations of intelligence tests   In Chapter 1, the writer pointed out that there are numerous instances of zero correlations between tests that logically belong in the intellectual category and that a zero correlation between two tests indicates that they have nothing in common. To make this point more strongly here, it can be said that over 7,000 intercorrelations among tests of an intellectual nature were examined (Guilford, 1964c). If any coefficient in the range below $+.10$ is taken as being essentially zero, about 18 percent of the coefficients were in that category. Including only the rs that do not differ from zero significantly at the .05 level, the percentage of zero rs rose to about 24. Whether one accepts the idea of aptitude factors or not, it is still true that if one test of a pair that correlates zero is a measure of intelligence, the other definitely is not. If it is recognized that both tests belong in the category of intelligence, a much simpler interpretation is that both measure different components of intelligence but components that are independent *in the population.* This does not mean that such components are completely isolated in the functioning of the individual.

Having adopted some standard battery of tests as *the* measure of intelligence, one does not have to go far to find that some other tests that seem logically to belong in the intellectual category fail to correlate with that measure of intelligence. Presumably, it would be generally accepted that learning a foreign language is an intellectual enterprise. And yet Carroll (1962) found that a vocabulary test, which is recognized as a good representative of verbal-intelligence scales, did not predict achievement in learning a language at all well, whereas a battery of specially developed language-aptitude tests predicted achievement (in a one-week trial language course) with a multiple correlation of .75. Carroll concluded that facility for learning to speak and understand a foreign language is a fairly specialized talent or group of talents relatively independent of intelligence. There is no need to rule those talents out of intelligence if the latter is amply conceived. In another kind of study, Edwards (1950) found that his test of ability to think critically proved to be relatively independent of an intelligence-test score. A large category of evaluation abilities is now known to exist and has not been heretofore envisaged within the traditional scope of intelligence.

Even composite scores for "general intelligence" obtained from different scales—Stanford-Binet, Otis, Wechsler, California Test of Mental Maturity, American Council on Education Psychological Examination, and Raven's Progressive Matrices test—intercorrelate far from perfectly. Even after correction for attenuation, each correlation would very likely be short of 1.0, which means that although these batteries may overlap in factors sampled, each has something unique about it. And all of them put together undoubtedly fall short of encompassing the whole range of intellectual abilities as we now know them. In this connection one needs only to mention tests of divergent-production abilities (see Chapter 6) or the so-called creativity tests. There are many others of various kinds.

A class of tests that some investigators have taken to be measures of intelligence but which have almost always been found to correlate low, zero, and even slightly negative with IQ tests is the category of infant and preschool tests. Since the same types of tests given later could not be applied to children below the age of two, other kinds of tests had to be brought into use for assessing mental status. These tests can be readily granted the status of "psychological" tests, for they pertain to behavior; but this does not make them intelligence tests. During the first year, for example, the tests are heavily weighted with measures of attention and motor functions. Some obviously different ability factors would be involved in the early-year tests, as Stott and Ball (1963) and others have shown, and this has been suspected by many others (e.g., Bayley, 1955). Other circumstances that probably contribute to the low correlations between preschool tests and school-year tests have been mentioned, such as the effects of emotional reactions to tests at the tenderer ages and changes in environmental features. But the difference in factorial content is probably the strongest determiner.

Prediction of achievement   Binet's original scale was designed for prediction of achievement in school, and the school was at an elementary level. Prediction at that same level remained for many years the main objective in validation of intelligence tests, while the widening specializations more obviously found at the high-school and college levels were very much ignored. The forms of college-aptitude tests have remained very much the same for many years and have shown few departures from the contents of the original intelligence tests, which were designed for children. Failures to predict achievement at the college level have often been hidden by the faulty practice of using grade-point averages as criteria of achievement. Even then, correlations in the .30s are often reported. But for single courses there may be complete failure to predict. The instance of predicting achievement in foreign language (Carroll, 1962) has already been mentioned.

Predictions of achievement in mathematics courses offer other examples. Hills (1957) applied a variety of factor tests, many of which are not represented in common college-aptitude tests, to 23 small classes of mathematics students at upper-division and graduate levels to relate scores with criteria of achievement, including ratings as well as grades. A vocabulary test had no significant correlations, and a numerical-operations test had only 4. Two of the six new factor tests (not ordinarily used in aptitude examinations) had 6 and 10 significant validity coefficients.

At the ninth-grade level Guilford, Hoepfner, and Petersen (1965) used a more extensive list of factor tests and had available also the scores from three standard aptitude batteries (California Test of Mental Maturity, Differential Aptitude Tests, and the Iowa Tests of Basic Skills). In four mathematics courses (two levels of general mathematics and two levels of algebra) it was found that multiple predictions of achievement-test scores were as good (or better) for combinations of factor tests as for the standard tests and that adding the factor tests to the standard tests yielded increased muliple correlations, especially in the algebra courses. Even so, it is likely that this study did not include all the intellectual factors that would be relevant to prediction of achievement in ninth-grade mathematics.

With rare exceptions one should not expect a score for a test of any one factor to show as high predictive validity as could be found for a composite score such as an IQ score. Criteria of achievement in any academic school subject is likely to be factorially complex when achievement is sampled with sufficient breadth. The best use of factor scores is therefore in well-chosen combinations, covering in the composite the most relevant abilities represented in the achievement measures. Shaw (1949) demonstrated this principle when he dealt with predictions of achievement from the six PMA tests at the ninth-grade level, with 13 different criterion measures involved. Whereas the typical validity coefficient for IQ-test scores was found to be .45, the multiple correlations for various combinations of the PMA tests were generally higher. With all six scores combined, the multiple Rs ranged from .45 to .82. Combinations of two to five PMA scores did about as well. There are many more factors and their tests available now, of course, that offer possibilities of adding unique contributions to prediction of achievement.

Prediction of occupational success The fact of the differential success of different kinds of tests in predicting criteria of success in various kinds of work assignments also attests to the need for predictors of various factorial compositions. In their survey of the degrees of prediction to be obtained from different kinds of tests for workers in work assignments such as recording, computing, protection, and personal service and as vehicle operators, repairmen, electrical and machine workers, inspectors, and packer-wrappers, Ghiselli and Brown (1951) found the tests variously predictive. The same test is not equally predictive in all such occupations, and not all tests are equally predictive in the same occupation. The United States Employment Service's General Aptitude Test Battery was designed along factorial lines and in recognition of these principles (Dvorak, 1947), but apparently not much information concerning its differential-predictive properties has been made public.

Perhaps the most outstanding success of vocational prediction with multiple-test batteries was in connection with the selection and classification of aircrew personnel in the Army Air Forces during World War II, and this prediction has continued successfully since. By using 20 different scores, which represented perhaps half that many factors, most of them in the intellectual category, it was found that one combination of scores with unique weights would predict best in pilot training, another combination in navigator training, and still others in bombardier and in flight-engineer training. It was possible to account for the good prediction obtainable in each case in terms of common factors shared by training criterion and the collection of tests and to account for the differences in predictive batteries on the rational basis of underlying abilities (Guilford, 1948).

Studies of brain functions Throughout the history of psychology and even before, there has been considerable interest in relations between psychological functioning and the brain. Nowhere has a need for a good taxonomy of abilities been more apparent. The use of single composite scores from intelligence scales has told investigators very little except that there is or is not a difference in mean scores with a change in brain condition. The working of the brain was never conceived in the nature of more or less of one unitary function. The great number of intricate structures and their organizations have always been suggestive of multiple types of function; yet a single intelligence score has had considerable use in brain research.

As long as twenty-five years ago, Lashley (1941) pointed out that whereas local brain lesions seemed to have little correlation with stimulus-response variables of classical psychology, they might show better correspondence with unitary behavioral parameters that come out of factor analysis. Herman Harvey (1950) was one of the first to follow up the implications of Lashley's suggestion in a systematic way. He pointed out that failure to find differences between means of test scores from brain-damaged and normal subjects might be due to the confounding of factor variables in the tests that were used to assess psychological deficit. Still later, de Mille (1962) demonstrated that tests designed along the lines of factors were more sensitive to differences between lobotomized and non-lobotomized paranoid schizophrenics than were tests of the traditional types, as represented by the Wechsler scales.

After an extensive review of studies in which tests were used to determine the nature of mental defect associated with brain damage, Haynes and Sells (1963) ended with a plea for a multivariate approach to the problem. Orbach (1959) had earlier expressed a similar view. In the report of a study of effects of topectomy (removal of frontal-lobe cortex area), A. Smith and E. F. Kinder (1959) concluded that intellectual loss is clearly dependent upon the kind of test used.

Years ago, Halstead (1947) concluded that the best approach to the measurement of mental deficit in connection with types of brain damage was to use factor tests. He proceeded to perform his own analysis, which although it did not yield factors in line with those usually accepted in the domain of intelligence, provided him with tests whereby differential losses of function could be investigated (Shure & Halstead, 1958). Reitan and his associates (Matthews, Guertin, & Reitan, 1962; Matthews & Reitan, 1964) have used the parts of the Wechsler adult scale to good effect in studies of hemisphere functions and in comparing different pathological groups.

The use of special tests in studies of brain disorders works both ways. If the practice gives the brain investigator more information and better insights, the finding of special symptoms of intellectual weakness also provides the multivariate psychologist with hypotheses as to what possible new differentiable abilities he might investigate. For example, the wealth of observations of Kurt Goldstein (1948) are very suggestive, and it is relatively easy for the psychologist who knows the intellectual factors to see where they probably apply. Such parallels provide the hope for finding new hypotheses as well as a kind of construct-validity information with regard to factor concepts.

Nowhere is the possibility of one-to-one connection between symptom and factor clearer than in the area of agnosias and aphasias, as Elmgren (1958) has pointed out. Such correspondences will be discussed in Chapter 15. Critchley's book on the temporal lobes (1953) is rich with accounts of symptoms that are suggestive of certain factors of intelligence. It is true that observations in recent years have thrown some doubt upon the neat classificatory schemes for agnosias and aphasias. It is also true that two factor analyses involving test scores and symptoms have failed to support the classical forms of these disorders (L. V. Jones & J. M. Wepman, 1961; Schuell, Jenkins, & Carroll, 1962) and have also failed to reveal intellectual factors such as are usually found in tests. The two analyses in question must be regarded as faulty, however, the latter for lack of hypotheses about factors, the former for the wrong kind of hypotheses, and both for inadequate selection of experimental variables. It is the writer's opinion that new factor analyses are not so much needed at this stage of investigation of the agnosias and aphasias as experiments relating symptoms to already-known intellectual factors.

There is a definite place for factor analysis in studies of brain disorders for a somewhat different purpose, as suggested by de Mille (1962). He pointed out that when one applies the same tests to different pathological groups and to normals in order to compare means and variances, it may be well to question whether each test measures the same ability in the groups being compared. His two populations were composed of paranoid schizophrenics who had been lobotomized and those who had not, his samples being matched in other respects. The tests on which he wanted to compare them were factor-analyzed in a larger battery that included enough tests of each factor to determine its role in his tests, in the two populations separately. If a test does not measure the same underlying variable in two populations, there is little point in finding a difference between the means derived from samples from those populations. To do so would be like subtracting temperature from body weight, if comparable scaling for the two variables were assumed, and the difference would be as meaningful. Most of the tests came out with major loadings on the same factors for which they were intended and as found in normal samples, but there were one or two discrepancies that rendered comparison of means somewhat dubious.

Studies of heredity   The investigation of the relative effects of heredity versus environment upon the development of mental ability has had persistent interest. After reviewing the many conflicting results and conclusions up to 1940, Harold E. Jones issued a call for more basic theory and information on intelligence and its components and on the many influences in the environment that should be recognized. Too little attention has been paid to the influential variables in the environment as well as to intellectual components. Jones thought that each of the environmental and intellectual variables should in turn be considered in studies of heredity. A little later, Mandel Sherman asserted that most investigators believe that inherited aspects of intelligence are not a unit character but a complex affair (1945, p. 246). They have not particularly shown this conviction, if it does exist, for in a review of 52 studies involving the intercorrelations of test scores of children and adults in 99 groups, it was found that two-thirds of the investigators used IQ tests and the others used special tests, including some who used factor tests.

To show how it may be highly misleading to use any one test, simple or not, to stand for intelligence in the study of heredity, the classical study of Tryon (1929) may be cited. Tryon bred selected rats who were "bright" or "dull," respectively, in terms of performance in maze learning, in order to see whether extreme strains could be developed. In terms of maze running, two extreme groups were developed, and the two strains have been kept apart for further experiments over the years. Twenty years later, Searle (1949), tested 10 from each strain and 15 typical rats in several tasks as well as maze running. He found no evidence that there was any generalization of ability to perform in the other tasks, which included an elevated maze, two other mazes, and discrimination learning. Major differences noted in the descendants of the two strains were in motivational and emotional rather than intellectual traits. The indication is that Tryon's maze test may have been emphasizing some rather special ability not indicated by other tests that might have been used and that his selection was inadvertently achieving some hereditary differences that were not intended.

Using a number of special aptitude tests, Stafford (1961; 1963) has been intercorrelating all possible pairings of parent and child in each test in order to find answers regarding, by inference, the relation of abilities to genes and to sex linkage. With special tests such refinements are possible. In studies of twins, Vandenberg (no date) has been using PMA tests in a novel experimental design, from which he concludes that heredity is a determining source in connection with certain abilities and not with others.

Factors and education In her very insightful book on special talents and defects, Leta S. Hollingworth (1923) presented conclusions from long study of special strengths and weaknesses as she saw them in children taking various school subjects. The special talents and weaknesses that she noted were observable by virtue of the fact that many children could have one of the talents alongside a weakness, such as being an excellent reader and a very poor speller; or, within the subject of reading, being able to read the printed page fluently and yet not know what was said; or, in arithmetic, being able to compute rapidly and accurately and yet be unable to solve arithmetical problems. As one goes through her lists of talents and defects, one can clearly see their logical relationships to intellectual factors found in recent years. Her book would have been a gold mine of hypotheses for the factor analysts had it been better known.

A more recent example is a survey of special abilities believed to underlie reading disabilities in college students (Holmes, 1954). Here, also, the list is strongly reminiscent of factor concepts that we shall meet later.

In psychopathology It has long been known that in most psychoses there is some degree of intellectual impairment and that the impairment takes different directions somewhat characteristically in different categories of pathology. The coming of special tests of an intellectual nature, from Kraepelin to the Wechsler adult scale, has made possible studies of differential impairments. The use of factor tests in this connection does not seem to have caught on much as yet, except as the Wechsler tests approach factorial salience. An exception, mentioned before, was de Mille (1962), who found factor tests revealing more decisive differences between lobotomized and nonlobotomized schizophrenics than did the Wechsler tests. The comparison was not quite fair to the Wechsler tests, since the sample for the factor tests was larger and the two groups had been matched on the Wechsler total IQ. It should be noted, however, that differences were found in tests for factors not in the Wechsler scale, thus showing that the survey of possible differences can be considerably extended when new kinds of tests are used.

In studying differences between paranoid schizophrenics and normals in verbal-intellectual status, Moran (1953) matched two groups on the Wechsler Vocabulary score, age, and education and administered a variety of verbal-ability tests. The tests were not described in factorial terms, but one can discern the probable roles of several verbal factors in those tests. There were a number of significant differences in these special tests, even when the two groups were matched for the factor of verbal comprehension (on the Wechsler Vocabulary test).

It has sometimes been noted that schizophrenics seem deficient in ability to understand other people. No standard intelligence test covers what may well be called the ability of social cognition, unless there be some of this kind of ability represented in the Davis-Eells Games or in the Wechsler Picture Arrangement test. Vandenberg (1962) tested the hypothesis in question by administering a special test of "social understanding," involving the recognition of expressions in photographs of faces by choosing one of two names of expressions in each item. In comparing two groups, 37 schizophrenics and 14 nonschizophrenic patients, on this test, he found the schizophrenics significantly lower. The paranoids tended to do better than the rest of their group. Factor analysis shows social cognition to involve abilities quite differentiated from other intellectual factors of intelligence (O'Sullivan, Guilford, & de Mille, 1965).

Experiments on drugs In recent years we have seen a new surge of interest in the effects of drugs on mental functioning in studies under the general heading of psychopharmacology. Where intellectual aspects of functioning are involved, again, it is believed that factor tests will be found to be the most informative instruments. In discussing the possible finding of drugs that might facilitate mental growth (having in mind the remarkable benefits of thyroid treatment in the case of cretinism), Goodenough (1940) pointed out the need of understanding the basic components of intelligence. Harvey Nash (1962) has paid attention to this principle in his studies of effects of alcohol and caffeine. Evans and Smith (1964) have also taken this route in studies of effects of *d*-amphetamine and morphine sulphate. In both instances, certain differential effects were observed. There is no known chemical correlate for any of the intellectual factors as yet, but chemical theories are looming in connection with one class of these factors, in the attempts to relate memory to the RNA molecule. Other affiliations are not beyond the range of possibilities.

Advantages of the factor approach

We have just seen by incidental references some of the points at which the use of factor tests can be advantageous. Let us now generalize somewhat and also consider the advantages of using factor concepts.

Economy in number of variables   The advantage of economy in number of variables has been almost universally recognized. There are hundreds of tests, all with claims to membership in the category of "intellectual," but only approximately eighty factors of intelligence known at the time this was written and at least one hundred and twenty predicted by the structure-of-intellect theory as now constituted. Wechsler is among those who recognize that an aim of factor analysis is ". . . to account for the major variance of a large battery of tests in terms of a minimal number of primary abilities or factors" (1958, p. 128). He spoils it all by saying immediately: "There seem to be more factors than available tests." The two statements are obviously inconsistent. Wechsler does qualify the second statement by adding: ". . . certainly than good tests of intelligence."

If Wechsler had in mind his own scales when he said "good tests of intelligence," he is definitely right; there are more factors than tests, even far more intellectual factors. His adult scale very likely represents about as many factors as tests, although not entirely on a one-to-one basis. The numerous factor analyses of his scale tests by themselves have been entirely erroneous if the aim was to find out how many and what basic intellectual abilities are represented. It is impossible to solve for as many factors as there are tests. The only adequate way of analyzing the Wechsler-scale tests is to add to the analyzed battery about twice as many marker tests as there are common factors represented in the scale. The only suitable analysis that has been made of the Wechsler tests, to the knowledge of the writer, was that of P. C. Davis (1956), the results of which support the statement made above, that there are about as many factors as tests in the Wechsler scales.

Wechsler's apparent distaste for numerous factors of intelligence seems to rest on a misapprehension. He presents (1958, p. 128) two propositions: (1) with a few factors, each factor accounts for large proportions of variances; and (2) with many factors, each accounts for 1 to 3 percent. From these propositions he draws the conclusion that numerous factors would be of little or no importance. There is a confusion here in the base of the argument. If all the intellectual factors were by some miracle represented in the same test and equally so, the proportion of the common-factor variance attributable to each factor would indeed be exceedingly small. But what would this have to do with the general importance of each factor? There are particular tests in each of which a factor can represent as much as 60 percent (let's face it, such tests are very rare and hard to achieve), and there are particular activities in the laboratory and in daily life in which the factor may also be all-important. The frequency with which those activities arise may even be limited; yet when they do arise, outcomes may be vital. To a basic scientist, one factor is just as important as another, as a scientifically elicited finding. As a scientist, he should not be concerned about social or other criteria of value; such evaluations belong to technology, not to science.

Resistance to the fact of numerous intellectual factors is sometimes expressed in another way. It is pointed out that additional factors come about by the splitting of already-known ones. One implication is that there is no end to splitting, and another implication is that the splinters cannot be of much consequence. The conception of "splitting" is erroneous; things only sometimes look that way. What has usually happened is that early attempts at analysis did not represent all the factors adequately, as in the analysis of the Wechsler-scale tests. Put additional (marker) tests in the analyzed battery with the Wechsler tests, and it will be found that the verbal tests go off in different directions along with selected marker tests to form new groupings to indicate other factors of narrower scope. The verbal "factor" that appears to "split" is simply a confounding of a number of basic factors. When do we know that we have found a basic factor and that there will be no further splitting? When we reach the point where the list of tests representing a factor persists in hanging together on a factor in spite of efforts to differentiate among them. While recognizing that apparent splitting (of confounded factors) often appears, the writer can cite many instances in which what are believed to be basic factors refuse to split when given ample inducement to do so.

Increased amount of information   In several places in earlier discussion of the employment of tests the point was made that the use of composite scores loses information where such information might be especially helpful. This point was mentioned in connection with the derivation of growth curves and curves of decline of mental ability. It was mentioned also in connection with comparisons of populations, as in studies of sex differences and pathological groups. In later chapters, it will be emphasized repeatedly that the concept of information plays a very important role in connection with all intellectual factors. *Information* is defined as that which an organism discriminates. Making new discriminations means that we have achieved new information. For certain technological purposes, it may well be unnecessary to make certain discriminations: the problem does not call for them.

But a scientist usually is, and certainly should be, if he merits that label, concerned with achieving new information, new discriminations. He never knows but what the next discrimination he makes may be of great significance. How many times has some whole new field of investigation opened up because someone in physics or biology or astronomy detected an unusual trace of some kind on a photographic film or in a microscope or a telescope which turned out to be of foremost importance? The history of science has been the story of man's making finer and finer discriminations. To turn one's back on new discriminations because they make life more complicated is to deny the desire for scientific progress. If the new discriminations cannot be replicated or if the implications from them prove not to be important, that will be found out sooner or later.

On a more workaday level, the question of ambiguity of information can be raised. For purposes of communication and of prediction of behavior and also in the operations of applying treatment, we need univocal or unambiguous information; otherwise someone is misled or someone is self-deceived, or both, and predictions are off the mark when they need not be. Let us assume the case, not unusual, in which a certain test measures factors

A and *B* equally strongly. Person K makes a score moderately above average in the test. Such an outcome could actually represent a great many combinations of positions on the scales of factors *A* and *B*. K might be at the very top in *A* and below average in *B*, or vice versa, or he might be equally high in the two factors. If our advice to K rests critically upon his having very high status in factor *B*, we would lead him seriously astray if his test score really stands for a below-average status on factor *B*. The same principles apply whether we are talking about two factors or about any two other variables that are relatively independent in the population.

Broad versus narrow view of intelligence   As suggested earlier, numerous tests have been found that correlate close to zero with scores from composite intelligence scales. Such tests may well successfully lay claim to the label of "tests of intellectual qualities." By tradition, certain kinds of tests have been favored in intelligence scales. Unfortunately, Boring was right in another sense when he said that intelligence is what intelligence tests test. With the adoption of component tests of intelligence scales, the concept of intelligence became circumscribed within the limits of such collections of tests.

In spite of the fact that scales have included quite a variety of tests, for which we owe thanks to Binet, the variety has still not been wide enough to encompass the ranges of intellectual abilities as we know them today. The writer's inspection of the most recent revision of the Stanford-Binet, Form L-M, suggests that among the 140 single tests, including the alternates, some twenty-eight of the intellectual factors are represented, each by at least 1 test, as compared with about eighty that are regarded as known and more than one hundred that are probable when all are known. The most notable group of factors that have been missed in all intelligence scales consists of the divergent-production abilities, of which 24 are represented in the structure-of-intellect model and 16 have been demonstrated by means of tests. History shows many examples in which too restricted views of an area of investigation have hampered progress. It is doubtful that views that are too broad have ever done so.

Factors provide a frame of reference   We come to what is probably the most important feature that factors have to offer: *frames of reference*. Let us see what a frame of reference means and what it can do for an investigator or a user of the fruits of science.

The meaning of factors   Before speaking about frames of reference with the implication that they have psychological significance, it is desirable to say something about the psychological significance of the factors from which frames of reference are constructed. It should be remembered that the term *factor* is used in a double sense, at least. There is the mathematical factor that is extracted from intercorrelations and that helps to represent those intercorrelaions in a shorthand manner. After an analysis, we have the correlations of *n* tests with *k* factors, where *k* is less than *n*, whereas we previously had a much larger matrix of intercorrelations of *n* tests with one another. From the recognized properties of the tests that are strongly correlated with a mathematical factor, in distinction from the properties of tests *not* correlated with the factor, the investigator intuitively extracts an idea as to what psychological variable may be represented by the mathematical factor. That psychological variable is the psychological factor. It is a genotype, whereas the mathematical factor is a phenotype. It is an intervening variable, conceived by the investigator, and has a status like that of *drive* and *habit*, which are also inferred from observed data. An investigator can be mistaken. But this is no more true, in principle, of the one who factor-analyzes than it is of any other kind of investigator. The support for the investigator's intuition is empirical replication of his results or the finding of other empirical evidence that points toward the same conception of a genotype.

Stability of intellectual factors   Replicated results in factor analysis have two useful functions. One is that duplicated findings, in extracting information from data, convince us that something other than chance is operating to produce the results. The other is that a concept that is derived from the results stands for something in a stable manner and therefore lays claim to dependability and potential usefulness.

Under appropriate conditions, there is considerable stability or constancy of factors and factor loadings in tests that represent them. The most favorable condition for demonstrating invariance of factor loadings relating certain tests to certain factors is to analyze exactly the same test battery in a different sample from the same population.[1] Such replications were applied in repeated analysis of the United States Army Air Forces Aircrew Classification battery during and after World War II. Even when extra tests were added to the analyzed battery and when some substitutions of factor tests were made from one period to another, duplications of factorial results were very good, as reported by Guilford (1948) and Zachert and Friedman (1953).

There are three other examples in each of which the same test battery was analyzed with a slight change of population. In a battery composed mainly of divergent-production tests, in four samples of ninth-grade boys and girls, 11 intellectual factors were identifiable as being the same, with some differences in tests that represented them best, and 1 factor that appeared for the boys' sample but not in the girls' (Guilford et al., 1961). In another such battery, emphasizing other divergent-production factors, 12 intellectual factors were identified as the same in a sample of ninth-grade students and a sample of male adults, with a thirteenth found only in the ninth-grade sample (Gershon, Guilford, & Merrifield, 1963). In the study of prediction of achievement in ninth-grade mathematics, referred to earlier, a battery of 25 tests was first analyzed in two groups, those taking general mathematics and those taking algebra (Petersen, Guilford, Hoepfner, & Merrifield, 1963). The same 13 intellectual factors were found, but the loadings differed sufficiently to lead to the selection of some different tests to represent some of the factors in the multiple-regression studies.

The general conclusion from these illustrations is that if populations are much the same in age, in amount of education, and in culture, one can expect to identify the same psychological factors, with some variations in the way in which different tests represent them. The most extensive support for this conclusion is to be found in John W. French's monograph (1951), in which he has assembled the factor-analytic studies up to that time, drawn from many authors, many different batteries, and somewhat different populations. French could conclude that there were multiple supports for most of 45 different factors, 19 of which can be considered to be intellectual, 7 perceptual, 7 psychomotor, 20 other psychological, including personality traits other than aptitudes and achievement in certain areas, and 2 nonpsychological, e.g., chronological age.

The question often arises about the existence of factors to be found alike in different populations with different cultures. There is suspicion that the poser of this question may be a strong believer in the hereditary determination of all intellectual abilities and hence expects to find the same factors in all human populations, if they represent genuine abilities. If he did not find this to be the case, he would regard factor analysis to be dis-

---

[1] Also presupposed are appropriate procedures in rotations of axes in a factor-analytic solution. There is not space to go into the issues on rotation methods here. For a treatment of the issues, see Guilford and Zimmerman (1963).

credited as a method. Now the result of an ordinary (R) factor analysis by itself tells us nothing about how psychological factors came about in a population; they could be determined entirely by heredity, entirely by environmental influences, or by some combination of both. They could, in fact, be heavily determined by the culture in which the individuals have lived. In the last-named case, some factors might be evident in one culture and not in another. This fact would in no way discredit factor analysis but would extend its usefulness in comparing cultures.

Some evidence of the effects of variation in culture can be found in several analyses with much the same test battery. Frank J. Dudek (1948; 1949) analyzed the USAAF Aircrew Classification battery with a group of WASPs (Women's Auxiliary Service Pilots) who were in flying training. The obvious population difference was sex membership. Another was that all the women pilots had had some flying training before taking the tests. The men had been preselected on a qualifying examination in which about 50 percent usually failed; the WASPs had not taken the qualifying examination, but of women like them who had taken it, about 30 percent had failed.

The results showed that five factors were common to the two populations in the battery of tests in question. A notable difference was that male pilot students always showed a mechanical-knowledge factor but that the women showed none. This was clearly attributable to the fact that the women's mean and variance in scores in the mechanical-knowledge tests were distinctly lower than those for men. Female culture does not introduce variance with respect to mechanical knowledge that boys gain to different degrees. There must be substantial variance in a factor in a population if it is to be evident in the analysis. While there were some differences in factor loadings in the two populations, Dudek concluded that this was likely to be true for tests that more nearly approach purity for a factor.

Using the same classification battery, Michael (1949) carried out analyses in connection with West Point Army cadets and with a group of Negro pilot trainees in the Air Force. Less invariance of factors and their loadings might have been expected, for of the 15 printed tests in the battery, 8 had been replaced by new ones. These were mostly new forms for the same factors, however, and the 6 psychomotor tests were the same. The most notable difference was a factor identified as "kinesthetic sensitivity" for the Negro students that did not appear for the West Point cadets. This factor was prominent in one test in which it was important for the examinee to keep his balance by making quick readjustive movements. The well-known verbal and numerical factors came out confounded for the Negroes, refusing to separate, which might indicate a wider range of educational achievement in that population. Thus, such striking differences between populations can often be accounted for by reference to cultural circumstances.

In a more drastic variation of cultural milieu in populations, Vandenberg (1959) administered 20 of the 57 tests that Thurstone (1938a) had used in his first major study of primary mental abilities to students who had grown up in China and were studying in several universities in the United States. To this battery were added 4 tests translated into Chinese. Rotations were made to see how close the factor structure in the Chinese sample came to that found by Thurstone for the same tests. Of seven interpretable factors, five were very congruent with Thurstone's corresponding factors. One was a factor based mostly on the Chinese tests, and one was some kind of reasoning, not clearly indicated. There were indications that the verbal factor, in particular, was dependent upon culture, in that tests for that factor correlated with several indices of acculturation.

An even more extensive study was made by G. M. Guthrie (1963) with a sample of Philippine women college students whose native language had been Tagalog in most cases but whose education had been in English. He used many tests from the Educational Testing Service's standard factor battery, which is made up of tests that have fairly well-established factorial content from analyses in the United States. Different forms of a few of the verbal tests were also given in the Tagalog dialect. Fifteen of the twenty-two factors extracted and rotated can be identified with factors obtained from the same tests in the United States. There was a strong factor of verbal comprehension in Tagalog, separate from the usual verbal-comprehension factor that is marked most strongly by an English-vocabulary test. The English-verbal-comprehension factor was loaded .35 for grade-point average, interestingly, because instruction was in that language. There was some suggestion of two word-fluency factors, one for each language. There were a few uninterpretable factors, but that would probably have been true had the same battery been given to native English-speaking subjects. Again, there are not many cultural differences in factor structure where all groups are tested in the same language, and such differences as occur can be accounted for in terms of cultural variables.

Stability of profiles of factor scores An implication of multiple measurement of individuals is that profiles of scores rather than composite scores should be used to describe them quantitatively. There is some appropriate concern about how stable an individual's profile is from one time to another. Leona E. Tyler (1958) investigated this problem with respect to four Thurstone PMA tests, comparing the same children's scores obtained when they were in grades 1 and 4 in one group and in grades 4 and 8 in another group. There was some risk in making these comparisons because the form of the test battery had to be changed from one age to the next. But to the extent that the factorial composition of each test for a factor is fairly consistent from one age to the next, some useful information should be forthcoming.

The correlations for single test and retest scores were only moderate. Between grades 1 and 4 and between grades 4 and 8 they were:

Grades 1 and 4			*Grades 4 and 8*
Verbal	.48	.65	Verbal
Number	.42	.82	Number
Space	.51	.41	Space
Perceptual	.53	.65	Reasoning

These correlations are essentially retest reliability coefficients, but with alternate forms, after an interval of about three years in the one case and four years in the other. But this information does not tell us about the stability of *profiles*. This is a matter of *intra*individual differences. For this purpose, Tyler determined each child's IQ on his total score and something equivalent to an IQ on each of the four tests for that child. The children were then scored in terms of their deviations from their own total IQs, and each was given a plus rating if he was 5 or more points above his total IQ in the test, minus if he was 5 or more points below his total IQ, and equal if between those limits. Having placed the children in 3 deviation categories at the first-grade level and also at the fourth-grade level, she set up a contingency table 3×3 (3 rows for first grade and 3 columns for fourth grade) and computed a chi square. There were thus four chi squares for the four tests in the 1-4 comparisons, one for each test, and four in the 4-8 comparisons. Only the chi square for the Verbal test was significant in the 1-4 comparisons, but in the 4-8 comparisons chi squares for the Verbal and Number tests were significant at the .01 level, that for the Space test was significant at the .02 level, and that for the Reasoning test was not significant.

Several conditions work against evidence of uniformly good stability of profiles. Intra-individual differences are expressed essentially in difference scores, in each case a difference between a factor score and the mean of all the others. In Chapter 1, it was pointed out that difference scores can be very unreliable unless the correlation between the two terms for which the difference is obtained is very low and both terms are very highly reliable. The reliabilities of the single PMA test scores were probably not so very high, and there would necessarily be a substantial correlation between a part and the total of four scores, of which the part is a component, in addition to some correlation among the parts themselves, in spite of their representing mainly four different factors. Thus, the correlations of unreliable deviations should not be expected to be strong. From another point of view, logically one should not expect near-perfect stability of profiles even under perfect measurement conditions, for there are individual differences in rates of growth in the different factors.

One should expect some stability of pattern in each person's unevenness in a list of intellectual factors, however. Tyler did find some significant stability in going from grade 4 to grade 8. W. J. Meyer (1960) made a similar type of study with samples from grades 8 and 11, with a 3.5-year interval, using the same form of the Thurstone PMA tests. The retest reliabilities of the test scores ran a little higher: .81, .73, .66, .75, and .43, for the tests Verbal, Numerical, Spatial, Reasoning, and Word Fluency, respectively. Applying the same kind of chi-square test of intraindividual differences for each test, Meyer found all correlations to be significant at the .001 level. How much to attribute this increased stability to age and how much to the use of the same form of PMA tests are not known.

The psychological nature of intellectual factors

A good frame of reference, for a scientist or a technologist who is concerned with tests, should have some general psychological significance beyond a mere collection of aptitude variables. Too often, if the technologist finds his tests work, that is sufficient for his purposes. He may be a confirmed pragmatist, not concerned with theory. But it is theory that gives meaning and significance to what one is doing. The basic scientist, of course, cannot so well insulate himself from theory.

People do sometimes ask: "What sort of thing is a psychological factor, anyway?" This is an encouraging sign. There is no univocal answer, but there are some helpful suggestions that can be offered. As a factor is demonstrated, by virtue of a small cluster of tests that share the factor in common, it is conceived to be an underlying, latent variable along which individuals differ, just as they differ along a test scale on which there are various numerical values. Test scales along which individuals differ are manifest variables. We can observe the test, and we can observe the set of scores for a sample of individuals. We cannot observe the factor, and we cannot observe the positions of individuals along the scale of the factor; but we can estimate factor scores, and we sometimes do.

Factors and functions   But what do the factor scores mean? Whereas observed scores from a test indicate how well individuals do in taking the test, factor scores indicate how much of a certain attribute individuals have. What is that attribute? The test may present a list of figures with the instruction that the examinee is to memorize them so that later he can show that he does remember them by drawing them or by recognizing them when they are mixed with figures not in the memorized list. In this example it is reasonable to say that if the score is high, the person has good visual memory; if low, poor visual memory. It happens that there is a known factor of visual memory. In this example, the association of latent with manifest content is quite clear.

In other instances the association is not so direct or so clear. For example, suppose we give a test composed of items like the following. Which of these letter combinations does not belong with the rest?

PXNO   VRIM   AQES   GUVC
  1   2   3   4

It is combination number 3, because it contains two vowels, whereas the others each contain one. If you were to ask almost any psychologist what ability such a test measures, he is likely to be ready with a suggestion. It measures abstracting ability, inductive-reasoning ability, discrimination ability, and so on. These suggestions are all hypotheses, nothing more. Furthermore, they are untested hypotheses. Too often an investigator or other test user, having adopted a hypothetical ability for a test, sticks with it and draws deductions from results with it, forgetting his flimsy theoretical foundation, if it can be called a foundation.

It is only by correlating this letter-combination test with other tests that we can test any hypothesis as to what it measures psychologically. It would be found that this test correlates substantially with at least two others but low with almost everything else. One with which it would correlate is called Number-Group Naming, with items like:

What do these numbers have in common: 15, 110, 85

to which the answer is "multiples of 5." Another test with which both of these would correlate substantially is the Number-Relations Test, with items like:

Which pair of numbers does not belong with the rest:
A. 2-6   B. 3-9   C. 4-12   D. 6-15

The answer is D, because in all other pairs the relation is that the second number is three times the first.

By now it should be clear that the thing that these tests require in common is the cognition of classes. In the first and third tests, it happens that one has to see a class applying to three members, of letter combinations in the one case and number relations in the other, excluding the fourth member that does not belong to the class. In the second test, one indicates that he knows the class by naming it. How much farther does the ability go? Does it apply to classes of all kinds, including classes of figures and classes of meaningful objects? This question can be answered only by including in the factor analysis also some similar tests with figural and meaningful elements, to see whether those tests go along with these letter and number tests or whether they determine separate factors.

It can be reported that they do not; there are three different factors for cognition of classes, for the three kinds of information. Will number and letter tests of these kinds separate if we have enough of both kinds in the analysis? Thus far they have not; quite commonly, number and letter tests are almost interchangeable in tests of the same factor. The inference is that in considering these two varieties of information we really have only one kind, which has been recognized as "symbolic" information.

In our search for the meaning of aptitude factors, we can take one more easy but very significant step, for it ties factors (properly isolated) to psychological theory. This step is to say that such a factor is also a psychological function. If people are found to differ from one another with respect to visual-memory ability, they must have in their repertoire of functioning a process of remembering figures. If they differ along a continuum of ability to cognize symbolic classes, they function in a way that can be identified as cognizing symbolic classes. It is readily granted that there are other ways than factor analysis of arriving at conceptions of particular psychological functions. The history of psychology is of course filled with instances. Taxonomy of functions has always been recognized as a legitimate and necessary task of the theoretical psychologist. But probably no single research method ever devised is better suited than factor analysis, properly used, to the task of answering psychology's taxonomic questions.

Ferguson's transfer theory of factors   If we grant that aptitude factors have scientific status and that they pertain to isolable psychological functions, how do they come about within individuals? Full answers (and the plural is required here) will call for the most exacting studies of hereditary and environmental conditions that can possibly make contributions. We have one significant theory that suggests how environmental influences make their contributions, offered by George A. Ferguson (1954; 1956).

First of all, Ferguson regards learning as the acquisition of abilities. All learning generalizes somewhat; transfer is the rule, not the exception. Thus, abilities are generalized, and the generalized effects become relatively stable because of overlearning. The individual thus develops status in each generalized ability approaching his asymptote for performances in that particular class of activities. The asymptote is a limit set by heredity and maturation.

Transfers take place within limits, which set the boundaries for the factors. The culture within which the individual develops largely determines what he shall learn and what transfers will occur; hence culture has much to do with what the factors will be. Transfers are differential, but on this point Ferguson is not very explicit. He cites the instance of development of the number factor, which comes from practicing number combinations. It is a good example for his theory, but elsewhere it is more difficult to see how factors become so thoroughly circumscribed. The theory developed in the chapters to follow will help to show how this may be. Ferguson's theory seems to be in the right direction.

Relation of practice to particular factors   One line of evidence that supports the theory is from experiments on the effects of certain kinds of training upon certain factors. An obvious deduction from the theory is that practice in exercises similar in the activities involved to tests that measure the factor should yield increases in scores in those tests. An example is a study by Blade and Watson (1955) on the effects of taking certain engineering courses upon the factor of visualization. They found that whereas engineering students during the first year increased their mean score in a visualization test to the extent of 1 standard deviation, nonengineering students had an increase of ½ standard deviation, giving a difference with a t ratio of 6.38. They found that higher initial scores were associated with mechanical hobbies and mechanical-drawing courses during high school. The initial and final scores in the visualization test correlated .28 and .37, respectively, with grades in the course in engineering drawing and .46 and .52 with grades in descriptive geometry. It is interesting that the final scores in each case correlated a little higher than the initial scores, suggesting that, at the end, the courses had brought the students closer to their respective asymptotes for the visualization factor.

More recently, Heinonen (1962) asked the question whether practice designed to improve status in a certain factor would have transfer effects to performance in tests of two other factors. He gave pretests and posttests for three psychomotor factors. One of the tests was chosen as the practice task. He factor-analyzed both pretest and posttest batteries of 16 tests. His significant finding was that gains in the different tests were negatively related to the angular separations of their vectors from that of the practice test, in the common-factor space, which means the more there was in common in terms of factors between a test and the practice test, the more transfer was apparent. This might suggest that if practice is in a test for a single factor, transfer is relatively limited within the area of performance related to that one factor. There is other scattered evidence that this principle applies. In a number of studies designed to increase the level of creative-thinking performance, where the emphasis is on cleverness or originality, there is likely to be improvement on tests of originality but not on tests of some other factors (see Chapter 14).

Factors and comprehensive psychological theory   Not the least feature of attractiveness of intellectual factors as a frame of reference is the fact that since they have been organized in a single, unitary system—the structure of intellect—considerably more significance can be attached to them. The next chapters will be devoted to an exposition of the system, with supporting evidence, and of the way in which its concepts can account for a great range of common psychological phenomena. There is considerable meshing of findings from factor analysis with those from experimental psychology and other sources.

Summary

The major approaches to the understanding of intelligence have been through experimental psychology, genetic investigations, and multivariate methods, particularly factor analysis.

Experimental psychologists originally contributed numerous tests of considerable variety upon which Binet and others drew for their test batteries. Through the years experimental psychology has continued to investigate problems of perception, cognition, learning, memory, and problem solving, all of which have direct relevance to the understanding of intelligence, but the outcomes have had little use by mental testers. On the other hand, experimental psychologists could have utilized considerable assistance from factor analysts, who have had much to offer in the way of empirically based, taxonomic concepts.

From the genetic point of view, the most useful information about the nature of intelligence has come from Piaget and his coworkers. A very brief introduction was given to Piaget, his methods, his types of findings, his major concepts, and the relations of these outcomes to what is known about the factorial nature of intelligence.

Most attention was given to the multivariate approach of factor analysis: some of the characteristics of the method, conditions that are favorable for an effective factor analysis from a psychologist's point of view, and reasons for needing factor analysis. These needs are seen in connection with accounting for unevenness of abilities within persons, sometimes unevenness of dramatic proportions. Unevenness is also evident in growth curves and curves of decline in old age. Numerous tests of an intellectual nature correlate zero or near zero with one another and with composite scores from recognized intelligence scales. The different IQ scales themselves fail to correlate perfectly, even allowing for errors of measurement.

Tests measuring factors have their places in investigation of brain functions and brain disorders, in studies of heredity of intelligence, and in assessing intellectual deficits in psychopathology. The advantages of using factor tests have been evident in multiple predictions of achievement and of job success. They could be utilized much more than they have been in connection with special talents and defects found in the educational process.

More general advantages include economy of measurement, where measurement of differential aptitudes is concerned; and providing a much more comprehensive coverage of intellectual qualities, going well beyond traditional intelligence scales. Not the least of the advantages is the psychological meaningfulness provided, based on empirical fact and on general psychological theory, to which factor analysis now makes its contributions.

3 General theory of intelligence

This chapter has much more to say about frames of reference and will present the general theory of intelligence that prevails in the following chapters. Other theories will be considered, and since it is basic to most of the theories, factor analysis will receive some attention from a more technical point of view.

Frames of reference and theory

Needs for theory   Any serious investigator, in basic science or in technology, finds a good frame of reference very helpful. A frame of reference may be as broad as a philosophical point of view or as circumscribed as a limited scientific theory. The kind that is at least close to a scientific theory is most useful to the investigator of some particular domain such as intelligence. Why do we need scientific theory?

Without scientific theory, the investigator lacks major goals or directions; it is almost a case of the proverbial ship without a rudder. It is not enough just to have a strong desire "to do research." Undirected effort is often futile. An investigator without focused efforts is likely to pick away at minor problems, here and there, as fancy of the moment dictates or as opportunity comes his way. There may be occasions for this "browsing" type of approach, but only more or less by chance is the investigator likely to work on significant problems and to make a lucky strike, if he ever does.

A scientific theory is a source of significant problems, each problem a question, to which an answer is sought. Progress depends very much on being able to ask questions, furthermore, to ask the significant questions. Theory generates questions and also provides a basis for determining whether questions, however generated, are significant ones. Obtaining answers to questions by way of empirical testing or research should be expected either to support the theory or not to support it. In the latter case, a change in theory may be called for. The need to change a theory is no disgrace. In research, one cannot afford to be afraid of making mistakes in theory. Such fears put a damper on creative production. Correction of mistakes at least eliminates blind alleys and holds the prospect of progress in other directions. Finding out what *is not* true is often as informative as finding out what *is* true. There is no need for expecting that any theory will stand for all time. It is often said that the history of science is strewn with discarded theories; they are means to ends, not ends. In all probability the theoretical models favored in this chapter will sometime be replaced with better ones. For the time being, they seem very fruitful. Fruitfulness is an important criterion by which a theory should be judged.

Requirements for a good frame of reference   A good frame of reference for an investigator's purposes has three important specifications: it should be comprehensive, it should be systematic, and it should be empirically based.

Saying that a frame of reference should be comprehensive does not mean that it should be vague because it is broad. It should be sufficiently pointed to generate questions that can be answered by making empirical tests by empirical procedures. But it should not be so circumscribed that one loses sight of the larger picture, for all phenomena have significant ramifications. Understanding one item in a complex of items depends in part upon knowing interrelationships. Keeping a broad view is needed to ensure that some item, perhaps an important one if not a crucial one, may not be overlooked. In previous chapters the point has been stressed that the vision of mental testers has been all too restricted, and for the most part there has been too little interest in theory.

Some investigators, in their legitimate efforts to simplify things, in their dutiful application of the principle of parsimony, are likely to eliminate from possible view some of the phenomena that should come within the scope of their observations. Too many psychologists, at least, have overdone the urge to simplify, with the result that significant phenomena have been excluded from consideration.

A good frame of reference is systematic. The only hope of human understanding of natural phenomena is the fact that there are regularities in nature. Such regularities are what we are seeking within the sphere of our investigations. They offer the possibilities of principles and scientific laws. Principles and laws provide a shorthand type of apprehending information, enlarging the scope of our understanding and our powers to operate with phenomena. In the pursuit of further simplification and at the same time larger grasps of information, model building becomes possible. Model building is theory construction.

Types of models   It appears to be in the nature of human thinking to resort to one or more of a few standard types of models, which can be quickly pointed out. In the psychological investigations of children, Inhelder and Piaget (1964) point out that there is growth in conceptions of what they call "seriation." By seriation they mean the arrangement of items of information in linear order, each item related to the next in line in the same manner, e.g., larger than, harder than, or more beautiful than. In the adult, particularly the educated adult, thinking in terms of abstract dimensions becomes more or less natural. Thus we have *dimensional* models, which are most widely applied in mathematics and the physical sciences.

Inhelder and Piaget (1964) also point to a parallel development in the recognition of classes and of classes within classes, in other words, *hierarchical* systems or models. Such models have been relatively more common in the biological sciences, in the classification schemes of Linnaeus. They are not unknown in psychology and psychiatry, and we shall see that this type of model has been strongly advocated for an encompassing theory of intellectual abilities and other traits of personality. It is the type of conception to which mathematical set principles readily apply.

To a third type of model, not nearly so well known, has been applied the term *morphological* by the astronomer Zwicky (1957). Basically, this model is a cross classification of phenomena in intersecting categories, rather than in categories within categories, as in the hierarchical model. The most notorious example in science is the chemists' periodic table introduced by Mendeleev, in which the chemical elements are arranged in rows and columns, each row and each column representing a different category. It could also be referred to as a "logical matrix." An ordinary matrix, as in mathematics, has two dimensions, formed by rows and columns. There is no reason for not extending the use of the morphological type of model to three or more dimensions, if necessary. The writer has advocated the use of the morphological-type of model in psychology. It is this type of model that is proposed to organize the intellectual-aptitude factors in a unitary system. It has also been applied to the psychomotor abilities, factors of temperament, and factors of psychopathology (Guilford, 1959a).

A fourth type of model owes its promotion, if not its origin, largely to the communication engineers and to the fields of cybernetics and computer technology. It is well named an *operational* type of model, for it conceives of events in terms of interconnected series of transmissions of information. In the course of time, some steps have been made in this direction by psychologists in attempting to account for sequences of events in behavior. The steps in problem solving proposed by John Dewey (1910), the steps in creative thinking proposed by Graham Wallas (1926), and the steps in producing an invention proposed by Rossman (1931) are rough examples of this type of model.

But, for the most part, the operational models utilized by psychologists have been highly oversimplified, constituted of stimulus and response, as in conceiving of Pavlov's classical conditioning episode. Taking their cues from computer technology and the efforts to simulate human thinking and problem solving by means of computers, some psychologists are now proposing more complex, more sophisticated, and more descriptive operational models. A model of this type designed for a generalized description of problem solving will be presented in Chapter 14.

The requirement that a model be empirically based should be an obvious one for the scientifically minded. It is not easy to say when any proposed model has enough empirical support to justify serious attention to it. It is not necessary to have empirical support at every point, but there should be enough empirical foundation to support the superstructure that is built upon it. What is more important, there would be some possibility of testing the model at all crucial points. Its chief utility is in the testable problems that it generates and in the reasonable implications that flow from it for technological practices.

Factor-analytic models and methods

Basic equations in factor analysis   Factor theory is in the form of dimensional models, with mathematical descriptions of their properties. The basic equation, which is a kind of axiom or postulate, from which other things flow by implication, is often stated as follows:

$$z_{ij} = a_{j1}z_{i1} + a_{j2}z_{i2} + a_{j3}z_{i3} + \cdots a_{jq}z_{iq} + a_{js}z_{is} + e_{ij} \tag{3.1}$$

where

z_{ij} = standard score made by individual I in test J and also = $(X_{ij} - M_j)/\sigma_j$

a_{j1} = factor loading of test J for factor 1, a_{j2} = same for factor 2, and so on for all *common* factors 1 through Q

z_{i2} = score for individual I on scale of factor 1, and other z terms for factors 2 through Q indicate corresponding values

z_{is} = score for individual I for *specific* component in test, in other words, for test's unique contribution; and a_{js} is its weight, just as other a terms serve as weights for their respective components

e_{ij} = error contribution or component for particular individual I in taking test J

Translated into English, this equation means that a person's obtained score (in standard form) is a linear combination of weighted contributions from his status on common factors, a specific factor, and an error component. It is the main objective of a factor analysis to find the values for the a coefficients (factor loadings) for the common factors. In all this discussion we are concerned only with the case in which the factors themselves are uncorrelated (orthogonal), for that is the case to which the equation applies.

It has been proved mathematically that the a coefficients or factor loadings bear a functional relation to coefficients of correlation between tests, a fact that provides the basis for determining the factor loadings from intercorrelations of tests. For the correlation between two tests, J and K, the equation is

$$r_{jk} = a_{j1}a_{k1} + a_{j2}a_{k2} + a_{j3}a_{k3} + \cdots a_{jq}a_{kq} \tag{3.2}$$

where the a terms are the same as in equations of the type (3.1) for the tests J and K. The same kind of equation applies to correlations between other pairs of tests; hence in a table of intercorrelations the same factor loadings are represented in many of the coefficients, the condition that provides the basis for extracting the information as to how large those loadings are. With orthogonal factors, a factor loading is the coefficient of correlation between a test and a factor.

One deduction from equation (3.2) is that tests correlate to the extent of the factors that they share in common. If any a_{jq} or a_{kq} is zero, which means that a certain factor has no relationship to one test or the other (or to both), that term drops out of the equation and adds nothing to the size of the correlation. If two tests have no factors in common, their intercorrelation is zero. Coefficients of correlation are large when pairs of a_{jq} and a_{kq} coefficients are large, with the limit that no r_{jk} can exceed 1.0, of course. The more nonzero terms there are in equation (3.2), the larger the correlation is likely to be. This means that two tests that are both factorially complex have a better chance of correlating highly with one another. Tests each with one common factor will be likely to correlate low or zero with all except other tests loaded on the same factor.

Geometry of factor theory; dimensional models   The models just mentioned are expressed in the form of algebraic equations. They can also be expressed in geometric form. Each factor can be represented as a single dimension, and since the factors are assumed to be mutually independent, the dimensions can be placed at right angles to one another. Figure 3.1 illustrates the intersection of three factors, each represented by its own dimension. The factor axes are drawn so as to intersect at the means of a population of persons or at standard scores z of zero. The same idea could be extended to four and even more dimensions, but three are all that can be shown in this manner. The three factors A, B, and C determine a sphere, which defines a *factor space*.

In Chapter 2 mention was made of the simple fact that each person to whom a factor applies can be placed somewhere as a point on the scale (dimension) for that factor. In a space of three factors, each person would have three factor positions or scores, each conceived as a perpendicular projection on its factor axis. Persons P and Q have been located as points within this factor space. Each person's point position is theoretically unique, unless two persons (such as identical twins) justifiably occupy the same point location.

The same factor space, with its three reference axes, can be used for the descriptions of tests. But a test is better represented by a line than by a point, for it has a continuous scale, to which numbers can be attached. Let us say that we are concerned with test T_j, which measures common factors A, B, and C and no others. The position of the line for test T_j in the three-factor space depends upon its three factor loadings or weights as in equation (3.1). The larger the factor loading of the test on a factor, the nearer the test line lies to that factor. In Figure 3.2, the line for test T_j is shown drawn so that the mean of the population on its scale is also at the origin. The direction of the line for T_j is closest to the dimension for factor C, next to that for factor A, and farthest from that for factor B. A score on the scale for T_j would indicate most the person's status for factor C and least his status for factor B.

There is a third way in which the factor dimensions can serve as a frame of reference,

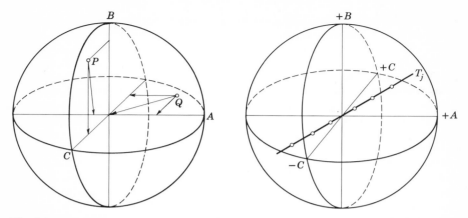

Fig. 3.1 Representation of three hypothetical independent factors, standing for three personality traits, as a reference frame of three orthogonal dimensions. Persons P and Q are represented as points within this reference frame, each with trait positions represented by projections of those points on the three dimensions.

Fig. 3.2 A three-dimensional model, with the same dimensions as in Figure 3.1, as a frame of reference for tests, showing a particular test T_j, represented by a vector.

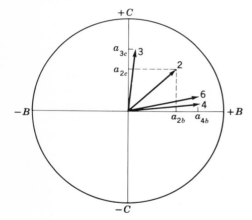

Fig. 3.3 Representation of four tests as vectors within a two-dimensional reference frame, the two axes representing two factors.

as indicated in Figure 3.3. Here we have only two of the factors represented, B and C, as a two-dimensional frame, with four test vectors shown within that frame: tests 2, 3, 4, and 6, about which we shall see more later. Each test is represented as a vector (a line having a certain length and a certain direction from the origin). The circle is drawn at a distance of 1.0 from the origin, providing an upper limit for any test vector. The shortness of the test vectors here is due to the fact that only the contributions of factors B and C are represented.

The scale for each factor is used to represent factor loadings. Test 2 has about equal loadings of .48 and .44 on factors B and C, respectively, indicated by the projections of a_{2b} and a_{2c}, respectively. Test 3 has projections of .07 on factor B and .75 on C, the latter indicated by a_{3c}. Tests 4 and 6 have loadings on factor B of .76 and .73, respectively, the first of these two values being coefficient a_{4b}, and loadings of only .08 and .16 on factor C. We shall see the usefulness of such a geometric representation shortly.

Extraction of factors   A factor analysis begins with a correlation matrix, such as that in Table 3.1, and ends with a factor matrix, such as that in Table 3.3, which was derived from the correlation data in Table 3.1. The two major steps are (1) the extraction of factors, yielding a temporary factor matrix, as in Table 3.2; and (2) a rotation of factor axes. There are a number of ways of achieving both steps. The simplest procedure to explain is Thurstone's extraction of centroid factors by using a temporary orthogonal reference frame and graphic rotations of axes, keeping them orthogonal. The details of extraction procedures will not be described here; descriptions can be found in several places (R. B. Cattell, 1952; Fruchter, 1954; Guilford, 1954; Harman, 1960).

The set of nine tests represented in Table 3.1 was carefully selected for illustrative purposes. One rarely finds a case with such a clear factor structure (as seen either in Table 3.3 or in Figure 3.4). A more typical analysis would involve from 30 to 50 test variables, 12 to 15 factors, and the calculations would be turned over to a high-speed electronic computer, which shortens the actual computing operations from several months to a few minutes.

The first thing to be noted about Table 3.1 is the unusually large number of zero coefficients. Such a condition is most favorable for a clear separation of factors and for many test vectors that lie close to factor axes in the final solution, as seen in Figure 3.5. The nine tests were chosen because it was known that they represent three factors univocally, except for one or two. One of the exceptions represents two of the three factors about equally well, and the other shares its variance with a factor not represented in the

Table 3.1   Correlation matrix for nine aptitude tests *

					Tests				
	1	*2*	*3*	*4*	*5*	*6*	*7*	*8*	*9*
1		.38	.55	.06	−.04	.05	.07	.05	.08
2	.38		.36	.40	.28	.40	.11	.15	.13
3	.55	.36		.10	.01	.18	.13	.12	.10
4	.06	.40	.10		.32	.60	.04	.06	.13
5	−.04	.28	.01	.32		.35	.08	.13	.11
6	.05	.40	.18	.60	.35		.01	.06	.07
7	.07	.11	.13	.04	.08	.01		.45	.32
8	.05	.15	.12	.06	.13	.06	.45		.32
9	.08	.13	.10	.13	.11	.07	.32	.32	

* *Nature of the tests:*

1. AAF Vocabulary (a multiple-choice synonym test)
2. Technical Vocabulary (composed of terms such as an aircraft pilot learns)
3. Reading Comprehension (based on short paragraphs of material such as a pilot student has to read)
4. Tool Functions (on knowledge of uses of common tools)
5. Biographical Data Blank (Pilot) (containing items regarding past experiences, emphasizing mechanical experiences)
6. Mechanical Information (mostly about knowledge of automative equipment and repairs)
7. Spatial Orientation I (requires rapid matching of aerial photographs)
8. Speed of Identification (requires rapid matching of outline drawings of airplanes)
9. Pattern Assembly (a paper form-board type of test)

other eight tests. Close inspection of Table 3.1 suggests three factors, one for tests 1, 2, and 3; one for tests 4, 5, and 6; and one for tests 7, 8, and 9. If we follow the diagonal from upper left to lower right, it is clear that three clusters of moderate correlations stand out from the others, which are distinctly smaller and even zero.

By means of Thurstone's centroid method of factor extractions, one factor at a time is pulled out. The first centroid factor has the largest mean of loadings, and each successive factor has a smaller mean of (absolute) loadings, as a rule. The first factor has all positive loadings when the correlation matrix has essentially all positive correlation coefficients. Each centroid factor after the first has a balance between positive and negative loadings, which means that the factors after the first are bipolar. These features are merely circumstances of the procedure of factor extraction. Most factor analysts do not regard the centroid axes as having any direct indications of psychological meaning, as is true of the original correlations, although signs of the final structure to be found are somewhat clearer in the centroid factor matrix. Examination of Table 3.2 suggests that each of the three triplets of tests has similar patterns of factor loadings, except for tests 2 and 5, which differ somewhat from their mates.

Some investigators, especially those who are determined to have a g factor, point to the fact that the first centroid factor is a universal one; it has all positive, nonzero loadings. Some have even interpreted it as g. If they do, they are left with bipolar factors for the other dimensions, which are not very easy to interpret psychologically or to defend logically. Most analysts do rotate, and the reasons for rotating are convincing.

Rotation of axes   First, the centroid method is an arbitrary procedure, applied for convenience and because the mathematics of a correlation matrix makes it possible. This cannot be simply explained. But there is general agreement as to the arbitrariness of the centroid factor matrix. Second, when the experimental variables analyzed are scores for tests of abilities, Thurstone has properly argued that it would be very unreasonable to accept the idea that any factor ability could have a negative contribution to make to performance, which would mean that the more of the ability a person has, the poorer he would do on the test. Consequently, Thurstone adopted as one important criterion, his condition of *positive manifold,* which means no negative loadings in the final solution, except very small ones, which might well be negative due to chance.

But the criterion to which Thurstone gave most attention is known by the term

Table 3.2   Centroid factor matrix with nine tests and three factors, with communalities H^2

Tests	A_c	B_c	C_c	H^2
		Factors		
1	.42	.21	−.59	.57
2	.62	.25	−.03	.45
3	.50	.18	−.51	.54
4	.55	.30	.43	.58
5	.38	.09	.33	.26
6	.55	.37	.38	.58
7	.39	−.53	.06	.44
8	.42	−.51	.01	.44
9	.37	−.36	.07	.27

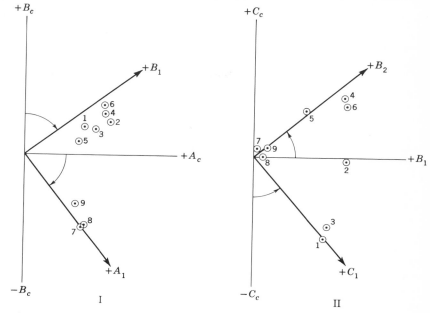

Fig. 3.4 Rotations of axes for the small AAF test battery, first, with the pair of centroid axes A_c and B_c rotated, in Diagram I, then axes B_1 and C_c, in Diagram II. The goals included making as many loadings (projections) as possible positive and as many loadings as possible near zero.

simple structure. If one plots the centroid factor loadings in planes, for two factors at a time, it will usually be observed that the points tend to cluster (see Figure 3.4, Diagram I, which is for centroid axes A_c and B_c). There are two small areas of high density and larger spaces of low density. Thurstone regarded this condition as highly significant and scientifically convincing. One should rotate with axes close to such clusters. In Figure 3.4 it can be seen that both goals, positive manifold and simple structure, can be closely approached by the same rotation of the two axes, keeping the axes at right angles.

For this illustrative problem, rotations were performed for one pair of axes at a time, ignoring the third axis. Since all axes are completely independent of one another, what happens to the two that are rotated has no effect upon the third, in that rotation. There are three possible pairings of the three centroid axes: *A-B, A-C,* and *B-C.* It is usually most expeditious to begin with a rotation in the plane for the pair *A-B*. The first rotation was made in that plane, and it is shown in Figure 3.4. A clockwise rotation was made over an angle of about 45 degrees, which is rather typical in the case of the first two centroid axes.

It can be seen that in the extraction of factors the first centroid axis went out in a central position with respect to the total configuration of test vectors. In fact it goes through the center of gravity for the whole set of points. The center of gravity is a *centroid;* hence the centroid method. In Diagram I, we see the configuration only from one point of view, down along axis C_c as our line of sight; so there appears to be some lopsidedness, which is more apparent than real, for the points are actually spread above and below the plane of *A-B.*

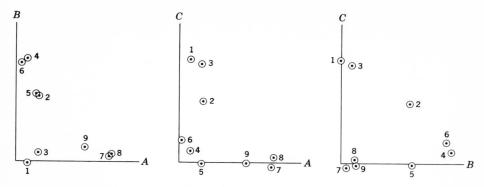

Fig. 3.5 Plots of the test vectors with respect to the three pairs of rotated factor axes, showing how positive manifold and simple structure have been achieved.

After we have made the first rotation, moving axes A_c and B_c to the new positions A_1 and B_1 (with subscripts to indicate one rotation for each axis), it appears that a good solution has been achieved for the new factor A; so the decision was to rotate the new B (B_1) against C_c, as shown in Diagram II. In this plot, we see the configuration of test points by sighting along axis A_1, and it is obvious that the six test points that appeared in Diagram I are separated into two clusters, with tests 4, 5, and 6 in one, 1 and 3 in another, and test 2 left in the middle. By using the new reference frame of all the rotated axes, we have the three plots as in Figure 3.5, representing graphically the final factor structure seen in Table 3.3.

Things do not always work out so well as in this problem with its preselected tests. Selection was possible because of much prior information about these nine tests and their major factors. Ordinarily, after rotation that is carried out according to the criteria of simple structure and positive manifold, factors are interpretable, more or less, each factor

Table 3.3   Rotated factor matrix *

		Factors	
Tests	A	B	C
1	.08	−.01	.75
2	.16	.48	.44
3	.15	.07	.72
4	.08	.76	.08
5	.15	.49	−.01
6	.02	.73	.16
7	.64	.04	−.03
8	.66	.05	.02
9	.47	.10	−.01

* The centroid matrix of Table 3.2 has been transformed to provide a new reference frame within which there are simple structure, positive manifold, and psychological meaningfulness.

vector, by virtue of its high and low loadings on groups of tests, suggesting some underlying psychological variable that the strongly loaded tests measure in common. Some factors are still puzzling, however, and sometimes some information about the tests and what factors they have represented in the past or some hypothesis or other as to what psychological factors ought to be represented may help to modify the rotations so as to clear up the picture.

Any subjectivity in decisions on where to rotate is undesirable, but the facts of life in factor-analysis procedures are such that it is often necessary; otherwise strict adherence to the rules of best simple structure may lead one astray psychologically. The writer has discussed these issues at greater length elsewhere (Guilford & Zimmerman, 1963). Since it is psychological information that the psychological factor analyst presumably wants to achieve and not exercise in completely objective following of rules of a method by which he may be misled, the exploration of abilities under relaxed rules seems defensible. The investigator can always test the hypotheses about psychological factors derived from an analysis by planning a better test battery and applying the procedures of analysis in a completely objective way in a later analysis. The writer often feels that the chief virtue of factor analysis is that it enables us to turn complex data around, in simpler views, so as to achieve better looks at the data, from which new insights may arise.

Interpretation of factors   In interpreting the three factors in the illustrative problem, we note first that for factor A three tests, 7, 8, and 9, stand out with relatively high loadings and all the rest have very low ones. What do these three tests have that the rest do not? The most obvious thing is that they are figural tests, whereas the others are verbal tests. The separation of verbal from nonverbal is one of the easiest discriminations to achieve. The many analyses of the Wechsler-scale tests by themselves almost always yield a verbal and a nonverbal "factor."

As far as this illustrative battery goes, we could extract little additional information about any special kind of nonverbal ability. But we know from analyses of larger batteries, with more nonverbal tests in them, that there are more than one nonverbal factor ability; in fact, there are quite a number. Tests 7 and 8 provide the best clue to the nature of this factor. Both require rapid matching of pairs of pictorial material, photographs in the one case and line drawings in the other. Furthermore, they are like tests in which a factor called "perceptual speed" has been found repeatedly. By using this additional information, it would be safe to identify factor A as perceptual speed. This interpretation is not belied by the moderate loading of test 9, Pattern Assembly, on the same factor. Some figure comparisons and matchings may well be involved in Pattern Assembly, but it is apparently more than that, for its loading on factor A is small enough to expect that, if reliable, it must have some significant relationship to a factor not in this analysis. Other analyses have shown that a factor of visualization is an even stronger component in such a test. No other visualization test was in this small battery to help bring out that factor.

Factor B is supported by tests 4, 5, and 6, as expected, but also by test 2. Tests 4 and 6 obviously sample the examinee's mechanical knowledge, each in its own way and in its own emphasis upon different mechanical areas. Test 2, Technical Vocabulary, appears on the mechanical-knowledge factor for an obvious reason. The words in this test involve technical terms, and an examinee who has in his memory store a good supply of mechanical concepts has an edge in this test. The Biographical Data Blank (test 5) is an inventory primarily about the examinee's past experiences. The items were selected because it had been found that each contributed to prediction of success in pilot training, and such items often pertain to life experiences of a mechanical nature, such as the existence of a good workshop at the examinee's home when he was a child and his having owned a motorcycle or a car. Other tests of mechanical knowledge all helped to predict passing versus failing to learn to fly an airplane.

Factor C is strong in tests 1 and 2, both vocabulary tests, one a general vocabulary and one a more special vocabulary. The Technical Vocabulary test differs from the general vocabulary test in sharing as much of its variance with factor B as with C, reflecting its special nature. Reading Comprehension is a faithful test for the verbal-comprehension factor but usually is not so strongly related as are simple vocabulary tests. Reading Comprehension usually shows some relation to reasoning factors when such factors are also in the analyzed battery.

Attention should be called to the fact that after rotation the sizes of loadings in the different factors are rather evened up as compared with the situation in the centroid factor matrix. Whereas the centroid method of extraction throws high loadings toward the first centroid factor, rotation takes some values away from that factor. This point will be brought out in later discussion, where its significance is more apparent. One other comment that should be made in passing is that some investigators do not rotate orthogonally, keeping the mutual separations of axis at 90 degrees; they permit that angle to become greater or less, allowing each axis to rotate its own amount. Such rotations are called "oblique." The significance of oblique axes will also come out later.

Spearman's g and s

Charles Spearman, the father of factor analysis in psychology, started out with the simplest possible factor model. In equation form, by analogy to equation (3.1), he held that

$$z_{ij} = a_{jg}z_{ig} + a_{js}z_{is} \tag{3.3}$$

where the subscripts g and s stand, respectively, for the universal factor g and the component specific to test j. Any test in the intellectual category has only one common factor g, plus a unique, specific component s. Spearman was very liberal in accepting the kinds of tests that he regarded as intellectual, all the way from judgments of difference in pitch of sounds to grades in Latin. The weight of g in tests a_{qg}, where q stands for any test, varies from large to small but is never zero.

Eventually, Spearman had to admit that something in addition to g is helping to produce correlation coefficients and this something is a different, additional component in different groups of tests; hence he recognized "group" factors. This would be represented in the equation by adding a few (sometimes only one) extra terms like those for common factors in equation (3.1). Spearman never gave much credit to the group factors, however, although the group factors that he identified and interpreted psychologically appear to bear much resemblance to some of the multiple factors found today.

In two previous places, this writer has indicated that any genuine zero correlations between pairs of intellectual tests is sufficient to disprove the existence of a universal factor like g. The staunch supporters of g have maintained that by rotation of axis, as in Thurstone's multiple-factor procedures, g is rotated out of existence; it is the major determiner of the first centroid factor. Rotation robs it of variance that belongs to it. If one demands a g factor, he can almost always have one. But it would seem illogical to insist upon it in the face of zero correlations.

As to the loss of g by rotation, with an implication that rotation will always lose it, the writer one time invented two artificial factor matrices, each with a g factor; a factor with all nonzero loadings. By working backward, it is possible to generate the correlation matrix from which such a factor matrix should be found by the ordinary processes of factor analysis. To make the problem more realistic, two different sets of random errors were added to the intercorrelations. Without knowing that a g factor was present, four students were given the two correlation matrices for analysis, with rotations by Thurstone's method. In every case the g factor was found, indicating that in the normal processes of rotation a g factor can still be found if it is, in fact, present. This does not mean that one is certain to find it in spite of rotating, but it does mean that one is not certain to lose it just by rotating (Guilford, 1941).

Spearman's psychological theory This writer has always felt that Spearman's psychological theory was better than his factor theory but that his psychological theory was also limited. In his view, the best tests of his g are concerned in some way with relations. Relations are perceived connections between things. The things between which the relation occurs Spearman called "fundaments." For example, the ideas HOUSE and ROOF are related as whole to part or as enclosure to cover, two different relations. In one kind of test we give the two fundaments, the examinee to see what the relation is, as in item A in Figure 3.6. This process Spearman called the "eduction" (not education) of a relation. In another kind of test we give one fundament and a relation, the examinee to supply the other fundament, as in item B in Figure 3.6. The item might read: "The opposite of COLD is _____?" This process Spearman called "eduction" of a fundament. His examination of many tests (Spearman, 1927) involved his finding items of these two types and his discriminating among different classes of relations. Although it is necessary to go well beyond these limited conceptions of intelligence, we shall see later that the idea of fundaments and relations is very sound, and we shall see how they are handled in a more comprehensive theory.

Hierarchical models of factors

The Burt model Followers of Spearman have held tenaciously to the g factor, but they have given relatively more attention to group factors. As the newly discovered factors increased in number, the need for putting them into some kind of logical interrelationship became a recognized problem. Sir Cyril Burt (1949) was one of the first to attempt this kind of exercise. Being a good Aristotelian in many ways, he conceived of a hierarchical type of model, which is like an inverted tree, as seen in Figure 3.7. The model as shown there applies to the whole of the human mind, with the first major dichotomy between intellectual characteristics, or g, and "practical" or behavioral characteristics. Among the practical abilities he placed psychomotor abilities and abilities for dealing with space and mechanical affairs.

Burt conceived of an ideal hierarchy with successive dichotomies, each subdivision of a higher factor to give two immediately lower (see Figure 3.7). The various levels of bifurcation he identified as "relations" at the highest level, "associations" at the second level, "perception" at the third, and "sensation" at the fourth. In fitting group factors into the model, however, Burt had to depart from strict dichotomization, for many subcategories contain more than two factors. At the association level, for example, he recognized a division into memory, with a general retentiveness, under which are group factors of visual, auditory, kinesthetic, and verbal-memory factors; and productive association, with a general factor of inventiveness, under which are group factors of fluency and originality. Other general-association factors include verbal ability, language ability, and arithmetical

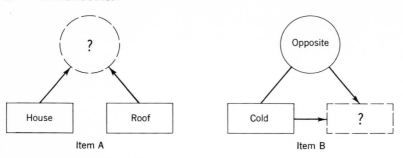

Fig. 3.6 Graphic illustration of Spearman's conceptions of eduction of relations (item *A*) and eduction of correlates (item *B*).

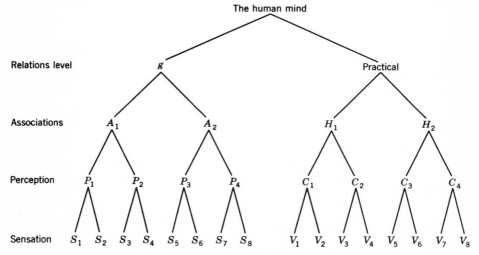

Fig. 3.7 Burt's conception of an idealized hierarchical model for aptitude factors, with successive dichotomizations at different levels of mental generality. (*Reproduced by permission from Burt, 1949.*)

ability, under each of which are two or three subfactors. These examples will give the general picture of Burt's hierarchical model.

The Vernon model   Before considering an evaluation of the Burt model, let us take a look at the Vernon theory, which is pictured in Figure 3.8 (Vernon, 1950). Under *g* are two major factors, *v:ed,* for verbal-educational, on the one hand and *k:m* on the other. The latter is called "practical," as in the Burt model. The former, *v:ed,* subdivides into verbal and numerical, while the latter, *k:m,* subdivides three ways, into space ability, manual ability, and mechanical information. Beyond these are specific factors, each of very narrow scope and considered by Vernon to be of trivial importance. Presumably, many of what Burt recognizes as small group factors belong in this category.

Evaluation of hierarchical models   Evidence has been cited against the idea of a *g* factor, which is a key concept of the hierarchical models of Burt and Vernon. Still another argument can be offered. It is the fact that where *g* is demanded and found, it is not an

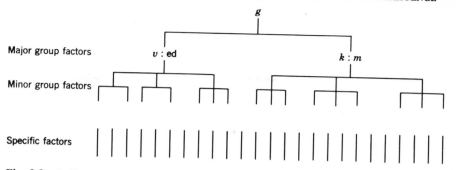

Fig. 3.8 A diagram of P. E. Vernon's hierarchical conception of aptitude factors. (*Vernon, 1950, p. 22; reproduced by permission.*)

invariant variable but changes almost with every battery of tests that is analyzed. This is particularly true when the first centroid factor is taken to be *g*. Change the battery, and the location of the centroid changes. Even when there is rotation from this dimension to locate *g*, it is difficult to see how its location can be invariant from one analysis to another.

Finding g as a second-order factor Realizing that his new methods of factor analysis would probably not, in fact did not, find a *g* factor, Thurstone proposed a special variation of his method that would make this possible. This is the practice of oblique rotation of axes. When axes are allowed to depart from orthogonality, which represents zero correlation between them, they have nonzero correlations. With nonzero correlations among a set of factors, usually positive because the angles of separation between axes that represent rotated factors are less than 90 degrees, the factor intercorrelations may themselves be subjected to factor analysis to find second-order factors. Thurstone said that *g* was to be found in the second-order domain, among the second-order factors.

But the trouble with this way of finding *g* is that in a large battery of aptitude tests, and it does not have to be so very large at that, more than one second-order factor is found (for example, see Matin & Adkins, 1954; Rimoldi, 1951). Which second-order factor is then to be recognized as *g*? Probably none is actually universal to the first-order factors. Furthermore, each second-order factor, embracing ultimately so many heterogeneous tests, which are the empirical referents for the factor, is difficult to interpret. The chances are it is not invariant with changes in test battery.

The second-order–factor route to *g* does not seem to have worked out. It would seem that the best strategy for testing the hierarchical organization of factors, as represented by vectors in space, would be through correlations of the factors in the population concerned. Ideally, we should know all the basic, or first-order, factors first. Determining their intercorrelations, we could then find the second-order factors and so on, through as many levels as we needed to go in order to arrive at one factor and one only. There are two difficulties in the way of carrying out this strategy. One is that we do not as yet know all the basic factors, and the other is we have as yet no good way of estimating intercorrelations of factors at any level.

The writer has never been able to accept the locations of oblique factor vectors and their angles of separation as the basis for estimating factor intercorrelations. We do not know, as yet, how to construct the tests that would be needed to locate these axes exactly. Many times it appears that a relatively small angle between two factor vectors, for factors

L and M, let us say, is due to the fact that we cannot construct a test for L from which all the relation to M is experimentally ruled out or we cannot construct a test for M with all the relation to L ruled out. Until we can be reasonably sure that this much experimental control is accomplished, the correlation between the two factors cannot be well determined. It will also probably be true that the intercorrelations of factors will differ from one population to another. And if there are some completely independent factors at the first-order level, there may be some completely independent factors at higher-order levels. A complete hierarchy would thus be precluded.

Evidence from the centroid factors As support for his type of model, Burt has cited what happens when factors are extracted from intercorrelations by his summation method, which is essentially the same as Thurstone's centroid method. From earlier paragraphs we saw how the first centroid factor is completely general with no zero loadings: a good-looking candidate for g. In the second column of factor loadings about half the values are positive and half negative. This looks like the first dichotomy or bifurcation of tests. Each of these two sets of tests will tend to have a further subdivision in the third column of loadings with two subgroups of loadings, one positive and one negative, and so on in later factors. Things do not work out as neatly as this but relatively so. This picture suggests a kind of hierarchy.

But should the mere nature of an arbitrary method of extracting temporary factors be used as a foundation for a psychological theory? In fairness to Burt, inspection of the rotations in Figure 3.4 gives first a separation of verbal and nonverbal tests and then a subdivision of the verbal tests into verbal-comprehension tests and mechanical-knowledge tests. But this was an incident to the choice of the first rotations. Had we rotated axes A_c and C_c first, the first separation would have been between the verbal-comprehension tests on the one hand and all the rest on the other, and the second set a *combination* of verbal and nonverbal. With much larger batteries, such wholesale dichotomies do not occur at any stage of the rotations. Furthermore, there are so many factors among the verbal tests and so many among the nonverbal tests that, ordinarily, at no stage does one find all verbal tests on the one axis and all nonverbal on the other. It is when the battery analyzed is a relatively small one, with quite heterogeneous tests and with too many factors actually present for the number of tests to separate them satisfactorily, that the major dichotomies occur, as in a study by Moursey (1952).

The structure-of-intellect model

Reasons for choosing a morphological model   When the writer first faced the problem of organizing the intellectual factors into a system, almost 40 such factors had been demonstrated (Guilford, 1956a; 1956b). Several facts based upon experiences in factor analysis of intellectual tests in the United States had cast doubt upon the applicability of a hierarchical structure. Almost no one reported finding a g factor; in fact, the tendency has been for each factor to be limited to a small number of tests in any analysis.

Furthermore, there has been little or no tendency to find a few broader group factors (represented each by a larger number of tests) and a larger number of narrow group factors. The factors appear to be about equally general in this respect, being strongly represented by small numbers, and relatively equal numbers, of tests. In part this may be attributed to the fact that the investigator who approaches analysis problems in a sophisticated manner starts by drawing up a list of hypothesized factors that he expects to find in an area of functioning, and he sees to it that each hypothesized factor is represented by a minimum of three tests. The extra loadings often come out in the analysis because tests designed for one factor so often unintentionally show significant relationships to other factors. The absence of a *g* factor and the apparently comparable generality of all the factors does not give support to a hierarchical conception of their interrelationships.

A third and most important consideration is that many factors have obviously parallel properties. For example, if one collects a half-dozen verbal factors in one set and an appropriate collection of a half-dozen nonverbal factors in another, it is clear that the factors in the two sets can be paired off in a meaningful manner. The psychological operation is the same in each pair; only the content of the test items is different. Yet the members of each pair come out of an analysis as separate factors. Historically, there seems to have been a belief that a psychological operation is the same whether it is performed with verbal-meaningful information or with visual-figural information, and gestalt psychologists have contributed to fixing this assumption. Extensive factor-analytical results have proved wrong the belief that the same ability is involved regardless of the kind of information with which we deal.

Categories in the structure of intellect

Content categories   The major distinction should not be confined to verbal versus nonverbal, for there is a third category of factors represented by tests composed of numbers or letters that seem completely parallel to factors in the figural and verbal sets, respectively. There is nothing to tie the three sets together except the fact that they are recognized as all being in the general category of intellectual abilities; nor is there a more general factor that would tie together the members of a set of factors. Even if this had been true, a hierarchical model does not take care of parallel members, nor are parallels needed to form a hierarchy, except for the parallel levels of generality; and there are no apparent levels of generality among the factors obtained. Thus it was that three distinct, parallel content categories were recognized and called by the terms *figural, symbolic,* and *semantic.*

As far back as 1933, G. M. Smith did a factor analysis in which he selected tests so that the analysis could cluster the tests either in terms of similar material (space tests, number tests, and verbal tests) or according to formats with similar kinds of items. The results definitely favored factors along the lines of material or content. Over the years since that time, factors of space, number, and verbal abilities have been consistently easy to differentiate.

With the three kinds of content well supported, a fourth kind of content was added (Guilford, 1958a). This step was taken on purely logical grounds, for there were no known factors at the time to support the idea. The kind of content called by the term *behavioral* was added to take care of the kind of information involved in cognition and in other operations pertaining to the behavior of other people. We know that we know to some extent what the other person is perceiving, attending to, feeling, thinking, and intending to do. We draw inferences from this information and we utilize such information in efforts to control his actions. The addition of this kind of content was also influenced by the proposal of E. L. Thorndike (1920) that there is a social intelligence, distinct from the traditional kind of intelligence. Logical support for the other content categories was welcomed from the same direction, for Thorndike and his associates came to recognize a distinction between concrete and abstract intelligence (Thorndike et al., 1927). They failed only to make the further distinction of two kinds of abstract intelligence, as accounted for by the distinction between symbolic and semantic information in the structure-of-intellect model.

Operation categories   Before these distinctions as to content became evident, there had been some tradition for classifying the intellectual factors in another way, i.e., according to the supposed kind of operations involved. There were recognized perceptual factors, memory factors, and reasoning factors. New investigations in the 1950s pertained to creative-thinking abilities, planning abilities, problem-solving abilities, and judgment or evaluation abilities. New factors were found in each of these heuristic categories. Classification of the same factors, which could be grouped according to kind of information or content, as just indicated, was attempted independently according to operation.

It became obvious that in addition to memory and evaluation, new operation categories were needed. Reasoning proved to be a poor categorical concept because it could not be uniquely defined. Creative-thinking abilities seemed to have properties of their own, involving fluency, flexibility, and elaboration abilities; so a class of factors was given the title of "divergent-thinking" abilities. The representative tests are all of completion form, and the examinee makes a good score for the number and variety of his responses and sometimes for high quality. It was recognized that there were other tests in which the examinee has to generate his own answer to each item but that it must satisfy a unique specification or set of specifications. A set of these abilities, parallel to the divergent-thinking abilities, suggested the title of "convergent thinking"; in accordance with the information given in the item, the examinee must converge upon the one right answer. To avoid the ambiguity of the term *thinking,* the later substitution of the term *production* was made. Thus, two operation categories, divergent production and convergent production, were adopted.

With four categories of operation accounted for, including the memory and evaluation abilities, a fifth category was found to take care of the remaining factors: the *cognition* category. Tests of many factors simply determine how much the examinee knows or can readily discover on the basis of what he knows. Such factors of knowing or discovering were recognized as cognitive abilities. In adopting this label for the category, a very apt and descriptive one for the purpose, it was realized that reference has traditionally been made to *cognitive abilities,* a term that is meant to include all intellectual abilities. The use of the term *cognition* in the more limited way seems more appropriate. After all, we do have the term *intellectual* to use for covering the whole range of abilities; there is no point in having two labels for the larger class of abilities.

The product categories   A third way of looking at the abilities and a third way of classifying them came to view more slowly. It came about because of the need for taking into account the parallels that appeared across both the content and the operation categories. That is, if we take a set of factors having in common one of the content properties, say semantic, and also one of the operation categories, say cognition, we have a set of semantic-cognition abilities, not just one. There are parallels to these abilities if we change either to a new content category, say divergent production, or to a new combination of both content and operation, such as figural–divergent-production abilities.

A way was found to integrate all these parallels (Guilford, 1958a; 1959b) by putting the known intellectual factors in a single, solid model, with the five operation categories arranged along one dimension, the three content categories along a second dimension, and the six product categories along the third dimension. Thus, content, operation, and product became three parameters of a three-dimensional model. The structure-of-intellect model (hereafter often referred to as the SI model), as shown in Figure 3.9, is the same as when presented in 1958.

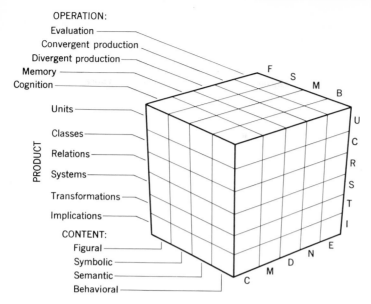

Fig. 3.9 The structure-of-intellect model, with three parameters (other parameters may need to be added).

The order of the categories along each dimension of the model has some logical reasons behind it but without any great degree of compulsion. Placing the symbolic category between figural and semantic depends upon the relation of symbols to both those two kinds of information. Symbols are basically figural but take on symbolic functions when they are conventionally made to represent something in the semantic category. They do, of course, also represent information in the other categories.

As for operations, cognition is basic to all other kinds; hence it appears first. If no cognition, no memory; if no memory, no production, for the things produced come largely from memory storage. If neither cognition nor production, then no evaluation. From front to back of the model, then, there is increasing dependency of one kind of operation upon others.

Of the products, units are regarded as basic; hence they appear at the top. Units enter into classes, relations, systems, and also transformations and implications. There might be some sense in putting implications immediately below units, since implications are the simplest and most general way in which units can be connected. There is reason for putting systems below units and relations, since both enter into systems; but implications do also. The unique character of transformations would be a reason for putting them last, since a transformation involves one item of information (possibly any other kind of product) becoming something else. The transformation of a transformation would not be unthinkable, for transformations, too, can be revised.

The concept of "product" pertains to the way or form in which any information occurs. An appropriate synonym for the term *product* could be the term *conception,* which also pertains to ways of knowing or understanding (see Figure 3.10 for illustrations of figural products). Information can be conceived in the form of *units*—things, segregated wholes, figures on grounds, or "chunks" (G. A. Miller, 1956). Units are things to which

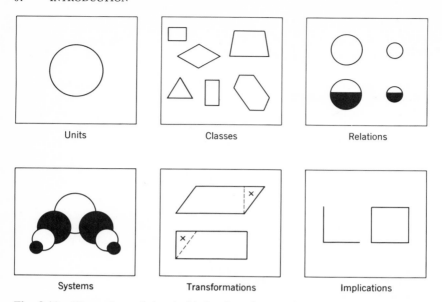

Units	Classes	Relations
Systems	Transformations	Implications

Fig. 3.10 Illustrations of the six kinds of products, using visual-figural examples.

nouns are normally applied. *Class,* as a kind of product of information, is near to the common meaning of the term. A class is a set of objects with one or more common properties; but it is more than a set, for a class idea is involved.

A *relation* is some kind of connection between two things, a kind of bridge or connecting link having its own character. Prepositions commonly express relation ideas, alone or with other terms, such as the expressions "married to," "son of," and "harder than." *Systems* are complexes, patterns, or organizations of interdependent or interacting parts, such as a verbally stated arithmetic problem, an outline, a mathematical equation, or a plan or program. *Transformations* are changes, revisions, redefinitions, or modifications, by which any product of information in one state goes over into another state. Although there is an implication of process in this definition, a transformation can be an object of cognition or of thought like any other product. The part of speech that we ordinarily apply to a transformation is a participle, a verb in noun form, such as shrinking, inverting, or reddening. It has been impossible thus far to treat transformation as an operation category; that is not the way the factors fall.

Finally, an *implication* is something expected, anticipated, or predicted from given information. Behaviorists who admitted the concept of "expectation" or "anticipation" to their lexicons have been talking about much the same idea. Any information that comes along very promptly suggests something else. One thing suggesting another involves a product of implication. Of all the six kinds of products, implication is closest to the ancient concept of association. But something more is involved in the concept. It is not that one thing merely follows another but that the two have some intimate way of being connected. This does not make an implication the same as a relation, for a relation is more specifiable and verbalizable.

These informal definitions of the category terms of the SI model will have to suffice for now. Meanings of the terms should grow as various factors and their tests involved in those categories are displayed in the next five chapters. Much more logical consideration will be given to all the 15 categories in Chapters 9 and 10, after illustrative factors and tests have been passed in review.

General status of the SI model   Since its conception as a frame of reference for the intellectual abilities, the SI model has served the heuristic function of generating hypotheses regarding new factors of intelligence. Additional factors were found in the literature and were readily given logical places within the model. The placement of any intellectual factor within the model is determined by its three unique properties: its operation, its content, and its product. The factor might be a matter of cognition of symbolic transformations, of evaluation of figural units, or of the convergent production of semantic systems, and so on.

New factor analyses have been directed toward testing hypotheses of abilities not yet demonstrated by factor analysis. The construction of tests for a factor not yet demonstrated is guided by the three specifications for that ability, as defined by its position in the model. At the time this was written, the number of demonstrated SI factors had grown to 82, with others under investigation. Of the total of 24 hypothesized cognition abilities, all have been demonstrated, including the 6 abilities for the cognition of behavioral products of information. The finding of these 6 behavioral-cognition factors vindicates the addition of the behavioral category to the other three content categories. Thus, whether the SI theory is the last word (and probably it is not), it has served well its purpose of guiding research. We shall also see that its concepts can add considerable new meaning and significance to old and new psychological findings by other methods.

Relation to other theories   It is possible to show how the SI model takes care of some of the features of other theories and other models. Spearman's "fundaments" are SI units; his "relations" are also SI relations. Spearman's concept of "eduction of relations" is equivalent to the cognition of relations. Where he thought this is one of the two major operations most characteristic of g, however, the SI model presents four distinct abilities for "educing" or cognizing relations, one for each kind of content: figural, symbolic, semantic, and behaviorial. Curiously enough, Spearman recognized several different kinds of relations, also along the line of different kinds of information, even including "psychological relation," which is rather clearly equivalent to the SI concept of behavioral relations (Spearman, 1927).

Spearman's conception of "eduction of correlates" belongs in the SI category of convergent production, in which relations are concerned. The typical test for the relations category with the convergent-production operation fits exactly Spearman's paradigm for eduction of correlates; i.e., given one unit and a relation, the examinee is to supply the one correct unit that fulfills the requirements of the given information. There are four such abilities, however, one for each of the four kinds of information. These comparisons indicate how narrow Spearman's psychological conception of g was, after all. If eduction of relations and correlates taken together are accepted as the *sine qua non* of g, then g embraces only 8 of 120 intellectual abilities represented in the SI model.

Vernon's first major bifurcation, between $v:ed$ and $k:m$ major group factors, is in a way parallel to the distinction between semantic and figural categories of information. His $k:m$ factor is much broader than the SI figural category, however, for besides space abilities it includes mechanical-information and psychomotor abilities. His further bifurcation under $v:ed$ between verbal and numerical is parallel to the SI distinction between semantic and symbolic information. He has nothing that suggests behavioral information.

And he has nothing to suggest operations or products, except incidentally in his further breakdowns, and it is probably true that he would regard most of the SI factors as being in his level of "specific" factors, which he thinks are of little consequence.

Burt's first, major bifurcation is so much like Vernon's that much the same parallels apply between this part of his hierarchy and SI categories. But because of much elaboration below that level, parallels are not so clear. Many of the same factors are identifiable, but their arrangements in his system have little in common with interrelationships of factors in terms of placement in the SI model.[1]

Other structural theories of intelligence

A chapter on current theory of intelligence would not be complete without mention of some other views. We are limited here to theories that offer ideas concerning the organization of abilities under the general heading of intelligence. This excludes conceptions offered from scattered psychoanalytical sources, which, in terms of psychometric standards, are exceedingly naïve. There are two other models that deserve mention. One is the facet type of model proposed by Louis Guttman (1965), and the other is known as "Bloom's taxonomy" (B. S. Bloom, 1956).

Guttman's facet model   The exact nature of the facet model has not been fully stated, except to say that it is an orthogonal system geometrically on the order of the structure of intellect. Guttman has been struck by the fact that, with the proper selection of tests, one can find matrices of intercorrelations that conform to one of two patterns. One satisfying his "simplex" model has highest coefficients along the principal diagonal, from upper left to lower right in the matrix, and diminishing values as one goes away from the diagonal to the corners at the upper right and lower left. A matrix of intercorrelations satisfying his "circumplex" model also has high coefficients along the principal diagonal but higher coefficients at or near the upper-right and lower-left corners, with two low troughs between the diagonal and the corners. In such patterns of correlations he sees important significance. But it should be said that such patterns are quite rare; most matrices do not conform to them, even after the order of variables has been rearranged. It is a question what Guttman would do about the many correlation coefficients that do not conform.

From the application of these models, Guttman (1965) concludes that there are three categories of tests, composed of pictures, symbols, and meaningful words, which are in line with the content categories of figural, symbolic, and semantic. He insists, however, that there are no other categories of content, overlooking the behavioral area of information. The three kinds of content form one facet of his complete model, yet to be constructed. He suggests that another facet will be found to involve the distinction between analytical and achievement items. By "analytical" items he means those that offer the examinee information from which he is to "deduce" a rule. From structure-of-intellect conceptions, this describes the set of four factors concerned with the cognition of systems, one for each kind of information. By "achievement" items he means those that present a rule with which the examinee is to operate. The SI equivalent is not so clear in this case, but the description suggests some productive-thinking activity.

In a general treatment of the organization of abilities, Humphreys (1962) at first espoused the hierarchical type of model and marshaled arguments in support of that type. He abruptly rejected this type, however, in favor of the Guttman facet model. His objec-

[1] An excellent review of the history of the application of factor analysis to the understanding of intelligence and a comparison of the theoretical models are given in French by Oléron (1957).

tion to the SI model offered the belief that tests of the SI factors are too simple and that more complex tests will demonstrate a model of the facet type.

Bloom's educational taxonomy   Bloom's taxonomy, as it has been known, was the joint product of a number of educators who were concerned about achieving a more widely accepted set of concepts and categories of concepts that could be more profitably used for communication and for guiding research in connection with curricula, teaching, and examining in education (B. S. Bloom, 1956). The well-known type of taxonomy that has prevailed in biology was the pattern toward which the efforts of his group were aimed. Although it was not proposed as a basic psychological theoretical system, the chief concern of its innovators was with psychological matters, including such activities as "remembering, recalling, knowledge, thinking, problem solving, and creating" (Bloom, 1956, p. 2). The many parallels with category concepts in the SI model are of interest here.

Of the six major categories in the taxonomy, four can be related to the operation of cognition. They are called "knowledge" (naturally the most inclusive, in the context of education), "comprehension," "application," and "analysis." From the point of view of psychological functioning as indicated by the 24 cognition factors in the SI model, there is an enormous amount of redundancy in the four major categories. Perhaps it would be unfair to say that only cognition is involved; there are some implications for memory and production.

But productive-thinking operations have the most obvious place in the taxonomy's major category, called "synthesis." Subcategories are production of communications, plans, relations, and sets of operations. These latter conceptions suggest the products of relations and systems. The sixth major category of "evaluation" comes nearest to a one-to-one parallel with an SI operation category, one having the same name. For some reason, the operation category of memory was given little attention; perhaps emphasis was desired on other things.

Summary

Frames of reference or theories are important because they are needed to provide significant goals and directions. They generate problems and hypotheses and help to interpret and evaluate results of investigations. A good frame of reference should be comprehensive, permitting the envisagement of much territory for exploration and excluding nothing that might be not only relevant but also significant. It should be systematic, taking advantage of all possible logical connections. It should be empirically based so as to yield communicable concepts.

Of certain somewhat standard types of models in human thinking, three have been applied in connection with the factor-analytic approach to the investigation and theory of intelligence. Factor theory itself utilizes a dimensional type of model, in which each factor is represented by a unique dimension in common-factor space. This model provides a reference frame for describing individuals and also tests; individuals are represented as points in the common-factor space and tests as vectors.

The factor analysis of a matrix of intercorrelations from among a set of tests involves the step of extraction of factors and the rotation of the axes for those extracted factors. Extraction determines the number of dimensions needed to account for the intercorrelations. Rotations are needed to place the reference frame of factor axes in a position such that each factor is psychologically meaningful. Illustrative steps were given.

A number of models have been proposed to provide organized systems of the many intellectual and other factors that have been found by investigators. Burt and Vernon have proposed hierarchical models, with Spearman's g at the top and with successive subdivisions in an inverted-tree design. Further evidence was cited against the acceptance of g, a key concept in those models, and against the kind of support that is sometimes offered for a hierarchical model for this purpose.

The writer's structure-of-intellect model was presented, with reasons for the need of a morphological type of model, particularly to take care of the obvious parallels that occur between series of factors. Some relations to other theories were pointed out. Brief mention was made of Guttman's facet type of model, which is in the early stages of development, and to Bloom's taxonomy of educational concepts, which attempts to cover a large range of intellectual activities without benefit of factor analysis.

II The structure of intelligence

4 Cognitive abilities

This chapter and the next four present the known evidence in support of the structure-of-intellect theory and model and of the concepts and categories involved, but they do much more than that. They supply the empirical referents for the many concepts and hence for the theory. In doing so, they lay a basis for the further general psychological theory to follow.

The division of the model for exposition purposes is first along the line of the five operation categories; hence the five chapters. Each chapter will begin with the presentation of a matrix of the SI factors for the operation category in question, with 4 columns for the 4 kinds of content and 6 rows for the 6 kinds of products. Reference to Table 4.1 will show this kind of matrix. Each of the 24 cells of such a matrix represents a single factor, with minor exceptions in the cognition and memory matrices, in which some cells have more than one factor, the reasons for which will be explained.

Each factor has a trigram symbol that stands for its unique combination of operation, content, and product, symbolized in that order. The letter symbol for each category is the initial letter for that category name, except in a few instances in which there are substitutions to avoid confusion. Thus, the symbol CBU stands for the cognition of behavioral units, and CMI stands for the cognition of semantic implications.[1]

Table 4.1   Matrix of the cognition factors (C) represented in the structure of intellect

Content				
Figural (F)	*Symbolic* (S)	*Semantic* (M)	*Behavioral* (B)	
CFU-V N 3, 14	CSU-V S 14	CMU N 2, 4, 6, 7, 9	CBU 2 14	*Units* (U)
CFU-A 1	CSU-A 2	10, 11, 13, 14		
CFC S 14	CSC S 13	CMC S	CBC 1	*Classes* (C)
CFR S 1, 3, 4	CSR S 14	CMR S 3	CBR 1	*Relations* (R)
CFS-V N 3, 4, 7, 9, 14	CSS S 14	CMS N 4, 6, 13, 14	CBS 1	*Systems* (S)
CFS-K S				
CFS-A 1				
CFT N 4, 13, 14	CST 1	CMT S	CBT 1	*Transformations* (T)
CFI S 4, 13	CSI S 14	CMI S 14	CBI 1	*Implications* (I)

[1] Quick reference to the SI model and its categories to be found inside the front cover may be helpful in many places in the chapters to come.

The trigram for the factor appears in the upper-left corner of the cell. Following it is a digit or letter to indicate the number of known analyses in which it is believed that such a factor has been demonstrated. The identification of a factor has been the writer's own, and in some instances it does not agree with the investigator's opinion. A factor that has been demonstrated only once or twice has a 1 or a 2 following the factor trigram. If it has been demonstrated more than twice but less than 10 times, the letter S (for several) follows the trigram; if 10 or more times, the letter N (for numerous); and if there has been no analysis, a zero.

On a second line numbers will sometimes be seen. These numbers indicate the chronological-age levels at which the factor has been demonstrated, no age below one year or above fourteen years being exhibited. Almost all the factors have been demonstrated at senior-high-school ages or for young adults. Years below three are mentioned with hesitation, because the tests for those ages are so different from those used in later years that there is risk in deciding the factors are the same. A number of the SI factors have been reported for ages even lower than one year by Stott and Ball (1963) and others. They are not noted in these matrices.

Within each chapter, the presentation of the factors will be by rows of the matrix; that is, the units factors will be mentioned first and the implications factors last, going from figural to behavioral factors in each row. An effort has been made to show much variety in kinds of tests have have been found to measure each factor, to give an impression of the breadth or scope of meaning that justly belongs to that factor. The reason for this, besides attempting to convey the meaning of the factor, is to help to reduce a common impression, sometimes expressed, to the effect that if there are so many factors, each one cannot be of much importance. There is even some inclination to regard some of the factors as specifics. No factor is genuinely specific unless it is represented only by alternate forms of the same test. A variety of tests mentioned for a factor should help to dispel any idea that it might be specific.

There will be no effort to mention all tests that have been found significantly related to each factor, where "significantly" means with a loading of .30 or greater. Such information can be found for the years to 1950 in J. W. French's very informative monograph (1951). Information of later origin can be found in the various *Reports from the Psychological Laboratory,* from the Aptitudes Research Project at the University of Southern Calfornia. One reason for not mentioning all tests is that it is apparent that many factors reported in the literature are confoundings of SI factors, in which case the factor to which the loading refers is ambiguous, and loadings are also sometimes inflated (Zimmerman, 1953a). Another reason is that there would be much redundancy in some instances, some tests not adding materially to the information about the properties of a factor. In general, factor loadings will not be mentioned, but in some instances they are stated to illustrate certain points. Some discussion of certain tests will occur where this serves to add information.

Cognition of units

Since these next five chapters are devoted to building up the experiential background for the concepts connected with the SI model, unelaborated definitions of those terms will be given as starting points, leaving more extensive generalizing discussion for Chapters 9 and 10. *Cognition* is defined as awareness, immediate discovery or rediscovery, or recognition of information in various forms: comprehension or understanding. *Units* are relatively segregated or circumscribed items of information having "thing" character, perhaps equivalent to the gestalt "figure on a ground." The gestalt concept of "closure" describes very well the process by which units are set off from other information.

Figural units (CFU)   As we look at the cell in Table 4.1 for figural units, we see not one but two factors represented. Figural information has sensory character, hence differs along the lines of the various senses. Most of the figural cognitive abilities we know have been demonstrated by using visually presented tests; and, what is more important, the examinee (E) processes his information in visual form. There is reason to believe that there are intellectual abilities for dealing with other kinds of sensory information, at least auditory and kinesthetic, for which some evidence is given here.

Cognition of visual-figural units $(CFU\text{-}V)$ This factor was evidently first reported by Thurstone (1944) and interpreted by him as "speed of perception." It should not be confused with the factor he earlier called simply "perceptual." J. W. French (1951) later called what is now identified as CFU-V "gestalt perception."

Letters of the alphabet can be used as figural units, and they constitute the material for four of Thurstone's tests:

Perceptual Span S (E identifies letters flashed in the periphery of vision)
Dark Adaptation (speed of seeing dim letters after bright stimulation)
Peripheral Span D (E reports whether the peripherally flashed letter is the same as the letter fixated)
Mutilated Words (E recognizes words with parts of letters erased; see Figure 4.1)

The word-recognition feature of Mutilated Words makes it in part a measure of factor CSU-V, the cognition of visual-symbolic units, since words are symbolic units whereas letters can also be quite readily processed as figural units. In large part, the recognition of the words in this particular form of test is dependent upon recognition of letters as such; hence it is a two-factor test.

Thurstone also used the Street Gestalt Completion test (see Figure 4.2), which has been the most univocal representative of factor CFU-V in more recent analyses. The use of either mutilated words or mutilated objects reduces the amount of sensory input, thus making the cognition task sufficiently difficult for testing purposes. Mooney (1954) has used his own Closure Test, which is based upon the same principle, to good effect for the same factor.

Cognition of auditory-figural units $(CFU\text{-}A)$ The only report qualifying a factor for interpretation as CFU-A was made by Fleishman, Roberts, and Friedman (1958) in an analysis in connection with code-aptitude tests. The definitive tests were:

Copying Behind (E marks the digits 1 to 5 on an answer sheet, following the hearing of the scrambled digits read in rapid succession)
Army Radio Code (after twenty-five minutes of instruction and practice in discriminating the code signals for the letters I, N, and T, E is tested for discrimination of the three signals given in rapid succession)
Dot Perception (either at the beginning or at the end of a series of code signals, E hears a set of one to five dots, to report how many there were in the set)

By analogy to the Thurstone letter tests, the codelike signals in these tests would seem to represent figural auditory units. Recognition is made difficult by forced pacing in the code tests, rather than by omission of parts, as in the parallel visual tests. With the tests limited to digit sounds and code elements, we do not know how general this ability may

Fig. 4-1 Sample items from Thurstone's test Multilated Words. The words FOOTBALL, KITCHEN, and STORY may be more or less readily perceived.

Fig. 4.2 A sample item from the Street Gestalt Completion test. What is the object?

be, but it may be suggested that phonemes could be used successfully in similar tests for the same ability.

Symbolic units (CSU)   Symbolic information is in the form of tokens or signs that can be used to stand for something else. In the cell for CSU we also find two factors, one visual and one auditory. Again, the two seem to be quite parallel.

Cognition of visual-symbolic units (*CSU-V*)   The unit involved in all tests of this factor has been the printed word. It is one thing to see printed letters, as figural units, and another to recognize familiar letter combinations, an obvious hurdle as the child learns to read. The kinds of tests have been quite varied, as shown by those described below.

Disemvoweled Words presents words with blanks where vowels normally appear, e.g., S C __ P __, T R __ V __ L, M __ D __ C __ N __, which should be read as scope, travel, and medicine.

In Omelet Test, an anagrams test, *E* is to tell the correct order for the four letters in a very familiar word, e.g., P A N L, C E I V, E M O C, which should be read as plan, vice, and come. Other forms of anagram tests have also been suitable.

Word Combinations tells *E* to make words out of the end of one word and the beginning of another, as in the item:

1. bridge   *A.* duress
2. beam   *B.* zero
3. open   *C.* pledge
                D. need
                E. None of these

answers:
1, D (gene)
2, C (ample)
3, A (endure)

Four-Letter Words contains lines of capital letters without breaks, within which appear at random four-letter words that *E* is to encircle, as:

A M G E (W I N D) T E Y K O C (R O C K) W Z L U (T E A R) A V N I

Mutilated Words is pictured in Figure 4.1. It typically shares its variance about equally between CSU-V and CFU-V. Both letters and letter combinations must be recognized.

Correct Spelling presents *E* with a list of English words that are commonly misspelled, half of them spelled correctly, half not. *E* is to say whether each given word is correct. Such a test measures CSU-V (Hoepfner, Guilford, & Merrifield, 1964). Spelling in general seems to depend in part on word recognition, but in this case it is more than knowing what word is meant, for *E* could probably *read* correctly the word misspelled. Recognition of the kind assessed by CSU-V tests evidently includes awareness of all letters present and in their proper positions in the word. It is probable that with different forms of spelling tests other factors would be involved, depending upon the kind of task.

Reversed Reading was found by Mooney (1954) to represent a factor that can be interpreted as CSU-V. It presents statements with the words spelled backward, with *E* required to extract the meaning from the statement and to state whether it is true or false. The test is almost as strong for a factor that can be interpreted as being CST (cognition of symbolic transformations), which would be quite reasonable, for *E* must see the transformation of what is given into the normal view of the word before it is recognized. The appearance of such a test on CSU-V suggests that reading print upside down or in mirror image might also do as measures of that factor, but CST might also be involved.

New Words is another Mooney test that came out on CSU-V. The given information is a condensation of two words, e.g., SKRINK, which is to be decoded as "skating rink." This test also involved substantial variance from factor CST.

A test that failed for CSU when it might have been expected to go along with the preceding tests is Five-Letter Words (Mooney, 1954). In this test, *E* is to draw a line through every five-letter word that contains the letter *S* in a long list of words. Sometimes a test that fails to measure a factor tells us a great deal about what a factor is not. This test differs from the preceding ones in that it does not call for the identification of a *particular* symbolic unit. What it does do is to specify the class to which the correct words belong by stating two attributes: containing five letters and containing the letter *S*. Such a test should measure the factor ESU, not CSU, since it calls for judgment of how well symbolic units fit a class specification. We shall see later that a successful test for ESU merely gives one specification: words containing the letter *U*. All the words in such a test are very easily recognized; there is no missing information, no distorted information, or no extra information to distract or interfere with particular units.

Cognition of auditory-symbolic units (*CSU-A*)   Like printed words that we see, spoken words that we hear are also units of symbolic information. Karlin (1942) discovered a factor that fits such an idea. Some tests were:

Haphazard Speech (*E* writes words that are spoken with unusual inflections)
Illogical Grouping (*E* writes words or phrases spoken out of order)
Singing (*E* writes words heard in singing)

In all these tests, *E* has to derive word structure in auditory terms from given stimulation that is designed to make the process abnormally difficult, again, for testing purposes. The kind of difficulty appears to be important, for two other tests that appear to fit this category did not do at all well for this factor. They were:

Intellective Masking (*E* hears words against a background of continuous talking)
Sensory Masking (*E* hears words against a buzzing background)

Thus, masking stimulation, although it lowers intelligibility of words, does not serve as good material for measuring factor CSU-A. The important difference seems to be that the successful tests for this factor present distorted sound patterns that deviate from conventional speech symbols without interferences. Apparently the singing of words does not provide interferences. The unsuccessful tests mentioned provide distracting and interfering stimulation, not simple distortion. Hearing words on distracting backgrounds might be a kind of successful measure of a hypothetical factor NFT-A, convergent production of auditory-figural transformations, by analogy to tests of seeing hidden figures, which measure factor NFT-V, or seeing hidden words, which measure a factor NST-V. Two tests mentioned above, Four-Letter Words and Word Combinations, are inclined to have a little variance from that factor.

Carroll (1962) has made reference to a factor that he calls "phonetic coding ability," which might well be CSU-A. He defines it as the ability to code auditory phonetic material so as to be able to recognize and to remember it for a few seconds. The mention of memory and the fact that a test of memory for syllables and paralogs was involved on the factor suggest that he might have been dealing with a confounding of CSU-A and a possible MSU-A. Earlier, Carroll (1953) had pointed out that there are very large individual differences in hearing speech on the background of noise, but in view of Karlin's finding that tests of this kind did not go with his factor CSU-A, Carroll might have been talking about a possible factor NFT-A, as previously suggested.

Semantic units (**CMU**)   Under this heading we come to the best-known and most widely replicated of all the intellectual factors. Probably its first announcement should be credited to Cyril Burt (1915).[1] The most dependable and most univocal measure of CMU is a vocabulary test of some kind, some kinds being better than others. The completion type, in which *E* provides definitions or other kinds of responses indicating that he has speaking acquaintance with the concept for which the word stands, is usually quite successful; so is a multiple-choice form of test.

Note that it is cognition of the meaning attached to the word label, not of the label

[1] It is likely, however, that the factor reported was a verbal-composite factor, as Burt himself later implied (Burt, 1917; 1949).

itself, that is important for factor CMU. Thus, from one point of view, the size of the examinee's listening or reading vocabulary can be claimed as the variable measured. There have been many investigations of the level of understanding indicated by E's responses, whether they be synonyms, or descriptions, or some comments about the words presented. The problem of level of response will be discussed at length in Chapter 9.

One type of vocabulary test that tends to go off to some extent on factors other than CMU presents the definition of the word, with E to supply the word. Hints of the word may be offered to E in terms of an initial letter or the number of letters in it, or both. There is a factor NMU that has as its special province the supplying of a meaningful word to fit prescribed information: a naming or word-finding ability. A vocabulary-completion test of the type described is likely to go somewhat in the direction of NMU. The content and the product are the same, but the operation is different from that with tests of CMU.

Recent information throws some new light upon the nature of CMU. Two tests that were designed for the factor EMU (evaluation of semantic units) emphasize appreciation of exact meanings or distinctions between fine shadings of meaning (Nihira, Guilford, Hoepfner, & Merrifield, 1964). The words themselves are rather familiar, so that very few examinees should miss them in an ordinary vocabulary test.

In Word Substitution, E substitutes what he thinks is the best of four alternatives for an underlined word in a sentence. A sample item is:

He was a good doctor, but alcohol was his ruin.
A. plague B. undoing C. fate D. destruction

Synonyms was designed in accordance with the same principle, with the word to be replaced not given in a sentence, e.g.:

LAMP
A. torch B. burner C. candle D. lantern

Neither of these tests measured factor EMU significantly; both measured CMU, which means that this important ability involves more precise knowledge of familiar words as well as breadth of knowledge of less familiar words.

The thinking that led to construction of Synonyms, especially, since it looks like an ordinary multiple-choice vocabulary test in format, suggested the hypothesis that the multiple-choice format itself in a vocabulary test might turn the test in the direction of measurement of the factor EMU to some extent. A typical multiple-choice vocabulary test was put in the analyzed test battery, together with a defining vocabulary test, to see whether the multiple-choice form would show some relation to EMU where the completion form would not. The result was that both forms showed strong relation to CMU; the multiple-choice form showed no relation to EMU.

It is a common finding that CMU comes out with significant loadings in many kinds of verbal tests, such as verbal analogies, verbal relations, and following directions, where those tests are designed to measure factors other than CMU. It is good policy to keep the vocabulary level low in all such tests, in which one may be wanting to emphasize semantic relations, classes, and implications, rather than units. The writer has found that following that policy has helped to differentiate other semantic factors from CMU.

To illustrate what may happen where vocabulary level is not controlled and one wants a reasoning test, we have the well-known Miller Analogies Test. This test was designed to be useful at the graduate-student level. The analogies form of item ordinarily involves relations as the kind of product. But in attempting to make the test difficult for testing purposes, the vocabulary level was apparently stepped up, which shifted the factorial nature of the test toward CMU, which is already well represented in academic-aptitude tests. No factor analysis of the Miller Analogies Test is known to this writer, but its correlation with a good vocabulary test at the college level was reported to be about .85.[1]

But in view of the studies with evaluation tests (for factor EMU) just mentioned, it is apparent that in addition to keeping words familiar, with vocabulary level low, for tests of factors other than CMU, one must also see that the meanings required on the part of E are not too precise. An exception might be in the area of convergent-production abilities.

It should be said that the common loadings for a verbal factor like CMU on verbal tests that are not vocabulary tests may not necessarily mean involvement with variance from CMU. It is suspected that many a verbal factor reported in the literature is not simply CMU but is a varying confounding of CMU with one or more other semantic abilities. One reason for this kind of outcome in an analysis is that the semantic tests of other factors are not sufficiently numerous or sufficiently strong on their respective factors to effect a separation from CMU. Another reason may be that a number of verbal tests are all factorially complex, by virtue of relations to other semantic factors. If the combination of other semantic factors is about the same in all tests, they cannot help coming out together on the same common factor, which is a composite, as Zimmerman (1953a) has pointed out.

Tests other than a vocabulary test that often load significantly on CMU or a CMU-like factor are general-information tests, such as the one in the Wechsler scales and in the Army Alpha, and achievement examinations in various school subjects, which are special-information tests. Tests of special vocabularies can also measure CMU, as demonstrated with the United States Air Force's Technical Vocabulary test, whether scored for predicting navigator success or for predicting bombardier success (Guilford & Lacey, 1947). This suggests that specialized and general vocabularies are likely to vary together.

It is often stated that the dominant factor, by far, in traditional intelligence scales of verbal composition is CMU. This generalization is well supported by citations from J. W. French (1951). The Henmon-Nelson Test of Mental Ability was reported to have a loading of .76 on the verbal factor, and the Otis Self-Administering Test of Mental Ability had a loading of .69. These loadings are of the same order of magnitude as for the Thurstone PMA Verbal score, with a loading of .74. The College Entrance Examination Board test, Verbal score, was reported to have a loading of .79. There is a real question of how much prediction such scales are giving over and above that obtainable from a good vocabulary test that might take one-quarter of the time. This question hinges on the univocality of the "verbal factor" involved when these verbal loadings have been found: whether the factor was a verbal composite or CMU, and whether there is enough of other relevant factors involved to add to predictions.

Behavioral units (CBU)   Since the concept of behavioral information is quite new, some of the general characteristics of that kind of content need attention before the first behavioral factor is introduced. For discussion purposes, *behavioral content* is defined as information, essentially nonverbal, involved in human interactions, where awareness of attention, perceptions, thoughts, desires, feelings, moods, emotions, intentions, and actions of other persons and of ourselves is important.

As early as 1920, E. L. Thorndike had proposed that there is a social intelligence, apart from ordinary intelligence, and he defined it as ". . . the ability to understand and

---

[1] Personal communication from R. G. Watt, former director of the Testing Bureau, University of Southern California.

manage men and women, boys and girls—to act wisely in human relations" (1920, p. 228). He went on to express doubts as to whether pictures could be used in the place of real-life situations as test material, saying that ". . . for most of the activities of intelligence in response to the behavior of human beings, a genuine situation with real persons is essential. . . ." Recent developments may have proved him to be quite wrong in making the last statement. The evidence will soon be presented.

To make the discussion more concrete, information about some varieties of subject matter of behavioral tests will help. Most of the sensory cues from which behavioral information is generated are visual or auditory in character, instigated by the behavior of persons. It is the expressive aspects from which the cues arise: the postures, movements, vocalizations, and verbalizations that people show. The expression can involve the entire body, a part of the body, or a combination of parts.

For testing purposes, most of the material is presented in pictorial form. This does not mean that the tests measure figural abilities, although the absence of figural-factor content should not be taken for granted. The fact that the information processed by the examinee and the information about which he is being tested are behavioral makes the tests behavioral. The pictures are in the form of photographs or line drawings. Some of them show just one person; others show two or more persons interacting. Verbalization on the part of the examinee is generally avoided, so as to prevent the involvement with semantic information. Tests that require E to name expressions or to make or to accept comments about them should be avoided for the same reason. Even then, one should not take for granted the elimination of all semantic content. But as will be seen, verbal material can be used effectively in proper ways as carriers of behavioral information, avoiding semantic content.

There has been very little precedent in the way of factor analysis of social-intellectual abilities. The first report of such an analysis was by Robert L. Thorndike (1936), who analyzed the parts of the George Washington Social Intelligence Test along with five tests of verbal content. He extracted three centroid factors but unfortunately did not rotate axes. Because the first centroid factor had such large loadings on all tests, he concluded that a verbal factor would account for most of the variances of the social tests. There appear to be indications in the centroid matrix, however, that as a group the social tests had something unique; at least a second dimension seemed called for.

A second attempt was reported by Woodrow (1939b), who also analyzed the parts of the same social-intelligence scale along with 47 other tests of very heterogeneous nature. Four of the five social tests went strongly on a verbal factor (undoubtedly a composite), and the fifth, Memory for Names and Faces, went on the spatial factor (also evidently a composite), for some unaccountable reason.

The first analysis to report a behavioral factor was done by Wedeck (1947), who introduced into his analysis eight new behavioral tests of his own. Four of them employed pictures from paintings by contemporary artists, with verbal answers called for to indicate understanding. Two portrayed temporary mental states, and two indicated cognition of personality traits. One test required matching character sketches with traits. Another required E to say whether the heard answers to questions were truthful or false. Still another presented social-situational problems for E to solve. There were seven nonverbal tests and four verbal tests in the analyzed battery.

Wedeck reported three factors, of which one had to be g (on which only seven tests had loadings of .3 or higher, incidentally), one was a verbal factor, and the third was identified as behavioral cognition. On the last-named factor, the four tests involving cognition of immediate mental states were strongest. Extraction of more factors and further

 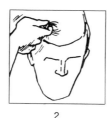  

| 1 | 2 | 3 | 4 |

Fig. 4.3   An item from the Expressions test. Which of the four alternative expressions conveys the same information about the state of mind of the person as in the lone figure above? Answer 4 is keyed, because it also gives the impression of emphasizing a point.

rotation of axes would probably have cleared up the picture considerably. Wedeck might be given credit for finding the trace of a CBU factor.

Recently, El-Abd (1963), in a study designed to test a number of structure-of-intellect hypotheses concerning abilities, found something that might be CBU, for a sample of boys but not for a sample of girls. Defining test for the factor was Faces, which involves naming expressions of faces, and Old Figures Persons, which is composed of symbols from Egyptian picture writing with multiple-choice names of things signified. Presumably the symbols have behavioral reference.

From one analysis aimed at the area of behavioral cognition (O'Sullivan et al., 1965), we have results to show several tests loaded on factor CBU, although not so strongly as should be desired. The test Faces, composed of photographs of faces from the Frois-Witt-man (Hulin & Katz, 1935) and the Lightfoot (Engen, Levy, & Schlosberg, 1957) series, was designed by analogy to a vocabulary test. One face depicts a certain mental state, and with four other faces given as alternatives, E is to choose the alternative that indicates the same state of mind or nearly the same. Here the tester has to be very careful lest figural properties of the faces give away the answer, by making judicious choice of alternatives.

Expressions is another multiple-choice form of test, with outline drawings of expressive behavior, using faces, hands, arms, and general postures in various combinations (see Figure 4.3). The variety of body parts represented in this test helps E to infer that the ability is not confined to facial expressions, for faces are emphasized as sources of information in the other CBU tests used in the analysis.

In each item of Questions, the face of the well-known French comedian Fernandel is shown, and with it are four questions which might have been asked of him just before he looks the way he does. In one item, with a surprised, leering look on Fernandel's face, the questions are:

1. Can you remember the first line of the Constitution?
2. Don't you think that girl's short skirt is a scandal?
3. Isn't that your wife's car?
4. Did you enjoy your vacation?

Inflections presents vocal stimuli by means of a tape recording. Six short verbal utterances are used, e.g., "Yes," "I did it," and "Really." Each is spoken with five different inflections, for each of which E has four faces in line drawings to use as alternative answers, to say which face goes with the vocal stimulus. It would take one or more additional vocal tests and some with all-sound information to determine whether the visual and auditory tests cohere on a single CBU factor or whether they separate as they do for factors CFU and CSU. It would be a reasonable hypothesis that CBU is more like CMU in this respect, that it does not matter what the kind of sensory input is: there is but one CBU.

Cognition of classes

Classes can be somewhat operationally defined as recognized sets of items of information grouped by virtue of their common properties. One thinks of *items of information* as units, first, for they form the most commonly known types of classes in our experience. But there is evidence, which will be presented, that classes may be formed of relations and systems as well as of units. There are also classes of classes, as in hierarchical models. But before all this takes on too much of an appearance of complexity, let us get right to examples of abilities to know classes. The definition puts the emphasis upon things that may be observed. The crux of classes, psychologically, is in the form of class ideas or class concepts, and this puts the emphasis upon attributes or properties, where it more properly belongs.

Tests of abilities pertaining to the cognition of classes can be of several standard types. In one format, a set of similar items of information is given, with E to tell which member of the set does not belong to the class. This is the *exclusion* format. An *inclusion* format can take several forms, but a matching test is a common example. Given single items of information on the one hand and several groups, the members of which belong together by reason of certain common properties, on the other hand, which item goes with which group? A discrimination format provides two sets, each of a different class, with E to say to which class a given item of information belongs or whether it belongs to neither. Another kind of classes test that has not done so well calls for the naming of classes. It has been found that naming tests become involved with the naming factor, NMU. Such tests are often of complexity 2: they measure significantly two different factors.

Figural classes (CFC)   The more or less successful tests for CFC are described below.

In Figure Classification, E assigns each given figure to one of five classes, each defined by three examples of their class. This is a short matching format, as shown in Figure 4.4 (see page 82).

Figure Exclusion asks E to select the one figure in a set of five that does not belong to the class. Another exclusion test used by Canisia (1962) was called Figure Grouping.

Figure Matching presents a figure and five alternative figures, the problem being to say which of the five has the most features in common with the single figure, as shown in Figure 4.5 (see page 82). Although this test has apparently been successful for factor CFC, because of its similarity to certain evaluation-ability tests, it may share its variance with factor EFC. This possibility is yet to be tested.

Symbolic classes (CSC)   It has been difficult to construct tests for CSC that do not also significantly measure other factors. One of the more successful has been Number Classification, which provides short matching sets, as in this sample item:

Which one of the five alternative numbers, *A* to *E,* fits into each of the classes?

Classes			Alternatives	
I. 44	55	33	*A.*	421
II. 10	45	70	*B.*	53
III. 23	83	31	*C.*	219
IV. 89	49	109	*D.*	22
			E.	25

answers: I, *D;* II, *E;* III, *B;* IV, *C*

Number-Group Naming asks for statement of the class property, as in the example:

15   27   42

answer: divisible by 3

Although this is a strong measure of factor CSC, with a loading as high as .60, it has a substantial secondary loading on the naming factor NMU, a common fate of tests requiring naming.

The test Best Number Pairs was designed to measure the parallel factor of ESC, but it proved to be a fairly good measure of CSC instead. A sample item is:

Choose one of the three pairs of numbers that makes the best class (where "best class" is defined by the rank order: perfect square, multiples in common, odd or even numbers, and no common properties) :

A. 6-4   *B.* 4-9   *C.* 9-6

answer: B   (perfect squares)

This test could perhaps be made to measure ESC by invoking decisions of the yes-no type, e.g., "The pair is or is not a set of perfect squares."

The Number Relations test is a good example of a principle stated earlier, that classes can be composed of relations as well as of units. A sample item is:

Which number pair does not belong with the others?
A. 1-5
B. 2-6
C. 5-8
D. 3-7

answer: C   (in all other cases the difference is 4)

The relation, as such, is very easy to see; hence the loading on CSR was very low (Guilford, Merrifield, Christensen, & Frick, 1961). But unfortunately for a test of CSC, an equal amount of variance on factor CMS came into the picture. This should indicate that examinees use a strategy that involves verbalizing and find it useful to grasp some kind of semantic conception in order to solve the problems.

Another test for CSC must be mentioned for two reasons. It is a letter test, whereas the others mentioned in connection with this factor are number tests. The presence of this test tends to show that the generality of CSC is such as to apply to letter material as well as to numerical. Such generalizations quite often apply to symbolic abilities. The other reason is that the test, Letter Grouping, illustrates the point that classes of systems occur, as well as classes of units and of relations. This test was originated by L. L. Thurs-

Items   Alternatives

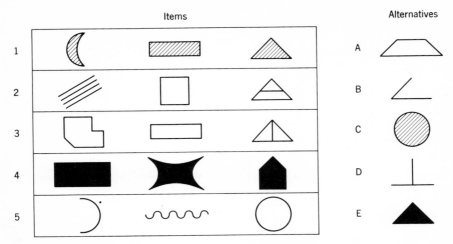

Fig. 4.4 Some matching items from the test Figure Classification. Which alternative belongs to the same class as the three given in each item? *Answers:* 1, *C* (striated); 2, *A* (contains parallel lines); 3, *D* (contains a right angle); 4, *E* (solid black); 5, *C* (contains curve).

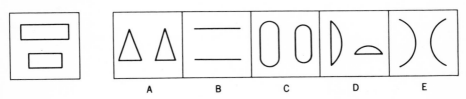

Fig. 4.5 Item from the Figure Matching test. Which alternative at the right is most nearly like that at the left? *Answer: C*, because it has the most attributes in common—similar large and small figures in parallel positions.

tone and helped to establish his "induction" factor. But it appears that his induction factor might have been a composite, a confounding of CSC and CSS. A sample item for Letter Grouping is:

Which letter group does not belong with the rest?
1. A A B C   *2.* A C A D   *3.* A C F G   *4.* A A C G

answer: 3   (the others contain two *A*s)

Letter Grouping has a significant loading on factor CSS (Guilford, Merrifield, et al., 1961), which could be the reason it went along with Thurstone's induction factor, which was probably closer to CSS. Letter Grouping could probably be slanted more toward CSC by making the principles that identify the letter groups absurdly simple to see, with relatively less certainty regarding class membership.

Another CSC test utilizing letter material is Word Groups, a sample item from which is:

What do the following words have in common in terms of letter content?
read   retire   rearming   restless

The answer is that they all begin with *re*. The absence of NMU from this test is interesting, for it is not strictly a naming test in the sense of producing one right word; the answer can be expressed in a number of ways, all acceptable. *E* has freedom to use different words.

Semantic classes (CMC)   Tests for CMC, like those for CSC, have also suffered from secondary factor variances, indicating that in both instances it has been difficult to apply the proper experimental controls to focalize tests upon CSC and CMC.

Verbal Classification is a test adapted from Thurstone, illustrated by the following item:

Check the class to which each of the words in the middle list belongs, leaving the spaces blank if the word belongs to neither class:

COW	_____	desk	___✓___	TABLE
HORSE	___✓___	sheep	_____	CHAIR
GOAT	_____	rocker	___✓___	BOOKCASE
DOG	_____	tree	_____	LAMP
	___✓___	cat		
	_____	nose		
	_____	dresser	___✓___	
	___✓___	donkey		

With some consistency this test has some variance from factor CMR. The most obvious kind of relation is that of member to class or class to member: supraordinate or subordinate. The test's relation to CMR may be due to the need for seeing the genus-species relationships.

Word Classification is of the exclusion type, with items like:

Which word does not belong?
A. horse   *B*. flower   *C*. mosquito   *D*. snake

Tests of the exclusion type have been at least moderately successful for measuring cognition-of-classes abilities, but there have been better tests for this purpose.

The Word-Group Naming test is another classes-naming test, which suffers the common fate of having much NMU variance. A sample item is:

What is the nature of the following class?
knife   pan   bowl   rolling pin   strainer

to which the term *cooking utensils* would be the most expected answer, but similar terminology would be acceptable as long as it fits the class concept.

Behavioral classes (CBC)   Only recently demonstrated (O'Sullivan et al., 1965), the ability to apprehend classes of behavioral information has been represented fairly well by two tests and not by two others. The best test in the one analysis was Expression Grouping. In each item (see Figure 4.6) three line drawings of expressions, of hands, of face, or of the whole body, form the basis for a class. The task is to find from four alternatives, also expressions from different body sources, the one expression that belongs to the class; the others do not. In the illustrated item, the three class representatives should convey the idea of approval or approbation, so that alternative number 1 is correct.

Picture Exclusion presents a set of four photographed expressions in each item, two based upon head and shoulders, one on hands, and one on body posture (the face being

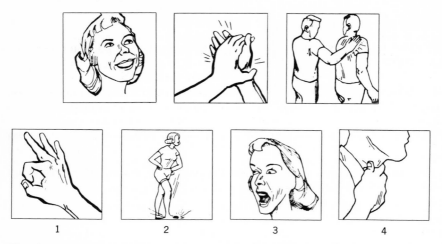

Fig. 4.6   An item from the Expression Grouping test. Which of the four alternatives is the best candidate for membership in the class of three? *Answer:* 1 (indicates approbation or approval).

blocked out). Which one of the four does not belong to the class? The exclusion type of item works with behavioral information as well as with other kinds.

One of the tests that failed to measure CBC was recognized as a gamble, for it deals with classes of systems, in a pioneer territory. Odd Strip Out is an exclusion type of test in which three cartoon strips are presented in each item. Two of them have some psychological significance in common, such as a character (Ferd'nand) doing harm to someone but showing nonchalance about it, whereas the third cartoon strip does not have these features. The difficulty with the test is that the situations portrayed in each strip are at a high level, so that the strip emphasizes grasping a behavioral system. Thus the test's variance went most strongly on the CBS factor. There was incidentally a small but significant variance from CBT, which means that some reinterpretations of the situations came in handy, for some of the examinees, at least. Those who might have stayed with their first impressions were possibly led into error.

The other test that failed is of the group-naming type. The group of expressions to be named in the Sound Meaning test are vocal but not verbal, given from tape recordings. They include such expressions as sighs, moans, whistles, applause, and laughter. A set of three such expressions, belonging to the same group because they represent a class, is presented in each item, with E to select the best word label from a set of four in his booklet. The main trouble with the test is its very low reliability (about .30). Its higher loadings were on CBC and NMU, as one should expect, with a similar loading on CMU (all loadings about .23), the latter suggesting some difficulty with word meanings.

The limited experiences with sound-presented tests of behavioral cognition indicate that the art of constructing such tests has not yet been mastered. One of the inherent difficulties is that with sound presentations the stimuli must be spread out in time and the examinee cannot prolong, or reexpose himself to, sensory inputs of the item, as he can with printed items. Some memory is very likely involved. On the other hand, such time-controlled stimulus presentations may be definite assets in connection with other kinds of abilities, especially memory abilities.

Cognition of relations

We come now to the kind of product—relation—on which Spearman appeared to stake everything pertaining to g and its dominant role in intelligence. It may be that he had in mind a broader conception of the term *relation* than that used in SI theory, in which it is defined as a recognized connection between two items of information based upon variables or upon points of contact that apply to them. The term *variables* is included in the definition in recognition of the fact that many relations are of a quantitative or ordered sort, as described in such statements as "*A* is more *X* than *B*" or "*D* is less *X* than *B*." In their conception of "seriation," Inhelder and Piaget (1964) give most of their attention to this type of relation, which is so conspicuous in mathematics. The many kinds of relations that actually exist psychologically will be given more attention in Chapter 10. We shall see some examples of certain kinds incidentally in what follows.

Although relations between classes, between systems, and even between relations may occur, as well as relations between units, we shall be concerned mainly with the last-named case, which is the only one represented in relation tests thus far. The kind of relation-cognition test of longest standing is in the form of analogies. Such a test, of verbal analogies, appeared in the Army Alpha, and it has been more or less popular in standard intelligence scales to the present time. The multiple-choice format is the most favored because of the conveniences of answer-sheet recording and scoring.

A completion form of analogies test would almost certainly represent two relations factors. There would be recognition of the relation between the first two items of information, figures, words, and so on, which would emphasize factor CFR or CMR or their parallels. After having grasped the relation, if he does, *E*'s next task is to think of an item of information that fits the third given "fundament," as Spearman called it, and his own cognized relation. The latter event should depend mostly upon factor NFR or NMR. If the words needed to complete the analogy are uncommon or hard to think of precisely, some NMU and CMU variance would probably enter the measurement picture. But the two main factors, CFR and NFR (with figural items) or CMR and NMR (with meaningful-verbal items), would fit Spearman's concepts of "eduction of relations" and "eduction of correlates," respectively.

A completion form of analogies test, then, should be of complexity 2. The supplying of alternative responses as in a multiple-choice form should materially reduce the convergent-production variance, but this would also depend upon the prevailing strategy of the examinees. If, quite generally, the *E*s actually produce their own correlates before examining the alternative answers, the convergent-production variance would be substantial. If *E*'s general strategy is to look at the alternatives to see how each is related to the third element in the analogy and to match these relations with that seen between the first two, the cognition variance would be enhanced. This is an example of how prevailing strategy of examinees can help to determine what is being measured. J. W. French (1965) has recently investigated "response styles" and strategies and how they affect factor composition of tests. He found that some tests are more open to effects of such examinee-instituted conditions than others.

Another form of test for relation-cognition abilities is of the trend type. It presents a set of items of information of a certain content category in serial order. A continuum or dimension of some kind is represented for *E* to grasp if he can. This type of test comes closest to the Piaget concept of seriation, although it was developed independently of that idea. In such a series, if the items of information are in perfect order, each item is con-

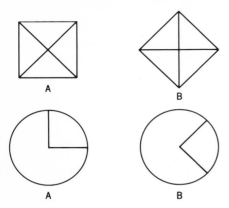

Fig. 4.7 An item from Perceptual Relations Naming. The two *A-B* pairs illustrate the same relation. What is it? *B* is advanced clockwise 45 degrees with respect to *A*.

nected to the next in the series by some relation. Some series could be out of order, in some test items and not in others, for *E* to say which are in correct order; or *E* could be asked to shift the order where necessary to make it correct. A trend test is thus a kind of succession of analogies. A special variant of the trend test has a matrix type of item, in which a different kind of trend occurs in columns and in rows; there may be only three steps in each trend.

Figural relations (CFR)   As might be expected, one of the best types of CFR tests is a figure-analogies form. A test called Figure Analogies used by Kettner, Guilford, & Christensen (1959a) was clearly superior and relatively univocal for measuring CFR. In the Air Force use of a Figure Analogies test, although its salient loading was on the factor called Reasoning II, which can now be interpreted as CFR, it had significant secondary loadings on three other factors. The Abstract Reasoning test of the Differential Aptitude Tests proved to have a strong and clearly univocal relation to CFR in one analysis (O'Sullivan et al., 1965). It is ironical that the test was entitled Abstract Reasoning, however, since it represents a *figural*-reasoning ability and might better have been entitled "Concrete Reasoning."

A test called Perceptual Relations Naming (see Figure 4.7) performed in the direction expected (Kettner et al., 1959a). From hindsight, it might have been expected to show significant loadings on factor NMU, the fate of most naming tests, but it does not always do so. Reference to Figure 4.7 may show why NMU would not be so important. In describing the change in going from *A* to *B* in the two pairs, *E* has much liberty in the choice of words; he does not have to converge very much on one and one only, as is true of NMU tests in general.

The Figure Matrix test (see Figure 4.8) has consistently measured factor CFR, usually with fairly satisfactory, univocal strength. In the Air Force research (Guilford & Lacey, 1947) that kind of test was a good measure of Reasoning II, which was probably CFR.

A simple figural trend test, simple because it is composed of items with one-dimensional trends rather than two-dimensional items as in Figure Matrix, is the Series part of R. B. Cattell's Culture-Fair Test. This test should be a measure of factor CFR. In one analysis in which it was known to be used (Berger, Guilford, & Christensen, 1957), Series had no significant loadings on any factor that was found. No CFR factor was identified

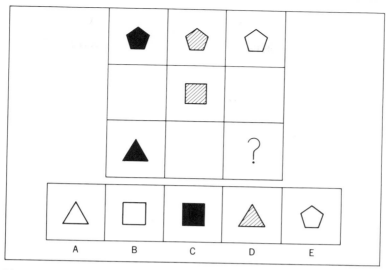

Fig. 4.8 A sample item from the Figure Matrix test. What kind of figure should appear in the cell with the question mark? *answer: A.*

in that analysis; so it could still show that relationship. In a later rotation of the same matrix, in which a CFR factor was permitted to appear, Series had a moderate loading on it.

If the Series test proves to be a measure primarily of CFR or some other figural ability, as should be expected, it would be likely to miss the intention of the author, who probably had something much broader than figural abilities in mind in proposing the test as a measure of intelligence. In attempts to construct "culture-free" or "culture-fair" tests, it is a common trend to settle on nonverbal ones, to circumvent the language barrier encountered in the use of verbal tests. The result is that semantic abilities go largely unassessed, and they are precisely the ones that would probably be of greatest interest to the tester. The stark implication from the findings in testing the SI theory is that the content areas of abilities are the least easily bridged by means of homogeneous tests. The indications are that if and where there are correlations between factors, they are least likely to be across content boundaries.

Symbolic relations (CSR)   Seeing Trends II, as its name suggests, is a trend test, modeled after Seeing Trends I, in which the trends are verbally meaningful. In Seeing Trends II, the systematic series of words is based upon a relation that pertains to spelling. For example, what is the principle in the item:

rated   crate   morning   dearth   separate

---

answer: The letter *R* moves one place to the right each time.

Seeing Trends II has been a fairly dependable but not always strong test for CSR. Twice in six analyses it has had a significant secondary loading on CMU, for which there is no ready explanation, except that before *E* can write an answer, he must make a translation of the symbolic relation into a semantic idea. Limitation in vocabulary may be a handicap in some instances.

Word Relations is in the category of an analogies test of the multiple-choice type, with the minor variation of presenting two pairs of words to help pinpoint the intended relation that is to be applied in the third pair of words. A sample item reads:

on-no	*A*. art
top-pot	*B*. pat
part-___ ?	*C*. rapt
	D. tar
answer: E	*E*. trap

A secondary loading for this test on DSR in one analysis would suggest that a common strategy in that case might have been a resort to a trial-and-error approach (divergent-production tactics) in filling the blank with the question mark, checking with the given alternative answers in the process. In such a manner, secondary loadings give leads ·to hypotheses as to what examinees may do with items of a test.

Another analogies test failed to measure CSR strongly. It is Letter Analogies, in which items of information to be related are single letters, pairs of letters, or triplets, two examples being:

m-o	*1*. k	ij-jk	*1*. fe
f-h	*2*. l	op-pq	*2*. uv
j- ?	*3*. u	ef- ?	*3*. gi
	4. i		*4*. fg
	5. p		*5*. bc

answers: 2, 4

It is not the figural properties of the letters that are used in forming the relations; it is alphabetical position or order. Letter Analogies is parallel to Word Relations in format, the obvious difference being that the latter uses words as items of information and the former uses single letters or letter combinations. The failure of Letter Analogies to go strongly on CSR cannot be attributed to its low reliability, for its communality was .50 (Guilford, Merrifield, Christensen, & Frick, 1961).

Semantic relations (CMR)   We might expect a verbal-analogies test to be one of the best for factor CMR, and this seems to be the case. In Verbal Analogies I an effort was made to emphasize variance in CMR at the expense of variance in NMR by making the apprehension of the relation between the first pair of words relatively difficult and the satisfaction of the relation in the second pair relatively easy. Verbal Analogies II was constructed with the relative difficulties reversed so as to stress NMR variance. In no analysis of Verbal Analogies I was there a serious threat of NMR variance. But there has been some extra CMU variance, which may mean that in making the first relations difficult to see in the items, some precision of meaning was introduced. It was stated earlier that the Miller Analogies Test probably gets its dominant CMU variance from the fact that the vocabulary level was raised in order to achieve test-item difficulty. Vocabulary level was kept low in the construction of Verbal Analogies I.

By analogy to the Figure Matrix test, a Word Matrix Test was constructed, with two rows and three columns, as in the item:

Which word should go in the blank space to fulfill relationships that call for it?

ground   street   automobile
air   route   ?

A. airplane   *B.* bird   *C.* kite   *D.* balloon   *E.* cloud

answer: A

This test performed very well in one analysis (O'Sullivan et al., 1965) but had two additional significant loadings in another analysis (Green, Guilford, Christensen, & Comrey, 1953). A secondary loading on NMR is reasonable, in that in spite of being given alternative answers, *E* might produce his own conclusions to the analogy before considering the alternative answers given.

A stray test named Word Linkage seems to have done better than either of the two just mentioned. Word Linkage was actually designed as a measure of a parallel evaluation ability, EMR, because it requires that *E* consider carefully a relation for adequacy or its correctness in some respect. But in one analysis this test turned out to be a strong and univocal measure of CMR (Nihira et al., 1964). Consideration of the kind of item should suggest why this may be so:

Which of the three alternative words is most related to both of the other two words?
JEWELRY-BELL   *A.* ornament   *B.* jingle   *C.* ring

answer: C

In constructing evaluation tests, the policy has been to keep the cognition problem at a low level of difficulty, in order to rule out that kind of variance in total scores. The relations of RING to JEWELRY and also to BELL are not so very difficult, but the two relations differ in kind, and one may block the recognition of the other. At any rate, the result shows that there was a real cognition-of-relations problem in this test and not much of an evaluation problem. Apparently, once the cognition problem has been solved, the evaluation problem is almost taken care of. Further light on the kinds of tests that stress evaluation of semantic relations will be provided when that subject is reached in Chapter 8.

Another unexpected bonus in the form of a CMR test occurred in the study of planning abilities (Berger et al., 1957). One hypothesis was that a good planner must be keenly aware of the order of things: he must realize when things are not in good order. The test Sensitivity to Order, along with others, was constructed with that hypothesis in mind. Under the instruction to indicate the change, if needed, to correct the order of a series of words, two items read:

TREE   LOG   WOOD   PAPER   ASH
FLOUR   BREAD   DOUGH   CRUMBS   TOAST

The first order is correct; the second needs a reversal of CRUMBS and TOAST, also of BREAD and DOUGH. The relations in the sample items might be conceived as "made into" or "before-after." There were other items each of which suggested a dimension, e.g., of hardness, height, or brightness of light. This test appears to be in the seeing-trends category, a type that often measures relations factors.

Behavioral relations (CBR)   In the O'Sullivan analysis, of four tests that were designed for CBR and analyzed, two came out fairly well and two not so well, but all significantly and univocally for CBR. Two tests emphasized relations between pairs of individuals; a

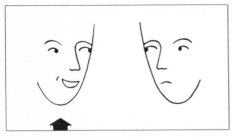

1 I'm glad you're feeling a little better.

2 You make the funniest faces!

3 Didn't I tell you she'd say "No"?

Fig. 4.9 An item from the Social Relations test. In view of the two expressions taken together, what is the person marked by the arrow saying to the other person? *Answer:* 3. The second person does not look as if he were feeling better, and he is not making a funny face. Both expressions fit the third answer.

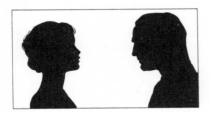

1	2	3

Fig. 4.10 Which of the three female faces below most likely goes with the girl in silhouette, in view of the two postures? The skeptical expression of number 1 seems to satisfy the two related postures. The girl is not just thoughtful, nor is she agitated. (*Silhouettes used in this test were adapted by permission from Robert H. Knapp.*)

third was an analogies test; and the fourth dealt with expressions of opposites within the same person, represented by stick figures.

In Social Relations (see Figure 4.9), just parts of faces in near-profile views are shown in outline drawings for two individuals facing one another with certain expressions. *E* is to choose from three alternative verbal comments what the marked person is saying to the other. Here it can be seen that the use of verbal information does not necessarily involve the test with semantic variance, for five of the semantic-cognition factors were represented in the analysis, CMR being among them, without Social Relations showing semantic variance.

Silhouette Relations is based upon silhouettes of head-and-shoulders portions of a young man and a young woman facing one another (see Figure 4.10). Impressions of different relations between the two can be given by raising or lowering each silhouette in

Fig. 4.11   Which of the three stick-figure alternatives expresses a mental disposition most nearly opposite the one above? The opposition seems to be between an alert, active disposition and the relaxed, fatigued disposition of number 2.

the field and by tilting either one forward or backward in various combinations. With the pair of silhouettes E is given three photographs of faces in different expressions, faces of women in half the items and faces of men in the other half. He is to select the face that he thinks belongs to the woman (man) in view of the relationship suggested by the silhouettes.

The Cartoon Analogies test has a misleading name, for the analogies are not formed of cartoons but of single expressions, of face, hands, or other body parts. The analogy format is the customary one, with three alternative answers. The finding with this test verifies the expectation that an analogies form of test applies to testing for cognition of behavioral relations as well as of relations with other kinds of content. But the behavioral-analogies test is apparently not the best kind for the purpose.

Stick Figures Opposites was the only analyzed behavioral test using stick figures. It proved to be difficult to show many kinds of relations by means of stick figures; so one of the easier relations to represent, opposites, was chosen and used in every item. Some risk was taken by confining the test to one particular relation, but the test was at least minimally successful. A sample item is given in Figure 4.11.

Cognition of systems

A *system* may be defined as an organized or structured aggregate of items of information, a complex of interrelated or interacting parts. Environmental energies to some extent enforce certain organizations upon us by the nature of the stimulation. Gestalt principles pertain to stimulating conditions that favor realistic groupings. The organism has much freedom, however, to produce its own organizations, and in this capacity lies an important basis for creative production.

Figural systems (CFS)   In Table 4.1 (p. 70) we find in the cell for CFS three distinct abilities, distinguished along sensory-input lines: visual, auditory, and kinesthetic. Of these, the visual-spatial ability has received an overwhelming amount of attention and confirmation; yet its nature has been rather controversial (Michael, Guilford, Fruchter, & Zimmerman, 1957).

Cognition of visual-figural systems (CFS-V)   Probably the first report of a visual-spatial factor can be credited to Truman L. Kelley (1928). El Koussy (1936) devoted attention to conceptions of space from a factorial point of view, and L. L. Thurstone (1938a) reported a space factor in his first primary-mental-abilities study, defined as facility with spatial and visual imagery. Since that time, there have been numerous studies, particularly in the AAF Aviation Psychology Research Program during World War II (Guilford & Lacey, 1947). The important contribution from the latter source was the differentiation of the factor of visualization [later identified as factor NFT (Guilford, 1959a) and still later as factor CFT], separating it from its common confounding with CFS. Also differentiated was the space factor now identified as CFS-K, a kinesthetic ability.

Good tests of CFS-V are numerous, too many to mention. A list of only those that give a conception of variety, that contribute to the meaning of CFS, and that are more familiar will be presented.

Thurstone's tests called Figures, Cards, and Flags have been very commonly used in analyses where space abilities have been involved. Operationally, they are so much alike that they might well be regarded as alternate forms of the same test. This suggestion is supported by the fact that when the three are in the same analysis separately, their loadings are quite high (.65 to .75, as reported by J. W. French, 1951), but when one appears alone or the three are combined to give one score, the loading is much lower (in the neighborhood of .45, as reported by Michael, Zimmerman, & Guilford, 1951, and in the AAF research). The higher loadings in the first case suggest a confounding of CFS-V with a specific variance for the three test forms.

A typical item in these tests presents a pair of like objects—figures, cards, or flags— the two members of the pair being in different positions. Sometimes this difference involves turning one of the two over; sometimes it involves only a rotation. E is to say whether or not the same side of the two objects is showing or whether one has been turned over, with the reverse side showing. These three tests represent one distinct type of spatial-relations test. According to the AAF research, they are loaded also on the second space factor, CFS-K; especially is this true of Flags.

Because of the relative importance of the CFS-V ability for learning to fly an airplane, the AAF research involved trying out quite a variety of space tests, most of them successful for the factor and successful for predicting the criterion of pass-fail in flying training. Other tests not particularly designed for the spatial-relations factor, as it was commonly known then, were found to measure it to some extent. Some were psychomotor tests, and some were printed tests.

Two psychomotor tests that measure CFS-V, as well as other factors, were the Complex Coordination test and Discrimination Reaction Time. The former was designed to simulate what a pilot does with a stick and a rudder-control bar. A panel in front of E displays three red lights, each of which is in a different position in different trials. By moving his stick right or left to different extents, E can bring a green light close enough to match one of the red lights. By moving his stick forward or back, he can bring another green light in matching position to a second red light. And by moving his rudder control by pushing with right or left foot, he can match the third red light. When the three matches are perfect, the machine automatically sets up a new pattern of red lights and a new test item begins. The score is the number of complete matches made in eight minutes.

There is obviously a space problem in this test. The three red lights establish a spatial pattern, and the three green lights that E controls have to be manipulated in space to achieve the matchings. From this test alone, one cannot tell whether the aspect of the problem that is significant for the space factor is a purely cognitive one, whether it is primarily one of motor adjustment or control, or whether it is a problem of coordinating movements with cognition.

The same question arises regarding Discrimination Reaction Time. In this test, E has four toggle switches arranged in a diamond formation, upper versus lower and right versus left. The stimulus on the panel before him, when it comes, is a pair of lights, red and green. Sometimes the pair is horizontal, sometimes vertical. If the red light is above the green one, E is to react by using the upper switch; if it is below the green one, E is to react by using the lower switch. Red light on the right means using the right-hand switch, and red light on the left means using the left-hand switch. The score is the total accumulated time in making a series of 80 reactions.

Other tests indicate that the spatial ability is a cognitive one; they do not require adjustive movements in space corresponding to the stimulus pattern. One printed AAF test was called Instrument Comprehension II. There had been an Instrument Comprehension I, but it was not acceptable because its scores contained some CMU variance and because, for the range of CMU ability represented in the aviation student group, a CMU test had no validity for predicting the pass-fail criterion in flying school. The test had some CMU variance because it presents views of combinations of instruments such as appear on a pilot's panel and E is to show that he understands the meaning of those indicators by choosing a verbal description of how the airplane is flying. The test has had some spatial-ability variance, but the presence of the CMU variance reduced its validity. In Instrument Comprehension II, two instrument readings provide the given information and the alternative answers are nonverbal, in the form of pictures of model airplanes flying in different attitudes and directions, one of which is in accordance with the instrument readings.

An even better CFS-V test is Aerial Orientation. The first view presented in an item is what a pilot would see if he were flying over a shoreline separating water from land. In each of the alternative answers is an airplane flying in a certain direction and with a certain attitude, with a glimpse of the shoreline (the same for all alternatives) below it. From which of the airplanes would the pilot see the first view?

Among commonly known types of tests of CFS-V is Spatial Orientation, Part V of the Guilford-Zimmerman Aptitude Survey. Figure 4.12 presents two items like those in the test, with an accompanying explanation. Another test of CFS-V is the Block Counting test, which asks E to count the number of blocks in a pile. This test is likely to share variance with factor CFT. Thurstone's Cubes shows two cubes with markings on their faces in common to the two. E is to determine from the similarity of interrelations of the markings whether or not the two cubes could be identical. Other common tests, such as Minnesota Paper Form Board, Block-Design, Pursuit, and Copying, were mentioned by J. W. French (1951) as having strong loadings on the "space" factor, but it is suspected that in some of the analyses the factor was a confounding of CFS-V and CFT (visualization), and the latter may indeed have been the dominant component.

It now seems rather clear that CFS-V is an ability to apprehend visually the spatial arrangements of things in one's psychological field. It is a cognitive ability and not a psychomotor ability, although the management of one's movements in space is dependent

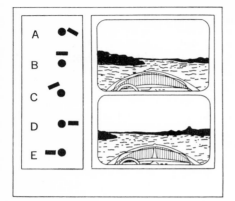 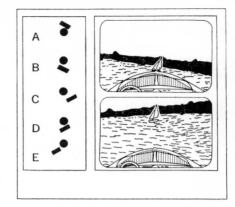

Fig. 4.12 Two sample items from a spatial-orientation test. As the position of the boat changes with respect to the background when we go from the upper to the lower picture in each item, which alternative symbol should show what the change is like? The dot in each alternative answer indicates the position of the prow of the boat in the upper picture, and the rectangle indicates the position of the boat in the lower picture. *Answers: D* and *B,* for first and second items, respectively. (*From Part V of the Guilford-Zimmerman Aptitude Survey, courtesy of the Sheridan Psychological Services, Inc.*)

upon such cognition. The general question of the relationship of motor arrangements to cognition will come in for attention in Chapter 12.

It can be said, further, about CFS-V that the frame of reference for cognized spatial arrangements is primarily the person's own body, in his personal three-dimensional scheme with himself at the origin. His experiences have evidently led him to conceptions of up-down, right-left, and forward-backward dimensions. In the development of this frame, it is most reasonable to assume that his movements had much historically to do with the matter. This agrees with Piaget's account of development of conceptions of space, as discussed in Chapter 17. While the person's own frame of reference remains fundamental, he does also acquire a more general conception of space that is not restricted to that frame, and other frames can be adopted. How far factor CFS-V extends to other frames of reference is still an unanswered question.

Before leaving the CFS-V factor, it is tempting to propose that when Tolman (1948) concluded that the rat in the maze learns ". . . sets which function like cognitive maps," he was talking about visual-figural systems. He cited rather convincing evidence for this conclusion: the fact that rats learn something by merely exploring the maze; the fact that after learning to run through the maze, if the cover is removed, the rat skips directly across to the goal; and the fact that after learning one path to food and another path to water, the rat takes off in the direction of food when hungry and in the direction of water when thirsty. Van Steenberg (1939) has reported a factor for rats that he interpreted as "visual insight," but which seems to fit the definition of a spatial-orientation factor, or CFS-V.

Cognition of kinesthetic systems (CFS-K) A number of analyses by different investigators have forced the recognition of a second space factor, limited to a narrow range of tests. Most faithfully representative is Thurstone's Hands test, which presents pictures of the human hand, right or left, in many varied positions, with *E* to say whether he is looking at a right hand or a left hand. Another test in this group is Thurstone's Bolts, which shows pictures of a bolt protruding from a block of wood. The bolt always has a right-hand screw, but each item shows a view from a different direction, with E to say in which direction the bolt should be turned to screw the bolt into the wood. Thurstone's Flags, Figures, and Cards also have loadings on this factor, especially Flags.

From consideration of these related tests, the thing in common seems to be a right-left discrimination. People who are easily confused as to which is right and which is left would have trouble with these tests. A common observation of individuals taking these tests, particularly Hands, is that the examinee resorts to manipulations of his own hands, perhaps attempting to get the "feel" of the right-left arrangement. This observation is an important basis for labeling the factor as kinesthetic. It might be a special, one-dimensional visual-space ability, but it is not entirely reasonable to believe that although a person is good at three-dimensional visual-space problems, he could be poor in one of those dimensions.

Another space factor found in one analysis (Roff, 1952) may be a candidate for identification with CFS-K. One of the leading tests was Compass Orientation, with the following type of items:

You are flying	and turn	New direction
North	left	_____
West	right	_____
East	left	_____

The items appear to be absurdly simple, but the average percentage of wrong responses was about 12. Much of the variance comes from speed of responding. Another type of test that went with this one on the factor is Following Oral Directions, in which there are spatial problems. The left-right decisions involved in these two tests suggest that the factor is CFS-K.

Cognition of auditory systems (CFS-A)   A factor that appears to qualify for identification as CFS-A was reported by Fleishman et al. (1958). Two leading tests on the factor involved cognition of rhythms and of melodies, two clear cases of auditory systems. Rhythm Discrimination is an adaptation of Seashore's test, in which two rhythmic patterns are given in immediate succession, with E to say whether the two are the same or different. In Hidden Tunes, pairs of short melodies are presented, the second member of the pair being slightly longer, with E to say whether the second includes the first. If these two tests alone were strong on the factor, it might be claimed as an evaluation ability, EFS-A, since they are very similar in format to other successful evaluation tests, as we shall see in connection with factors EFU and ESU. But a nonmatching, noncomparison type of test, Dot Perception, is also strongly loaded. Described previously in this chapter, this test presents series of code dots and dashes, with a run of a few dots at the beginning or the end, E to say how many dots in the run. With minor loadings were two other tests, also clearly cognition tests, not evaluation tests. One was the Copying Behind test mentioned earlier, and the other was the criterion test for the rate of learning to receive code messages early in the course. It therefore seems that Fleishman et al. may be credited with the first reporting of factor CFS-A. The only remaining possibility, other than this conclusion, is that their factor is a confounding of EFS-A and CFS-A. Clear separation of corresponding cognition and evaluation factors is not always easy to achieve.

Symbolic systems (CSS)   A symbolic system is an organized pattern or gestalt composed of letters or numbers or other sign material. As stated earlier, it is believed that

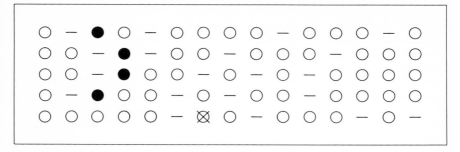

Fig. 4.13   A sample item from the test Circle Reasoning. What is the rule by which the circles in the first four rows have been blackened? It is the first circle after the first dash. The last row has been marked accordingly with an X. (*Adapted from the Circle Reasoning test by Robert I. Blakey, 1941.*)

Thurstone's induction factor is in part the ability CSS. He adopted Letter Series, which was a strong one for his induction factor, as his Reasoning test in his PMA battery. Sample items for Letter Series are:

What letters are needed in the blank spaces in order to extend the series?

A   R   B   R   C   R   __   __
N   O   O   P   Q   Q   __   __

Two links have been found between Thurstone's induction factor and CSS. Kettner et al. (1959a) found Letter Series coming out strongly on CSS. They also found even larger variances for two other factors, CMS and NSR, but subsequent rotations of axes have shown Letter Series to be essentially univocal for CSS. The same solution showed a Number Series test also to be strongly and univocally loaded on the same factor. In this form of the test, E is asked to state the nature of the principle involved in the item. For example, the series might read: 24 48 12 24 6 12 3 _____, to which E should respond by writing in the blank: $\times 2$, $\div 4$. Another link between Thurstone's induction factor and CSS is in a study by Canisia (1962), who found Thurstone's PMA Reasoning loaded on a factor with Number Oddities, which involves seeing a principle in a set of equations.

In the Aptitudes Research Project at USC, a consistent marker test for factor CSS has been Circle Reasoning. A sample item from Circle Reasoning is shown in Figure 4.13. Although the circles and dashes are not letters or numbers, they are signs of entities and hence qualify as symbolic elements. Seeing rules, principles, or structures, as in Circle Reasoning, is the essence of a cognition-of-systems ability.

Another marker test has been Letter Triangle, although it has not always done so well consistently as a CSS test, apparently because it is more susceptible to cognitive styles on the part of examinees. A sample item from Letter Triangle is shown in Figure 4.14.

Semantic systems (CMS)   The much-investigated ability identified as factor CMS has had an interesting history. In his first major PMA analysis, Thurstone (1938a) found a factor on which the test Arithmetical Reasoning was most heavily weighted. He concluded that the common feature of tests loaded on that factor requires E to solve problems under restrictions. Tests of quite a variety were found related to it.

In the AAF research, such a factor was found repeatedly, with an arithmetic-reasoning test usually leading the list of variables loaded on it. Again, there was heterogeneity among

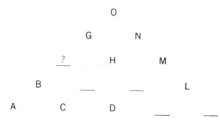

Fig. 4.14 A sample item from the Letter Triangle test. What is the system by which the letters are arranged in alphabetical order? According to that system, which letter belongs in the space with the question mark? *Answer:* F.

the other tests; consequently the factor was called "general reasoning." With such heterogeneity of tests for a factor, it is difficult to pinpoint the essence of the ability represented.

In his review of studies of this factor, J. W. French (1951) came to the unjustified conclusion that it should be called "deduction." Although it is true that, except for the several AAF analyses, very few studies cited by French had used an arithmetic-reasoning test, Thurstone's original deduction factor was well separated from his factor headed by Arithmetical Reasoning. Yet French recognized that an arithmetic-reasoning test had been the most consistent marker for his deduction factor. That his deduction factor had been a complex and varying thing is indicated by the fact that various achievement scores and grades were cited as being strongly loaded on it.

The factor known as "general reasoning" was given much sharper definition by analyses done by the Aptitudes Research Project. By trying out a number of hypotheses as to the nature of this factor so common to arithmetic-reasoning tests, it was demonstrated that the important aspect of solving such problems that should be attributed to the factor of general reasoning is the understanding or structuring of the problem (Kettner, Guilford, & Christensen, 1956).

Two tests especially designed to test this hypothesis were Necessary Arithmetic Operations and Necessary Facts. These tests were designed to see how well E understands the nature of a problem, nothing more. He does not have to go through the operations of solving the problem. In the former, E is to determine what operations are required to reach a solution, as in the item:

A city lot 48 feet wide and 149 feet deep costs $79,432. What is the cost per square foot?	A. Add and multiply B. Multiply and divide C. Subtract and divide D. Add and subtract E. Divide and add

answer: B

In Necessary Facts, a certain fact is missing from the statement of the problem. In each problem, what is the needed fact that is missing? For example:

A rectangular tank is being built to hold water. It is to be 5 feet high and 9 feet long. How many cubic feet of water will it hold?

Both these tests were significantly loaded on the general-reasoning factor, and rival hypotheses were not supported. Hence it can be concluded that the factor is a cognitive ability and that understanding the structure of the problem is the crucial aspect. Any

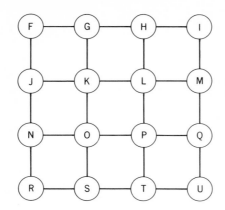

Fig. 4.15 The lettered positions in the grid of the Ship Destination Test indicate either ships or ports, in different problems. The distance between any two neighboring positions is 2 miles. Sailing with (against) the wind or with (against) the current reduces (increases) this distance 1 mile. Other conditions increase or decrease distances in more difficult problems. (*Courtesy of the Sheridan Psychological Services, Inc.*)

kind of deduction seems to be noncritical. As a matter of fact, CMS has as much claim to being an inductive ability as has its parallel ability CSS. We shall see later that there is another place for deduction in the structure of intellect and that, as with induction, more than one factorial ability qualifies for that label (see Chapter 9).

Arithmetic-reasoning tests have consistently had some variance from the numerical-facility factor, which comes from the necessary steps of computation. Necessary Facts, which implies no computation, had a loading of −.11 on the number factor (Kettner et al., 1956), but Necessary Arithmetic Operations had as much of a loading on that factor as the usual arithmetic-reasoning test. The reason might be that the kinds of alternative answers called E's attention to doing some figuring as a check on his consideration of the alternatives. It has been found possible to construct an arithmetic-reasoning test in which number-facility variance is reduced to a minimum, as in the Guilford-Zimmerman General Reasoning test (Guilford & Zimmerman, 1948), by making the needed computations absurdly simple. The same principle was applied in constructing the Ship Destination Test (Christensen & Guilford, 1955), in which additions and subtractions of 1 or 2 points are the only computations needed and answers are 1 to 5 (see Figure 4.15).

Since it was realized that comprehending a system, semantically conceived, is the essence of the factor of general reasoning and the SI model had been developed, it was easy to place this factor in the cell for CMS. Tests of types other than arithmetic problems have not been developed especially to determine whether a nonarithmetical type of system would serve as metric material for CMS. The factor has, of course, appeared in many purely verbal, nonarithmetical tests to some extent.

Copyright 1961 United Features Syndicate, Inc.

Fig. 4.16 Sample item from the Missing Cartoons test. Which of the four alternative scenes should be put in the blank section to make the best sense? Number 4 makes the most reasonable completion for the story. Each scene is a behavioral system, as is the total story. (*Courtesy of the Sheridan Psychological Services, Inc. and the United Features Syndicate.*)

Behavioral systems (CBS)   Again, because of the newness of this area of research by factor-analytical procedures, this factor must rest for the time being on only one analysis (O'Sullivan et al., 1965). Three tests were designed for CBS, and all were successful, with one having some secondary loadings on other factors. The factor receives additional support from two tests designed for other behavioral abilities, which tends to indicate how relatively easy it is to measure CBS.

By far the best and most univocal test was Missing Pictures. Items in this test, as in others, utilize a sequence of events as the kind of system that is to be cognized. Each item is designed to tell a little story in four successive scenes, with one of the four left blank and with E to fill it with one scene selected from three alternatives. The pictures in the scenes were photographs of posed actions of people (students) who were directed in their actions. The episodes often involved boy-girl problems, with one, two, or three persons appearing in each scene.

Missing Cartoons is a parallel type of test, with four successive scenes in cartoon drawings as the basis for each item, one scene being missing. Figure 4.16 is a sample item. Although almost as strong for CBS as was Missing Pictures, this test had secondary loadings for CBU and CBI. Apparently, in E's sizing up the situations and the sense of the whole story in this test, his examination of particular expressions, thus deriving helpful information about *units* of behavioral information, was of assistance. The CBI variance could mean that E often decided what kind of a picture should go in the blank, perhaps from the scene immediately preceding or the one immediately following, even without much impression of the total story. Because of its factorial complexity, such a test should have superior predictive validities where the criterion to be predicted also features the same three factors: CBS, CBU, and CBI. But it would not be so meaningful in research, where unambiguous measurement of any one of those abilities is wanted.

Facial Situations was the third test designed for CBS. It was rather univocal in this analysis but not so strong as the other two. An item shows photographs of two people, a man and a woman (from the Frois-Wittman and Lightfoot series, respectively), each with his or her own expression. The task is somehow to tie the two together or to see what the two expressions taken together mean. *E* is to show that he understands the situation by choosing one of three alternative verbal explanatory remarks. For example, in one item, she looks aloof and he looks pleased. The three comments are:

1. He has finally found a job.
2. They are watching a beauty contest.
3. The water is too cold for swimming.

Alternative 2 is keyed as correct.

The Odd Strip Out test, mentioned earlier, designed for CBC, came out as a strong measure of CBS. Cartoon Implications was designed for factor CBI. In each item it shows one cartoon scene, not the entire strip. For example, in one item Ferd'nand is in a kind of store and he has just torn his coat on a protruding nail. The proprietor rushes up with hands in air. Which of four alternative statements tells either what happened just before or will happen just after?

1. The man recognized Ferd'nand as a friend.
2. The salesman will bring a better-fitting jacket.
3. The man will say how sorry he is.
4. The man was looking all over for Ferd'nand.

Number 3 is keyed as correct. This test had a minimally significant loading on CBI but a stronger loading on CBS, probably because getting the answers hinges too much upon interpreting the entire situation. With four different kinds of tests (the first two being similar) to represent CBS, something of its scope is indicated.

Cognition of transformations

Transformations are changes of various kinds, of existing or known information in its attributes, meaning, role, or use. The most common transformations in figural information include changes in sensory qualities and quantities, in location (movement), and in arrangement of parts. Variations on a theme would be a case in music. In symbolic information, the best examples may be found in mathematics, as in factoring expressions or in solving equations. With semantic information, changes in meaning, significance, or use are found. In behavioral information, changes in interpretation or in mood or attitude would be examples.

Figural transformations (CFT)   The kind of figural transformations with which we are concerned here is confined to visual information. Factor CFT was first isolated in analyses in the AAF investigations. It was difficult to differentiate from its near neighbor CFS-V for the reason that so many space tests had both factors as components.

One of the most successful tests for CFT in the AAF research was called Spatial Visualization I (Guilford, Fruchter, & Zimmerman, 1952). This is a multiple-choice paper-folding-and-cutting test. *E* is shown in line drawings how a sheet of paper is folded, with one or with two or three folds in succession, and how one or two holes are cut at

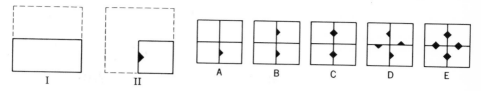

Fig. 4.17 A sample item from Spatial Visualization I, an experimental AAF test based on a test designed by the writer (Guilford & Lacey, 1947). Diagrams I and II show two steps in folding a square piece of paper and cutting a notch in a certain location. Which alternative shows how the paper would look when unfolded? *Answer: C.*

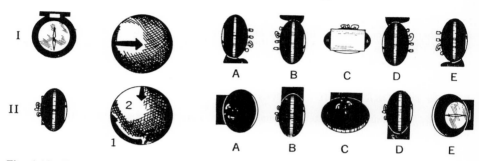

Fig. 4.18 Two items from a test of visualization. In each item, imagine how the clock at the left is turned in accordance with the arrow or arrows shown on the sphere. Which clock at the right shows how the clock would look after making the turn or turns? The first and second turns in Item II must be made in the 1-2 order. *Answers: B and C, respectively. (Courtesy of the Sheridan Psychological Services, Inc., from Part VI of the Guilford-Zimmerman Aptitude Survey, Form B.)*

certain places. Five alternative drawings depict how the paper might look when unfolded, with creases and holes showing (see Figure 4.17).

A quite different type of test, Spatial Visualization II (Guilford et al., 1952), has done about as well. Each problem describes a block of wood of certain dimensions, perhaps 3 by 3 by 3 inches, the wood being of a certain color, painted on the outside with another color. With *E* imagining the block cut into 1-inch cubes, he is asked questions concerning how many cubes have one color only or how many have one or more sides of the outside color. The interesting thing about this test, unlike most of the others, is that the object is verbally described rather than presented explicitly in pictorial form. This means that *E* must operate with visual imagery or some other surrogate for visual perception. In both these tests, *E* has to follow in his own thinking what is happening and to come out with correct knowledge about the final state.

In the AAF setting, various kinds of problems involving plane formations and mechanical movements were used. Most of these were successful as visualization tests, but some of them readily involved much of factor CFS-V because of some emphasis upon orientation.

Some commonly known tests of CFT include paper form boards; Thurstone's Punched Holes, a version of paper folding and cutting in which *E* gives responses by *drawing* creases and holes; surface-development tests, in which *E* must match a solid figure with a diagram of its surfaces unfolded; and Mechanical Principles, like Bennett and Fry's Mechanical Aptitude Test. The last-named type of test also measures a factor of mechanical knowledge about as well as it measures CFT. A current form of visualization test with some unique features is the Guilford-Zimmerman Spatial Visualization test, Form B, for which sample items are given in Figure 4.18.

At one time the writer (Guilford, 1959a) placed visualization in the cell for NFT, for the convergent production of figural transformations, thinking that in performing the solutions to items for the factor E has to be active enough to produce the changes himself. Later, another factor was found that filled that cell better, for in tests of that factor there is no doubt that E actually has to produce the transformations. In visualization tests, evidently enough information is given so that mostly all E has to do is to keep abreast of what is going on.

Symbolic transformations (CST)   Factor CST has not been investigated specifically as a hypothetical intellectual ability, but a factor that might well qualify for this spot in the SI model has been reported (Mooney, 1954). One of the leading tests on it is Spoonerisms, which gives nonsense in print that can be transformed into meaningful discourse. An example is:

LIVERS   MOKE   THE   LOON

which, by interchanges of letters, becomes "Lovers like the moon." Another test is Disjointed Sentences, which calls for regrouping letters, such as

BEE   RCONTA   INSAL   COHOL

which, by regrouping, becomes "Beer contains alcohol." Both these tests understandably have some secondary variance from factor CSU-V, due to the difficulty of cognizing familiar words in distorted form. The test New Words that was mentioned in connection with CSU-V is about equally loaded on these same two factors.

A serious reservation about accepting this factor of Mooney's as CST is that the leading tests bear resemblance to tests for the factor NST, in which E has to do a little more work on the transformations because he starts with the words undistorted but buried in a meaningful context. In the two leading tests just mentioned, E starts with nonsense, or partial nonsense. It may require better tests for both CST and NST to separate them clearly.

Semantic transformation (CMT)   The situation with respect to CMT is a little better than for CST, in that such a factor has been found in the Aptitudes Research Project efforts (Kettner et al., 1959a; Marks, Guilford, & Merrifield, 1959; Wilson, Guilford, Christensen, & Lewis, 1954), although not at first recognized as CMT. The most consistent marker tests for it have been Similarities and Social Institutions. The former is somewhat like the test by the same name in the Wechsler Verbal scale. E is asked to state as many as six ways in which two common objects, such as an apple and an orange, are alike. The transformation is thought to be a matter of redefinition of the objects in emphasizing one attribute or another. Social Institutions asks E to state things that are wrong with social institutions such as divorce or elections. In giving different things wrong, it is believed that E revises his conception of the institution as he deals with different aspects of it.

Sometimes other tests, which, like Social Institutions, were designed for a hypothesized ability to see problems, for example, Apparatus Test and Seeing Problems, have loadings on CMT, but they more often have loadings on a factor now recognized as CMI, a near neighbor of CMT (Nihira et al., 1964). More research needs to be done on CMT, with tests aimed more directly at the hypothesis as generated from the SI model.

1   2   3

Fig. 4.19 An item from Expression Exchange. Imagine the head at the top placed on the body at its right. Then decide which of the three heads below would change the behavioral meaning of the body most if it replaced the first head. Head number 2 would effect the greatest transformation, from a tense, annoyed stance to a coquettish one.

Behavioral transformations (CBT)   The one analysis of tests for CBT was eminently successful; with five tests aimed in that direction, all five were more or less correctly aimed, with only one having a significant secondary loading (O'Sullivan et al., 1965). It is true that two CBT tests were much alike, with photographs in the one case and cartoon pictures in the other. In both Picture Exchange and Cartoon Exchange, four scenes are intended to tell a little story. One of the four is marked with an arrow. Below are four alternative candidates for substitution for the one with the arrow. One of the four candidates, if used as a replacement, would make a genuine change in the story; the other three would not materially change it. The changed story is also reasonable, but it puts quite a different slant on things in the whole sequence of events.

The other CBT tests are rather different from these and from one another. Expression Exchange presents a line drawing of a face and alongside it a headless body with a certain posture (see Figure 4.19). If the head were put on the body, it would give the body posture a certain behavioral meaning. Three alternative answers are other faces, each a candidate for going with the body. The "correct" face is the one that would make a genuine alteration in the behavioral meaning of the body.

Social Translations is the only entirely verbal test that was tried in connection with behavioral factors, with satisfactory results. A short statement is quoted as having been made between two specified people, as in the item:

Parent to child   *1.* Teacher to student
"I don't think so."   *2.* Student to teacher
answer: 2   *3.* Student to student

The problem for *E* is to decide in which other person-to-person relation the same statement would change materially in significance, three alternative pairs being supplied for

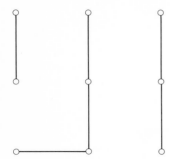

Fig. 4.20   An item to illustrate the test of Competitive Planning, an AAF experimental test. The examinee is to play the game for both opponents. Each opponent, by adding one line at a time according to rules, attempts to complete as many squares as possible. The examinee is given credit to the extent that he plays the game efficiently. (*See Guilford & Lacey, 1947.*)

his choice. Social Translations had a small secondary loading on factor CBR, probably because of the relational implications in the pairs of people described.

From the common features of the successful tests for CBT, it seems that this factor conforms well to the concept of transformation and that wherever it is necessary for the examinee to revise his conception or meaning of a behavioral event, a behavioral transformation is involved. Flexibility in dealing with people must surely depend upon the ability to realize such transformations.

Cognition of implications

The definition of *implication* emphasizes expectancies, anticipations, and predictions, the fact that one item of information leads naturally to another, for reasons which we need not go into here. The implication, as a product, must be the connection, which is not a relation, although it comes close to the type of relation that is described as cause and effect. Logic supplies a formal paradigm that roughly applies, as in the proposition: if A, then B. A difference is that in logic there is an ironclad connection, whereas in psychology only a probability statement can be made, including the special formal-logical case with its probability of 1.0, that is, certainty.

Figural implications (CFI)   In the AAF research, some efforts were directed to the problem of "foresight and planning" because it was reported that many a student pilot failed in training because he lacked foresight and planning adequate to the task. With the knowledge that the pilot's foresight and planning involved concrete problems in mastering flight patterns, landings, and so on, the tests constructed in this area were of figural content.

Route Planning (Guilford & Lacey, 1947) and Maze Tracing (Guilford et al., 1952) are both in the form of paper-and-pencil mazes, varying in complexity from simple to complicated. It is interesting that Porteus (1956) has long championed this kind of test as a good measure of intelligence, in which he believed that foresight should be emphasized. He has reported a history of successful use of the test in connection with studies of effects of drugs and in connection with brain insults (Porteus, 1957; Porteus & Peters, 1947). But it must be remembered that maze tests are far from being complete measures of intelligence and that as measures of foresight they are restricted to concrete, visual content.

Other CFI tests (visual, of course) include the AAF test of Competitive Planning, a sample item for which is shown in Figure 4.20; and Planning a Circuit, as shown in Figure 4.21. In all these tests, E must look ahead, seeing where each step he takes may

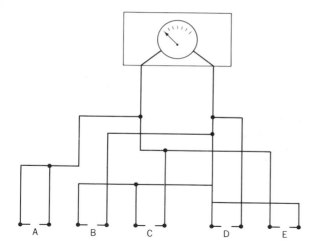

Fig. 4.21 An item from Planning a Circuit, another AAF experimental test (*Guilford & Lacey, 1947*). The problem is to find the pair of terminals at which a battery should be placed in order to complete an electric circuit through the meter. Dots indicate that two crossing wires are joined at those points.

lead. Anticipating consequences in concrete material is a matter of perceptual foresight or CFI.

Symbolic implications (CSI)   Only the work of the Aptitudes Research Project has demonstrated an ability to extrapolate with symbolic information (Guilford, Merrifield, et al., 1961; Hoepfner et al., 1964). Word Patterns was designed for this ability, and it has been fairly successful. The task is something on the order of developing crossword puzzles. Given the words BATS, EASY, HOT, TEA, THE, E is to arrange them with letters in rows and columns so as to spell all the words, making every letter possible do double duty. The most efficient way of arranging the five given words is:

```
    b
t e a
h o t
e a s y
```

Another test designed for CSI is Symbol Grouping, which has not been so satisfactory, but the principle of it is sound. Items go like this:

Given: X – O X – X

rearrange these symbols in as few moves as possible to get them in the systematic order: *X X X – – O,* moving one or more adjacent symbols at a time.

E shows his moves by encircling the elements moved and by making a check mark to indicate where each one goes.

Another test had been designed originally to test the hypothesis of a factor of "sensitivity to problems." It was called simply the F Test, the F standing for "frustration," a common reaction of examinees, for the test gives only a little information in each item, usually symbolic in character, telling E simply to "do something" with each item, whatever he sees fit. He had to initiate his own problem with each item.

The test did not go with others designed for the same hypothesis. It was realized later that the probable reason was that the other sensitivity-to-problems tests are semantic in content. On the basis of SI theory, it was realized that what E does in the test is to see implications in the form of things to do and that it should be a measure of CSI, which proved to be the case in a recent analysis, in which it was renamed the S Test (Hoepfner et al., 1964). Sample items might be:

$$\frac{A \qquad D}{B \qquad C} \qquad \text{and} \qquad O \; C \; B \; C$$

Semantic implications (CMI)   Eight studies in the Aptitudes Research Project support a factor of CMI. We have just seen that a symbolic test designed for a supposed factor of sensitivity to problems went with CSI. The verbal tests designed for the same ability have gone to CMI, as recent developments have shown (Nihira et al., 1964). The tests were called Apparatus Test (what two things are wrong with each given common appliance), Seeing Problems (what difficulties arise in using a common object, e.g., as candle), Social Institutions (described in connection with factor CMT), and Seeing Deficiencies (what is wrong with described plans). The sensitivity-to-problems factor was for some time assigned to cell EMI in the SI model, with the thought that seeing things wrong is a matter of evaluation. But an even better factor was recently found for cell EMI; so sensitivity to problems was moved to cell CMI, which gives to that factor added importance in the form of cognizing things wrong, in addition to more general seeing of implications.

The first recognition and definition of CMI was in connection with a study of planning abilities (Berger et al., 1957). The key test, then and frequently since, has been Pertinent Questions. In this test a certain action is proposed, such as setting up a new hamburger stand. E is asked to state as many as four things that should be considered in the choice of site for the new business venture.

Other tests that have measured the factor, rather univocally but not so strongly, have included one called Effects. Given some present-day trend, E is to forecast future events. For example, if he is told that for the past five years there have been more girls born than boys, he is to predict things that should result twenty years hence, giving as many as four effects.

In Alternate Methods, a problem situation is described, such as a fire to be put out, with contingent aids in the form of water supply, number of men, and kind of equipment, with E to give as many as six ways in which he would employ the resources.

A test developed later for a study of problem-solving abilities (Merrifield, Guilford, Christensen, & Frick, 1962) is known as Contingencies. E is to state the conditions that might require the use of specified objects in a described situation. For example, for two girls going berry picking, what might arise that would call for the use of ointment, pins, etc.? It is rather clear that in all these tests E has to go beyond the information given in terms of awareness of causes, effects, and concomitant conditions. The concept of implication fits all these cases.

It should be said, however, that to keep the ability featured in the category of cognition, it is necessary to stay within the bounds of things that E has experienced in connection before, either personally or vicariously. The tests sample his store of knowledge of such connections. If items call for connections he has not experienced before or cannot readily see, if he has to invent connections, the test gets over into the production areas, more likely the divergent-production area, where there is some degree of novelty in the implication that E comes out with: he produces it by way of transfer. We shall, of course, encounter implications again in dealing with the production abilities.

Behavioral implications (CBI)   Of the six behavioral-cognition abilities, CBI is least well supported in terms of the number of tests loaded on it (O'Sullivan et al., 1965). Al-

Fig. 4.22 An item from Cartoon Predictions. Starting with the scene above, state which of the three alternative scenes below is most likely to come next, all visible cues being considered and human nature being what it is. (*Courtesy of the Sheridan Psychological Services, Inc.*)

though three tests were designed for CBI, only one came out univocal and strong for the factor: Cartoon Predictions (see Figure 4.22). In each item, one cartoon scene provides a readily grasped situation, with three alternative sequels to it; which one shows what will most likely happen next? Comments were made earlier about the test Cartoon Implications, which turned out to be more of a CBS test, because the situations presented are not so very clear.

The third test, Reflections, should be rather appealing to clinical psychologists, particularly, had it worked better. Each item presents a comment that is purported to be made by a counselee. One such comment reads: "I'm just wondering how I'll act, I mean how things will turn out." *E*'s task is to choose one of three alternative behavioral interpretations of the comment. The three alternatives for this item are:

1. She's looking forward to it.
2. She's worried about it.
3. She's interested in how things will work out.

answer: 2

Preliminary tryout of this test showed that it was too difficult; there were apparently not enough sensory cues in the purely visual-verbal input. Consequently, the statements were put on tape, and each was sounded for the examinee as he read the statement. The oral inflections helped a great deal, but the test turned out with as much of a loading on CMR, a semantic ability, as on CBI. Factor CBI may be regarded as having been demonstrated, however, and there is information as to what kind of test best measures it.

Other possible cognition factors

If we accept the most uncertain candidates for the cognition category of intellectual abilities, we see that every one of the 24 cells of that part of the SI model is accounted for, with 4 additional abilities distributed among three of the cells, CFU, CSU, and CFS. The 24 completely parallel factors were found by the use of tests that employ visual input almost exclusively. The 4 extra factors are affiliated with tests with auditory and perhaps kinesthetic information. What is the meaning of this?

One implication is that if auditory tests were analyzed more extensively, we should find still other factors having auditory affiliation. It is not unreasonable to hypothesize a complete set of six auditory-figural abilities. It is not quite so reasonable to expect to find six auditory-symbolic factors. Nothing has happened to suggest that there should be any auditory-semantic or auditory-behavioral abilities, for semantic and behavioral information seems more removed from sensory input. This is more true of semantic information than of behavioral. As indicated when we discussed one or more of the behavioral-cognition abilities, the possibility of auditory-behavioral information should be tolerated as a hypothesis; such information should not be assumed to be nonexistent.

How about tactual- and kinesthetic-figural abilities? We already have one ability tentatively identified as being kinesthetic-figural, namely, CFS-K. Logically, the probable answer to this question hinges on the extent to which somatic-sense information is structured in the form of products. For some guide in considering this point, we would do well to give attention to experts in the field of somatic perception, for example, Revesz and Berkeley (1950), who have devoted years to studies of such problems, much of their work being with the blind.

Revesz and Berkeley do not make much distinction, operationally at least, between tactual and kinesthetic perception, treating them together under the category of "haptic." They point out a number of parallels between haptic space and visual space, but they conclude: "Haptics is completely independent of the sense of vision and creates its world through its own activity and its own laws, irrespective of whether in this process it makes use of the aid of the sense of vision" (1950, p. 36), just as visual and acoustic worlds develop independently.

There is haptic recognition of objects, which suggests a hypothetical ability CFU-H, for dealing with haptic units. There is awareness of internal organization of objects (p. 77), which suggests haptic systems. Because the blind person cannot touch many objects all at once, he builds up a total impression from exploration of the parts, which he organizes. The blind person aims to find representative features of objects and fits them into typical groups of forms. In other words, he has haptic classes. Revesz also speaks of the individual's making transformations in the form of transpositions. The extent to which the seeing person does all this also is uncertain. One might well predict a much clearer and fuller haptic factor structure for blind than for seeing individuals and perhaps a quite limited one for the seeing population.

Summary

Because of the enormous amount of detail in this chapter, it is a very difficult one to summarize with any pretense of conserving much of the information presented. Some generalizations will be extracted from this information.

Of all the operation categories in the SI model, cognition has been the most extensively and intensively explored, and the most is known about cognitive abilities. And yet, we have just considered some possible abilities that may have been overlooked, largely owing to the fact that such abilities have not been thought of in the context of intelligence. But the SI model demands a much more comprehensive view of that context and prevents our ignoring those potential contributions to intellectual functioning.

The finding that all 24 cells of the cognition matrix appear to be occupied with differentiable abilities is good support for the informational category concepts of the SI model and a source of encouragement to push investigations into all parallel areas. The verification of the expected parallels is additional support for the choice of the matrix type of model for the entire domain of intellectual abilities.

It is true that some cognitive factors are much better established than others. Five of the factors have been demonstrated 10 or more times, by different investigators in different contexts. Twelve of them have been verified by being demonstrated from 3 to 9 times. Eight have been demonstrated only once each, but five of these are in the behavioral or social-intelligence area, where investigation has only very recently begun.

As to the ages at which the various factors have been demonstrated, it can be asserted that probably all of them are differentiable at high-school and adult levels, in Western European types of cultures, at least. Nine have been reported at elementary-school levels, and some even at younger ages. For the most part, the 28 abilities that were presented have not at all been knowingly investigated below the high-school years. At the preschool levels, one should not expect much in the way of visual-symbolic abilities until after the age of six or much in the way of semantic abilities until after the age of two, but one might well expect to find some figural and behavioral abilities differentiated below the age of two. Testing these hypotheses will depend upon the ingenuity of those who invent the tests that would be needed for the purpose.

5 Memory abilities

It may be recalled from Chapter 2 that Binet recognized ability to remember as being a distinct area of intelligence and that, furthermore, he hypothesized several distinct kinds of ability in this area. In what follows we can see how nearly right he was, particularly which of his hypothesized memory abilities have been supported by the results of empirical analysis.

Early evidence for memory factors

The empirical data regarding distinct memory abilities go back some forty years, at least. Spearman (1927) arrived at a number of conclusions about memory abilities that have later been supported when he discussed this subject under the heading "retentivity." He cited the fact that there were correlations among memory tests that could not be accounted for in terms of his *g* factor. Furthermore, such tests correlated close to zero with tests related to *g*. The tests called for memorizing lists of numbers and words and associations between paired numbers and words. Even tests of memorizing sentences and paragraphs gave similar results. Spearman was more or less forced to read memory out of the concept of "intelligence," for he regarded tests involving "eduction" (which we can translate to include both induction and deduction) as the empirical referents of *g*, hence as having to do with intelligence.

It is of interest to note that Spearman recognized a separation of verbal and nonverbal memory, even separate memory abilities for visual and auditory information, although he also thought that there was a more general sensory-memory ability that tied the two together. He concluded that there was no separation of abilities for immediate **versus** delayed memory or for recognition versus recall memory, conclusions that seem to have been consistently supported (Brown, Guilford, & Hoepfner, 1966; Christal, 1958; Kelley, 1964; Tenopyr, Guilford, & Hoepfner, 1966).

Not long after Spearman's announced conclusions regarding memory abilities, Anastasi (1932) reported finding a memory factor. The lack of variety of tests in her analysis precluded finding differentiated memory abilities. She drew one pertinent conclusion to the effect that the factor represented a certain type of material rather than a particular method of testing. During the 1930s there were a few other mentions of memory factors, without adding much in the way of information regarding them.

An exception was Thurstone's first PMA analysis (1938a), which brought out an ability he called "rote memory," on which the strongest loadings were for paired-associates items with meaningless associations. The fact that a Figure Recognition test and a Word Recognition test had significant loadings on it suggests that it was a confounded factor. A Picture Memory test of the report type had a loading that just missed being significant. Thus, several of the SI memory factors now recognized were probably represented, each with one test, not permitting separation along SI-factor lines.

The Army Air Forces analyses distinguished between two memory abilities: visual memory, pertaining to recognition or recall of exposed pictorial material; and a paired-associates memory, which was probably equivalent to Thurstone's factor of rote memory but was more limited to the learning of paired items of information and hence was probably more nearly a unitary ability (Guilford & Lacey, 1947).

By 1951, J. W. French could accept a well-replicated associative-memory factor and three other memory factors less well verified. The associative-memory factor has always been best indicated by paired-associates tests, with E memorizing pairs of items of information, then later being given the first member of each pair, to supply the mate to it. Almost always the items of information were in symbolic form, as shown by these examples: color-word, Turkish-English, English-Turkish, word-word, initials-names (E given name to supply initials), picture-number, number-number, word-number, and first name–second name (E to recall the first). In two cases there was auditory presentation of the pairs to be learned; otherwise presentations were visual. From the list of pairs used, it is probable that the SI factor most represented was MSI, the memory for symbolic implications, in which the first member of a pair implies the second member.

Span memory was accepted by French as a separate factor, since memory-span tests, with either digits or letters, or both, commonly generated a factor of their own, not going with paired-associates tests. With essentially alternate forms of the same test representing the span factor, however, the factor could have been a memory-span specific. The possibility of an additional relationship of memory-span tests to other memory factors would not be precluded, but in earlier analyses those appropriate other memory factors were evidently not sufficiently represented.

From the AAF analyses, visual memory was regarded by French as being weakly supported. The best tests had to do with the examination of maps of local terrain, with a recognition test of segments of that terrain later or a test involving verbal questioning about graphic features.

The musical-memory factor accepted tentatively by French had been found by Karlin (1941). It rested on tests of memory for melodies, rhythms, and musical forms. This factor and two others mentioned by French have appeared to fit into unique places in the SI model. The traditional span-memory factor was tentatively considered for cell MSU, since the list that is fully grasped with a single exposure is a kind of unitary event (Guilford, 1959a; 1959b), but the writer has also entertained the hypothesis that span tests should share variance with the hypothesized factor MSS, since memory for *order* of symbols suggests memory for symbolic systems. There are some very recent results bearing upon span tests and their possible relations to factors MSU and MSS, which will be brought out later.

Still another factor that was listed by French but was not identified by him as a memory ability is a candidate for that category. It is the factor found in the Air Force research and called "Integration I." The typical kind of test for this factor provides some detailed instructions for what E is expected to do. No one detail in the instructions is difficult to follow, but the E who can keep in mind several things to do in the task has an advantage. The term *integration* had been applied to such tests with the hypothesis that the significant ability involved is the coordination of the subtasks in the whole task. But memory for the subtasks could be regarded as a matter of MMU, the memory for semantic units, each subtask idea being a semantic unit.

Some special problems in memory testing

Before we go into the parade of memory factors, what follows will be more fully appreciated if a few general comments are made concerning some special problems that arise in connection with memory tests and the kinds of difficulties they entail. Some more special features of memory tests will be mentioned as we come to certain factors.

The chief difference between memory tests and tests for other psychological operations is that the former involve a two-stage process: (1) memorizing and (2) testing for how much is retained. In tests of operations other than memory, only the testing step is involved. In an ideal memory test, we should like every examinee to have had equivalent cognitive experience with the information on which he is to be examined. Individual differences should then reflect variations in the memory ability in question and not variations in cognitive abilities. To the extent that we cannot standardize input information for all examinees, the variance in memory-test scores should represent cognitive abilities.

The input information should in some sense, at least, be new to the examinees: new in substance, as when nonsense figures are presented; or new in connections, as when paired-associates material is presented; or new in organization, in linear order or in other kinds of order or systematic arrangement. Since these aspects are new, there are some cognition problems. We want all Es to be able readily to cognize all information as the items were intended that they should. This means that all Es must be depended upon to have the necessary basis for cognition, in terms of previously stored information, and the necessary cognitive ability to effect adequate input. The input material must be relatively unambiguous, except where the product of transformation is concerned. If aids to correct cognition are provided for E, we must see to it that the aids do not go further and differentially affect retention. That is, verbal aids might mean verbal memory where nonverbal memory is being tested.

The double-stage nature of memory tests almost inevitably offers occasions for the examinee to alter his intended task by injecting some strategies of his own devising. The same danger exists in other kinds of tests, but in memory tests E has two chances for this kind of deviationism. The interval between memorizing and testing provides a little additional time. E can take each test and each item as special problems to be solved, calling for invention of his own methods for dealing with each problem. The longer the delay, the more open the conditions for loss of experimental control. These features are not confined to the psychological-testing context by any means; they also beset the path of the laboratory experimenter who works on problems of human memory.

Some variations used in memory tests   Although the group-testing approach that is almost necessary for efficient factor-analytic investigation puts some limitations upon the kinds of techniques employed, some of the common variations of conditions are possible in the memorizing and testing phases. The presentation of information to be memorized can be made through either the visual or the auditory channel, although a choice does not exist for all kinds of information that might be presented. If the presentation is visual, there are some alternatives as to placement on a study page where the items of material are exposed. The items of information may be scattered haphazardly, or they may be ordered in some way, in a list or in pairs or in matrices. The total exposure time for a set of printed study material can be controlled and varied, but the timing of exposure of particular items of information cannot be controlled as in a laboratory experiment, except for auditory presentation. In the latter instance the order is fixed, except where there are several exposures, with changed order each time. There are many ways of exposing visual material with time controls on a screen or on flash cards, of course, but the convenience of study pages often makes the last-named technique relatively attractive.

In the testing phase, we may give recall tests or recognition tests. As stated before, experience shows that this variation has historically made little difference in the factors that are measured. For different products of information, however, those two methods must be applied with discrimination. The use of paired associates has been a very popular method, as in the laboratory, undoubtedly favored because of the prevailing association theory. With presentation of pairs of items of information for study, the testing task can be varied in terms of completion, multiple-choice answers, or matching. A recall test should be expected to involve some memory for units as well as for implications, whereas the other two kinds of tests should emphasize implication variance more nearly uniquely. In the latter procedures the unit, as such, need not be remembered.

In testing for retention of systems, as distinct from units, relations, or implications, a little-used method known as "reconstruction" suggests itself. Since E has memorized items of information in a particular order or pattern, his retention of the system should be more nearly univocally measured by presenting him with the items of information for him to construct the proper arrangement. Such performance is not easy to score. We may avoid this difficulty by using a kind of pair-comparison procedure in which pairs of items are presented, with E to say which came first in order.

Some special difficulties   Some difficulties have already been implied in the preceding discussion of conditions and variations. There are a few others that call for our attention. They have to do with translations of information, with other behavior on the part of the examinee that come under the general heading of violation of instructions, and with the phenomenon of interferences, well known in the psychological laboratory.

The phenomenon of translation of kind of content of information has been found troublesome elsewhere, but it can be especially so in connection with memory tests, where there are more opportunities and where there is more possible payoff. It is well known that we memorize and retain (semantically) meaningful material much more readily than either symbolic or figural material. This means that wherever we can readily translate the last two kinds of information into semantic terms, we stand to gain by that strategy. For example, Christal (1958) reported that one individual took a certain figure composed of simple lines to be a telescope, another figure as a cannon firing five shots, and still another as an arrow flying toward a tree. It is not easy to prevent an examinee from adopting this kind of practice if he is so inclined. To give a prohibitive instruction would probably call the attention of additional examinees to the possibility of translation and would not be effective in preventing translation.

The confusion of products of information is also common and difficult to control, but regulation is not beyond reach. As is true in other operation categories, there is danger of confusion between units and systems. In fact, retention in unit form may become a feature of tests designed for a number of the other products. For example, a relation may be verbalized or named and remembered as a semantic unit. But there is abundant evidence that information is retained in forms other than units.

There is also some tendency toward confusion between relations and implications. Relations and implications are not so very far apart in terms of definition. Both are connections between pairs of items of information. The main difference is that relations have meaningful characteristics; the connections possess qualitative differences. Implications are simpler, more incidental connections of less definitive nature. An implication can become a relation if the individual injects some known or meaningful kind of connection between members of a pair. Particular instances of such confusions will appear in connection with discussions of the various factors.

Another instance of violation of instructions has been found in connection with E's memorizing and recalling items of information in given orders in spite of the instruction to report items without regard to order. This is probably more a matter of habit than of invented strategy. The habit could be counteracted somewhat by presenting the material more than once, as in auditory stimulation, with the order changed in each presentation. To the extent that order is maintained, however, we might expect some system or implication variances to be introduced when the interest may be in other products.

The group-testing situation, in which one test is given after another for a period of two or more hours with little interruption, is favorable for the formation of interferences between the items of information in one test and those in other tests or between two parts of the same test. This situation is relieved somewhat by the fact that tests containing similar items of information are not given in immediate proximity, and nonmemory, marker tests are interspersed with memory tests. Since the tests are administered in the same sequence for all examinees, the conditions for interferences are rather standardized for all individuals, except for possible interaction effects between persons and tests.

Memory for units

A brief look at Table 5.1 will show that memory factors seem to have been demonstrated for 14 of the 24 cells of the memory matrix, with a second factor in the cell for MFS. In 9 instances, only one recognized analysis has been responsible for each factor, and all 9 were from two analyses completed only recently. Where the number of analyses is indicated by an S (for several), only three or four analyses are involved. Only the two recent analyses were conducted on the basis of SI hypotheses, in the columns for semantic and symbolic abilities. Where more than one analysis is indicated, other, independent sources have also deserved credit, except that factors MMU, MMS, and MSI have been much better supported and more clearly defined in the recent analyses.

Figural units (MFU)   Although there are moderately supported suggestions of a visual-memory ability in four analyses, the evidence leaves something to be desired (Christal, 1958; Guilford & Lacey, 1947; H. P. Kelley, 1964). In two Air Force analyses, the two forms of the test Map Memory were similar in each case; so the factor could have been a confounding of a general MFU factor with a Map Memory specific, or it could even have been a map-memory specific, which is less likely, because probably no test is

Table 5.1   Matrix of the memory factors (M) represented in the structure of intellect

Figural (F)		Symbolic (S)		Semantic (M)		Behavioral (B)		
MFU	S	MSU	1	MMU	2	MBU	0	*Units* (U)
				13				
MFC	0	MSC	1	MMC	1	MBC	0	*Classes* (C)
MFR	0	MSR	1	MMR	1	MBR	0	*Relations* (R)
MFS-V	3	MSS	1	MMS	2	MBS	0	
6								*Systems* (S)
MFS-A	2							
MFT	0	MST	1	MMT	1	MBT	0	*Transformations* (T)
MFI	0	MSI	S	MMI	1	MBI	0	*Implications* (I)

confined to a specific. The Map Memory tests of one AAF analysis present a line drawing of a limited geographical area like two or three blocks of a town, with landmarks labeled. In one multiple-choice test each item presents a segment of the map, with E to choose its name or label. In the other form, E answers questions about locations, directions, and distances, in multiple-choice verbal items. In a second analysis, a new form of Map Memory was introduced, along with one of the former type. The new form provided a recognition test, in which the five alternative answers were all similar versions of some selected segment of the total map. A notable result was the clear separation between the visual-memory factor and an associative-memory factor, in spite of the fact that tests for the latter involve visual-figural items of information paired with one another or with names, as of lakes, rivers, and airplanes.

The H. P. Kelley (1964) analysis used what would appear to be a better test for factor MFU, a test called Reproduction of Designs. Each of 10 designs was exposed for five seconds, with E to reproduce them later by making sketches. This test strongly headed the list for a factor but with two other tests, with little logical claim to involving MFU, having minimally significant loadings. A Recognition Test III should logically have gone on factor MFU with Reproduction of Designs. It did not do so, although one of its two strongest loadings [1] (.26) was on that factor. Its communality was very small (.32). This figural-recognition test presented 40 designs that were to be studied for one minute and were mixed with 40 others for recognition in the retention test. One difficulty with the test may have been that such a form offers too many opportunities for interferences.

Most surprising of all, in the Kelley analysis, the three Map Memory tests, one a reproduction form, one a verbal-quiz form, and the third a recognition form, had "loadings" of only .18, .24, and .12, respectively. The second and third forms are similar to two AAF tests in which it had been thought that a MFU factor had been found. The communalities of these tests were quite low, however, being .34 and .39, respectively. The communality for the third form was only .18. Perhaps a new rotational solution could bring all these tests more nearly on the same factor, but the low communalities would almost preclude high loadings.

Christal's analysis (1958) was directed mainly at the general area of visual memory. For one thing, he hypothesized two separate abilities that might fall in the cell of the SI model for MFU: a memory for colors distinguished from a memory for form. Two memory-for-colors tests that could potentially represent a units factor were designed. In one, E is shown, for a duration of two seconds each, 20 objects, each in a different color. Later he is given the names of objects to identify their respective colors. In the other test, following a color-discrimination test in which 30 sets of three colored objects each are presented, E is given a multiple-choice test. A third test involving colors presents colored objects, each paired with a word in a paired-associates format. It should be predicted that this test would not go with any units factor but with other paired-associates tests on an implications factor. It did the latter. The first two color tests did determine a factor, and it was separate from any form-memory factor. But it is best to regard this color factor not as a special MFU ability but either as a specific or as a sensory or perceptual factor. The memory involved is for a sensory quality or attribute, not for an organized object, as is true of figural-units abilities in general.

Christal had three tests designed for memory for visual forms, but they did not determine a factor. The reasons for this outcome can be readily surmised. A Pattern-Word

---

[1] Because of Kelley's oblique rotations, one should say "coefficient" rather than "loading," for technical reasons. The term *loading*, in the context of these discussions, will be better understood.

Association Test should have gone with other paired-associates tests, and it did. A Picture Detail Recall test was a verbal quiz on some aspects of figures exposed earlier in another test, an incidental-memory test. It went with the test from which observations were obtained because of an experimental dependence between the two. That left the third, Pattern Detail Memory Test, which should have been a good test for MFU, except that the multiple-choice alternatives were so much alike that evaluative ability should have come in. The test had a significant loading on a factor that was apparently a confounding of EFU (an evaluative ability) with CFS-V (a cognitive ability). Little variance would be left to support a MFU ability, especially E with little or no help from other good MFU tests.

Symbolic units (MSU)   In approaching the subject of memory for symbolic units, we have a special problem to consider, namely, the possible recognition of the often-found memory-span factor as MSU, as mentioned earlier in this chapter. It was pointed out that in earlier analyses the memory-span factor had been found to be limited very much to memory-span tests and that more than one memory-span test, such as letter-span or digit-span tests, had been included in the same analysis. There has been a growing belief that E's having to recall the symbolic elements (letters or digits) in correct order should involve factor MSS, memory for symbolic systems, the systemic aspect being temporal or spatial order, depending upon whether the elements are exposed in sequence in either auditory or visual form. Giving a short list in the backward direction might emphasize the systemic nature of the task even more.

Incidentally, the elements (single letters or digits) in lists of memory-span tests should not ordinarily be regarded as symbolic units; it takes more than one such element to form a symbolic unit, as we saw in connection with factor CFU-V and its parallel factor CSU-V and also the pair of factors CFU-A and CSU-A, treated in Chapter 4. A letter or a digit has figural properties, and such elements have been used in tests of figural-units abilities. Visual-symbolic units have usually been syllables or words, and auditory-symbolic units have been spoken words, at least in tests in which factors CSU-V and CSU-A have been demonstrated (see Chapter 4).

The abilities MSU and MSS are testable by tasks other than those in memory-span form, as we shall see. A study of the question regarding the involvement of MSU or MSS, or both, in memory-span tests should be answerable by giving those other kinds of tests designed for the two abilities along with a memory-span test to see in which direction the latter goes. Several kinds of outcome would be possible. The memory-span test could go toward MSU or toward MSS, or it could share its variance with the two factors, evenly or unevenly. Another possibility, if there were more than one memory-span test in the analysis, would be a separate memory-span factor, distinct from MSU and MSS. With more than one symbolic memory-span test in the analysis, we should expect a factor common to those tests in addition to MSU and MSS where the latter are accounted for. The memory-span tests might or might not share common-factor variances with MSU and MSS, in addition to that shared with other memory-span tests.

The analysis by Tenopyr (1966) was designed, among other things, to answer these questions about memory-span tests and their common factor or factors. In the analyzed battery were four memory-span tests. Two were composed of consonants, but they differed from one another in certain ways. One other test was composed of digits, and one of nonsense syllables. Also in the battery were at least four nonspan tests designed for MSU and four nonspan tests designed for MSS. No way was found to give a backward-span test in group form, for in writing his answer, E could readily defeat the intention of the test by writing the elements in backward order on his test page, which could permit him to remember them in the forward direction as presented.

It was fairly clear from the examination of the intercorrelations that the span tests shared variances over and above, and even separate from, tests designed for either MSU or MSS, although there seemed to be more affinity of span tests for MSS than for MSU. The factor identified as MSU will be described first, and then the span factor. Factor MSS will be treated in its regular turn.

One of the strongest tests for MSU was Memory for Nonsense Words—Free Recall. E studied a list of 15 nonsense syllables and immediately afterward was told to write as many of them as he could remember in any order. A marginally significant loading on factor MSI probably came from the fact that E studied the list in its given order. The evidence that he did so is that most reported lists followed that order. Although this circumstance was apparently not sufficient to introduce a significant amount of variance from MSS, it was sufficient to introduce some significant MSI variance. This suggests that the effect of studying the list in order was to form implications from one syllable to the next but not to form a conception of a system.

Another strong MSU test, designed for the purpose, was Memory for Listed Nonsense Words. The study task was like that for the preceding test, memorizing 15 syllables presented in a list, but the test of retention was a yes-no recognition task. This test was univocal for MSU in the Tenopyr analysis, without significant MSI variance. The recognition test presented the same syllables in haphazard order, mixed with as many new syllables. In such a task the incidentally formed direct forward connections or implications should be of no help, and the results bear out this hypothesis.

A third successful test for MSU was Memory for Digital Units. In this test E studied two-digit units in lists of 15 and then was given a recognition test such as was just described for the preceding test. Apparently the two-digit combinations functioned as symbolic units. It would be of interest to know whether three-digit units would have served the purpose for measuring MSU any better. The three-letter units appear to have been better for that purpose. Perhaps a two-letter unit would serve less well.

A Related Number Association test was designed for factor MSU, but besides having its leading loading on MSU, it was factorially complex to the extent of marginally significant loadings on both MSR and MSC. This test was intended for MSU with the idea that a number pair might be processed as a unit in memory. Number pairs like 3-6, 800-200, and 70-10 were presented in a list of 15 for study, the two numbers of each pair being related by a simple ratio. The test of retention was a four-choice affair, with the first member of a number pair being given and the alternative answers all having simple ratios with it, for example:

3-

A. 15
B. 9
C. 30
D. 6

One could predict that there should be some MSR variance in this test, and there was: almost as much as for MSU. Because of the paired-associates type of task, one might predict some MSI variance, but the loading on that factor was only .15, whereas it was minimally significant for MSC. The reason for the latter affinity is not clear, except that pairs related by simple ratios are similar in having a common denominator and hence belong to the same classes.

A special span factor   We next consider what happened to the span tests in the Tenopyr analysis. They definitely did not come out loaded on factor MSU. Such an affiliation was precluded by the fact that whereas the span tests intercorrelated in the range .30 to .46, they correlated with MSU tests in the range .12 to .26. A clear-cut span factor did come out of the analysis by rotating to it. The four span tests were all loaded significantly on it.

The four tests can be briefly described:

Consonant Span I, as its name implies, gave lists composed only of consonants. The presentation was in visual form, one letter at a time, with *E* instructed to write the letters in the correct order.

Consonant Span II was similar, except that presentation was auditory and *E* was told that he could write the letters in any order. As was quite common under such an instruction, however, most listing was in order of presentation.

Digit Span was typical of common span tests, with auditory presentation and with *E* instructed to report digits in correct order.

Nonsense Word Span presented lists of nonsense syllables, in visual form, one syllable at a time on flash cards, *E* being told that he might report the syllables in any order.

In another rotational analysis of the Tenopyr data (Tenopyr et al., 1966), the four span tests were combined to give one memory-span score. In this case, a special span factor would not be expected, and none emerged. The composite span score had a fairly strong but not high loading on factor MSS, indicating that the best SI placement for a memory-span test is for factor MSS rather than MSU. Since a memory-span test is a kind of limiting case of one-trial learning of a serial type, an inference would be that MSS should be a common component in serial-learning tests composed of symbolic elements.

When all four span tests were in the analysis separately, only Digit Span had a significant loading on factor MSS, and that loading was minimally significant. It may have been that the higher intercorrelations among the span tests, which are essentially alternate forms of the same test, prevented each span test from showing its full relationship to factor MSS. It is also likely that the summing of the four span tests gave a substantially more reliable score, which could correlate higher with other MSS tests and thus show a higher loading on that factor.

Semantic units (MMU)

An earlier sign of an MMU ability may have been found in the analysis by H. P. Kelley (1964), in a factor that he chose to call "unidentified." Two tests were loaded significantly on it. Memory for Ideas involves *E* in reading the story *The Marble Statue* for fifty seconds, then reproducing in his own words ideas from the exposure he has had. Each idea can be regarded as a semantic unit. Memory for Limericks involves *E* in studying 30 limericks for five minutes, then being tested by his supplying the idea of the last line in each limerick.

There is some doubt of the interpretation of this factor as MMU, for two tests that should have been expected on such a factor did not go there. One test called for *E*'s recognition of words heard earlier in lists. Another, called Memory for Instructions, in which *E* heard two to five instructions to be carried out, failed to appear on the factor. It should be noted that both Memory for Ideas and Memory for Limericks went significantly also on another factor that could possibly be identified as MMS. The fact that the expressions to be reported in these two tests are a little complex evidently gives them some systems variance.

An even earlier analysis may have detected a factor that qualifies as MMU. In his rerotations of the first Thurstone PMA analysis, Zimmerman (1953) found a factor, led by Picture Memory, in which E, having been exposed to a complex picture, answers questions about its content. In the Theme test, E is to describe a friend. A third test, Disarranged Sentences, does not obviously involve memory, unless it be an extremely short-term memory. From the two memory tests alone, it is not possible to say whether the Zimmerman factor pertains to visual memory (MFU-V) or to semantic memory (MMU), or both; the content aspect was not fully controlled. Zimmerman was partial to the visual-memory interpretation.

The strongest evidence for a factor MMU is provided by the Brown analysis. In that study, four of five tests designed according to specifications of the MMU cell of the SI model came out substantially on the factor. Picture Memory presents a study page with 20 familiar pictured objects on it, with E almost immediately to recall and list the names of as many objects as he can. No MFU tests were in the Brown battery; so we cannot tell how much some Es might have depended upon visual memory. In view of the generally strong preference for memorizing material semantically, it is likely that the dominant variance was for MMU.

Test Name Recall was as strong as Picture Memory on the factor. The score was derived by asking E to list the names of the tests he had just taken in a test booklet that contained six or seven different tests. He was told to list them in any order. In contrast to the situation with most tests in the battery, there was unusual delay in the recall test, up to about fifty minutes for one of the test names.

In Recalled Words, E studies 20 words scattered about a page and is later told to recall as many as he can. Such a test might involve some MSU variance, less likely some MFU variance; but, again, the natural preference for semantic memory may have helped to keep the test in the semantic category. Word Recognition presents a list of 15 words on a study page, with a recognition test later, the 15 words being dispersed among 15 other words.

The test that did not work for MMU was Memory for Word Meanings. In this test, an experimental attempt was made to eliminate possible variance in MSU, the symbolic parallel to MMU. The retention test required neither recall nor recognition of each word but provided a list of 30 short definitions or synonyms for the 15 words on the study page. With a loading of only .22 for MMU, the test went mainly on factor MMT (.45) and slightly on factor MMC (.32). The hypothesis was that since it is the semantic meaning that is to be stored and tested, less direct ways of indicating retention for a unit should be adequate to show that there is retention. Discussion of the test's involvement with MMT will be delayed until we come to that factor. The involvement with classes in connection with the MMC variance must have come from the use of word substitutes, especially synonyms, which are, of course, members of classes along with the words studied. We shall see that a good MMC test also involves naming members of classes previously studied.

Memory for classes

Symbolic classes (MSC)   Symbolic classes are formed on the basis of common attributes in literal or numerical items of information. This means similar sets of syllables, words, or numbers. One analysis (Tenopyr et al., 1966) has demonstrated that memory for such classes is a unique ability, with four tests designed for it found to be at least minimally effective.

Memory for Name Classes presents sets of three given names each for E to study, for example:

Iris, Irene, Irving   (beginning with *Ir*)
Robert, Gomer, Louise   (containing letter *O*)

The class idea must be easy to grasp; otherwise cognition variance enters the picture, in this case, CSC. The test of retention presents a list of names, some of which belong to the memorized classes and some not, for example, Molly and Ira, which do belong to the two illustrative classes, and Ida, which does not.

Memory for Word Classes is like the preceding test, with common words as material. Examples of word classes are:

plate, rate, grate
jury, just, jump

With 10 such sets on the study page, there are 20 single words on the test page, 10 of which belong to the classes and 10 not.

Memory for Nonsense Word Classes is similar to the two tests already described but has four-choice items in the retention test. Class sets such as NEG, NEP, and NEF or GUZ, GAZ, and GYZ are followed in the test by such items as:

1. NOP		*1.* GIS	
2. NAP	(*answer: 3*)	*2.* GOZ	(*answer: 2*)
3. NER		*3.* LOZ	
4. NUP		*4.* MOZ	

Another test for MSC is Memory for Number Classes—Recall, and its presence in the list helps to indicate the generality of the obtained factor, the fact that the factor extends beyond literal material. In this test, *E* studies lists of sets of three numbers each, and later he indicates retention by writing the names or descriptions of classes that he has studied. The kinds of number classes are indicated by these examples:

5, 10, 25   (divisible by 5)
307, 602, 704   (second digit is 0)
621, 821, 521   (end in 21)

Any answer showing that a certain class was remembered was accepted, and the classes could be described in any order. It is possible that this test would contain significant variance in factor NMU, the naming ability, since parallel cognition tests do so. That factor was not represented in the analysis.

Semantic classes (MMC)   Before the analysis by S. W. Brown et al. (1966), no memory-for-classes factor had been hinted anywhere. Only from SI theory would such an ability be expected. Of five tests designed for MMC, five could be regarded as at least minimally loaded on that factor. The highest loading, however, was .48, with three of the tests having significant secondary loadings, two on MMT and one on MMI. In view of the general role undoubtedly played by classes in the processes of storage and retrieval of information, it would not be surprising to find such secondary loadings. Remembering the class within which a certain product falls helps one to remember that product.

Classified Information presents for study 15 sets of three words each, the words of a set forming a readily recognized class, such as SILK, WOOL, NYLON. The recognition test that follows does not present the same words, as such, for fear that this would involve MMU variance; remembering the units might be a great help in remembering the class ideas. Instead, sets of three words, each set representing one of the classes appearing on the study page, are presented for recognition, the same 15 classes being interspersed among

15 others. For the illustrative class given above, the corresponding class to be recognized is RAYON, COTTON, FELT.

In Picture Class Memory, there were three pictured objects of a class, for example, pictures of three kinds of fruit, in each set on the study page. There were 11 such groups. In the recognition test, 22 pairs of objects appear on a page, 11 of them being classifiable with corresponding trios on the study page. One object of each pair was common to the corresponding pair and trio. Some experimental work is needed to find the optimal numbers of class members to use on study page and test page and to learn whether or not the repetition of an object introduces some semantic-units variance. In the use of pictured objects, also, there is danger of involving the test with some figural variance, as found with tests of cognition of classes (see Chapter 4).

In Remembering Classes, E studies 15 sets of four words each, e.g., BOOTS, SHOES, STOCKINGS, SLIPPERS, in 15 classes, and he is tested by his recognizing the class names among 15 others. A minimal loading of .30 on MMC was this test's highest in the battery. If the test has any strong variances from other factors, those factors were not present in the analysis.

Another minimal loading appeared for Concept Recall. In the latter test, classes represented by three words each, e.g., BANANA, APPLE, ORANGE, are given on the study page, with a recall test calling for the names of classes. A higher loading for factor MMT was found for this test. The role of transformations in this test is not clear, unless we hypothesize that as E inspects a class, he undergoes a transformation of class idea and that when he recalls the class, he undergoes the same transformation.

Memory for relations

In earlier considerations of memory factors, the writer (Guilford, 1959a; 1959b) concluded that the rote-memory factor or associative-memory factor that has been found so commonly with paired-associates types of tests belongs in the cell MSR in the SI model. The logical support for this hypothesis was that in memorizing pairs of items of information E invents relations that serve as aids to recall. To the extent that the units connected involve semantic information, factor MMR should be featured. It was recognized that the relation-forming strategy might be difficult when the information lacks relation-forming possibilities, as with nonsense syllables and numbers.

In the studies by Tenopyr and Brown, there was a shift of expectation: that the paired-associate tests with *arbitrary* pairings of units would tend to go with the implications factors MSI and MMI unless fairly readily recognizable relations were possible. Efforts were made to keep a clear distinction between pairings that were readily relatable in some tests and pairings that were not in other tests, with the expectation that the former would go on memory-for-relations factors and the latter would go on memory-for-implications factors. This expectation was strongly borne out, as the next discussion will show.

Symbolic relations (MSR)   In one analysis (Tenopyr et al., 1966) four of five tests designed for factor MSR helped strongly to determine that factor. In Similar Word Changes Cross-out, the test and study pages are combined. A list of 40 pairs of words is given, with some relation readily discernible within each pair. Some of the pairs given later on the page repeat the same relation in a new pair. For example, an early pair might be BRINK-BRINE, and a later one might be SINK-SINE, where the endings of three letters bear the same relation, -INK and -INE. Another example is the pair NIT-TIN, followed later by the pair RAT-TAR. Although E could refer back to earlier pairs, in a speeded test he would do much better if he remembered the relation and did not have to refer back to it.

Memory for Letter Series presents for memorizing some series of letters containing trends, with relations between successive pairs of letter combinations. Examples are:

```
aa     aaa    aa     aaa    aa     aaa
b      bbb    bbbbb  bbbbbbb
```

The test page is composed of four-choice items, with one of the four series in each item presenting the same trend or relation as one of those on the study page. The letter composing the correct series in the test item is a different one from that in the series studied.

Memory for Name Relation presents for study sets of three names of persons, such as:

Sam Martin	Robert Reading
Tom McTavish	Rose Rearson
Pam Merton	Roger Renshaw

A relation between the given name and the family name is repeated in each set of three. The repetition is not to establish a class but to facilitate cognition and to confirm the relation. The first set of names features the identical letter for the end of the given name and the beginning of the family name. It is this relation that E is to remember and to look for in the test that follows. In the second set of three names, the initial letter of each given name is identical with the initial letter of the family name followed by the letter O in each given name and by E in each family name. In the retention test, a given name is presented with four alternatives for the family name. The test items going with the relations illustrated above are:

Tim: *Roy:*

A. Thompson   *A.* Rollins
B. Traver   *B.* Revere
C. Mensch   *C.* Radford
D. Tolman   *D.* Young

answer: C   *answer: B*

Memory for Word-Number Relations is the only test involving numbers in relationships that succeeds as a measure of MSR. It is not easy to present pairs combining words and numbers that have some natural basis for relationship within pairs. This test has to depend upon some arbitrary pairings of word and number in ways that emphasize the transposability of the relation, for the test items offer alternatives in which the relation is transposed to new units. Examples of material for study are:

| dead-285 | neck-412 |
| read-685 | neat-419 |

E has to note that -EAD goes with -85 and that NE- goes with 41-. Test items for these relations are:

lead: *next:*

A. 682   *A.* 312
B. 784   *B.* 416
C. 685   *C.* 482
D. 786   *D.* 498

answer: C   *answer: B*

The cognition problem was not made sufficiently easy in this test, for its loading on factor CSR was .34, secondary but significant. There also appeared a small loading of .35 on factor MSU, which means that memory for symbolic units was of some relevance in the task. This must mean that although there was transposition of the relation, there were, after all, a number of combinations of symbolic elements in common between studied relationship and test relationship, which might aid Es differentially.

The test intended for MSR that failed used numbers only. Memory for Numerical Relations presented for study two pairs of numbers for each relation, for example, 2-8 and 3-12, the relation being ×4. Another example is 14-8 and 10-4, with the relation -6. The test of retention is in the form of a verbalized statement of all relations remembered, completing the statement: "The second is _____ the first." The loading on factor MSR was insignificant. Although the test is a simple-appearing one, its variance scattered rather widely, among CSI, CSC, CSR, MSI, MSC, and MSR. Thus, cognition variance was not fully reduced, and product control was not effected. It is interesting that in both cognition and memory the strongest loadings involved factors for classes, relations, and implications. This is obviously not the way to construct a univocal test or a memory test without cognition variance. It is probably not the fact that the material is numerical rather than literal that caused the test to fail for its intended factor. The kinds of relations available in simple form are rather limited in the case of numbers, which may preclude the possibility of constructing a good numerical MSR test.

Semantic relations (MMR)   Experience with tests designed for MMR (S. W. Brown et al., 1966) gives a picture parallel to that for factor MSR. Three of the four tests designed for MMR helped to define it, with some additional help from two tests designed for other factors but readily rationalized as MMR tests.

Remembered Relations presents on the study page 15 short sentences explicitly stating relationships, for example:

Gold is more valuable than iron.
Tar is blacker than cement.
Lead is heavier than sand.
Diamonds are harder than coal.

The retention test is in multiple-choice form, for example:

Coal is _____ than diamonds.
A. softer
B. blacker
C. less valuable
D. none of these   (*answer: A*)

Sand is _____ than gold.
A. harder
B. blacker
C. lighter
D. none of these   (*answer: D,* a relation not given)

It should be noted that in the test items the relations can be reversed and that the fourth alternative is always "none of these," permitting the correct report of recognition that there is no stated relation. Also to be noted is that the same relation words are used a number of times, so that a partial matching test is involved.

Memory for Word Relations was successful but had a significant secondary loading for factor MMC. The study page involves some cognition or discovery of relations, e.g., the information SCISSORS-HAIR. The test provides multiple-choice items with alternative pairs. The correct pair does not have the same members, but it involves the same relation. The four alternative answers for the pair just given read:

A. Mower-lawn
B. Nail-clipper
C. Knife-cut
D. Break-hammer   (*answer: A*)

The involvement with classes might come by awareness that the relation is a generic idea that has general application. But the same should be true of memory for almost any concept having generality. It needs to be explained why MMC variance creeps into this test and not into some others.

Like many other tests, Recalled Analogies takes advantage of the general principle of constructing tests for unknown factors by analogy to those for known parallel factors. Analogies of one form or another have worked well almost across the board where relational abilities are concerned, and well they might. The study page presents an incomplete analogy, such as:

Native-Tourist: Resident-   ?_____

In a retention test, *E* is to complete the analogy, with only the third term supplied as a cue, for example:

Resident-_____

with *E* to fill the blank with something like VISITOR. The given RESIDENT by itself could have a number of things related to it. *E* is likely to be correct only if he remembers the relation between the first two words.

The Outcomes test was first conceived as a measure of MMI, but it turned out otherwise. On the study page, *E* reads statements of cause-and-effect types, e.g., "When a driver does not stop for a traffic signal, he usually gets a traffic citation." The first idea implies the second, but evidently the connection is too meaningful to provide a MMI test. In a multiple-choice retention test, the first part of the statement is presented paraphrased, for example:

Ted did not stop for the red light.
A. He probably didn't see the signal.
B. He must be in a hurry.
C. He got involved in an accident.
D. He will probably get a ticket.

answer: D

It may be noted that the right answer is also paraphrased, to get away from memory for particular words. Although this test was eventually hypothesized for MMS, on which it proved to have a minimally significant loading, MMR was found to be the leading source of variance. The cause-effect relation is probably accountable for this result. There was also a minimal loading on MMT, the reason for which is not obvious, unless *E*'s reinterpretation of the studied statements foreshadowed the paraphrasing that occurs in the test items.

The MMR-designed test that failed was Memory for Definitions. In this test the study page gives 15 words, each with a short definition, for example:

NEUTRAL—Neither one thing nor another

Most of the words are definable in quite different ways. The multiple-choice test of retention gives items like the following:

NEUTRAL:

A. Not engaged
B. Neither plus nor minus
C. Not harsh
D. Neither of two things   (*answer:* *D*)

As in many of the semantic-memory tests, the answers are paraphrased. The major loading was on the cognition factor CMU. The uncertainties concerning the exact definitions of the words may have been responsible for this result (see the discussion of factor CMU in Chapter 4).

It was mentioned earlier that there was some recognized risk of confusing relations and implications and that tests designed for the one might be involved with the other. Descriptions is a good example; designed for MMI, it proved to be much better for MMR, and it is easy to see why. This test calls for the study of pairs of word meanings, such as:

HOUSE-TENT   ELEPHANT-MOUNTAIN

There are reasons why each of these words should imply its mate. There is a meaningful connection, without the connection being obviously in the nature of a relation. The retention test given following the study of these pairs is in recognition form, with stated words that might tie the pairs together mixed with as many other words. The two words listed to take care of the two pairs just given are LIVABLE and BIG. Apparently, the connecting word, which stands for some common property, puts the pairs in the form of being related by reason of the relation of similarity. We saw how, in another test (Outcomes), a cause-and-effect relation in all pairs of ideas was sufficient to inject variance from factor MMR, in a similar manner. This test, like some others, shows how *E* takes advantage of observable relations when he can.

Memory for systems

An individual having cognized or constructed systems should retain such structures as such in memory storage. Four memory-for-systems factors have been demonstrated with some degree of satisfaction in three of the four SI systems categories for memory abilities, whereas for other products usually only two have become known.

Visual-figural systems (MFS-V)   For a likely factor of MFS-V, H. P. Kelley (1964) may have found some evidence, but his factor was probably confounded with other figural factors, such as CFS, CFT, and EFU. There were two memory tests on it, his Map Memory III, a recognition form of the AAF test of the same basic name, and a test called Memory for Relations, which presented for memorizing some arrangements of words, letters, figures, and numbers in a matrix, to be associated with their locations within the matrix. The multiple-choice recognition form of Map Memory provides segments from the map along with alternatives that are distinguishable in terms of arrangements of objects and lines, each arrangement being a system.

A clearer and more restricted factor that qualifies for cell MFS-V was reported by Christal (1958) in his study of visual memory. Position Memory asks *E* to recall the position on a page at which he has studied certain number-word pairs (in connection with another test of paired-associates form), the recall test being given four hours later. Position Recall I provides four study pages on each of which 12 figures are scattered, with E later to recall the positions. Space Memory presents five squares, each divided in five sections, with an object in each section. Later, E is to report in which section each object appeared. The emphasis upon memory for positions would seem to make these tests parallel to the cognitive tests for factor CFS-V. Memory for the mutual orientation of the objects is an obvious feature. It is noteworthy that all three tests bore some significant relations to a paired-associates factor that might be a confounding of MFI with MSI, the other tests not being of purely figural pairings. The implications variance probably came into the three Christal tests because the retention tests call for supplying *position associated with object.*

Auditory-figural systems (CFS-A)   In two analyses, Karlin (1941) found and replicated a factor that seems to qualify for the designation MFS-A. Although the factor was confined to tests of a musical character, which justified J. W. French (1951) in calling the factor "musical memory," in the light of SI theory we may venture to give it a broader interpretation.

The tests that identified the factor involved memory for melodies, rhythms, and musical form. Seashore's Tonal Memory test was one of the supporters for the factor. In this test, short melodies are repeated with one tone changed, with E to say which one. The Rhythm test asks E to say whether two given rhythms in immediate succession are the same or different. If it were not for the fact that other tests on the factor are described as measuring memory for compositions and musical form, we should hesitate to eliminate alternative hypotheses that the factor might be either CFS-A or EFS-A. It is probably unwise to reject those alternatives without further information.

Symbolic systems (MSS)   It was reported above in the discussion of span tests and their factor that only one of the four span tests in the Tenopyr analysis showed significant variance on factor MSS, and that was a relatively small amount in the Digit Span test. Other tests designed for MSS were successful in defining that factor, although not strongly so. All of them depended upon temporal order as the systemic principle, which leaves the generality of the ability in some doubt.

Memory for Order of Listed Numbers presents on the study page a list of 12 numbers each of one or two digits. The test page is composed of 15 four-choice items in answer to the general question, "Which number came first?" In this connection, "first" means earliest in the list. This format of the test was designed to avoid the scoring difficulties that would arise in a reconstruction test, in which E would be presented with the 12 numbers scrambled, to put them in correct order.

Memory for Nonsense Word Order presents a list of 15 syllables on the study page, then tests E with two-choice items of the type: "Did GER come before XAM?" Although supporting the hypothesis of a MSS ability, this test had a small significant loading on MSR. Alternative hypotheses for this are that (1) E is sometimes able to invent relations between successive pairs of syllables and (2) the before-after type of question in the items of the test of retention emphasizes observations of that kind of relation in studying the list.

In Memory for Transpositions the examiner reads two four-digit numbers in immediate succession, then repeats them immediately with a pair of neighboring digits interchanged in one of the numbers or in neither, with E to report what has happened. E is not asked to report the digits themselves, only whether a transposition has occurred and, if so, in which number. The change-in-order aspect should be the test's reason for measuring MSS.

Another test involving memory for the order of numbers was named Memory for Number Order. A total of 60 five-digit numbers appear in four columns on a page with corresponding five-digit numbers on the back of the same sheet. Half the numbers are identical, and in half there has been some rearrangement of order, with E to mark an answer sheet with alternatives S (same) or D (different). Some forgetting was expected to occur during the process of flipping the page. This test barely achieved the significance level of .30 for MSS. Because the test resembles tests for factor ESU, the evaluation of symbolic units (see Chapter 8), except for the need to turn the page in comparing two multidigit numbers, it had a larger loading on factor ESU than on MSS. Because such a relationship was somewhat anticipated for this and one or two other tests, two good marker tests for ESU had been put in the analysis.

Although we may say that the factor of MSS has been demonstrated and although we learn from the analysis that span tests have some relation to it, much stronger tests need to be developed for that factor. Systemic principles other than order need to be used so as to establish that MSS has relevance for systems of other kinds.

Semantic systems (MMS)

Semantic systems (MMS)   There is evidence from three sources regarding the existence of a factor for cell MMS. Christal (1958) found three tests loaded on such a factor, all of which emphasize memory for temporal order of events. Order has been a consistent kind of organization for systems factors in other operations categories, but other kinds of systems have been relevant, also; for example, spatial arrangement for visual-figural systems and matrix arrangements for semantic systems.

One of Christal's tests was Sequence Memory. Three days after the airmen subjects of his study had taken their classification battery, they were quizzed on their memory for the order in which the tests had been administered, a pair-comparison format being used. In Christal's Position in Succession test, E was given a pair-comparison testing on the order in which color cards had been presented in the Color Memory Test. In Position Recall II, E was asked to recall on which of four successive pages of a booklet each of 48 figures had been shown. The loadings for the factor were limited in size (around .35), but there was definitely a common factor. The content was probably mainly semantic, but we cannot be sure about this point because of the limited number of tests and the opportunities they could offer for memory in terms of other kinds of information, particularly visual-figural.

H. P. Kelley (1964) reported a factor involving quite different tests, but from their properties the factor that they represent in common could be MMS. Sentence Completion involves the study of some sentences and later filling one-word blanks in the same sentences. Since only one word is to be recalled, it might be expected that this test would measure factor MMU. It could have been that this factor is a confounding of MMS with MMU, except for the fact that under the discussion of factor MMU above it was tentatively suggested that another of Kelley's factors could qualify for MMU. Other tests in the same list with Sentence Completion more definitely look like MMS tests. Merely adding a deleted word to a sentence may involve some system memory, for each word has a role in a system, the entire sentence.

Memory for Limericks, which had a small but significant loading for the factor identified above as MMU, had a larger loading on the Kelley factor just identified as MMS. The idea of the entire last line of the limerick and the key word had to be reported in order to receive credit. In Consequences II, Verbal, E hears two sentences in succession, stating a condition and a consequence. In the retention test, E hears only the first member of the sentence pair, to supply the idea of the second in his own words. This test is reminiscent of the Outcomes test used by S. W. Brown et al., which went most strongly on MMR, although hypothesized for MMS, as related before. One difference was that in the Brown test E studied the condition and its consequence in one sentence rather than two, and another difference was that the test was a multiple-choice recognition test of retention rather than a recall of the consequent idea.

One test in the list for Kelley's factor that is under discussion looks more like an implications test. Known as Memory for Words II, it is in a paired-associates format, which also suggests an implications test if the words of the pairs are unrelated. But a fifth test again looks more like a systems affair, in which E makes a nonverbatim report of the ideas in a story that he reads. The test, Memory for Ideas, loaded much more strongly on the factor identified as MMU. The ideas are organized in the story; hence the systems variance. From the presence of the two tests that look like MMI tests, Kelley's MMS factor might be a confounding of MMS with MMI. Or it might even be MMI almost exclusively, for in Sentence Completion we can say that the given incomplete sentence implies the missing word and in Memory for Limericks we can say that the first four lines given imply the last line. Further analyses are needed of the same tests along with more clearly known marker tests of MMS and MMI in the battery.

With the tests in the Brown analysis especially designed for MMS, the obtained factor is much more readily identified as MMS. One of the leading tests, but not quite the strongest, was Memory for Test Order, which used the same format as that for a test that helped to identify the MMS factor attributed to Christal. The pair-comparison items pertained to the order of the tests just completed within the same booklet, whereas Christal's items pertained to a longer battery taken four days previously.

The leading test in Brown's analysis, Learned Information (System), was a recall test for six short paragraphs of expository material about the structure of intellect. In taking the retention test, E has a given list of the major technical terms about which he is to write a coherent account, covering ideas in the reading material in the order in which they were presented.

In a test called Memory for Facts, E studies 15 short statements of fact, after which he has a verbal quizzing about the facts, something like a delayed reading-comprehension test. Putting the description in such terms suggests that some CMU variance would enter the picture, and it did. The loading on CMU was .40, and on MMS the loading was .35.

A fourth test designed for MMS just barely failed to show itself significantly on its intended factor. Sentence Memory, based upon the previous experience that a sentence is a kind of semantic system, although not always, went very strongly on factor CMU. Seven sentences of increasing length and complexity are read to E, who is told to report the ideas contained, in the proper order. Evidently the level of verbal comprehension is higher than it should have been for the eleventh-grade students who took the memory battery. Some of the sentences became rather long and complex.

Memory for transformations

Symbolic transformations (MST)   Memory-for-transformations tests should somehow ensure that E experience certain given transformations and then be given a test for retention of those transformations. The kinds of transformations that have been most common with symbolic information have dealt with changes in spellings of words or with breaking words into parts and recombining the parts in new ways. Three such tests were moderately successful, and a test of a different character was not (Tenopyr, 1966).

Memory for Misspelling presents for study words that are misspelled, such as BOAN, KETLE, SKURT, and FASEN. The misspelling provides a symbolic unit that, when pronounced, gives a familiar word sound. It is not possible to control E's way of perceiving the printed word, whether he sounds it or takes it purely visually. On the test page, E is given the word in its correct spelling, to which he must respond by giving the misspelled form that he studied. An assumption could be that if E saw what real word was intended, he also saw the transformation from the correct to the incorrect spelling that was given.

Although this test led the list on factor MST, it had an even higher loading on factor CSU. Evidently, the difficulty of perceiving what word was intended from inspection of the study page was so great as to introduce strong individual differences due to differences in ability to cognize symbolic units. This would suggest that most Es did not take advantage of the phonetic approach, which would have helped in recognition of the words. The high loading (.62) on CSU may have been inflated, however, for another test in the battery that has a history of helping to mark the CSU factor also involves the recognition of misspelled words. Correct Spelling lists words half of which are misspelled, with E to tell which are correct and which incorrect.

Memory for Word Transformations presents on the study page a string of consecutive letters spelling two words in two ways. With the words divided in one way, one pair of words can be made; with the words divided at another point, two other words appear. Examples are:

BIND/ARE   EARN/ICE   FIR/STRING   LIGHT/ENTRANCE

On the test page, the same letter sequences are repeated, some transformed and some not, with E to say which ones are and which are not transformed. The relatively low loading of this test on MST indicates that although some memory-for-transformations variance is involved, it is not very strong. This is probably due to the fact that no transformations were actually required to be cognized in studying the material, although E could readily produce some and possibly did. No tests for factor CST were in the analysis; so we cannot estimate the strength of the possible relevance of that ability.

Memory for Hidden Transformations was constructed in resemblance to Camouflaged Words (see Chapter 7). In the latter, each item presents a meaningful sentence within which a name of a sport or a game is hidden. Such a name can be made by combining the ending of one word with the beginning of the next word in the sentence. In the memory test, E is given the sentence with the hidden word marked off so as to ensure cognition of the transformation on the study page. Such sentences are:

Don't leap in before you look.
You must not burden the teacher.

Can E recognize the transformed words any more easily in new sentences because he has already experienced the same transformation product?

The new words must be formed by making the same combination of letters. The test sentences including the same transformed products as those illustrated above were:

He will stop in the evening.
They loaded entire trucks.

The first transformation is exactly the same as that on the study page, but the second is not. The word PIN came by joining P and IN, but the word DENT was previously formed by joining the DEN with T, not D with ENT. Showing E the actual transformations in both study material and test material should keep both the CST and the NST variances low. The effects of these kinds could not be checked in the Tenopyr analysis because those two factors were not represented. There was not a significant loading on factor MSU, as might have been hypothesized.

A test, Memory for Decimal Point Shifts, which involved numbers, did not do so well for factor MST. For this test, a shift in a decimal point in a number is regarded as one kind of transformation. On the study page, pairs of numbers like the following are presented:

8.167   514.3   61.94
81.67   5.143   6.194

On the test page, some pairs are given with the same shift in decimal point and others are given with different shifts, with E to say which are the same and which are different. This unsuccessful test for MST was the only one that used numbers as material, but from this fact alone we cannot conclude that transformations involving numbers are not related to MST. Other candidates for MST with number material should be tried out. Transformations as in numerical equations, if examinees are sufficiently sophisticated for such tests, should be effective.

Semantic transformations (MMT)   Only one analysis has demonstrated a factor of MMT (S. W. Brown et al., 1966). With five tests designed for the factor, all five contributed to bringing it out, with the aid of two other tests not designed for it. One of the two tests that tied for first place on MMT was Double Meanings, and the other was Unusual Answers.

On a study page of Double Meanings, 15 pairs of sentences are presented for a learning exercise, each pair containing a word in common but with different meanings in the two. One example is:

She brought the groceries home in a paper bag.
The hunter planned to go out and bag a deer.

Another pair is:

The calf was born yesterday.
The athlete strained a calf muscle.

The word in common to the two sentences is underlined. The transformation from one to the other meaning is obvious, being well determined by the contexts of the sentences. The retention test is in recognition form, with the 15 pairs represented among 15 other pairs. In each item, a pair of words (synonyms for the two meanings) or of short definitions is given. The correct pairs for the two transformations given above are:

Sack-Obtain   and   Baby cow–Lower leg

Too commonly, the MMT tests have secondary loadings with weaker contributions. The secondary loading for Double Meanings was for factor MMC. It can be surmised that the generic properties of the words make some contributions. The MMC variance occurs perhaps because the words in common in the sentences share class memberships with the answer words.

Unusual Answers is based upon riddles and answers to riddles. On the study page are presented a riddle and an answer, involving a transformation, such as:

What can never be beaten?   (*answer*: a broken drum)

In the retention test *E* is to answer questions like:

What is special about a broken drum? _____

This test is unusually complex factorially. Besides the loading of .53 on MMT, it has loadings in the .30s for each of the factors MMS, CMU, and EMC. Evidently the completion problem in an item leaves a great deal uncontrolled. Other types of retention items should be tried out for this test.

Homonyms presents in a pair of sentences two words that are homonyms, as in the sentence:

There is a hole in the wall.
He ate the whole pie.

The retention test presents a synonym for one member of such a pair, with alternative answers, one of which is a synonym for the other. The item pertaining to the two words just given underlined reads:

ENTIRE
A. Nut   *B.* Ship   *C.* Hollow space   *D.* Operation
answer: C

The appropriate pair of homonyms must be remembered in order to do the item. No significant secondary loading appeared for this test.

Substitutions was developed analogously to the test Gestalt Transformations, an NMT test that asks what object can be adapted to some unusual purpose, the transformation being in its use, which is one kind of meaning. In Substitutions, the study page contains statements about unusual uses, e.g.:

A gummed label may be used as a bandage.
A cigaret filter may be used as a pin cushion.
A mop may be used as a wig.

The retention test is in matching form, unusual uses (paraphrased) to be matched with given objects that appeared in the list of statements. A short matching test will illustrate:

A. Cigaret filter	*1.* To dress for Halloween	(*answer: C*)
B. Gummed label	*2.* To clean a floor	(*answer: D*)
C. Mop	*3.* To help straighten out a sewing box	(*answer: A*)
D. None of these	*4.* To dress a wound	(*answer: B*)

Answer *C* to item 2 would not be acceptable, for it is not an unusual use; no transformation is involved. Each test page contained 15 object names plus "None of these" and 16 uses. There was a small secondary loading for factor MMU. In spite of the fact that paraphrasing was used or perhaps because it was, some verbal-comprehension variance also crept in.

Puns are well-known examples of semantic transformations and hence were readily considered for use when MMT tests were being constructed. The study page for Remembering Puns presents 15 sentences, each containing a pun, for example:

A bird-loving bartender was arrested for contributing to the delinquency of a mynah.

The retention test is in completion form, giving the underlined pun word, with E to supply the transformation, as in the item:

Mynah-_____

The secondary CMU variance indicates that there was some vocabulary trouble with this test. This trouble could probably be avoided in revisions of the test.

Whereas CMU tended to creep into tests designed for MMT, a certain test designed for MMU came out instead to be strongest on MMT. This test was Memory for Word Meanings. On the study page appear 15 familiar words. On the test page are 15 synonyms or definitive phrases, mixed with 15 other such expressions. If the words to be studied are:

WINTER   KNIFE   WISH

the answers to be recognized as representing them are, respectively:

A season of the year
Used to cut
To hope

It is difficult to see that any transformation would occur or need to occur at the time of learning the concepts presented; therefore there should be no occasion to retain such products. Transformations might have to occur at the time of finding a good synonym or a definitive expression, since the latter could represent a somewhat different meaning than occurred at the time of study. It does not seem that this involvement with transformations is enough to put the test in the MMT camp. This particular result might not be replicated with the same test in a similar battery, but if so, further possible hypotheses for the MMT variance would be called for.

Memory for implications

Symbolic implications (MSI)   With factor MSI, we come to another special and interesting situation, because of some involvement of the numerical-facility factor and because of the history of rote-memory or associative-memory factors and their logical claim for consideration as implications abilities. There has been a growing confusion concerning the factor long known as numerical facility. Recent analyses of symbolic-memory abilities have helped to clear up the picture, but some long-held notions concerning that factor are in need of changes.

Background of the number factor   In his monograph, J. W. French could feel secure in saying, "The *Number* factor is the clearest of them all," since he could cite 35 analyses in which number factors had been found even before that time (1951, p. 225). He went on to say that the factor's characteristic tests obviously involve numbers and the nearer the tests' problems come to purely numerical-operations form, the higher the factor loading. In Thurstone's first PMA analysis, for example, his four numerical-operations tests and four others were loaded as follows:

Multiplication	.81	Number Code	.62
Addition	.76	Numerical Judgment	.43
Subtraction	.67	Tabular Completion	.39
Division	.62	Arithmetical Reasoning	.38

In the four other tests the numerical computations are more or less incidental, except for Number Code.

Among the 19 tests found loaded on number factors in the literature by French, 11 are strictly computational and others involve computing incidentally, but 1 or 2 seem not to require numerical operations at all. Dot Counting involves simply counting, and Dial and Table Reading appears to involve mainly perception and interpretation of numbers. Highest Number involves locating the highest number in a column of numbers. Incidental mentions of number tests in Chapters 4 through 8 of this volume provide quite a few examples of number tests that do not involve the number factor. Although we do not know clearly the features that differentiate number tests that do and do not involve the number factor, the need for computation or its incidental involvement seems to have much support as the distinguishing mark.

But more recent experience has called for reassessment of what have been called number factors. The first placement of the typical number factor in the SI model was in cell NSI, for the convergent production of symbolic implications (Guilford, 1959a; 1959b). Logically, any simple numerical operation appears to involve an implication that E must produce from his memory store. For example, the information 2×4 implies 8 to the person who has mastered the art of multiplication.

But two independent findings, one supporting the other, changed the idea that the traditional number factor is NSI, at least exclusively. Both P. C. Davis (1956) and de Mille (1962) found that the Wechsler Digit Symbol test went strongly with a number-operations test on a factor that could be identified as numerical facility, a result that was verified in a second analysis by de Mille. But because of the probability of the memorial character of the Digit Symbol test, these factors could be identified as SI factor MSI. The Wechsler test clearly appears to involve memory for implications: digits implying symbols. It was also recognized that there was another good candidate for cell NSI of the SI model; so the number factor could readily be vacated from that place without any loss.

One important difference between the Digit Symbol test and a test of numerical operations is that for the former the period of retention is extremely short, whereas for the latter it is very long, since it depends upon implications learned in childhood. Another difference is that the Digit Symbol test involves some poorly practiced implications, whereas numerical-operations tests involve well-practiced connections. Numerical-operations tests violate one important feature of good memory tests, the condition that all Es should have equivalent amounts of practice. In spite of all these differences, a numerical-operations test can be regarded as a measure of memory for symbolic implications.

In some of the more recent analyses, a numerical-operations test has been found to share some of its variance between what has been recognized as MSI, following the Davis and de Mille findings, and factor NSI, which has been identified by means of other tests (for example, see Petersen et al., 1963). Thus, a numerical-operations test, which has seemed to be the epitome of univocality, has more recently appeared to be complex factorially.

Numerical-operations tests and MSI   In the three analyses in which the Wechsler Digit Symbol test joined with a numerical-operations test to determine a factor, only one test of each type was present. In Thurstone's original analysis and in many others following it, two or more numerical-operations tests have usually been present. When this has been true, the tests have functioned much as alternate forms of the same test, having relatively high intercorrelations and also relatively high factor loadings on their common factor. The conclusion seems clear that with more than one numerical-operations test in the analyzed battery those tests have loadings reflecting a confounding of a common factor (common also with non-numerical-operations tests) with a factor specific to computation tests.

In the Tenopyr analysis (1966), two tests of the digit-symbol type were included. One, Digits and Symbols, was essentially another form of the Wechsler test, with new symbols. The other was Symbols and Letters, in which E is to write the letter that goes with its symbol as given at the top of the page. These two tests intercorrelated .65. The four numerical-operations tests—Addition, Subtraction, Multiplication, and Division—intercorrelated from .61 to .69. The correlations between the two digit-symbol tests and the four numerical-operations tests ranged from .34 to .48, distinctly lower than the intercorrelations just cited but high enough to suggest much in common between the two kinds of tests.

A rotational solution that took cognizance of the higher intercorrelations of the numerical-operations tests gave them an opportunity to have a factor of their own, leaving opportunity for any remaining variance to go with the other tests recognized as being more clearly MSI tests. The result was that the two digit-symbol tests helped to determine a factor recognized as MSI. The four number tests determined their own factor, with no other tests significantly loaded on it, even though there were several memory tests in the battery that contained numbers in the items. Only one of the numerical-operations tests (Addition) was loaded significantly also on the factor identified as MSI, with moderate strength, the other three having loadings only a little below the magic significance level of .30.

In a modified analysis of the Tenopyr data (Tenopyr et al., 1966) with the four numerical-operations tests combined to give one composite score and with the two digit-symbol tests also combined, a factor for MSI was found, but the numerical-operations score had a barely significant loading on it. We are accordingly left with the present conclusion that the factorial picture of single numerical-operations tests in general includes rather small relations to factors MSI and NSI, with an unusually large specific component. Second thoughts suggest that such tests could not be strong representatives of either MSI or NSI. The fact that an equal amount of practice, a necessary condition for good memory tests, does not apply should preclude much variance from MSI. The fact that convergent production requires more than a replicative recall of items of information (see Chapters 7 and 13) should preclude much variance from NSI.

It should not be surprising to find that numerical-operations tests have a strong specific component. From studies of the relation of practice to factor content, it is commonly found that there is a specific component in the variance of scores from a task and that this component grows in importance with practice (see Chapter 12 for examples). Number-operations skills are overlearned habits; hence tests that measure them should be expected to have a strong specific component. The same is somewhat true of activities like the span tests, for which acts like memorizing phone numbers and the like should yield individual differences in that kind of skill.

MSI tests and the factor ESU   It was stated before that tests of the traditional paired-associates type would go on a memory-for-implications factor if that factor were sufficiently determined in an analysis. This expectation was given support by the fact that the test Number Letter Association helped very much to determine the factor adopted as MSI, along with Digits and Symbols and Symbols and Letters. In fact, it led on the factor, whereas Symbols and Letters was loaded with minimal significance. A paired-associates type of test should do better than a digit-symbol type of test for MSI, because in the latter E has the right answers before him at the top of the page. In the Number Letter

Association test, E studies two-place numbers each of which is paired with a letter. On the test page he is given the numbers to which he is to supply the appropriate letters.

The correlation of .65 between the two digit-symbol types of tests was by no means fully accounted for by their loadings on factor MSI. There happened to be in the battery two good marker tests for factor ESU, which was expected to crop up in two other tests. In one of those marker tests, Symbol Identities (see Chapter 8), E compares two letter or digit sets that are presented side by side, to say whether they are the same or different, different when letters or digits are replaced or transposed. ESU was expected to appear in two memory tests in which E compares something on the front of the page with a corresponding something on the back of the page, to say whether they are the same or different. It turned out that both Digits and Symbols and Symbols and Letters also came out with loadings on ESU as strong as or stronger than their loadings on MSI. Evidently, in doing a digit-symbol type of test, E does considerable checking back and forth between his answers and the code.

From this result we draw the inference that the Wechsler Digit Symbol test is a two-factor test and that it should be expected to measure factors MSI and ESU about equally well. If one wants a good MSI test without involvement with factor ESU, a paired-associates format should be used, as in Number-Letter Association or in several tests of the kind developed for MMI, to be mentioned next.

Semantic implications (MMI)   As indicated historically a number of times, factors have been found common to tests in paired-associates form, but none of them qualifies as an unconfounded factor MMI. The analysis by S. W. Brown et al. (1966) provides such a factor. To keep MMI tests clear of factor MMR, it was found necessary to use connections between paired units that are clearly on the arbitrary side. Three of four tests designed for MMI were exceptionally strong and univocal for the same factor; the fourth failed, going primarily on MMR.

Paired-Associates Recall is a typical paired-associates task with pairs of unrelated but meaningful words. It resembles the typical laboratory task except for the matter of controlled exposure times for the pairs in the laboratory case. E sees 12 pairs on a study page looking like:

SUCCEED . . . HEAVY

and in the recall test, items like:

SUCCEED-_____

Related Alternatives uses family names paired with occupations, such as:

SMITH-Bricklayer   JONES–Radio announcer

The test of retention is in multiple-choice form, the correct alternative answer naming something obviously used in the occupation, not the name of the occupation itself, for example:

SMITH-   JONES-

A. Piano   A. Microphone
B. Microphone   B. Watch
C. Brick   C. Tire
D. Typewriter   D. Brick

answer: C   answer: A

It may be noted that the right answer in one item is sometimes included among the wrong answers in another item, so that there can be little dependence upon memory for particular words. The tendency is toward a matching format, which should be ideal for memory-for-implications tests, as stated before.

Books and Authors is similar to the preceding test. To a family name is arbitrarily attached a book title that the person was supposed to have written. The title includes a clue to the author's occupation, for example:

Adams—Great Moments in Baseball
Brooks—Pictures I Have Painted

In contrast to the method of the preceding test, E is to recall enough about the title to be able to write the name of the occupation when the name of the author is given.

The test Descriptions failed for measuring MMI, evidently because the connections between pairs were too meaningful, that is, not sufficiently arbitrary. Only one test not designed for MMI was loaded on it, and that was a minimal and secondary relationship, namely, the test Classified Information, which was designed for MMC. In that test, it might be that during the study of the three-word class, such as SILK, WOOL, NYLON, there were automatically some implications of other class members that happen to be in the three-word set to be recognized: RAYON, COTTON, FELT. Such implications cognized during the study operation could be retained and could thus help E to recognize the second set and its class.

Summary

The finding of quite a number of memory abilities as forecast by the SI model vindicates the recognition of a special operation category for memory and the hypothesis that memory abilities would parallel those in other operation categories. Memory abilities have been found quite separable from cognitive abilities on the one hand and production abilities on the other.

Memory abilities are distinguishable from cognitive abilities operationally by subjecting examinees to comparable, if not equivalent, exposure to certain quantities of information and testing for retention of that information later. Cognitive abilities are functions of the quantities of information possessed, without regard to how or when obtained.

The distinction between memory abilities and production abilities means that retention and retrieval of information are distinctly different operations. Of course, if there has been no retention, there cannot be retrieval. Tests of production abilities have emphasized, as an experimental control, information that examinees are likely to have retained in common.

Although a few memory factors had been reported from various sources, some of which fit logically into the SI model, in the light of new findings a number of those early factors now appear to have been confoundings of SI factors.

In spite of unusual difficulties with respect to experimental controls in applying memory tests, separation of retentive abilities for different kinds of content and different kinds of products has been demonstrated. All of the semantic- and symbolic-memory abilities have now been indicated, and there are signs from earlier sources of at least two figural-memory abilities. No investigation has yet been made regarding behavioral-memory abilities, but experiences in other content areas lend some confidence to the expectation that such abilities can also be demonstrated.

Recent analyses have thrown much light upon the factorial nature of two well-known and popular kinds of tests, memory-span tests and numerical-operations tests, neither of which now appears to be factorially strong and both of which appear to have substantial specific components. The latter feature is probably a reflection of the fact that they are overlearned, special habits.

Experience with factoring memory tests suggests that those who experiment with human memorizing in the laboratory would do well to pay much attention to the SI categories of information, in terms of kinds of content and product. Some of the apparently conflicting results of the past might be reconciled if this suggestion were followed. More significant experimental studies should be initiated, they should be more meaningfully controlled, and the results should be more significantly interpreted.

6 Divergent-production abilities

With items of information cognized and put into memory storage, they are more or less available for retrieval when occasions call for them. Reviving items of information from memory storage in order to meet certain objectives is the basis for psychological production, either divergent or convergent. Divergent production is a concept defined in accordance with a set of factors of intellectual ability that pertain primarily to information retrieval and with their tests, which call for a number of varied responses to each test item.

Certain hypotheses about abilities that should be of special relevance for creative thinking (Guilford, 1950) led to the search for abilities having to do with *fluency* of thinking and *flexibility* of thinking, abilities concerned with the ready flow of ideas and with readiness to change direction or to modify information. The first large factor analysis that was aimed at the investigation of those hypotheses (Wilson et al., 1954), and others that have followed, have found not one kind of fluency factor but three, not one kind of flexibility factor but two, besides a factor that was called by the term *originality*. It was recognized that the three fluency factors were probably the same as had been found before: word fluency (Thurstone, 1938a), ideational fluency (Calvin W. Taylor, 1947), and associational fluency (Fruchter, 1948, in a reanalysis of Thurstone's 1938 data). For the two flexibility factors there were no known precedents.

For the originality factor there were two historical precedents. Garnett (1919) found a factor he called "cleverness" in a study of ratings of many personality traits. The full identification of this factor with one found only in aptitude tests cannot be effected on the basis of the evidence. Hargreaves (1927) found a distinction between a fluency factor and an originality factor, of which he thought the latter to be a combination of *g* plus fluency (without its speed aspect) plus memory. Hargreaves was able to conclude, correctly, that creative imagination is by no means an undifferentiated ability.

In a study of planning abilities (Berger et al., 1957), there was hypothesized an ability to elaborate upon ideas, to fill them out with details. The results added another kind of ability, *elaboration,* to be considered along with fluency, flexibility, and originality, to make up the set that was to become known as divergent-production abilities.

A fourth kind of fluency had been added to the list by Taylor (1947). He called it "verbal versatility," but it became known later as "expressional fluency," an ability to produce connected discourse. Carroll (1941) had found a factor earlier that he called "speed of production of meaningful discourse," which describes expressional fluency very well, but the listed tests representing it were mostly different from the usual markers for the expressional-fluency factor.

Since divergent-production tests require examinees to produce their own answers, not to choose them from alternatives given to them, it is not surprising that any such tests would be conspicuous by their absence in modern group tests of intelligence, particularly after machine scoring came into the picture. Their absence from individual tests is also well known, a fact that can probably be traced to Terman's early experience (1906) with his seven "bright" and seven "stupid" children that were not discriminated by a test of creative imagination in line with other tests. In recent years it has become known that children of high IQ can be either high or low on divergent-production tests. With only seven cases in his "bright" group, Terman could have had an adverse selection on divergent production, which precluded any superiority of his group over his low one, particularly if the judges who selected the bright children did not include imagination among their signs of brightness. For whatever reasons, the divergent-production abilities have historically been outside the domain of intelligence tests and conceptions of intelligence.

The divergent-production matrix   Table 6.1 presents the matrix of the 24 cells for the divergent-production (DP) abilities as envisaged by SI theory. At the time this was written, of 16 DP factors that had been investigated, 16 had been demonstrated. Curiously, 1 factor was found in a ninth-grade population but not in an adult population. DP abilities in the behavioral category were under investigation when this was written, with preliminary testing giving some indications that those factors, too, could be demonstrated.

The symbols within the matrix in Table 6.1 mean the same as they did in previous tables (see Chapter 4). As previously stated, all except 1 have been demonstrated in adult samples and all 16 at the ninth-grade level. Some of these have been found at the fifth- and sixth-grade levels (Lauritzen, 1963; Merrifield, Guilford, & Gershon, 1963), although with not so much strength and clarity as should be desired. Two have been found at the age of six (McCartin, 1966), and two others have been proposed in interpretation of factors found at the six-month level (Stott & Ball, 1963).

Divergent production of units

The main characteristic of tests that have brought out DP factors where units are the products generated is that they present tasks each of which specifies some class property or properties, with E to list members of the class so specified. It is characteristic, also, that the specifications should be neither too broad nor too narrow. If the specifications narrow the class to one member, we have *convergent* production rather than divergent production. The moderate breadth of class must have some psychological significance, concerning which there will be some speculation later.

*Table 6.1   Matrix of the divergent-production
factors (D) represented in the structure of intellect*

Figural (F)		Symbolic (S)		Semantic (M)		Behavioral (B)		
DFU 14	2	DSU 13, 14	N	DMU 6, 10, 13, 14	N	DBU	0	*Units* (U)
DFC 14	1	DSC 14	S	DMC 11, 12, 14	N	DBC	0	*Classes* (C)
DFR 14	0	DSR 14	S	DMR 11, 12, 14	S	DBR	0	*Relations* (R)
DFS 14	2	DSS 14	S	DMS 6, 13, 14	S	DBS	0	*Systems* (S)
DFT 14	S	DST	0	DMT 11, 12, 14	N	DBT	0	*Transformations* (T)
DFI 11, 14	S	DSI 14	2	DMI 11, 12, 14	S	DBI	0	*Implications* (I)

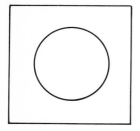  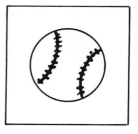

Fig. 6-1   Given a simple, familiar form, e.g., a circle, the examinee is to make as many real objects as he can with a minimum of addition of lines, as in the Sketches test.

Figural units (DFU)   Tests for DFU were constructed with its SI properties in mind and by analogy to successful tests of DSU and DMU, which had been known for a considerable time. A difficulty that was not anticipated was encountered in constructing tests that differentiate clearly between factors DFU and DFS. In the figural-content category, especially, it proved to be difficult to construct units tests that are entirely free from systems involvement and even more difficult to construct systems tests free from units involvement. The difficulty is perhaps due to the fact that in the visual-figural area a unit can readily be treated as a system and a system can readily be conceived as a unit. Experience throws a little light on how this distinction can perhaps be improved.

In both adult and adolescent populations, the strongest and most nearly univocal test for DFU was Sketches (Gershon et al., 1963; Guilford & Hoepfner, 1966). In this test, E is given a simple basic figure and told to add just enough to it in order to make a recognizable object. For example, the sample item in Figure 6.1 provides a circle, and E is shown two possible, acceptable responses. Not very much production-of-systems variance should be involved, because the familiar objects are already organized as units in E's experience. It is interesting that the loadings for adults and adolescents were so similar (.53 and .52, respectively) on DFU for this test.

Another relatively univocal test, although not so strong on DFU, is Make a Mark. This test calls for lines with a single specification, such as "Draw some open figures in dotted lines," samples of which are given, as in Figure 6.2. The loadings on this test were .44 and .46, with no significant loadings on DFS. Organizing is minimized, since only one or two lines are to be produced. In each problem, two specifications for the class, e.g., open figures made with straight lines in one task and closed figures made with curved lines in the other, are given.

A test that is especially strong for DFU at the ninth-grade level but that allows DFS variance to creep in is Make a Figure Test. In this one, E is given two or three line elements with which he is to construct different figures, as shown in Figure 6.3. In the test proper, three elements are given in each section of the test. The DFU loadings were .61 and .41 for adolescents and adults, respectively; the DFS loadings were .41 and .36. In arranging the line elements in various ways, organizing ability comes in, thus DFS.

A test that was designed for factor DFS but which shared its variance in the two ways is of interest, especially because of the age difference in this respect. Monograms presents three capital letters, such as A, V, and C, with E to arrange these letters, as if they were initials of his name, so as to make a variety of monograms. The two DFU loadings were .52 and .36 for adults and adolescents, respectively, and the two DFS loadings were .36 and .54: almost exact reversals. An interesting hypothesis to investigate would be that the

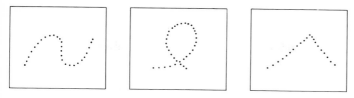

Fig. 6.2 In the Make a Mark test, the examinee is to make as many simple line figures as he can, keeping within a class specification. The examples given were in response to the instruction: make different simple, open figures in dotted lines.

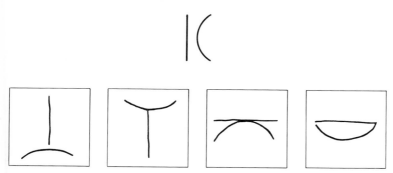

Fig. 6.3 In Make a Figure, given two line elements, the examinee is to combine them in a great variety of ways to make figures.

adults conceive of monograms more in the nature of units, and adolescents more in the nature of systems. The one group may emphasize total effect; the other, internal arrangements.

Symbolic units (DSU)   The factor that Thurstone called "word fluency" has been investigated probably more than any other DP ability. It is one of the easiest to test univocally and with a rather wide variety of tests. It probably does not have the significance that Thurstone attached to it, when he put it in his PMA batteries, being limited to generating words, as letter patterns, from memory storage to fulfill certain class requirements. As in the case of other symbolic abilities, meanings of the words are of no consequence. For word meanings, DMU is the corresponding ability.

Among the better tests, with loadings on DSU in the region .55 to .60, are:

Suffixes (E writes words ending in a specified suffix, e.g., -TION)
First and Last Letters (e.g., write words with the first and last letters R_____M)
Tests with first letter only specified
Tests with one letter specified (e.g., the letter E)
Tests with two letters specified (e.g., the letters C and A)
Tests with three letters specified (e.g., the letters $M, U,$ and B)
Rhymes (E gives words rhyming with a specified word, e.g., ROAM)

There is a general tendency in DSU tests for some CMU variance to come into the picture when the specification is more restrictive, as in the case of the last two tests mentioned: in giving words with three specified letters or in giving rhymes. In these instances it pays to have a larger vocabulary, for probably it is necessary for E to go into some of the less familiar words to gain length of list.

Some of the kinds of tests that have not done so well, with loadings on DSU of .40 and lower, include:

Anagrams tests (which probably have significant secondary or even primary loadings on factor CSU, the cognition problem becoming a source of individual differences in scores)

Tests specifying the number of letters (e.g., write three-letter words)

Word-listing tests (without any further specification), one of which had a loading of only .22 on DSU (Christensen & Guilford, 1963)

It has been remarked before that symbolic tests may utilize letters or numbers almost interchangeably. At least it is usually true that both letter and number tests of a certain kind otherwise are loaded on the same factor. Perhaps because the factor has been known as *word* fluency, very few investigators have ever thought of determining whether there would be a number fluency and whether it would also be loaded on DSU. The SI placement of the factor in the cell for DSU calls for testing the hypothesis that fluency in producing number information would also go with factor DSU. Fortunately that hypothesis has already been incidentally tested by Canisia (1962). In a battery that included the PMA Word Fluency test she had a Number Fluency test, in which E is to think of numbers that satisfy certain class specifications. The two tests went together on a factor. This result supports the redefining of word fluency as DSU.

Semantic units (DMU)   Following the principle that for testing abilities of divergent production of units the task should prescribe class properties, with the examinee to list class members, several tests of DMU have been of that type. Christensen and Guilford (1963) made an experimental study of the optimal number of specifications for a class to be used in such a test, with some rather decisive results. When there is a low degree of restriction, as in the task calling for the naming of metals, fluids, or kinds of fish, the loading on DMU has been about .35. A number of other tests of this type, including Things Round, Adjectives, Things to Eat, and Animals, have given loadings on DMU on the order of .40. With some restriction added, as in a form of Thing Listing that calls for two specifications, such as solid and soft, fluid and flammable, or white and smaller than a football, the loading is in the range .50 to .55. With more restriction, as with three specifications, such as soft, white, and edible, the loading dropped to .20. Thus, the optimal range of restriction for good measurement of DMU with a thing-listing test is very narrow.

Tests of different kinds that have done well for DMU include:

Consequences (obvious) (E lists consequences of a given event, such as people's no longer needing or wanting sleep, only the more direct or obvious responses being counted)

Plot Titles (nonclever) (E lists possible titles for a given short story, only the nonclever ones being counted)

Utility Test (fluency) (E lists uses he can think of for a common brick, a wooden pencil, or a wire coat hanger, the total number of relevant responses being counted)

The loadings in such tests have been of the order of .50 to .55. Occasionally a score from Consequences (obvious) has had a significant secondary loading on CMI, cognition of semantic implications, which is reasonable: consequences are implications.

The reference to "obvious" consequences and "nonclever" plot titles, together with the fact that a fluency score in all these tests is merely a count of the total number of relevant responses, indicates that DMU is measured by sheer quantity of relevant output in a limited time. We shall see later that the quality of output or, more accurately stated, the quantity of high-quality responses is an indication of flexibility in production.

Another type of DMU test involves theme writing on given topics. There is one type of test called Topics and another called Theme, in either of which E is to write on a subject such as "A Man Going up a Ladder" or "The Parcel." As a rule, the score is the number of words written. Variations of such tests ask E to write in response to a picture, describing or telling a story about it. Such tests have had exceptionally high loadings (.55 to .70) on factors identified as ideational fluency. But there has usually been more than one test of the same kind in the analysis; so there is reason to believe that the loadings are inflated, either by specific variance, arising from two forms of the same test, or by the concurrence of factors other than DMU shared by such tests.

Tests calling for responses to inkblots also have substantial loadings on factors like DMU. This is true, too, of the R score (total productivity) from the Rorschach inkblots, as found in an unpublished study in which the writer took part.

Divergent production of classes

Before we consider particular factors for divergently producing classes, it is desirable to give a bit of background information. In the first major analysis of creative-thinking abilities (Wilson et al., 1954), the hypothesis about flexibility factors led to the development of several tests involving flexible behavior, including Brick Uses. The list of uses for common bricks that E gives in eight minutes is scored in two ways, for fluency by counting all relevant responses and for flexibility by counting the number of different *categories* of uses, or, alternatively, the number of times that E shifts category of use. An E who says bricks could be used in building a house, a barn, a silo, a school, a store, a bank, a walk, a wall, a floor, a barbecue, or a chimney would have a fairly good score for fluency but a zero score for flexibility. Another E who says bricks could be used to build a house, throw at a cat, drown a cat, make a doorstop, make bookends, make red powder, write a message, make a filter, make a baseball base, or make a tombstone for a bird would have equal length with the other E, but he would also have a large number of categories or shifts, hence a high score for flexibility.

The factor was called "spontaneous flexibility" because there is nothing in a task of the Brick Uses type that either instructs E or suggests to him that he should be flexible; if he is flexible, he shows this on his own initiative. A qualifying term such as *spontaneous* was also needed in order to distinguish this kind of flexibility from another that was qualified as *adaptive*. After the structure-of-intellect theory had been developed, it was realized that the category score or the shift score indicates the number of changes from one class to another: E is producing varied *class* responses. Following this decision, tests more obviously calling for varied class responses were developed for all the DP abilities in which class is the critical product.

Figural classes (DFC)   This was true when it came time to construct tests for the hypothesized factor of DFC. Alternate Letter Groups presents a set of capital letters, such as A H V T C, with the examinee to form subgroups each of which makes a class according to the *figural* properties of the letters. He might select the set *A H T* (all having horizontal lines), A H V T (all straight lines), or H V C (open sides), and so on.

The same principle is true of Figural Similarities (see Figure 6.4). By grouping the figures by sets of three, quite a number of different classes can be formed. These two

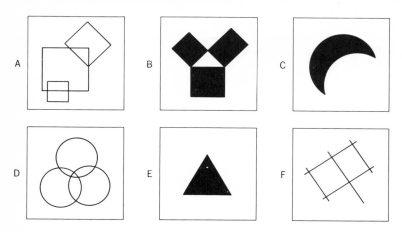

Fig. 6.4 Figural Similarities presents six figures each having a number of attributes. *E* is to find as many classes, in sets of three figures each, as he can. Some classes are BCE (black), ABD (three parts), ABF (straight lines), etc.

tests determined a factor for an adolescent group but failed to do so for an adult group. The failure may be attributed to a radical departure from the principle in DP testing that *E* should *produce* his answers. The test Figural Similarities was put into essentially multiple-choice form by presenting all possible triads, with *E* to say which triads form real classes.

A third test (Varied Figural Classes) intended for factor CFC was very weak, even for the ninth-grade sample. Figure 6.5 shows a sample item. The three objects presented serve as definitions of two or more different classes, since they have more than one property in common. Each of two or more alternative figures could satisfy the qualification for one of those classes. Perhaps the number of potential classes is too limited in this test for a good measure of DFC.

While on the subject of flexibility in reclassifying figures, it is of interest to cite a striking result obtained by Goldstein and Scheerer (1953). In their Color Form Sorting test, after the subject has sorted the objects according to the principle he has chosen (by form or by color), he is asked to reclassify them in another way. Many brain-injured subjects find it impossible to do this, even after they are shown that it can be done. It might be suggested that such patients are showing a very low degree of CFC, if not a zero quantity.

Symbolic classes (DSC)   Three analyses support a unique ability of divergent production of symbolic classes, with two faithful but not always strong markers. One is Varied Symbols, which asks *E* to find a number of different properties that sets of letters have in common and to show this by adding in turn other letter sets. One problem reads:

E P Z T	A P C T O U M D T		
answers: 1	(starts with a vowel)	*1.*	A C B E
4	(contains the letter *T*)	*2.*	R O S
5	(has three consonants)	*3.*	C O M
		4.	G A T U
		5.	Z M O D

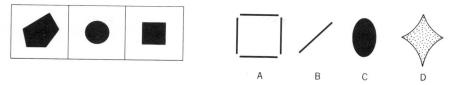

Fig. 6.5 A sample item from Varied Figural Classes. Which of the four alternatives at the right can be classified, for different reasons, with the set of three at the left? Both *C* (black figures) and *D* (closed figures) qualify.

The other test is Name Grouping, in which, presented with a short list of given names, *E* is to classify and to reclassify them in different ways. A sample problem reads:

1. GERTRUDE	*answers (alternate classes):*
2. BILL	
3. ALEX	*1, 3, 4* (two syllables)
4. CARRIE	*2, 4, 5* (double consonants)
5. BELLE	*1, 4, 5* (begins with consonant, ends with vowel)
6. DON	

For some unaccountable reason, a Number Grouping test has thus far refused to go with these two tests on factor DSC. It is apparently an analogue to Name Grouping but does not behave that way, dispersing its variance in different directions though all on symbolic factors. A list of numbers to be classified in different ways might be: 2, 3, 4, 6, 17, 23, 36, from which could be formed a class of odd numbers (3, 17, 23), prime numbers (2, 3, 17, 23), or multiples of 3 (3, 6, 36). Possibly the limitations on kinds of classes are too great; possibly number classes are less familiar. Number Grouping has gone with small loadings on factor DSR, a neighbor in the SI model, in two analyses and on ESS in the third. It can be seen how classes of numbers can be formed by relating them by trial and error (hence DSR); it is not so easy to see how systems would be involved to give variance from ESS. In such discrepancies lie opportunities to find out more about tests and their factors, with new hypotheses and new analyses to test them.

Semantic classes (DMC)   Previous discussion mentioned the role of the Brick Uses test, flexibility score, in the discovery of the spontaneous-flexibility factor and this factor's eventual identification with DMC in the model. The same score has been a faithful marker for that factor, as has the later Utility Test (shifts), which also contains another part on uses of a wooden pencil.

Another faithful marker test for DMC has been Unusual Uses, which was later renamed Alternate Uses. This test contains many more problems than the Utility Test and puts a limit of six on the number of responses to each problem. *E* is asked to state uses, other than the common one, which is stated, for objects such as a newspaper, an automobile tire, or a shoe. The unusual-use instruction excludes repetitious responses and essentially demands a change of use category with every response. One of the effects, however, is to introduce some variance from factor DMT, for the reason that in adapting an object to some quite different purposes, some drastic transformations occur. This involvement with transformations does not bother the Brick Uses or Utility Test, probably because the transformations are easier to make and they are not forced upon the examinee.

The shift-score principle has also been used successfully for DMC by Frick, Guilford,

Christensen, and Merrifield (1959) in the test Object Naming, in which E is to list names of objects in a broad class, such as building material, and the score is the number of clusters of objects each representing a subcategory of the main class. Laboratory experiments on the clustering of verbal responses in recall thus appear to be involved with the phenomenon of class shifting and the ability DMC.

After spontaneous flexibility had been identified as factor DMC, a new test called Multiple Grouping was constructed to satisfy the SI cell for DMC with its three specifications. This test is analogous to others we have just seen in connection with factors DFC and DSC. A sample problem reads:

From the list of words at the left, make some small subclasses of objects:

1. arrow	*alternate classes:*	
2. bee	*1, 2, 5, 7*	(found in the air)
3. crocodile	*3, 4, 6*	(found in the water)
4. fish	*2, 3, 4, 7*	(animals)
5. kite	*3, 4, 5, 7*	(have tails)
6. sailboat	etc.	
7. sparrow		

The finding that this test goes along with the Utility Test and Alternate Uses on a factor (Guilford & Hoepfner, 1966; Lauritzen, 1963) supports the placement of spontaneous flexibility in the SI model.

Divergent production involving relations

The heading of this section is stated in an unusual manner for a reason. For the production categories, both divergent and convergent, the early tests involving relations and also revealing relational abilities do not actually call for the producing of relations; they call for the producing of what Spearman called "correlates." As mentioned in Chapter 3, relations exist between correlates. Relation-cognition tests pertain to *seeing* a relation, given two correlates, or what Spearman called "eduction" of a relation. But production tests have commonly presented one correlate and a relation, with the other correlate to be produced to fulfill or complete the relationship. The term *relationship* is well reserved for the complete structure of two correlates and their relation. Completing a relationship was known as "eduction of a correlate" by Spearman. The heading above might have been "Divergent production of correlates," but the product-category name is "relations"; hence the particular wording used.

But later tests have attempted to determine whether the production of multiple *relations* in a task would also qualify as a means of measuring divergent production where relations are concerned, and we shall see that they can do so. Thus, DP abilities dealing with relations can be measured by tests that require the production of either relations or correlates.

Symbolic relations (DSR)   Alternate Additions was designed especially for factor DSR. It presents problems of the following type:

Given the numbers 1, 2, 3, 4, and 5, combine (relate) them in several different ways to achieve a total of 7, using each number only once in each answer.

possible answers: $2 + 5 = 7$, $3 + 4 = 7$, $1 + 2 + 4 = 7$, $3 + 5 - 1 = 7$

The conception was that the plus and minus operations are kinds of relations that can be applied between numbers. In two analyses this test failed to help demonstrate a DSR factor, going on the number-facility factor instead (Gershon et al., 1963). In three other analyses Alternate Additions was the leading test for DSR with strong loadings (Guilford & Hoepfner, 1966; Guilford et al., 1965).

A test designed for DSR that was successful in three analyses is Number Rules. In this test, E is told to start with a given number and by applying other numbers and operations to arrive at a second given number in different ways. For example, starting with 2 to reach 6, E might respond with $+4$, $\times 3$, $\times 2 + 2$, $+5 - 1$, and so on.

A test called Number Combinations was designed for the factor DSS, but in one analysis it turned out to be in part a measure of DSR (Guilford & Hoepfner, 1966). In this test, given a set of numbers, e.g., 2, 4, 5, 6, 7, E is to write a number of equations within the limitations of certain rules. The equation-formation activity is shared by the two tests just mentioned; so there is reason for it to go with them on DSR.

It may be noted that no letter test has been mentioned in connection with DSR. Appropriate letter tests should be possible for DSR, but none is known to have been constructed.

Semantic relations (DMR)   A factor known as "associational fluency" was latent in Thurstone's first major PMA analysis (Thurstone, 1938a) but did not emerge. Reworking of Thurstone's data yielded such a factor (Fruchter, 1948; Zimmerman, 1953b), with two tests among the leaders in both instances. The tests were Controlled Associations and Inventive Opposites. In the former, E is to write as many words as he can, similar in meaning to each of eight given words, in sixteen minutes. The relation is obviously similarity, E to produce multiple correlates. In the second of these two tests, E is given words for which he is to produce two words each, opposite in meaning to the given words. The first letter of each of two opposites is given as a hint. The relation in this case is obviously opposition in meaning.

These tests have served consistently as markers for DMR, but there have been others that help to tie associational fluency with DMR. Before we mention other types of tests, it might be said that Christensen and Guilford (1963) tried experimentally to determine the relation of a controlled-associations test to factor loading when E's responses from different working-time intervals are used in scoring: the first 0.5 minute, the next 1.5 minutes, the next 1 minute, and the next 2 minutes. They found that the loadings were highest for the first two working periods and tapered off slightly during the next two, suggesting that two minutes' working time for each problem would be optimal.

Of a somewhat different type, Simile Insertions has also been a consistent measure of DMR. Each item gives the beginning of a simile, e.g., "His smile was as wide as a[n] _____," the blank to be filled with as many different alternate words as E can think of in limited time. The relation is between an attribute and its object, and the given correlate (attribute) is WIDE, the object to be supplied in each answer. There is additional information in the form of a context, the key to that context being the word SMILE in the illustrative item. With the figure-of-speech setting, E can be encouraged to do considerable wandering to obtain responses.

Multiple Analogies was constructed with the SI cell DMR in mind, to check on whether the kinds of tests just mentioned do belong to a factor that qualifies for that cell. This test presents analogies in which there are several possible relations between the first two words. For example, in one problem there are four possible relations to be seen and used:

ATHLETE is to SCHOLAR as BRAWN is to _____
ATHLETE is to SCHOLAR as PRACTICE is to _____
ATHLETE is to SCHOLAR as GYM is to _____
ATHLETE is to SCHOLAR as INNING is to _____

Of five analyses in which this test has appeared, four of them at the ninth-grade level, in only two of them did it come out significantly on DMR; so the tie between associational fluency and DMR is still not so well supported as one should like. One difficulty is that Multiple Analogies comes out substantially on factor CMU in all analyses, the probable reason being that in order to see all the analogies between the first two words E has to have a rich supply of meanings for the words that make up the pair. Precision in the meaning of the word to be supplied may also be a feature. On a logical basis, associational fluency has no better place than cell DMR, and Multiple Analogies does lend some support.

Divergent production of systems

An incident reported recently is a very good example of divergent production of systems. A resourceful student, however else he might be described, in college physics was given the problem: "Show how it is possible to determine the height of a tall building with the aid of a barometer." The instructor evidently had a particular answer in mind. The student's answer was to take the barometer to the top of the building, attach a long rope to it, lower the barometer to the street, bring it back, and measure the length of rope needed to reach the ground.

The answer was not what the instructor was evidently expecting, and he asked the student to try again. His second plan was to take the barometer to the top of the building and drop it to the ground, timing its fall with a stopwatch. By using the formula $S = \frac{1}{2} gt^2$, one could then calculate the height of the building. Other answers he gave were also ingenious. One was to take the barometer out on a sunny day, measure its height and the length of its shadow and the length of the shadow of the building, and use the simple ratios. His fourth method was simplest of all. Take the barometer to the superintendent of the building, promising him that he will receive a gift of a nice barometer if he will tell the height of the building.

All these plans are systems, semantic systems. They involve rational sequences of pertinent meaningful steps. The instructor probably thought he was asking a question that would lead to convergent production of the plan he had in mind, but the information he gave the student left the door open for alternative plans, and the student, who was evidently set to be original, took advantage of the situation. The student should score high on a test of divergent production of semantic systems. As the relative independence of DP abilities involving systems in different areas of content suggests, we should not necessarily expect him to be high in other system-producing abilities. We have information concerning three different factors for producing systems and the tests that measure them.

Figural systems (DFS)   The figural-systems abilities known thus far in terms of factors are mostly of visual nature. Tests for DFS emphasize the organizing of visual-figural elements into wholes; for example, the test Making Objects. Figure 6.6 illustrates the kinds of items in this test. Using two or more of several given simple geometric forms, E is to organize them to construct an object that is named. The object is named, which should reduce the DFU or DMU variance that would come in if E had to think of the objects that he is to make. The DFU variance was controlled for a ninth-grade population but

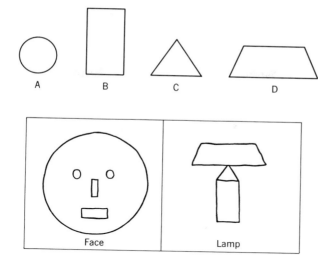

Fig. 6.6 Items as in the Making Objects test. The four simple figures at the top are to be combined in various ways to make named objects. Two examples of organized objects are shown. (*Courtesy of the Sheridan Psychological Services, Inc.*)

not completely for an adult population (Gershon et al., 1963). For the younger group a bit of secondary variance was from factor DFI, which could mean that to succeed with the items of this test they found elaborating their product (one thing leading to another) to their advantage.

It is of incidental interest to know that Making Objects was originally constructed with the factor DFT in mind. In the case of DFT, to which we shall soon come, it was believed that one important feature of its tests is that the examinee must redefine the functions of lines or line elements; in other words, produce transformations. In Making Objects, it was thought that using a given element for different purposes in the various objects would constitute a transformation. But two analyses (Gershon et al., 1963) agree that this test does not go with the other transformation tests but with the systems tests. After reexamination of other DFT tests and also NFT tests, in both of which groups of tests transformations do play roles, it was concluded that the crucial difference is that *before the change an element has a role in some other composite.* In Making Objects the element does not; it is presented apart from any organized whole. By means of another experimental miscarriage for a test, we thus learn more about a concept, "transformation."

In discussing DFU, we mentioned that tests measuring DFS tend also to measure DFU, and the instance of Monograms, which proved to be a better systems test at the ninth-grade level and a better units test at the adult level, was pointed out. This test, coupled with the Making Objects test, suggests that age and experience may contribute to this difference.

Another DFS test that succeeded but which shared heavily its variance with DFU is Designs. Given in each problem were a few simple line elements, such as an angle, a circle, a bow, and a dot, with E to organize these elements into patterns such as one sees in fabrics, wallpaper, or linoleum. Perhaps the DFU variance comes in because E first conceives of the kind of repeated effect he wants to produce; then fitting the elements into it is not so much of an organizing problem.

Symbolic systems (DSS)   DSS is one of the most poorly supported of all the DP factors that are regarded as having been demonstrated. It came to light in only a half-hearted expectation but has had some degree of opportunity, though not much, in five analyses. The circumstances must be told.

The factor previously identified with cell DSS in the SI model was known as "expressional fluency." The best tests of this factor ask E to construct a variety of sentences, following certain rules and restrictions. Although such tests stress ability to produce organized verbal discourse and could thus lay claim to being semantic, it was thought that the organizing of words in sentences is a matter of syntax and is therefore a symbolic proposition. Doubts about placing expressional fluency in the cell DSS mounted until it was decided to construct some more clearly symbolic system-production tests that would be free from semantic involvement. The result was in the form of only two tests, Make a Code and Number Combinations. It was thought that if these two tests would correlate with one another substantially, as expected, but not much with expressional-fluency tests, a separation of two factors would be effected. If a separation did not occur, the conclusion could be that expressional fluency had been properly placed as DSS.

Since the separation of the two factors hinged very much upon one coefficient of correlation, there was a fair chance that their separation would not occur. The separation did barely occur, in three analyses out of four at the ninth-grade level (Guilford, Merrifield, & Cox, 1961), with Make a Code effective in all three but Number Combinations effective in only one, for boys but not for girls or for a mixed sample.

The Make a Code test asks E to use the alphabet and the number system to construct as many different code systems as he can, substituting numbers for letters. The Number Combinations test calls for the production of simple numerical equations, using a set of given digits. In a more recent analysis (Guilford & Hoepfner, 1966), also at the ninth-grade level, Make a Code came out strongly on the factor designed to be DSS but Number Combinations came out instead on CSR and DSR, two relations abilities. Obviously, some much better tests for DSS need to be constructed; they can probably not be found in existence.

Semantic systems (DMS)   There was considered to be enough evidence to make a transfer of expressional fluency to the spot DMS. In the writing of sentences, apparently the organization of meanings outshadows the organizing of syntactical structures in demands upon human resources. In the production of short sentences, perhaps organized ideas are very automatically translated into grammatical sentences in educated individuals; the syntactical problem is of minimal importance. That would be a deduction from the results of factor analysis of sentence-construction tests.

Sentence-construction tests have been the mainstay in the measurement of DMS, and this reliance extends to sentence construction in the more open-ended theme-writing types of tests. But let us consider first an experiment designed to determine what kind of sentence-construction test is optimal for measurement of DMS. In many sentence-construction tests, short sentences have been favored, for this permits Es to achieve a greater number of completed sentences in the same amount of testing time and thus has a chance of enlarging the variance of the total scores. Carroll's Letter-Star test (1941), for example, asks for four-word sentences in response to information like Y*N*, to which E is to use the Y and N as initial letters of two words and is left more free to choose words to replace the stars. A constant number of words per sentence also standardizes the task, thus exerting some experimental control.

The experiment referred to (Christensen & Guilford, 1963) varied the number of words per sentence, two-word sentences in two tests and four-word sentences in two others.

In one test of each length, all the initial letters were specified and were the same for a list of sentences in each part of the test. In the other test of each length, no initial letters were specified. The four tests were:

Two-Word Combinations (no initial letter specified)
Two-Word Combinations FL (e.g., L_____ T_____)
Four-Word Combinations (no initial letters specified)
Four-Word Combinations FL (e.g., W_____ C_____ E_____ N_____)

With the same initial letters to be used in a number of different sentences (no word to be repeated), the response to the last item might be "We can eat nuts," "Who colored Eve's nose?", or "Why cannot elephants navigate?"

The results of this experiment were very illuminating. The best of the four tests was Four-Word Combinations FL, with a loading of .59 on DMS. The Two-Word Combinations form was next best (with a loading of .50), but it had a substantial loading (.43) on a psychomotor factor recognized as writing speed. The latter factor was marked by a test of speed in making Xs in squares. Third in order was Two-Word Combinations FL, with a DMS loading of .43 and a loading of .35 on DSU (word fluency). Last was the plain Four-Word Combinations, with a DMS loading of .37 and a writing-speed loading of .36.

The secondary loadings in these tests could have been predicted; hindsight is better than foresight. Note that the two forms without first-letter designations involve some writing-speed variance while the two with first-letter specifications do not. The likely reason is that with no initial letters specified, E can think of sentences faster than he can write them. With the first-letter restriction, he can keep his writing up with his production; hence writing speed does not contribute to variance in total scores. Note that the Two-Word Combinations FL form has secondary variance in word fluency. One popular form of DSU test asks E to write words each beginning with a specified initial letter. Choosing two words in combination, each beginning with a specified initial letter, is not so very different as a task. The Four-Word Combinations FL is relatively free from variance of this sort, its DSU loading being only .22. The reason is probably that the organizing problem, with four words to be combined versus two, is more difficult and takes relatively more of E's attention to organizing effort.

Other tests of DMS have been less controlled, with E simply to write a theme on some subject and the score to be the quantity written in terms of number of words. Such tests were used by Carroll (1941), in a Words Score test; by C. W. Taylor (1947), in an Unfinished Stories test; by Fruchter (1948), in Thurstone's Free Writing test; and by C. A. Rogers (1953), in Unfinished Stories.

Two tests of somewhat different kind were C. W. Taylor's Sentence Fluency (1947), in which E is to restate the same given idea in different ways; and Word Arrangement (Christensen & Guilford, 1963), in which E is to write sentences each containing four given words, such as SEND, ALMOST, SHORE, LARGE.

In the same study (Christensen & Guilford, 1963) and subsequently, a Simile Interpretation test has been successful as a measure of DMS but with small secondary loadings on DMT. In each problem in this test, a simile is stated, with E to make explanatory additions in a variety of ways, e.g., "A woman's beauty is like the autumn, it _____," to which E might say: ". . . passes before it is appreciated," ". . . is a feast for the eyes," or ". . . calls for colorful changes in dress." The small DMT component may come from some incidental reinterpretations.

It is unfortunate that all the successful tests for DMS have been composition or writing tests. There are semantic systems other than sentences; for example, there are story plots, arithmetic problems, and scientific models and theories in general. Does the same ability that is tested by sentence construction apply in these other connections? Getzels and Jackson (1961) composed a test that asks for the writing of a variety of arithmetic problems, given the same basic information, but there is no indication that it has ever been analyzed or even correlated with known DMS tests so as to determine its construct validity for measuring DMS. Since *comprehending* arithmetic problems is mostly a matter of the ability CMS, it seems reasonable to expect that the Getzels-Jackson problem-construction test should be a measure of DMS.

Divergent production of transformations

Figural transformations (DFT)   In the first major analysis of abilities believed to be important for creative thinking (Wilson et al., 1954), a factor labeled "adaptive flexibility" was found, with a test of Match Problems its leading indicator. Such an affiliation has persisted through a number of analyses since that time. The original match-problems test, of which there have been a number of versions, was a 12-item affair, with items like that shown in Figure 6.7. Most items were composed of collections of adjacent squares, like that shown, with each side representing a removable matchstick; a few items were composed of equilateral triangles. In speculating about the nature of the psychological factor involved, there were two hypotheses. One was that each problem probably involves considerable trial and error. Failing in one attempt, E must revise his tactic and try another approach. If he is too firmly set on one approach, he is handicapped in doing the test. The other idea was based on the fact that some of the items in the test require E to desert what was probably a common assumption, e.g., that the remaining squares or triangles should all be of the same size. Figure 6.8 shows such an item. In either case, a kind of flexibility is involved, for a change of direction in the one case and for a relaxation of restrictions or a revision of the rules in the second. In contrast to the factor of spontaneous flexibility in the same analysis, this factor was qualified as "adaptive" because the flexibility is essential in order to solve the problems and to do so rapidly.

In the analysis of planning abilities (Berger et al., 1957), Match Problems II was introduced, bringing in a third principle. This test includes problems each of which can be solved in four different ways; E is so informed and is given four opportunities. Match Problems III uses the multiple-solution principle but also emphasizes problems that can have unusual solutions, with final squares of different sizes, one within another, and overlapping each other. Match Problems IV differs from the other forms in that it specifies only the number of squares to remain, the number of matches to be removed being left to the examinee. Match Problems V reverses the instructions of Match Problems IV with respect to specifying the number of matches to be removed but not the number of squares to remain. In all forms the remaining squares must be complete, with no dangling matches left over.

In some of the more recent analyses, in which two or more forms of match-problems tests have been present, it might appear that the factor is more or less a match-problems factor but for the circumstance that at least one test of a different character has been present. All the forms of Match Problems have done about equally well, with Form III probably slightly in the lead. A second faithful marker for DFT has been Planning Air Maneuvers, an adaptation of an Air Force test. This test involves the planning of sky-writing with an airplane. E is shown where his plane starts, where it is at the finish, and

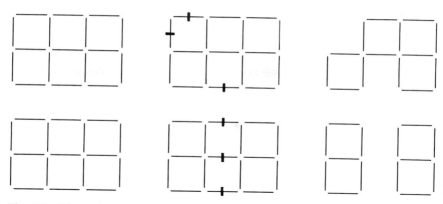

Fig. 6.7 Illustrative item from Match Problems in which two different alternative solutions are given, the problem being to remove three matches, leaving four complete squares and no excess lines.

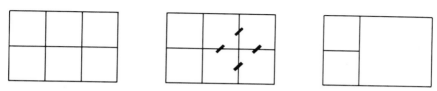

Fig. 6.8 Another item from Match Problems, calling for the removal of four matches to leave three complete squares. The solution requires the unusual resort to a square of larger-than-normal size.

how sharply it can make turns. The plane is to be maneuvered so as to write two capital letters in succession as efficiently as possible. A good deal of trial and error is necessary, with revisions of steps.

Other tests that have incidentally been found to be related somewhat to DFT are Insight Problems, Squares, and Dot Systems. Insight Problems, used by Frick et al. (1959), consists of 12 puzzler items, about half of the items being of figural content. Squares, used in the same analysis, presents several replications of a checkerboard, with E to place a specified number of Xs in different arrangements so that no two are in the same row or column. Dot Systems presents rows and columns of dots, within which E is to locate two letter Ts in varied ways (Gershon et al., 1963).

It can be seen that all these tests contain problems requiring shifts of tactics as E indulges in trial and error. The placement of the adaptive-flexibility factor in cell DFT is in line with this emphasis on "shift," but we need to examine more closely the nature of that shift to be sure that it is a figural matter. This can be rationalized by saying that every time E thinks of one tentative solution to a problem he is making a change in the configuration of lines that he sees to a new configuration of the kind that he thinks he wants. If we want to be more analytical about this, we may say that as a transformation occurs, lines in the configuration change roles, the main kind of change being from a line that stays to a line that is removed, or vice versa.

Semantic transformations (DMT)   Aptitude DMT is the ability known for some time as the originality factor. The early mentions of such a factor by Garnett and by Hargreaves have been noted previously in this chapter. Even before those events, Chassell (1916) had proposed a number of tests of originality and had experimented with them. Some of his tests are of interest here because they foreshadowed some of the more recent forms that have proved successful. His Chain Puzzle (cutting and welding a minimum number of links) is like items in the Insight Problems tests just mentioned in connection with DFT and would undoubtedly go with that factor if analyzed. So would his Triangle Puzzle (making four equilateral triangles with six toothpicks). His Novel Situations test is a form of what is now known as a Consequences test. One of his test-construction principles that could have been used to advantage much more than it has been in constructing DP systems or transformations tests is to ask E to write test items of certain kinds. Chassell had examinees write items for an analogies test. It might be that some examinees could not even get started on such a test, but this has to be determined by experiment.

In the first major analysis of creative abilities (Wilson et al., 1954) it was hypothesized that originality could be assessed by means of tests constructed on the basis of one of three principles. An originality test should emphasize either (1) ability to produce responses that are statistically rare in the population, (2) ability to produce remotely related responses, or (3) ability to produce clever responses. Tests were constructed to fit all these principles, and all have come out together on the same factor. In spite of opportunities for tests of these three kinds to go off in two or three ways on different factors, we have been left with one factor.

The unusualness tests   A test built on the principle of rare responses is called Quick Responses. It is based on the familiar word-association test made prominent by Kent and Rosanoff many years ago. In Quick Responses, 50 stimulus words from the K-R list are presented orally, E being given five seconds in which to write each response before the next word comes. In keying the tests for scoring, frequency counts were made for all responses to all stimulus words and weights were assigned to the responses; the more rare the response, the greater the weight. In the first analysis this test proved to be loaded on the factor identified as originality, but it failed almost completely on a second attempt (Kettner et al., 1959a), with a loading of only .18 and a communality of only .28. It has not been analyzed since; there have been more successful tests and tests more easily keyed for scoring. The only virtue of the test in comparison with others in this group is the possibility of completely objective scoring.

There has, however, been some evidence of construct validity for the uncommon-associative-response score of word-association tests. Licht (1947) found that an uncommonness score distinguished two groups of professional people. Those groups tending to score low (for uncommonness) were executives, salesmen, teachers, and politicians. Those tending to score high were scientists, artists, musicians, engineers, and writers. Maltzman, Belloni, and Fishbein (1964) have capitalized on the uncommonness principle in a number of studies of originality training with some success (see Chapter 14). J. J. Jenkins and D. S. Palermo (1964) have made experimental studies of different ways of scoring association tests for uncommonness, so that perhaps, after all, ways will be found to make a word-association test function better as a measure of originality.

Remote-associations tests   The principle of remote associations was applied in the test called Consequences (remote). A problem in this test asks E to list all the consequences he can think of as a result of some unusual event, such as everybody's suddenly going blind. If the response is of the kind "Everybody would stumble and fall" or "Nobody could read," it is categorized as "obvious." The total number of obvious responses is a good score for DMU, ideational fluency, although there is recent evidence (O'Sullivan et al., 1965) that it shares some variance from CMI, which is a "foresight" type of ability, a matter of cognition of implications. Recognized consequences are certainly implications. Responses of the type "Those previously blind would become the leaders" or "Light and power companies would become bankrupt" are scored as "remote," and the total number given is a measure of DMT, as a number of analyses show. This score has been successful for all groups except some at the ninth-grade level (Guilford, Merrifield, & Cox, 1961). This finding is curious, because the Consequences (remote) score helped to define a DMT factor in the sixth grade (Merrifield et al., 1963) and even in the fifth grade (Lauritzen, 1963). For three of four ninth-grade samples (Guilford, Merrifield, & Cox, 1961), Consequences (remote) became a weak DMC test instead of a DMT test. For some reason, for these examinees, being able to shift classes was an important contribution to success in the test. It is not clear how this should be. There was no sign of such involvement with DMC in the fifth- and sixth-grade analyses.

In order to achieve a word-association test that would force E to give remote associations, a number of test forms, called Associations I, II, III, and IV, have been tried out in various analyses in which the writer was involved. In Associations I, E is told merely to give a single word that is associated with both of two stimulus words, as in the items:

Indian_____penny   (*answer:* copper)
movie_____fishing   (*answer:* reel)

Associations II is similar, but a multiple-choice format, in which the answers are alternative initial letters one of which is for a word that is correct, was used in writing it. This form did not work well; so nothing further will be said concerning it. But it is another example of how a multiple-choice form of test fails to measure a divergent-production ability.

Associations III is like Associations I, with the added stipulation that the response word must have the relation of *similarity* to each of the two stimulus words, e.g.:

nonsense_____bed   (*answer:* bunk)
recline_____deceive   (*answer:* lie)

Associations IV is the same except that the relation is not confined to similarity; it can vary, with E left to find the relation for himself. Sample items are:

jewelry_____bell   (*answer:* ring)
skin_____conceal   (*answer:* hide)

The fate of these tests is of interest. Associations I had its highest loading where it was intended, on originality, but that was only with a minimally significant value (Wilson et al., 1954). Associations III and IV behaved similarly but not much like Associations I. In four analyses in which they appeared, in no case was the relation to DMT significant (.30 or higher). In two analyses (Kettner et al., 1959a), the significant loadings were modest on DMR, the ability to produce varied relations or correlates. These two forms of Associations emphasized relations, as stated above. In two other analyses these tests were loaded significantly on factor NMR, for the convergent production of semantic relations or correlates (Christensen & Guilford, 1963; Kettner, Guilford, & Christensen, 1959b). The fact that only one response is called for in each item should tend to put these tests in the class of convergent production. The product is again a relation. The appearances on DMR may be accounted for on the basis that the NMR factor was confounded with DMR in the first two analyses referred to, there being no other tests of NMR to separate that factor from DMR in those two analyses. It is more reasonable to expect these two Associations tests on factor NMR than on DMR.

Mednick and Mednick (1964) carried the principle of multiple stimuli in word association a step further by employing *three* stimulus words to each of which the response should be related. To make the items less difficult, they favored very familiar language-habit types of associations; for example, the three stimulus words FLOWER, BERLIN, PAPER are expected to elicit the response "wall." The three words are tied to the response in our speech habits in the combinations wallflower, Berlin wall, and wallpaper. In spite of these speech-habit possibilities, if each stimulus word were to be given alone, it would not be so likely to elicit the same response except where the response word is second in the habitual sequence, as in the case of Berlin wall.

Some quite varied predictive validities have been reported for the Mednick Remote Associates Test (RAT) in connection with criteria of creative performances. RAT has apparently never been factor-analyzed, and the predictive validities in connection with creative-performance criteria tell us very little about its probable factor composition, since a large number of different abilities contribute to success in creative performances of various kinds. We shall go into some general problems of validity later in this chapter. Since RAT is most like Associations III and IV, one guess would be that the main factor in the test is NMR, but this would be risky because the "relations" in the RAT are of a more superficial, perhaps symbolic, type.

Cleverness tests   The most commonly used test based upon the cleverness principle is Plot Titles (clever). This test presents a short story like the following:

A man had a wife who had been injured and was unable to speak. He found a surgeon who restored her power of speech. Then the man's peace was shattered by his wife's incessant talking. He solved the problem by having a doctor perform an operation on him so that, although she talked endlessly, he was unable to hear a thing she said.

The nonclever titles suggested by *E* for this story and for others like it are counted to give a DMU score that has worked well. The number of clever responses is a score that has done well for DMT. Examples of nonclever responses are "A Man and His wife," "Medicine Triumphs," "A Man's Decisions," and "Never Satisfied." Examples of clever responses are "My Quiet Wife," "The Deaf Man and the Dumb Woman," "Operation—Peace of Mind," "Doctor Quiets a Home," "A Happy Deaf Man," and "Yack, Yack, Hack."

Other tests constructed on the cleverness principle are Cartoons and Riddles, both of which were successful in their limited uses (Christensen & Guilford, 1963; Frick et al., 1959; Kettner et al., 1959a). Cartoons presents cartoon pictures adapted from magazines, with *E* to write the punch line for each one. Riddles calls for two solutions to each riddle, one of the solutions to be clever. For example, to the riddle "Which city is most preferred by movie actors?" the commonplace response could be "Hollywood," and the clever one could be "Publicity." Puns are quite common where responses are clever. A pun is an example of a transformation: a sudden shift of meaning occurs. One variety of humor found by factor analysis (T. G. Andrews, 1943) is pun humor, which is instigated by transformations.

A test of a rather different character asks *E* to represent by means of simple line drawings the ideas expressed by words. Alternate Signs is illustrated in Figure 6.9, where to the stimulus word HEAVY *E* is to produce as many as six different pictorial representations that attempt to convey the idea (Guilford, Merrifield, & Cox, 1961). An earlier test

Heavy:

Fig. 6.9 Alternate Signs asks for representing a verbalized concept in the form of varied pictorial symbols. The four figures given were in response to the concept "heavy."

of the same type was Symbol Production, in which E produces only one figural representative for each word. Both tests did well for factor DMT. These tests go into the semantic category instead of the figural category, very likely because although figural responses are produced, the transformations come in terms of turning the word meaning over and over in order to find an aspect that is amenable to figural representation.

Roles of transformation in DMT tests   In placing originality in the cell DMT, we need to be clear that transformations are actually involved in all the kinds of originality tests that have been mentioned. The clearest case is the category of cleverness tests, whose relation to transformations has already been mentioned. Tests involving remote associations, such as Consequences (remote), probably involve transformations in that the event to which E gives consequences must be turned around in various ways and reinterpreted in order that the remote responses be generated. Lack of such revision of conception of the event can only lead to a limited number of more obvious responses.

It is most difficult to see where the tests based upon the unusualness principle, for example, the Quick Responses test as the best representative of this principle, involve transformations. One rationalization would be that unusual word-association responses are also remotely associated responses. Let us say that for every semantic unit, represented by a word, there is a core idea that is touched off immediately by the stimulus and there is a context of connected ideas, with different degrees of connectedness.[1] The nature of the connections will be discussed in Chapter 10; the term *association* is studiously avoided. Sarnoff A. Mednick (1962) has proposed the theory that there is a gradient of connectedness of the various contextual units in relation to the core, to paraphrase his statement of the theory. The more creative individual tends to have flatter gradients, with all degrees of connectedness more uniformly distributed than is true of the less creative person. Hence, responses more unusual in the population have a better competitive basis.

But this theory has no use for the concept of transformation. An alternative hypothesis would be that when the stimulus word comes, the higher-DMT person runs over the various aspects of meaning very rapidly, so rapidly that he has come to a remotely connected unit of information in time to give expression to it. The unit's chances of coming out overtly in a very short time are fairly good. Along with this disposition there may be a tendency to avoid the usual and the trite response, but this may be a temperamental trait rather than an aptitude trait of personality. Such a tendency without ability to produce transformations rapidly would lead to relatively long reaction times in a word-association test.

[1] A core-context theory of meaning will be elaborated in Chapter 10.

Other possible originality measures   Before leaving the originality factor, it is not out of order to consider some other potential sources of measurement for that trait. In the Rorschach projective technique, there are two indicators that have commonly been proposed for originality. One is the movement score, in connection with which some scorers place the emphasis upon human movement; and there is an unusualness score, which seems in line with one of the principles of originality measurement discussed above. A large number of animal responses is taken as a negative indication, since animal responses are so common to the Rorschach inkblots. Owing to the very limited numbers of responses ordinarily obtained from application of the Rorschach inkblots, however, one should not expect high reliability for an unusualness score from that source.

In a study of 20 male painters of high artistic rank, Roe found that both the Rorschach and the Thematic Apperception Test (TAT) failed to indicate the presence of a high degree of creative ability (Roe, 1946). In a study aimed at validation of movement responses, Griffin (1958) obtained movement scores in a test known as the Levy Movement Blots from two selected groups of women students. There were 20 regarded as "creative" and 20 as "uncreative" from nominations by teachers and fellow students. No difference in movement scores was found between the two groups. Similar results can be cited from Rust (1948) and Burchard (1952). There is evidently little support for the claim that an indication of originality or of creative potential in general can be gained from administration of the Rorschach. Special uses of stories obtained from the TAT have yielded indications of originality that correlate with other scores for originality (Barron, 1955).

The Luchins Water Jar Test   Since tests of divergent production of transformations are under discussion and since abilities in this category have been referred to as traits of flexibility, factor DFT being recognized first as adaptive flexibility, the question can naturally be asked whether the much-used Water Jar Test introduced into psychological research by Luchins (1942) is a measure of factors DFT or DMT. Frick et al. (1959) considered that possibility, including a group form of this test in a factor analysis along with many tests designed for flexibility factors not only in the divergent-production category but also in convergent production. The analysis showed that total scores on the Water Jar Test were correlated .45 with the factor of logical evaluation (EMI), .42 with general reasoning (CMS), and only .18 with adaptive flexibility (DFT). Oliver and Ferguson (1951) had previously reported a loading of this test on general reasoning. There is another possibility that the test might be related to hypothetical factor DST, which has not yet been demonstrated, or to factors NFT or NMT. In the study by Frick et al., however, it was related to factor NST only .19 and to factor DMT —.09. Thus the Water Jar Test looks most unpromising as an intellectual-flexibility factor. Much doubt has been cast on its being a measure of other kinds of flexibility by Leavitt (1956).

Flanagan's Ingenuity test   Desiring to bring the measurement of creative talent within the realm of answer-sheet testing, Flanagan proposed his Ingenuity test, which is sometimes referred to as a creativity test. Each item presents some kind of predicament the solution to which can be stated in one or two words. In a mechanical problem, for example, the solution is to turn a piece of equipment upside down. Alternative answers give only initial and final letters of each word, as for this problem, U____E D__N, among four similar alternatives.

From the fact that productive abilities involve the examinee's actually producing something and without the aid of irrelevant hints, it is questionable that the Ingenuity test measures any divergent-production ability to an appreciable extent. Flanagan (1963) has gone to great pains to show that this test measures something unique, something not covered by other tests in his FACT battery, but the question of what that something unique is remains open. The test seems not to have been factor-analyzed, and there is little or no direct evidence concerning construct validity. It correlates moderately with a number of other tests, and it may well predict some practical criteria, but where it does, this could be by reason of measuring traits other than ingenuity or any of the divergent-production abilities.

Divergent production of implications

Figural implications (DFI)   The first elaboration-ability factor was found in a study of planning (Berger et al., 1957). It was represented by both semantic and figural tests, one of the latter being Figure Production, in which E is given one or two lines with which to make a meaningful object by adding lines. His score is dependent upon the amount of detail he adds to what is given. It could not be decided, because of the meaningfulness of the objects to be produced, whether the factor was semantic elaboration or a confounding of semantic and figural elaboration. The elaborating in the test is surely in terms of figural information.

In a later analysis (Guilford, Merrifield, & Cox, 1961) two additional figural-elaboration tests were added to see whether two factors would be found, one figural and one semantic, and if there were two factors, whether Figure Production would stay with the semantic-elaboration tests or go with the new figural-elaboration tests. The second alternatives were decisively supported; there were two factors, and Figure Production went with the new figural tests.

Of the two new figural tests, Production of Figural Effects resembles Figure Production. That is, with a line or two given, E is told to add lines, but he is told *not* to make a meaningful object. The other is Decorations, in which outline drawings of common objects, like pieces of furniture and articles of clothing, are given, each two times, with E to fill them in with decorative additions. A sample problem is given in Figure 6.10. The score is a function of the quantity of additions, where repetition of the same decorative theme is not accepted, as E is forewarned. All three tests are fairly strong for DFI and relatively free from secondary factors. There seems little doubt of characterizing their common factor as the implications ability, DFI, because what is given in the way of lines suggests by implication what to add and what is added suggests further additions, as in doodling. It would be an interesting hypothesis that a productive, versatile doodler is relatively high on the factor DFI.

Symbolic implications (DSI)   Factor DSI is one of the more poorly demonstrated dimensions of intellectual aptitude. In two analyses (Gershon et al., 1963; Guilford & Hoepfner, 1966), Symbol Elaboration has been a consistent representative of it, but there has been little else. In this test, two very simple equations are given, with E told to deduce other equations from them, as many as he can. For example, if the two given equations are

$$B - C = D \qquad \text{and} \qquad Z = A + D$$

E might offer these equations:

$$D = Z - A \qquad B - C = Z - A \qquad A = Z - D \qquad \text{and so on}$$

The test was tailored in view of the SI definition of DSI.

Fig. 6.10 Decorations is an effective measure of the factor of divergent production of figural implications. Given outline pieces of furniture, implements, or clothing, *E* is to embellish them with varied decorative lines, two opportunities being afforded with each object. Sample decorations are shown for a chest and a knife. (*Courtesy of Sheridan Psychological Services, Inc.*)

Another tailored test, Limited Words, has not worked so well. It had a loading for DSI in a ninth-grade population but not for adults (Gershon et al., 1963). And for the younger group it had a slightly significant loading on DSR. It is a kind of two-word anagram task, with two given words to be made over by rearranging letters to make other pairs; e.g., given the words

SHIRT-BEAN

E might make the new pairs HAIRS-BENT, BEARS-THIN, etc. It is clear that a couple of good tests for DSI are badly needed. Because of the similarity of Symbol Elaboration to operations in algebra, the relevance of this test and perhaps of the factor CSI for success in mathematics would seem to be rather clear.[1]

Semantic elaboration (DMI)   The first finding of an elaboration factor (Berger et al., 1959) followed the testing of the hypothesis that ordinary planning entails an ability to think of details, and the factor centered in two planning tests. One was called Planning Skills II, in which, following a model planning test by Irving Lorge,[2] *E* is told of a prob-

---

[1] Because of the transformations involved in these two tests, recent thinking suggests that the factor may be DST rather than DSI.

[2] Personal communication.

Fig. 6.11 In Possible Jobs, a test of divergent production of semantic implications, E is given a symbol, such as an electric-light bulb, to name groups of people or occupations for which the object could stand as a symbol. Some responses to the symbol given have been "electrician," "manufacturer of electrical appliances," "communication," "teacher," and "gifted students." (*Courtesy of Sheridan Psychological Services, Inc.*)

lem situation that calls for an organized plan to meet the difficulties, such as might be involved in a situation of low morale in a military installation. If scored for the number of ideas or steps, such a test almost inevitably assesses the amount of detail or elaboration E adds to his presentation. Another test, Planning Elaboration, was aimed more directly at elaboration by offering the examinee the outline of a plan, including all major steps needed, with E to add detailed steps needed to make the plan work.

Other tests that went with these two planning exercises to support the factor included Effects and Unusual Methods. Effects shared its variance equally between DMI and CMI, as reported in discussing that factor. From this fact we conclude that the test calls for both cognition and production of implications. Since as many as four predictions of future events are called for in each problem, the production is divergent.

Unusual Methods was designed for a hypothesized factor of ingenuity which did not materialize separately from originality. E is asked to suggest two different and unusual methods for dealing with a problem, such as boredom of employees, other than the usual practice of rest periods or coffee breaks. E might suggest that employees change their kind of work at intervals or that a four-hour shift replace the eight-hour shift, for example. Since these suggestions are essentially steps in plans, Unusual Methods might well go along with planning tests; but apparently little or no elaboration is involved. This suggests that there was something in common in the first elaboration factor in addition to elaboration.

After it had been recognized that the elaboration ability is really DMI, the test Possible Jobs, emphasizing meaningful implications more explicitly, at least more explicitly to the psychologist, was designed and written. Figure 6.11 shows a sample item. Given a pictorial design with realistic meaning, E is to suggest what occupations or groups of people the picture might stand for. The thing E gives in response is an implication. Possible Jobs has failed to help bring out DMI in one of five analyses in which it has appeared, and in one it had a little relation to CMI, indicating that some of the ninth-grade students had some difficulty in *seeing* the implications. It would be a fair prediction that if only one or two responses were called for in every problem, the CMI variance would increase for other groups as well. There might be an optimal total number of responses per item that would emphasize DMI to the disadvantage of variance from CMI.

Some special problems with divergent-production abilities

Divergent-production abilities represent such a new class of intellectual resources that many special questions arise concerning them. Many of these questions stem from the common linkage of the DP abilities with creative potential and from the high current interest in creativity. How far do the DP abilities go in accounting for creative potential? In part, this is a question of construct validity. The validities of the DP factors as psychological constructs and the validities of the tests for measuring those variables are largely covered by the operations of factor analysis. But the question of attaching the construct label of "creative abilities" to the DP factors calls for other operations in obtaining an answer. The relations of the factors and their tests to other indices of creative performance must be demonstrated.

There is also the major problem of the relation of DP abilities to the traditional concept of intelligence and to measures of that construct in terms of IQs. Does the traditional IQ reflect divergent-production abilities to any extent, in spite of the obvious fact that IQ tests do not contain much at all of the kinds that measure DP factors?

DP factors and creative potential

Creativity and content area   A subsidiary question must be faced. The range of creative performances in daily life is very great. Among recognized groups of productive people are writers, scientists, inventors, mathematicians, artists of various kinds, and choreographers, as well as composers, planners, and manipulators of people. Would it be possible for the known and predicted DP factors to account for creative potential in all these varied directions?

If we consider the four content areas in which DP factors have been found and are expected, it would seem that most of these areas of creation could be accounted for with the exception of musical composing and arranging. Writers, scientists, and planners should find most of their support from resources in the semantic area. Inventors should depend heavily upon visual-figural content, and so should those in the visual arts. None of these statements means of course, that the same creator may not cross content boundaries, as when the artist conceives of his theme in semantic terms and translates such ideas into form and color on a canvas. Much of such translation obviously goes on. Mathematicians would depend heavily upon symbolic information, and so would mathematical scientists and cryptographers. For the creative musician there would presumably be some auditory DP abilities, probably paralleling the visual DP abilities, just as we have already seen a few signs of such parallels in the areas of cognition and memory.

There is already some evidence that content categories have an important bearing in creative people of different kinds, as the writer had predicted (Guilford, 1957). Welch (1946) gave four DP tests to a group of 30 professional artists and a group of 48 college students, the latter presumably representing the run-of-the-mill range with respect to creative potential for art. The four tests involved the following tasks:

1. Compose sentences from 10 words randomly presented.
2. Form many letters of the alphabet from a few given lines.
3. Given 20 words, construct a story using them.
4. Given 10 blocks of different shapes and sizes, design home furniture.

It would appear that Welch had two measures of factor DMS (1 and 3) and two of DFS (2 and 4). At any rate, two were semantic, and two were figural. The two figural tests separated the two groups, artists and students, significantly, whereas the two semantic ones did not. This outcome could have been predicted from knowledge of the factorial separations between figural and semantic abilities.

Fisichelli and Welch (1947) followed with another experiment using the same four tests, with 25 art majors brought into the comparisons. The art majors were significantly higher than unselected students on tests 1, 2, and 4. The unselected students were higher than the art majors on test 3.

C. A. Jones (1960) has made a much more systematic study of the same kind of problem. The purpose of the study was to determine whether the creative quality of a writing product could be better predicted from semantic DP tests and that of an artwork product from figural DP tests. His subjects were sixth-grade students. He used criteria of creative performance in the form of writing on the one hand and of artwork on the other. Each child produced three samples of each kind, and each child's best product of each kind was evaluated by several judges. For both the drawing and the writing samples, three variables were rated: creativeness, freedom in use of material, and amount of detail. The correlations between the corresponding pairs of criterion variables were .25, .14, and −.03, respectively, indicating the relative independence of excellence of creative performance in the two areas of creation, figural and semantic.

Using as the criterion a combination of the first two of the three variables (creativity and freedom), Jones found that verbal-test composites correlated with the creative-writing criterion .46 (with four DP tests in the composite) and .58 (with six tests in the composite). A verbal composite correlated .32 with the drawing criterion. Figural-test composites correlated with the creative-drawing criterion .50 (six tests) and .54 (seven tests). A figural composite correlated .40 with the writing criterion. Some differential validities were thus demonstrated, not absolutely but definitely in the direction predicted.

It is not so strange, then, that Brittain and Beittel (1961) and Beittel (1964) should have found mostly insignificant correlations between a number of semantic DP tests and criteria of creative performance in art students at the college level. They did find that a figural test—Punched Holes, a measure of factor CFT, and hence, also, a transformations test—correlated .40 with their criterion in a sample of 50 students. In accordance with the results of Jones, Kincaid (1961) found that eight DP tests, mostly in the figural category (with the factors CES, CFT, DFS, and DFI and with DMS also probably represented), had promising correlations, with high multiple Rs in small samples of 29 art students (children in grades 1 to 4) and 46 adults. The criterion in question was a rating for creative imagination based upon three crayon drawings.

Creative potential in childhood and youth   Correlations between DP-test scores and criteria of creativity during the years through high school have not been spectacular, to say the least. There are just enough significant correlations to indicate that both the tests and the criteria lie in the same general direction. Torrance (1962b), who has done more than anyone else in the development of DP tests for children and in research on creativity in education, reports considerable information on this point. High-scoring children on DP tests in the lower grades are conspicuously nominated for having wild, silly, and sometimes naughty ideas; especially is this true of boys. By grades 5 and 6, high-DP children are more often nominated for having "good" ideas, and their teachers report that they have unusual ideas, ideas so unusual sometimes that they are hard to evaluate by ordinary standards. Experiments showed that when a high-DP child is placed to work on a problem in a group of five, the other four being lower, the high-DP child initiates ideas far out of proportion.

In high school, Torrance found a correlation of .24 between DP-test scores and a nomination criterion. Yamamoto (1964) reported correlations of about the same order of magnitude between various DP-test scores and teachers' nominations. Piers, Daniels, and Quackenbush (1960) obtained ratings of creativity of students in grades 7 and 8 and gave the students a number of DP tests from among those described in this chapter. A combined originality score correlated .23 with the criterion, and a combined score for semantic fluency correlated —.02. Merrifield, Gardner, & Cox (1964) also reported generally low correlations between DP-test scores and teachers' ratings.

Teachers' ratings of creative disposition of students can be readily questioned on logical and empirical grounds. It is very doubtful that the ordinary schoolroom offers opportunities for observing all the significant aspects of creative behavior that would provide an adequate basis for making judgments. It is doubtful that the average teacher knows just what to look for or understands fully the characteristics to be rated, even when the variables are broken down and explained. Indirect evidence for these propositions is to be seen in the low intercorrelations of different observers when rating or nominating for creativity and the very high intercorrelations of ratings for different trait variables as evaluated by the same teacher.

In a very large sample of fifth-grade children, Lauritzen (1963) found that a score for originality predicted teachers' ratings of originality of the children with a correlation of .48, but a score for ideational fluency predicted very poorly, with a correlation of .17. These results could mean that these teachers had some basis for observing originality and knew the signs of originality but for some reason did not assess ideational fluency at all well.

Correlations of DP tests with criteria are generally much higher when the criterion is based upon some standardized performance, as found in the work of C. A. Jones (1960), cited earlier. Another example in which the criterion was based upon actual performance of the subjects is from A. R. Bass, G. L. Hatton, T. J. McHale, and L. M. Stolurow (1962). With a small group of 21 high-school students, one criterion, called Experimental Design I, asked the student to design an experiment on transfer of training, the product being evaluated. A composite score from the DP tests Consequences, Unusual Uses, and Plot Titles correlated .41 with the criterion, which is significant in a one-tail test.

Creative potential in adults   A performance criterion will not always be predictable from a DP test, because it may emphasize abilities quite different from those that are featured in the DP test or tests used. For example, Jacobsen and Asher (1963) found the correlation between Consequences (obvious and remote) and a work-sample criterion to be .07 and .21, respectively, for 85 college students. The work-sample criterion was a total score in four tasks requiring the listing of ideas for improving an office desk, an advertisement, and the human hand and for getting more foreign teachers to visit the United States. One legitimate conclusion could be that the criterion had no DMU variance and very little DMT variance. Without a factor analysis of the criterion or without having its correlations with a great many factor tests, we cannot know what *its* construct validity is. From descriptions of the criterion task, it would appear that the dominant factor involved is DMI, which would require tests other than Consequences to make good predictions. If other tests do predict the criterion, one can depend upon it that they have factors in common with the criterion; in no other way could there be nonzero correlation between them.

Barron (1955) has given much attention to the construct validities of a number of tests for the measurement of originality. In one study, he correlated scores from three DP tests (Unusual Uses, Plot Titles, and Consequences) with various other assessment variables designed for originality in a sample of 100 Air Force captains. The tests correlated .30, .36, and .32, respectively, with the assessment-staff ratings for originality. Between a composite of eight apparently DP tests, including the three mentioned, and the rating criterion, he found a multiple correlation of .55. Subjects scoring high in DP tests were assessed generally as being verbally fluent, conversationally facile, clear and effective communicators, and effective leaders (Barron, 1957).

Zaccaria, Chorness, Gerry, and Borg (1956) used as a criterion a score derived from biographical information that stressed signs of previous creative performance and found significant correlations with it for 11 of 15 DP-test scores. In a study of research scientists, Calvin W. Taylor, W. R. Smith, and B. Ghiselin (1963) found little predictive validity for DP tests, but very few DP tests were actually used in the investigation. F. E. Jones, on the other hand, using a detailed rating system by which to obtain criterion measures of about one hundred chemists and chemical engineers, found correlations of .54 for Consequences (remote) and .34 for Ideational Fluency for factors DMT and DMU, respectively.[1] In combination with three other tests (Ship Destination, a CMS test; Logical Reasoning, an EMI test; and a fifth test), the multiple correlation was .65. The contributions of tests from outside the DP category to the prediction of a creative-performance criterion is not unusual and shows how varied and numerous the contributors to creative success may be.

C. W. Taylor et al. (1963) have highlighted the enormous complexity of the evaluations of performance of creative scientists by factor-analyzing over 50 obtainable variables of assessment of research scientists' achievements in their work. As many as 15 different factors were found, indicating the rather high dimensionality of "success" in creative scientific research. It is possible, even so, that not all possible relevant variables were assessed.

There is some evidence with respect to creative performances of other occupational and professional groups. Wallace (1961), using the Minnesota creative battery, which is composed of DP-like tests, found that saleswomen in "high customer service" assignments obtained a significantly higher mean score than those in "low customer service" assignments. The highest third of the 61 saleswomen, with respect to sales records, also obtained a significantly higher mean test score than the lowest third.

In studies of governmental administrators in 30 agencies of the United States government, Forehand and Libby (1962) found for a group of 60 "group-centered" administrators that DP tests and flexibility and implications tests correlated near .30 with superior ratings of innovative behavior and also with peer ratings of the same variable. From the nature of the tests, the factors involved could have been CMT, DMU, DMT, NMT, and CMI.

Elliott (1964) has provided some of the strongest predictive validities for semantic DP tests yet reported, in connection with the performances of public-relations personnel and advertising copywriters. From two public-relations firms he assembled two criterion groups by nominations from their superiors, a group of 25 nominated as more creative and a group of 17 nominated as less creative. The two groups were significantly discriminated on the basis of each of five of the eight tests used, most of which were semantic DP tests, with two tests doing particularly well.[2] Using a multiple-cutoff method, in which each subject was scored in terms of the number of cutoff points he exceeded, 23 of 25 of the more creative, or 92 percent, had 5 points or more (two tests were double weighted), whereas only 1 of 17 less creative, or 6 percent, reached that level.

In another population composed of advertising personnel, Elliott gave the same battery of tests. The sample was selected from 40 persons working in the copy department, where ideas are generated and advertising material is written. Four raters agreed upon the

---

[1] From a personal communication.
[2] Among the tests were Ideational Fluency, Alternate Uses, Associational Fluency, and Consequences.

14 most creative and the 14 least creative. One result was that 12 of the 14 most creative scored favorably on four or more of the five tests that were predictive, whereas only 1 of the 14 least creative made such scores. If we take the highest and lowest halves of the 40 in the department, 16 of the high group and 4 of the low group made favorable sets of scores. In a comparison of the 25 most creative subjects in the copy department with 24 employees in a department considered noncreative, 22 of the 25 made 4 or more points, whereas 3 of the 24 others reached that standard.

Evidently, both public-relations workers and advertising copywriters in these organizations were doing the kind of work and were evaluated by their superiors for that work in ways that emphasize some of the semantic DP abilities. Even when one makes allowances for the fact that the correlations are inflated by using cutoffs established in favorable positions in this same group and that no cross validation was made, the demonstration of relevance of DP tests and their factors for certain kinds of creative performance indicates substantial validity.

Creative potential is complex   By now it should be clear that creative potential is not a single variable, any more than intelligence is. Creative performances in daily life are enormously varied in the demands that they make on intellectual resources. The performances singled out for their more obvious signs of creativity—novelty, ingenuity, inventiveness—probably involve one or more divergent-production abilities as key aspects, or transformation abilities, outside the DP-operation category as well as within it. But there is a distinct possibility that almost any other ability, in neither the DP nor the transformation categories, may make important contributions to the creative act, whatever it may be. The term *creative potential,* like the term *intelligence,* needs qualification wherever it is used if communication is to be at all precise.

Relations of DP abilities to IQ   Since DP factors are relatively independent of cognition factors and the intercorrelations between tests of these two categories are also low and since IQ tests emphasize cognition abilities, particularly CMU and CMS, we should not expect to find much correlation between DP-test scores and IQ, and we do not. Such a state of affairs was known long before DP tests were recognized as a special group. It had been noted by Dearborn (1898), Chassell (1916), E. G. Andrews (1930), and Welch (1946). Since the recognition of the category of DP abilities and their assumed relation to creative potential, there have been quite a number of studies of correlations between them and IQ tests. Getzels and Jackson (1961) dramatized the hiatus between DP abilities and traditional intelligence by pointing out that electing high-school students in the highest fifth (of a high-IQ group) in terms of IQ would miss about 70 percent of the highest fifth on DP tests. In spite of many criticisms of the studies made by these two investigators, such a result has been replicated a number of times by Torrance (1962b) and others.

In Table 6.2 is assembled some correlational information from different sources, with different ages and educational levels represented and also different measures of intelligence by traditional methods. In the writer's experience (see the last two rows of Table 6.2), in a sample of 204 ninth-grade students, the mean of 45 correlations was +.32. It should be noted that these correlations are Pearson rs, with linear relationships assumed, whereas, as a number of writers have pointed out, such relationships are apparently curved. More will be said on the regression problem later.

Figure 6.12 shows a kind of general case of a scatterplot with DP score as a function of IQ. It is such that those with high IQ may be found almost anywhere along the range on a DP test; those who are low on the DP test can also be almost anywhere on IQ, but

Table 6.2   Some representative correlations between traditional intelligence-test scores and assessments of creative potential and performance

Investigator	Type of subjects	Intelligence test	Creative assessment	Correlations
Torrance (1962b)	Elementary grades	Stanford-Binet	DP-test composite *	.16, .17
		Otis		.32
		Kuhlman-Anderson		.26
		California TMM		.24
Yamamoto (1964)	High school	Lorge-Thorndike	DP-test composite	.30
Torrance (1962b)	Graduate students	Miller Analogies	DP-test composite	−.02, .11
Torrance (1962b)	Graduate students	Ohio State PE	DP-test composite	.10
D. W. Taylor (1960)	Engineers	Terman Concept Mastery	Ratings	.20, .07
MacKinnon (1961)	Architects	Terman Concept Mastery	Ratings	−.08
	Scientists		Ratings	−.07
Ripple and May (1962)	Seventh grade	Otis	DP-test scores	.11–.73
Razik (1963)	College	Ohio State PE	DP-test scores	−.04–.37
Guilford and Hoepfner (1966)	Ninth grade	California TMM	45 DP-test scores	−.04–.70 (M = .32)
		C-Z Verbal Comprehension		−.15–.52 (M = .21)

* DP stands for divergent production.

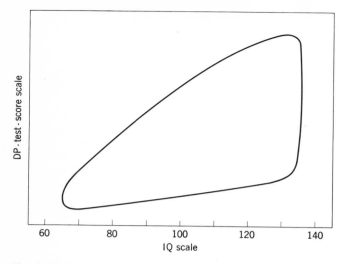

Fig. 6.12 Illustration of a somewhat typical scatter of individuals when scores for divergent-production tests are considered in relation to IQ. One striking feature is the scarcity of cases combining low IQ with high status on divergent production; the other is the incidence of conjunction of low divergent-production ability and high IQ.

those high on the DP test have a high probability of being above average on IQ. As it turns out, however, the nonlinear eta coefficients between IQ and DP scores are not very different from the Pearson rs for the same scatterplots and are very rarely significantly higher than the Pearson rs. This is due in part to the generally low correlation of either kind and in part to the peculiar shape of the scatterplot. It can be seen that the scatter of cases within many arrays can be rather broad. Dunn (1962) also reports such triangular scatterplots in relating scores for DP factors to scores from achievement tests in physics and chemistry.

The pattern of bivariate distribution of the cases suggests that although high IQ is not a sufficient condition for high DP ability, it is almost a necessary condition. Among outstandingly creative producers in the general population a high proportion of high-IQ individuals is usually noted where the fields have been science, writing, or architecture, for example. This relationship is to be expected, for a college education is almost essential for individuals to enter such professions in these times. The members of the creative professions have therefore passed over some high academic hurdles, which they could not have done without having above-average IQs. But passing those hurdles is no assurance of creative success. And it is still possible for an individual to become distinguished in some areas of creative endeavor, such as inventing and composing, perhaps painting, without passing high academic hurdles and presumably without an exceptionally high IQ.

In the case of children and youths who have yet to reach the higher academic hurdles, the low proportion of children with high-DP status and low-IQ level calls for some speculation. It could be that the present DP tests are inadequate measures of DP abilities when IQs are low. The weakness of the low-IQ individuals in many DP tests can hardly be attributed to failure to understand instructions, for the tasks in DP tests are usually quite simple. It is true that the tasks are somewhat novel, and perhaps the low-IQ child is slower in adapting to the new types of tasks.

But a more likely hypothesis is that IQ tests emphasize cognitive abilities, which deal with the person's stock of information that might be available for use. If the information is not there in memory storage, it obviously cannot be produced. Dunn (1962) has favored this hypothesis. If we recognize that there are four general kinds of information, the four content categories, a typical IQ test, which favors semantic information, might be expected to correlate higher with semantic DP tests and lower with DP tests dealing with other kinds of information. Correlations of the three kinds of DP tests with the CTMM IQ averaged .22 for figural DP tests, .40 for symbolic DP tests, and .37 for semantic DP tests.[1] Thus, one difference (semantic versus figural) is as expected; the other difference (semantic versus symbolic) is not. The test samplings are not, however, strictly comparable.

The triangular bivariate distribution, such as is illustrated in Figure 6.12, might be expected when semantic tests are correlated with verbal IQ but not for tests of other content. Actually, figural DP tests in relation to CTMM IQ give about the same kind of bivariate scatter.

The picture is thus not very clear. At any rate, we may well raise the question whether the high-IQ and low-DP individuals are really creative underachievers and whether anything could be done about it. They are apparently not able to make full use of what they know in taking DP tests. What is preventing this? Can anything be done with it?

Summary

The conception of divergent-production abilities came about through investigations of certain hypotheses regarding the component abilities most relevant to creative performance. A factor of fluency was expected, and three kinds of fluency were found; a factor of flexibility was expected, and two kinds were found; and an expected factor of originality materialized. Later, in a study of planning abilities, a factor of elaboration was expected and was demonstrated.

But factors of fluency and flexibility have been found in nonverbal tests as well as in verbal tests. Search among nonverbal tests revealed the parallels essentially complete in figural and symbolic areas of information alongside those in the semantic category. In other words, there are factors of fluency, flexibility, originality, and elaboration which fit into the SI model. The three kinds of fluency are concerned with the products of units, relations, and systems; the two kinds of flexibility are concerned with classes and transformation, into which category originality fits; and elaboration has to do with implications.

Tests of DP abilities must call for examinees actually to produce information, in quantity and in variety, and sometimes with alterations in that information. Experimental work with some tests has demonstrated the forms and conditions needed for optimal factor measurement.

Quite a number of studies have lent support to the claim that DP factors and tests have relevance in connection with the measurement of creative potential, but creative potential is very complex and at times and in different ways involves abilities outside the

---

[1] Correlations of DP tests with a vocabulary test give a similar picture, except that the correlations are lower (see Table 6.2) and the triangular form of bivariate distribution is not so marked.

divergent-production and the transformation categories, which are most important in that connection.

Relations between divergent-production–test scores and IQs are generally quite low, but it appears that although a high IQ is not sufficient for doing well in DP tests, being above average in IQ is almost necessary.

7 Convergent-production abilities

The operation category of convergent production is one of the less explored regions of intelligence, as Table 7.1 will show. Of the 24 hypothesized abilities, 13 have not been investigated. The symbol S in the table usually means only three or four investigations in which signs of the factors have been revealed. In 5 instances, convergent-production (CP) factors have been suggested at an age as young as fourteen (El-Abd, 1963), and in 2 instances at an age as young as six (McCartin & Meyers, 1966). Stott and Ball (1964) were able to interpret a few factors found in infant and preschool tests as convergent-production abilities. In view of the logical possibilities of the *figural CP* abilities for potential in the fields of geometry, engineering, and architecture, it would seem to be a severe oversight not to have investigated that particular set of hypothesized abilities, only 2 of 6 having any known empirical support.

Convergent production is in the area of logical deductions or at least the area of compelling inferences. Convergent production rather than divergent production is the prevailing function when the input information is sufficient to determine a unique answer. In terms of the kinds of tests that measure the two kinds of productive abilities, there is sometimes a twilight region, if not an apparent continuum. For example, if we ask, "What is *the* opposite of HARD?" we should give credit only for the response "soft." The ability measured by such items should be NMR. But if, as in Thurstone's Inventive Opposites test, we ask E to give two words both meaning the opposite of HARD, the score for such a test should become more of a measure of DMR. It may be recalled from the preceding chapter that there are indications that Associations III and IV, which call for response words each associated with two given stimulus words, divide their variances in the two ways, toward both DMR and NMR.

Table 7.1   Matrix of the convergent-production factors
(N) represented in the structure of intellect

Figural (F)		Symbolic (S)		Semantic (M)		Behavioral (B)		
NFU	0	NSU	0	NMU 6	S	NBU	0	Units (U)
NFC	0	NSC	1	NMC	2	NBC	0	Classes (C)
NFR	0	NSR 14	S	NMR	S	NBR	0	Relations (R)
NFS	0	NSS 14	S	NMS 6	S	NBS	0	Systems (S)
NFT	S	NST 14	S	NMT	S	NBT	0	Transformations (T)
NFI	0	NSI	S	NMI 14	S	NBI	0	Implications (I)

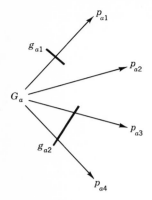

Fig. 7.1 Graphic illustration of the conditions under which convergent versus divergent production occurs, with and without the restrictive information provided by g_{a1} and g_{a2}.

It is commonly found that for a test calling for the naming of things, particularly of abstract ideas such as relations and classes, the ability in question is NMU. It can be predicted that if we asked for alternate names for the same items of information, the test would go in the direction of DMU. This experiment has apparently not been attempted.

We may visualize the difference between convergent production and divergent production by using a simple diagram as in Figure 7.1. Let G_a be some particular given information, as a certain item in a test. With instructions sufficiently open, such as "Give words opposite in meaning," the productions could be p_{a1}, p_{a2}, p_{a3}, and p_{a4}. But if supplementary information specifying limitations, in the form of g_{a1} and g_{a2}, such that g_{a1} excludes p_{a1} and g_{a2} excludes p_{a3} and p_{a4}, is given, then the only possible production is p_{a2}, a convergent output.

Convergent production of units

Semantic units (NMU)   It was mentioned earlier, in connection with tests designed for cognition of classes and relations, that because some of these tests call for the naming of the class or relation, variance in a naming factor came into the results. That naming factor was later identified as NMU.

Much earlier, Carroll (1941) had found a factor common to two tests, Color Naming and Form Naming. The writer at one time considered this factor of Carroll's to be NFU in the SI system (Guilford, 1959a), but subsequent considerations suggest that this factor might better be treated as a confounding of NSU, DSU, and NMU. One reason is that in the Color Naming and Form Naming tests it is not actually figural units that are being produced; it could be either symbolic or semantic units, depending upon whether E's productions are merely signs or involve color or form ideas. A third test helping to define the factor for Carroll was Giving First Names (listing boys' and girls' names), which should emphasize factor DSU. A fourth test, Phrase Completion, in which E gives a word to complete a phrase, suggests factor NMU. Present thinking is that an NFU test should require E to generate figural units to satisfy completely certain given specifications.

Since no study has been aimed specifically to investigate factor NMU, no tests have been developed intentionally for that factor. It has happened that tests developed for certain cognitive abilities have contributed to the finding of this factor. Tests strongest for NMU have been Picture-Group Naming and Word-Group Naming, designed for CMC;

Verbal-Relations Naming, designed for CMR; and Number-Group Naming, designed for CSC. Less strongly loaded tests on factor NMU have been Seeing Trends, designed for CMR because it calls for naming the principle of the trend, a repeated relation; and Vocabulary Completion, which Thurstone (1938a) had designed as a vocabulary test.

This wealth of experience definitely shows that the act of naming cannot be safely used as a criterion of whether or not a class or a relation has been cognized. Although a number of these tests have been found strong for factor NMU, most of them have secondary significant loadings; they are not inclined to be univocal for NMU. Sometimes the secondary loading is for the factor that was intended, sometimes not. Whether the naming of objects and attributes, as in the Color Naming and Form Naming tests, will be found loaded on factor NMU remains to be seen. It was suggested above that they may go on factor NSU. This in turn suggests another reservation about interpreting the naming factor as NMU: it might possibly be NSU. A logical reason in favor of identification with NMU is that classes and relations are abstract items of information while colors and forms are concrete. We might therefore expect the two classes of tests to separate in a factor analysis.

Convergent production of classes

Figural classes (NFC)   Some years ago, David Rapaport, M. Gill, and R. Schafer (1945) drew a sharp distinction between "active" and "passive" concept formation. The Rapaport modification of the Goldstein-Scheerer Object Sorting Test (Goldstein & Scheerer, 1941) accordingly has two parts. The first part, for active sorting, requires E to sort objects into classes, after which he is to define his classes. The second part, for passive concept formation, requires E to watch a sorting being done and then to define the class the examiner has produced. From the standpoint of SI theory, one should expect the active-sorting score on Part I to involve factor NFC and the defining score to involve factor NMU (perhaps also CMU). The score for Part II should involve factor CFC (perhaps also CMU).

Silverstein and Mohan (1965) have done a factor analysis to determine whether Parts I and II of the modified Goldstein-Scheerer test would go on different factors. Using intercorrelations given by Rapaport, involving 13 score variables from the sorting tests and the Wechsler full-scale IQ, with scores obtained from three populations—normal subjects, schizophrenics, and neurotics—the factor analyses yielded some interesting results. Part I did go on two different factors, for the two pathological samples but not for the normal one. This could suggest that the defining task was too easy for the normal group but yielded greater individual differences within the abnormal groups. One of these factors could have been NFC, and the other NMU. These two factors were distinct from a third factor that applied to the score for Part II. The latter factor could have been CFC. If these interpretations are correct, in this study we have the first empirical sign of factor NFC.

Semantic classes (NMC)   Factor NMC was found, but very poorly represented, in only one analysis (Merrifield et al., 1962). Tests were designed for an ability hypothesized as the production of classes, in connection with an analysis of abilities believed to be pertinent to problem solving. The successful test of a pair was Word Grouping. A problem in this test presented a list of about a dozen common words, with E to classify them in a specified number of classes. The words were so chosen that there is only one reasonable set of classes and no word is to appear in more than one class. Such a list is:

1. blue	2. cutter	3. driver	4. heavy
5. larger	6. light	7. little	8. long
9. opener	10. orange	11. redder	12. short

From this list the classes of words, by number, are 1, 10, 11; 5, 7, 8, 12; 4, 6; and 2, 3, 9. It may be recognized that Word Grouping is a good analogue for the test Multiple Grouping, which was designed for factor DMC and in which to make a good score E must reclassify the same word in more than one way.

The test that failed is called Sentence Pairs. Since failures are often informing, the test will be described. It is in a short matching format, with four given short sentences, each to be classified with one of five alternative sentences, grouped by virtue of similar ideas. A sample item is:

1. He walked home every night.
2. Some animals make good pets.
3. Artists are sometimes well paid.
4. The train gathered speed as it left.

for which the alternative matching sentences are:

A. Cats are real companions.
B. Deer are excellent game.
C. Exercise promotes good health.
D. The storm approached rapidly.
E. The picture sold for twice its true value.

answers: 1, C; 2, A; 3, E; 4, D

Sentence Pairs divided its variance mostly between CMC (.39) and CMS (.28); in other words, in the one analysis it appeared to be a cognition test rather than a convergent-production test. Whether this is due to the small number of members (two) for each class is hard to decide. The test might have done better had the eight classifiable sentences been listed mixed together as in Word Grouping, with E to pair them off. A longer list, with more members per class, might have been even better.

The test helping to determine factor NMC in the analysis referred to was Figure Concepts. This test presents a relatively large number of pictured familiar objects, with E to form as many classes composed of two or three members each as he can. Since E may use the same object in more than one class, the test would appear to favor factor DMC rather than NMC. The obtained factor might have been a confounding of NMC with DMC, but in that particular study the time limit had been reduced, making the test more of a speeded affair. One effect was for E not to take much advantage of the possibility of reclassification; he also had great latitude in the number of objects given, so that reclassification would not be needed in order to make a high score in the time allowed; thus this test could have been a measure of NMC.

Convergent production of relations

Symbolic relations (NSR)   The most consistent test indicating factor NSR has been Correlate Completion II. In an early analysis of reasoning abilities in the Aptitudes Research Project (Guilford, Green, Christensen, Hertzka, & Kettner, 1954), a test Correlate Completion was employed. It was designed after the abstraction test in the Shipley-Hartford scale for the assessment of intellectual deterioration (Shipley, 1940) with curiosity as to what type of reasoning might be involved in that kind of test. The test helped to determine a factor that was described as "eduction of correlates" and that was named in line with Spearman's terminology, which seemed very appropriate. When the distinction between semantic and symbolic abilities became apparent, it was realized that Correlate Completion contained items of both kinds of information; so Correlate Completion II was designed, with all items involving symbolic information only. One unusual result with this test, however, is that in different analyses different kinds of tests have tended to come out with it; sometimes they have been tests that might be expected to do better for other factors, such as NFR and NMR, to the right and left of NSR in the SI model, and CSR and CSS. Obviously, another strong test for NSR is needed to help clear up that factor.

Canisia (1962) has found in two quite different kinds of tests a factor that appears to fit the definition of NSR. One of her tests was Algebraic Inequalities, which requires E to deduce an inequality from two given algebraic statements. The other was Formulas and Figures, which asks E to associate an algebraic statement with a given figure. The latter seems a little like a cognition test but perhaps requires productive thinking. It is obvious that if such tests are measures of NSR, this factor has good potentiality for relevance to aptitude for mathematics. The measurement of NSR would be made easier with examinees all of whom had had a course in beginning algebra. Canisia's subjects were eleventh-grade girls who had had some algebra.

Semantic relations (NMR)   As stated above, the first form of Correlate Completion was instrumental in bringing out a factor of eduction of correlates, which may have been a confounding of NSR and NMR. After the semantic items had been eliminated to produce Correlate Completion II, the latter continued as a marker for NSR but had no further apparent relationship with NMR. No semantic-correlate-completion test was constructed. Instead, dependence was placed upon Verbal Analogies Completion, in which, as the title implies, E has to supply his own answers. He still has to cognize the relation for the first pair, however, and this requirement naturally has shown up in the form of significant loadings on CMR (Kettner et al., 1959a).

In order to keep the CMR variance in such a test at a low level, Inventive Verbal Relations was designed. In this test, E is told what the relation is between the first two words. A sample item reads:

(a) is the opposite of (b)
(a) black : (b) _____ : : (a) strong : (b) _____

with E to fill the blanks. But then some secondary variances have come into the test; it is not univocal for NMR. There is still no univocal test for NMR, but there seems little doubt about the separability of this factor.

Convergent production of systems

Symbolic systems (NSS)   The first factor to be found that called for an interpretation in line with the idea of convergent production of systems was called "ordering" ability. In the study of planning abilities it was hypothesized that there should be an ability to order a sequence of steps so as to complete a complex task (Berger et al., 1957). Two subhypotheses were investigated. One was that temporal ordering would be one kind of such ability; so temporal-ordering tests were written. The other was that another kind would be represented by hierarchical ordering, of which the outlining of ideas with headings, subheadings, and subsubheadings is an example. Two outlining tests were constructed. Under the same subhypotheses, a matrix-building test was constructed, although it represents still another kind of system. The significant outcomes will be discussed in connection with factor NMS. The finding of a semantic-ordering ability suggested that there should be a symbolic-ordering ability. That was one factor hypothesis investigated in a study of symbolic abilities (Guilford et al., 1961).

Factor NSS has been demonstrated in four analyses, with a specifically designed test, Word Changes, serving to mark it each time. This test was based upon a somewhat familiar game, which asks E to go from a given word to another given word by changing just one letter at a time. The same kind of problem is given in Word Changes, with the needed intervening words also presented in mixed order, E to say what the order should be. A sample problem reads:

Terminal words		Intervening words
BELL		*1.* bail
————		*2.* ball
————		*3.* mail
————	(*answer: 2, 1, 3*)	
MAIN		

Word Changes has not always been free from secondary factor variances, which have not been consistent, except that they have always been symbolic.

Operations Sequence has been univocal for NSS in the two analyses in which it has appeared (Guilford et al., 1961; Hoepfner et al., 1964). It is a number test in which each item asks E to state the needed order for a given set of operations in starting from a given number and reaching another given number in three steps. A sample item is:

Start with 6, obtain 18   *A.* $+ 3$
                            B. $\div 2$
                            C. $\times 3$

answer: B, A, C

The same test under the name Right Order worked well in one group of ninth-grade students but not for another (Petersen et al., 1963), for no apparent reason. This test, especially, suggests the probable importance of factor NSS in potential for computer programmers, who must organize detailed sequences of symbolic operations. There is already some indication that this is a good prediction.[1]

Semantic systems (NMS)   To come back to the planning study, six system-making tests, three under the heading of temporal ordering and three under the heading of hierarchical ordering, were tried out. The outcome was that three temporal-ordering tests headed the list on a factor, along with the matrix-ordering test, plus two others which will be mentioned later. The two outlining tests failed to go with the ordering tests. With communalities of about .25, those tests failed to go on any factor in particular in the planning analysis. This does not rule out the possibility that they have other common-factor component variances or that other tests calling for the organization of hierarchies will not be found to be loaded on factor NMS.

The leading ordering test on the factor was Picture Arrangement, a test borrowed from Adkins and Lyerly (1951), which also has usually led in identifying factor NMS

[1] From a personal communication from Raymond M. Berger and Robert C. Wilson.

since the planning analysis. Picture Arrangement presents problems of putting the parts of a cartoon strip in correct sequence, as in a part of the Wechsler scale. In each problem the four parts of a cartoon strip are presented in randomized order, with E to indicate what the correct order should be.

Another test, Sentence Order, was also adapted from Adkins and Lyerly, with some alterations. It gives three sentences each of which is a natural step in some series of events, such as:

————— She bought some food at the market.
————— She returned home and cooked some of the food.
————— She went to the market.

E indicates the correct order of events by writing 1, 2, and 3 in the appropriate blanks. This has been a fair test for NMS.

Essentially as good in the planning analysis, but not utilized since, is the test Word Matrices. This test presents nine lines in three rows and three columns, on each of which is to appear a word. Three words may be given already placed correctly in the matrix, with the remaining six words to go into it, for example:

minnow	—————	net
—————	—————	rod
—————	—————	—————

lake, whale, ocean, bass, harpoon, pool

A test called Temporal Ordering was next best. This test presents a problem that takes a number of successive steps in a logical or practical order. The steps are listed in scrambled order, with E to answer such questions as:

The steps that should precede step d are ————— ————— —————.
The first two steps, in order, should be ————— —————.
The next to the last step should be —————.

One problem was the changing of a flat tire, with seven steps; another was the preparation and seeding of a new lawn, with more than seven steps.

Matrix Order was designed to examine the hypothesis of an ability of "sensitivity to order." A matrix of words 3×3 is completely presented. A logical sequence of three words can be seen in any one row or column or along either diagonal, E to indicate by drawing a line through the words where the sequence is and to show the direction by an arrowhead, if there is a natural direction, or by two arrowheads if the order is a reversible one. One might expect this test to be in the area of cognition, particularly for factor CMS. But even with CMS identified in the analysis, Matrix Order came out on NMS, suggesting that the typical E has to do some work to bring about an order.

Procedure Applications was designed without any particular factor hypothesis in mind; it was of interest to know, in connection with operations in planning, how well an individual can take a method or procedure that he learns in one context and apply it to serve some purpose in some other context. For example, one problem in the test describes a method involving successive crystallization in chemistry, and E is asked to state four other situations in which methods following the same principle might be useful. There is an implication of successive steps in this kind of problem, which may account for the test's significant but minimal loading on NMS.

If we were to focus attention upon only the two leading tests mentioned for the ordering or NMS factor, we might have to admit that the factor might be merely one concerned with producing temporal order, other kinds of systems not being pertinent to the factor. But as we saw, other kinds of systems are involved in tests loaded significantly on the factor, the matrix type of model being the prominent one. The failure of the two hierarchical-systems tests to go along with the rest might be due to the special kinds of items of information that were to be organized. They were statements such as could be readily expanded into a theme. The hierarchy was not a neat, classes-within-classes affair. There were opportunities to organize the headings in various ways. With instructions to reorganize, the test might be fair for the parallel factor DMS. Everything considered, the ordering factor seems to have considerable generality, qualifying it for NMS.

Convergent production of transformations

At first thought, the intersection of convergent production with transformations might appear to be incongruous, the one suggesting a kind of rigidity, the other definitely a flexibility. But such a conjoining of the two concepts in psychological economy is forced upon us by the results of factor analysis. In fact, we have demonstrations of three such factors, as compared with only one or two in other product categories, as Table 7.1 shows.

When the matter is put in terms other than flexibility and rigidity, the convergent producing of transformations can be made to seem more reasonable. There are situations in which some kind of change in information is needed in order to achieve a certain goal and no other change will do. As we saw in the preceding chapter, transformations may very well be divergently produced where the way is open and breadth of search is desirable. But, under other circumstances, the conditions can be so restricted that only one particular transformation will do. Then we have convergent production, just as for any other kind of product. In solving a mechanical puzzle, for example, one particular twist of the linked parts must necessarily be accomplished to get the links apart. That twist is a transformation, a transformation of the system of interrelated parts of the puzzle.

Figural transformations (NFT)   The first hint of a factor of NFT came in Thurstone's analysis (1944) of what he called perceptual abilities (most of those factors have found places within the intellectual realm). One of his factors, which he called "gestalt flexibility," was characterized by Hidden Pictures and by two forms of Gottschaldt-figures tests. There were also two other tests with strong to moderate loadings on the factor, which suggests that it was a confounding of NFT with something else, the nature of which is not clear. One has to disregard the leading test (Two-Hand Coordination) to interpret the factor as NFT.

Subsequent to Thurstone's experience with his gestalt-flexibility factor, when a Gottschaldt-figures test has appeared in analysis without sufficient support from other tests of NFT, like Thurstone's Hidden Pictures or the AAF Penetration of Camouflage, a hidden-faces task, it has gone in different directions, none of them recognizable as NFT (Green et al., 1953; Guilford & Lacey, 1947; Guilford et al., 1954). The loadings of what is now recognized as NFT for the various forms of Gottschaldt-figures tests, including the writer's Hidden Figures (see Figure 7.2), which dates back to 1940, have been sufficiently low (around .40) that there is much room for other common-factor variance, but no other factor has shown up consistently for it.

Wherever a Gottschaldt-figures test and a hidden-pictures or hidden-faces test have appeared together in an analysis, a factor that can be called NFT emerges (Botzum, 1951; O'Sullivan et al., 1965; Roff, 1952). Thus a factor characteristic of this kind of pair of tests seems replicated sufficiently to accept it. It fits cell NFT because only one trans-

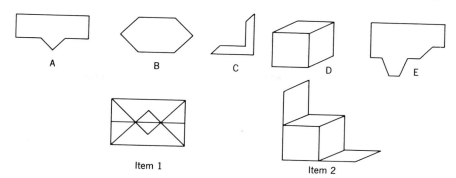

Fig. 7.2 Sample items from the Hidden Figures test. Which of the five simple figures at the top is concealed in each of the item figures? *Answers: 1, A; 2, D. (This test is based upon figures originally designed by Gottschaldt, 1926.)*

formation is acceptable for each item (hence it is convergent); a transformation does occur, in the form of revision of the interpretation or definition or use of lines. Before the hidden figure or face appears, the lines are parts of larger structures. After it has appeared, the lines are boundaries of new figures. Old forms give way to new ones.

At one time the writer (Guilford, 1959a) believed that the well-known factor of visualization belonged in cell NFT, on the ground that in taking a visualization test the examinee has to be active in producing the changes required for an answer. But the hidden-figures type of test takes more "doing" on the part of the individual. In a visualization test, the examinee need only follow what is given through prescribed or resulting operations. In a hidden-figures test, E must tear a new organization out of an old one. He must redefine objects or parts of objects. This is also true for tests of parallel abilities of NST and NMT, to be given attention next.

Hidden figures and field dependence   Witkin, Dyk, Faterson, Goodenough, and Karp (1962) have used a Gottschaldt-figures test extensively in connection with their studies with a series of tests of a trait that they call "field independence-dependence" (let us abbreviate it by saying FID) and that Witkin (1964) regards as a "cognitive style." Because of the connection of the Gottschaldt-figures tests to NFT, there is reason to consider the possible relation of NFT to the FID variable. The score on Witkin's Embedded Figures Test, which is based upon the Gottschaldt figures, is the total time E takes to see the hidden figures in the set of items. The tests of FID include:

Rod-and-Frame (E sees a luminous rod inside a luminous frame in a dark room, both rod and frame being tilted; E is to adjust the rod until he thinks it is at the true vertical)

Body-Adjustment (The small room into which E looks, E's chair, or both are tilted in various ways; E is to bring his chair to what he considers the true vertical)

The FID score indicates the extent to which E's judgments of the vertical are determined by his visual information. A high score indicates field dependence; a low score, field independence.

Witkin et al. (1962) report correlations between the Embedded Figures Test (time score) and the FID score to be from .36 to .64 for men and from .21 to .51 for women (with Ns of about 50). Thus, the field-independent individual does better on the Embedded Figures Test, which is reasonable. The person who pays too much attention to what he sees and who holds onto it should be less likely to see changes in the figures.

To what extent does an FID score measure factor NFT? On this we can only speculate for the most part. Both a FID score and a Gottschaldt-figures–test score correlate with so many other variables that they both give the impression of being factorially complex. That leaves us wondering which of several common factors accounts for their intercorrelation. In one place, Witkin (1964, p. 180) identifies his FID "factor" with adaptive flexibility (DFT). Karp (1963) tested this hypothesis by correlating FID scores with two DFT tests, Match Problems and Insight Problems. There were relationships, but by a small factor analysis Karp found that these two tests have something in common that they do not share with FID scores. This something might well be DFT. It would be more reasonable to expect NFT variance in the FID scores than DFT variance, because there is little apparent involvement with multiple responses in the FID tests. Performance is scored on how much E conforms to a realistic standard, the vertical.

Both Karp and Witkin report correlations between FID scores and the Wechsler tests of Object Assembly and Block Design. P. C. Davis (1956) found that the leading factors in these two tests were visualization (CFT) and perceptual speed (EFU). From this indirect evidence, also, the FID scores appear to be factorially complex. Only a factor analysis of FID tests, along with appropriate marker tests in order to examine hypotheses concerning the most likely intellectual factors, will clear up the mystery. Because the FID scores derived from different sources tend to correlate differently with aptitude tests, we should expect some different factor compositions for those sources. FID scores may measure nonaptitude traits also, as suggested by Witkin et al. when they classify their "factor" in the category of cognitive style.[1]

Symbolic transformations (NST)   The first inkling of a factor NST was seen in an analytical study of flexibility (Frick et al., 1959). A test called Camouflaged Words, designed by analogy to the NFT test of Penetration of Camouflage, led on a doublet factor with Hidden Figures. The factor was probably a confounding of NFT and NST, but it was a promise of the possibility of demonstrating NST. In three later analyses (Guilford et al., 1961; Hoepfner et al., 1964; Petersen et al., 1963), Camouflaged Words and Word Transformations have together marked a factor NST. Sample items for the former, in which E is to find and circle the concealed names of sports or games, are:

Cowardice is not a soldierly attribute.   (dice)
I did not know that he was ailing.   (sailing)
To beat the Hun, tin goes a long way.   (hunting)

In Word Transformations, only phrases or parts of sentences are given, with E to make complete regroupings to form new words, as in RINGS OF THE, which by regrouping becomes RING SOFT HE; and THE RED OLIVE, which becomes THERE DO LIVE. In both of these tests E must break up words in natural contexts to form new words. That the context need not be meaningful, however, is suggested by the fact that the test Four-Letter Words has some loading on NST. In this test, which is a bit stronger for factor CSU-V, four-letter words are buried in continuous lines of capital letters that are randomized except for the occasional word. Even the fact that the cognized word must be torn out of a letter-sequence context is evidently sufficient to involve NST.

In theorizing about the nature of the FID variable, Witkin (1964) concludes that it is an ability to break up or to analyze a perceived visual structure. It is not analysis in the usual sense, of arriving at significant parts that help one to understand a totality. The

---

[1] For a discussion of cognitive-style factors, see Chapter 9.

emphasis should be on *breakup;* even *destruction* would be a better word with which to describe what happens with words in connection with NST or with figures in connection with NFT.

Semantic transformations (NMT)   In the investigation of abilities entering into creative production, a hypothesized factor was termed *redefinition,* a concept borrowed from gestalt psychology (Wilson et al., 1954). One of the tests designed for this hypothesis was Gestalt Transformations, in which E is asked to select one of five objects that could be used in whole or in part to accomplish some unusual purpose for that object. For example, asked which object could be best adapted to starting a fire, the alternatives are (A) fountain pen, (B) onion, (C) pocket watch, (D) light bulb, and (E) bowling ball. $C,$ pocket watch, is the keyed answer, since its cover glass could be removed and presumably used as a lens for condensing light rays. A second test designed for the hypothesis was Object Synthesis, in which E is given two common objects with which, by combination, he is to make something else that is useful, e.g., pliers and a shoestring, from which a pendulum would be a good solution. The third test, Picture Gestalt, shows a photograph of an ordinary room in a home, such as a kitchen or dining room, with the usual kinds of objects visible, and E is told to suggest what object he would use for accomplishing each of several purposes, e.g., "to protect your hat in the rain" or "to tie a package."

These three tests performed as expected, and in later analyses one or more of them have helped to mark the recognized factor NMT, but in no case have the loadings been more than moderate in strength. Evidently the best test for this factor has not yet been written. One question to which we need to know the answer is whether items that require the use of a part rather than the use of the object as a whole give a better measure of NMT. From the fact that the good tests for NFT and NST call for destruction of units in the process of transformation, it would seem that the same principle would apply in the case of NMT.

Convergent production of implications

Symbolic implications (NSI)   A characteristic of tests of both the known factors NSI and NMI is that they involve drawing logic-tight deductions from given information. In the realm of logic, of course, only such deductions exist. In psychology, such deductions exist only in the convergent-production area of abilities and functions. In the case of divergent production, there are also deductions or inferences, but the truth value for such an implication is free to vary, with all degrees of probability of being sound. This is one of the distinctions that is important to keep in mind in considering the differences between psychology and logic; there are others, of course, which will be discussed in Chapter 10.

The first trace of factor NSI appeared in the first exploratory analysis of reasoning abilities in the Aptitudes Research Project (Green et al., 1953). The factor was marked, almost alone, by the test Form Reasoning, which had been previously used by Blakey (1941). Figure 7.3 shows how the test was structured. E is presented with a set of simple equations based on the combinations of figures, two at a time, to give other single figures. Using this information, E is to solve problems that consist of combinations of *three* figures each, in a multiple-choice type of item. The first two of these figures imply another figure, as specified in the definitions given, and this other figure combined with the third implies still another.

A second test has helped to mark factor NSI in more recent analyses. This test is Sign Changes. In Sign Changes, E is to solve simple arithmetical equations under the

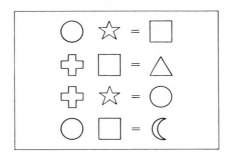

Fig. 7.3 Sample item from the Form Reasoning test. Given the simple equations at the top, each one indicating that a given figure is implied by a combination of two others, what figure is implied by the combination of three figures in the item? In solving the item, combinations of two figures at a time are taken in turn. *Answer: A.* (*Adapted from a test designed by Blakey, 1941.*)

special instruction that he is to replace one of the operation signs with another, for example:

Replace $-$ by $\times$ *Equations to be solved:*
Replace $+$ by $-$

$$3 - 6 = \underline{\hspace{1cm}}$$
$$6 + 2 = \underline{\hspace{1cm}}$$
$$4 - 3 = \underline{\hspace{1cm}}$$

The completion form is in recognition of the need to have E produce the answer himself.

As mentioned in connection with factor MSI, for some time the long-known number factor was recognized as NSI. This meant forcing the factor headed by Form Reasoning into the neighboring cell of NFI, on the slim basis that the test is composed of figures, while recognizing that the figures have only symbolic significance; their figural properties have no utility except that of identification. When it was found that a number test, Sign Changes, also marked the factor, then known as "symbol substitution" (Kettner et al., 1959a), the NFI interpretation became untenable. It was also found (P. C. Davis, 1956; de Mille, 1962) that numerical-operations tests were loaded on the same factor as the Wechsler Digit Symbol test, which is generally recognized as a short-term memory test. Numerical-operations tests could be defended as long-term memory tests, and since the two kinds of tests went together, the numerical-facility factor could be defended as MSI. Numerical-operations tests have more recently tended to divide their variances between MSI and NSI (Petersen et al., 1963), but they also have a strong specific component, which can be regarded as an overlearned skill, acquired through education (see Chapter 5).

Semantic implications (NMI)   There are only slender threads of evidence for factor NMI, one which seems so close to the popular psychological concept of "deduction" that it is strange that it has not been more assiduously investigated. Thurstone (1938a) named one of his first-discovered factors "deduction," with two syllogistic-reasoning tests leading on it. For some reason, J. W. French (1951) chose to designate as "deduction" another factor which seems to be a composite dominated by CMS, the characteristic factor of arithmetic reasoning.

Studies by the Aptitudes Research Project have consistently found a factor prominently led by syllogistic-type tests, but the interpretation has always been that the factor belongs in the category of evaluative abilities, since the syllogistic tests have been of the true-false or multiple-choice types, in which E does not have to draw his own conclusion; it is given to him. But he must evaluate the conclusion, whatever else he may do. In one analysis (Hertzka, Guilford, Christensen, & Berger, 1954), a syllogistic test in completion form was included, but all by itself it could not have determined a production ability NMI separate from the corresponding evaluative ability with which that test went. This was not unreasonable, since besides producing his own conclusions in that test E probably did some evaluating of his answers.

The test that has marked a factor that can be defined as NMI in three analyses is Sequential Associations, which was designed for a study of problem-solving abilities (Merrifield et al., 1962). This test presents an item like this:

pen	pig	read	write

E tells into what sequence, from 1 to 4, these words should be put in order that there be a natural connection from the first to second, second to third, and so on. The keyed order is pig, pen, write, read. It was thought that the keyed order is sufficiently determined that the task is convergent and that each word best implies the one that follows it.

A second test very weakly helped determine this factor. This was Attribute Listing II, in which E is to list the *essential* attributes of an object that is needed to achieve a stated purpose, e.g., driving a long nail into a thick block of wood. The attributes implied by these specifications apply to an object that can be held in the hand, is harder than the nail, has a flat striking surface, and is light enough to be operated with the arm.

A factor with Sequential Associations leading has been reported in two analyses, with boys and girls separately, by El-Abd (1963). Additional kinds of tests are needed to verify the factor and to check on its degree of generality. A syllogisms test in completion form might go with the tests already mentioned to help define the factor.

Additional comments

Tests of convergent-production abilities feature the drawing of deductions from given information, deductions that are logic-tight, in that they are essentially uniquely determined by the given information. In divergent-production tasks there is considerable freedom, but not complete freedom, in producing information to serve a purpose. In convergent production, there is no freedom, if the individual's productive processes are functioning properly and if he has the information available or can readily construct it.

The CP category of abilities and functions has been relatively neglected in explorations by factor analysis and rather slighted in traditional intelligence tests. In view of the apparent importance of CP abilities for any activities of life in which rigorous thinking is involved—mathematics, logic, science, engineering, and law, to name a few—there is a need to push forward in the exploration of this whole area.

In recent psychological and educational literature, there are occasional confusions of the concepts of cognition and convergent production. Although cognition tests are commonly keyed for one right answer, this in itself is not sufficient to justify reference to cognitive abilities and tests as convergent-production abilities and tests. Cognition means *having* information and comprehending it, more in the nature of observing it. We might say that, in the terminology of Heidbreder (1924), cognition is like "spectator behavior" and convergent production is like "participant behavior," in order to distinguish these two operations.

All content areas except behavioral, where no investigation has occurred, are represented by known CP factors, and all six product areas are represented; hence there is promise of a complete set of 24 CP abilities. The question of whether there will also be some CP abilities where auditory and other nonvisual senses are involved has not been seriously raised, but it is a question to be tolerated.

There is an interesting question concerning the role of evaluation abilities in connection with convergent production versus divergent production. We shall look into the area of evaluation abilities next; the question of their possible relations to convergent production will have to wait until later.

8 Evaluative abilities

Evaluation has been another neglected aspect of intelligence. Binet thought that one of the important kinds of abilities is concerned with critical judgment, but his test scales did not reflect that view to any great extent. The framers of the Army Alpha Examination adopted a test they called Common Sense as one of its eight components, thus giving some recognition in the direction of evaluation.

During World War II, at the beginning of the AAF Aviation Psychology Research Program, pilot instructors were consulted as to what they thought were the reasons why 1,000 students failed in learning to fly. The most frequent reason given was "poor judgment." When further enlightenment was sought as to what the instructors meant by poor judgment, however, it was found that they might be referring to anything from errors in judging distances to errors in choice of flight pattern. This should have been a hint of the fact that *judgment* is not any one thing. As so often happens, it is a term that covers a variety of things.

In trying to gain a better conception of judgment and ways of measuring an aptitude of that kind, the AAF psychologists constructed some judgment tests, and by factor analysis they found what could be called a "judgment" factor (Guilford & Lacey, 1947). The most common type of test in this category was Practical Judgment, a test that presented problems of a common, everyday type: a predicament of some kind, with five-choice answers in the form of solutions and E to say which is the best of the alternative solutions. Such tests had typically low reliability and low factor loadings. The tests did tend to make some prediction of passing in flying training, but this could be accounted for largely in terms of the mechanical-knowledge factor variance in the tests. The tests drew heavily upon that area of information.

The first systematic investigation of judgment, for which the term *evaluation* was preferred, was conducted in the Aptitudes Research Project (Hertzka et al., 1954). Two major analyses have been completed more recently (Hoepfner et al., 1964; Nihira et al., 1964). Search of the literature reveals that a number of factors found previously can also be interpreted as evaluation factors, identifiable with some found recently.

On the basis of the information obtained from these sources, evaluation is defined as a process of comparing a product of information with known information according to logical criteria, making a decision concerning criterion satisfaction. The mention of "logical criteria" is deliberate, for it has been found that the more nearly tests emphasize criteria of identity, similarity, and consistency, the more likely they are to measure evaluative abilities. Other important kinds of criteria of evaluation, such as aesthetic and ethical, are used in behavior, but there has been no factor-analytic experience as yet with tests that emphasize these criteria. It may yet be found that such criteria apply in connection with abilities for evaluating figural and behavioral information, respectively, but this is still to be determined.

Evaluation of units

Of all the product categories, that of units has received by far the most attention in connection with evaluation, mostly without realization that evaluative abilities were being investigated. Reference to Table 8.1 will show that only in the units row have as many as three evaluation abilities been reported, and these with multiple investigations. One of these factors (EFU) has been found to apply to young children (Meyers et al., 1964), and the other two at eighth- and ninth-grade levels. Stott and Ball (1963) have interpreted a few factors found in infant and preschool tests as belonging to the evaluation category.

Figural units (EFU)   Factor EFU is another of the Thurstone firsts. Thurstone characterized it as being perceptual and as being "a facility in perceiving detail that is imbedded in irrelevant material" (1938a, p. 81). In the last qualification he was wrong, for this expression better describes another factor, NFT. Thurstone's perceptual factor later acquired the label of "perceptual speed," by which it was known for a long time. The reasons for identifying it with EFU will appear in the following discussion.

A favorite and faithful marker test for perceptual speed has been Thurstone's test Identical Forms, sample items from which are shown in Figure 8.1. The essential task is saying whether or not each figure is identical with a model figure. Air Force tests that consistently marked this factor were:

Speed of Identification, in which short matching items are given, the objects to be matched being line drawings of airplanes. The differences between planes within a matching set are small, but the nonmatched pairs have supraliminal differences. A "civilian" form of the same test is the Guilford-Zimmerman Perceptual Speed, which is illustrated in Figure 8.2.

Spatial Orientation I presents a large aerial photograph of a city or other terrain with a number of small circular patches taken from that same view alongside it, to be matched with lettered locations within the complete photograph. This test is unique among perceptual-speed tests because the information consists of photographs; ordinarily, line drawings prevail.

Spatial Orientation II presents segments of aerial photographs to be matched with positions in an aerial map rather than in a large photograph as in the preceding test. The change to a map is associated with a consistently smaller loading on perceptual speed.

The appellation of "perceptual speed" for this factor arose from the fact that items in an EFU test are typically easy, so easy that if E had sufficient time he could complete all items with almost no mistakes. The typical test of EFU is therefore highly speeded.

Table 8.1   Matrix of the evaluation factors (E) represented in the structure-of-intellect model

Figural (F)		Symbolic (S)		Semantic (M)		Behavioral (B)		
EFU 2, 4, 6, 13, 14	N	ESU 14	S	EMU 13	S	EBU	0	*Units* (U)
EFC	0	ESC	1	EMC	1	EBC	0	*Classes* (C)
EFR	0	ESR	S	EMR 14	S	EBR	0	*Relations* (R)
EFS	0	ESS	1	EMS	S	EBS	0	*Systems* (S)
EFT	0	EST	1	EMT	1	EBT	0	*Transformations* (T)
EFI	0	ESI	2	EMI	S	EBI	0	*Implications* (I)

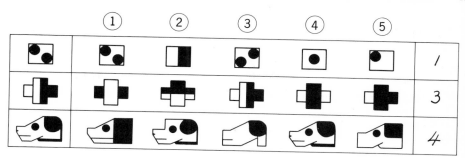

Fig. 8.1 Items like those in Thurstone's test Identical Forms. Which figure in each row is exactly the same as the one at the left? The answers are marked.

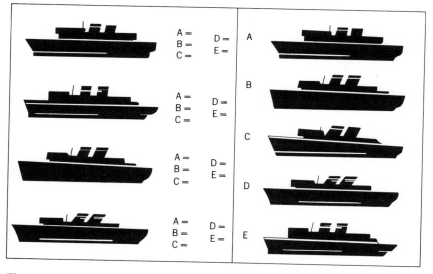

Fig. 8.2 Items in a short matching set of items for the factor of evaluation of figural units. Identical pairs are to be matched exactly, where there are small but supraliminal differences among the objects. (*From Part IV of the Guilford-Zimmerman Aptitude Survey, courtesy of the Sheridan Psychological Services, Inc.*)

The reason for identifying the perceptual-speed factor with EFU is that matching and also decision as to identity versus nonidentity are involved. These characteristics (comparison and decision concerning some criterion satisfaction) conform to the definition that applies to all evaluative abilities. There was an implication in the early interpretation of the factor that visual-figural recognition is involved. But a telling argument against this view is that there is another factor that better deserves that description, which is the factor CFU-V, or *cognition* of figural units. Mere recognition is involved; there are no matching and no accepting or rejecting of matches. We shall see that certain tests for the parallel factor ESU are similar to those for EFU except for content, as they should be.

It will be noted in Table 8.1 that factor EFU has been identified in analyses at mental ages of six, four, and even two years, in tests very much like those used with adults (C. E. Meyers et al., 1964; Orpet & Meyers, 1965).

Symbolic units (ESU)   Over the years, there have been a number of analyses in which certain letter and word tests went with marker tests for EFU and again they did not but determined a separate factor. It is clearer now that some of the early factors found in this area were confoundings of EFU and ESU. When enough tests of the two kinds in the analysis, purely figural and purely literal, both calling for decisions as to identity versus nonidentity, are given in the same analysis, there are two distinct factors. One of the most successful types of tests for ESU is Symbol Identities (Hoepfner et al., 1964), which conforms to the type so common in tests of clerical aptitude. Pairs of letter, number, or name sets are to be compared. Members of some pairs are identical, and members of others have a minor discrepancy, a change of a letter or digit or a transposition. Items are of the following type:

    6410739 _____ 6410729
James M. Urban _____ James M. Urban
    VDNIYOP _____ VDNIYUP

E is to write S if he thinks the two are identical and D if he thinks they are different.

Another good test of a different type is Letter "U," in which E is told to mark every word in a list that contains the letter U. It should be noted that this test is analogous to a kind of test for factor DSU, in which E is instructed to *list* words each of which contains a specified letter. In the latter instance E *produces* words containing a specified letter; in the former he evaluates words given to him as to whether they contain a specified letter. Presumably other types of DSU (word-fluency) tests could be made into evaluation tests in the same manner. In fact, we can propose a general principle to the effect that the operations of scoring production tests, divergent and convergent, involve evaluation abilities parallel to the abilities needed for producing the answers to be evaluated.

A test that failed to go more than minimally on ESU is very interesting, because of its educational implications and because its failure adds to the understanding of limitations to ESU. A test Correct Spelling was designed for ESU, but it elected to go mostly elsewhere in the analysis (Hoepfner et al., 1964). Such a spelling test may be somewhat standard for measuring achievement in spelling. The test gives a relatively long list of words that are commonly misspelled, about half of them spelled correctly and about half with errors.

The hypothesis was that an important characteristic of evaluation is a sensitivity to errors. In Correct Spelling, E is to say whether or not each word is spelled correctly. The main common-factor contributor to this test was found to be CSU-V, the cognition of visual-symbolic units. Thus, it may be that detecting errors, as such, is a matter of cognition, in this area of information at least, but the principle may be broader than that. If so, an important general principle has been uncovered. From this finding, it would appear that to involve evaluation, there need be some kind of model for comparison. Without a model, we are dealing with cognition. This would be one reason for including comparison in the definition of evaluation.

Another test that failed was Familiar Letter Combinations (Hoepfner et al., 1964). In an item in this test, E is presented with two alternative three-letter syllables, such as LOY and NIS, to say which one is more frequently encountered in ordinary English writing. The syllables have been calibrated for frequency (Underwood & Schulz, 1960), and pairs between which the difference in frequency is known to be rather large can be used. In this test, we may say that the criterion is degree of frequency. The test might have failed for factor ESU by reason of a criterion that does not apply, but it is more likely that it failed because no models are available for comparison: another reason for emphasis upon comparison.

The question of models is an interesting one: do models have to be present to the senses or in immediate cognition? Such a condition is true of Identical Forms, Perceptual Speed, Symbol Identities, and other versions of the last named, including Identical Numbers (C. W. Taylor, 1947), and Number Comparison and Name Comparison of the United States Employment Service (War Manpower Commission, 1945). But in Letter "U," the model is not presented for perception; in fact, there cannot be exact models, since only a class specification—words containing the letter *U*—is given. It could be said that the model *is* just the letter *U,* for which *E* has to look. But it is doubtful that looking for a particular letter is a symbolic task; it is more like a figural task. "Look for words containing *U*" is a different set than just "Look for letter *U*." In this kind of test, it may be that the class idea serves as the model. It can be regarded as the "search model," of which more will be said in Chapter 14. The question of models also applies to kinds of products other than units.

A factor that looks very much like ESU was found for a sample of six-year-old children (Orpet & Meyers, 1965). One strong test for it was Finding the O's, which, like Letter "U," asks *E* to mark all words containing the letter *O*. Another strong test was Number Comparisons, which is like Symbol Identities but involves only digits to be matched. A test called Word Comparisons called for matching of words, but its loading was only minimally significant on ESU and much higher on EFU. It is possible that with children for whom words as visual-symbolic units are not yet very familiar, the matching is done primarily in terms of figural appearances. At least that is what the relative loadings for EFU and ESU in the Orpet-Meyers analysis suggest.

Semantic units (EMU)   In the most recent analysis and the only one that aimed specifically at finding a factor EMU, the most successful test, Double Descriptions, was modeled after a good type of test for DMU, substituting an evaluative task for a divergent-production task (Nihira et al., 1964). In the Ideational Fluency test, *E* may be asked to *list* all the objects he can think of that are round and hard. In Double Descriptions, *E* may be asked to say which of four given objects comes nearest to satisfying the descriptions ROUND and HARD, the alternatives being (1) gold, (2) record, (3) steel, and (4) coin. The keyed answer is 4. It will be seen that Double Descriptions is analogous to Letter "U," both of which specify attributes and thus the class to which the potential members belong. In the latter test, it is a matter of belonging or of not belonging: in the former, it is a matter of degree: which comes nearest to satisfying the given attributes. Rather generally, in the Nihira analysis of semantic-evaluation abilities and in the Hoepfner analysis of symbolic-evaluation abilities, it was found that absolute judgments and relative judgments work almost equally well. The absolute-judgment type of test makes possible a simpler kind of problem, which should work more toward univocal measurement.

Looking further back in time, we find examples of what appears to be the same factor. Hertzka et al. (1954) found a factor characteristic of two similar tests, Word Checking I and Word Checking II. They are like Double Descriptions; in fact, the latter was adapted in part from Word Checking II. Word Checking I has only one specification to determine the class, and it had a distinctly smaller loading: .46 versus .62 for Word Checking II. This difference is interesting in comparison with a similar change of conditions in Thing Listing tests (Christensen & Guilford, 1963), with which it was found that for measuring factor DMU, the task with two specifications of class properties is superior to that with one specification.

Going further back, we find that other word-checking tests have been successful for factors that may now be recognized as EMU or close to it, for example, in Bechtoldt's 1947 analysis (reported by J. W. French, 1951); in an analysis by Thurstone and Thurstone (1941) at the eighth-grade level; and by Thurstone (1938b), in his first analysis of perception. The last two analyses mentioned showed that a test Verbal Enumeration is also quite effective. This test asks E to check all the words in a column that belong to the class named at the top of the column. Not enough was said about how the class was presented, whether it was merely named or defined with specifications; so it is difficult to compare this test with Word Checking or Double Descriptions.

Two other tests of Thurstone's appear to be in the same category, namely, Concrete Association and Abstract Classification. In the former, E is to mark words in a column that are closely "associated with" the word at the heading of the column, including such cue words as garage, student, estate, and radio. In the latter, there is a similar task, the cue words being "abstract," e.g., lightness, within, angular, again, etc. E is to check the words in each column that come under the category indicated by the cue word. The latter is more like the word-checking type of test, in that decisions are concerned with class membership; the former is not so clearly in the word-checking category, unless the relations of response words to cue words are in the nature of subordinate to supraordinate. Both tests had significant loadings on a factor that can be identified as EMU.

Still other kinds of tests were used by Bechtoldt (1947). Size Comparison told E to mark the larger of two named objects. One could bring this test also under the word-checking category by saying that the class designation is "larger than." The test Unfurnished House asks E to mark words of things associated with an unfurnished house. This is more readily brought under the class-member–identification task when we consider that the class is composed of all things in the "unfurnished-house" category. A test called Opposites requires E to mark every pair of words that are opposites in meaning. Here the class specification is the relation "opposites." But such a test might do better for the evaluation of relations, or factor EMR. Boys' First Names, in which all such terms in a column are to be marked, would seem to get nearer to ESU than EMU, but it went along with the other EMU tests mentioned. It can be seen that with a little broadening of the concept of identifying class members versus nonclass members, most of the tests mentioned for EMU thus far can be brought under the same principle. But this entails the problem of determining the conditions under which such a task pattern exists.

A couple of instances in which there was failure to measure the intended factor EMU will be mentioned. The tests were designed more in line with the principle of EFU tests and of the ESU test Symbol Identities. That is, semantic units (verbal meanings) were presented for matching, calling for decision about identity of meaning between them. This is different from the task to say whether or not a word fulfills a class specification. One of the tests was Word Substitution, which was mentioned in connection with factor CMU, for that is where it went (see Chapter 4). E is to say which of four given words comes closest in meaning to an underlined word in a sentence. For example, if the sentence is "The lecture lasted so long that I fell asleep," which of the following words comes nearest in meaning to the underlined word?

1. extended   *2.* remained   *3.* continued   *4.* endured

The other test was Synonyms, which calls for a similar judgment, except that the stem word is not given in a sentence. Both of these tests went on the CMU factor along with ordinary vocabulary tests; they are not evaluation tests.

In the same analysis (Nihira et al., 1964), a test designed for the evaluation of semantic systems came out on EMU instead. It was called Sentensense. Because under other circumstances, as with factor DMS, a sentence behaves like a semantic system, Sentensense was designed to see how well E can judge a sentence for internal consistency. Previously it had been found that consistency within a system, such as a pictured situation, serves as a workable criterion for evaluation of systems. Half the given sentences in Sentensense are internally consistent, half not. One with internal inconsistency reads: "Johnny, who is seven, went to Europe with his mother ten years ago."

Sentensense's coming out on factor EMU in one analysis might have been an event that will not be replicated. But assuming that it actually measures EMU, we have something that needs to be explained. It is not the first instance in which there has been some confusion between units and systems in constructing tests, as was brought out in connection with DFS tests that sometimes behaved at least in part as units tests (see Chapter 6). It is probable that in Sentensense the unit is not the entire sentence but, rather, each of the two facts within the sentence is a unit, and what E is judging is the compatibility of the two units. If so, we have evidence that a criterion of consistency, compatibility, or congruity also applies in the evaluation of units.

Another test not intended for EMU also came out with a low but significant loading on it. The test, Product Choice, was designed for factor EMT. This test was suggested by the test Object Synthesis, which has worked for the parallel factor NMT. In the latter, E is given the names of two objects and asked to make some other object by combining the two. Product Choice gives in addition three alternative solutions, with E to rank them for suitability in terms of how well they would function. For example, given a wire coat hanger and a lace curtain, with the possibility of making (1) a Christmas wrapping, (2) a mop, and (3) a butterfly net, which one is best and which is poorest? It was expected that the transformation of the two given objects into a third would be the thing evaluated, but the factor analysis tells us that it was apparently the final product that was evaluated, not the transformation. But, if so, we have an instance in which the criterion for judgment is not well specified (workability). It is certainly not a sharply defined criterion like identity, class membership, or consistency, all of which are logical in nature. It may be, however, that comparisons with models for similarity do apply in this test. The models are concepts of the requisite properties of a Christmas wrapping, a mop, and a butterfly net, with each of which the composite object is compared.

Evaluation of classes

The essence of evaluation of classes would seem to be in answer to the question of how good a particular class is in meeting certain criterional requirements. The emphasis should be upon the class *idea* rather than upon collections of particulars, upon denotative aspects rather than on connotative aspects. Criteria might be in terms of whether the class idea represents all the pertinent common properties of the members that compose the class or in terms of whether irrelevant properties have been permitted to help determine the class idea. There would be a possibility of applying the criterion of identity, as in the case of evaluation of units, but the criterion of consistency is not so obviously applicable. The range of criteria for evaluating classes has not yet been clearly delineated.

Symbolic classes (ESC)   In the one analysis that has demonstrated for the first time a factor of ESC (Hoepfner et al., 1964), three tests designed for that ability were found loaded on the same factor but along with a number of other tests. Those other tests added nothing toward understanding the nature of ESC; so they can best be ignored here. The more or less successful tests are listed below.

In Best Number Class, E judges into which of four specified number classes a given number fits in order to win the most points. He is instructed that even multiples win 1 point, odd multiples 2 points, squares 3 points, and prime numbers 4 points. Given the number 100, the best he can do is to assign it to the class "squares." In one respect, this test is a reversal of a good type of test for evaluation of units. In that case, E says which is the best unit to satisfy a given class, whereas in Best Number Class, he says which is the best class for a given unit.

Sound Grouping, originated by Thurstone, is a test that has been used a number of times in different analyses, largely because it deals with classes. It has had a history of going on different factors at various times. Inspection shows that it is probably best for a hypothesized SI factor of CSC-A, an ability to cognize classes of auditory information. It presents four words in each item, one to be selected because it does not rhyme as well with the others. A sample item is:

1. COMB   *2.* HOME   *3.* FOAM   *4.* COME

in which word 4 should be excluded because it does not sound quite like the rest. In an evaluation analysis (Hoepfner et al., 1964) the test did come on factor ESC, for which there was some anticipation, but in view of its history of going hither and yon (probably for lack of another good CSC-A test to go with it and to mark such a factor), its "support" for factor ESC must be regarded as incidental. It might eventually be shown to have some variance in a hypothetical factor ESC-A; the consideration here is ESC-V.

Word Choice presents three words that obviously provide a class idea based upon spelling, e.g., the words SCHOOL, FLEET, DOOMSDAY. Which of three following words best fits with the word class:

A. delete   *B.* relate   *C.* expect

None of these words exactly fits the class, which is characterized by words having double vowels. All three of the alternative answers have the letter E repeated but not adjacently as in the specified class. Answer A is keyed as correct, since it does better than repeat a vowel: it has the same vowel three times. The principle of having no exactly correct answer was applied in several tests; it is uncertain whether application of this principle has any advantages.

A first analysis designed for any factor must have some exploratory function. There is still much room for a better test for ESC, and a number of possible criteria for evaluation of symbolic classes have not yet been investigated.

Semantic classes (EMC)   For information concerning evaluation of *semantic* classes we are also limited to the results from one analysis (Nihira et al., 1964). Two tests designed for the factor succeeded univocally, and a third failed. The two successful tests were Class Name Selection and Best Word Class.

In Class Name Selection, E is to say which of three class names best fits a class represented by four given members. The criterion has to do with whether the class name is too restrictive or is not restrictive enough. A sample item is:

Class members	Class names
CAT	A. farm animals
COW	B. four-legged animals
MULE	C. domestic animals
MARE	

Class name A is too restrictive, since CAT is found elsewhere than on a farm, which is also sometimes true of MARE. B is much too general, since it would include numerous other cases than those given. C is broad enough to include all four and yet sufficiently restrictive; so it is the keyed answer.

Best Word Class differs from the preceding test in giving only one word to be fitted into a class, e.g., the item:

PALM

answer: C

A. plant
B. flower
C. tree
D. leaf

Here PALM would not fit into two class concepts at all, namely, B and D, although it has some association with either. A, plant, is too broad. C is more descriptive, hence correct.

Best Word Pairs, the test that failed, presents three pairs of words, each pair a potential class, with E to say which pair forms the best class. The three pairs are confined to the same three words in all possible pairings, e.g.:

1. CHINESE-ORIENTAL
2. ORIENTAL-JAPANESE
3. JAPANESE-CHINESE

where 3 is the best pair, since it includes two *members* of a class, whereas each other pair contains a class name and a member name. Reflection on the failure suggests that what is being tested here is an appreciation of when a term is a class name and when it is a member name. Different kinds of pairings might do better as an EMC test.

Evaluation of relations

In considering the evaluation of relations in general, the two criteria of identity and consistency seem obviously to apply. We can ask whether the relation of A to B is the same as that of C to D. We can also ask whether the relation of P to Q is consistent with the relation of K to L. If we are told that P is greater than Q and that Q equals K, then it would be inconsistent to say that K is greater than P. Tests constructed on the basis of these principles have been successful for factors ESR and EMR.

Symbolic relations (ESR)   Most of the evidence regarding ESR comes from a recent analysis (Hoepfner et al., 1964). But going back to earlier analyses, we find that a certain test, Symbol Manipulation, persisted in marking a factor that was called by the name of the test—"symbol manipulation." The test was designed for exploratory studies of reasoning abilities. It is essentially a syllogisms test in symbolic form, containing items like the following, preceded by some relational definitions:

Definitions:

    l = larger than
    s = smaller than
    e = equal to
    nl = not larger than
    ns = not smaller than
    ne = not equal to

Items:

If *X* s *Y* (*X* is smaller than *Y*), then which other statements are true and which are false?

1. *X* e *Y*
2. *X* nl *Y*
3. *X* l *Y*
4. *X* ns *Y*
5. *N* ne *Y*

In the recent analysis referred to, some new tests, listed below, helped to mark factor ESR, as anticipated.

Related Words I gives a pair of words with a rather obvious relation in terms of spelling, then three alternative pairs, with *E* to state which of the three has a relation that is most like that of the given pair.

Given pair: GRAND-RAN   *Alternative pairs:*

        1. country-cot
        2. respite-sit
        3. loving-log

Although no alternative presents exactly the same relation as in the given pair, 2 (respite-sit) comes nearest, in the sense of making a short word from letters in the middle of the given word. In answers 1 and 3, terminal letters are used in the short words.

Similar Pairs presents in each item two pairs of either familiar words or nonsense words, with *E* to say whether the relation represented in the second pair is the same or not the same as that in the first pair; examples are:

1. kire-lire   fora-gora
2. brake-rake   greed-reed
3. moan-noam   toes-seot

The relations are the same in items 1 and 2, not the same in item 3.

In these three tests, the criteria of both identity and consistency were found to work. Also it was found that the criterion of similarity was successfully applied, with judgments of relative approach to identity, where no alternative answer achieves complete identity.

Semantic relations (EMR)   In three analyses, three tests for EMR have quite successfully marked that factor (Nihira et al., 1964; Petersen et al., 1963). Except for format, Matched Verbal Relations is an analogue for Related Words I. It presents a pair of words with an apparent relation between them and four alternative pairs, with *E* to say which of these comes nearest to expressing the same relation. A sample item is:

Given pair: BIRD-SONG   *Alternative pairs:*

                   1. fish-water
                   2. man-letter
answer: 2   3. pianist-piano
                   4. horse-ranch

The reason for choice of answer 2 is that it makes the closest analogy: bird produces song as man produces letter.

Verbal Analogies III was designed as a traditional verbal-analogies test, except that the alternative answers are close together in competition for completion of the analogy in each item. A sample item is:

TRAFFIC : SIGNAL as RIVER : _____?_____

A. bank   *B.* dam   *C.* canal   *D.* sandbags

The flow of traffic is regulated by a signal, as the flow of water is regulated by a dam. Other relations could readily call for one of the other alternatives, but only *B* gives a really tight analogy. For example, another relation might be "confined by," which would give *A* and *D* about equal claim. But a signal also releases traffic as a dam releases a flow of water.

A third successful test is Best Trend Name. In the discussion of factors of *cognition* of relations (see Chapter 4), it was suggested that seeing trends should be an appropriate type of test. For a trend test that would assess evaluation, *E* is asked to say what conception of the trend is best. That one is best which most exactly expresses the relation or the variable within the trend. Best Trend Name attempts to achieve an evaluation task by presenting a series of words that might represent different trends and alternative names descriptive of those trends. For a sample item we may use the problem:

Word series: HORSE—PUSHCART—BICYCLE—AUTOMOBILE
Alternative names: A. speed   *B.* time   *C.* size

The best answer is *B* (time). The four words are not in the best order for either speed or size. As means of transportation the four came historically in about the order given.

It is noteworthy that trend tests worked for factor EMR whereas they were rather poor for CMR and other cognition factors. The reason is fairly obvious. The trend tests for cognitive abilities, where the trends had to be named, became instead tests of NMU, the convergent production of semantic units. In Best Trend Name, the elimination of production was achieved by the fact that trend names are provided.

Evaluation of systems

Symbolic systems (ESS)   This factor is supported by evidence from a single analysis (Hoepfner et al., 1964), in which four tests intended for it succeed in marking it, one rather weakly, and one other test that was not intended for it helps.

Series Relations uses number series as the kind of system to be evaluated. Each item presents a set of three numbers in order. Such a set might be *17, 9, 2. E*'s task is to choose one of three given alternative arithmetical operations that best describes the principle of the series (or near series). The alternatives to go with the illustrative set are:

A. −8   *B.* ÷2   *C.* −7

in which *A* comes closest to describing the principle, starting with the number in italics.

In Way-Out Numbers, *E* is to choose the one of the four given numbers that is farthest numerically from the rest. For example, in the set

31   36   45   47

31 is the farthest from the others. It is difficult to see what systems property is being evaluated in this test and how. It might be an observation by *E* of symmetry versus asym-

metry pertaining to the first two and last two numbers in the set, for often a decision as to which of these two differences is larger can give the answer.

Two tests made use of letter and number series as the systems to be evaluated. Correct Letter Orders announces the principle for a series and then presents a set of five-letter series, E to say whether each one does or does not follow the announced principle. A sample item is:

Rule: Alternate letters in the alphabet (skipping one)

1. M O Q S U W   (correct)
2. P R S U W Y   (incorrect)

The announcement of the principle is to preclude the necessity for E to discover the rule, thus attempting to minimize cognitive variance. Items for Correct Number Series are much the same, for example:

Rule: Alternately add 1, multiply by 3

A. 2 3   9 10 30 31   (correct)
B. 5 5 15 16 49 50   (incorrect)

These two tests, particularly the latter, did not do quite so well as measures of factors ESS. The reason may be that E's task boils down to the checking of particular elements rather than consideration of systems as organized patterns to see whether they conform to descriptions of principles.

There was a minimal loading on ESS for the test Word Changes, which had been designed for factor NSS and was described in connection with that factor in the preceding chapter. E is to say in what order three short words should be placed in going from a starting word (not among the three) to a terminal word (also not among the three) by changing one letter at a time. E has to *produce* an order (system), but the ESS variance for the test suggests that he may approach the problem by trying out one order after another, testing each one for satisfaction of the criterion of the goal idea. The trial-and-error aspect might suggest that there should be some divergent-production variance, but there are only three ways in which the three words can be ordered; the variations would be too easy to make.

Semantic systems (EMS)   A factor qualifying later for cell EMS in the SI model was brought to light by Hertzka et al. (1954). It was then labeled "experiential evaluation," because the judgments required seemed to depend very much upon E's past experiences. The leading test, which continued to be its chief marker, was Unusual Details. This test is based upon the familiar game of "What's wrong with this picture?" A picture is presented in which there are two things wrong, usually inconsistencies, as in Figure 8.3. In Unusual Details, E is to write descriptions of the two things wrong. In a recent version of this test, renamed Unlikely Things, E selects the two things wrong from among four given alternatives, in an answer-sheet format. It is reasonable to take the presented situation as a system or any major part of it and to say that the criterion for evaluation is consistency: consistency with known information or internal consistency.

A second test that has functioned with much less satisfaction is Social Situations. It has done better for EMS with two samples of schizophrenics than it has with normal examinees (de Mille, 1962). Each item presents a kind of dilemma involving social interaction. A sample item presents this situation:

Fig. 8.3 Unusual Details is of the type that asks, "What is wrong with this picture?" In the picture given, two things are incongruous or incompatible: the shining light bulb is not plugged in, and some numbers on the clock are out of order.

You are on a weekend trip with a group of friends. Most of them would prefer to spend the day hunting, but you prefer to go fishing.

You should:

A. Go hunting with them.
B. Tell them to go hunting, while you go fishing.
C. Try to convince them that they would have a better time fishing.
D. Offer to toss a coin to decide whether the whole group goes hunting or fishing.

The situation, including the alternative actions, is a kind of system, a set of people with interrelationship and a solution to go with the set. It may be that the system involved is more behavioral than semantic, in which case the test would be a better one for hypothesized factor EBS.

In the most recent analysis Social Situations was not present, but there were four new tests of which only Word Systems was substantially successful.[1] This test presents for evaluative judgment three alternative arrangements of words in a matrix of order 3×3, with E to say which is the best system in terms of internal consistency and which is worst. A fully consistent system reads:

child	play	toys
youth	study	books
man	work	machines

The two alternative arrangements in the item have one or two interchanges of words. The cognition problem seems to have been controlled in this test. The matrix form did not involve relations as a kind of product, probably because real trends are not very common in the items.

[1] Found in a revised rotation of axes by Ralph Hoepfner for the data in the Nihira analysis (Nihira et al., 1964).

Two tests were developed for EMS with the idea that a sentence is a good example of semantic system. Complete Thoughts is composed of statements half of which are complete sentences and half not, in mixed order, E to say which is which. One of the difficult things in English writing is for the writer to realize when he has a complete sentence and when not. Is this a matter of factor EMS? Judging by the failure of Complete Thoughts to go with the EMS factor, it is not a matter of evaluation of systems. The criterion of evaluation in this test is completeness of a system. Sample items are:

The parrot with his bright feathers.
Light breaks in secret places.

This test went strongly on factor EMI rather than EMS, for reasons that are not obvious. It may be that the partial sentence implies something else that is not present and the complete sentence fulfills in the last part what is implied in the first part. Thus, fulfillment of an implication would be the criterion for evaluation, which would put the test in the EMI list.

The second sentence-system test designed for EMS was Sentensense, which went strongly on factor EMU and helped to determine it, as related under that factor. Inconsistency of two facts (units) apparently turned out to be the major feature of that test. It might be that longer and more involved sentences would work better for EMS.

Evaluation of transformations

In this particular area, evaluation of transformations, it can be reported that there is evidence for two factors, but the evidence for one of them, EMT, is very limited; for EST there is more support.

Symbolic transformations (EST)   Three tests were designed for the hypothesized EST; all three were at least minimally loaded on it, and only those three. The strongest was Jumbled Words, in which E is to judge whether or not the given words can be made just by mixing the letters of another given word. Notice the sample items:

Given word: START   *Possible new words:*

        1. stare   (cannot be made)
        2. stars   (cannot be made)
        3. tarts   (can be made)

Only the letters given can be used, and none may be omitted. The transformation is a rearrangement of letters, and the judgment has to be whether the transformation satisfies the rules.

Decoding is a rather complex test. E is given five rules regarding the coding system, in which the digits 1 to 5 are to be substituted for letters as follows:

1 for all double letters (oo, gg, etc.)
2 for all pairs of vowels (ou, ai, ea, etc.)
3 for all pairs of consonants (sh, bl, pr, etc.)
4 for single vowels
5 for single consonants

Operating under these rules, E is given in each item two words and he is to say which one, if coded under the rules, would be the more readily decoded. A third alternative is "neither." The transformation in this test is that of coding or substitution. The criterion has to do with the interpretability of the coded word.

Typing Errors has to do with the decisions regarding mistyped words; the transformation is in the form of substituted letters. From knowledge of the typewriter keyboard, which is pictured on the test page, what substitution would most likely have occurred? If the given typed word is FHEE, what was most likely intended?

1. thee   *2.* tree   *3.* free

answer: 1

There is much yet to be learned about optimal tests for measuring EST and about the kinds of criteria for evaluation that apply when transformations are concerned. At least a beginning has been made.

Semantic transformations (EMT)   In the only attempt to demonstrate factor EMT, with three tests designed especially for it, such a factor at first failed to appear (Nihira et al., 1964). The test Product Choice was designed by analogy to the test Object Synthesis, which had been successful for factor NMT. The latter called for objects that could be made by combinations of pairs of given objects. Product Choice gave not only a pair of objects but three alternative objects that could be made from them, *E* to say which is the best and which the worst; for example, the item:

Given objects:	*Alternatives:*
lace curtain and wire hanger	*A.* Christmas wrapping
answers: C (best)	*B.* mop
A (worst)	*C.* butterfly net

This test turned out to be only a fair but a univocal measure of factor EMU, the evaluation of semantic units. Apparently, what was evaluated in this test is the end result, not the transformation.

Another failing test for EMT was called Story Plot, which was constructed by analogy to Plot Titles, for which clever responses are scored for factor DMT. For the evaluation measure, three alternative titles are given for a story, *E* to choose the best and the poorest in terms of cleverness and appropriateness. The leading variance for this test proved to be CMU, which must mean that the alternatives presented some problems of precise meanings of words. Difficulty in understanding some of the subtleties involved in clever titles might have been determining as to factor composition.

The third test, Useful Changes, was constructed by analogy to the NMT test Gestalt Transformations. In the latter test, *E* is asked which is the object among five that could be adapted in an unusual way to a use such as starting a fire. The five alternatives include only one object that could very well do the job.

In Useful Changes the three alternative objects could all be used for the purpose, with *E* to say which would serve the purpose best. A sample item is:

Specified task: To slice cheese	*Given objects:*
	A. guitar
answer: A	*B.* plate
	C. paper clip

In the first rotational solution this test went with factor CMU, which did not seem reasonable, for there is nothing difficult about comprehending the alternative words given as answers. In a subsequent rotation, in which room was made for an additional factor and an axis was aimed at this test, it came out with a loading of .55 on a factor that might be EMT. The loading on CMU dropped from .46 to .26. New tests designed for EMT will be needed to confirm that factor and its apparent relation to Useful Changes.

Evaluation of implications

Since common synonyms for *implication* are conclusion, inference, or expected consequence or outcome, these are the kinds of mental events that call for evaluation. Are conclusions sound; are they in all probability correct; do they follow from the given information? There is some evidence for a factor ESI and much evidence for a factor EMI.

Symbolic implications (ESI)   In a recent analysis (Hoepfner et al., 1964), three tests designed for ESI came out together on a factor, but a test designed for ESS was slightly in the lead, of which more later. The three ESI tests included Abbreviations, which asks E to say for what word a given abbreviation best stands. An abbreviation implies a word or words for which it stands. Some abbreviation-word conjunctions are more reasonable or apt than others. For example, the abbreviation CRNT might stand for (1) crescent, (2) coronation, or (3) current. For the person who had not been told the word, answer (3), current, would seem best represented by CRNT. Although the alternative answers are meaningful words, it is their spelling features that determine the fitness of the abbreviation; hence the implication is symbolic rather than semantic.

Symbol Reasoning is composed of letter-and-number expressions involving statements of equality and inequality and deductions therefrom, with E to say whether each deduction is correct or incorrect in terms of the given information. Some sample items are:

Given: $2x > 3y > 2z$, is each of the following true, false, or uncertain?

$x = z$ (false)
$y < x$ (true)
$z = y$ (uncertain)

Letter Problems was fashioned by analogy to Form Reasoning, a good measure of NSI (see Chapter 7). Letters are used as symbolic elements in place of familiar forms, and, of course, E is to evaluate answers instead of producing them. But E is not merely to say whether the answer is true or false; instead he is to say whether the problem in the item is solvable, unsolvable, or solvable by transposing two elements.

Let us turn to the test that headed the list for ESI, Best Letter Set. This test was designed for factor ESS, with the assumption that a set of three or four letters in sequence is a kind of system, for it can represent a principle. E is to say which of three letter sets most resembles a given set, in terms of some principle, for example:

Given set: UVW   *Alternatives:* *1.* JFI
                                   2. KLN
                                   3. DFH

answer: 2   (comes nearest to having three consecutive letters of alphabet)

For the present, the presence of this test on ESI will have to remain a mystery. The best suggestion for now is that this result represents a bit of confounding with another factor.

Canisia (1962) may have caught a trace of factor ESI in her study of mathematical abilities. Two tests that resemble ESI tests came out together, but along with others that do not, in what is probably another case of confounding. The two tests are Conditions I and Statement Translation. The former asks E to judge whether a conclusion is true or false under a given set of conditions. The conclusion is an algebraic type of statement. In Statement Translation, E is to choose the algebraic statement that best represents a given verbal statement of a problem or situation. In both of these tests the act of evaluating implications would seem to be very prominent.

Semantic implications (EMI)   Factor EMI has a double history, one aspect negative and one positive. In Chapter 4 it was related how for some time a factor first interpreted as "sensitivity to problems" was assigned to cell EMI on the basis that "things wrong" that are seen with respect to appliances, institutions, and common objects are implications and that something wrong involves evaluation. It should have been clear, as it is now, that it is not that implications are *evaluated* in such instances; instead, they are cognized. The factor called "sensitivity to problems" is now in its more appropriate place, CMI.

The positive story pertains to a factor previously known as "logical evaluation." From the first analysis in which it was recognized as such (Green et al., 1953) through a number of subsequent studies, tests of a syllogistic nature have marked a factor by that name. This part of the history actually goes back to Thurstone (1938a), who found such a factor with two syllogistic tests prominent on it, but along with quite a number of other types of tests, including Mechanical Movements. The first placement of logical evaluation in the SI model was in the cell EMR, on the belief that the propositions involved in the syllogism state *relationships* and that consistency of relations is the criterion for evaluation.

A recent analysis (Nihira et al., 1964) led to the double shift, of sensitivity to problems to cell CMI and of logical reasoning to cell EMI. More reasonable tests fitting the definition of EMR were found to determine a factor distinct from logical reasoning, as shown earlier in this chapter. And the syllogistic test, Logical Reasoning, went along with new tests designed for factor EMI. It did retain a significant trace of variance from EMR, indicating that its earlier logical placement was not entirely without foundation.

One of the new tests, Sentence Selection, a kind of informal syllogistic test, was quite successful as a measure of EMI. In this test, E is to judge inferences drawn from a single premise, with items of the following type:

Given statement: In the mid-Pacific, on Buna-Buna, the game of ticky-ticky is played out-of-doors.

Alternative conclusions:

A. People in Buna-Buna like to play games.
B. Ticky-ticky is a difficult game to play.
C. There is an island called Buna-Buna.

answer: C   (most fully covered with information in the given statement)

With some stretching, all the alternatives might be regarded as permissible conclusions from the given statement, differing in the degree of likelihood that they can be truthfully deduced from the given statement.

The test Word Extension was another new one designed for EMI, but it was not found to be univocal or strong for that factor. It contains items such as:

Given: A *radio program* always involves

A. an announcer
B. a sponsor
C. sound
D. a commercial

answer: C   (a radio program might occur without any of the others)

This test shares its common-factor variance about equally with EMR, indicating a more general principle, which has sometimes been suggested elsewhere, that it can be difficult to provide the experimental controls that cut sharply between relations and implications. Word Extension might have avoided this complexity by emphasizing cause-and-effect relations rather than risking involvement in a variety of other possible relations.

Summary

Explorations thus far in the operational domain of evaluation leave no doubt about the need for such a category of abilities and functions. The greatest operational difficulty is in differentiating evaluative abilities from corresponding cognitive abilities. This can be done by employing the principle of making the cognitive problems as simple as possible in evaluation tests.

Evaluation tests have often employed forms analogous to those for divergent or convergent production. In the latter, E is to produce answers; in the former, E is given some alternative answers among which he is to choose the best, and sometimes also the worst, in terms of suitability according to certain criteria of goodness.

Evaluative abilities have been found for every kind of product in the SI model and for every kind of content except behavioral, for which there has been no investigation. Most of the figural-evaluation abilities hypothesized by the model still call for investigation. They should be important in connection with the field of geometry.

It has been found that evaluative abilities may be measured by tests that call for either absolute judgment of the yes-no, disjunctive type or relative judgments of the "which-is-best" type. The former probably has the advantage of providing better experimental control of what is measured.

One of the most important remaining general problems is concerned with what kinds of criteria for judgment are usable in tests of evaluation. The more precise criteria of identity, consistency, and similarity work well in some instances; it is not certain whether they can be universally applied among the different products. Tests with looser criteria of various kinds have been variously successful, indicating some breadth of generality with respect to criteria for evaluation. No criteria of an aesthetic or ethical character have been applied. It is possible that they involve new dimensions of evaluative behavior.

Nothing was found to account for the AAF factor called "practical judgment." Tests of it do not go consistently with any of the SI factors, nor do the tests persist in supporting a unity of their own.

9 Categories of operation

In the preceding five chapters we have been concerned mainly with the evidence for the SI model in terms of demonstrated factors of intelligence that it implies. We have seen considerable detail concerning the kinds of tests that represent each factor and give it empirical referents. In this chapter and the next we shall try to bring things together in a more comprehensive look at the theory, and we shall do it by emphasizing the 15 major categories of abilities represented in the model (5 operation, 4 content, and 6 product categories) and the three parameters along which those categories are dispersed.

In the course of things, we shall take closer looks at the 15 category concepts, which were only partially characterized in preceding chapters. We shall try to see what each concept denotes and what its connotations are. We shall find that some similar distinctions have been made in the past in other connections, and we shall see how some of the historically honored concepts can be given new and better-based interpretations, including such concepts as "induction," "deduction," and "meaning." We shall also see that the informational categories in the SI model, treated in the chapter to follow, can serve as a kind of psychologic on the one hand and a kind of psychoepistemology on the other.

The factors of intelligence, the primary mental abilities, as Thurstone called them, first of all, serve a taxonomic purpose, as pointed out in Chapter 2. In terms of the roles of those concepts in the functioning organism, it is preferable to think of them in terms of processes. If there are unique ways of behaving intellectually in which individuals differ from one another, there are also unique ways of functioning. The five operation categories pertain to unique general ways of functioning.

Cognition

Meaning of cognition   Defined in the light of the kinds of tests needed to represent cognition factors, cognition is *awareness, immediate discovery or rediscovery, or recognition of information in various forms; comprehension or understanding.* The various alternative terms in this definition reflect the fact that cognized information is in the form of different kinds of products. Some terms apply better to certain kinds of products, and other terms apply better to other kinds of products.

Cognition and memory   The most general term, *awareness,* emphasizes having active information at the moment or in the present. The long-term possession of information, which is one dictionary meaning of "cognition," is sufficiently broad to cover both cognition and memory. The distinction between cognition and memory has to be in terms of manifest information right now (cognition) versus latent information held over the long term (memory). But what an organism does in the current moment in the way of cognition most certainly depends upon what is in his memory storage. His memory storage is an essential condition or determiner of his cognitions, but this does not make cognition the same thing as memory.

In assessing how well the individual does in the way of cognitive activities, we are indirectly assessing the extent of his memory store. This is easily illustrated in connection with a vocabulary test. A vocabulary test that is designed so as to sample well the whole range of words of a language yields a score that is a good estimate of the number of words whose distinguished meanings are within the possession of the individual. An ordinary vocabulary test approaches this potentiality for assessment. What has just been said regarding vocabulary, which pertains to semantic information, also applies in other areas of content. A test of figural units like the Street Gestalt Completion test indicates something about the person's stock of recognizable visual objects. A test of anagrams samples his stock of known words, as letter patterns. And a test dealing with facial, manual, or postural bodily expressions samples indirectly his store of behavioral units.

Cognition and learning   The other side of the picture is facility for gaining new information. Brunswik (1957), for example, defines cognition as the acquisition of knowledge, and Heidbreder (1945) defines cognition as perception and the attainment of concepts. Whatever the person's store of a certain kind of information, has he not, in addition, a facility or readiness for acquiring new information, a kind of learning-skill constant? And does not status with respect to this learning skill differ from person to person? And do not scores from cognition tests indicate individual differences in this facility?

A score on a cognition test does not tell us how the individual was prepared for receiving it. We do not know whether he earned it by virtue of a memory store of a certain degree of completeness alone or by virtue of a facility for bringing that stored information to bear upon the acquisition of new information. We do not know whether two people who have the same fund of pertinent information in memory storage might still differ in readiness to cognize some new information. Having a large store of information of a certain kind may reflect a facility for gaining new information, a facility that was responsible for the accumulation of that store. And yet, readiness for learning is undeniably dependent upon information already possessed. The acquisition of information is something like a snowballing phenomenon: the more the person has, the more ready he is to acquire more. This implied positive acceleration could not continue indefinitely, of course, for as the upper limit of available information in an area is approached, there should be diminishing returns.

Recognition and discovery   In popular usage, the term *recognition* is applied to knowing the same *particular* on second encounter. In the context of psychology, it more often applies to knowing the member of a class. Some degree of generality is implied.

In the given definition of cognition, the distinction between *recognition* and *immediate discovery* is a very fine one. Let us use an example, illustrated in Figure 9.1. If we present the examinee with the few lines given there and if, after some hesitation, he says "It's a cat," is he recognizing a cat or discovering it among disconnected lines? There is some room for quibbling over terminology here. The distinction is best made in terms of the speed with which the successful cognition comes: if cognition is practically instantaneous, call it "recognition"; if it comes with a slight delay, call it "immediate discovery."

The qualification of "immediate" before "discovery" is intended to exclude productive and evaluative activity. By a process of productive operations, E might come to a conclusion that "It must be a cat, although I do not see it." He would have made an equivalent semantic discovery, but he would not cognize the cat as a visual-figural unit. In the ordinary test of cognitive abilities, the timing or other conditions are made such that there is little chance of gaining score points by bringing in other operations. In a vocabulary test, if it is univocal for factor CMU, the examinee knows a word or he does

Fig. 9.1   What common object is represented? Lines designated to illustrate the "immediate discovery" of a familiar object (cat) from limited figural cues.

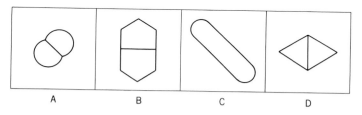

A   B   C   D

Fig. 9.2   Which figure does not belong to the class determined by three other figures? Sample item from a common form of test for the cognition of figural classes, illustrating immediate discovery and recognition of a figural class.

not; he cannot arrive at the correct answer by reasoning or other noncognitive operations. The expression "recognition" applies best to units of information, as subsequent discussion will show.

Immediate discovery can also be illustrated with cases of relations or classes. Given the item shown in Figure 9.2, which asks E to say which figure does not belong, he is to discover the common property of three of the objects not shared by the fourth. When he observes that in three of the figures there are two parts, one a mirror image of the other, he has made a "discovery." He may never have encountered such a class before, although he has seen many bilaterally symmetrical figures, providing him with stored information that no doubt facilitates the discovery. The next time an item comes along in which a class depends upon the same common property, E will know at once what makes the class (recognition) or he will "rediscover" the class idea, seeing the class concept more promptly than he did the first time.

We can also speak of discovery in connection with the seeing of principles, sequences, patterns, or structures; in other words, systems. But the possession of a system is more naturally referred to as comprehension or understanding. The individual knows what comes after what; what interacts with what, and how; and what organizational pattern, principle, or rule applies. When the student follows the instructor's demonstration of the solution to a mathematical problem so that he can reproduce the solution, he has cognized the system. When he follows the instructor's factoring of an algebraic expression, he is understanding or cognizing a transformation. When the instructor suddenly stops and asks the class "What is the natural next step?" and the student sees what it has to be, he has cognized an implication.

With the overlapping of the terms used in the formal definition, we have some redundancy, but the use of all of them in the definition helps to communicate the connotations of the operation of cognition. Its denotation is best expressed by saying that to cognize is to be aware of some product of information. A formal treatment of the concept of "information" will be postponed to the next chapter. With the several kinds of information mentioned (kinds of content and products) and the numerous examples of test items that represent particulars, it has been assumed that enough has been communicated regarding information for current purposes.

Induction and the structure of intellect   The concept of "induction" has never found a stable place in psychology, nor has it been empirically defined. Most definitions or explanations say something about "going from the particular to the general," but when it comes to pointing to any particular event that epitomizes induction, there is likely to be difficulty. The trouble, again, is that there is no constant referent for the concept because it has been used to cover a variety of things, which can now be delineated.

Kinds of induction   "Induction" has always implied abstraction, which means going beyond the immediately given and the particular event. In a previous publication, the writer (Guilford, 1961) proposed that we recognize four kinds of induction. He arbitrarily adopted units of information as the "immediately given" and regarded what the organism makes from them in terms of classes, relations, systems, and implications as being the results of induction. They are the kinds of information to be had by "going beyond" the given. We would then have the kinds of induction called classificatory, relational, systemic, and implicational.

Once such products are derived, they are *transposable*. That is, a class idea applies not only to certain members that give rise to the class idea but also to other members that share the pertinent class properties with them. This extension is the generalizing aspect of induction. A relation that is seen to exist between a cat and a mouse can be extended to pursuer and pursued for predatory purposes in any other such pair of units. The system that applies to the organization of a certain set of units and relations can also be applied to another set of units and relations.

But further thought suggests that a transformation is also transposable, and, in a sense, this is also true of units. Every conception, and every conception is a generalized product of information held in memory storage with some degree of permanence, is built up on the basis of a succession of particular occurrences of similar nature. Every experienced product has general as well as specific aspects, the former aspect being transferable and having transfer effects and the latter not.

The concrete and the abstract   But there is another interpretation of the "immediately given," which has some vogue. This meaning of the expression emphasizes the contrast between the concrete and the abstract. In SI terminology, the concrete can be defined as figural information, and other kinds, particularly symbolic and semantic, can be considered abstract. In a sense it is true that figural information is basic and that other varieties of information are built upon it as a base, to form a complex superstructure of conceptions. But it should be remembered that there are figural conceptions as well as other kinds, in the form of figural products. Other kinds have the advantage of being more generalizable, for they can be freed from the restrictions imposed by the nature of stimulation.

Still another kind of distinction between concrete and abstract information is closer to popular views. It regards as concrete those informational products tied to figural products that can be seen or heard or touched, other products being abstract, such as the concepts of "truth," "justice," and "beauty." Such a distinction between concrete and abstract may be useful in certain practical situations, but it is of doubtful scientific significance.

The upshot of this discussion is that with the more elaborate and systematic conceptions provided by the SI theory, there appears to be little further need for the concept of "induction." It can be replaced with concepts that are more precise and richer in meaning and have ties to empirical referents.

Inductive logic   Before leaving the subject of induction, however, it is of interest to note modern efforts that have been made to develop what is called an "inductive logic." Carnap (1951) has been a leader in this movement. It should be said at the outset that psychology and logic are very different disciplines, with very different goals and methods. As a science, psychology is concerned with observations of how products of information come about and develop toward stability and how they are utilized, with the objective of description of these processes. The aim of logic, on the other hand, is to develop a set of arbitrary rules by which knowledge can be tested. The subtle distinction between information and knowledge will be explained later, when additional discussion of psychology and logic will be given.

Traditional (deductive) logic provides rules whereby the truth or falsity of propositions can be decided. There are only two truth "values," true and false. Inductive logic recognizes gradations of truth values, on a scale of probability.[1] One example of an inductive logic that is applied by scientists is mathematical statistics, which is seen in use in the testing of statistical hypotheses, according to rules developed by R. A. Fisher and others. Alternative rules derived from the Bayes theorem have more recently been gaining some favor. The goal in an inductive logic is to be able to decide with some degree of confidence C how well certain evidence E supports some hypothesis H. This statement of the goal implies the Baysian approach more than it does the Fisher approach.

Levels of cognition   Some attention has been given to the question of how *thoroughly* items of information are known; particularly is this true of semantic units, in connection with vocabulary tests. It had often been noted that on vocabulary tests there is much less decline with advancing age beyond middle life and less deficit on the part of pathological individuals, as compared with tests of "reasoning" or learning. Some doubts have been raised about the use of a differential score, such as the Shipley-Hartford measure for the assessment of intellectual deterioration, leading to a number of studies.[2] The doubts have pertained to the awareness that if the standards for accepting responses to vocabulary items were low, this might give an unwarranted advantage to the elderly and the pathological, and that if standards were raised, more decline would be apparent in vocabulary tests.

Differential scoring of vocabulary tests   Feifel (1949) was one of the first to attack this problem. He recognized several levels of response to vocabulary items, given here as adapted by Thomas (1964):

Synonym (showing conceptualization of meaningful classification)
Usage (showing knowledge of function or application)

[1] If logic is defined in a way that tolerates only two truth values, of course, then the expression "inductive logic" is a misnomer (see Werkmeister, 1948).
[2] Further discussion of deterioration scores will be found in Chapter 18.

Description (giving details and characterizations)
Example (relating to other members of the same class)
Insufficient (indicating some meaning without enough elaboration for certainty of any knowledge)
Failure (provides no information)

Comparing normals and abnormals with respect to different levels of response given to words, Feifel found that differences were not very great, but there was some tendency for normals to give more synonym responses and for younger subjects to give more synonym responses than older subjects. When Moran (1953) matched normals and schizophrenics with respect to age and education, however, he found no differences in frequencies of types of responses given.

In another study, dealing with relations to age, Thomas (1964) was concerned with elderly and senile subjects. Two methods of scoring vocabulary tests were used: qualitative and quantitative, arbitrarily named. The qualitative scoring used differential weights, empirically derived, for the different levels of responses listed above. The quantitative method gave points of 2, 1, and 0: 2 for a synonym, description, or classification; 1 for an example, use, or pointing; and 0 for failure. Subdividing his sample of patients into a highly deteriorated group (call it D) and a group of elderly with perhaps some deterioration (call it E), Thomas found that the D group gave significantly more insufficient responses and the E group gave significantly more synonym and description responses. The qualitative score correlated .83 with a criterion of general mental level, and the quantitative score correlated .77: not a great difference, but it was significant. The correlations of the two scores with the quantitative score on a different vocabulary test differed in the opposite direction, however: .81 for the quantitative score and .66 for the qualitative score. Appropriately, Thomas took this to mean that the two scores measure something psychologically different. That something different must mean some difference in factorial content of the score variables.

Scoring and factor content   Change in factorial content for vocabulary scores is suggested by results of other investigators. C. Graham (1963) used three scores for each of two vocabulary tests, the one from the WISC and the other the Mill Hill Vocabulary Scale. One score was differential, weighting higher-quality responses 2 and lower-quality responses 1; one was called "lenient," weighting all responses alike; and one was called "strict," counting only high-quality responses. The criteria with which these three scores were correlated included the Stanford-Binet vocabulary, the Watts Vocabulary, the Otis Quick-Scoring test, and the Raven Progressive Matrices test. The averages of correlations of scores from the WISC Vocabulary test with these four criteria were .77 for the differential scoring, .60 for the lenient scoring, and .43 for the strict scoring. For the scores from the Mill Hill Vocabulary Scale, the correlations were .80 for differential scoring and .62 for the lenient scoring. Without knowing that the reliabilities of the scores were very similar, we cannot say for sure, but there is some implication of change of factorial content.

A more indicative finding was reported by Nyssen and Crahay (1960). They gave a vocabulary test in two forms, one presenting a word to be defined (definition score) and the other presenting a definition with E to supply the word defined (evocation score). Subjects were tested in every decade of life through the eighties. For the definition score, decline was noticeable beginning at forty but was not very marked. For the evocation score, decline was noticeable after thirty, with a faster decline after forty than for the definition score. From the preceding chapters, we know that the definition score should measure factor CMU and that the evocation score should measure factor NMU, perhaps as strongly as CMU, perhaps more strongly. The two primary abilities evidently have different decline curves.

Variation of kinds of understanding and factors   Moran (1953) gave even more extensive evidence of change of factor content of scores as one asks E to do different things with words. Moran was interested in evidence of word knowledge as one asks for different things to be done with words, to indicate breadth of understanding, precision of understanding, ability to form concepts, conceptual level of concepts, and abilities to communicate and to reason with words. The later qualifications of "understanding" in this list obviously get away from CMU and into the dimensions of other semantic factors. Moran hypothesized that schizophrenics would show more or less defect as compared with normals, depending upon the level or kind of understanding that is being measured. He designed tests to assess the different aspects of word knowledge, as he thought, but each variation can be interpreted as bringing in another (hypothetical) factor:

Recall Synonym (E gives synonyms for each word; factor DMR)
Recognition Synonym (NMR)
Sentence Construction (DMS or NMS)
Similarities (E puts words in classes; NMC)
Analogies (CMR; NMR)
Word Associations (Responses weighted for meaningfulness; DMT in reverse)

As one should expect from the suspected factorial emphasis in each test, there was room for differences between schizophrenics and normals (matched for vocabulary, age, and education) to vary from one test to another. If the guesses concerning emphasized factors given above are correct, from the results one may conclude that the paranoid schizophrenics were not different from normals in factors DMR and NMR; normals excelled in measures of DMS, NMC, and the Analogies test (for a two-factor test a unique factorial conclusion cannot be made); and if a high score on Moran's Word Associations meant low originality (DMT), the schizophrenics were more original! On the latter point, one has to consider relevance of the responses before such a decision can be made.

Vocabulary tests and CMU   In conclusion on this point about levels of cognition, it appears that "level," at least as applied to cognition of word meanings, is not purely a quantitative matter. Word meanings are semantic units, and it seems that anything beyond acquaintance with a unit tends to involve other products, such as classes and relations. Mention was made in Chapter 4 to the effect that two tests emphasizing precision of meaning of words went along with ordinary vocabulary tests that were in both definition (completion) and multiple-choice form. The precision tests were not highly loaded on factor CMU, in fact, not so highly loaded as regular vocabulary tests. No allowances had been made for possible differences in reliability, however. From all these indications, if one wants a univocal measure of CMU, it would appear to be acceptable practice to score a vocabulary test in any way that indicates a high probability of E's acquaintance with a word meaning, acquaintance to the extent that it is a member of his stock of semantic units in memory storage. If one wants evidence of how functional this information is in different ways, he is interested in knowing about abilities other than CMU. Calls for additional information about uses of word knowledge, in testing, extends measurement to other semantic factors, sometimes one, sometimes another.

Cognitive dispositions   Before leaving the connotative aspects of cognition, we should not overlook a line of investigation that has been directed to some features of cognition that have been emphasized by Riley W. Gardner and others. These features have been variously referred to as "cognitive strategies," "cognitive styles," and "response sets." Until more is known about their nature as a group of characteristics, it is best to put them under the more general heading of "cognitive dispositions," for they do pertain to individual differences and have the character of personal traits.

Among the categories of personality traits (Guilford, 1959a), they probably come closest to fitting the concept of attitudes; thus they might be called "cognitive attitudes." As such, they may represent another fruitful approach to the investigation of cognition, in addition to the aptitude approach, which is of primary interest in this volume. They can hardly justify the label *strategies,* because that term implies something in the way of plans of operation, as in solving problems.

A list of cognitive attitudes   Gardner and Long (1960) provide a summary list of the cognitive-attitude traits that are said to have been found by factor analysis. There is space here only to mention them by name and to characterize each one very briefly:

Selectivity of attention pertains to control of sensory input, and in this sense is a pre-cognition affair or condition. But apparently it is more than what was formerly known as "concentration of attention," or the set to narrow attention, for those authors speak of it as being a more general trait than, and inclusive of, Witkin's "field-articulation principle."

Extensiveness of scanning pertains to the breadth of search, so to speak, within the perceptual field. But the authors say that it applies to search for ideas as well as for sensory input. One scanning test mentioned is in the form of a recording of eye movements of a subject while looking at figures that he is comparing for size (Gardner & Long, 1962).

Breadth of equivalence range has to do with extensiveness of category concepts, for persons, objects, and events. Some individuals are said to have characteristically narrow ranges, and others have broad ranges; the former evidently restrict connotative meanings, while the latter freely extend them.

Tolerance of unrealistic experience shows itself in response to the Rorschach inkblots. Tolerant subjects are more comfortable with the inkblots, less dissatisfied with the task, and less critical (G. S. Klein, R. W. Gardner, & H. J. Schlesinger, 1962). Less tolerant subjects allow themselves little freedom in responding to the blots. There are other signs, found in other contexts.

Leveling-sharpening as a concept is reminiscent of the gestalt psychologists' contrasting phenomena that occur in memories for figures and other information. It applies both to perception and to memory. Sharpeners are inclined to learn and remember more. Levelers are likely to confuse information in general (Gardner & Long, 1960). In this description we can read a trait variable representing a general need for sharp discriminations of information versus a tolerance for blurred contours.

Cognitive attitudes and aptitudes   It is quite obvious that there is nothing like a correspondence between these factors of cognitive attitude and the factors of intellectual abilities in the area of cognition. They come from very different kinds of evidence, representing different aspects of cognitive processes. Cognitive operations in daily life may well reflect the joint effects from both sources.

It is not known how such nonaptitude traits may affect performance on aptitude tests. In their studies of risk-taking behavior, Kogan and Wallach (1964), finding correlations between some of their risk-taking scores and intelligence-test scores, conclude that risk-taking attitudes may have much to do with scores on aptitude tests, particularly tests of the multiple-choice type. The nature of the particular test should determine whether risk taking has any appreciable effect upon individual differences in scores.

Memory

Definition of memory   The SI definition of the memory operation is that *it is retention or storage, with some degree of availability, of information in the same form in which it was committed to storage and in connection with the same cues with which it was learned.* Traditionally, psychology textbooks have treated under the subject of memory the topics of memorizing, even learning in general, also evidences of retention in the form of recall and recognition. More often in recent years, the concept has been narrowed to the retention phase, a change that the analogy to computer memory has perhaps helped to bring about.

"Availability" is a concept pertaining to retention that is growing in recognition and in use. Scattered information, but particularly the observations of Penfield (1958) to the effect that "forgotten" experiences can be revived vividly by direct electrical stimulation of the cortex of the brain, have led to the inference that no memory trace is ever completely lost in connection with a living, intact brain. Such memory traces as Penfield thus revives are generally regarded as unavailable. We may say that memory traces are available when normal empirical evidence can be found for the continued existence of the information these traces have held. Direct electrical stimulation of the brain would not be considered "normal." There are some writers, such as Asch (1964), who limit the definition of *availability* operationally to *free recall* of the information, with the application of appropriate cues; but such a restriction is arbitrary. This much restriction would lead to conclusions that certain unavailable traces are having their effects upon recognition and upon transfer effects (positive or negative) when there is, in fact, this kind of normal empirical evidence for their existence.

In the stated definition, the expression "retention . . . in the same form in which it was committed to storage" does not rule out the possibility of alterations in memory traces, such as have been claimed by gestalt psychologists. "The same form" here means in the same kind of content and the same kind of product. Within those limits there is room for some changes, but it is difficult by experimental procedures to determine whether such changes as have been reported come during the latent retention period or at the moment of revival, when revised and new products may come about. The deeper significance of the expression "the same form" is that things are stored much as they are cognized, and this means that a full set of 24 kinds of memory should parallel the 24 kinds of cognition.

The expression "in connection with the same cues with which it was learned" is needed to distinguish memory from convergent and divergent production, particularly convergent production. If an examinee memorizes a complete syllogism, with its premises and conclusion and if later he is given the premises to which he responds by giving the same conclusion, merely because he has previously memorized it, he is only showing that he has retained a memory trace and that it is available in response to the appropriate cue. But if he is given two other premises, two propositions that he has never seen or heard before in conjunction, then if he gives the correct conclusion, he is engaging in convergent production. The cue statements are new for that particular item of information that he generates from his memory storage. Because the cue is new, there is *transfer recall.* Transfer recall is a more obvious feature of divergent production, which is accordingly more easily discriminated from memory.

Relation of memory to cognition   There is memory if, and only if, there has been cognition. Cognition need not have been highly conscious. The issue of cognition or learning without awareness will be treated at greater length in Chapter 11. Here we need to consider the phenomenon of incidental learning, for this question has been given some attention in connection with memory abilities in a factor analysis by Christal (1958), who expected to find a factor of incidental memory but did not. The matter is perhaps worth some further consideration, but a good prediction at present is that the same factors would be found for incidental memory as for intentional memory. There would probably be some motivational aspects to blur the picture, since whether memory is incidental or more than that depends upon attention, and attention depends upon motivation. This is not to say that retention is no better with intentional than with incidental memory. It merely means that, given the same level of attention or vigilance, at either high levels or low levels, the same memory abilities and functions should apply.

Short- and long-term memory   Are different memory abilities or functions involved in immediate or short-term memory than in long-term memory? Much experimental effort is directed at this time to questions of memory immediately following stimulation versus memory with some appreciable duration. There is a question as to whether there is a short-term storage mechanism separate from a long-term storage mechanism. The long-standing debate over whether forgetting over the long term is due to decay of traces or to interferences has been recently focused upon immediate memory. The two durations of storage are also being compared with respect to other features. There is no doubt about short-term–memory phenomena, and a study of them may throw much light on how some cognized products become firmly fixed in long-term retention and why others do not. Some writers feel the need, also, of an intermediate-term memory, during which perseverative activities seem to have some bearing on more permanent fixation of traces.

We shall return to these questions and others on memory in Chapter 13, where suggestions will be offered as to how SI concepts might be of some service. An important consideration here concerns the relation of duration term to memory factors. Are different abilities involved in short-term memory and long-term memory, not to mention a possible intermediate-term memory? Almost all the memory testing for factor analysis has involved very short long-term memory, that is, a matter of a few minutes. The typical test asks E to study the information to be memorized for a couple of minutes; he is then to turn the page and take some kind of retention test on what he has just studied. One might say that the test is of E's intermediate-term memory.

There would have to be some one-way relationships between longer and shorter retentions, at least. For there cannot be good long-term retention unless there has been good intermediate-term retention, and there cannot be good intermediate-term retention unless there has been good immediate retention. There could, of course, be good immediate retention without good intermediate- or long-term retention, and good intermediate retention without good long-term retention.

Imagery   Most attention to the subject of imagery went out the window when behaviorism came in the door, but no amount of ignoring or denial could make it vanish. There are even voices calling for its return (Holt, 1964). Images are memory phenomena, but where do they fit into SI theory? This is an easy question to answer. To the extent that images are revivals of perceived experiences, they are in the category of figural information.

This is not to say that all figural memory is imagery. The revival of figural information may or may not carry with it observable images. Evidence of retention of certain figural products gives us inferential knowledge that something figural in nature has been retained. We might say that where the individual cannot report images but still functions as if certain figural information were in his memory storage, he has imageless figural information, by analogy to the Würzburgers' imageless thoughts. The problems of imagery are still with us, but recognizing their figural character may be of some help.

What is remembered?   Ask almost any of today's psychology students what it is that we retain when we remember, and if he has read his textbook well and if he does not give a neurological answer, he will probably say "associations." Twenty years ago he would have said "stimulus-response connections." Both answers reflect the overwhelmingly strong indoctrination with associationism, which has been with us in one form or another for centuries. Gestalt voices on this subject cried in the wilderness. Today, other voices are taking up the protest, and they are being heard more effectively. Some of the recent voices have been those of Whorf (1956), Snygg (1959), Asch and Ebenholtz (1962), and Rock and Ceraso (1964).

Memory for products   As this writer has asserted a number of times in recent years, the things remembered are products of information, and they come in the six kinds of the SI model. This is not to say that the principle of association is entirely wrong; it means that the time-honored and very useful concept that has done yeoman's service for psychology for so long must be superseded by new and more generally serviceable concepts. All the phenomena that were legitimately accounted for by means of the association principle can be accounted for more fruitfully by the product concepts. Among them are implications and relations, plus a great many more phenomena for which the association principle accounted very poorly, if at all. Some of the same voices that have objected most strongly to associationism have also proposed something like products as substitute principles: the "schema" of Frederick C. Bartlett (1932), the thought structures of O. Selz (1924; 1927) and of Mandler (1962), and the "chunks" of E. B. Hunt (1963), not to mention the concepts of Piaget, which are productlike mental structures. The ways in which products play their roles in mental functioning will receive much attention in the next and later chapters.

Divergent production

In Chapter 6, some general discussion was given concerning the general role of divergent-production functions in connection with creative thinking. Here we are more concerned with the psychological nature of those functions. A formal definition of "divergent production" reads: *generation of information from given information, where the emphasis is upon variety and quantity of output from the same source; likely to involve transfer.* This definition arose directly from consideration of the kinds of tests needed to measure the various divergent-production abilities. We need to give it more general interpretation and to fit divergent production into the context of psychological theory.

Divergent production and recall   The earlier treatment of divergent production (Chapter 6) placed it in the category of the operation of retrieval of information from memory storage, or what has been more familiarly known in psychological terminology as "recall." DP tests present the examinee with the need to present, in quantity, lists of items of information falling within prescribed categories. The items may be in the form of any of the six products of information. The cue for recall is therefore some kind of class designation, which sets the limits within which search for the needed information is made and which also directs the search in favorable directions. The search in memory storage for information is sometimes likened to scanning operations, as in radar, television, or computers (Gomulicki, 1963; Yntema and Trask, 1963). Whether or not such analogies will hold up as we gain more psychological knowledge about recall as a process remains to be seen. The subject of recall will be treated at much greater length in Chapter 13.

At this point, it is well to raise the question as to whether in divergent production something more than recall is involved. In the production of units of information, as in response to the instruction "Name things that are soft and white," the class specified is a conjunction of things soft and things white, and once retrieval has been achieved, nothing more appears to be needed. The same is true with regard to producing what Spearman called correlates, something satisfying a given relation and a given unit. But when it comes to producing systems, as in writing sentences, the construct or system that is the complete sentence is more likely never to have existed before, as such. In that event, the constituent ideas and symbolic parts constitute the stored information that is retrieved, but the particular combination produced is new. In such instances, some organizing activity has occurred in addition to retrieval. This is not to say that a system, once formed, cannot be put in memory storage for future recall or that there are no previously formed systems, any one of which could be the object of recall.

Transfer recall and the search model   It may be that the concept of transfer will account for this kind of organizing activity. Things are recalled in connection with cues with which they were not experienced before. The recall is forced by the circumstances of the demands of the task. Duncker's concept (1945) of a "search model" applies very well in this connection. The task, as comprehended or cognized, is a system, pattern, or model that guides the search or scanning activity. Such a model has the cue value or potency to seek out and to activate the needed items of information in memory storage. In this manner organisms are freed from the restrictions of recalling information only in response to cues with which it was learned.

Convergent production

Comparisons of convergent and divergent production   Convergent production shares some characteristics with divergent production, but it offers much more in the way of contrasts, as the two terms imply. Both involve the generation of information from given information, and the generated information draws very heavily upon the memory storage. This does not exclude the use of new input information that may be handy or that may have been sought by the individual. Both terms involve transfer recall of information, in response to cues provided by the given information, which, with sufficient comprehension, provides search models. The information produced is more or less fitting in the light of the search model.

There are characteristic differences between divergent and convergent production with respect to the problem situation that ordinarily instigates the two kinds of activity. In the former case, the problem itself may be loose and broad in its requirements for solutions; or the problem, if properly structured, may call for a unique solution, but the individual may have an incomplete grasp of it; or he may comprehend the problem fully, but he is unable to find the unique answer immediately, resorting to trial-and-error behavior, which means divergent production alternated with evaluation. In convergent production, the problem can be rigorously structured and is so structured, and an answer is forthcoming without much hesitation. In the former case, restrictions are few; in the latter they are many. In the former, the search is broad; in the latter it is narrow. In the former, output is in quantity; in the latter it is limited. In the former, criteria for success are vague and somewhat lax and may, indeed, stress variety and quantity; in the latter, criteria are sharper, more rigorous, and demanding.

In everyday life, of course, the middle ground between these two kinds of functioning is not excluded, and the individual very frequently engages in much divergent production on the way to a convergent answer, as when he puzzles over a mathematical problem and tries one solution after another. The differences mentioned reflect the contrasts between the kinds of test that have worked best for the two kinds of production abilities and have discriminated between them.

Deduction and convergent production   We saw that the operational category of cognition is the proper place for what has been called induction. Convergent production is the proper place for deduction, if we adopt the definition of this term given by logic, where it means drawing necessary conclusions. The specification of "necessary" rules out divergent production. Because in daily life we are very rarely drawing *necessary* conclusions but are perpetually drawing conclusions nevertheless, the category of divergent production opens up possibilities for describing the typical event of going from information to information. We might say that in divergent production we are generating the logical *possibilities* from given information, whereas in convergent production we are generating logical *necessities*.

Of the six kinds of CP abilities dealing with kinds of products, the most obvious kind justifying the definition of deduction is that of implications, for conclusions are implications. The writer has argued for the application of the label "deduction" also to the convergent production of correlates, as occurs in reasoning by analogy, where rigorous conclusions are also reached (Guilford, 1961). It is doubtful whether the concept applies beyond these two kinds of products, but with the addition of the four other kinds of CP abilities and functions, we have a much enlarged approach to the description of rigorous thinking. Taken together, the CP abilities and functions provide a richer and more precise language for describing logical thought processes than has been possible with the single concept of deduction.

Thinking interests and attitudes

Factors of interest in thinking   From a review of the properties of DP and CP functioning, one might expect to find that there would be some personal attributes of nonaptitude types to go with them, that some individuals might be inclined to favor one type of thinking and some inclined to favor the other. Such a general hypothesis was investigated by the writer and his associates (Guilford et al., 1961). It had been previously found by factor analysis of experimental inventory-variable scores that certain dimensions of interest connected with thinking could be differentiated. According to factor-analytic results, there is an interest in the meditative, reflective type of thinking; an interest in rigorous or logical types of thinking; and an interest in the autistic, wish-fulfilling type of thinking (Guilford, 1959a).

The new analysis found evidence for three additional interest factors pertaining to types of thinking. One of these new factors could be called interest in divergent thinking, marked by a score variable called Adaptive Divergent Thinking, containing items of this type: "You like to examine a new idea from all possible angles"; and "When members of your group are looking for novel ideas, they would do well to come to you." It was marked also by a variable called Transitional Thinking, which was based on items like "You like conversation that easily flits from one thing to another" and "Some people seem to think you are a scatterbrain."

Another new factor could be called interest in convergent thinking, with one score variable on it called Goal-Directed Thinking, which involved items like "When you have a problem to solve, you like to have a clearly defined goal toward which to work"; and "You like to choose one method of solution to a problem and follow it through." Another marker variable was Decisiveness—in Others, with items like "It is hard for you to sympathize with a person who is always doubting and unsure about things" and "A strong person will be able to make up his mind even on the most difficult questions." A third variable was Decisiveness—Personal, with items like "When shopping for some article, you usually know just what you want, find it, and buy it"; and "You have no difficulty making up your mind regarding your own affairs."

The third new thinking-interest factor, although not immediately relevant, is noteworthy: tolerance for ambiguity. Two of its related score variables were Black-White Thinking and Need for Definiteness, which are fairly well described by their titles.

Relations between interest and aptitude factors   In an extension of the study of thinking-interest factors (Merrifield et al., 1961), relations between some measures of those factors and measures of aptitude-factor scores were obtained for a young adult population in military service. Scores were available for four fluency factors (DSU, DMU, DMR, and DMS) and two flexibility factors (DFT and DMT), one of the latter being known also as originality. While these six DP factors were represented in this study, there were only two CP factors, NMR and NMT. The latter, unfortunately, because it involves flexibility, has tests that look more like DP variables.

The correlations between the interest-inventory factors on the one hand and the aptitude-factor scores on the other were all very low, almost all below .3, but because of the very large samples, with Ns over 200, quite a number of the correlations were significantly different from zero. Briefly, with results for the interest-factor scores only, the following significant correlations were found:

Tolerance of ambiguity with DMR	.15
Meditative thinking with DMS	.21
Logical thinking with DMU	.11
Meditative thinking with DMT	.25
Tolerance of ambiguity with DMT	.12
Interest in convergent thinking with NMR	.18
Interest in convergent thinking with NMT	−.25

The score for interest in divergent thinking did not correlate significantly with any of the DP-factor scores used in the study, although some of the other thinking-interest–factor scores did correlate with the DP scores in reasonable ways, with the exception of the correlation of the score for logical thinking with DMU. The score for interest in convergent thinking correlated positively with the score for NMR but negatively with the score for NMT. The latter result could be explained on the basis already mentioned: the tests for NMT look more like DP tests.

Enough has been shown of the results from thinking-interest scores and thinking-aptitude scores to indicate that there is very little in common between them and that contrasts between divergent- and convergent-production abilities cannot be accounted for in terms of contrasting interests or attitudes. Even making allowance for the fact that scores from personality inventories never seem to achieve even moderate correlations with aptitude tests and that this may be largely attributable to the difference in medium of assessment, the correlations do not appear promising of much in common.

Evaluation

To repeat a definition given in Chapter 8, evaluation is *a process of comparing a product of information with known information according to logical criteria, reaching a decision concerning criterion satisfaction.* Sometimes the comparison is between two or more given products of the same kind, and sometimes it is with some goal idea that is given or implied. In the three major analyses of evaluative abilities thus far, there was much exploratory effort, hence no very systematic application of kinds of comparisons or coverage of kinds of criteria. It is much more feasible now to initiate such systematic studies.

In what follows there will be a survey of the different kinds of criteria for judgment involved in tests for evaluative abilities, to give an impression of the range of relevant criteria and to yield some assessment of their relative importance. There will also be a major section that attempts to put evaluation as an operation in an appropriate larger context in behavior.

Varieties of criteria   A consideration of the various tests mentioned in Chapter 8 suggests the kinds of criteria involved with different factors and different tests for the same factor. We shall take each known factor in turn, putting the criterion in the form of a question.

EFU   Is this figure identical with that one?
ESU   Is this letter set, number set, or name identical with that one?
       Does this word belong in the specified class (e.g., does it contain the letter U)?
EMU   Which word best fits the class specifications (attributes given)?
       Does this word belong in the class specified by name?
       Does this pair of words belong to the prescribed class (e.g., opposites)?
       Which sentences contain inconsistent ideas?
       Which function or use is best fulfilled by a combination of two objects?
ESC   Which is the best class for a given number (where four classes are ranked for value)?
       Which word gives the poorest rhyme?
       Which word best fits a class formed by a set of three given words?
EMC   Which class name best fits the class of a set of four meaningful words?
       Which class name fits a single word best?
       Which pairing among three words makes the best class?
ESR   Which relations between letter symbols are consistent with two stated relations?
       Which pair of words has a spelling relation most nearly similar to that of a given pair?
       Do two pairs of words or letter sets have the same relation?
EMR   Which pair of objects has most nearly the same relation as the given pair?
       Which word best completes an analogy, where all alternatives are related to the third word?
       Which name best describes the trend among four words (a trend repeats a relation)?
ESS   Which rule best applies to a given number series?
       Which number in the set is farthest numerically from the rest?
       Do letter orders follow stated rules?
EMS   What objects in a situation are inconsistent with others?
       What is the best solution, among given alternatives, to a problem in a social situation?
       Which matrix of words presents them in the most logical arrangement?
EST   Which word is merely a rearrangement of letters in a given word?
       Which coded word can be most readily decoded?
       Which word was most probably intended by this wrongly typed word?

EMT   Which object could be best adapted for some unusual purpose?
ESI   Which word is most probably intended by the given abbreviation?
       Which symbolic statements are consistent with an inequality statement, and which cannot be decided?
       Which symbolic problems can and cannot be solved?
EMI   Which conclusion follows from the given premises?
       Which item of information is most fully implied by a given statement?
       What object or condition is always found in connection with a given object?

Among the instances in which a test featuring a certain kind of criterion failed to measure its intended factor or did so minimally are the following:

ESU   Is this word spelled correctly?   (came out as a CSU test)
       Is this syllable more familiar (appears more frequently) than that one?
EMU   Which word is closest in meaning to that one?   (came out on CMU)
ESC   Which pair of numbers makes the best class?   (came out on CSC)
EMS   Is this a complete sentence?   (came out on EMI)
       Are the two ideas in this sentence consistent with one another?   (came out on EMU)

To summarize all this information, we may say that the criteria that were used most often and were most successful were identity, similarity, satisfaction of class membership, and consistency. Although there were three instances of failure for tests constructed with use of the criteria of identity and consistency, it was probably not the fault of the criterion selected in each of those cases. Other criteria did not happen to be used more than once or twice, but in the great majority of the cases their tests were successful, thus indicating that quite a variety of criteria can be used in evaluation tests. We are not sure that the most popular ones thus far can be applied successfully for all products. It can be noted that the criterion of identity worked for EFU and ESU but not for EMU. Class membership worked as a criterion for both ESU and EMU but has not been tried as yet for EFU. There are numerous unanswered questions of this kind that remain to be investigated.

Evaluation and decision making   The definition of evaluation includes the term *decision*. In recent years considerable attention has been given to the subject of decision making, decision theory, game theory, and related topics. Is there any connection between evaluation as an operation and what commonly goes under the heading of decision making in psychology?

There seems to be a connection, but it does not go very far. It is safe to say that some of the strongest and most univocal tests of evaluative abilities have involved quite simple decisions of the yes-no type. Not a great deal of uncertainty is involved, and there is no risk taking in the sense that the individual makes some payment for his wrong decisions, except loss of score points. It is probable that when E is wrong on simple-decision items, he has some feeling of assurance that he is right, thus little feeling of risk.

It is probable that when decisions become more difficult, the tests are relatively poorer for measurement of evaluation abilities, especially when difficulty involves complexity. In the latter case, especially, E's behavior is more like the activity of problem solving, with a number of different factors entering the picture. The phenomenon of problem solving is treated in Chapter 14.

Evaluation and values   The operation under discussion suggests values. Leaving to the philosophers the knotty problems regarding values as such, psychology can deal with values only in terms of behavior that occurs where values are concerned. The involvement of values is inferred where there is advancing versus retreating or repelling behavior, where there are choices and rejections, and where there are expressions of preferences. None of this behavior seems to be in the same category with that observed in examinees who are taking tests of evaluative abilities. Even though there are multiple-choice items, one would not attribute choices of answers as indicating liking or disliking, as would be the case when a man purchases one necktie and not others. Such choices and preferences are personal, whereas the choices in evaluation tests are keyed for right answers to which there would be close to unanimous agreement among competent persons.

There appears to be no overlap between evaluative functions of the kind represented in the SI model and value behavior of the personal-preference type. Even judgments of moral or aesthetic kinds appear to be excluded. But to the extent that there can be conventional consensus, there might be a place for some parallels with what we know of evaluation on the basis of logical criteria.

Cognitive dissonance   The mention of consistency as a criterion for evaluation brings to mind Festinger's concept (1957) of "cognitive dissonance," for a condition that is said to arise when an individual's action is not in accord with his belief. A man believes the medical evidence that cigarette smoking contributes to development of lung cancer, yet he smokes. The hiatus between belief and action is seen as incongruous; there is cognitive dissonance, which the individual attempts to reduce. He may attempt this by changing either his action or his belief so that they become less dissonant.

The point of contact with the kind of evaluation under discussion in this chapter might be a sensitivity to incongruity, much as a person is sensitive to other inconsistencies, where evaluative abilities are known to be concerned. Since actions and beliefs are involved, the kind of information is in the behavioral category. When studies are made of evaluation abilities dealing with behavioral information, the Festinger conception should be remembered.

Evaluation and cybernetics   When the days of guided missiles arrived, they brought into being a discipline known as cybernetics, which was to have some significant consequences for psychology. Cybernetics deals with the principles of self-regulated machines (de Latil, 1957). A guided missile is given a target toward which it is aimed, but if it is off the path that would take it to its target, it has devices for sensing the error and for correcting its course. If there is overcorrection, it can also correct the correction. The sensing device is said to provide feedback information.

Another example of a self-regulating, self-correcting mechanism is found on a steam engine in the form of a governor. With the main control set for the engine to operate at a certain speed, should an increased flow of energy start to speed up the engine, the governor is immediately affected and automatically lowers the output. Should the speed drop, the governor automatically releases more energy. A thermostat keeps a room or a house at an even temperature for which it is set. A lifting crane regulates the expenditure of energy according to the weight of the load to be lifted. A water heater turns the gas on and off to keep the water in the tank uniformly hot or nearly so.

There are a number of analogies between a self-regulating machine and a self-regulated organism, some of which will come out later. At this point it is desirable to see how evaluation can be illuminated by applying ideas from cybernetics. When the sensing mechanism of the machine detects a discrepancy between the direction or the expenditure of energy that ought to prevail and the direction or the expenditure of energy that is actually occurring, it is going through an operation of comparison and matching, such as occurs in the operation of evaluation. The guided missile has its target "goal," which is preset; the engine has its goal rate, which is preset; and the room thermostat has its goal temperature, which is preset. The discrepancy between the two conditions, the goal and the actual, is referred to as a discrepancy between input and output information, the goal condition being the input condition and the actual condition being the output condition. The machine's evaluation consists of a matching of input and output conditions.

In a test of evaluation abilities, the "input" and "output" items of information are provided in the instructions and the information given in the items. The examinee reports whether or not there is a discrepancy or which of two or more discrepancies is greater. Even the term *information* is used in cybernetics to refer to that which provides communication between parts of the machine. In fact, it is a key concept. We shall give considerable attention to information as a concept in psychology in the next chapter.

Summary

Considerations were given to the meanings of the five major kinds of mental operations, with elaborations upon their definitions and some attention to possible relations to other known psychological processes.

Cognition was identified mainly with awareness or possession of information in the present, although it is very dependent upon information in memory storage. It also includes quick learning in the form of immediate extensions and transformations of already-known information. The cognitive factors account for all the traditional inductive phenomena and more. Depth of understanding of units, such as verbal meanings, involves more than knowledge of units; it involves other products. Cognitive-attitude factors that have been proposed involve an approach to cognition other than that concerned with aptitudes.

Memory is defined as storage of information only, and it is indicated empirically by means of memory tests, which give all individuals equal opportunity to memorize. There are still unanswered questions as to whether there are different memory abilities for immediate memory and for long-term memory, as well as for incidental and for intentional memory. Present meager evidence is against the probability of additional memory factors for those special conditions.

The distinguishing characteristic of divergent production is the phenomenon of transfer recall: revival of information in response to new cues, which are in the nature of search models. Search models furnish cues for recall and also make recall selective.

Whereas divergent production is a matter of generating logical possibilities, convergent production is a matter of generating logical necessities. It is the category in which the time-honored concept of deduction, as a psychological process, belongs, although deduction applies clearly to only two subgroups of convergent-production abilities. There is much evidence of factors of interest in different kinds of thinking but no indication that any of them accounts for the difference between divergent and convergent production or for the development of those abilities.

Evaluation is a process of comparing and matching items of information according to different logical criteria and of making decisions with respect to satisfaction of those criteria. It has no promise of accounting for all of decision making or risk-taking behavior in general, which is better conceived as problem solving. A new place in psychological theory seems badly needed to take care of self-regulating activities, with principles analogous to those of cybernetics, in which evaluation should have a prominent role.

10 Categories of information

The categories of content and of products of the structure of intellect can well be treated together, since they both pertain to kinds of information. The four content categories are the very broad, *substantive* areas of information, whereas the six intersecting product categories are *formal* types of differentiation. The philosophers' distinction of substance versus form seems to do very well here. Items of information differ as to content and as to product. Taken together, the 24 intersections can serve as a systematic basis for what may be called a psychoepistemology. They provide the basic classes for all the things that we can cognize, remember, produce, or evaluate.

We shall first give attention to the question of the general nature of information, as seen from a psychological point of view. The psychological concept of information will be distinguished from the communication engineer's concept of information and from the philosopher's concept of knowledge. Some historical precedents will be cited for the need of content and product differentiations, and some conceptions parallel with those of SI theory. Attention will then be given to particular content and product categories and problems that arise in connection with them. The relevance of the products for a kind of psychologic will be pointed out.

The nature of psychological information

As envisaged by SI theory, "information" is defined in the broadest possible terms as that which an organism discriminates. Although this definition does not necessarily imply conscious experience, it is convenient to talk as if we were dealing with a conscious field. Actually, it would be more accurate and more general to use the expression "psychological field," which includes both conscious and unconscious components.

Information and discrimination   If the psychological field of an organism at the moment were a uniform gray, with nothing else in it, there would be zero information. The simplest and most primitive discrimination would be some kind of division of that field into A and not-A regions: the first analytical event. One of these regions is likely to have some degree of dominance, and what we have is the gestalt psychologist's figure on a ground. The figure emerges with the character of a "thing"; it is a psychological unit of information.

Further discriminations give rise to two figures on the ground, one darker than the other, a condition that may become a second kind of item of information. If so, a relation has come into existence: a synthetic event. Still darker units emerge, also still lighter ones, giving a basis for generalizing the relation and abstracting a variable, as well as a realization that things have properties or attributes. The darker units can be cognized as a discriminated group, also the lighter ones, and the product of class comes about.

Then, in time, the organism cognizes the fact that the smaller units tend to be darker and the larger ones tend to be lighter. This correlation need not be perfect, but there is sufficient basis for noting a bivariate trend, in a way reminiscent of partial reinforcement. Thereafter, the organism expects small units to be dark and large ones to be light. Implications, another kind of product, have come into the picture. It is also eventually noted that a smaller unit may expand, growing larger, and as it does so, a larger one grows smaller. In this event, two other products, transformation and system, are illustrated, not that they always occur in conjunction. The changing in size is the transformation, and the principle of reciprocity in size and brightness is the system.

Thus, discriminations of information may be between items of different kinds of product and also between items within the same kind of product. The different kinds of products serve different purposes in the psychological economy. Unless there is differentiation, there is no information. But as we noted, not all development of information comes by way of analysis; synthetic steps also play their roles, as in the formation of classes, relations, systems, and implications. We can gain new information, new discriminations, by combining old information in new ways, different from other combinations.

Information and knowledge   The terms *knowledge* and *information* are not synonymous, the latter having greater extension than the former. "Knowledge" has so much common usage that it is best not to attempt to give it definition for scientific use. It has been defined for philosophical use, in connection with logic and epistemology, by Werkmeister, when he says that knowledge is "warranted belief" (1948, p. 3). A belief is statable as a proposition, which has a subject and a predicate. The distinction between knowledge and awareness is given by examples. We are aware of blue, pain, bitter, fragrance, all of which can be regarded as figural information. We perceive a rose, a house, or a motorcar, all of which are units of information. But when we say that we know that the rose is red, that the book is heavy, or that sound came from a bird, we are stating propositions and we are expressing beliefs. These events are still within the realm of information, semantic in nature. The "warranted" component of Werkmeister's definition of knowledge pertains to truth. He states that a proposition is warranted if there is sufficient reason for believing it, which may need further specifications, some of which can be found in formal logic.

Categories of knowledge   Philosophers who have given special attention to problems of knowledge, in other words, epistemology, have attempted to arrive at basic categories; for example, Immanuel Kant. This exercise has had to be speculative, for lack of any empirical method by which categories as such could be demonstrated. Examples of such categories are presented by Werkmeister (1948). They are of interest here because of the possibility of comparing them with the categories of information provided by SI theory. The SI categories *were* derived by an empirical method, namely, factor analysis. It is because the lists were designed for similar purposes that the suggestion was made above that the SI categories of information might serve as a psychoepistemology.

The Werkmeister list of categories, in large part, is as follows:

Quality-quantity
Unity-manifoldness
Form-matter
Universal-particular
Relation-substrate
Continuity-discreteness

Unity versus manifoldness is suggestive of the distinction between units and systems. Universal versus particular is suggestive of class versus unit. Relation is mentioned, as such, but there is no parallel in SI theory for "substrate," which presumably refers to things related, which would usually be units but could be other products between which relations can be cognized. Continuity suggests implication, which has sometimes been characterized as an extrapolation, but "discreteness" merely suggests lack of implication.

The form-versus-matter category does not suggest any particular kind of product but rather the distinction between product and content, as two of the three parameters of the SI model, those pertaining to information. Quality and quantity have no counterpart, unless quantity is treated as seriation, which implies a relation. If we consider that the two lists of categories (that of knowledge and that of information) were designed for somewhat different purposes and by different methods, they have some similarities and, to that extent, mutually supporting parallels.

Information theory and psychological information   What is generally known as information theory (and information measurement) was developed by communication engineers to solve some of their problems of the transmission of information over communication channels. Their problems were concerned with how much information is to be transmitted at the source, how much information the channel can accommodate, and how much information comes through to the receiver. The emphasis upon "how much" obviously calls for measurement of information, and that is mostly what information theory is about.

Information measure   As an illustration of how information in a source of a communication is measured, let us take the case of guessing how the events of tossing a coin 3 times in succession came out. Your friend tosses the coin and you are guessing how the combined events came out, with the aid of questioning. You are allowed 3 questions to which your friend answers by yes or no. There are altogether 8 possible ways in which the experiment of tossing the coin could turn out:

| HHH | HHT | HTH | THH | HTT | THT | TTH | TTT |
| A | B | C | D | E | F | G | H |

The 8 cases, *A* through *H*, are all the possible ways, of which, let us say, *F* was the actual outcome. Your most efficient way of questioning would be:

Was the first coin H?   (no)

This question eliminates half the cases, *A, B, C,* and *E*.

Was the second coin T?   (no)

This question eliminates half the remaining cases, *G* and *H*.

Was the third coin T?   (yes)

With only cases *D* and *F* remaining, the third question eliminates *D*, leaving *F* as the correct outcome.

Note that, starting with 8 possible alternative ways, each question eliminated half the number of alternatives remaining at the time the question was answered. Every answer is said to transmit 1 unit of information, called a "bit," which is a contraction of the expression "binary digit." It is defined as the amount of information that reduces uncertainty by one-half.

Note, also, that with 3 coins tossed, the total number of alternatives is $2 \times 2 \times 2$, because for each of the 2 ways that the first coin falls there are 2 ways the second one falls, and for each of these 4 combinations of 2 coins each there are 2 possibilities for the

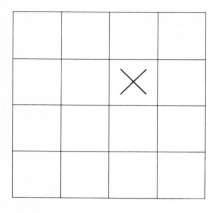

Fig. 10.1 A criminal is hiding in the city square marked with an X. It takes a minimum of 4 bits of information to locate him.

third coin. $2 \times 2 \times 2$ can be written as 2^3. In this special kind of situation, the exponent of 2 is the number of bits of information involved.

To take another example, let us assume that a hunted criminal is in one of the 16 city blocks shown in Figure 10.1, the one marked by an X. A detective has apprehended an accomplice, who knows the location of the hunted man. The accomplice refuses to answer questions except by saying yes or no. By efficient questioning, the detective can gain all the information he is seeking by asking 4 questions and getting 4 "messages." The 4 questions would be of the type:

Is he in the right half of the map?   (yes)
Is he in the lower half?   (no)
Of the upper-right quarter, is he in the upper half?   (no)
Is he in the left half?   (yes)

Each message carries 1 bit of information, and there are 4 bits altogether. There are 16 logical alternatives to start with, and 16 is 2^4. Again the exponent of 2 is the number of units (bits) of information. As a general rule, the number of bits of information is measured by the logarithm to the base 2 of the total number of equally probable alternatives. Where probabilities are not equal for the possible categories, the same principle of measurement still applies. For our purposes here, however, we need not go into these more general cases.[1] The number of bits of information is not always an integer.

Information and uncertainty The important thing to be noted is that the larger the number of categories within which an item is to be found, the more *uncertain* the location of that item. For this reason, some investigators have used the term *uncertainty* rather than information, as Garner (1962) does. The index in number of bits is a measure of uncertainty rather than information in the usual sense. It is unfortunate for psychology that this switch in meaning occurred. The conception of "information" in SI theory agrees with that in information theory with respect to the importance of discrimination, but from that point on the two theories part company, for the SI meaning of information is in the direction of certainty, not uncertainty.

According to information theory, a well-structured figure contains little information because it entails little uncertainty. On the other hand, organisms strive toward good structure, for good structure makes possible the steps needed for coping with objects. It

[1] For an excellent introduction to information theory, see G. A. Miller (1953).

may well be that better coping with the objects may require additional information in the form of further discriminations, but, again, it is well-structured discriminations that are desired. One might also say that the further discriminations add information of the SI type as well as of the information-theory type, which means that there is not a perfect negative correlation between the two conceptions of information.

Uncertainty and SI information   For the living organism, depending upon its purposes and its success or failure, certain moderate levels of discrimination are often optimal. There are also optimal levels for preference. It appears to be a general principle that the individual prefers a level of complexity that is within his range of possibilities of mastery and yet which holds his interest because it is not too commonplace and offers some challenge. He likes structure, but he also likes the satisfaction of achieving new structure. The degree of uncertainty that he accepts or enjoys depends upon his capacity for reducing it.

Other comparisons may be made between the two conceptions of information, in addition to the certainty-uncertainty contrast and the difference on the structured-unstructured continuum. In information theory, information is discriminated in terms of categories; in SI theory, in terms of contents and products. In information theory there is essentially one kind of content, symbolic; in SI theory there are four kinds. Information-theory approaches in psychology have had some success by translating figural information into symbolic form but have not succeeded as yet with translations of semantic information, except through language symbols. There is much semantic information that does not get translated into language symbols. In information theory, information differs only in amount; in SI theory it differs in kind as well as in amount. Insofar as other kinds of information can be translated into symbolic form, it may be that uncertainty measurement will have a great deal to contribute to the quantitative treatment of information in general. Garner (1962) has been demonstrating achievement along these lines.

Categories of content

Before we take up particular categories of content, some attention will be given to non-factor-analytical sources in which similar differentiations of categories have been made. In a general theoretical discussion of intelligence, Viaud (1960) distinguished between "practical" and "conceptual-and-logical" types of intelligence. The former deals with concrete problems and is exhibited by lower animals, which are almost entirely confined to this type. Conceptual-logical intelligence depends upon the use of symbols (representations of things). Viaud does not make the further distinction between purely symbolic and semantic information.

Categories of content and communication   Most of the distinctions that have been made among three kinds of content, prior to SI theory, came about through the consideration of language and the information for which it stands. It is necessary, therefore, to treat the three kinds together, for they grew together in their historical background.

Thought-and-thing triangle   Ogden and Richards (1930) were among the first to point out the threefold distinction of *referent* (the thing perceived), *symbol* (speech sign of the thing), and *reference* (the thought about the thing). The relations among these three aspects of communication were conceived in the form of a "thought-and-thing triangle." A version of that triangle is represented in Figure 10.2. The relation between the referent and the reference is considered to be of a causal nature, in the sense that experi-

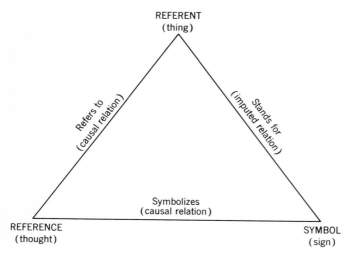

Fig. 10.2   The semanticist's thought-and-thing triangle. (*Adapted from a model originally presented by Ogden & Richards, 1930, with modifications by Cherry, 1957. Reproduced by permission.*)

ence with the perceived object gives rise to certain thought (semantic information). The reference refers to the referent. Through the need to communicate the thought to others, there develops a conventional connection between the reference and a symbol. More recent writers prefer the term *sign* to *symbol,* and with this change this writer is in agreement. *Symbol* is a more general term. For example, some writers speak of the thought or idea, the semantic event, as a "symbol," because it stands for or represents the real object (referent). Then, again, there is the reference to such things as flags, coats of arms, and flowers, as symbols for nations, families, and states, and so on. *Sign* can be more restrictively defined as a language unit, visual or auditory, that serves as a substitute for either the referent or the reference. The relation of sign to referent is an "imputed" or arbitrary one, which is more in the nature of an implication than a relation. In fact, all the connections in the Ogden-Richards triangle are more like implications than relations in the SI sense.

Writers since Ogden and Richards, among them being Carnap (1946) and Cherry (1957), have elaborated somewhat upon those authors, in discussing three disciplines that are associated with the threefold distinction. The most common mention is of *semantics,* defined by Carnap as the study of the meaning aspects of language. This has been the basis for naming one kind of information in the SI model "semantic." According to Carnap, however, semantics, as a discipline, is a metalanguage, a language about language. According to Cherry, syntactics is a discipline concerned with signs and relations between signs. It studies language from the point of view of symbolic structure. A third discipline, not so well defined, is called "pragmatics." It has to do with relations between language and its users. Cherry recognizes that mathematics belongs in the category of symbolic information, having to do only with signs. But when mathematics is applied, there is substance for the study of pragmatics. To pragmatics he also allots questions of value and usefulness.

In the definition of pragmatics, there is just a hint of reference to behavioral information. Korzybski (1950), a leader in the field of semantics, pointed out that two kinds of events are on what he calls the "silent" level, by which he probably meant nonverbal. One kind of event on this level is environmental, which can be equated to figural information, and the other is psychological, which can probably be equated to behavioral information. He says that we can speak *about* the silent level but not *on* that level. He made a great deal of the human weakness of confusing verbal and nonverbal levels, that is, of attaching verbal labels and of then treating those labels as realities. There will be a little more on behavioral information later.

Figural information   There is little to be said here about figural and symbolic information, except to present formal definitions and to add a few superficial comments. *Figural information is in concrete form, as perceived or as recalled in the form of images.* The term *figural* implies some degree of structuring, even if only in the form of figure and ground. Different sense modalities—visual, auditory, kinesthetic, etc.—may be involved. Some speculation was offered in Chapter 4 concerning whether the visual-figural abilities now known or hypothesized will be paralleled generally by abilities in the auditory and kinesthetic areas. Already one or more such factors have been demonstrated in each area.

In the visual area, we encounter such properties as color, shape, texture, size, continuity, and dimensionality. Shapes may be geometric or quasi-geometric, rectilinear or curvilinear, and contours may be rough or smooth, with an almost infinite variety possible, realistic and nonrealistic.

Figural meaning Garner (1962) has made some interesting suggestions concerning what he calls "meaning" in figural information. This is not semantic meaning but meaning indigenous to figures and dependent upon figural properties. It is meaning as structure, by which Garner means the "totality of relations between events" (p. 141). The structure may be internal or external. The arrangement of dots in a picture is an example of internal meaning. One of the important aspects of internal structure is constraint, which means interrelatedness within the structure, or correlations between parts. Constraints put limitations upon amount of information (uncertainty). For example, a bilaterally symmetrical figure has less uncertainty than an irregular figure. On the other hand, we must recognize that its significance, or power to evoke semantic information, is enhanced by improved structuring.

Symbolic information   *Symbolic information is in the form of signs, materials, the elements having no significance in and of themselves, such as letters, numbers, musical notations, and other "code" elements.* The alphabet and the number system provide code elements that can be combined in endless ways as seen in license-plate numbers, telephone numbers, etc., and in words, prices, and statistics. Oral (English) speech also has its code elements in the form of about forty phonemes, elemental sounds from which all spoken words can be formed. For the blind who read braille, there is a code of tactual symbols. Deaf-and-dumb persons converse with hand-movement symbols.

Semantic information   It is concerning semantic information that most is known, because of the great amount of research allotted to it. Semantic information is in the form of meanings to which words commonly become attached; hence it is most notable in verbal thinking and verbal communication. Although words do commonly become attached, we must recognize that much semantic information is also nonverbalized. In actuality, it, too, can be on Korzybski's "silent" level.

Semantic content and speech   A number of writers have expressed convictions on this point, some taking violent exception to John Watson's erstwhile assertion that thinking is subvocal talking. For example, Vygotsky (1962) maintains that language and thought develop more or less independently, with the developments intersecting at points along the way. In giving evidence for this view, he points out that primates think (which can be interpreted as using semantic information) but have no language in the sense of verbal signs standing for ideas.

In support of this view, Vygotsky could well have cited the work of Harlow (1949) on learning sets. It is probable that the learning sets in monkeys' learning how to learn new discriminations can be regarded as semantic information. Particularly is this true of monkeys' learning how to cope with reversal principles. Thus, in phylogeny there is a prelinguistic phase of development of thought. There is also a preintellectual phase in the development of speech, in that the earliest communicative utterances of animals have affective significance. The same principles are true of ontogenetic development. Speech and semantic content become affiliated through the child's realization of how one can serve the other, as in his questioning stage. By that time he has gone quite a way in development in both respects.

Another voice against the belief in an intimate tie between intellectual and speech development, where "intellectual" can probably be interpreted as semantic information, is that of Furth (1964). After reviewing the evidence from studies of development of deaf individuals and its bearing on the significance of speech for intellectual development, Furth concluded: "Language does not influence intellectual development in any direct, general, or decisive way" (p. 160). The influence of language is indirect and specific. Individuals without linguistic experience, such as the deaf, are not permanently or generally retarded, although there may be temporary retardation during development and they may be deficient in specific skills.

Semantic meaning   Although one ordinarily thinks of meaning as being semantic and hence this heading may seem redundant, the qualification is used in recognition of the discussion above, in which meaning of a kind was attributed to figural information, following Garner's suggestion. In the preceding chapter we considered the question of the "level" of meaning of verbal concepts in connection with vocabulary tests, without going into the meaning of semantic meaning. Here we cannot dodge that issue.

Almost all treatments of this subject have been in the context of communication, and hence they have emphasized relations between items of semantic information and their signs. There is an impression that some confusion results from the fact that signs and things signified are not well distinguished, in spite of the fact that writers often give lip recognition of this distinction. The worst confusion comes with those of S-R bias in theory, who do not know what to do with meaning but who cannot get rid of it. A common solution is that offered by Osgood (Osgood, Suci, & Tannenbaum, 1957), who treats semantic meaning as a "mediation process," a little s-r connection that is formed from the individual's (usually repeated) S-R behavior in connection with a sign and the object for which it stands. The little r becomes a substitute stimulus to which the individual reacts. Both s and r are parts or aspects of S and R. This conception would apparently preclude the development of any semantic information apart from language responses, an inference that is contradicted by abundant evidence, some of which was given earlier.

One of the important difficulties in defining semantic meaning and in research upon it is that, as such, it can never be on display. We can get at it only through its figural (real-object) or its symbolic (sign) affiliates, which *can* be on display. What little we can observe of semantic information is through introspection, which gives very meager data, or by inferences from behavior. Our approach must be very largely indirect. This fact accounts for the heavy emphasis upon signs and upon deductions about meaning from the manipulation of signs. The results from such investigations are likely to be more revealing about the individual's processing of symbolic information than about semantic information.

Denotative and connotative aspects Another difficulty with definitions and with much research on semantic meaning is that little distinction is made between denotative meaning and connotative meaning. A denotative meaning is restricted to what Werkmeister (1948) calls "lexical" or dictionary meaning, meaning that applies to a concept in isolation from any context. Since the time of Aristotle, a dictionary definition attempts to specify genus and species for a word. This means giving a class and differentiation within some subclass. As Vygotsky has stated (1962), a word (ordinarily) does not stand for a single object; it stands for a conception, a generalization. It is probable that many psychologists are more than willing to hand denotative meanings over to the logicians and philosophers, for the reason that they believe that those events cannot be dealt with in empirical science. It is ostrichlike to dodge such problems; denotative meanings must surely have something significant to do with behavior. Since they are events, there must be ways of dealing with them.

Most of the thinking and research on semantic meaning on the part of psychologists has dealt with connotative meaning. The interpretation of meaning of this kind is generally an associative one. Connotative meaning affiliated with a certain sign is the composite of all things associated with that sign. The crux of this statement is the nature of "all things associated." Does this rightfully include other signs? Operationally, research on this problem seems to proceed as if this were the case. The operational definition of connotative meaning is often in terms of a free-association task, in which all the signs given by individuals in response to a given sign are taken to establish the meaning attached to that sign. Probably, most investigators who use that approach are properly thinking in terms of the semantic meanings that are carried by those signs, the given sign and the response sign.

A core-context theory of meaning A definition of meaning that fits the view of the writer was suggested by Werkmeister (1948), who defined meaning as *expectancy*. An object or a sign carries semantic meaning because it points to something beyond itself. This statement is precisely the definition of the kind of product known as implication. The "something beyond itself" is information other than that involved in a core product; it is context. A verbal sign implies a core product, which is semantic information, and this, in turn, implies other products as a penumbra or context (see Figure 10.3). The core is the denotative, identifying aspect of meaning, which acquires an almost one-one connection with the sign. It consists of implied classes, classes such as are necessary for a lexical definition of the concept. The context is implied by the core, and in it may be any other kinds of products and even any kind of content, such as images and feelings, the latter to be classified as figural and behavioral information, respectively.

And speaking of behavioral information in this connection, we are reminded of the psychologists who have insisted that concepts of objects, at least, include all the motor actions that would be pertinent to the object, as shown by definitions in terms of use (e.g., a chair is to sit on and a spade is to dig with, etc.). Patterned motor reactions can be regarded as products of behavioral information, a view that will be mentioned a number of times in chapters to follow. An important departure from the view of those who

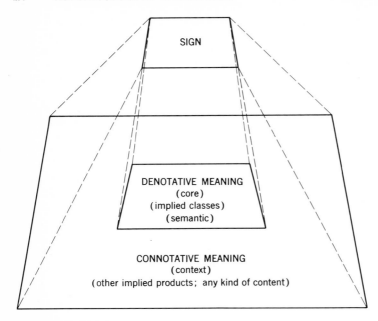

Fig. 10.3   Diagram representing the core-context theory of meaning, in which the core is the denotative aspect and the context is the connotative aspect, both affiliated by implications with the sign (a symbol).

espouse the motor theory of meaning is that the behavioral-product implications in the context that makes up the connotative aspect of meaning are only part of the context, not all of it.

To add some general qualifications, it should be noted that a sign cannot exist as such without something for which it stands, for that is the definition of a sign. A semantic meaning, however, can exist without a linguistic sign, as in prelanguage stages of development. A linguistic sign is symbolic. There can also be visual-figural or auditory-figural signs, which became phylogenetically the basis for primitive picture writing, in a transition to symbolic information and symbolic signs.

In passing, it is interesting to note that the denotative aspect of a concept is convergent in nature, whereas the connotative aspect is divergent. Thus, the denotative aspect becomes conventional, whereas the connotative aspect shows considerable variation from person to person and from time to time in the same person. Although the lexical definition is dependent upon class specifications, dictionary definitions do not always comply with that form. They often give synonyms and use other information that should more properly be regarded as connotative, in an effort to achieve communication.

Let us take a specific example to illustrate the core-context conception of semantic meaning. The sign is TAPIR, for which the usual definition states that it is a large, nocturnal ungulate, most commonly found in South or Central America. The statement may add that a tapir is shy, gentle, and harmless, that it is related to the horse and the rhinoceros, and that one variety is found in Malaya. Applying the core-context paradigm, we may diagram this as in Figure 10.4. The main class involved in the denotative core is ungulate, which is sufficient for one important discrimination if the individual knows that this means

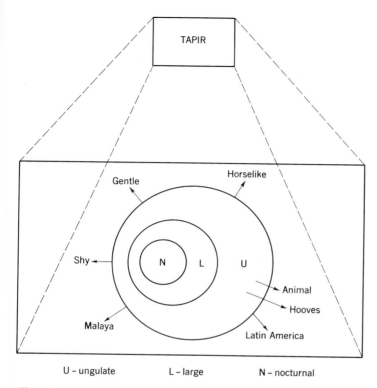

Fig. 10.4 Diagram representing the core-context theory of semantic meaning applied to the denotative and connotative implications connected with the sign TAPIR.

an animal with hooves. To those who know this, to add "animal" or "mammal" would be redundant. The qualifier "large" makes a further restriction in the class ungulate, and the qualifier "nocturnal" is perhaps sufficient restriction to pinpoint more nearly the nature of a tapir. The other qualifiers add to richness of meaning but may be redundant.

In the successive specification of restrictions, we can see how each added item of information reduces uncertainty by an appreciable amount, unless it happens to be completely redundant. We cannot apply the operations of information measurement, however, because we do not know the proportion p by which alternatives are eliminated. In any particular case in which the probabilities are known, we could state the average amount of information in a definition.

The classes-within-classes system represented in the core of the meaning in Figure 10.4 suggests the hierarchical type of model for denotative meaning. If the successive principles of classification are mutually independent, a morphological model would also apply. There would be one dimension or parameter of the model for each of the class distinctions: ungulate versus nonungulate, large versus medium versus small, and nocturnal versus diurnal. Such classifications would avoid redundancies and would thus reduce uncertainties efficiently.

In communication, the speaker who wishes to convey to his listener a certain semantic meaning starts with a semantic product that he wishes to encode by finding an appropriate sign or signs, hoping that the sign or signs will be decoded by the listener to arrive at very much the same semantic product as that with which the speaker started. The speaker no doubt takes advantage of the context in which speaker and listener find themselves and organizes his symbolic information so as to have the best effects. Under normal circumstances, the speaker's brain organizes a symbolic pattern in split-second operations, and vocalized signs spill out in amazingly good order and with amazing efficiency. If speaker and listener have similar sets of implications in connection with the signs used by the speaker, there will be reasonably good communication.

Measurement with semantic information   Motivation for scientific studies of meaning, or studies in which meaning is an important consideration, has led to a number of attempts to apply measurement where semantic meaning is concerned. This problem first arose when it was questioned whether Ebbinghaus's nonsense syllables were really all nonsense, with suspicion that many of them are bearers of meaning. This question can be put in SI terms by saying that Ebbinghaus's intention was to have symbolic information exclusively involved in his material to be memorized, with a realization that variations in semantic involvement would not permit good control of the learnability of his units of material.

The efforts of early investigators who tackled this problem are generally known (Glaze, 1928; Hull, 1935). They used association methods, determining the association value of a syllable in terms of the proportion of the subjects who gave associated words in limited time. The method would fail to measure generally familiar words, however, for *every* subject would have associated responses for them; so Noble (1952) introduced another associative method, in which the index of meaningfulness (not meaning) is in terms of the number of associations given to a word in sixty seconds, disregarding affective responses. Applying his index m to 96 word signs, some being two-syllable paralogs, some infrequently used words, and some frequent words, Noble found average values from 0.99 for the paralog GOJEY to 9.61 for KITCHEN. From two groups of subjects the averages over the population of words correlated .975, indicating high average intersubject agreement. It should be noted that all these methods pertain primarily to the connotative aspects of meaning.

Another approach suggested by Noble (1953) was aimed at an index for familiarity of a word. He defined *familiarity* empirically as frequency of exposure to the word sign. He asked observers to rate each exposed word for degree of familiarity on a 5-point scale. It should be expected that the more frequently a word is exposed, the more opportunities there are for forming implications or associations, and hence there should be a positive correlation between Noble's familiarity index f and his meaningfulness index m. Using the same words evaluated for f and for m, Noble found a very high correlation (.92) between those two indices, the relationship being nonlinear but monotonic. The value of such indices has been limited thus far to the calibrating of words for use in experiments on memorizing.

An experiment on perception of word signs also used the m index to advantage. Kristofferson (1957) used 20 words of known m values for a recognition study. Each word was exposed to S in a tachistoscope, starting with an exposure time too short for recognition and stepping the time up by small increments until S could recognize the word. The mean time score for each word was determined and the time scores correlated with the m values and f values. The correlations (Kendall tau) were $-.56$ with m and $-.61$ with f, showing that the richness of connotative meaning of a word is related to the speed of recognition in perception. In more general terms, the results indicate that cognition of symbolic units is facilitated by the richness of connotative meaning that is largely semantic.

Osgood's semantic differential Probably the best-known and most widely used application of measurement in connection with semantic information is that of Osgood (Osgood et al., 1957). Osgood's conception of meaning has already been mentioned. In approaching the problem of measurement (which he regarded as the measurement *of* meaning, the possibility of which can be logically questioned), he rejected the associational methods, for reasons that need not be repeated here. Instead of utilizing the free-association responses of individuals, which are subject to so many determiners other than meaning attached to the stimulus word, Osgood sought to standardize reactions to words by asking S to describe the word quantitatively by means of a standard set of adjectives in what he called the semantic-differential method.

The theory is basically that of the factor-analytic dimensional model referred to in Chapter 3. Osgood assumed a semantic space of an unknown number of dimensions, each orthogonal dimension representing an independent variable along which words could be allocated. With the proper dimensions determined, it would be possible to describe the meaning of a word as a point in this n-dimensional space, much as individuals can be described in a space representing factor abilities, as illustrated in Figure 3.1.

The idea was ingenious and promising of quantitative descriptions of semantic concepts. In order to find out what the reference axes in the semantic space should be, he applied quite a number of "tests" to quite a number of words. His "tests" for words were graphic rating scales, each with 7 units, at the ends of which were paired adjectives with opposite meanings. An example follows.

Word to be rated: MOTHER
Scales:

small	____:____:____:____:____:____:____	large
black	____:____:____:____:____:____:____	white
happy	____:____:____:____:____:____:____	sad
slow	____:____:____:____:____:____:____	fast
strong	____:____:____:____:____:____:____	weak
sour	____:____:____:____:____:____:____	sweet

With 20 words rated on 50 such scales by 100 subjects, each scale was arbitrarily given numerical values from 1 to 7 so that the scales could be intercorrelated and the intercorrelations subjected to factor analysis. In such analyses, three strong factors have consistently come out, with a few other weak ones that have not been easy to interpret and have been generally disregarded.

The three strong factors have been interpreted as:

Evaluation, with certain scales heavily loaded, including good-bad, beautiful-ugly, sweet-sour, happy-sad

Potency, with leading variables of large-small, strong-weak, heavy-light, thick-thin

Active-passive, with fast-slow, active-passive, hot-cold, sharp-dull

Other rating scales were likely to be loaded on more than one of these dimensions.

To determine how any word stands on the three dimensions, ratings on a few of the scales, such as those just mentioned, can be combined to give an estimate of the word on each factor. This can be done for an individual or for a group of individuals. Each word would then have three values rather than one, such as Noble's m or his f. The Noble values are highly correlated and hence give about the same information concerning a word. Osgood's values for a word, being essentially independent, provide information regarding three different aspects of the meaning of a word.

It is also possible to determine the difference between two words in the factor space if we know their factor "scores." The difference is the linear distance between the two. It is also possible, if we know such interword distances for an individual, to see how he conceives of different concepts and their similarities in the factor space. Quite a number of such applications have been made.

What is it about semantic meaning that is measured by means of the Osgood semantic differential? It is definitely not the denotative meaning of a word. If one were told the three values of a word on the factor dimensions, he could almost never guess what word had been evaluated. It is possible for words very different in denotative meaning to have very similar sets of values on the three reference axes: they occupy very nearly the same spot in the Osgood factor space. Examples are the words HERO, SUCCESS, NURSE, SINCERE. There is a probable reason why the Osgood values miss denotative meaning. Denotative meaning does not call for a dimensional model to represent it. A much more appropriate model would be a hierarchical one, since classes play the crucial role in the denotative aspect of meaning.

Does the Osgood method measure *connotative* aspects of meaning? If we recall the great mass of implications that are likely to have places in the context of a concept, as illustrated in Figure 10.3 and as indicated by the large number of associative responses likely to be given to a word, it seems unlikely that three dimensions would be sufficient to take care of the variety of information thus clustering about the denotative core.

Examination of the three dimensions that Osgood found suggests that they are actually dimensions of *feeling*. With slight change in terminology, evaluation becomes pleasant-unpleasant; power, or strong-weak, becomes tense-relaxed; and active-passive becomes excited-calm. Old-timer psychologists should recognize these as Wundt's three dimensions of feeling. It thus appears that Osgood's factors represent only the affective connotations in the context of a word, as shown in Figure 10.3. If feelings are properly classified as behavioral information, we can say that a lot of words have behavioral information in common in their connotative contexts.

There is much in the semantic contexts of words that the semantic differential misses, in addition to missing the semantic cores entirely. This is probably because contextual information other than the affective aspects does not conform to a dimensional model. It is true that some investigators have found strong correlations between semantic-differential values of words and other indices aimed at some aspects of meaning, such as Noble's m for the same words (Staats & Staats, 1959). But this may mean that Noble's m is also in part a measure of affective aspects of meaning contexts. Words are given in response to other words in free association because they share contexts, including affective similarities.

Measurement of similarity in semantic meaning   It was mentioned in passing that with the three semantic-differential values known for each word, it is possible to estimate the linear distance between any two words in the three-dimensional space. Other methods based upon word-association responses have been tried out for achieving a more comprehensive measure of interword distance. Two principles, one using the frequencies with which two words share the same word-association responses and the other using information as to how frequently the one word elicits the other in free association (Deese, 1962;

Garskof & Houston, 1963; 1965), are commonly applied. Marshall and Cofer (1963) review other methods.

Such methods probably emphasize the connotative aspects of meaning, but there is a chance that denotative aspects also enter into the measurement, for some of the word associations given are in the category of species-genus or genus-species connections. It might be suggested that if the desire is to emphasize the distance between denotative meanings, the associations should be restricted to this kind of connection. If the writer is correct in hypothesizing that denotative meanings are confined to *class* products, then the attempt to measure linear distances between concepts is inappropriate and some other kind of separation is called for, possibly in terms of hierarchical levels and branchings.

The logic of similarity Noble (1957) has done much to clear up the problem of similarity in general (and his reasoning applies to similarity of meaning, also) by examining its logical aspects. As a logical concept, similarity is a relation between two elements, which can be expressed as a proposition of the sort A_1 resembles A_2, symbolized by $A_1 \sim A_2$. The properties of the relation "resembles" can be stated as follows:

1. It is nontransitive: i.e., if $A_1 \sim A_2$ and $A_2 \sim A_3$, A_1 may or may not resemble A_3. Figure 10.5 shows in terms of a Venn diagram a universe of discourse U_1, in which three elements A_1, A_2, and A_3 have some overlapping properties and some nonoverlapping properties, with the relation of A_1 to A_3 in this case expressible by $A_1 \not\sim A_3$; A_1 does not resemble A_3.
2. It is symmetrical: the relationship applies in both directions; i.e., if $A_1 \sim A_2$, then $A_2 \sim A_1$.
3. It is irreflexive, which means that the relation does not include the case of identity. To say that $A_1 \sim A_1$ has no meaning. From this we infer that similarity implies some difference. Similarity and difference are logically two sides of the same coin. The logical proof that identity is not the limiting case of similarity is that the relation of identity *is* transitive and it *is* reflexive.

Putting similarity of two concepts in terms of overlapping with common properties provides one basis for a quantitative evaluation of degree of similarity. This requires the further assumptions that different properties of an element are mutually independent and are of equal weight. With these assumptions satisfied, a coefficient of correlation can be applied with the equations:

$$r_s = N_{(1+2)}/\sqrt{N_1 N_2} \tag{10.1}$$
$$r_s = \sqrt{N_{(1+2)}/N_P} \tag{10.2}$$

in which

r_s = index of similarity, a correlation coefficient
$N_{(1+2)}$ = number of common properties in the two concepts
N_1 and N_2 = numbers of properties in the two elements, respectively
N_P = number of properties in the larger concept, where it entirely includes the properties of the smaller one

It will be recognized that a correlation index is not a measure of linear distance between two things. The applicability of these formulas is in much doubt, for lack of ways of counting properties in most situations to which they might apply and for lack of satisfaction of the necessary assumptions. The logic and the method are presented because they represent a novel way of thinking about the problem of similarity. Other methods can be built upon the theory.

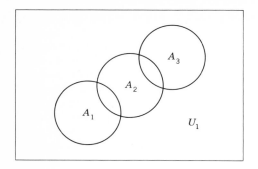

Fig. 10.5 Representation of similarity between units or concepts by means of overlapping circles. A_1 resembles A_2, which resembles A_3, but A_3 does not resemble A_1. All are in the universe of information U_1.

Other approaches to similarity measurement   The problem of measurement of similarity has recently been treated by Ornstein (1965). His immediate problem is concerned with similarity of blood samples. By a certain technique it is possible to determine the proportion of each kind of protein present in a sample of blood, in terms of 400 attributes, with measurements on every attribute.

For two such assessments of two blood samples, the measurements could be treated as score profiles, such as are common in psychological-testing practices. Ornstein suggests that a coefficient of correlation between two profiles can be transformed into a linear distance by finding the negative logarithm to the base 2 of the obtained r. A difficulty with this procedure is that two profiles could correlate $+1.0$ and still not be identical, owing to different means and variances.

An alternative procedure considered is an index suggested by Tanimoto: his "similarity coefficient" (1961). This is simply the ratio of the number of nonzero identical attributes to the total number of pairs of attributes, and it varies from 0 to 1. A distance value is obtained by transforming to the negative logarithm to the base 2, which puts the value in the context of information measurement. The index was first designed for the binary case, in which an attribute is present or absent, but has been generalized for the case of continuous measurements on the attributes. The index then becomes the sum of the smaller of the paired values on attributes divided by the sum of the larger paired values.

The problem of similarity of items of information is becoming more important where more precise categorizations of information are wanted, as in the classification of blood samples. The problem is crucial to the operations of storage of information that utilizes computer equipment.

Satiation of meaning with repetition   If one repeats a familiar word aloud for a period of some fifteen seconds, he may find that the semantic meaning of the word tends to weaken and perhaps entirely disappear, leaving only the sound of the word apparent. In the extreme case, the semantic content has vanished but the figural content (auditory) remains. Some studies have attempted to see what effects there are upon semantic-differential values of such words and words of similar Osgood values, without decisive results (Floyd, 1962; Reynierse & Brach, 1963). Recovery of meaning may occur rapidly, but the method may have some possibilities of determining what aspects of the core and context are affected most in the satiation process.

Behavioral information   A formal definition of behavioral information and some discussion of it were brought into Chapter 4, in connection with cognitive abilities. There is little to be added here, for this is the least explored area of information. Some precedents for a category of behavioral information will be mentioned, however, for they contribute to understanding of its scope and its meaning. A new model including behavioral information will be proposed as a substitute for the thought-and-thing triangle.

Psychological relations   Spearman (1927) was sometimes better as an insightful psychologist than he was as a factor theorist, as was shown when he recognized the need for a concept such as behavioral information. In reviewing the basic kinds of "relations," which were regarded as all-important in his conceptions of intelligence, he included a category of "psychological relations" among 10. The other categories do not concern us here. Spearman pointed out that an individual can generate for himself the thoughts and even the percepts of other persons around him, by analogy with his own inner experience. Since this information comes about as the completion of an analogy, he regarded the awareness of the mental states of others as a case of "eduction of correlates," therefore as an act exhibiting intelligence.

Spearman believed that ability to know the mental states of others could be measured by such tests as Binet's Interpretations, Decroly's Sequence, and Healy's Pictorial Completion, which involve some personal interactions. The interpretation of pictures involves seeing what is going on, inferring what went before, and predicting what comes after the pictured event. Spearman reported some analytical results from such tests, which, he concluded, measure something in common in addition to their involvement with *g*. There was no further evidence to show that the additional component was behavioral.

Person perception   More recently social psychologists have speculated about problems of person perception in instances of human interaction. Bruner and Tagiuri (1954) represent the views of others when they recognize three classes of problems. One problem pertains to the cognition of emotions from observed expressions. The second pertains to judgment of personality traits from external signs. The third is concerned with the formation of impressions of other individuals. The second and third problems are, of course, highly related. The first problem is concerned with awareness of the current mental states of persons observed at the moment; the other two problems pertain to decisions concerning the long-term characteristics of persons. In the latter connection there have been a number of studies of what it takes to be a good judge of personalities, for example, the studies of Taft (1956).

Sensitivity training   Psychologists and others who have been concerned with what is called "sensitivity training" of personnel, usually in organizational settings, come close to the first problem. The interest has been more on training procedures, but there has been some attention to basic problems, as in the work of Massarik and Wechsler (1959). Some of the particular problems that they envisage are rather suggestive of some behavioral abilities hypothesized by the SI model. For example, there is need for an observer to penetrate the defenses of another person, which might well involve SI ability NBT. Penetrating defenses would surely entail producing a revision of the impression of what the observed person's actions really mean. "Connecting cues with that which they indicate" suggests factor CBU, and so does "organizing impressions from fragmentary cues." Sizing up a group situation is an excellent description of CBS, the cognition of behavioral systems. Thus, some of the behavioral abilities hypothesized by SI theory appear to be relevant to problems of those who are directly concerned with person perception.

Information of self   In addition to the kind of information involving the awareness and management of others, there is information concerned with the awareness and management of ourselves. We not only know, but we know that we know, and we know that we have feelings, emotions, intentions, and actions. It is possible that there is another set of functions pertaining to such information. It is possible that it would be fruitful to regard our personal plans of action, our strategies, and our tactics, all of which have to do with what we do and how we do it, as forms of behavioral information, also occurring in the form of the usual kinds of products of information. Our repertoire of plans, emphasized by Miller, Galanter, and Pribram (1960), would constitute systems of behavioral information. With this conception, skills, psychomotor as well as intellectual, can be brought into the realm of information.

The informational tetrahedrons   With three kinds of information, a triangle is sufficient to represent their interrelationships, as illustrated in Figure 10.2. But with a fourth category of information added, a tetrahedron is needed, as shown in Figure 10.6. This model indicates the possibility of going from one kind of information to another. Behavioral information, as well as figural and semantic, can be communicated in terms of signs; hence its connection with symbolic information. It is common to conceive of the behavior of others less directly in terms of semantic understanding; hence the need to represent the connection with the semantic category. There are numerous implicational connections between observed expressions and behavioral information; hence the figural-behavioral connection has a real basis.

But if the hypothesis of a separate self-observed behavioral category of information is sound, there would be need for another corner in the model, which can be achieved by the double tetrahedron shown in Figure 10.6. The direct connection between other-behavioral and self-behavioral categories suggest the interesting possibility of representing the phenomenon of empathy.

Products of information

In preceding discussions the point was brought out that content categories are substantive whereas product categories are formal. In this section we give attention to the formal aspects of information. The six product categories were defined in Chapter 3, and we have seen numerous examples of what constitute the different kinds of products in Chapters 4 through 8. Here we can perhaps sharpen the conceptions of the product categories and also see in what respects they are parallel to some historical psychological conceptions and to conceptions in formal logic.

Units of information

Units and the other products   A unit of information is a "thing." It is not enough to say that it is segregated or that it is a "chunk" of information, for other kinds of products are also segregated; they are discriminated, otherwise they would not be information, as that term is defined in this volume.

A unit has properties, each unit with a unique combination of properties. Unlike other kinds of products, it can exist without other products; differentiation of figure from ground is sufficient. It would be better to say that a unit need not imply any other product, although it may do so, of course, whereas other products, such as relations, classes, and systems, do imply more than one product.

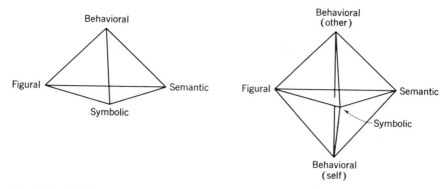

Fig. 10.6 With the addition of the fourth category of information (behavioral), the thought-and-thing triangle must be extended into a third dimension to form an informational tetrahedron. With the distinction between *self-* and *other-*behavioral information, a double tetrahedron is needed.

Other kinds of products can become units, as they acquire "thing" character. A relation can become an object of interest as an event; so can a class or a system. We saw in earlier chapters instances in which there was some uncertainty as to whether examinees process the given information or the produced information as units or as systems. To generalize this principle a bit, we also saw some uncertainties in places with regard to implications and relations. What may start out as simply an implication, without definitive connection, becomes a relation as the connection takes on relational significance. This transition between products is an example of the general versatility in information processing and indicates possibilities for change, which is learning. It is analogous to the changes from one category of content to another, which are like translations between languages.

Units as revealed by tests   A quick glance over the tests involving units in preceding chapters should be informative regarding the kinds of things that deserve to be regarded as units.[1] Among the visual-figural units utilized in tests have been single letters, where their figural properties are crucial to the test problems, as in unit-recognition tests and in classes tests where classes are formed in terms of common figural properties of the letters. Pictured familiar objects have been utilized in connection with both cognitive and evaluative tests. Monograms proved generally to be units for adults but generally systems for adolescents, in a divergent-production test (Monograms).

Auditory units used in tests have been dot-dash code signals, spoken digits, and runs of dot signals, the number of the dots to be reported. It is probable that phonemes will be found to serve as auditory-figural units.

Visual-symbolic units have been in the form of familiar printed words for both cognitive and evaluative tests, and syllables have also served as units in memory tests. Auditory-symbolic units have been in the form of spoken words. In the area of evaluation, letter

---

[1] The fact that certain things have served as a certain kind of product in test examples should not be taken to mean that there are no other possible kinds of material that would not also serve. Also, when something fails to serve as a certain kind of product in a test, there is no necessary inference that it cannot so serve; failure might have been due to other features of the test, e.g., its being entirely too easy or too difficult so as to fail to detect individual differences.

sets, digit sets, and the names of persons or firms have served as units to be compared for judgments of identity.

The best example of a semantic unit is a word meaning. But from earlier discussions we saw that there is much semantic information to which words do not become attached. Varieties of tests that have come out on semantic-units factors also reveal that single words cannot express many such units. It appears that a semantic unit may be as broad as a fact, which would perhaps require a whole sentence to express it, as seen in general-information tests, which are habitually loaded on factor CMU. In tests of DMU (ideational fluency), an "idea" is a unit, as in a Topics test, such as requires listing ideas in connection with "a man going up a ladder." Named objects are semantic units, naturally; so, also, are the particular uses of objects. Titles for stories and stated consequences of events also count as units in other divergent-production tests. From an evaluation test (Sentensense) we also gain the impression that a stated proposition can be a unit, in a sentence that contains two propositions to be judged for consistency with one another.

Behavioral units are more difficult to circumscribe. Tests for CBU have used faces with expressions and other body parts (arms, legs, hands, etc.) and their combinations, some of which are more complex. The behavioral unit is not the thing seen on the printed page; it is what that cue material arouses in the observer, who identifies something that can best be described as a particular state of mind or a particular intention or action. Further experience with tests designed for CBU will have to be gained before the more precise nature of a behavioral unit can be stated.

Classes   As a product of information, a class is an abstraction from a set of units that hold class membership by reason of common properties. The number of properties that determine a class may vary from one to a large number. Common properties imply similarity among class members; so we shall have to take a further look at that concept and its logical implications.

Classes as revealed by tests   Since classes are determined by similar units, once we have decided what are legitimate units of various kinds, we have fairly well decided also what classes can be formed. A brief review of kinds of classes that have been represented by factor tests will be helpful, however, without any necessary implication that other kinds of classes could not also be used.

Tests for factors CFC and DFC have employed quasi-geometric figures of simple constitution, utilizing properties of shape, size, shading, and so on, also letter groups, in which the classes depend upon figural aspects of the letters.

Tests of factor CSC have utilized number sets, in which the examinee is to see and to report the common number property, and also sets of pairs of numbers, in which a class of number relations is to be cognized. Sets of letter sets (each set having four letters) have been used, the common feature being similarity of letter sets in terms of some principle to which the latter conform. In the last two illustrations we have classes of relations and classes of systems involved. In a test for factor DSC, sets of boys' and girls' given names are presented, for E to group and regroup them in various ways by reason of spelling principles.

Semantic classes naturally depend basically upon meanings for which words are the operational signs. Named objects or adjectives have commonly been used to form class sets. One test that calls for classification of short sentences failed, but theoretically such a test should work if properly constituted.

In the behavioral area, tests utilizing sets of expressions from different body parts and also sets of vocal expressions were used, the former successfully, the latter with some doubt. An improved test with vocal expressions may still be useful for factor CBC.

Classes in experimental psychology From Hull's classic study of concept formation (1920) to the present, there has been continued interest in problems of concept formation and concept attainment, which pertain specifically to the product of class. Heidbreder's long series of studies is of special interest in connection with SI theory, because she came to the conclusion that there is a systematic order of difficulty in learning concepts, with classes of concrete (pictured) objects easiest, classes of forms second, and those of numbers most difficult. She was apparently dealing with semantic versus figural versus symbolic information. Dattman and Israel (1951), however, found that the order of difficulty that Heidbreder had obtained could have been due to some confounding with another condition, that of clarity with which attributes of the objects to be classified stand out. When they took steps to hold constant this condition, the Heidbreder order no longer applied.

More recent experimental studies of concept formation have taken into account potentialities for simulating that kind of psychological event using computers (E. B. Hunt, 1962). Such thinking has made us more aware of the potential role of classes in memory storage and in retrieval of items of information from storage. Search operations would undoubtedly be served in retrieval if the desired item of information were properly classified within a hierarchy of classes and subclasses. Woodworth (1938) cited what he called Wenzl's law of recall, which is to the effect that the search for something, such as a person's name, proceeds from general class properties to more special class properties. This somewhat casually derived principle deserves experimental attention. There is also a need to establish other principles of class formation, as proposed by Binder (1955), who has suggested the application of information measurement to problems of classes.

Logic of classes Such theorizing about classes would be greatly facilitated by considering the logical aspects of classes. Piaget (1953) has given some attention in this direction. A very natural logical model for classes is provided by set theory. Since semantic concepts also represent classes, the same kind of logic as that mentioned previously (Noble, 1957) in connection with similarity applies to classes. Classes can be represented by Venn diagrams, as in Figure 10.5. In this connection, U_1 represents a larger class within which A_1, A_2, and A_3 are subclasses, with various degrees of overlapping to represent members in common.

Class, subclasses, and subsubclasses can also be represented as hierarchies, in which the operations of division, addition, and subtraction apply: division when classes are subdivided, addition when subclasses are combined to form larger classes, and subtraction when a subclass is removed. Piaget cites the case of cross classification as being an operation of multiplication. Having classified animals as vertebrate and invertebrate, we can reclassify animals according to another principle into aquatic and terrestrial. A third basis would be whether they are edible or inedible, and still another basis whether they are domesticated or nondomesticated. The result can be readily recognized as what was called earlier a morphological model, of which the structure-of-intellect model is an example. Either a hierarchical or a morphological model is an example of a system, a system of interrelated classes.

Concrete versus abstract classes in psychopathology The problem of classification in relation to category of information seems to have some bearing on organic psychopathology. Kurt Goldstein has long maintained that a most notable defect in brain-injured cases is a loss in what he has called "abstract attitude." Evidence for this loss has been sought mainly by means of tests involving the classifying of objects as to color and as to form (Goldstein & Scheerer, 1953; Hanfmann, 1953). The difference between normal and pathological individuals, giving rise to the concrete-abstract hypothesis, however, appears not merely to be a loss of semantic-classification abilities but involves a number of abilities. One of them may be DFC, as shown in inability to make a shift in principle of classification. Others may be semantic, including CMU and CMS, as shown in inability to understand what is wanted in the classification test, and NMU, the ability to name a class once it has been formed. The weaknesses shown in taking classifying tests may be with respect to all these abilities. The abstract-concrete dichotomy does not seem to apply very well.

Relations   The number of possible relations is very great. The variety of relations can be seen by examination of an analogies test. In figural-analogies tests, any variable that can be applied to figures—size, position, distance, shading, texture, and so on—can be utilized as a relation. Also utilized are inversions, rotations, and reversals. In verbal-analogies tests, any of the standard relations, including opposites, genus-species, part-whole, action-agent, verb-object, and the reverse of most of these, plus many others, are used. With numbers, any of the fundamental operations is a way of relating them, as are connections of equality and inequality.

One type of item that has successfully yielded measurements of relations abilities has been in the form of trends. A trend entails a variable and hence involves a relation between neighboring items of information within the series making up the trend. For example, the series ANT, MARBLE, SHRUB, ELEPHANT, TREE, HOUSE represents the variable of size, with the relation "larger than." A trend is in the nature of what Piaget calls "seriation" (Inhelder & Piaget, 1964). Seriation is not the only instance of relations. It might be regarded as a category of quantitative relations, which leaves a great many "qualitative" relations to be considered.

Systems   There has been no lack of recognition of the need of a concept like "system" in psychology in spite of the associational tradition, which has not coped at all well with systems or structures. Goss (1961) reminds us that forerunners of what may be called systems have been Descartes's "innate ideas," Kant's "categories" and "schemata," Locke's "abstractions," Frederick Bartlett's "schemata," and, of course, the gestalt conception of "configurations." To this list of originators of concepts in this category we may add Helen Peak (1958), who emphasized "structures," by which she meant "systems of relationships between identifiable parts," inferred from observed events. Murphy and Hochberg (1951) also made a great deal of "structures" in connection with theory of perceptual learning.

Behaviorists have commonly recognized "behavior patterns," which can be regarded as behavioral systems, in SI terminology. F. H. Allport (1955) wrote a large volume about structure, as a pervasive concept in psychology. Tolman (1948) concluded that even rats learn spatial systems called "cognitive maps," as well as motor patterns (1949). Others have recognized that there can be modification of components of motor patterns to suit the particular occasion, indicating some conception of a goal to be accomplished and a generalized scheme as to how this may be achieved (E. R. Guthrie & G. P. Horton, 1946; Muenzinger, Koerner, & Ivey, 1929). Such authors point out that an animal, rat or cat, having learned to achieve a certain end effect, such as tilting a vertical pole to obtain food, may accomplish the same result by nosing the pole, pawing it, or rubbing against it, and so on. The animal must have had some general conception of an end to be achieved and behavioral systems for accomplishing it.

Systems found in tests   Tests used to demonstrate factor abilities for dealing with systems reveal quite a variety of examples of systems. In the visual-figural area orientation in space is regarded as a system. There is appreciation of the orientation of an object and of positions of objects with reference to one another and with reference to the observer, as well as appreciation of patterns of lights in relation to movements that must be made. Another example of a visual system is seen in a test that requires the examinee to organize elementary figures so as to construct a familiar object. Examples of auditory-figural systems are rhythms and melodies.

Symbolic systems involve arrangements of symbols in space or in temporal sequences. Tests of these abilities may involve letter series or number series in which principles of organization are involved, as well as systematic sequences of dashes and circles. One DSS test calls for the production of alternative code systems, substituting letters for numbers. One NSS test calls for putting in correct order a series of words so that by changing only one letter at a time one may go from a starting word to a final word. Another test for the same factor asks for the sequence of numerical operations needed to go from one number to another.

Semantic systems in tests have involved verbally stated arithmetic-reasoning problems and word matrices with meaningful sequences in columns and rows. DMS tests have called for the construction of sentences and the completion of stories both in varied ways. NMS tests have emphasized temporal order of events, as in rearranging the cartoons in a cartoon strip so as to make the story most reasonable and as in rearranging verbally described steps in achieving a practical goal. Construction of a word matrix has been a successful task for measuring factor NMS, but a test asking for outlining of an exposition was not. In an EMS test, noting discrepancies within the layout of a pictured situation served to measure that factor.

Behavioral systems have also involved comprehension of situations of interacting individuals, and have called for completion of a four-part cartoon strip by selecting a fourth cartoon picture. A dyad of persons reacting in common to an absent person has also been a successful kind of CBS-test item.

Transformations   There has been no discoverable precedent in psychological literature for the concept of transformation as a product of information. In fact, there has been little precedent of any kind, with the exception of the gestalt concept of redefinition, which was the key starting point from which the discovery of transformation abilities took place (Wilson et al., 1954). One of the important transformation abilities had been known, without recognition that in that factor of spatial visualization transformation is a key definitive concept.

In certain visualization tests, following in imagination the folding and cutting of a piece of paper and the subsequent unfolding is the problem. In tests of mechanical principles or mechanical movements, being able to imagine the positional changes of parts is the problem. In other visual-figural–transformation tests, the transformation is in the form of altered roles or functions of lines, as in tests involving hidden figures, where the same lines before and after seeing the hidden figure serve different purposes. The same is true of the match-problems tests, where multiple changes must occur.

Examples of symbolic transformation appear in a test that calls for decoding a spoonerism to see what the speaker intended to say, for example on seeing or hearing "the fix-soot man." Other symbolic transformations have been in the form of breaking up old words to make new ones and in judging whether one word can come from another merely by rearrangement of letters.

Semantic transformations have involved shifts of meanings of words, revising interpretations of stories and of situations, and changing the use of objects. Behavioral transformations have involved the revision of a story as told by four consecutive scenes by making a substitution for one of the scenes, changing the expression given by a body by giving it a different head, and changing the meaning of the same stated comment by attributing it to another speaker and listener.

The demonstration of so many transformation abilities, as predicted by the SI model, should lend good support to the treatment of transformations as products of information. The substantial variety of changes that can be used as transformations in tests also attests to the generality of the concept.

Implications   A good synonym for implication is "expectancy." When Tolman (1932) announced the view that what the rat learns in the maze and even what Pavlov's salivating dog learned are in the form of an expectancy, he was implicitly recognizing the product of implication. Tolman reiterated the view a number of years later (1949). His conclusion was based upon such observations as seeing a rat, having been trained to run a maze to a food box with sunflower seed as the incentive, on finding a substitute food there, rejecting it and searching as if looking for the accustomed reward. There were other such observations.

Rejection of the expectancy view by Tolman's critics probably arose from their interpretation of "expectancy" in mentalistic terms, as if a lower animal showing this quality should do so with the full awareness and complexity that would be true of a human individual in similar circumstances. Tolman's conception did not gain much acceptance, in a psychological milieu in which theory was restricted as much as possible to peripheral, stimulus-response concepts.

Implications in tests   The concept of "implication" may fare better than that of "expectancy," especially as applied to human subjects, in that there is much empirical evidence on which to base the concept. The variety of behavioral events in which implications appear to play roles lends some support to this expectation and also contributes to its connotations.

Tests of figural implications involve looking ahead with respect to routes in mazes and with respect to moves in a game. Presumably factor CFI would be of great importance in games of chess and checkers and in athletic games of many kinds. Tests for factor DFI involve adding lines to already-existing line drawings, each one suggested in some degree by what is already there. The artist who shows considerable embellishment in his product would be producing implied information.

In the symbolic area of information, cognition of implications is tested by tasks that call for efficient use of symbols, where efficiency depends upon seeing ahead. CSI is also tested by giving a few symbolic elements and asking the examinee to do something with them; he does something reasonable that is suggested by what he has to start with. A test of DSI asks E to draw as many inferences as he can from two very simple algebraic equations. An NSI test calls for drawing the right conclusion to two defined operations with pairs of symbols. A test of ESI asks E to say whether or not conclusions can be drawn from some stated inequalities.

Implications dealing with semantic information are common in tasks that involve foresight with respect to meaningful events. Cognition tests, for CMI, may ask E to say what defects, deficiencies, or difficulties he foresees in connection with common appliances and common social institutions. Other tests ask him to say what contingencies or consequences he sees in connection with certain events that are specified. DMI tests call for elaboration of a plan in the one case and for different things that a design may symbolize in the other. Tests of NMI should call for unique conclusions to given meaningful information. One test asks E to put in the proper sequence four words so that each is associated with the next. Another asks him to name the necessary attributes of an implement that is to be used to serve a certain purpose. An evaluation test involving semantic implications is of the syllogistic type, in which conclusions are stated, to be judged as true or false.

For behavioral implications, we know only what kinds of tests will work for the operation of cognition, but they fit the expected picture. Given one pictured scene with two or three people interacting in it, what is the next event likely to be? In a different kind of test, E is asked to decide what a statement made by a counselee really means (implies) with regard to his attitude or mental state.

Psychology and logic

At the beginning of this chapter, mention was made of the possibility of relating the products of information to formal logic. Now that we have reviewed the characteristics of the kinds of products, let us see how this might be done. Along the way, we saw how Noble has pointed out some logical properties in connection with the similarity between semantic concepts or units. Since almost any semantic unit, with any degree of generality, is also a class, the same reasoning applies to classes. Treating classes as sets composed of class members, we have a very natural way of representing them logically in the form of Venn diagrams, an example of which is given in Figure 10.7.

Logical properties of relations   It can also be said that H. M. Johnson (1959) has pointed out some of the logical properties of relations. But in connection with this kind of product, we find that there are varieties of relations, some satisfying one logical property and some another. For example, some relations possess the property of symmetry, as when we say that John is the brother of Richard and that Richard is also the brother of John. The symmetry can be expressed by the symbols $a\ R_1\ b$ and $b\ R_1\ a$, where R_1 stands for the same relation. In other relations there is asymmetry, as when we say that Bob is the son of Tom but the reverse does not hold. These relations can be symbolized as $a\ R_2\ b$ and $b\ \bar{R}_2\ a$, where the bar over the R indicates "not so related."

There can also be both transitive and intransitive relations. A transitive one is best found in the case of a quantitative relation, such as "harder than." The symbolic statement would be: If $a\ R_3\ b$ and $b\ R_3\ c$, then it follows that $a\ R_3\ c$. If a diamond is harder than iron and iron is harder than aluminum, then a diamond is harder than aluminum. An intransitive set of relations would be symbolized: $a\ R_4\ b$ and $b\ R_4\ c$, but $a\ \bar{R}_4\ c$, which would fit the case in which, in games of tennis, a defeats b and b defeats c but a does not defeat c.

Relations can also be either reflexive or irreflexive. In a class of words that are all synonyms, we can express the relation $a\ R_5\ a$, where a indicates class membership. But in the class of numbers, no two numbers have the same value; hence the relations are irreflexive. These examples are sufficient to show that a beginning has been made toward a logical treatment of relations.

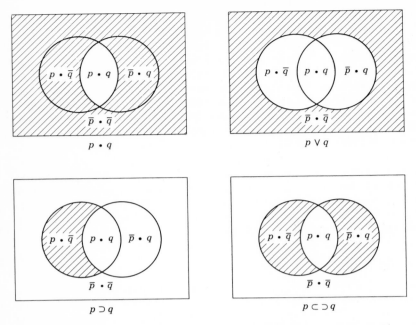

Fig. 10.7   Representation of classes as well as propositions and their combinations by means of Venn diagrams.

Differences between psychology and logic   Before going further with this kind of application of logical principles, we should be clear as to what belongs to psychology and what to logic. Psychology is an empirical science, one of whose aims is to describe in terms of general principles or laws what actually happens when individuals think. Its approach is that of observation and induction; its operation is mainly cognitive; it seeks to understand. Formal logic, on the other hand, is not an empirical science. Like mathematics, it starts with axioms, statements that it assumes to be true, and it aims at sets of rules for thinking whereby it is possible to determine whether inferences are true or false. Both mathematics and logic exist in the realm of pure ideas. Both can be effectively applied as aids to accurate and effective thinking. Both provide models for rigorous thinking.

Piaget makes some interesting points regarding the relations between psychology and logic. He maintains that in the relating of *mental structures,* which we may paraphrase as "products," to logic, it is necessary to develop intermediate systems that can constitute a psychologic (Piaget, 1953). Some formalization can be introduced in steps before arriving at the complete formalization that must be achieved in logic. The possibility of doing this suggests that formal logic may be to psychology what mathematical theoretical physics has been to physics.

A necessary step, before formal logic can be fully applied, is the stating of psychological events in terms of propositions, for formal logic can deal only with propositions; only where information becomes knowledge, in Werkmeister's sense (1948), can the logical calculus be applied. Not every statement is a proposition: only those that can be either true or false. A proposition cannot even be partly true and partly false, for logic operates under the principle of the excluded middle; in the excluded middle, part truths dwell.

This poses a problem that has to be overcome or circumvented, or it leaves us with a limited application of logic to psychological events.

Piaget (1953) points out other difficulties. He comments that even much of the usual thinking of an adult is unformalizable in logical terms. Only mathematical thinking is completely formalized. In normal thinking, genetically, propositions come first and axioms last, just in reverse order to that of logic. Furthermore, *systems* of information do not lend themselves to step-by-step treatment such as is characteristic of logic. As F. H. Allport (1955) has emphasized, mental structures (systems) defy mathematical and logical treatment. We shall have to wait to see whether the approach through information measurement, as proposed by Garner (1962), is found to work.

Basic operations with propositions   Let p and q be two simple propositions, such as "This boy is creative" and "This boy is intelligent," where in each case the statement means being above the mean, for a composite divergent-production score in the first case and for an IQ rating in the second. Either of these statements can be true or false. Let us symbolize false statements by $\bar{p}$ and $\bar{q}$, which is to say, not p and not q. Using a dot to indicate conjunction or "and," we have four combinations of these two propositions, each with two truth values. They are:

1. $p \cdot q$
2. $p \cdot \bar{q}$
3. $\bar{p} \cdot q$
4. $\bar{p} \cdot \bar{q}$

These four cases are often represented pictorially by means of Venn diagrams, as in Figure 10.7. Ignore the shadings for the time being. Case 4 is the area within the rectangle but not in either circle. The circle at the left in each case stands for p, and the circle at the right for q. Case 1 ($p \cdot q$) is indicated by the overlapping portions of the two circles. Cases 2 and 3 are shown by the nonoverlapping portions of the circles.

We can make certain statements about the propositions which automatically group the cases in various ways. If we make the statement p and q ($p \cdot q$), we can mean case 1 only. If we say p or q, symbolized by $p \vee q$, we actually mean p or q, or both, which involves cases 1, 2, and 3; in other words, all cases except 4. See the Venn diagram for the case of $p \vee q$, with only the $\bar{p} \cdot \bar{q}$ region shaded.

A third general statement is of special interest, for it is concerned with an implication. If we say p implies q, symbolized by $p \supset q$, we are logically referring to three cases, 1, 3, and 4, case 2 being false. If p is true, then q has to be true (case 1), but $p \supset q$ says nothing about q if p is false. If p is false, q could still be either true or false; hence cases 3 and 4 apply.

A fourth kind of statement is that p implies q and q implies p. Said in conditional form, the statement reads: If, and only if, p, then q. The "only if p" rules out case 3 as well as case 2, leaving only cases 1 and 4. This is shown in the last diagram in Figure 10.7.

Implications and correlation   Psychologically, implications are predictions. One way of representing predictions mathematically is by means of a correlation scatter diagram. To go along with the two-valued truth scales adopted in formal logic, we may artificially dichotomize correlated continuous variables to obtain a 2×2 contingency table. Thus, the two propositions ("This boy is creative" and "This boy is intelligent") can be represented as two variables in a correlation table shown in Figure 10.8. The plus and minus signs mean true and false, respectively, with respect to the two propositions. When we say that p implies q, we are saying that if the boy is creative, he is intelligent (case a in this

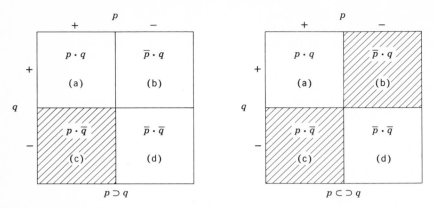

Fig. 10.8 Representation of implicational statements by means of a 2 × 2 correlation diagram.

diagram). If he is not creative, he could be either intelligent or not, which means that cases *b* and *d* are true. But if he is creative, he can only be intelligent; he cannot be unintelligent case *c*.

The one-way prediction of intelligence from creativity, with no prediction in the reverse direction, is in rough agreement with the obtained facts, as related in Chapter 6. Let us take a case in which prediction is possible in both directions, which is the more common finding with variables in psychology, with a linear relationship between the two variables. The parallel logical case is the conditional statement "*q*, if and only if *p*." This leaves only the *a* and *d* quadrants (see Figure 10.8).

Observed correlations But note that the application of the logical operations presupposes perfect correlations. In everyday life, correlations of events are almost never perfect. As a part of an individual's normal cognition of things in the world about him, he observes what he thinks are correlations between events. It may take only one conjunction of two events *p* and *q* to lead him to expect *q* when *p* comes. Subsequent experiences may correct that implication, but it will usually only modify confidence in the expectation to something on a probability basis, where the probability is less than 1.0. The empirical correlation might be on the order of .2, but because he senses some relationship, the individual may have the confidence that should go only with a higher degree of correlation. He may talk as if the correlation were perfect, in which case he is applying naïvely the logical calculus.

Furthermore, the individual is likely to conclude that *q* implies *p* as well as that *p* implies *q*, when as a matter of fact only one of these propositions is sometimes true. Much faulty reasoning stems from this kind of fallacy. In more common terminology, the individual mistakes a sufficient condition for a necessary condition, or vice versa, or either of these conditions is regarded as both sufficient and necessary. In correcting such mistakes, formal logic can be of great value. But as for representing what goes on in the form of correlational impressions in cognition, the mathematics of correlation seems to provide a more realistic model, since it allows realistically for both the *p* · *q* and *p̄* · *q̄* cases no matter what the implicational statement happens to be.

Inhelder and Piaget (1958) concluded that after the individual reaches the stage at which he indulges in formal operations that conform to the rules of logic, he may also show a naïve conception of correlation. Inference of such a conception is based upon the behavior of the subject, from the fact that he recognizes the four possible cases, as represented in Figure 10.8, to the effect that cells a and d contain confirming cases and cells b and c contain nonconfirming cases and that there is a positive relationship if $a + d$ exceeds $b + c$. This achievement was found to be reached commonly by ages fourteen to fifteen. The experimental material consisted of sets of pictures of faces with varying numbers of combinations of blue versus brown eyes with blonde versus brown hair. The subjects could readily be aware of the frequencies of $a, b, c,$ and d cases.

With adult subjects, however, Smedslund (1963), H. M. Jenkins and W. C. Ward (1965), and Ward and Jenkins (1965) have found that there is little support for the conclusion that there is a conception isomorphic with the principles of correlation, where the person has no technical information on the subject. There is a strong tendency for subjects to ignore negative cases and to be influenced almost entirely by the positive cases, that is, the a cases, where both p and q are true. This means considerable ignoring of the nonconfirming cases and failure to recognize that the d (or $\bar{p} \cdot \bar{q}$) cases are also confirming.

In considering this behavior, we are reminded of the phenomenon of partial reinforcement in classical conditioning. Conditioning can be established even with a small proportion of reinforced stimulations, which are the $p \cdot q$ cases. We are also reminded of the fact that in experiments on attainment of concepts, the subject frequently makes little use of negative instances. But in conditioning of discriminations, where stimulus A is given with reinforcement and stimulus B without reinforcement, negative cases become very effective. It is surprising, then, that human subjects do not pay more attention to negative instances. Under the appropriate modes of presentation, they may be found to do so.

Summary

In SI theory, information is discrimination within the psychological field, with no implication that that field is entirely conscious. It is different from philosophy's conception of knowledge, which is in the form of propositions, and hence is more limited in scope; and from the conception in the discipline of information theory, which views information as equivalent to uncertainty and as lack of structure, although also emphasizing discriminations.

Precedents for the distinctions among the content categories of figural, symbolic, and semantic information are to be found in disciplines dealing with verbal communication, but only incidental precedents for behavioral information can be found.

It was concluded that semantic information is not completely tied to verbal signs, in fact, that there is much independence of the two, in development and in adult functioning. There is a generally unrecognized need to distinguish between denotative and connotative aspects of semantic concepts. A core-and-context theory of semantic meaning was proposed. Methods of measuring in connection with semantic meaning have been limited to connotative aspects.

Considerable attention was given to the relation of psychology, and particularly the products of information, to modern formal logic, in view of the many parallels and the steps already taken to apply logical operations to units, classes, relations, and implications. It was proposed that the products provide a basis for a psychologic and that the multiplication of product and content categories provides the basis for a psychoepistemology.

III Implications for psychological theory

11 Perception and cognition

In the preceding chapters we were concerned first with the general taxonomy of intellectual abilities, emphasis being placed upon the categories within which those abilities are logically classified. Although the category concepts and their implications took us into certain problems of how the psychologist's organism operates, there is much more to be considered in this direction. In this chapter and those immediately following, we shall adopt more completely the operational point of view and try to see how the new information about intellectual abilities helps us to understand some of the perennial psychological problems, suggesting some new types of problems.

The general point of view is an informational type of psychology, in line with the emphasis upon information in Chapter 10. A reading of the writings on psychological theory during the past twenty years leaves a definite impression that there is a trend away from stimulus-response psychology and toward some form of cognitive theory. It is more commonly realized that what is inside the "black box" is, after all, the most important subject matter about which psychologists should be concerned.

Cognitive theory emphasizing information is not new, for a number of investigators and writers have chosen to follow this emphasis in their own ways. Among them are James G. Miller (1955), J. McV. Hunt (1961), Broadbent (1958; 1962), Crossman (1964), Treisman (1964), and Gaito (1965), to mention a few. Others, including Murphy and Hochberg (1951), F. H. Allport (1955), and Peak (1958), have emphasized informational structures, not unlike the SI products. In Chapter 9, the operation of evaluation was connected logically with cybernetic principles, which will be related to perception and cognition in this chapter. Among others who have found use for those principles are Slack (1955), Solley and Murphy (1960), K. U. Smith (1962), and D. P. Andrews (1964).

In this chapter we shall be concerned with distinctions between perception and cognition, but the chapter will be mostly about perception, since cognition was treated extensively in Chapter 9. We shall be concerned with some of the problems of sensory input and attention and with questions of consciousness and the possibilities of unconscious perception and cognition. And, finally, we shall consider the matter of perceptual development. The general subject of learning is reserved for the chapter to follow, and intellectual development in general will be the subject of Chapter 17.

Input operations

The concept of perception   In the operations of perception and cognition we are concerned with sensory input and with what happens almost immediately subsequent thereto. This places those two concepts in their proper context but does not differentiate them. The distinction can best be achieved by considering the typical sequence of events following stimulation of a sensory surface like the retina. Gaito (1965) has clearly proposed an "information-extraction" model to describe those events. What the individual has in the way of information consequent to a certain stimulation depends upon how much information he "extracts from" the input from the receptors.

Let us say that the visual input is from the printed word sad and that the stimulus is exposed tachistoscopically, beginning with very subliminal exposure times and increasing by small steps until the observer reports and understands the word. The amount of information "extracted" would begin with a minimum of just a brightness variation, a mere noticing that something is present. Such reports from the observer would be the basis for finding his detection threshold. The next increment of information might be that the nature of the stimulus is in the form of lines, no letters being perceived. The next level would possibly be the recognition of one letter of three, then two of three, then three letters and the realization that they form a familiar word; finally the meaning of the word arises. Whether we call the progression of events an increasing "extraction" of information, "decoding" of information, or "development" of information is a matter of preferred terminology, determined by general theoretical views. Let us see how we can use this picture of psychological events to help differentiate perception and cognition.

In terms of structure-of-intellect categories, recalling from Chapter 4 some examples of units of information that are cognized, we see that at the stage of seeing single letters and identifying them as such, the cognition of figural units is involved. At the stage at which the three-letter combination is recognized as a word symbol, a symbolic unit is involved. At the final stage, when the meaning is attached to the word, a semantic unit is developed. Thus, the steps from recognition of letters upward are properly placed under cognition. It seems to be common usage to say that letters are *perceived,* however, and there is no good reason for discontinuing this practice. It would be stretching the meaning of perception too far to include awareness of semantic meaning, although this is sometimes done. Even realizing that SAD is a sign for something beyond itself is probably carrying the meaning of perception too far, from a technical point of view. With some arbitrariness, then, perception may be said to overlap cognition where figural information is concerned.

But the illustration pertains to units of information only and to no other kinds of products. Shall we say that an individual perceives classes, relations, systems, transformations, and implications when they are figural? All these products go beyond the immediately given, much as semantic meaning does. If we restrict perception to information that is immediately given by sensory events, it applies only to the cognition of figural units. In the other direction, farther toward the initiation of input, it can be said that perception goes all the way to the point of first discrimination. But from an earlier discussion of the meaning of cognition in Chapter 9, it was implied that cognition goes that far also. We are thus left with a definition of *perception* that makes it synonymous in part with cognition of figural units of information. The only reasonable alternative would be to say that cognition begins only when there is some degree of structuring of the input. This decision would raise the question of criteria for structuring, which would not be easily answered.

This conception of perception still leaves much territory that is covered by the term. There are numerous problems concerning the way in which figural units come about. The principles of sensory organization proposed by gestalt psychologists—the laws of proximity, continuity, similarity, and common fate—were designed for this very purpose. Efforts to extend this list and to apply it more generally beyond the visual modality seem to have lapsed. Other principles must surely be involved. Some help in this direction may be derived from new information concerning sense-organ operations. For example, W. H. Miller, F. Ratliff, and H. K. Hartline (1961) discussed interaction of receptor cells within the retina and the way in which some cortical control is exerted over receptor activity. Recordings of neuron activity show how successive stimulations become fused, how border contrast develops, and how boundary lines are sharpened.

Factors of sensation and perception   Factor analyses of certain perceptual tests have brought out some special abilities that have little or no claim to recognition as intellectual abilities. For example, there are three factors representing sensitivity to colors: red sensitivity, green sensitivity, and blue sensitivity (F. Nowell Jones, 1948; 1950). There are also three dimensions representing sensitivity to sounds: long-wave sensitivity, moderate-wave sensitivity, and shortwave sensitivity (Henry, 1947).[1] There are also a factor for pitch discrimination and one for loudness discrimination (Karlin, 1942). There are a factor of kinesthetic sensitivity (R. I. Bass, 1939; Fleishman, 1954) and one or more factors of sensitivity connected with the static sense (Bass, 1939; McCloy & Young, 1954).

All these factors have to do with sensory functions and probably depend more upon sense-organ structures than upon brain structures. From the psychological point of view, the kinds of information involved pertain to *properties* of objects or units rather than to units as such. Units become known by virtue of combinations of such properties or attributes. Attributes also play roles in connection with figural classes and relations. Classes are distinguished by virtue of common properties, including sensory properties of qualitative and quantitative kinds. Relations of figural information also depend upon such sensory attributes. In spite of the fact that sensory properties play such important roles, no satisfactory way has been seen as yet for incorporating sensory factors into structure-of-intellect theory, except in the incidental ways mentioned.

Two other known aptitude factors in the perceptual area go beyond sensory qualities. One is length or size estimation (Guilford & Lacey, 1947), and the other is sensitivity to visual movement (Roff, 1952). The first of these deals with a certain quantitative relation (greater size), which suggests that it might belong in the category of cognition of visual-figural relations, as an ability of narrow scope. In spite of its narrow scope, it could be very important, as in parking a car. The second, since it pertains to movement, could be included as a transformation ability of a special kind, placeable in the category of CFT-V. It is not the same thing as the visualization factor.

Other factors of perceptual kinds will probably be found when appropriate tests for them have been constructed and analyzed. As more of them become known, they might call for a structure or model of their own, or the SI model might be expanded to take care of them.

Filtering operations   One interesting feature of recent history of psychology is the rediscovery of the phenomenon of attention. With the domination of stimulus-response behaviorism, the concept of "attention" went into discard. The organism was regarded more or less as a passive victim of environmental forces acting upon it. A number of circumstances, however, have brought the phenomena of attention back into consideration. One event was the discovery of the functions of the reticular formation, an important part of the brainstem, through which incoming impulses from most of the sensory inlets must pass on their ways to higher centers. One of the behavioral features clearly traceable to this organ is that of general wakefulness, vigilance, or activity level. Interest in problems of vigilance, in connection with watch-standing activities in the military services, was a parallel development that called for the concept of something like attention.

Another aspect of attention to receive new notice is selective activity in perception. New experimental studies of perception, especially in England, have demonstrated the severe limitation in the capacity of an individual for handling incoming information. To adopt language from communication engineers, it was realized that the "channel capacity"

[1]For some additional information on sensory factors, see Guilford (1959a).

of the individual for handling incoming information is very limited. In order to keep the amount of effective information at levels that can be handled, some kind of valve or "filtering" device has to be assumed, as suggested by Broadbent (1957b). Thus, the level idea connected with the former concept of attention was replaced by the concept of "vigilance," and the selective idea was replaced by the concept of "filtering." Both concepts are improvements, in that they are more operational in nature.

The competition of sensory inputs and the need for selection because of limited capacity is easily illustrated in daily life. If two people are speaking simultaneously, it is possible to follow the thread of communication from one speaker but not from both simultaneously. The listener may alternate between the two, and he may even store temporarily in his immediate-memory system information from one source while attending to the other and come back to the stored information a moment later. Thus, temporary memory storage helps to extend input capacity somewhat. Another way of enlarging input capacity is to gain familiarity with information. Inputs usually provide an overabundance of sensory cues from the same source of information, a phenomenon known as "redundancy." With increased familiarity, only a segment is needed to represent the total. Another device for enlarging intake in spite of limited capacity is *chunking*, which means unitizing, or making larger units out of smaller ones, or making units out of systems.

Many experiments in which stimuli are applied by means of earphones to the two ears separately but simultaneously, under varied conditions, have been done by Broadbent and others. We shall be concerned with the memory aspects of this kind of experiment in the next chapter. Here we can note some of the conditions that reduce the effects of competition at input.

If two voices are speaking, it helps the auditor if they are very different in tone quality (e.g., one is a man's voice and the other is a woman's), if they are in different languages, or if they are talking about different subjects. Similarity of either the figural or the semantic components of information is a condition for confusing the two messages and of making it difficult to ignore the one while listening to the other. It is not a matter of sensory masking, for successful attention to the one voice brings it in unfused with the other.

Simultaneous inputs from different sense channels can also have interfering effects, unless the two are integrated as in viewing television or cinema. But if one were required to extract special information about either the sound track or the picture, interference would again be experienced and there would need to be selection of the one and filtering out of the other. Even within the same sense, if special information is to be extracted regarding one aspect, e.g., color, the observer almost has to ignore properties other than color.

Conditions of attention   Such discussion brings us to an old-time topic, long dormant during the de-emphasis of the subject of attention. Madison Avenue advertisers have not ignored the subject but have utilized effectively the principles governing prepotency of information competing for input. The principles pertaining to the nature of stimuli are well known. They are the formerly recognized "objective" conditions of attention: intensity, size, position, isolation, change, suddenness of onset, movement, and repetition. The so-called subjective conditions of attention have their foundation mainly in motivation. Stimuli gain prepotency to the extent that they fit in with the motivational condition of the organism at the moment.

There is one subjective condition that has been given special attention in recent years: novelty of the input. Novelty is a function of the individual for whom the stimulus is novel, and it is novel because it departs significantly from the ordinary or the expected. In this connection, Treisman (1964) speaks of the principle of habituation, which applies to the fact that input from a stimulus tends to diminish and to disappear on prolonged repetition of the stimulus. Broadbent (1958) put this in the form of a principle that the attention filter favors passing novel messages. After habituation to a certain stimulus, which shows up also in terms of failure to block the alpha rhythms of the brain and failure to produce a GSR (galvanic skin response), a slight change is likely again to elicit a brain response. A cybernetic type of interpretation is that the altered input fails to match what is stored in memory. Failure to match is a call for activity. Another interpretation is in terms of Helson's adaptation-level theory (H. Helson, 1964). According to this theory, prior stimulation establishes a condition of neutrality, and in general it is departure from adaptation level to which organisms react. So potent are conditions following this principle that when a stimulus level steps down in intensity, it arouses attention; even when we have become habituated to a barely supraliminal stimulus, its cessation arouses attention.

A flow chart for perception Crossman (1964) has presented an excellent diagram that illustrates many of the features under discussion and others in the process of perception, a modified copy of which is shown in Figure 11.1. The input source is the visual apparatus. Each fixation in vision covers only about 0.1 percent of the visual field with resolution sufficiently good for detailed vision. Fixations may last from 25 to 400 milliseconds, at which rate it would take several minutes to cover the whole visual field with close inspection. As fixation shifts, the input from the previous fixation persists in temporary storage and is experienced as an image if one pays attention to it or returns to it. A kind of ghostlike representation hangs suspended for a second or two. Titchener (1915) one time called this the *memory afterimage,* a term that went out of vogue with his existential psychology but which could well be used again in connection with temporary memory storage. It is to be noted that the observed information in this image is figural and that any other kind of information to be extracted from it requires some further activity—cognition. It is possible to derive other information, e.g., semantic, from the memory afterimage by reexamination.

Crossman (1964) cites an experiment to illustrate how the memory afterimage can be used. If a matrix of letters in three rows of four letters each is exposed for fifty milliseconds, the typical subject can report, on the average, 4.5 letters, correctly, coming from scattered places in the matrix. If immediately after the exposure a tone signal is given, indicating to S which row he is to report, S can usually report the four letters in that row perfectly. This means that he has been able to "read" those four letters after the exposure; he evidently reads them from the memory afterimage. To return to Figure 11.1, the filter is shown cutting out most of the potential input information and passing only a small portion of it. The next block shown in the path of the incoming information represents the temporary memory store from previous fixations, from which additions are made to current incoming information.

At this point, information in permanent memory storage makes some contributions toward recognition of properties of the pattern represented in the input. This store contains elementary pattern information from previous experience. This stage might be what gestalt psychologists have called "sensory organization." Recognition of an element is represented in the figure by a narrowing to one item of information, for which there is another temporary memory store. At this stage the permanent memory store is called upon for information regarding more complex patterns, and the complete object is recognized and held in another temporary memory store. If recognition of the object is the only problem,

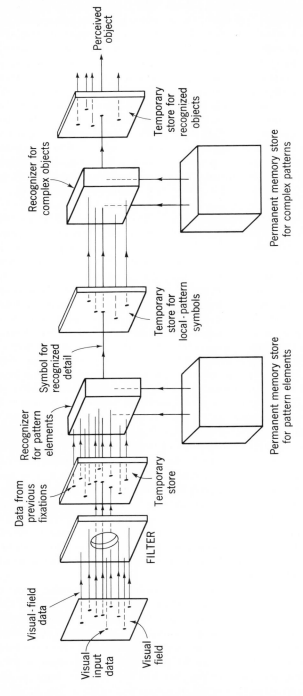

Fig. 11.1 A hypothetical flow chart or operational model for input of information in perception and cognition. (*From Crossman, 1964, reproduced with permission.*)

things may stop there; if something is to be done with that object or if further reflection is in order regarding it, the permanent memory store may make further contributions.

Although one might question some of the details of this picture, its general nature has considerable merit and probable validity. We shall have occasion to refer to this kind of operational model in later chapters, in dealing with motor activity and with problem solving and creative production.

Conscious and unconscious information

The basic definition of *information* given in Chapter 10—that which the organism discriminates—says nothing about whether information is conscious or whether it may also be unconscious. We must now face that question. This is particularly necessary because of the great number of studies in recent years dealing with the phenomenon often known as "subliminal perception," some of which claim to have demonstrated that there can be perception and also learning without awareness. Then, of course, there is the vast psychoanalytical literature with numerous descriptions of what happens mentally but unconsciously. And often inferences are drawn that we are more capable unconsciously than consciously, as if we had a chained genius hidden somewhere in our being.

As the definition stands, information could be either conscious or unconscious. Wherever discriminations are made, including discriminatory conditioned responses, the definition would be satisfied. Whether or not the conditioned dog or rat has conscious discriminations we cannot know. Conditioning experiments with human subjects offer some basis from the subjects' own reports concerning perceptions during conditioning.

If we consider the wide range of psychological tests given to human subjects, as described in earlier chapters, it is obvious that whether or not there can be unconscious discriminations, conscious representations provide an enormous range of possibilities for making discriminations, which would appear to be precluded at an unconscious level. It may be said of consciousness that its reason for being is that it furnishes to the organism a representation of his environment with point-at-able components.

Studies of perception and learning without awareness   Before we can decide that anything happens without awareness, we must have criteria of when there is awareness and when there is not. A verbal description or report is evidence that there is awareness, but there is much awareness that is not and cannot be verbalized. Correct choice of alternative stimuli beyond a chance level provides one nonverbal criterion. There need not be complete veridical recognition of objects in order to satisfy such a criterion of awareness. For example, geometric figures may be exposed with such minimal time or illumination that the subject cannot report verbally which figure was exposed; yet he may be able to say that the exposures were different. In other words, there are different levels or degrees of awareness. The psychologist's general problem is to determine what can and what cannot be done at different levels of awareness.

Conditioning experiments   Experiments on this subject have been of a few standard types. Some of them have been conditioning experiments, in which the interest has been in seeing whether conditioning can be effected to a stimulus too weak to arouse visual or auditory awareness. Baker (1938) reported producing a pupillary response to a sound stimulus below the absolute threshold, but according to Ericksen (1960) a number of other investigators were unable to replicate this finding.

Others have used the GSR as the response to be conditioned. Lazarus and McCleary (1951) and McCleary and Lazarus (1951) used nonsense words such as YILIM, GAHIW, and VECYO as stimuli, the subliminal exposure of some of these words being consistently reinforced and that of others not at all. They placed much emphasis on the finding that even when S gave a wrong (verbal) recognition response to a conditioned stimulus, he was likely to show a GSR. They took this to mean that there was unconscious discrimination of stimuli, or what they called a phenomenon of "subception." It should be pointed out that this does not necessarily mean that there was unconscious *perception of symbolic units;* the discriminations could be based upon very crude figural differences. One significant finding that we shall use later is that the less subliminal the stimulus, the greater the percentage of conditioned GSRs when recognitions were wrong.

The results of Lazarus and McCleary might be taken to mean that we can discriminate stimuli better unconsciously than we can consciously, since there were GSRs when there were errors of verbal report. The trouble is that we also have to consider the mistakes in the GSR when verbal responses are correct. The two discriminative responses, GSR and verbal, are obviously not correlated perfectly, but there is evidence that such pairs of responses are positively correlated.

The results with this kind of experiment have not always been positive. F. W. R. Taylor (1953) used visual forms as stimuli and obtained significantly more GSRs for the reinforced stimuli than for the others in only two of eight subjects. Voor (1956) repeated the Lazarus-McCleary experiment, using eight syllables, to four of which reinforcement was applied and four not, in conditioning the GSR. In the test trials, three levels of illumination were used, the highest giving the GSR in 50 percent of the trials. His subjects rated on a 3-point scale their degree of confidence in their naming of the exposed syllables. Voor was able to conclude that there is a definite relationship between the amount of information received from a stimulus and the ability to discriminate in terms of the GSR. When no reportable information of any kind is received from the stimulus, the subception effect is not significantly greater than chance. There was no evidence from his results that there could be autonomic discrimination without some kinds of awareness.

Subliminal suggestions A different kind of experiment provided subliminal suggestions while subjects were making psychophysical judgments, comparing rectangles for size by the method of constant stimulus differences (P. Davis, 1964). A standard size of rectangle and two larger and two smaller rectangles were compared with the standard. Whenever the standard was compared with itself, the word SMALLER or the word LARGER was flashed on the screen just before the second rectangle of the comparison pair was exposed. When pairs were actually different, a wordlike figure was flashed on the screen. The results were that the Ss' judgments agreed with the "larger" and "smaller" suggestions from 8 to 19 times out of 24 for the various Ss, the mean being 13.2, which was just barely significant. No S reported having seen the flashed suggestions, although Ss had been instructed to note and describe anything unusual.

In a somewhat similar experiment, Calvin and Dollenmayer (1959) exposed two circles, one labeled "Right" and the other "Left," with S to choose one or the other in a set of 10 trials. Each of 60 Ss was told that it was an experiment on extrasensory perception. Half were told whether they were right each time and half not. During the exposure of the two circles, there were flashed on the screen for 0.01 to 0.03 second the suggestions "Choose right" or "Choose left." The result was a mean near 5.0, or just a chance number of guesses in accordance with suggestions, under all conditions.

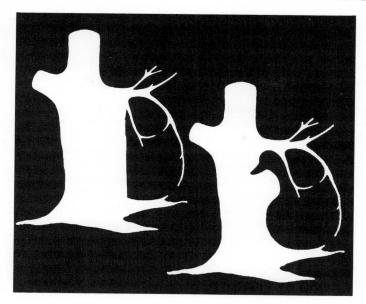

Fig. 11.2   One of the tree figures contains a hidden duck. (*After Eagle, Wolitzky, & Klein, 1966; reproduced with permission.*)

In a class on advertising, Champion and Turner (1959) showed a thirty-minute film about advertising. At 10-second intervals, a lantern slide was flashed for 0.01 second, showing a spoonful of rice and under it the label "Wonder rice." A control group had a comparable exposure of some nonsense lines. After the motion picture, Ss were shown the spoonful of rice supraliminally without a label and were asked two questions: "Did you see this on the screen at any time during the motion picture?" and "Whether you saw the picture or not, which is the most likely brand name of the rice, Monarch or Wonder?" There was no significant difference between the two groups of Ss in frequencies of responses to either of the questions.

Associative responses without awareness   Even though an individual may be unaware of a visual object when the stimulus conditions make this possible, items of information that are ordinarily associated with that object may be aroused, as shown by Eagle, Wolitzky, and Klein (1966). They exposed one of the two tree pictures shown in Figure 11.2 to each of two groups of students. One picture had a hidden-duck figure; the other, not. The exposure times were either 0.01 second or 1.0 second, in a few repeated trials. After each exposure, S was to draw a sketch of what he had seen and to write the names of the objects in it.

It had been determined in another large group, to which a picture of a duck was exposed five times, what kinds of verbal associative responses such individuals give. Such responses were looked for in the sketches drawn by the Ss in the main experiment. The group having the hidden-duck exposure gave significantly more instances of duck-connected responses than those exposed to the other tree picture.

Other experimental steps elicited the information that it was unlikely that those exposed to the hidden-duck tree actually saw the duck. When Ss were later shown the tree with the duck for thirty seconds and were told to look for the duck, only about 50 percent saw it.

Unrecognized reinforcements   Other experiments have been designed to answer the question whether learning can occur when *S* is not aware of the reinforcing stimuli, presented either subliminally or supraliminally. A. Jones, M. Manis, and B. Weiner (1963) did three experiments in which the reinforcing stimuli "Right" and "Wrong" were applied subliminally. Five visual forms were to be classified in one of two categories, four in one and one in the other. With subliminal reinforcing stimuli flashed on the screen during 100 runs through the five stimuli, there was no significant evidence of learning either with or without monetary incentives. In the third experiment, *S* was to guess what number the experimenter was thinking of. Half the *S*s were reinforced for giving odd-numbered responses and half for even-numbered responses, with no evidence for learning found.

Essman (1957) applied verbal reinforcement supraliminally. *S*s were to sort 60 nonsense figures in four verbal classes: human, botanical, animal, and anatomical. Previous trials had shown the categories of human and anatomical to be most unpopular. In the experiment, the experimenter said "Good" whenever *S* placed a figure in either of the two unpopular categories. By questioning it was learned that 8 of 10 *S*s were aware that the reinforcing stimulus was being given, but none associated it with the two reinforced categories. *S*s were reported to have given a significant increase in use of those two categories. It can be inferred that although the *S*s did not form a self-recognized implication between category and reinforcement, the reinforcing condition was effective. Can we say that an unconscious implication was formed? Or is it simply unnecessary for such an implication to be formed? We cannot decide from the information available.

Extraction of products of information   Some experiments have called for possible unconscious discriminations of a less immediate sort. For example, Betke and Lighthall (1963) presented simple number series to be completed, such as 3, 4, ___, 6. The *S*s were unable to respond at better than chance level when the exposure of the series was at the detection threshold or below, leading to the conclusion that the stimuli at such levels did not convey enough information. One might say that it would be necessary for *S* to cognize a simple symbolic system in order to succeed with these items.

Dixon (1958) and, later, Fuhrer and Ericksen (1960) tested whether word meanings could be conveyed by subliminal exposure of a list of 10 words. *S* was instructed simply to respond with any word that occurred to him. At a later session, *S* was presented with the list of stimulus words along with the list of his own responses, with the instruction to match them as he thought most appropriate. His matchings were better than chance, but variations of the conditions showed that the success could have been due to figural cues, which throws doubt on *S*'s having achieved anything in the way of semantic information during the subliminal exposures.

Unconscious information   The general conclusion to be drawn from all such experiments is that there is no superior "unconscious" that has peculiar advantages in perception and cognition. Again and again, it is shown that the stronger the stimulation, in the neighborhood of the detection threshold, the greater the likelihood that information will be transmitted, either for autonomic or for verbal discriminations. Ericksen (1960) has pointed out that when a conditioned response has been established with a supraliminal stimulus, to be used later in determining an absolute threshold, the threshold is about the same whether the conditioned response is used or a verbal judgment is used as the indicator of information input. Any stimulus of some degree of complexity provides a great redundancy of possible information that can be utilized in making discriminations. Discriminations can be made to subliminal stimuli as long as any distinguishing aspects get through. And getting through sufficiently for making discriminations is about as effective for one purpose as for another, GSR or verbal response.

It is obvious that we do have many instances in which sensory cues are effective in terms of discriminative responses without awareness, e.g., the ocular cues to distance and depth perception. But in such cases the connections are very highly habituated, as they are in an innate reflex connection. The experiments cited all involve relatively *new situations in which at least some learning is involved.* In our highly skilled activities, such as driving a car, we continually react to cues that pass unnoticed. In problem solving, things in memory storage definitely have their effects upon present behavior, without our being aware of them. Awareness, then, has an eminent role in learning but not with respect to information already committed to memory storage.

Perceptual development

Hereditary versus environmental sources   The old nativist-empiricist controversy is still with us and must be considered here. It is no longer a question of which is the right view and which is the wrong one but of how much and what come by way of natural growth and what is the role of stimulation and experience. Much of the evidence comes from deprivation experiments (withholding normal environmental stimulation) in lower animals or from human individuals who have gained the use of their eyes after having developed without vision. Other experiments involving environmental enrichment of stimulation have been performed with human subjects as well as with animals. We shall confine our attention here mostly to effects on perception.

Discrimination experiments   Fantz (1961) has done experiments on the visual perception of infants, using their tendency to fixate exposed material as an indication of form perception. His technique (Fantz, 1963) has been to let an infant lie on its back looking toward the ceiling and to expose the stimuli on a horizontal display directly above it. The index he used for pattern vision was the length of time the child fixated the display. The displays included a figure of a face versus concentric circles, stripes, a checkerboard, newspaper print, simple geometric figures, and uniform color fields.

One general result was that infants looked at figured stimuli twice as long as at plain ones. The face was fixated usually longer than the circles and the circles longer than the newsprint. The results were about the same for infants under five days of age as for infants from two to six months of age.

In a special study regarding perception of the human face, three stimulus patterns were used: a stylized face in pink and black, a face composed of scrambled parts, and a face shape with pink and black segregated. Infants aged from four days to six months tended to look longest at the most realistic face, next at the scrambled face, and least at the other display. Fantz (1961) took this to mean that there is an innate disposition in human infants to recognize human faces. From the experiments in general he concluded that the infant's visual world is structured, not a confusion. Beyond this, however, it is difficult to decide how much structuring there is and of what kind.

Experiments on sensory deprivation   Riesen (1950) has reported that chicks kept in complete darkness for five days after hatching were able to peck 24 of 25 grains successfully, which was a record 12 percent better than that made by chicks tested immediately after hatching. This indicates pattern vision sufficiently good for accurate pecking, developed without practice in seeing. Chicks kept in darkness for fourteen days, however, did not peck at all and would have starved in the midst of plenty had not unusual steps been taken to feed them. If animals are kept in darkness for an extended time after birth, it is said that actual atrophy of the retinas may occur (Zuckerman & Rock, 1957). Atrophy may have contributed to the behavior of the chicks kept in the dark fourteen days, or it may be that failure to exercise the brain pattern involved in visual perception and pecking was responsible.

Also regarding chicks, Fantz (1961) reported that those kept in the dark a short time after hatching, given grains of eight different shapes, pecked at spherical grains 10 times as often as at pyramid-shaped grains. With grains in flat forms, circles were preferred to triangles regardless of size, and spheres were preferred to flat circles. These results appear to mean that form discrimination of some kind, including discrimination of three-dimensional objects from essentially two-dimensional ones, is innate. Fantz (1961) also found that young infants prefer looking at a sphere to looking at a flat circle of the same diameter, which he took to mean that there was some depth perception.

The work of Riesen (1950) is often cited in this connection. In spite of the fact that his sample of chimpanzees was exceedingly small, the results were so striking that some credence must be given them. Of three baby chimps, Debi was kept in complete darkness for seven months, Kora had only 1.5 hours of diffuse illumination daily, and Lad had 1.5 hours daily of full patterned stimulation. After seven months, Lad's performance was like that of normal chimps, while Debi and Kora were retarded to different degrees. Even a blink reaction in response to a moving object, which is often regarded as an innately determined reflex, came only after five days for Kora and fifteen for Debi. Following a moving person with the eyes came in fifteen days for Kora and thirty days for Debi. Even then, the eyes followed with jerky movements. Fixating a stationary person came in thirteen days for Kora and thirty days for Debi.

Another chimp named Falk was kept in normal lighting for seven months, then in the dark from eight to twenty-four months of age. His vision had developed normally during the first seven months. At the end of twenty-four months he had lost all use of vision, no longer recognizing objects, failing to look at people, and being unable to follow a light until the fifth day.

From these experiments, Riesen concluded that vision of the chimp must be put to use if it is to develop normally; that it takes several hundred hours of practice in seeing for normal development; and that if the beginning of stimulation is delayed too long after birth, there may be some permanent damage.

Fantz (1961) also cites experiments on maturation of input functions and learning in the case of monkeys. Monkeys raised in darkness for different time intervals from one to eleven weeks reveal some principles. The longer the delay of practice, the poorer the form perception and the greater the amount of practice needed for them to become normal. Fantz remarks that if form perception were entirely innate, it should appear regardless of the length of deprivation. This can be readily doubted, for degenerative changes may occur in the retina during the period of darkness. He also remarked that if form perception were entirely learned, it should require the same amount of practice regardless of the deprivation time. This can also be doubted, for the same reason.

Fantz concluded that the actual situation is that there is a complex interaction of heredity and learning in perceptual development. There appear to be critical times for the optimal development, with appropriate stimulation, of a particular function. If the needed stimulation is not available when the individual is ready for it, development may thereafter be deficient, without extraordinary experience or practice to make up for the deprivation. It is not known to what extent the same principle applies to human individuals. We shall see evidence on this point with respect to intellectual development in Chapter 16.

Experiments on enriched environments   If deprivation of stimulation is damaging to a young infant, will a supernormal environment lead to better-than-normal development? There is some indication that this is the case.

Forgus (1956) aimed to determine whether early perceptual experiences of rats with specific two-dimensional forms would aid in later discrimination-learning tasks. Some rats, in an early-exposure (EE) group, were exposed to four different forms—triangle, circle, cross, and square—from the time their eyes opened (at sixteen days) until they were forty-one days old. Rats of a second, late-exposure (LE) group were similarly exposed to such figures from forty-one to sixty-six days of age. Both groups were tested in a discrimination test at the termination of their exposure periods. Two matched control groups were similarly tested. Both the EE and LE groups were superior to the control groups. They also excelled in generalization tests, which involved rotating the figures 90 degrees. The mere exposure to visual figures appeared to give rats an advantage in discriminating those figures later, and it did not matter whether the exposure came earlier or later in the "childhood" of the individuals. Gibson, Walk, Pick, and Tighe (1958) confirmed these results and also demonstrated that the exposure helped in discrimination of similar figures but not of figures too dissimilar.

Human perceptual learning   It is often popularly expected that adolescents or adults who suddenly gain their sense of sight should be able to see as well as anyone else, but this is decidedly not true. Although we do not know in full what the life history of such a person has been, particularly how much opportunity he has had to learn through other senses information that may transfer readily to the visual medium, it is obvious that he has a great deal to learn. He does not recognize persons by sight who were well known to him by sound, touch, or odor; he does not recognize objects that had been familiar by touch; and many things are confusing to him. A young girl, known to the writer, who had been an accomplished pianist while blind, could not play the piano with her eyes open because the sight of movements of fingers and keys disrupted her playing habits.

Although the basic aspects of seeing, such as boundary lines, colors, and simple forms, are apparently present without practice, much of the remainder has to be learned. After reviewing the literature on problems of innate versus learned visual perception, Zuckerman and Rock (1957) came to somewhat the same conclusion, that color discrimination, form discrimination, and boundary lines have an innate basis but that experience contributes to further development of those innate powers and adds many new ones.

Subjects undergoing the experience of an inverted visual field show how ingrained visual-perceptual habits may be and yet how in time they may be drastically altered, as reported by Hochberg (1957). The visual field is inverted for these subjects by the wearing of prism lenses before their eyes. Some of the effects first reported are that objects and people appear strange, as if not seen before. The walking of people appears mechanical and unnatural. As time goes on, faces appear less unfamiliar and their features again take on meaning, but expressions are still strange. S is highly incapacitated with respect to movements in his upside-down world. In time, however, he learns to maneuver about the streets, but the world still appears inverted and stubbornly refuses to change. Visual inversion of upside-down views does ultimately begin to occur, but not all at once. Bodily movements and things along the vertical dimension are among the first to appear righted. On removal of the prisms, there is again a period of necessary readjustment to normal perception. These are examples of drastic perceptual learning.

The learning of constancies   One of the most important things learned by the growing individual is the nature of constancies. In spite of the fact that the infant's bottle looks different to him from different angles, he comes to recognize it no matter in what direction it is held and no matter whether it is far or near, within sight. Other objects must be mastered in the same manner. Connecting links are furnished by the senses of touch and kinesthesis. The process is undoubtedly facilitated by motor activity in connection with the object. Not only does the child run his fingers over the object as he sees it, but he squeezes it, lifts it, pushes it, and he drops it and sounds occur. He is thus building up connotative contexts of meaning, and thus semantic units are also formed. Later the child learns that the object has a name and an auditory label. According to Wohlwill (1960), there is evidence of some constancies in the child at the end of the first year, and numerous additional ones have developed by the ages of five to six. In these ways, the infant and child are stockpiling units of information in their permanent memory stores.

Children can also learn to extricate familiar objects from interfering, irrelevant material. This has been demonstrated by Elkind, Koegler, and Go (1962) in a study with hidden figures. With children of ages six, seven, and eight, they applied such procedures as telling the child what kind of object to look for and covering all the picture except the hidden object. Using 24 different pictures, they determined each child's score for seeing the hidden figures before training, after training, and again a month later. In every age group there was substantial gain, with mean scores becoming approximately doubled (from means of 6 to 8 to means of about 13 to 17). The status achieved essentially persisted a month later.

At all three testing times, there was a systematic increase of mean score with age. This result might be attributed to maturation or to added transferable experiences in older groups, or to both sources. The demonstration of gains from training, however, was clear.

Learning to read   The formation of such constancies (which are really units of information) is illustrated also in learning to read. Eleanor J. Gibson (1965) has given an excellent survey of the steps that a child takes in learning to read, following an essentially informational type of interpretation.

First, the child must learn to discriminate among letters (figural units). He must learn to recognize each letter in spite of ordinary transformations that it undergoes, as in viewing it from different angles, in rotated positions, with changes in size, and with distortions of different kinds. Distinguishing marks (properties) are in the form of straight lines versus curved lines and their various combinations and positions within each letter; angle of slant, from vertical to horizontal; open and closed portions; and so on.

The next problem is that of translating visual units into auditory units: graphemes into phonemes. One great difficulty with English is that the same grapheme has coded with it more than one phoneme. For this reason, only in recent years some methods of teaching reading have started the child with modified alphabets so there are one-one codings rather than one-many. The transition to the conventional alphabet can be made without very much pain later.

Next, the child learns to identify common letter combinations, or words; he is forming visual-symbolic units. Familiar syllables take on the same character with respect to information. Pronouncing the words is a matter of encoding in auditory-symbolic units. Translation is thus a kind of decoding-encoding process.

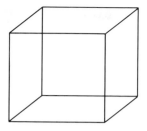

Fig. 11.3   The well-known Necker outline cube, an ambiguous figure used in some experiments on the role of reinforcement in perceptual learning.

Since by the time the child is learning to read he has already established a translation from auditory-symbolic units to semantic units, he readily acquires translation directly from figural symbols to semantic units, deriving meaning from what he sees on the printed page. Learning to read silently more or less successfully eliminates the auditory link, and speed is gained as such redundancies are eliminated.

According to Gibson, the child is still showing progressive mastery of discrimination among letters at the age of eight. Improvements in the other skills continue to go on for a much longer time, with no limit to the addition of symbolic and semantic units to the individual's memory storage, although self-imposed limits are often applied after the completion of schooling.

Reinforcement in perceptual learning   Reinforcement plays an important role in perceptual learning, as it does anywhere else in behavior. Some examples will be given from experimental sources. It is well known that the Necker outline cube (see Figure 11.3), an ambiguous figure, is seen with either the lower square or the upper square in front and that most individuals see a shifting back and forth as they continue to look at it. Solley and Santos (1958) tried to achieve a bias in subjects for seeing one view or the other, by applying verbal reinforcement. The cube was repeatedly exposed first for just two seconds each time, which was long enough to determine which view the subject saw at first glance. After the experimenter had determined which view the subject saw less often, the latter's reports of that view were reinforced 70 percent of the time in subsequent exposures and the other view was reinforced 30 percent of the time. The reinforcing stimuli were the experimenter's utterance of "Uh-huh," "Fine," and "Good."

The *S*s showed a systematic shift in frequency away from the less often reinforced view toward the more often reinforced view. After this training, a reversal of the application of reinforcements was followed by a shift back toward the initial status. Some *S*s noticed that the reinforcing stimuli were being given but were not aware of the differential application of them. The effects of this kind of training were detected later when *S*s viewed the cube continuously, with a tendency to hold the reinforced view and with some difficulty in shifting away from that view.

Solley and Murphy (1960) reported the results from another experiment in which the subjects were to adjust a rectangle to make it look square. Unless *S*s made the height too short, they were given electric shocks, with the result that their adjustments shifted to being perpetually too short, thus enabling them to avoid the shocks. It is not certain that they actually saw the resulting object as being perfectly square, but according to their own statements, they did see it as square.

In a third experiment (Solley & Long, 1958), things did not turn out as expected. The ambiguous figure was that of figure-ground perception, with a circle divided down the middle by a wavy line separating two distorted faces named Clem and Jake (see

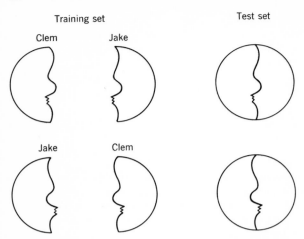

Fig. 11.4   The Clem and Jake figures used by Solley and Long (1960) in experiments on reinforcement in perceptual learning. (*Reproduced with permission.*)

Figure 11.4). In the training trials, some *S*s were trained to recognize Clem and were rewarded with two nickels when they succeeded and were punished by having to give up two nickels when they made an error, the two faces not being very different in profile. Other *S*s had positive training for Jake. Later, the two faces were presented in the complete circle. Before each exposure, *S* was to predict which face he would see first, and then after the exposure he was to report which one he saw as figure. In general, *S* expected the rewarded face more often, but there was no relation between what he expected and what he saw. Other *S*s, who were only punished for recognizing one face and not rewarded for the other, were more inclined to expect the neutral face, but not significantly so.

The role of feedback information   The ineffectiveness of applied reinforcement for determining perception in the last-mentioned experiment is probably due to the artificiality of the reinforcement, in its kind and in its manner of application. In daily life, reinforcement for much of our mental activity comes naturally, applied in the form of automatic feedback information. It is probably not so much the "reward" or "punishment" value of the feedback information that makes it effective, although these aspects probably make some contributions, as it is its informative value. We could not learn to talk without automatic, almost instant feedback information. We immediately hear what we have said and how we have said it, and we can match it with a model just heard or remembered. The deaf child does not learn to talk unless someone has the patience to give him other than auditory feedback information, which is much too slow and too crude a method to provide the shaping of good-sounding vocal expression.

The role of rapid feedback information can be dramatically illustrated to a hearing person in experiments on delayed feedback. His own voice can be fed back to him through earphones by putting his speech onto recording tape that plays his voice back to him with controlled amounts of delay, as described by K. U. Smith (1962). The general effect is a slowing down in the rate of speech (as if waiting for the feedback), an increase in both intensity and pitch of voice (a sign of greater effort), and some stuttering. The maximal effect comes with a delay of 0.2 second. This very short time shows how very rapidly the guiding effect of feedback normally occurs for speaking and hearing.

In the control of speech, feedback is concerned with the guidance and correction of motor responses. Perceptions are likewise automatically corrected as feedback information comes into play. What we feel is corrected by what we see, and vice versa. The impression of kinesthetic effects is corrected by visual estimates. It is the redundancy of information from these different sources regarding the same objects that helps to develop realistic representations of those objects. An infant subjects the same object to inspection with several senses, mouthing it, staring at it, manipulating it, and making it give off sounds.

D. P. Andrews (1964) speaks of error correcting intrinsic to the same sense organ. He asserts that much correction takes place within the retina, for example, as if the retinal elements went through a process of averaging excitations to arrive at an adaptation level. He suggests that such correcting activity accounts for phenomena like adaptation, figural aftereffects, and geometric illusions. Thus, learning to see and hear, and so on, is guided and shaped by ubiquitous operations of feedback and automatic correction. Cybernetic principles apply to perception as well as to other aspects of behavior.

Summary

Both perception and cognition are concerned with input information from sensory sources, perception the more immediately, with overlapping of the two concepts. Perception is concerned with sensory properties and with the cognition of figural units. Input of information involves filtering operations, which formerly went under the heading of "attention."

Quite a few experiments designed to show perception and even learning without awareness, as in discriminating subliminal stimuli in conditioned GSR, reactions to sub-liminal suggestions, and reinforcement from incidental and unnoticed stimuli, generally fail to show that there is more discrimination unconsciously than with awareness in the form of verbalized discriminations. This failure does not discount the role of unconscious information already in memory storage.

Experiments with both human and lower-animal subjects tend to show that there is some innate preparation for cognition of such elementary visual information as colors, lines, and simple forms but that on this very limited foundation there is an enormous amount of perceptual learning. This is shown by experiments with sensory deprivation in infancy and also with environmental enrichment. Perceptual learning comes about by way of developing constancies (units of figural information) and stockpiling them in memory storage. Reinforcement, in the form of feedback information, has a role in perceptual learning as well as elsewhere.

12 Learning

In connection with the review of intellectual abilities in earlier chapters, it should have been noted that no factor was interpreted as a learning ability. In fact, one could look a long way in the literature and not find such a factor. J. W. French (1951) does not list such a factor. Among other things, this means that learning is not identifiable as a kind of operation or a kind of information or as any unique combination of these categories. It is universally recognized as belonging in the intellectual domain, however.

With the single label of "learning," there has often been an implied assumption that all learning phenomena are in some way representative of a single kind of psychological operation. This deceiving simplicity has led to efforts to find a single principle or at least a very small set of principles by which to account for all learning events. This state of affairs has resulted in arrays of competing theories, with no resolution in sight. The situation is more serious than the competition of theories suggests, for, as Hilgard (1956) has remarked after thoroughly reviewing theories of learning, laws of learning have an uncertain status and most of the facts of improvement with practice and the effects of reward and punishment are still in dispute.

In viewing the problems of learning properly, one of the first needs is to recognize learning for what it is. It is *change* in behavior, not behavior. It is a transition from one behavioral status or condition to some other, and it is not always improvement. To say that it is improvement of behavior involves us in value judgments, which take us beyond basic science into technology.

In the preceding chapter we considered the role of learning in the development of perception. Since perception was defined so as to include the cognition of figural units, we may say that perceptual learning involves the formation of units of figural information. In this chapter we shall consider the problems of the formation of all kinds of products of all basic kinds of information.

Previously it was proposed (Chapter 9) that the six kinds of products of information be substituted for the concept of "association." Some further reasons for this decision will be brought out in what follows. We shall consider the roles of intellectual-aptitude factors in learning not only in the ways in which they contribute to learning but also in the ways in which learning affects the factors. We shall also consider the relations of products of information to motor activities and some of the problems of the conditions determining learning, such as frequency and reinforcement.

There will be no attempt to develop a full-fledged theory of learning or even to consider much of the multitudinous literature on learning. The major concern here is to show the relevance of the SI concepts for clarifying thinking about learning and for operations in the investigation of learning. Physiological bases of learning will be left for Chapter 15, which deals with the various physical bases for intellectual functioning. The psychological knowledge of such functioning so far outstrips the knowledge of correlations with physical bases that only incidental references to the latter need be made in exposition concerning the former.

What is learned?

Inadequacy of the association principle   Many of the traditional limitations and objections to the association principle are so well known that they will not be treated at length here. Some relatively recent suggestions and evidence will receive attention.

Associations and meaningful connections   Although he has been apparently willing to retain the term *association,* Wolfgang Köhler (1941) has insisted on giving the concept an important qualification. In his conception, two things become associated when there is some connection between the properties of the one and the properties of the other. For the traditional association theory, the properties of the things associated are irrelevant. Association by sheer force of contiguity is recognized by Köhler as a limiting case. Even in this instance, however, when two things become associated, there is some degree of unity about the outcome. Postman and Riley (1957) have investigated the Köhler conception by means of a series of experiments, with the results in general support of the Köhler view.

Whorf (1956) expressed a view very similar to Köhler's, but it was limited to association of verbal ideas as expressed by words. Such an association, he maintained, is more than a mere hooking together. Something meaningful or logical is involved. The context theory of semantic meaning presented in Chapter 10 can be applied in this connection. The meaningful or logical things in common are the constituents of the connotative meanings of the two semantic units that become associated. The easier linking of items of semantic information as compared with figural or symbolic items, a principle that is universally recognized, undoubtedly stems from the relative richness of common elements in the context of semantic items of information. Unfamiliar or unrealistic figures and symbols do not possess much in the way of connotative contexts. G. A. Miller and J. A. Selfridge (1950) suggested that the reason that meaningful material is easy to learn and to remember is that it conforms to expectancies. Expectancies can be readily interpreted as implications, which, according to the context theory of meaning, provide the basis for contexts.

Nonassociative animal learning   Not to be overlooked, by any means, are the six kinds of learning proposed by Tolman (1949), particularly his recognition of cognitive learning and his reasons for believing in the six varieties (1948). Certain phenomena in rat learning, e.g., latent learning, vicarious trial and error, search for stimuli, and the apparent use of hypotheses, have defied associative interpretations.

A recent report of rats' learning by observation has been given by Schaeffer (1964). Rats kept in restraining cages were moved bodily over the correct pathway in a Y maze into either a white or a black alley, in which they were then fed. When given the first opportunity to run the maze, 13 of 17 rats chose the correct turn.

Snygg (1959) cites another experiment in which opportunity for observation appeared to facilitate learning markedly. In the learning of a Warden U maze with 10 choice points, the mean number of trials required was 29. When 5 of the correct turns were painted white, the mean was reduced to 12. When all the correct paths were painted white and the incorrect paths were painted black, the mean was further reduced to 7.

Although the last two experiments cited are amenable to associational interpretations, other observations of rat learning more strongly lend themselves to a nonassociational description. One is the fact that rats appear to break up a total maze path into submazes and that they show anticipatory movements as if they had ideas of "ahead" and "around the corner," according to Snygg. Bruner (1957) also pointed out that a rat that has mastered the simple alternation problem with the sequence of turns RLRL more readily learns the sequence LRLR. The two systems have much in common, and the learning transfer appears to be in a class with that attributed to Harlow's learning sets.

Mandler (1962) has recently pointed out three phenomena that defy associational explanation. One is the phenomenon of "warming up," in which performing one task has a facilitating effect upon performing another task, even a quite disparate one, immediately following. In such cases, however, we are not sure whether the effect is confined to performance or whether it applies to learning. A second phenomenon is that an overlearned task has positive transfer effects even to another task in which there would be interference or negative transfer effects if it were not for the overlearning. Overlearning a set of "associations" should be expected to produce negative transfer, not positive. The third phenomenon is the learning of sets, as in the famous Harlow experiments (1949) with monkeys. Mandler favors the conception that what is learned is in the form of "structures," which could be in the nature of the writer's products of information.

Human serial learning   In human serial learning of lists of items, the usual associational interpretation has been that each item in the list becomes a stimulus for an S-R association with the one immediately following. The writer (Guilford, 1961) has proposed an alternative hypothesis in terms of informational psychology to the effect that the individual learns the items as units, the forward-immediate connections as implications or relations (if there is enough basis for forming relations), and the whole as a total system. There is scattered experimental evidence in support of these interpretations, some of which will come out later in this chapter.

Jensen and Rohwer (1965) have had subjects first memorize lists of trigrams and later learn paired associates that involve the same S-R sequences as were involved in the lists. In the early "relearning" trials they found little evidence of transfer. They concluded that in memorizing the lists something other than S-R associations was being learned, and they suggested that the "something other" seemed to be in the form of mastery of a kind of unity such as is shown when a subject in a memory-span task grasps the whole list correctly. This conclusion suggests the cognition and memory of a system.

In a study of the "initial reproductive tendency," G. Meyer (1939) tested the Müller-Pilzecker hypothesis to the effect that in learning a series of items each one on the list tends to instigate the *first* item in the series. This hypothesis could be interpreted to mean that a kind of looping phenomenon is involved, as if the list were being tied in a single package. In learning very short lists of three syllables each embedded within longer lists, when single items from a short list were later given as stimuli for free association, subjects tended to respond with the first item in the set. An associational intrepretation of this outcome would have to be that some backward associations were stronger than forward associations and the backward-remote associations were stronger than backward-immediate associations. Meyer concluded with the hypothesis that in learning a list of syllables, the tendency is to reproduce it as a system in correct temporal order.

Others who have dealt with serial learning also cast much doubt upon the importance of associative bonds' being formed between each item and the next. There are results suggesting that S learns items in response to serial position, as shown by the position effect, the fact that the end items are more rapidly learned than the central ones. Rock and Ceraso (1964) reported that they induced Ss to learn each item in connection with an assigned serial position. Without having had the items exposed in serial order at all, the Ss could recite the list correctly. Thus, learners *could* master a list in serial order without forming item-to-item connections, but this does not mean that learning with serial exposures is ordinarily not done by forming such connections.

There is no need to conclude from such experiments that serial learning is any one kind of event, either the formation of associations between items of information that are more or less contiguous *or* a matter of forming systems. The generally recognized association-formation phenomenon can be readily interpreted as the formation of implications. The formation of both implications and systems could occur in the same learning episode.

In free recall of items in testing the retention in serial learning, Ss are likely to mention first and last items before giving central ones, and the items recalled are often not in serial order, nor is the order of free recall the same on each test trial (Asch, 1964). The distinctive positions of first and last items give those items natural advantages in free recall. Doubt is expressed as to whether any remote associations are formed. Rock and Ceraso (1964) point out that intervening items should disinhibit the inhibition of delay that is supposed to account for remote associations according to Hullian theory. Slamencka (1964) remarks that the bowed position function is a better explanation for remote associations than the reverse, the latter being the common way of looking at this phenomenon.

Paired-associates learning In some of the recent investigations of paired-associates learning, there have also been a growing number of suggestions that one of the most important things learned is familiarization with the items themselves, particularly with the second, or *B,* members of the *A-B* pairs. The usual evidence of learning has been correct anticipation of the *B* member as the *A* member is presented, either during the learning trials or in later test trials. It has commonly been found that when the *B* members are given as stimuli in test trials, the score for giving *A* members is much poorer. The interpretation has been that forward associations are stronger than backward associations. Asch and Ebenholtz (1962) made the two items of a pair equally familiar (equally available as units of information) and found that backward-test scores were only slightly lower than forward-test scores.

Asch and Lindner (1963) found forward and backward scores to be equal under the condition of equal familiarity. They make the point that in the usual paired-associates experiment, because *S* anticipates the *B* member he is giving it greater attention and hence enhancing its familiarity; he does not need this familiarity for the *A* member, since he expects it to be given to him in the later test, as it is.

A supporting result obtained with different kinds of items has been reported by J. O. Cook and J. E. Brown (1963). Their familiar items (F) were letters of the alphabet, and their unfamiliar items (N) were in the form of an 8 × 8 grid with a dot in one particular cell. They constructed four kinds of lists of pairs, FF, NF, FN, and NN, where the first letter of a pair stands for the kind of *A* item and the second for the kind of *B* item, familiar (F) or nonfamiliar (N). The ease of learning was in the order of the four kinds of lists as just given, with FF lists easiest. Again, the importance of the learning of units of information was demonstrated. The learning of connections between pairs of items may be regarded as the formation of implications.

How products are learned

Since we have come to the conclusion that what is learned is in the form of products of information, the following discussion will attempt more explicitly to see how the interpretation of learning works out on this basis. Most learning studies that have emphasized the formation of connections may be interpreted as pertaining to implications. This is true when the connections are either between stimuli or between stimulus and response, particularly where expectations may be said to be involved. This means that by far the greatest amount of research has been devoted to the formation of implications as the products.

Another kind of product that has received much attention in experimental research is that of classes, as in studies of concept attainment and concept formation. Since concepts become units of information, such learning also applies to the (indirect) formation of units. Particular units are acquired through the process of familiarization, as suggested earlier. From the fact that almost any kind of product can also become a unit, it is quite common to find that units are formed indirectly through the acquiring of other kinds of product first.

Not much effort has been devoted explicitly to investigation of the learning of relations, systems, and transformations, but such learnings have not been neglected, by any means. Serial learning of almost any kind involves the formation of systems. The discovery of principles involves relations or systems, depending upon the complexity of the thing learned.

Receiving least attention, either directly or indirectly, has been the product of transformation. We come nearest to examples of involvement with transformations in learning in the gestalt-favored types of experiments in which insight is an important feature. The reorganization of a field is a transformation, or it involves a number of transformations. If we are to go fully along with gestalt theory of learning, we should see transformations in almost all learning.

It is also possible to see the product of transformation in the Piaget concept of "accommodation." By this term Piaget means that as input information is assimilated, there are readjustments. Readjustments may be kinds of transformation. Since Piaget is not very free with examples of observed events as referents for accommodation, it is difficult to say how much matching there is with the concept of "transformation." One difference between transformation and either reorganization or accommodation is that transformations are also regarded as products of information that can be remembered and utilized later. They are usable later in transfer recall because they are transposable.

The Learning of classes

Stimulus generalization   It might be said that the most rudimentary form of classification is seen in the conditioning phenomenon of stimulus generalization, in which the organism makes the same response to a range of similar stimuli, as if they were equivalent. From this point of view, stimulus generalization is simply failure to discriminate, indicating lack of information. And yet, superficially, it is not so very different from the behavior of a mentally deficient individual who groups things together because they are somehow similar, without being able to give any particular reason why they belong together.

One difference, of course, is that in the case of stimulus generalization there is no evidence of recognition of differences among the stimuli; in the case of classifying, there is. Also, whereas in experiments on stimulus generalization only one variable is usually involved, with a narrow range of values on that variable, in the case of classifying there may be more than one variable with well-discriminated values on each of them. If we define classifying in such a way that similarities are recognized in spite of divergences, then stimulus generalization is not an instance of classification, not even a limiting case. The usual conception of classification does appear to imply differentiated information prior to the classifying act.

Role of attributes In order to put the general problem of the learning of classes into perspective, let us consider the variety of activities in which an examinee or a subject for an experiment becomes involved where classifying or categorizing is concerned. He must be aware of a common attribute or a number of common attributes in a set of items of information, which is a matter of cognition of classes. The clearest case involving cognition only occurs when he is presented with an already classified set, all members being appropriate examples, to see what they have in common. What the subject sees in common may not be the same as what the experimenter sees in common, but he may have a legitimate class. It is not essential that the subject be able to name the common properties, but he must indicate somehow that he uses them appropriately.

If *S* is presented with a collection of objects representing more than one class and is asked to segregate them into categories, each a legitimate class, then he must not only cognize the class idea but indulge in some productive activity, divergent or convergent, depending upon the nature of the collection and the instructions he is given. If he is to name or describe the class idea, he is indulging in still another particular kind of activity known as convergent production of semantic units (where there is a well-recognized term for the idea).

From this line of thinking, it seems incorrect to insist that the classifying act is incomplete unless the subject has verbalized the result. Forming the class idea and verbalizing it are two quite different operations. Many a class idea is never verbalized. In fact, some are so incompletely developed that verbalizing would be impossible. A verbal response can therefore be taken to indicate that a class of a certain kind has been formed, but failure of verbal response is no sign of absence of a class idea.

The common elements that determine a class idea may be of different kinds. They may be simple properties or attributes, as of color, size, or shape, or they may be more complex. In Chapter 4 we saw examples of tests in which the classes were formed by virtue of common relations or common systems. In hierarchical systems, the common members of larger classes can be subclasses. Common *principles* are also sometimes utilized in experiments on what Bruner, Goodnow, and Austin (1956) call "relational" categories. An example of a relational class would be all those states in the United States in which the President-elect received a higher percentage of the votes than did those of his party who were running for Congress.

Kinds of classes Bruner et al. (1956) make a distinction also between conjunctive and disjunctive classes. A conjunctive class is one based upon a *combination* (conjunction) of attributes, for example, all congressmen who are under forty years of age and who were elected for the first time. Three attributes are pertinent: being a congressman, being under forty, and being elected for the first time.

A disjunctive class is one for which there are alternative specifications, such as all congressmen who are between the ages of forty and sixty, or are unmarried, or are bald. Such collections of specifications are sometimes rather arbitrary and would be used under special circumstances. To give a more realistic example, in civil-service examinations the alternatives of having a certain college degree or a certain number of years of a certain kind of experience may qualify an applicant. Admission to college is often in the form of a certain adopted minimum score on an aptitude examination or a minimum of a B average in high school as alternatives. If an individual is attempting to guess what the specifications are for a class, he finds the task much easier if it is conjunctive than if it is disjunctive. According to Bruner et al., most subjects proceed in learning the specifications for a class as if they assumed it to be a conjunctive category.

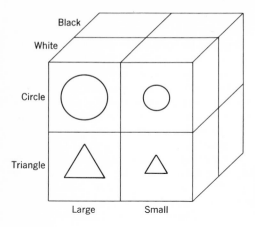

Fig. 12.1 Three visual-figural dimensions each with two values employed for generating objects usable in experimental studies of cognition and production of classes.

The same investigators make a distinction between *attainment* of a concept and *formation* of a concept. The attainment problem gives S some information regarding the class, and from a succession of exemplars (examples of class members) he is to arrive at a conception of the differentiating features of the class, the common attributes. A concept-formation task presents S with a number of exemplars, with S to decide what classes to form. In the attainment problem, S may select exemplars as prospective class members, each time being given information whether or not the exemplar is a member of the class; or he may be given a selected potential exemplar and be required to say whether or not he believes it to be a member. Most of this, either way, is hypothesis testing, in a problem-solving setting.

To make these problems more concrete, let us use a set of 8 objects that can be described in terms of 3 variables—color, shape, and size—with 2 values for each variable: black versus white, circle versus triangle, and large versus small. The 8 objects are made by combining these values in all possible ways, as shown in the model in Figure 12.1. The 8 objects thus generated are laid out singly in Figure 12.2.

Classifying these objects on the basis of 1 specification only, we could have 6 classes with 4 exemplars to each category: all white, all black, all triangles, all circles, all large objects, and all small objects. With the values combined by 2s, we could have 12 different classes of 2 exemplars each, such as small triangles, black circles, small white objects, and so on. Conjunctive classes with all 3 variables relevant would give us 8 classes, each with a single exemplar. We sometimes speak of a thing as being in a class by itself, and we see from the last comment that such classes are reasonable.

Logically there can also be empty classes, categories with no known exemplars. Such classes are often hypothesized by a scientist who thinks that a class having such and such properties should exist. Light waves and other electromagnetic waves were thus forecast as classes of phenomena; so were microbes, chemical elements, and nuclear particles. Before empirical demonstrations, these classes were empty.

Material such as that in Figure 12.2 has been used in sophisticated ways in experiments on concept learning, as by Shepard, Hovland, and Jenkins (1961). Although it is probably recognized that in daily life the alternatives are not so regular or so limited in complexity, such restrictions are necessary for experimental purposes. It can be expected that findings with such material can have more general relevance for understanding be-

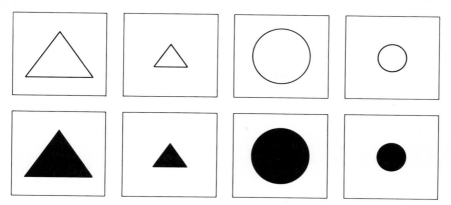

Fig. 12.2 Eight unique objects generated from the cross classification seen in Figure 12.1.

havior involving classes and concepts in daily life: a credo that underlies all experimental research.

Evolutionary levels of concept learning Harlow (1958) has given some attention to the complexity of concept-learning problems that can be mastered by species of different levels of intellectual functioning. The simplest problem that has been utilized experimentally is discrimination in terms of one variable where there is only one irrelevant variable. For example, if it is desired to test whether an animal can learn to respond to a triangle, rejecting a circle that is paired with it, the two are presented with triangle or circle on the right in random sequence. The shape variable is relevant, the right-left variable is not. The simplest case can be mastered by a variety of species: fish, mice, rats, pigeons, cats, dogs, monkeys, apes, and man.

At the next level of complexity, two variables are irrelevant, as in connection with the "oddity" problem. In this kind of task, *S* must learn to choose the one of the three objects that is different from the other two, e.g., a triangle in preference to two circles or a circle in preference to two triangles. The locations are irrelevant, and so are the shapes. The relevant variable is uniqueness. The task is like the exclusion type of test item used in measurement of abilities for cognition of classes (see Chapter 4). Harlow reported that no pigeon, rat, cat, or dog has been known to solve this kind of problem in the form described. The problem is beyond the young child, but the age at which success is common has apparently not yet been determined.

The concept-learning problem of next-higher complexity Harlow calls the "oddity-nonoddity" problem. In this type of problem *S* is to choose the odd object when the tray on which the objects rest has a green border and to choose one of the repeated (nonodd) objects when the border is orange. In this problem there are three irrelevant variables. Many human subjects, including adults, cannot master this problem. But even more complicated problems can be mastered by monkeys, and one chimpanzee has been reported to solve a problem with five variables.

From such an array of results, Harlow (1958) generated a theory that in learning in general the key is learning to inhibit responses to irrelevant variables. This generalization involves the assumption that before learning the organism has positive reactions to all objects, regardless of their properties, a highly questionable assumption. There is no doubt that some aspects of learning involve rejection of objects or hypotheses, but the acquisition of familiarity and of implications, as in classical conditioning, is definitely in the form of positive attainments. One should be suspicious of any theory of learning that stakes everything on a single principle.

Strategies in attainment of concepts   In arriving at the definition of a class, Ss may show different systematic modes of attack, as revealed by their succession of choices or decisions. According to Bruner et al. (1956), such strategies are designed to accomplish one or more objectives. S wishes to learn efficiently, i.e., by using as few examples as possible and undergoing as little "cognitive strain" as possible. By the latter expression the authors mean difficult decisions and difficult memory problems in keeping track of successes and failures in testing hypotheses. S also wishes to minimize the number of errors and to develop a maximum feeling of assurance of being correct. The various strategies serve to contribute to progress toward one or more of these objectives. For example, they may ensure that each trial elicits needed information and keeps the risk of error low.

In one type of strategy called "simultaneous scanning," S emphasizes getting the greatest amount of information on every trial in order to eliminate the largest number of wrong hypotheses. In the "successive-scanning" strategy, S tests a single hypothesis at each trial. This simplifies his task but does not make the maximum use of possible information. In the "conservative-focusing" method, having found a positive instance, S proceeds in the subsequent trials to change one attribute at a time, as in some common experimental methods. He is likely to get an answer to every test he makes, adding some information, but not always as much information as could be obtained by making other choices. The "focus-gambling" method, like the preceding one, starts with a positive case but takes much risk by varying more than one attribute at a time. If S is lucky, this operation pays off in quick solutions; if not, he may be in trouble.

The studies of Bruner et al. (1956) are very informative, particularly about the ways in which a problem solver seeks information in the environment when he faces a class-defining problem. Much is learned about the conditions affecting the individual's behavior during such problem solving, which involves not only cognition but productive thinking, divergent and convergent, as well as evaluation. Thus, the learning of class ideas can be a very complicated affair. The subject of problem solving will be given special treatment in Chapter 14. Here some further comments will be made concerning the phenomenon of strategies, as such.

In an informational psychology, such strategies and others may be regarded as behavioral systems, systems of behavioral information with regard to the problem solver's own plans and procedures. Each strategy is a kind of program of steps, learned by the problem solver or invented by him for the occasion. This will be the general view in what follows regarding the response side of behavior. The input side of behavior has the function of developing the appropriate representations in the form of cognized products of information. On the output side there is a stock of plans, strategies, tactics, and subtactics, as set forth by George A. Miller et al. (1960). The strategy called into play depends upon habitual implications (representational product implying an executive product) or newly formed implications by reason of recognition of class memberships of input and output products. The same conception holds for motor patterns as well as for thinking patterns. All this is not strange, in view of the fact that to a large extent the two (input products and output products) develop together in childhood.

Some generalizations on acquisition of classes There is space only to summarize some of the hard-earned conclusions that have been reached concerning concept attainment and concept formation. Vinacke (1951) has well summarized the experimental work to 1950. One of the important questions has concerned the usefulness of negative or misleading instances. These have sometimes been found to help and sometimes not. It depends on how much use S can make of such information. Bruner et al. (1956) reported that S hesitates to use negative cases, for such cases call for the transforming of hypotheses, something that S seems reluctant to do. There is agreement that when the differentiating criteria are clearly set forth for inspection, learning is facilitated. But giving the common elements (attributes) alone was found not to be very helpful (Hull, 1920). Alternating those elements with exemplars was helpful.

All investigators agree that a working concept may be attained without S's awareness of what it is. If S has erroneous preconceived notions, he requires more information to achieve the class idea: something that is easily observed in daily life. Subjects have a natural tendency to simplify the number and kind of relevant attributes, and when the going becomes difficult, they are likely to snatch at irrelevant information. The reasons for failure to achieve the concept are many, including failure to evaluate cues, i.e., to distinguish between criterional and noncriterional signs; poor structuring of the problem, hence testing the wrong hypotheses; choosing an inefficient strategy; and failure to use available information.

As to the continuity-discontinuity issue in connection with concept attainment, Vinacke (1951) concludes that this category of learning involves gradual learning. To outward appearances this is no doubt true, for S goes through a series of trials, and he may show increasingly better approximations if his progress toward the "correct" class idea and toward its full development is considered. But since progress is a matter of hypothesis testing, it can be said that the rise of a new hypothesis is a sudden, discontinuous event. Only the notable "brilliant" jumps in hypothesis generation would ordinarily be accepted as cases of insight. Minor insights are covered over in the general pace.

The learning of relations Studies aimed specifically at the problem of the learning of relations have been rare. One study that was labeled as such, an investigation by Kreezer and Dallenbach (1929), is naturally very relevant. The authors limited the study to one particular semantic relation, namely, the relation of opposition in meaning. Each of 100 schoolchildren in the range from 5.0 to 7.5 years of age, 20 in each half-year group, was first asked whether he knew the meaning of "opposite." Each child was then given the examples of GOOD-BAD and BIG-LITTLE, as preliminary tests. He was reinforced by the signals "Right" and "Wrong," whichever was appropriate, and he was told the right response. He was then tested with other familiar stimulus words. If he still did not succeed, he was given the two repeated examples and then another chance at the final test.

Nearly 90 percent either said they did not know the meaning of opposite or showed that they did not know it in connection with preliminary probing. But after having been given further instruction, with the same two examples and with reinforcements, 51 percent demonstrated that they knew the concept in taking the test and 18 percent more after further instruction. There was no indication that the concept came gradually or step by step, for when it came, it came suddenly and was not lost thereafter during the experiment. The investigators rejected the prevailing learning principles of frequency of exercise and gradual learning, in favor of insight as the mode of learning relations of this type.

Following the procedure of Kreezer and Dallenbach, Schooley and Hartmann (1937) extended the study of the learning of semantic relations to a variety of relations other than that of opposites. They also found that the learning of each relation came rather suddenly and once it came was not lost. The order of difficulty of learning the various relation concepts, from easiest to hardest, was action-agent, agent-action, attribute-substance, substance-attribute, genus-species, whole-part, part-whole, and species-genus. The age levels at which 50 percent of the Ss could learn the relations extended over a rather narrow range of one year and three months, around the age of six.

Piaget has a great deal to say about the development of class ideas at different stages of childhood but relatively little to say about development of relations, as such. What he does say about relations comes mostly under the heading of "seriation," which is concerned with quantitative relations only. Since most of what he has to say on these subjects pertains to genetic development and not specifically to learning, it will be treated in Chapter 17.

One of his principles of development is pertinent here, however. In the young child, according to Piaget, there is considerable sensorimotor interplay in behavior. In his development of classes and class ideas, for example, the child often groups objects in terms of what he can do readily with them. Objects are for noisemaking, cuddling, tearing, or rubbing, etc. (Inhelder & Piaget, 1958; Piaget, 1950). Conceptions of relation, also, may be seen to start in activities in which the child arranges things in order, e.g., blocks in order of size. It is probably because of his interest in logic and mathematics that Piaget seems generally to ignore the problem of development of nonquantitative kinds of relations.

The transposition phenomenon   A prominent experimental problem involving relations of the serial type was brought to our attention by gestalt psychologists. This is the "transposition" problem. In its simplest form, such an experiment involves training a chicken to eat grain from the lighter of two gray surfaces, A and B, B being lighter. The subject is then tested with another pair of grays, B and C, C being still lighter than B. When S eats from the new stimulus C in preference to B, to which it had been trained to react positively, it is said that a transposition has occurred.

Transposition behavior is variously interpreted. Most credit goes to the chicken by saying that it has learned to react to a relation "lighter than," perhaps with recognition of a brightness variable, rather than to an absolute level of gray. Next highest in terms of credit is to say that S has been responding to a step or a gradient. Presumably no one goes so far as to say that the chicken has a concept of a variable of lightness-darkness, an unverbalized idea of an abstract variable.

Spence (1942) developed an ingenious theory to account for the transposition event in terms of conditioning principles, on the basis of generalization and lack of reinforcement. This theory made it unnecessary to credit the animal showing the transposition reaction with having anything in the nature of a cognition of a relation, under the usual circumstances.

There have been other experiments, however, demonstrating that lower animals *can* apparently discriminate relations as transposable information. Lawrence and De Rivera (1954) trained rats to jump to the right if the top half of a display was darker and to jump to the left if the top half of the display was lighter. The conclusion was that the rats learned to discriminate between relations. This was supported by the additional fact that the lighter portion of the display was varied in three steps, which was also true of the darker portion.

The acquisition of systems   In an earlier discussion, a distinction was made between input and output systems, cognitive and executive. Some input systems are patterns, principles, rules, problem structures, orders, models, and theories. Examples of output systems are motor patterns, plans, strategies, tactics, methods, and programs. Numerous experimental studies have impinged more or less directly upon all such systems. A system has to be formed (excepting in human behavior those few simple, innate schemas, as recognized by Piaget) and can hardly come into existence full-blown from nothing in the way of basic information. The formation of systems depends upon prior possession of parts. The parts either are in memory storage or are derived from new input.

It is generally agreed that, as in the attainment of concepts, the generation of a system usually comes not in one fell swoop but in stages. There are enough examples, however, to indicate that at least some systems come by way of unusual jumps in the nature of insights, and many begin as vague outlines or sketchy "blueprints." Most of the steps in progress toward the final structure are small and not noteworthy, but some steps can be leaps, dramatic clickings into place of previously disparate contributors. Such have been some of the notable creative performances: Kekulé's benzene ring, Charles Darwin's principles of evolution, and Poincaré's Fuchsian functions. While recognizing such flashes of genius as being insights, we are likely to overlook the numerous other instances because of their inconspicuousness. Indeed, it is likely that in the formation of any product of information there are genuine discontinuities at many points.

The occurrence of transformations   There is no doubt of the unique nature of transformation as a product category of information. With a transformation defined as a change in information and learning defined as a change in behavior and with the theory that behavior is a matter of processing information, on both the input and the output sides of the organism, it follows that there must be some significant relationship of transformation to learning. Although much change in the organism's stock of information is brought about from new input, much other change in information comes about through transformations. The possible relations of transformations to the gestalt concept of reorganization and to Piaget's concept of accommodation were mentioned earlier.

If we understand the nature of transformations, how they come about and under what conditions, therefore, we should also know a great deal about learning. Experiments aimed at the conditions that are favorable and unfavorable for the occurrence of transformations might be more fruitful than those aimed at the less definite goal of understanding learning. Studies regarding such conditions will be cited in Chapter 14 in connection with creative production, which is also an instance of learning, for it is an example of a change in behavior.

The relations of transformations to freedom from certain kinds of rigidity, as demonstrated by Frick et al. (1959), also call for concentrated investigations on this kind of product. Such research would not solve all problems of rigidity, but it would cover many important problems of rigidity in thinking and, indirectly, rigidity in overt behavior.

Roles of factors in learning

In this section we give attention to particular factors and categories of factors as related to learning. There have been a number of investigations of what happens to factor loadings in a task in which there are practice and improvement, from first to last trials. All such studies demonstrate systematic shifts of factor loadings, with some general principles, from which significant deductions can be drawn. Studies of smaller groups have been concerned with the effect of certain kinds of training upon certain factor scores of individuals who have undergone the training. Related to this problem is the more general question of the extent and kind of transfer of skill to be expected when the training task emphasizes a certain factor. All these investigations have bearings upon principles of learning when learning is described in terms of the nature of factors.

Changes of factor importance with learning   The apparent pioneer work in this area was done by Woodrow (1938), in a series of studies of the relation of abilities to improvement with practice. These studies were also related to questions of learning ability, a subject that was discussed in Chapter 1. In one of Woodrow's studies, 56 students practiced over a period of thirty-nine days in seven tests in the intellectual category. Factor analyses, including the initial and final scores in these seven tests and scores in nine factor-marker tests, three given both before and after practice and six either before or after, were made. Although the nine factors obtained are not easily interpretable, Woodrow was able to conclude that factor loadings in a test do change incident to practice and that loadings on the verbal factor tended to decline, slightly but consistently, in all the tests in which practice occurred.

Changes of loadings in psychomotor tasks   In several studies, Fleishman and his associates have analyzed successive scores obtained during practice in each of several tasks, mostly in the psychomotor category, along with marker tests for factors known from previous experience to be involved to an appreciable degree in those tasks.

Some technical problems, one of which is the fact that correlations of successive scores in the same task are essentially retest reliability coefficients, are involved in such a procedure. Some of these coefficients become quite small, however, following the general principle that the more remote the two stages of practice, the lower the correlation. What these within-task correlations usually do in a factor analysis is to determine a factor specific to the scores in the learning task. Other aspects of the factor structure seem to be very reasonably interpretable.

When the learning task was the Complex Coordination (CC) test, eight stage scores, from 5 trials each, were selected along a practice curve that extended over 64 trials in all (Fleishman & Hempel, 1954). In the CC test, the examinee's task is to make a pattern of movements with arms and legs in accordance with a pattern of three lights. The score is the number of these adjustments he can complete in a given time interval. A number of common factors, both psychomotor and intellectual, are involved in the performance at the start. Figure 12.3 indicates graphically the relative contributions of five of the common factors and of the specific component to the total variances of scores at the eight stages of practice.

From Figure 12.3 it can be seen that at the beginning of practice the more important factors were multilimb coordination, as Fleishman calls it; [1] spatial orientation, factor CFS-V in the SI model; and visualization, CFT in the model. Both CFS-V and CFT decline in importance, the latter more rapidly at first, and contribute almost nothing to variances during the last four practice stages. It is as if these two cognitive functions served to guide the development of motor patterns or systems that could be touched off without the aid of such cognition in later trials.

Since the days of William James, it has been recognized that in mastering a psychomotor skill there is in early trials much conscious activity, which drops out as the skill becomes more nearly automatic. By the technique used by Fleishman and Hempel, we see

---

[1] The writer has identified this factor as "gross bodily coordination" and has placed it within a system of the psychomotor abilities (Guilford, 1958b).

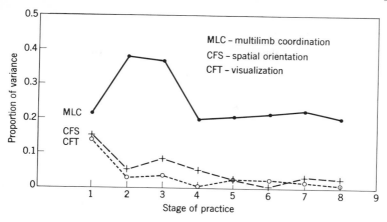

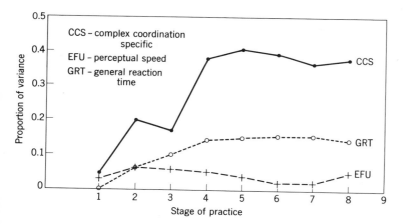

Fig. 12.3   Trends in the importance of six different aptitude factors in practice on the Complex Coordination test. (*From data presented by Fleishman & Hempel, 1954.*)

that it is possible to determine what form the conscious activity probably takes. It can be described in terms of cognitive functions.

The multilimb ability starts relatively high in importance, jumps to a status of prime importance in the next two practice periods, and never goes much below its initial status during the remainder of practice. It is apparently an ability that is much needed regardless of the amount of practice. But it would be of interest to see whether with still further practice even such a psychomotor factor also decreases in importance.

Another factor, which is intellectual but not cognitive, perceptual speed (EFU), contributes very modestly to variance throughout training, never losing all of what little value it has. This ability probably comes in because *S* has to match the given set of three lights with the three that he produces and to decide whether the match is close; hence the need of figural evaluation. No matter how much practice *S* has during the experiment, it appears that this kind of matching must continue.

The psychomotor factor of general reaction time has no importance in the initial trial but steadily increases in relative importance to a moderate plateau during the last five stages of practice. After some degree of smooth-running activity has developed, the number of matches S can make in a limited time depends relatively more on how promptly he moves in response to changes in the environment. It thus appears that simple reaction time sets an upper limit to the speed with which individuals can operate in this task. This does not mean that there are not other functions that also help to set limits. The so-called physiological limit that has often been given as the explanation for the fact that learning curves approach asymptotes may also yield to analysis in such a manner.

The most striking gain in importance is made by the specific factor, CCS, which starts very low and reaches a high plateau during the last five periods of practice. One interpretation of the CCS factor is that it is a genuine specific, unique to this particular task. From this point of view, it is presumably a nontransferable skill and individual differences in it cannot be predicted from any other measure of performance; in other words, no common-factor test would predict it. There is a real sense in which performance on the CC task is a unique kind of system.

Another interpretation would be that the factor is not a genuine specific: it is composed of variances of common factors not represented in the set analyzed with it. A third interpretation is that it is composed of a combination of a specific skill and some additional common factors yet to be determined. If it contains any common-factor variance at all, individual differences in it should be predictable to some extent.[1]

At any rate, it can be seen that it would take tests of different factors to predict performance in the CC test early versus late in the overall practice period. We can state the general hypothesis that cognitive abilities are more likely to be of some importance during the early stages of practice and that psychomotor abilities are relatively more important in later stages. Put in another way, input factors are relatively more important early in learning, and output factors relatively more important in later stages of learning. It can be inferred that the cognitive abilities make some contribution to learning but that the psychomotor abilities may be limited to contributions to performance.

In a later study with the same task (Fleishman, 1957), an effort was made to learn more about the possibility of predicting performance on the CC test late in practice, by bringing some additional factors into the picture. Four practice scores, each based upon 5 trials, were selected from 64 practice trials on the CC test. For six of the marker tests, practice was also involved over a series of trials, from each of which two scores were obtained, an early one and a late one. The hypothesis being tested by this arrangement was that late trials from a number of different tests will share common factors that become important with practice. The two complete analyses, involving the six early scores in the one case and the six late scores in the other, led to much the same factor structure, however, not supporting the hypothesis of late-score variables' sharing anything new in the way of common factors. This tends to support the hypothesis that the "specific" factor in a learning series of scores is unique.

The results of the experiment also verified the early decline in loadings for factor CFS-V and for CFT, the former declining from .35 to .16 from the first to the fourth practice score and the latter declining from .38 to .09. Two factors showed systematic increases of importance: arm speed, whose loadings increased from .04 to .40; and the CC specific, with an increase from .22 to .56. The loadings remained moderate and rather uniform for a psychomotor-precision factor (with first and last loadings of .41 and .42,

---

[1] Further information regarding such a factor will be found later in this chapter.

respectively) and for another psychomotor factor that Fleishman calls response orientation (loadings of .35 to .37). Response orientation might be the executive counterpart of the input factor CFS-V. In other words, it might be a *systems factor for psychomotor activity.* Loadings were consistently low for the factor of perceptual speed (EFU), as before, with first and last loadings of .21 and .11, respectively.

In a learning study with the Discrimination Reaction Time (DRT) test, another psychomotor test from the USAAF Aircrew Classification battery, similar results were found (Fleishman & Hempel, 1955). In brief, spatial orientation (CFS-V), most important at first, became progressively less important. Verbal comprehension (CMU), never very strongly represented, steadily declined in its contribution. Reaction-time variance increased throughout practice. The arm-speed factor increased rapidly in importance after the first two practice stages. Arm movement was involved because in every reaction in the DRT test S has to jump his responding finger from a resting place to one of four reaction keys. It takes a different kind of ability to initiate a movement than it does to carry out the movement rapidly, a difference beween being quick and being rapid (see Guilford, 1958b). The specific DRT factor increased systematically in relative importance but not so decidedly as the CCS factor did during practice on the Complex Coordination task.

Practice on the Rotary Pursuit test gave results with some noteworthy differences from results of other psychomotor tests (Fleishman, 1960). In its variance for the initial trials, this test was represented by almost nothing of an intellectual nature, its relevant factors of any consequence being psychomotor. It is therefore of special interest here. In such a case, will all psychomotor factors show increased proportions of variance with practice? For the control-precision factor (accuracy of arm movement), the relative variance started at about 30 percent, with practice dropped as low as about 15 percent, and then climbed again to about 25 percent. A rate-control factor started with about 10 percent of the variance and systematically declined in importance.

One unique finding was that there were two Rotary Pursuit special factors, RPS I and RPS II. The former started near zero in terms of variance and climbed systematically to about 50 percent. RPS II, on the other hand, started at about 35 percent of the total variance and declined to zero. Although they are very much confined to the Rotary Pursuit sources, two such factors cannot both be the Rotary Pursuit specific factor; one or both could represent one or more common factors unaccounted for by the tests that were put into the matrix for analysis.

Two such factors common to learning scores should be somewhat typical, if practice is continued long enough. The typical matrix of intercorrelations from a series of practice scores from the same task gives a pattern of coefficients that Guttman (1965) has called a "simplex." A simplex has its highest coefficients along the principal diagonal, a circumstance which follows the rule that the nearer together the trials from which the scores come, the higher the correlations between them. If one analyzed a simplex matrix, securing factor loadings only from scores obtained during practice, he would find two factors, an early-practice factor and a late-practice factor, which are difficult to interpret psychologically. The two factors probably represent some systematic shift from an early special strategy, unique to the task, to a late special strategy, also unique to the task. The task is a changing one psychologically as practice continues. One hypothesis might be that both mathematical factors represent confoundings of common psychological factors, one set important early and the other late in practice, changing in importance together so that they could not be separated. A genuine specific component would apply to one practice-score variable only. The early and late factors are quasi-common factors, shared by neighboring practice scores from the same task (the same, that is, in terms of physical require-

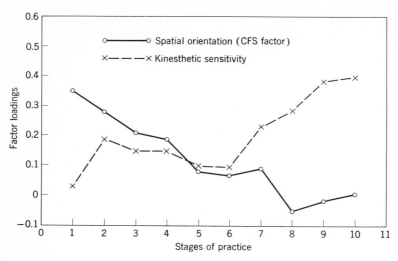

Fig. 12.4 Trends in spatial-orientation and kinesthetic-sensitivity involve-
ments in practice on the Complex Coordination test. (*From data presented
by Fleishman & Rich, 1963.*)

ments but not the same psychologically as practice continues). There remains the question
of why no early-practice factor appeared in the cases of Complex Coordination and Discrimination Reaction Time tests. Evidently the learning scores on those tests did not give
a simplex pattern of intercorrelations.

Fleishman and Rich (1963) have found that not all input factors lose importance
with continued practice. In further efforts to determine what common-factor variance
might be involved in late-practice scores in tests such as Complex Coordination, they
hypothesized that kinesthetic control might be important late in practice, whereas visual
control is important early. For the visual test they used a measure of spatial orientation
(CFS-V) called Aerial Orientation. For a kinesthetic-sensitivity test they used a measure
of sensitivity to difference in lifted weights. Such a test has not been analyzed; so whether
it is intellectual or perceptual in character is not known. A good guess is that it is the
latter, since no obvious kind of product of information is involved.

Ten successive scores were obtained from 40 trials with the Two-Hand Coordination
test, in which E attempts to keep a pointer on an irregularly moving button by manipulation of two lathelike controls. The hypothesis was that in early trials guidance of the hand
operations would be under control of visual input, involving factor CFS-V, which is a
known component of the initial trials with that test, and that this would shift later to
kinesthetic input. The hypothesis was clearly borne out, as seen by the trends of the
factor loadings in the factors represented in the two marker tests (see Figure 12.4). It
would thus appear that in this test kinesthetic feedback is more efficient and that some
kind of sensory control must be maintained for accurate performance. As an incidental
outcome, the investigators concluded that abilities may be regarded as ". . . capacities
for utilizing different kinds of information" (p. 10), which fairly well describes the nature
of factors as represented in the SI model. "Utilization" might be paraphrased as "operation with," and "kinds of information" are defined by conjunctions of content and product.

Changes in loadings in intellectual tasks   The only known studies in which the learning involved an intellectual task, no psychomotor components being involved, are the Woodrow study (1938) and a couple of others. One of these, by Fleishman and Fruchter (1960), pertained to learning to receive Morse code. The 4 learning scores were in terms of time required to achieve certain standards of reception, i.e., the time for reaching a reception rate of 4 groups per minute and the time taken in going from 4 to 6 groups, from 6 to 10 groups, and from 10 to 14 groups. All 4 learning scores were not factor-analyzed together along with the 14 marker tests, as had ordinarily been done. The tests were analyzed without the learning scores to determine the factor structure of the tests only. After learning scores (also regarded as criterion scores) had become available, the criterion variables were located within the reference frame already determined by the tests and their factor loadings. By this procedure, no *specific* code-reception factor was determined.

The factor loadings in the criterion variables show generally decreasing relationships to most of the factors. Curves for three of the factors are represented in Figure 12.5. One of these factors was interpreted by the authors as "auditory perceptual speed," but it has been identified by this writer as CSU-A, the cognition of auditory-symbolic units (see Chapter 4). Recognition was involved in the items, not matching, as is true of evaluation tests. "Auditory perceptual speed" should be factor EFU-A. In terms of information, such code signals are auditory-symbolic units. Another factor was interpreted as "auditory rhythm perception," but it has been identified by the writer as CFS-A, the cognition of auditory-figural systems, which seems to describe successions or patterns of dots and dashes fairly well.

The very weak factor represented in Figure 12.5 is a verbal ability, probably CMU, which is included here because of general interest in the factor that dominates verbal-intelligence scales. Its very weak contribution to the learning of code lends no support to it as "general learning ability." With the contributions of the common factors to achievement in learning to receive Morse code decreasing with practice, predictability of

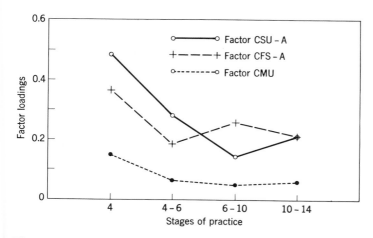

Fig. 12.5 Trends in the importance of three cognition factors in practice on the learning of the Morse code. (*From data presented by Fleishman & Fruchter, 1960.*)

the learning criterion measures also decreases with practice, the multiple correlations for predictions of the four practice-score variables being .59, .39, .29, and .33, respectively. Thus, only the early stage of learning was strongly predictable from the combination of tests in the study. Some other common factors would have to be brought into the prediction equation if the later criterion measures were to be well predicted.

Gagne and Paradise (1961) followed the correlations of certain selected tests, some of which measure recognized factors, with performance scores in the solving of simultaneous equations by seventh-grade students who had previously had programmed instruction on the subject. Tests of the two most relevant factors, numerical facility and a paired-associates memory factor, showed marked decreases in factor loadings as practice proceeded. From the beginning, less relevant tests, including a test of Following Directions, a vocabulary test, and a test called Speed of Letter Discrimination, had little change in factor loadings.

Thus, in tests not involving psychomotor-factor components, practice almost always entails decreases in relationships to common factors in which initial scores stand relatively high. Prediction from factor tests decreases with practice, but there is a possibility that when more is known about each task in which learning occurs, other common factors will be recognized and predictions can be kept higher for the later performance scores, as in the case of the kinesthetic-sensitivity factor in the Complex Coordination test, mentioned earlier. The latter is a psychomotor test. The application of this principle to nonpsychomotor tests is not clearly promising.

But it may well be that in every particular skill development the general, transferable features that can be attributed to the common factors help to shape the new special products, often in the form of systems, and that once the new systems have been well formed, much of the common-factor involvement is no longer needed or relevant, unless there is a change of method and reorganization occurs. The output, psychomotor factors, having less of a shaping function and more of a constituent function, aiding performance rather than learning, may well continue to have some importance.

Use of information regarding factor involvement Knowing that the relevance of factors changes with practice tells us that certain aspects of a problem or skill are ordinarily mastered first and other aspects later, Parker and Fleishman (1961) made use of this principle by applying appropriate training procedures. The learning task was a tracking operation, which meant keeping a white spot in the center of a screen by means of stick-and-rudder adjustments.

Group I practiced this tracking task with no formal instructions, but its questions were answered. Group II was given "common-sense" instructions, which included an initial explanation, a demonstration, and guidance, with critiques following certain trials. Group III was given the same instructions as group II and in addition some special information derived from the known involvement of aptitude factors. Since factor CFS-V (spatial orientation) was known to be of maximal importance for individual differences early, with decreasing importance, Ss in group III were told about this during trials 1 to 3. Since the multilimb psychomotor ability was known to be of maximal importance at trial 9, instruction about this ability was given beginning with trial 5.

In terms of both integrated-error score (summation of all kinds of errors) and a time-on-target score, the learning proceeded significantly more rapidly for group III and least rapidly for group I. Furthermore, the superiority of group III persisted in later tracking sessions without any further instructions. Companion experiments would introduce special instructions regarding either relevant or irrelevant factors at stages when those factors were not optimally relevant, to note effects upon the involvement of those factors in total scores.

Aptitude factors and transfer effects   In recent discussions it was suggested that when a factor appears to be having greater effects upon performance scores early in practice, the ability is aiding in the formation of new products of information. We may also say that it is having transfer effects. Some investigators have reversed matters by asking the question whether life experiences may have bearings upon the development of factorial abilities. An affirmative answer to this question would be in support of the Ferguson hypothesis mentioned in Chapter 1 (George A. Ferguson, 1956). We shall give attention to studies of this kind next; there have not been many.

Effects of learning upon status in factors   Will practice in visualizing develop an individual's level of ability in factor CFT, and will practice in tasks that call for hearing words on a background of sounds build up a person's status on factor CSU-A or factor NST-A? This kind of question has been investigated in a number of studies.

Faubian, Cleveland, and Harrell (1942) asked this question regarding mechanical aptitude, as measured by the tests Mechanical Movements and Surface Development. Two groups of 100 servicemen each were matched for intelligence on a test "like Henmon-Nelson." One was a group of new recruits, and the other had completed a six-week course of training, including the subjects of drafting, blueprint reading, electricity, shop mathematics, and Air Corps fundamentals. There was no significant difference in means for either of the tests. One might have expected that training in mechanical drafting and blueprint reading, particularly, would have a chance to promote development in visualizing ability, which is known to be a strong component of both such tests. In spite of the fact that the two groups were matched for verbal intelligence, we do not know but what the new recruits may have had greater average visualizing ability than the trained group had when it began its courses of instruction. We know that the correlation between visualizing ability and verbal-intelligence scores is very low.

Churchill, Curtis, Coombs, and Harrell (1942) asked about the effect of engineering training of a similar nature upon visualization as measured by a Surface Development test. Of two classes of about sixty men each in the AAF, one was studying drafting for nine weeks while the other was studying water purification. Both groups were tested with a form of the Surface Development test before and after training, also with a test involving mechanical information and comprehension. Both groups gained significantly in the Surface Development test. The difference between the two mean gains was also significant. Those who took the water-purification course gained more in the mechanical test.

Blade and Watson (1955) studied the effects of a year of engineering instruction upon scores in a test designed for visualization, in three different institutions. They found a mean gain in the test equivalent to 1 standard deviation, whereas nonengineering students showed a gain of ½ standard deviation, a very significant difference. Both initial and final test scores correlated moderately with grades in descriptive geometry and engineering drawing, indicating that such courses were relevant for training that might affect status in the factor.

Extent of transfer from training with respect to factors   The cited experiments on the effects of training upon factor status of individuals are only suggestive. The training was varied and complex and not well controlled. What is needed is training aimed at selected factors only. Woodrow (1939d) did the first such experiment when he asked whether practice in a verbal test would lead to positive transfer to other verbal tests. His study was done before it was known that there are so many different verbal abilities, and his tests undoubtedly involved a number of them.

The training was in two selected tests: verbal analogies, which could involve factors CMR, NMR, EMR, and CMU; and a test of categorical anagrams, which from appearances could involve factors CSU and DSU. Seven other verbal tests, involving various semantic abilities, were given as terminal (initial and final) tests. Experimental and control groups did not differ significantly in the terminal tests. It is difficult to say whether the end tests were appropriate to the factors involved in the training tests, and where so many factors are involved, there is bound to be ambiguity in the results. Woodrow's conclusion was that the effects of training were entirely specific, but his data were inadequate for that conclusion.

A much better-designed experiment of this type was performed by Heinonen (1962). His hypothesis was that training in a task will give transfer effects in other tasks in inverse proportion to the angular separations of the test vector for the transfer task from the test vector for the training task, in the common-factor space. The angular separation in degrees can be estimated from the cosine of the angle of separation, and the cosine of the angle is related to the coefficient of correlation between the two tests by the equation

$$r_{ab} = \cos \phi_{ab} h_a h_b \tag{12.1}$$

where

r_{ab} = correlation between tests A and B
ϕ_{ab} = angle of separation between vectors for tests A and B in common-factor space
h_a = length of vector for test A, also square root of communality for test A
h_b = similar constant for test B

From equation (12.1), solving for $\cos \phi_{ab}$ we obtain

$$\cos \phi_{ab} = r_{ab}/h_a h_b \tag{12.2}$$

and ϕ would, of course, be found in trigonometric tables. The expression on either side of equation (12.2) is known as a correlation corrected for uniqueness. Uniqueness is the proportion of non-common-factor variance (specific plus error variance) in the test. It is the amount of correlation existing between two tests if all the variance in both tests were attributable to common factors or if the test vectors were of unit length.

In testing this hypothesis, Heinonen used a battery of 16 psychomotor tests representing three known factors. One of the tests was chosen as the training test. A factor analysis was obtained for the battery that was given before practice and another for the battery given after practice, which provided the information needed in applying equation (12.2). Gains in means were found for all tests, and the mean gains were compared with the angular separations ϕ_{ab} for all tests, where A was the practice test and B varied over the other tests. The hypothesis was well confirmed. The increase in mean for a test varied systematically with the angular separation of that test from the practice test. This was true whether the angles were determined from the pretests or from the posttests.

A more recent study by Melametsä (1965) did not turn out positively. It was in the area of intellectual tests. Training was given on a Number Groups test, which was evidently a measure of both CSC and CSS. In each item of the task E was to recognize the common feature in four of five combinations of four letters each, excluding the one that did not embody the feature; hence the involvement with CSC. Seeing the principle that provided the common feature would probably involve factor CSS. Training included instructions concerning principles involved in the items, with practice on 12 forms of the test.

An experimental group and a control group repeated the battery tests after a six-week interval, during which training was given the experimental group.

Except for the Number Groups test, in which practice occurred, the experimental group gained more than the control group to such small extents that it was not possible to test the hypothesis of a positive relation between such differences and nearness of tests to the practice test in common-factor space. It is not clear why a control group is needed in making this kind of test of the hypothesis. Also, it is not clear that the other battery tests were well selected for a study of differential transfer effects. Three tests appear to represent factor CMU, three to represent CMT, and one each to represent factors CMR, CFS, CSC, and CSS. Although the last two represent the probably strong factors in the training task, the kind of training may have employed the wrong approach in that it emphasized the specific relations and systems used in the training test rather than general principles of cognition of symbolic relations and systems. Without very much confidence, we might conclude that the Melametsä results favor a hypothesis of very restricted transfer.

Krumboltz and Christal (1960) have presented some evidence that also favors a specific-gain hypothesis. They repeated the administration of two tests—Instrument Comprehension and Flight Orientation, both predominantly measures of factor CFS-V—sometimes in the same form and sometimes in a second form. In other groups of subjects the second testing was with the other test. The investigators found that administration of the alternate form of a test gave as much improvement as administration of the same form but that practice in the first administration of one of the tests did not yield comparable improvement in the other test of the same factor. It can be questioned whether one administration of a test of a factor is sufficient practice for adding personal stature in the factor. One administration might be sufficient for learning specific habits that transfer to another form of the same test.

The results of the four studies just mentioned are not very decisive, and their balance, leaning toward the hypothesis of specific gains only, runs counter to results from many other studies that will be mentioned in Chapter 14 in connection with divergent-production abilities in problem solving. Larger and more systematic studies of the kind done by Heinonen are needed in connection with this important problem. Such studies are crucial to the transfer theory of factor development proposed by Ferguson (1956), as related in Chapter 1.

The role of frequency in learning

It is not the intention of the next few paragraphs to go into the historical debate about the importance or unimportance of the condition of frequency of exercise. Emphasis will be upon recent studies that bear upon the learning of products of information. Attention must be given to the lively issue of "all-or-nothing" learning, or one-trial learning of products, which belongs under the general problem of frequency.

One-trial learning   The issue of one-trial learning arose in recent times primarily with the work of Irving Rock (Rock, 1957; Rock & Ceraso, 1964), who questioned whether repetition is a necessary condition for learning. His typical demonstration of unnecessity has been made in connection with paired-associates learning. In the traditional application of this procedure, S is given paired items of information, perhaps numbers paired with syllables, and receives enough trials so that eventually when the first member of each pair is given, he can respond with the second member, for all pairs. From one exposure trial to the next, there is ordinarily a progressive increase in the number of correct recalls of second members in response to the given first members when an anticipation test is used.

Rock varied the conditions in two ways. Using lists of eight pairs each, after the first trial, when, as usual, S could successfully respond in some of the pairs, he substituted entirely new pairs for those pairs in which S failed. Such replacements were made after each learning trial until all responses were correct. It was commonly found that with this substitution method, it took no longer to memorize the list of connections between all eight pairs than it did when keeping the same pairs in the list throughout. The inference was that S either learns a connection or he does not, on an all-or-none basis on any one trial.

A second variation involved not only making substitutions for the nonlearned pairs but composing the substituted pairs of the same items of information as had been presented before but in new pairings. The idea was that if there had been any partial learning in early trials, this re-pairing would introduce interferences that would hinder later learning and add to overall learning time. The time required to learn lists under this condition was about the same as under the conditions of no substitution and of substitution with all new items in the pairs. It is possible, however, that increased familiarity with the items of information (units) as such was a condition that tended to offset losses due to interferences.

Rock's hypothesis was that repetitions are necessary for overcoming the effects of interferences and thus for ensuring *retention* but are not necessary for learning. He cites the fact that if a person is given just one pair of items under normal conditions of observation, he can recite it with certainty. Given more than a pair of items in a list shorter than his memory span, the person is likely to pass the association test perfectly without repetition. He might master even 8 pairs in a list of 8, but if he were given a list of 10, he would probably succeed with less than 8 pairs. Interferences would be the probable reason.

Another interesting observation (Rock, 1958) is that anything beyond one exposure (with learning taking place in that one exposure) can be regarded as a case of overlearning, overlearning that may be needed to counteract the effects of interferences. This idea is supported by the fact that in a later retention test for a list of pairs learned by the replacement method, the pairs that are present from the first trial are better retained than those entered as replacements. They have had more overlearning.

Rock and Ceraso (1964) also point out that if S is merely asked to match given pairs as a test of retention, he is likely to do better than if he has to recall the second members. The matching test is like a recognition test for units; it is a recognition test for the retention of implications, in this case. A recognition test is generally easier than a recall test. From these facts it appears that there are degrees of availability of memory traces both above and below the threshold for one-trial recall.

A number of other investigators have given support to the all-or-none hypothesis of learning items of information implied by other items, as in paired-associates memorizing. John Brown (1964b), however, brings out arguments and evidence against the hypothesis and in favor of partial learnings. He cites the case in which further attempts to recall an item of information that could not be recalled on the first attempt apparently give it a greater-than-chance probability of being recalled. This fact indicates that a trace of some degree of strength was retained, even though it was not sufficiently strong to function in the ordinary anticipation test.

Brown also points out that even units of information may be complex in terms of the way in which they are stored and hence could be learned in parts or aspects. Some of the distinguishable aspects of a unit are its class memberships and, one might add, its possible relations and implications, such as are included in connotative meanings. Such aspects could be remembered or not remembered, each with some degree of independence; hence there is room for partial learning. One bit of evidence to be added in favor of partial learning is that when there is a multiple-choice test of retention of the pair member, S sometimes fails to select the right response but selects one that is similar from among the alternatives. According to Brown's theory, all learning involves an excess, a redundancy of information. A memory trace is complex to the extent of that redundancy. Thus, partial learning is always possible. Some parts may be lost by decay; some not. The probability of recall is a function of undecayed redundancy involved in the memory trace for an item.

The view taken earlier in this chapter on the continuity question is that learning can be both gradual and discontinuous, depending upon one's view regarding increments and accuracy of information. There are stepwise accretions, some of them very small, some large. This is almost a foregone conclusion when it is information that is developed and it is discriminations that make information. The major problem should be concerned with the kinds of increments that occur and under what conditions they occur. It is difficult for the writer to conceive of completely continuous changes, especially in view of the fact that at some level of nervous functioning an on-off principle must surely apply. Such a principle probably applies at different levels of complexity of functioning.

After considering various things that the expression "all-or-none" learning could mean, Restle (1965) has recently concluded that it must apply to the case, wherever found, in which "only one difficulty" is learned. If more than one source of difficulty is involved, there is opportunity for learning to be other than all-or-none. If all-or-none learning does not occur, we may infer that more than one source of difficulty is involved. Restle is not explicit as to what the sources of difficulty are, but it can be suggested that they are different products or parts of products of information.

Frequency and dissociative strength   The writer is in agreement with Ausubel (1965) when he points out that in learning a "dissociative strength" is developed as well as an "associative strength." Rock and Ceraso (1964) express belief in a similar conception. The products of information that we acquire in learning become more sharply defined as practice continues. By "dissociation" Ausubel means freedom of a learned item from subsumption or inclusion within a class so as to lose its identity. The writer would prefer to make the phenomenon more general and to regard it as freedom from confusion of information for whatever reason. Confusability of items of information is deficiency of discrimination and hence deficiency of information. In considering the findings of numerous studies of interferences in connection with spaced versus massed practice, Underwood (1961) came to a similar view, that interference means confusion of information.

It is well known that overlearning tends to "harden" information, to clarify it, to sharpen its boundaries. The information becomes less involved in interferences and negative transfer events. Repetition of cognition has the effect of modifying a product in the direction of lowered confusability. At each repetition of a unit, for example, a somewhat different (redundant) context comes with it, but certain more consistent elements come time after time, thus working toward a more denotative type of meaning. The rapid repetition of a word with loss of meaning context is probably a similar type of phenomenon. If consistent implications (associations) are also involved, they too become sharper and better defined with sufficiently spaced repetition. Thus, both associative strength and dissociative strength, as Ausubel calls them, are built up with repetition or practice.

We see similar phenomena in connection with learning psychomotor patterns or systems. M. B. Jones (1962) concluded that learning means simplification of the performance of the task. A large part of this may be the losing of irrelevant contextual information, as suggested in connection with the case of memorizing items of information.

Reinforcement as information

The writer has previously proposed the idea that the most comprehensive view of reinforcement is to interpret it in terms of feedback information (Guilford, 1961; 1965b). The view is sufficiently broad to include the explanatory principles of drive reduction, pleasure-pain, reward and punishment, confirming reaction, and knowledge of results. The last-named principle is a nontechnical description of the broader view of feedback information. This is a cybernetic type of conception, which seems to be growing in favor from different sources.

The view is very similar to that developed by George A. Miller et al. (1960). They regard behavior not in terms of stimulus-response sequences and patterns but as satisfying a TOTE model, which stands for the sequence of test-operate-test-exit. The sequence may be longer, expressed by TOTOTOTOTE, which would represent trial-and-error behavior. The test event determines whether or not things are all right; if not, some operation is performed to remedy the situation, and a further test determines the effectiveness of the operation. This is repeated until the test shows a satisfactory outcome, at which there is an exit (E) from the behavior pattern. Each test after the first one makes use of feedback information.

The similarity of the "test" concept to the operation of evaluation will be readily recognized. What Miller et al. refer to as "operate," could include cognition or either divergent or convergent production, the results of which are commonly evaluated. In the context of learning, a change in behavior yields feedback information which indicates either that the change is satisfactory from some point of view or that it is not satisfactory. If satisfactory, the change is likely to become a part of the memory stockpile; if it is unsatisfactory, some other change is tried and tested.

A striking instance of achievement of muscular control by providing feedback information was recently described by Basmajian (1963). It involved the development of voluntary control over a certain muscle element in the hand, served by a single axon from a cell in the anterior horn of the spinal cord. The subject would try to effect an isolated contraction in the particular muscle element, and when he succeeded, he received a visual or an auditory signal as feedback information. No contraction of that element, no signal. S could be trained also to increase or decrease the rate of rhythms of contractions, as well as to contract the muscle element in different rhythms. The skill remained after removal of the experimental feedback stimulus. Presumably, S learned to use a new feedback stimulus. S could also learn to suppress action in the same unit that he had previously learned to excite and to excite a new muscular unit.

The moral of all this seems to be that greater attention should be paid to looking for what feedback information is available and relevant in the self-testing of a particular event, muscular or not. In teaching others, it is desirable to find a way to see that feedback information of sufficient accuracy and completeness is available to the learner in his attempts to reach his goal and that it is available when most needed. Having a clear conception of the goal is very important, for evaluation is a matter of matching and comparing outcome with the goal condition: a comparison of output with input information, as the saying goes in cybernetics.

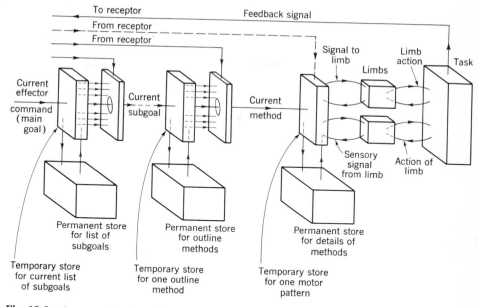

Fig. 12.6 An operational model representing steps in the flow of information connected with an intention and execution of overt actions. (*Adapted by permission from a model by Crossman, 1964.*)

Executive functions

Model for the human effector system   Previous discussions have made reference to motor patterns. Let us now consider a model designed by Crossman (1964), representing events on the output side of an overt activity that involves learned components. A view of Crossman's model is shown in Figure 12.6.

On the basis of input information and central operations with it, a general command is issued to the effector systems. The command might be: "Look in the morning newspaper to see what the Dodgers did in the game last night." This statement describes the main goal of the act, which calls into play a number of subgoals, including hunting for the newspaper, picking it up, turning to the sports section, and finding the appropriate column. Each of these part actions, in turn, calls into play subsidiary movements. Picking up the newspaper involves reaching, grasping, and lifting. Turning to the sports section includes possible looking at the index on the front page, separating the sections of the newspaper, and grasping the two edges preparatory to reading. Finding the desired column involves looking at various headlines. The total action is made up of a hierarchical organization of subactions and subsidiary movements, which are represented in the model in Figure 12.6.

The permanent memory store is shown as containing different levels of executive systems of different degrees of generality. In the course of development, the infant learns the detailed elements of movement first, in the form of waving, pushing, pulling, grasping, clasping, clutching, pinching, releasing, throwing, lifting, holding, dropping, shoving, and so on. Such events may be regarded as *units* of executive information. *Classes* are formed by virtue of the fact that collections of different movements have similar effects, such as increasing the distance between the object and the person, as in pushing, shoving, repelling, rejecting, and so on, which can be done with one hand or another, with legs, or with the head. *Systems* are formed by combining pieces of action into organized patterns and by producing hierarchical arrangements. There are possibilities of applying other product categories to movements. For example, a *transformation* would occur when a particular movement is adapted to some new use or when a system is reorganized. An *implication* would apply where one movement naturally leads to another.

It is not certain how far the structure-of-intellect categories can be applied to the area of executive functions, but it can be suggested that such parallels would furnish a natural link between cognition and action in behavior. A situation cognized in a certain way calls for organized actions of a certain kind, because of some degree of isomorphism that exists between input and output events.

One other feature of the model in Figure 12.6 that should be emphasized is the feedback signal represented. This provides a means of self-regulation, as in intellectual activity. Although feedback from the final act only is shown, it is probable that there is feedback from other points along the way, prior to the final act.

Summary

After citing recent examples of the growing discontent with the association principle and its inadequacies in accounting for learning, it was proposed that what is learned is in the form of new products of information. Classical studies of conditioning and other learning where the association principle best applies can be reinterpreted as dealing with the acquisition of implications.

In connection with the serial memorizing of items and paired-associates learning, there is a growing recognition that units of information must be learned as well as connections between units. A series also has systemic properties, which account for some of the phenomena in memorizing lists of items.

The many studies of concept attainment pertain to the formation of classes. Several of the SI abilities dealing with classes may be involved, depending upon the nature of the learning experiment. Studies of the learning of relations show that they are achieved suddenly, with insightful understanding.

The best examples of acquisition of systems in learning experiments have been on problems of development of patterns of movements. It was suggested that such systems are cognized in the behavioral (self-information) category but that on the output side they are executive systems. Thus, skills can be given informational interpretations. Strategies in such events as the learning of classes can also be interpreted as behavioral systems. A theoretical model for the operation of executive or motor systems, adapted from Crossman, was presented.

The role of transformation has interesting possibilities in theory of learning. The reorganizations of gestalt psychology are probably categorized properly as transformations, as is the concept of accommodation of Piaget. Transformation, as a product, however, is broader than either, for a transformation is an item of information that can be remembered and later be utilized. Like a relation or a system, it is transposable.

A good beginning has been made on the problem of how particular aptitude factors play roles in learning psychomotor and intellectual skills. In general, intellectual factors, particularly cognitive abilities, play roles in early learning trials in some psychomotor tasks, decreasing systematically in importance, while psychomotor abilities tend to increase in importance. A prominent "specific" task factor also increases in importance, but its possible constituents in terms of common factors are still unknown.

There is evidence that certain relevant kinds of experience may contribute to increased personal status in common-factor strength, but there is considerably more to be learned concerning the way in which experience contributes to the development of personal status in the various aptitude factors.

There is evidence that if items of input information are relatively free from interferences, they require only one-trial exposure for learning. There is increasing reason to regard interferences as confusion of information, and confusion means loss of discrimination or loss of information. An important role of repetition in learning is to sharpen discriminations, overcoming confusions. Another is to offer opportunities for transformations.

Reinforcement is given an informational interpretation. In one way or another, "knowledge of results" can embrace other conceptions of reinforcement. Feedback information provides an important key to reinforcement. This does not preclude the operation of other features, such as relative weighting of actions in view of motivational considerations.

13 Retention and recall

Although it is quite easy to make logical distinctions among learning, retention, and recall and although such distinctions are quite proper, the differential investigation of these three phenomena is exceedingly difficult. As is well known, the same conditions that affect one tend to affect all, and experimental conditions that permit drawing conclusions with respect to one of them very often apply to another. We cannot tell whether anything has been learned by a subject without evidence that involves some retention, and we often use some kind of recall test to indicate effects of either learning or retention. Certain variations of conditions, however, permit us to say whether one of the phenomena is predominantly involved.

In this chapter we shall focus upon the events and conditions that prevail in time after the cognition of information, dealing with its storage and its retrieval at some later time. We shall consider in what form information is stored and what may happen to it in storage. We shall consider the problem of short-term storage and of the loss of information in that connection. Principles of recall and some of the conditions affecting recall, particularly in connection with the operation of divergent production, will receive attention.

Retention

Storage in terms of products of information   Since we have found that cognition of information is in the form of products and that the information produced, either divergently or convergently, is also in the form of products, it is natural to assume that memory storage, too, is in the form of products. More direct evidence of this, of course, is the fact that memory abilities are also distinguishable along the lines of the same kinds of products.

The storage of units and systems   There is scattered opinion from different sources to this effect, also. For example, E. B. Hunt (1963) states that memory is stored in terms of "chunks" of information. He goes so far as to say, also, that each chunk is stored in a different location, something like books in a library, to use a metaphor, and that when activated, chunks can migrate to locations of other chunks. Postman (1963) comments that a memorizer may organize items in "chunks," producing systems. Gomulicki (1963) speaks of a double recording, generic and specific, which may be an implicit recognition of units' being stored as members of classes.

In addition to the evidence in the preceding chapter for things being learned as products and hence presumably being stored as such, some additional evidence for the storage of products can be cited here. Kintsch (1963), in developing a mathematical theory to account for paired-associates learning, regarded the latter as a two-stage process, involving the memory for units and the memory for connections (implications) between units. His experimental test bore out this distinction.

After reviewing the studies on memory span, Gabriel (1963) felt forced to conclude that a distinction must be made between memory for items in the memory-span list and for the order of the items. Order has been a useful kind of systemic principle in tests of abilities for dealing with systems, as indicated in earlier chapters. In his own experiments, Gabriel found that memory for order was lost more rapidly than that for items, along with other results, from which he developed the hypothesis that loss of memory for items is primarily due to interferences, whereas loss of memory for order is more due to decay of memory traces.

Representing the gestalt point of view, Katona (1940) has emphasized the hypothesis that memory for anything depends upon whether it is embedded within a total structure of some kind. We may say that total structures are likely to be in the form of classes or systems. The memory for a series of digits, 581215192216, could be facilitated by making of it a sum of money, like a Federal expenditure: 5, 812, 151, 922.16, for example. Or, inspection might show the possibility of making a number series of the digits: 5 8 12 15 19 22 26, with successive differences of 3, 4, 3, 4, 3, 4. Katona makes the interesting suggestion that two kinds of memory traces are ordinarily formed: those for specific items of past experience, which we can readily call units; and those for the whole character, in other words, the system, class, or relation. He says, further, that traces for individual items are rigid and fixed; the structural ones are flexible and adaptable. In saying this, Katona may be recognizing the fact that units of information are not subject to transformations, whereas the other, more complex, products are. He points out that individual traces are formed with a great deal of effort, whereas structural traces form quickly and with understanding. It would appear that if the "individual traces" he is talking about are in the nature of symbolic units, what he says hardly applies to semantic units. Even then, if symbolic products, like telephone numbers, are cognized clearly in isolation, one exposure may be sufficient. A further statement is that structural traces are retained longer, whereas individual traces need additional reinforcements for retention. Although there is undoubtedly much truth in the memory value of information that is encompassed within larger structures, the differences in memory traces are probably not so great as Katona's statements would suggest.

Schwartz and Lippman (1962) studied effects in retention when words are embedded in sentences and the effect of the degree of coherence of the sentence upon retention. Sets of sentences, each sentence containing four nouns, were read to the subjects. Sentences were of three degrees of coherence, high (H), medium (M), and low (L). Half the Ss were instructed to report later the nouns they had heard, and after writing nouns they were then told to list verbs, as a test of incidental memory. The other Ss were told to write complete sentences.

Both immediate and delayed recall of both nouns and verbs increased monotonically with increasing coherence of the sentences. Recall of sentences gave superior scores with respect to nouns and verbs; in fact, retention of sentences essentially doubled such recall scores. Even poor sentence structure (in the L sentences) appeared to be better than no sentences at all. It was suggested that S introduced better structuring of his own into these sentences.

Another aspect of this experiment is of considerable interest. This aspect has to do with the *clustering* of recalled items of information. S had a self-imposed option of recalling together either words that came from the same sentence or words that belonged to the same class in terms of meaning. A cluster was defined as two or more words in succession from the same sentence (system) or belonging to the same class. Ss tended to go toward one kind of clustering or the other. Clustering by classes tended to increase in the later recall (this was a matter of minutes). This fact suggests that the recency value of the sentence system was wearing off rapidly. It also suggests that retention tends to revert to class organizations. Classes are of a more permanent nature than are particular sentences.

The use of class membership as an aid in retention and recall is probably a very general strategy. Clustering showed itself in another way. Ss tended to forget words by clusters, particularly where sentence coherence was high. They were forgetting the system in which sets of units were embedded. This should be evidence that retention does occur in terms of larger wholes, namely, systems.

The loss of information in systems   Ausubel (1962) warns us that embedding of items within larger structures may be a hindrance as well as a help. Subsuming information may be an aid in retention early after learning, but it may help to lose information as time goes by. What happens depends upon the discriminability of the items within their larger carriers. Retention of something that is too well absorbed may mean loss of discrimination and hence loss of information. Although meaningful (semantic) information is more readily learned because it can be more readily subsumed within a system, it needs clear distinctions at the same time to ensure its separate recall at a later time. Similar effects with other categories of information, such as figural and symbolic, also should be considered.

A few investigations tend to show that there are significant individual differences with respect to the loss of information by leveling processes in retention. The terminology differs. Gomulicki (1956) speaks of individuals as "changers" and "condensers." Some individuals tend to make relatively more errors of commission after periods of retention, while others tend to make more errors of omission. The former apparently modify their memory traces, while the latter tend to lose details in larger masses of information. L. Berkowitz (1957) studied the relationship between the leveling tendency in retention (dropping out of details) and Frank Barron's variable of preference for simplicity versus complexity, with the hypothesis that the condensers prefer simplicity (in line drawings and other designs). Berkowitz found a significant relationship between two memory-leveling scores and also between those two scores and a score for preference for simplicity.

Gardner and Lohrenz (1960) made the distinction in terms of "levelers" and "sharpeners," evidently in consequence of the much earlier gestalt concepts brought out initially by Wulf (1922). The latter found that in reproductions of visual-figural units subjects showed two tendencies. One was to smooth over minor departures from continuity, and the other was to sharpen or accentuate the striking features of the object, somewhat as a cartoonist caricatures his subjects. Gardner and Lohrenz generalized these tendencies into opposite types of individuals who exhibit their own inclinations in both perception and memory. Of levelers they say that they ". . . show consistently great assimilative interaction among new experiences and related memories." Levelers consequently ". . . form relatively contaminated and undifferentiated memories of their ongoing experience" (p. 295). Sharpeners are ". . . characterized by little percept-memory interaction—experience new events in their own right, and consequently form relatively discrete and high differentiated memories." [1]

These authors hypothesized that there would be considerable difference in the way in which the facts of a story would be transmitted from one individual to another in a group of levelers versus a group of sharpeners. Two groups of each type were determined on the basis of a perceptual test involving judging the sizes of squares in inches, sharpeners making the more accurate judgments, thus having more discrimination. The levelers tended to confuse information.

[1] It is of incidental but somewhat exciting interest to note that the definition given for a sharpener seems to fit very well one of the extreme intellectual shortcomings of the infantile-autistic case as described by Rimland (1964).

Memory for ideas was tested by using a short story containing 25 "themes," or ideas. In each group, one S privately heard the story, then privately retold it to the second, and so on to the fifth S. The result was that the sharpener group retained more themes (116 versus 79), with a higher percentage correct. Levelers showed more transpositions. The number of imported themes was about the same in the two groups. The hypothesis seems to have been borne out, but in view of the fact that discrimination of squares and memory for semantic units are probably completely independent insofar as aptitudes go, any correlation between the two tasks of this study must have been due to a nonaptitude trait, such as an attitude.

D. R. Davis and D. Sinha (1950a; 1950b) contributed two related studies bearing on the same point, the loss of information during retention (also on changes in memory traces), starting from a different theoretical standpoint. They aimed to test Bartlett's theory that memory operates in terms of organized masses, not as a collection of items that maintain their specific characters. A schema is committed to memory storage, but it is plastic, subject to reshaping from the influence of subsequent experiences.

In the Davis-Sinha experiments, group A heard a story, then, four days later, saw a picture that had things in common with the story. Eight days later and also four weeks later, recall and recognition tests were given. The story was about a feud between two families that later had a marriage between two of their members. The picture was entitled "The Village Wedding." It was presented among six pictures, with S to select the one most closely related to the story. The recall performances were scored in terms of numbers of story elements reported. Group B had every treatment except exposure to the picture.

Group A recalled more items of information than group B, with medians of 50 and 43 items for earlier and later tests, respectively, against group B's medians of 45 and 24 items. In the results from group A, some items given in the first recall test were imported from the picture, and more were imported in the later recall. Thus, a related but different experience improved retention, but it also introduced some confusion of information. In another experiment with the same story and picture, one group exposed to the picture and the other not, a recognition test was given after about five weeks, as was a questionnaire concerning details. Again, the group seeing the picture showed many more confusions between picture and story.

The line of research in which Wulf (1922) was the first continued along much the same lines, using figural information. The results were both positive and negative, in a series of experiments too numerous to mention here. The more recent experiments just cited have used semantic information, with much more consistent and striking results. It would not be exact to say that all the changes thus demonstrated in retained information are in the form of leveling; some could be better described as a coalescing. There may be other varieties of changes that will come to light, but the influence of new experience on stored information can no longer be doubted. It cannot be described well in terms of associative bonds. It is better described in terms of transformations of products.

Short-term versus long-term memory   In Chapters 9 and 11, brief mentions were made of the phenomenon that is usually known as "short-term memory." We can now appropriately give fuller attention to that phenomenon. First, it is to be noted that there is some disagreement about the duration of short-term memory (STM), the length of time retention lasts after stimulation, about what the phenomenon should be called, about whether loss of information during its operation is attributable to decay processes or to interferences, and even about whether or not it is a genuine memory phenomenon at all.

In his earlier dealings with the subject, Broadbent (1957a) spoke of a perception system and a storage system; later he used the expression "short-term memory," which he said lasts during the first second after stimulation (Broadbent, 1963). John Brown (1964a) uses the same expression, but in passing he questions whether or not anything is stored at all. He likens the fleeting memory for things just exposed to a blackboard, which can be wiped clean at any moment. Again, he speaks of separate storage for visual and auditory information.

Many writers on the subject refer to what is remembered fleetingly as an image (this writer suggested in an earlier chapter that it is equivalent to Titchener's memory after-image), and Sperling (1960) avers that success in short-term memory depends upon the reading of that image. An image does seem to hang suspended for a moment or two, as if perception were persisting and one could attend to different parts of it, extracting further information.

Melton (1963) has concluded that there is really no break between short-term and long-term memory; a continuum, covering all the time following the stimulus, is involved, and the same principles apply all along it. His evidence was in terms of the effects of proactive and retroactive inhibition upon retention for what he considered to be short-term periods, but those periods ranged from three to thirty-two seconds, or beyond the usual time range that is considered to apply to short-term memory. Melton's assumption seemed to be that if retention is affected by interferences as it is for longer retention times, the kind of memory is the same. Broadbent had stressed the conclusion that short-term memory is affected by decay during the time lapse and not by interferences.

Waugh and Norman (1965) prefer the overworked terminology of *primary* and *secondary* storage. Information in primary storage is transferred to secondary storage if it is rehearsed, but it can be in both kinds of storage at the same time, if it has been recently perceived. Rehearsal helps to keep some information also in primary storage at the expense of other recent information and new-coming input. The authors regard the duration of primary storage as a matter of number of items of information rather than of length of time. The two are of course ordinarily correlated. New input displaces what is in primary storage, if it is assumed that attention is favorable to it and relevant cognition occurs.

Interference versus decay theories of short-term memory   Much debate and some research have been devoted to the issue of whether loss of information from temporary storage is due to decay or to interferences. Apparently all agree that the virtue of short-term storage is to compensate for the limited capacity for intake of information. Not all that is perceived can possibly become fixed in permanent storage, but by holding some of the input temporarily, as in an anteroom, as if prolonging exposure or achieving a rehearsal, which is next best to an actual restimulation, more information can be handled. The individual can take in successively what he could not take in simultaneously. Continuity of cognition is also thus facilitated. But the hold on the temporarily stored information is very tenuous, and the question is what makes it vanish, in part or in whole. The issue is a replication of that pertaining to long-term memory and one that has not been resolved, except that effects of interference have been well established. But this does not automatically eliminate the decay hypothesis, for which there is also positive evidence.

Evidence for the decay hypothesis   The chief advocate of the decay side of the issue with respect to short-term memory has been Broadbent (1957a; 1962; 1963). Broadbent initiated the type of experiment in which information is fed into two different sensory channels (eyes and ears or right and left ears) simultaneously or in rapid alternation. For example, he would put into the two earphones (in three different trials) the digits:

Right ear: 7 3 6 2 4 9   2 7 1 8 4 6   1 9 4 8 5 7
Left ear: 1 5   3 9   3 6

The digits were sounded at the rate of either two per second or one per second. Interest was in how well S could report the two digits exposed to the left ear when the delays differed. If the delay hypothesis is correct, the first of the three left-ear pairs should be easiest (least delay between exposure and recall at the end of the series of six digits) and the third should be most difficult. It worked out that way with the 0.5-second rate of exposure (but not for the 1-second rate), with scores of 40, 30, and 28.

It should be noted, however, that interference conditions are confounded with delay, with the number of digits exposed in the right ear after the two in the left ear increasing from none to two to four. Broadbent evidently assumed the opportunities for interference to be the same, since six items were present in competition to the two. But it is commonly agreed that information coming later is likely to wipe out that preceding it, which could be regarded as a case of retroactive inhibition. Another prediction would be that when the two digits are in the middle, they would be most difficult to recall because of the interference from both directions. This hypothesis includes possible proactive inhibition as well as retroactive inhibition. Broadbent's results from one such experiment (1957a) were in fair agreement with this prediction, with scores of 43, 30, and 43 at the slower rate.

Broadbent (1962) cites other evidence. In one experiment, several items were flashed on a screen, and after different small delays a pointer appeared, showing S the location of the items he was to report. The longer the delay, the poorer the score, even within a one-second period, in spite of the fact that longer delays would allow more time for rehearsal. Another observation was that Ss forget telephone numbers more often while dialing the number than they do when using the push-button form of calling a party on the telephone. The push-button method takes less time. What other conditions may have confounded the difference is not known. In another experiment (Broadbent, 1962), after an exposure of six digits, S was required immediately to speak the letters A, B, and C, synchronized with sound signals, at rates varying from all three in $\frac{2}{3}$ second to all three in 2 seconds. If equal degrees of opportunity for interference from the three letters are assumed, the principle of greater loss of information with greater delay of recall appears to support the decay hypothesis.

Evidence for the interference hypothesis   Broadbent (1962) admits that interference of certain kinds damages retention in short-term memory. He states that even dialing 0 before a telephone number may be enough to cause loss of the memory for the number. He also admits that distractions are effective, but he insists that such interference is different from the kind that affects retention for long-term memory (Broadbent, 1963).

Moray (1960) provides some evidence on the interference side of the issue. Moray used Broadbent's general procedure of presenting items to the two ears separately. He presented pairs of items at different rates in pairs per second, and he called for three kinds of reports: free-recall reports, successive reports (all from one ear, then all from the other), and alternating reports (RLRLRL). One finding, which runs counter to a decay hypothesis, was that the mean number of errors systematically decreased with *increase* in exposure time. More errors in recall came from the middle of the list of digits, also suggesting an interference theory. In order to support a decay theory, the most errors should occur for the first items in the list. Three-fourths of the errors were transposition errors, not omissions or substitutions, a fact that also suggests effects of interferences.

If we can accept the findings of Melton (1963), with delays of three to thirty-two seconds after the stimulus, as pertaining to short-term memory, there is additional support for the effects of interference. For example, he pointed out that when S has to do some brief counting immediately after the exposed items, there is loss of information. The phenomenon of intrusions, a common interference effect, also occurs.

As in the case of long-term memory, there is positive evidence for effects both of decay and of interference, and there is little reason not to accept both as determining influences. It is not necessary to make a choice between the two; one does not exclude the other either logically or empirically. It would be unreasonable to expect a memory after-image from stimulation to last indefinitely, even with zero sources of interference. And if we accept all poststimulus events, including distractions and simply new input of any kind, as sources of interference, everyday observation is convincing enough that these effects are genuine. It can be suspected that lurking behind the reluctance to accept interference as a determiner of information loss is the assumption that interference comes only from conflicting associations. From an informational point of view, interference is anything that tends to destroy discriminations and hence to lose information. The interfering sources can be regarded as noise, and there is a loss in signal-to-noise ratio, as the communication engineers say, even an overwhelming of the signal and its loss in the general melee of events. Rehearsals have the effect of building up the ratio, perhaps sufficiently for more permanent storage.

Conditions for permanent storage   With no interfering events, figural information may pass into permanent storage in figural form; if not available for recall or for recognition, perhaps it is revivable by means of Penfield's method of direct stimulation of the brain. If, as is probable, there is more than the image, something in the form of semantic recognition, permanent storage may be in that form. In the fixation of information for permanent storage, there is believed to be some perseverative activity, a kind of automatic rehearsal. Hebb (1949) has explained this theoretically in physiological terms as a matter of "reverberating circuits" in the cerebral tissues involved. The physiological basis of memory will be discussed in Chapter 15; it constitutes a very active subject of research at the present time.

To return to psychological matters, it seems that there is at work some selective mechanism that determines which cognitions are committed to permanent storage and which are not. The bulk of our ongoing experiences need not be stored, with availability for future use, and it would probably overtax our storage capacity if everything were so stored. The difference between intentional and incidental learning is one recognized condition. There must be others, and we need to know by what procedures intentional learning contributes to the probability of permanent storage. The intentional condition cuts more finely than the distinction between storage and no storage. We can intend to remember a telephone number just long enough to dial it, for as long as we know we are going to have to use it in the future, or for all foreseeable time; and such discriminations in intention seem to have positive results. The student who crams for examinations also knows this by experience.

Recall

The phenomenon of recall of information is interesting in its own right, but it takes on much-increased significance when its relations to the operations of divergent and convergent production are realized. The production of information in response to given information comes largely from stored information, an event that is, of course, recall or retrieval. If we understood the nature of recall mechanisms, we would know a great deal also about the production operations and about problem solving in general.

Conditions of recall   Although probability of recall of an item of information depends upon the goodness of retention and retention depends upon the thoroughness of learning, correlations of probability of recall with those other two variables are by no means perfect, as is well known. For example, sometimes you cannot for the life of you recall something that you say you know as well as you know your own name. The information is well recorded, but there is blocking of recall. On the other hand, things in memory storage that have been unavailable for many years may come out under unusual circumstances of hypnosis, drugs, or a crisis of some kind. We need to know when and to what extent the conditions of learning and retention also affect recall, when and to what extent those conditions do not, and what new conditions apply.

Among the well-known conditions that have been traditionally given for probability of recall are general relaxation, completeness of the instigating situation, overlearning, recency of exercise, and confidence on the part of the individual. We shall have some interest in most of these conditions here and shall consider some additional conditions.

Replicative versus transfer recall   But before we consider these conditions, it is important to make a new distinction between what will be called *replicative recall* and *transfer recall*. A replicative recall brings back stored information in its original form, or essentially so, in response to cues in connection with which it was committed to memory storage or at least to a part of those cues. Transfer recall is retrieval of information instigated by cues in connection with which the information was not committed to memory storage. Relatively too much research attention has been devoted to the former and too little to the latter. The reason has been the associational theoretical bias, under which it seems that nothing is expected to happen by way of recall that has not happened before. This situation should be corrected.

Relaxation and suspended judgment   A state of relaxation, often mentioned as a condition favorable for recall, has several different meanings. One variety is a general state of lowered muscular tonicity. There is also a more special relaxation of effort to recall specific information. Trying too hard to recall something often defeats the individual's purpose. Such effort may have its beneficial effects at some later time, as seems apparent in common experience; there is little experimental evidence on this point.

Another special kind of relaxation called to our attention in recent years is known as "suspended judgment" (Osborn, 1963). This condition can be described as reduction of evaluative operations, as in Osborn's well-known brainstorming sessions, in which all critical judgment is tabooed. The success of this procedure in bringing out quantity of ideas suggests that evaluation serves a filtering function as well as a matching-and-decision operation, unless the filter turns out to be of a nonevaluative kind.

Search and scanning operations   The condition of completeness of cues has been demonstrated in connection with replicative recall, but it undoubtedly has application also to transfer recall. In transfer recall the cue or cues are furnished by a search model, of which something has been said in an earlier chapter. It is becoming more common to think of information storage in terms of brain function as being in the form of some kind of pattern or template, whether in the form of neuron networks or molecular coding. This should hold true for any kind of psychological product of information, even a unit. The search model can also be conceived in the form of a pattern or template; it is a product of information that the searcher needs and for which he is searching. It is sometimes suggested that a kind of scanning operation analogous to that in radar goes on. The likelihood of activation of a certain template in storage depends upon the points in common between the search model and that stored template. There must be a certain degree of harmony, congruence, or resonance between the two, some degree of isomorphism. This description seems to fit evaluation. If there is a sufficiently good fit, the revived product not only is revived but is accepted; if there is not, the search goes on. Availability of certain stored items of information would depend to some extent upon the clarity and strength of the search model and how well the one pattern fits the other.

Overlearning and transfer   Overlearning is a well-recognized condition favoring replicative recall. We need to speculate regarding its role with respect to transfer recall. In both cases it should have the function of reducing possibilities of interference, that is to say, confusion of information. Overlearning sharpens discriminations and thus improves the coding of information. A consequence is a lowered danger of negative transfer from the information and a relatively better chance of positive transfer, even when there are conflicting aspects between tasks. There might be some danger of isolating the information too thoroughly, however, or of making it so clearly lacking in congruence with a search model that it would be passed by in the scanning search. There may be an optimal level of overlearning for different purposes. There could hardly be too much overlearning of the implications in number operations for almost any purpose, but where an object is to be used for some unusual purpose, there needs to be enough overlearning to ensure availability but not so much as to limit the object severely to one use or function.

There is some interesting evidence regarding the effect on recall of amount of original exposure, which has been pointed out by Deutsch (1962). When the number of trials in memorizing lists is kept constant, the recall score later will be constant, no matter how many such series of items the individual has previously learned. But as the learner improves in his rate of learning such lists and continues to practice each list to a criterion of complete mastery and as his number of needed learning trials decreases, his recall score also decreases. Underwood (1957) has taken such results to mean that proactive inhibitions are building up as the learner memorizes more series, but an alternative hypothesis is that the criterion of complete mastery is a changing standard with respect to retention and recall.

Recency of practice   Recency of practice can be a very powerful condition for recall of particular information. In fact, it can be too powerful under some circumstances, for example, when we do not want the information but it keeps intruding, to our disadvantage. The recently practiced information can thus provide a barrier against recall of information that we do want. One obvious remedy is to introduce a lapse of time, which may mean that we resort to a period of incubation with respect to the problem of the moment. In the next chapter we shall see how recency can be used effectively in aiding us toward the solution of problems. For one thing, it should pay to review information that is probably going to be needed in solving a problem, which means that there should be some way of anticipating what area of information may be needed, even in advance of analysis of the problem.

Both primacy and recency have long been recognized as favorable conditions, as shown by the bowed curve for memory as a function of position in a series of items. But whether the function applies only to recall, or applies to retention and therefore also to recall, or applies to learning and therefore also to retention and recall is difficult to say. However this may be with respect to primacy, there is considerable evidence apart from serial learning to show how important recency is for recall.

One of the recent kinds of experiments bearing such evidence is on the phenomenon called "priming." Storms (1961) hypothesized that revival of items of information (words) by preexposure shortly before a word-association test should increase the probability that such words would be given in response to stimulus words. For example, exposing the word JUSTICE and then a bit later giving the stimulus word PEACE would be expected to favor the response "justice," whereas otherwise the response might be "war" or "quiet."

Storms selected words from the Kent-Rosanoff list, whose first (most popular) responses had frequencies of 20 to 40 percent and whose third responses had frequencies of 8 to 20 percent. He made up an experimental list of 14 stimulus words and a similar control list, the two lists matching with respect to these associative characteristics. The third-response words for the list of 14 experimental words were read to 88 subjects, who then wrote their first associations for all 28 stimulus words. The result was that the popularity of the primed, unpopular responses increased in 11 cases of 14, but this happened to only 1 of the 14 control (unprimed, unpopular) words. For 9 of the 14 experimental words, the normally third response became the first response. This happened to only 1 of the control words. In a previous study, Storms (1958) had found, incidental to another experiment on paired associates, that such a priming condition increased the probability of S's giving *backward* associations.

"Localization" of a product   Asch and Ebenholtz (1962) speak of the *localization* of an item of information in memory storage as a condition affecting recall. By this term they mean the context within which the item was learned and stored. The specific reference was to an item within a series. That is, when S is trying to recite items given in a list, he tends to stay within that particular list, avoiding intrusions from without the list. Postman (1963) has remarked on the same phenomenon. The associative interpretation is that the item is associated with "this list." An informational interpretation is that the item is a part of a system. This would also be the gestalt interpretation. To the associationist the event is probably somewhat surprising, for he thinks naturally that the preceding item is the natural cue for the recall of an item, not the entire list.

The principle of localization goes beyond membership in lists or systems. It also applies to classes and hierarchies of classes, and undoubtedly more commonly so, because classes have much more general application than do systems. Computer people speak of the "address" of an item of information, which means much the same thing as location. As in the storage of information in libraries and other repositories, classification is the most natural convenient device for the location of the desired information. It is therefore natural that classes and systems should be brought into use in memory storage in the brain for the advantages in retrieval. At this point, however, we might refer back to the point raised by Ausubel (1965) to the effect that when an item is subsumed in a larger organization, it runs the risk of becoming lost. A sharpening of the item itself and its relation to the whole of which it is a part should help to reduce this risk.

It is suggested as a hypothesis that not the least important kinds of classes that aid in recall are the categories of information as provided by the structure-of-intellect model. Although the individual may not be aware of such categories as the 24-class epistemology implies, his brain could well be programmed to use such information about classes whenever it would be helpful. Classes *within* each of these SI categories would also be needed.

Clustering in recall   The individual's habitual use of class membership as an aid in cueing for recall can be seen in experiments on clustering of responses in recall. Bousfield (1953) has found that when S is given a free-recall test on a long list of words he has seen one or more times, he is likely to show runs of items belonging to the same class. Furthermore, the easier a class is to cognize in the list of words, the more likely S is to use it (Bousfield, Cohen, & Whitmarsh, 1958). These investigators first determined some taxonomic norms for a number of common classes. Given in turn 43 class names, e.g., fish, insect, human dwelling, each of 400 students was asked to list four members of each class. Frequencies with which items were given in each class were determined. From this information, lists of 40 words each were constructed for the recall experiment, some lists with high-frequency members and some with low-frequency members. These lists were exposed to new Ss, then a recall test was given, and a clustering score was computed for each student in responses to each list. The two major results of interest were that the numbers of words recalled were greater on the average for the high-frequency lists (23.6 and 26.0 versus 17.4 and 20.1, respectively) and that clustering scores were also higher on the average for the high-frequency lists (.52 and .57 versus .40 and .50, respectively). The conclusion seems to be that the more readily S can categorize groups of words, the more words he will recall and the more he will use classes as aids in recall.

These clustering experiments are of special interest in connection with one of the divergent-production abilities, spontaneous flexibility (factor DMC). A consistently good type of test for this factor, like Brick Uses and Naming Objects, asks for listing of words (objects or just words), and the score is the extent to which the examinee *avoids* clustering, for the measurement of spontaneous flexibility. The ability is defined in the structure-of-intellect model as the divergent production of classes. Clustering on the DMC tests indicates low status with respect to spontaneous flexibility. In the Bousfield experiments, apparently no attention was paid to individual differences in amount of clustering versus shifting from class to class. While some of Bousfield's subjects may have used clustering as an intentional strategy for enlarging their recall scores, on the other hand, to the extent that this clustering came naturally, it would seem to have definite kinship to the clustering in the DMC tests referred to. In these tests, too, some examinees may intentionally adopt clustering as a device for gaining length of list. These problems call for investigation in common.

Some principles of recall   We have just seen one example of how recall is logically related to a divergent-production ability; there are others, which we shall now consider. Some of the other experiments of Bousfield and his associates also have bearings of interest in this connection. One line of investigation has been on the relation of recall to working time in listing a number of recalled items (Bousfield & Sedgewick, 1944). These investigations have pertained to the recall of units of semantic information, but the principles found may be relevant to the recall of other kinds and products of information.

Recall as a function of working time   The typical early task given to subjects required them to list rapidly the members of a specified class with a single class property, such as the cities in the United States or the makes of automobiles. With S working for sixteen to eighteen minutes and marking how far he had gone at the end of every two-minute interval, a cumulative score was obtained at the end of each time interval. The cumulative scores were treated as a function of working time. The typical result is production at a decreasing rate so that n (the cumulative score) as a function of t (time in minutes) is negatively accelerated. The relation of n to t can be fitted well by an equation of the form

$$n = c(1 - e^{-mt})$$ (13.1)

where

c = total number of members available in memory storage
e = base of natural logarithms
m = constant related to rate at which supply of information in category is exhausted

and n and t have already been defined. The constants c and m can be determined for any particular set of data, and the equation applies to averages for groups as well as to individual subjects. The rate at which the available supply of information is exhausted is given by the differential equation:

$$dn/dt = m(c - n)$$ (13.2)

From this equation it can be seen that the rate of production at any time t is proportional to the rate constant m and also to the number of items yet available $(c - n)$.

The definition of *available supply* has to be the number of items of information that could be produced in infinite time, for as t becomes large, n approaches c as an upper limit. The constant c need not mean the number of items that the individual has ever known in the class, which probably exceeds c. It means the number of items that could be elicited under the conditions of the experiment. One interesting finding that supports this interpretation is that when subjects were given practice in listing members of a class, the constant m changed but c did not (Bousfield & Sedgewick, 1944).

Further enlightenment on these problems was added by D. M. Johnson and his associates (Johnson, Johnson, & Mark, 1951) in applying the Bousfield equation. One of their most pertinent findings is concerned with the interrelationships of n (defined as the number of items produced by the end of fifteen minutes), c, and m for different individuals and for different categories of information. Over a population of individuals, n correlated with c to the extent of .92 in naming cities and .74 in naming animals. The score n correlated with m to the extent of —.55 and —.59 in naming cities and animals, respectively; and c correlated with m to the extent of —.78 (cities) and —.48 (animals). These results mean that with liberal working time the score n is a good index of the available number of items of information of the kind possessed by the individual. C. A. Rogers (1956) reported correlations of .90, .95, and .97 between n and c in naming birds, words beginning with R, and animals, respectively, with shorter working times.

Incidentally, the negative correlations between c and m mean that the greater the individual's available supply, the lower his personal rate constant m for that category of information. A hypothesis offered for this finding is that the larger the supply, the more interference there is in recall (D. M. Johnson et al., 1951). Another hypothesis might be that limitation in writing speed may affect production on paper relatively more when c is large. But Rogers (1956) gave two of his tasks with oral responses, where motor restrictions should not be so important; yet correlations of c and m were —.67 and —.70, respectively. There could be some motor-speed restriction, of course, even in vocal responses, where S knows his long list so well that he cannot say its members as rapidly as he can think of them.

Width of category and recall   It is reasonable to think that in the individual's storage and retrieval of information his classification within categories must involve both narrow and broad classes, as in hierarchical classification. Helson and Cover (1956) directed a study toward the effect of breadth of category within which an item of information is classed upon recall, with the hypothesis that recall of an item is facilitated by its being in a narrower class. Items placed in broader classes should have more interferences, which should be evident in the form of more intrusions during recall.

Their items of information were names of famous people, four for each of six classes. One group of subjects was provided with six broad categories in which to classify each name as it was presented, such categories as musician, scientist, and writer. Another group had six more restricted classes, including opera composer, physicist, and playwright. Later, each S was to list all the names she could remember. Those having the broad classes recalled an average of 11.1 names of 24, and those having the narrower classes recalled 14.3, a highly significant difference. The average numbers of intrusions (names added, not among those given) were .59 and .33, for the broad and the narrow classes, respectively. The hypothesis seems to have been confirmed. The results are also in line with the finding of a negative correlation between c and m constants in the thing-listing experiments and support the interference hypothesis for that fact.

Principles applied to fluency tests   Of special interest is the relation of these recall principles to fluency tests, because of the similarity of fluency tests to the tasks involved in the experiments on recall. We may ask first the question as to which recall score, n, c, or m, would be best for indicating degree of fluency for a person. The score commonly used is n, which is also highly correlated positively with c and strongly correlated negatively with m. It would seem that in using n as the score, we should be measuring the examinee's amount of knowledge in a restricted area and therefore a cognitive ability. C. A. Rogers (1956) did find correlations of .42, .60, and .32, respectively, between the c score and a total score on the Thurstone PMA tests for his three thing-listing tasks. It should be said, however, that one of the tasks was a word-fluency test (listing words beginning with R) and that the PMA includes a word-fluency component. Score m, on the other hand, correlated .06, $-.38$, and $-.15$, respectively, with the PMA composite in the same three tasks. It would seem logically that m is a better score for fluency ability, since it emphasizes rate, but as we have seen, it is substantially correlated negatively with c and with n.

It may be remembered from Chapter 6 that Christensen and Guilford (1963) found that in thing-listing tests of factor DMU (ideational fluency), the type of task with only one class property given is not very good as a measure of the factor and that a task with two class properties specified appears to be optimal. But Bousfield and Sedgewick (1944) found that production curves when more than one class property is specified are much the same as when only one is prescribed. For example, one of their tasks called for the naming of four-legged mammals, and another called for the production of words containing the *three* letters M, T, and D.

The total length of working time allowed in a production task may make some difference in what the n score measures. The thing-listing tasks in tests for DMU have set much shorter time limits than sixteen or eighteen minutes. It may be that the n score for very short times is less highly correlated with c and it may reflect m to a greater extent. But Rogers (1956) found c and m correlated $-.67$ and $-.70$ (n and m would correlate similarly, since c and n are very highly correlated) in two tasks with total times of only 2.5 minutes. The responses were oral in these cases. Of course, the curve relating n to t might well have the same constants c and m no matter how short the testing time, if there were enough time to provide reasonable estimates of those constants.

In tests of associational fluency (factor DMR), Christensen and Guilford (1963)

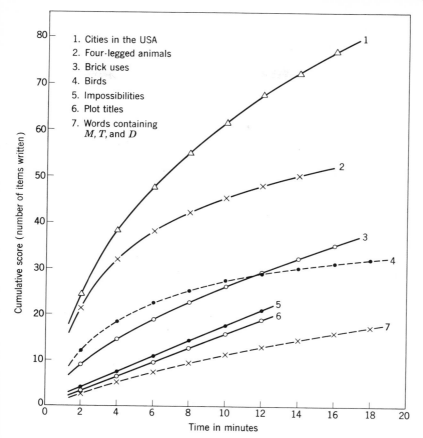

Fig. 13.1 Curves representing cumulative production scores in various multiple-response tasks, including some common tests of divergent production. (*From data presented by Bousfield & Sedgewick, 1944, and by Christensen, Guilford, & Wilson, 1957.*)

found the *n* score to be optimal for measuring that factor when it came from the first two minutes of work, which means that individual differences in *n* scores obtained where the curve is rising rapidly are better for measurement of that factor. How general this principle is, we do not know.

Rate of output in fluency tests   With different kinds of fluency tests other than thing-listing forms, the principle of diminishing rate of production was found to apply only slightly and sometimes hardly at all; the cumulative curves as functions of time were almost linear (Christensen, Guilford, & Wilson, 1957). Fluency scores for Plot Titles (two forms), Brick Uses, and Impossibilities (listing things that are impossible), taken at the end of every two-minute interval up to twelve minutes (sixteen minutes for Brick Uses), yielded cumulative production curves that are essentially linear for all except Brick Uses, which has just a trace of curvature (see Figure 13.1). This means that the production rate is virtually a constant: the average number of units produced per minute is uniform.

It seems reasonable that a law of diminishing returns would set in at some time, but it would have to be later than twelve minutes.

The difference between these tasks that call for rather imaginative responses and the other tasks may be that there is relatively more transfer recall in these fluency-test tasks and less of the direct, replicative type of recall. The novelty of the task would perhaps make the difference. These differences support the hypothesis stated earlier, that divergent production is something more than facility in recall and that the transfer aspect may account for that something more (see Chapter 9).

Originality and working time   Going to another divergent-production factor, DMT, known in common terminology as originality, we can also ask questions about production as a function of time; only here we are interested in quality of responses as well as quantity. Three different aspects of responses have been adopted as pertinent to quality: (1) the uncommonness of responses, i.e., the statistical rarity in the population; (2) the remoteness of association shown; and (3) the cleverness of responses as rated by observers. It might be predicted that in listing responses to test items, the examinee will come up with the more common responses first and the less common ones later, with the more direct associative responses first and the more remote ones later, and with the less clever responses first and the more clever ones later.

The first of these three hypotheses was supported by results of Bousfield and Barclay (1950), who found in three production tasks (naming birds, tools, and celestial bodies) that in recall tests the most commonly given words were written in the early stages of the production period. Christensen et al. (1957) found the same kind of result in tasks that had been designed as measures of divergent-production abilities. Two were tasks from the test Unusual Uses, for a button and for a pencil; one was the task in Figure Concepts, in which E is to group pictured objects by 2s or larger sets; and two were from the test Number Associations, in which E states what each number, e.g., 2, suggests. Weights were assigned to responses on an empirical frequency basis, and the responses were scored for uncommonness each on a 5-point scale. In every task, taking successive responses in order, the later the response in sequence, the higher the mean uncommonness score.

To test the hypothesis that the more remote the association between given information and response, the later it appears, four tasks from the Consequences test were used (see Chapter 6 for a description of the test). Degree of remoteness of each response was rated by five observers. Responses were divided into two groups for each examinee, those from the first half of his working period and those from the second half. In all four tasks the means of remoteness ratings were significantly higher in the second halves of the working periods.

Cleverness of responses in the Plot Titles test was also evaluated by means of observer ratings, two different plots being used and mean ratings being obtained for every two-minute period in a total of twelve minutes. In this test and with ratings of cleverness, it was found that the means remained surprisingly constant throughout the working period. This uniformity of cleverness as a function of working time was the same either when examinees had been instructed to "be clever" or when nothing had been said about being clever. Instructions to be clever had the predictable effect of reducing the total quantity of output of titles but of increasing the average level of cleverness of responses.

Parnes (1961) evaluated quality of responses by asking observers to distinguish "good" responses from others, where *good* was defined as "unusual" and "useful." In successive five-minute intervals, in a total work interval of either ten or fifteen minutes, the proportions of "good" responses increased with time. It is not known which of the three aspects—

uncommonness, remoteness, and cleverness—the ratings emphasized; apparently not cleverness, because the mean rating did not remain constant over time.

Summary

Although recall is dependent upon retention and retention is dependent upon learning, all these events present unique problems that can be investigated with some degree of separation. There is evidence, from factor analysis and from other sources, that information is stored in the form of products. Most is known, however, concerning storage of units, classes, and systems. Units are retained best when stored within classes and systems, with some risk that they become lost in the larger wholes. There is evidence that later experiences can have appreciable effects upon previously stored information.

Short-term memory seems to be an established phenomenon, lasting for a second or two in figural form after stimulation, to enlarge input by making it successive to fit a small input capacity. There is evidence that both decay and interferences account for the loss of information in short-term memory as well as in long-term memory. Permanent storage seems to require repetition or rehearsal.

The conditions that help or hinder recall of information are becoming better known. Besides a general availability level for an item of stored information, there is often a scanning of stored information with the aid of a search model, which contributes to availability of selected items. A distinction is made between replicative recall and transfer recall, the latter being more important for problem solving. The locating of needed information in storage is facilitated by the fact that items are organized in classes and systems.

In sequences of recalls of information to meet certain purposes, as in giving members of a certain category, there are principles relating rate of recall and quality of recall to working time during such a task. Significant relationships of these principles to divergent production (fluency, flexibility, and originality) were pointed out.

14 Problem solving and creative production

In this chapter we come to the most complex of recognized intellectual activities, for which the preceding chapters have been preparation. The two topics are treated together because they have so much in common that they are basically the same phenomenon. There is something creative about all genuine problem solving, and creative production is typically carried out as a means to the end of solving some problem. Both activities entail transfer recall; if only replicative recall were involved, there would be no problem solving and nothing creative about the behavioral event. These conclusions have been elaborated elsewhere (Guilford, 1963; 1964b). The reason for linking problem solving and creative production so intimately will become clear as we consider the ingredients of these two activities and find what they do have in common.

Similarities between problem solving and creative production

The great complexity of creative production was indicated in connection with the discussion of divergent-production abilities in Chapter 6. Something needs to be said here about the complexity of problem solving. One kind of evidence comes from the general psychological literature on problem solving. Those who have done experimental studies on problem solving have used a great variety of problem-solving tasks, including mechanical puzzles, anagrams, the game of 20 questions, concept attainment, syllogisms, the Maier string and hat-rack problems, and the Luchins water-jars problems. In animal psychology, we have seen varieties of puzzles boxes, mazes, discrimination tasks, and detour problems.

Factors and problem solving   The other main source of evidence comes from factor analysis. First, well-designed multivariate experiments involving recognized problem-solving tasks, such as the investigation by Merrifield et al. (1962), fail to find a unitary dimension that can be called problem-solving ability. The tests that were designed as problem-solving tasks in that analysis failed to generate a factor of their own but instead proved to be somewhat complex factorially, with variances accounted for by factors identifiable as CMU (verbal comprehension), CMI (conceptual foresight), DMT (originality), and DMI (semantic elaboration). The typical arithmetic-reasoning test, although having the factor CMS (general reasoning) as its salient component, commonly shares some variances also with factors of numerical facility, CFT (visualization), and CMU (verbal comprehension).

Actually, many an intellectual test, even among those approaching factorial univocality, can legitimately be called a problem-solving test, the problems usually being simple, each in its own way. Considering the great variety of such tests, we see that problem solving is about as broad as behavior itself, in the kinds of intellectual operations, contents, and products that are involved under one label. In spite of this diversity, there are enough aspects to episodes recognized as problem solving to enable us to draw a generic picture of it, as we shall see later, in the form of models for problem solving.

Steps in problem solving   As early as 1910, John Dewey proposed his classical steps or stages represented in common in different episodes of problem solving: (1) a difficulty is felt, (2) the difficulty is located and defined, (3) possible solutions are suggested, (4) consequences are considered, and (5) a solution is accepted. With minor modifications, these steps in problem solving have been rather persistent over the years, although they have not received much attention. D. M. Johnson (1955) simplified the "program" for problem solving by reducing the number of steps to three: preparation, production, and judgment. Merrifield et al. (1962) advocated return to a five-stage model with preparation, analysis, production, verification, and reapplication. The fifth term was included in recognition of the fact that the problem solver often returns to earlier stages in a kind of revolving fashion.

Steps in creative production   The classical model for steps in a complete episode of creative production is that proposed by Wallas (1926). The four steps are (1) preparation (information is gathered), (2) incubation (unconscious work is going on), (3) illumination ("inspired" solutions emerge), and (4) verification (solutions are tested and elaborated). After a study of more than 700 reputable inventors, Rossman (1931) proposed a more detailed set of steps, including:

1. Need or difficulty observed
2. Problem formulated
3. Available information surveyed
4. Solutions formulated
5. Solutions critically examined
6. New ideas formulated
7. New ideas tested and accepted

A noteworthy feature of the Rossman steps is the recognition of evaluative activity explicitly in steps 5 and 7 and implicitly in steps 1 and 3, which is reminiscent of the TOTE pattern of behavior in general suggested by G. A. Miller et al. (1960).

The similarities between the Wallas and Rossman models for creative production and the Dewey model for problem solving can be readily noted. Those similarities are more obvious when the steps are set out in parallel form, as in Table 14.1. There is not one of the Dewey steps that does not have its counterpart in the Rossman steps. There is one Wallas step, incubation, that has no counterpart in either of the other two lists. Logically, incubation does not belong in such a list, for it is in the nature of a condition rather than a kind of activity, which is a characteristic of each of the other steps. As a condition, incubation should be taken into account, as we shall do later. The parallels shown in Table 14.1 serve as one basis for concluding that problem solving and creative production are essentially the same kind of major operation and as a basis for the development of a single model that will serve to represent both.

A general model for problem solving

The proposed general problem-solving model, which also serves for most creative production, is shown in Figure 14.1. It takes into account the traditional models, the structure-of-intellect categories, and also some other considerations that have been mentioned in the preceding chapters. The model is considered to be a communication system, with inputs from the environment (E) and from the soma (S). The latter are concerned with behavioral information regarding the individual's own disposition, his motivational and emotional condition. The direction of flow of information is indicated by the arrows, sometimes in one-way connections and sometimes in two-way connections. The general time sequence is indicated in the horizontal set of blocks from left to right, following Input I at the extreme left.

Underlying everything is memory storage in the long rectangle at the base of the model. The four kinds of content are represented, and they are segregated only for illustrative purposes but not without some possibility of separate brain locations of some kind. Examples of different products, particularly units, systems, and some relations and implications, can be found in Figure 14.1. Transformations are not so readily exhibited, but modifications of any of the given items of information would qualify as transformations.

The arrows extending from memory to any other operations indicate effects that memory storage has upon all those events. Arrows extending in the direction of memory storage indicate some degree of search in memory storage for pertinent information; also, in the cases of cognition and production, such arrows indicate the committing of new or modified information to storage. Some of the transmission from memory storage to the central activities (cognition and production) is through evaluation, which may be said to have some filtering function. Some of the transmission is direct, bypassing the evaluation operation, as in the case of suspended judgment, or in wild outpourings of the mentally unbalanced, or in dreams.

The operation of evaluation is also quite generally distributed, for there can be testing of information at any step of the way. Some kind of evaluation occurs at the filtering stage, determining the selective action of the filtering mechanism. It is not certain whether this evaluation is of the same kind as that occurring in connection with cognition and production activities, which have been exhibited in the form of evaluative factors. The operation of evaluation is not shown as affecting memory storage. It is possible that such communication should be added in order to take care of the psychoanalytical phenomenon of repression. The evaluation function would then include the concept of a censor.

Input II and Input III are included to take care of the individual's active search for information in the environment, as shown by the arrow going up toward the input station,

Table 14.1   Steps in the solution of a problem, in creative production, and in invention, as seen by Dewey, Wallas, and Rossman, showing similarities and differences

Dewey	Wallas	Rossman
Difficulty felt		Need or difficulty observed
Difficulty located and defined		Problem formulated
	Preparation (information gathered)	Available information surveyed
	Incubation (unconscious work going on)	
Possible solutions suggested	Illumination (solutions emerge)	Solutions formulated
Consequences considered	Verification (solutions tested and elaborated)	Solutions critically examined
		New ideas formulated
Solution accepted		New ideas tested and accepted

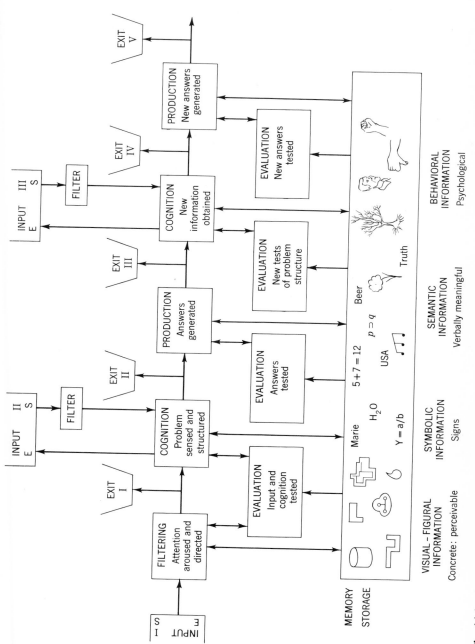

Fig. 14.1 An operational model for problem solving in general, based upon concepts provided by the structure-of-intellect model.

and also to take care of any incidental new input as the operations of cognition continue. Filtering action for the new input is indicated, but in connection with it arrows to and from memory storage and also evaluation, as for Input I, should be imagined. To add such arrows would complicate the illustration at too great a cost in confusion of information.

The exit stations indicate possible points of cessation of events in problem solving. The first exit may be a complete ignoring or rejection of the problem. The second exit may be due to a recognition that the problem is not important or that it is impossible to solve, or it may mean the postponement of problem-solving activity for the time being, possibly with an intention to renew the activity and with a condition of incubation occurring in the interim. Exit III might mean that a satisfactory solution has been reached.

One of the important features of the model is the liberal allowance for looping phenomena, with the involvement of feedback information. For example, with each cognitive phase and each production phase, there is the loop from cognition (production) to memory to evaluation, and back to cognition (production). This can be repeated many times. There are also larger loops, one including the first pair of cognition-production stations and another including the second pair, possibly followed by a third, a fourth, and so on. These looping phenomena permit some flexibility with respect to the order of events. Investigators who have tested the Wallas theoretical stages have found that his four steps do not always run off in 1, 2, 3, 4 order (Patrick, 1935, 1937; Vinacke, 1952). There is much overlapping of events and there is much backtracking, features that the new model takes into account.

One additional point needs comment. The model does not show any distinction between divergent and convergent production. The production stations in the model actually represent both. As pointed out in Chapter 7, some element of transfer must be involved in the recalled information in connection with both. The critical differentiation of the two kinds of operation is that the kind of response is completely specified in convergent production and not in divergent production. If you were asked to name American writers who lived in the first half of the twentieth century, you would have a number of logical alternatives and could write a number of names. If, however, you were asked the name of the American woman novelist living in the first half of the twentieth century who wrote a story about an archbishop, your answer should be "Willa Cather." The first case is divergent production, and the second is convergent production. Except for the difference in requirements, with a more restrictive evaluative filter in the second case, as determined by the number of specifications, the psychological events are the same.

It should be repeated that the model or flow chart represented in Figure 14.1 is of a generic nature; it may not fit any particular episode of problem solving. To fit better the solving of particular types of problems, special flow charts may be developed, as E. S. Johnson (1964) has shown. His problems pertained to the discovery of systems by which certain circlets in a row of five were blackened. When the simulation of problem solving by the use of electronic computers is attempted, flow charts represent a necessary step in the designing of a program, which instructs the computer what to do; i.e., it provides a strategy for the computer. Something more will be said about simulation problems at the end of this chapter.

The nature of problem solving and creative production

We shall now take some closer looks at the events taking place in an episode of problem solving, considering in some detail what occurs in different aspects of the general model just described. It happens that much more attention has been given to typical instances recognized as creative production than to cases recognized as problem solving; so the creative-production events will keep the center of the stage. Most of this discussion also applies to problem solving.

We shall follow events roughly through the temporal pattern implied by the model, stopping to note the roles of various contributing features. We shall consider the roles of motivation for creative production, of information, and of incubation; in connection with divergent production, the roles of insight or intuition and flexibility; and, finally, the role of evaluation.

Motivation for creative thinking   Thus far, in the review of psychological theory, we have not given any attention to the subject of motivation, except in the indirect way connected with theory of reinforcement. Since we are dealing with an elaborate pattern of events, if we are to have a satisfactory view of the behavior involved, we must consider motivational aspects. In the chapter on learning, the writer gave an informational interpretation of reinforcement, in terms of knowledge of results. Sometimes this is information about drive reduction and fulfillment of needs; sometimes it is feeling of satisfaction, of pleasure or its opposite. All this is considered behavioral information, information concerning need states and corrections of deficiencies and discrepancies. In Figure 14.1, the letter S at input is designed to recognize the origin of such information. Some of it, physiologically, comes from outside the central nervous system, but some also comes from within.

Intellectual drives   There has been a growing realization that the utilitarian drives of hunger, thirst, sex, and pain or fear are not by any means sufficient to account for much instigation of intellectual activity. Some animal psychologists who have observed exploratory behavior of rats and other animals have accepted a drive of curiosity; some have not been willing to go even that far. Others see even more than curiosity behind some animal behavior. E. L. Thorndike (1931) once suggested that the normal functioning of an organism in any respect is satisfying. The organism has certain equipment that is able and ready to accomplish certain purposes, and there is a natural urge to exercise that equipment. Having an unusual endowment of equipment in the form of brain cells, man has a natural urge to use that facility, as shown by an interest in having new experiences, in being the cause of movements, and in having ideas and playing with them to his satisfaction. Havelka (1956) noted that even rats sometimes show consistent preferences for solving problems on their way to reaching food. It may be recalled that some of Köhler's apes (1925), having solved a problem of making a long stick out of two short ones, seemed to take delight in using the new-found tool to rake in all sorts of things, letting the eating of food go until a bit later.

A number of psychologists have noted a similar source of motivation. White (1961) asserts that organisms have a natural desire to grow and develop, to master their environments by developing knowledge and skills. In other words, he posits a general drive to achieve competence. Berlyne refers to an "epistemic" curiosity, that ". . . activates a quest for knowledge and is relieved by acquisition of knowledge" (1962, p. 27). Epistemic curiosity is instigated by conceptual conflict, by discrepancies in beliefs, attitudes, and thoughts. In speaking of motivation for creative performance, Golann (1962) says that it is in the form of a desire to make the most of one's own perceptual, cognitive, and expressive potentials. J. McV. Hunt (1965) makes a good case for the thesis that cognition has its own intrinsic motivation and that drive is increased by discrepancies between input and stored information.

The study of recognized creative people demonstrates well the conclusion of Rossman (1931) that inventing carries its own intrinsic rewards. Inventors whom he studied often spoke of an exhilaration and a feeling of mastery and superiority on the successful conquering of problems connected with a new invention. So much is this true that the inventor looks for new problems so that he may again experience a similar reward. There is apparently little thought about the desire to benefit humanity, as much as some observers would like to think so. Roe (1952) found this to be true in general of her outstanding scientists, an exception being that some social scientists indicated the humanitarian kind of motivation. The creative producer probably derives secondary satisfactions from the fact that others do approve, and he experiences satisfaction from knowing that what he does is beneficial. On the other hand, there are those of other dispositions who derive sadistic satisfaction from the torture and destruction their inventions make possible.

Secondary sources of satisfaction   There are other secondary rewards derivable from creative productions. Hadamard (1945), in discussing creative people in different fields, remarked that artists often have the desire to do something different just because it is different. A similar hypothesis was tested experimentally by Houston and Mednick (1963). They hypothesized that highly original individuals have a strong preference for novel responses, as such. To express the hypothesis in a negative way, original persons have an urge to avoid the trite and the banal. The experimenters' results tended to support the hypothesis, but it was difficult to say whether the positive or the negative statement of the hypothesis is the more realistic.

Barron (1953; 1958) has found that artists as a group and other creative people in different professions exhibit preferences for complex visual designs over simple, regular, or symmetrical designs. One hypothesis is that the complex designs offer challenges to the comprehension abilities of the creative person and to his facility for establishing order out of disorder. This interpretation is close to the idea of a general drive for competence or intellectual mastery. From results obtained by Kincaid (1961) and Burkhart (1962), who do not find this kind of preference on the part of children, it appears that the preference for complexity is something that develops with age and experience. It may be that the individual at any age prefers a level of complexity that is neither so easy as to be beneath his coping powers nor so difficult as to be frustrating. The right level of complexity offers opportunities for the person to grow.

It has often been noted that creative people are likely to be independent thinkers. They have their own scales of values and are on the nonconforming side. Such a feature has been demonstrated experimentally by Crutchfield (1959), by use of the Asch-Crutchfield test of conformity. In this test, the examinee hears four of his associates render a judgment, e.g., of lengths of lines, before he gives his own judgment. By design, the four give a judgment that is in error. The score for the examinee is the number of times he goes along with group opinion. Crutchfield found a significant negative correlation between this score and an assessment of originality.

Factors of interest in thinking   Interests are motivational traits. They represent tendencies to be attracted to certain kinds of activities. A number of dimensions of interest in different kinds of thinking, including interest in reflective thinking, logical thinking, autistic versus realistic thinking, convergent thinking, divergent thinking, and a factor of tolerance of ambiguity, have been demonstrated (Guilford et al., 1961).

Scores for these interest variables and for other motivational traits have been found to correlate significantly but low with scores on some of the divergent-production tests

(Merrifield, Guilford, Christensen, & Frick, 1961). Associational-fluency tests correlated with need for adventure and with tolerance for ambiguity. It may be recalled that a leading test for factor DMR asks for a variety of synonyms. A long list can be obtained only if the examinee allows himself considerable leeway in accepting doubtful responses that occur to him. Expressional-fluency tests correlate with liking for reflective thinking. Originality tests correlate positively with liking for divergent thinking, tolerance of ambiguity, and reflective thinking; they correlate negatively with need for meticulousness and with need for discipline. These associations are all reasonable. Taken together with other sources of drive considered in previous paragraphs, these facts demonstrate the great complexity of motivation for creative thinking and problem solving.

The role of information   On the need for a good supply of information for successful creative production, there is practically unanimous agreement. Information is not sufficient, but it is necessary. Brain (1948) asserts that a genius excels ordinary men in his having a wealth of *schemata,* a term that we may translate as stored products of information. Agnew (1922a) concluded after studying composers that auditory memory is very important. After years of study of behavior in the visual arts, Meier (1939) concluded that visual memory is one of the most important assets for the artist.

As to the role of stored information, there are differences of opinion. Some seem to agree with Welch (1946) that there is nothing new in creative products except the arrangement: a kind of kaleidoscopic hypothesis. Such a view is favored by those who are partial to an associational theory. There is reluctance to admit that there is much change in the associative structure that is impressed upon the organism by his environment. There is preference for believing that most recall is replicative. As previous chapters have indicated, the informational view is that there is considerable transfer recall and there is considerable transformation activity in the emerging of new products of information.

The role of systems   Among the products of information, one of the most important in creative production is that of the system. In the field of mathematics, Hadamard (1945) advises that it is well for the mathematician to start with some kind of schema. It may be vague in form and outline, but it is needed to give unity to the thinker's efforts. In the field of music, Cowell (1926) asserts that the flow of music that the composer hears in auditory imagery centers in a theme. In her study of the writing of poetry, Patrick (1941) reported that about two-thirds of the poets had general ideas from the beginning of their periods of incubation and that all of them were involved with a general idea by the time of illumination. Those who began with some specific item, perhaps a single word, found a general conception growing out of such a beginning. Arnheim, Auden, Shapiro, and Stauffer (1948) also noted that poems typically begin in skeleton form; the poem is sketched out as a whole, with the structure becoming clearer with illumination later. In the paintings of artists and nonartists, Eindhoven and Vinacke (1952) found that a motif is established early. The subject matter and the composition may be changed a number of times, but the first steps involve an outlining of the working space, with rough arrangements, the details coming later.

The role of incubation   Observationally, incubation is a period during which there is no apparent activity on the part of the individual toward the solution of his problem but during which and at the end of which there is often evidence of material progress toward a solution. The period of incubation may be a matter of minutes, days, months, and even years. The evidence of some progress in the interim calls for explanation.

Such progress is associated with a persistent desire to solve the problem, perhaps with an intention to come back to it. Even without such an intention, problems seem to haunt some individuals, in a kind of perseveration.

The only known experiments designed specifically for investigation of the phenomena of incubation were those of Patrick (1935; 1938). She had subjects working on poems or on scientific problems in the laboratory. Periods of incubation occurred when an individual dropped one idea or strategy for a time and returned to it later. There was not complete cessation of problem-solving effort in these instances, but such pauses might be in somewhat the same category. Better examples were obtained when Patrick had half of the subjects planning experiments in the laboratory and the other half at home, with lapsed time for incubation. Although such an experiment runs great risk of losing control over conditions of work, the result was suggestive when she found that the group with the incubation period produced somewhat better ideas.

Hypotheses concerning incubation   Numerous creative people will testify to the benefits of incubation, if not to its necessity. In efforts to explain those benefits, many writers follow the lead of Poincaré (1913) when he stated that during incubation unconscious problem solving is going on. This hypothesis tells us practically nothing, of course. We still do not know what the unconscious psychological operations are, if nothing more is said.

A fatigue hypothesis has been suggested: the problem solver becomes tired, suffering a decrement in performance, and the period of incubation gives him a rest, after which his performance level is higher. The fatigue must be a very specific one, however, for the individual often turns to other work that should be just about as tiring. This hypothesis also fails to account for apparent benefits derived from delays of time intervals much longer than are needed to recover from fatigue.

Woodworth (1938) favored the hypothesis that taking up the problem again after a period of incubation provides an opportunity for a new start on the problem. Before the problem-solving effort has been dropped, certain wrong directions have gained such recency value that they inhibit the trying of other directions. During the lapsed time of incubation, such information loses its recency value and more fruitful recalls can be effected. This hypothesis is the same as that often favored in accounting for the benefits of spaced practice in learning. The two psychological problems, incubation and spaced learning, seem to have much in common. But it remains to be seen whether the same principles will account for both.

A transformation hypothesis   It can be proposed as a new kind of hypothesis that during incubation some transformations of information, transformations that take time to bring about, are taking place. In Chapter 13 it was concluded, largely on the basis of studies by D. R. Davis and D. Sinha (1950a; 1950b), that products of information in memory storage are not immune from interactions with new input. They may become modified or transformed. There is the possibility that interactions among stored products also occur, under the influence of somatic input from motivational sources. Bernard Weiner (1966) has assembled a great deal of evidence from various sources that indicates the effects of motivation upon memory traces.

That modifications take place unconsciously is incidental and gives no special superiority to an assumed "unconscious mind." The fact that so many so-called inspirations come into conscious view full-blown suggests that the transformations had occurred before the moment of inspiration or had been developing toward that moment. Such unconscious mental activity should not be surprising. Organized speech that rolls off the tongue so glibly is perpetually being formulated unconsciously.

Our best prospect of learning more about the role of incubation seems to be in the direction of discovering the principles governing the occurrence of transformations, conscious or unconscious. There must also be notable individual differences with respect to persistence of motivation to solve problems. There are "incubators" who do and others who do not carry around with them much unfinished business, making considerable difference between those who create and those who do not.

The role of insight or intuition   To most observers, the most dramatic aspect of creative production is the moment of "illumination," when the individual takes a notably large step in his thinking and it comes suddenly. Westcott (1961) refers to this step as the "intuitive leap." Although a number of experimental studies on the problem of intuition or insight can now be cited, we are still much dependent upon anecdotal information regarding the phenomenon in connection with what is called inspiration.

Emotional aspects   Many of the anecdotal reports regarding the moment of inspiration mention emotional accompaniments, sometimes with the implication that emotional aspects have something to do with the birth of the idea. C. R. Rogers (1962) speaks of the "Eureka feeling," also of a feeling of anxiety and an urge to communicate to others. Patrick (1937) reported that painters, professional and nonprofessional, during painting in the laboratory sometimes experienced emotional excitement along with insights, sometimes not.

It can be hypothesized that the amount of emotion occurring with illumination depends upon several conditions: the strength of motivation of the individual, the amount of frustration he may have endured for lack of progress, the size of the intuitive leap, and the importance of the outcome. How much the emotional component contributes to the success of the creator is problematical. Motivation, of course, should be a contributor.

The nature of insight or intuition   There can be no doubt about the fact of sudden arrival of increments of progress toward solutions, even when they are not complete. Intuitive ideas come with various degrees of clarity and completeness and with no apparent effort. Sometimes the intuited idea is only the nucleus of the eventual structure, but it is a key idea, and by working out the suggested implications the whole can be developed. Sometimes the intuited conception is rather evanescent, like a memory afterimage. It is apparently quite common for the idea to be overvalued rather than properly evaluated, but later corrections will possibly take care of that error.

Maier (1931) demonstrated some of the characteristics of insight in experiments with his famous string problem. In this problem, the subject is shown two strings hanging from the ceiling of a room, so far apart that when he attempts to tie the ends together, as instructed, he cannot reach both strings at the same time. Four solutions are possible: using a heavy object to anchor one string while the other is brought to it; lengthening one string temporarily with an extension; pulling one string over with a pole while holding the other; and, with the use of a weight, making a pendulum of one string, swinging it within reach. Various objects needed for these solutions are lying about, but some have to be put to unusual uses, e.g., using pliers as a weight to make the pendulum.

Maier reported that the solutions came as wholes in 75 percent of the cases. The self-observer rarely is able to catch any steps in his thinking immediately preceding the insight. The solution emerges like the hidden figure in a puzzle picture.

Mental state during intuition   From anecdotal information, there is unanimous agreement that there is an abandonment of controlled thinking, a resort to free association in a kind of daydreaming state (Beveridge, 1950). Composers, especially, speak of this type of experience (Griswold, 1939). Both Mozart and Brahms spoke of doing their best creations in dreamlike states or of ideas' coming as in vivid dreams. Tchaikovsky is quoted as saying: "There is something somnambulistic about this condition." César Franck is said to have been wandering in a trancelike state while generating his ideas. But there is also frequent mention of a very strong urge to create something and of much preparation and hard work preceding incubation.

It has long been known that relaxation is a favorable condition for recall of information. The dreamlike, dispersed type of attention may mean that there is a relaxation from a restrictive use of a search model, which results in a broadening of the scanning among stored items of information, providing a condition of improved probability of arriving at the needed information. The wide search may favor more remote transfers. This hypothesis needs investigation. Also to be answered is the question of why the relaxed and dispersed search does not bring about total recall. The creative product is, after all, a result of selective recall.

Environmental conditions   A number of creative people have attested to the need for complete quiet during the period of illumination, while others do not find this essential. There is greater agreement that lack of distractions and freedom from interruptions, even from threats of interruptions, are important conditions. Some idiosyncratic conditions are also reported. For example, it is said that Ben Jonson needed a purring cat, orange peel, and plenty of tea to drink; Balzac required much black coffee at night; Zola drew shades in the daytime and worked in artificial light; Kipling demanded black ink only; and Freud was a chain smoker (McKellar, 1957). Such conditions are often in the category of fetishes, something that many creators apparently get along without. Incidental stimulations may add their contributions, as in the case of Keats, writing "Ode to a Nightingale" after hearing one sing, and of Mendelssohn, who was inspired by the sight of a trumpet vine. Then there was Newton and the falling apple.

Some personality differences and intuition   Westcott (1961; 1964) has approached the problem of intuition from the standpoint of individual differences in personality traits other than intellectual aptitudes. He has been particularly interested in tendencies to take risks in reaching inferences on the basis of limited information. Westcott used problems of the following type:

4 : 2   9 : 3   25 : 5   100 : 10   64 : 8   16 : ＿＿＿

S is given these clues one at a time and is told to give an answer whenever he feels that he has had sufficient information. The number of clues that S requests is his *demand score*. The number of correct conclusions is his *success score*. The ratio of success score to demand score is an index of his efficiency of intuition. The demand and success scores correlated near zero; so there can be four types of individuals, those combining low demand with low success, low demand with high success, high demand with low success, and high demand with high success. The four categories of individuals are characterized as "guessers," "intuitive leapers," "poor problem solvers," and "steady, logical thinkers," in the order as just stated.

From independent assessments of personality traits of his subjects, Westcott (1964) found that those with high demand for information, regardless of success, were inclined to be cautious, conservative, and compliant. The high-demanding and successful Ss were not rigidly conservative or compliant and were willing to question things. The high-demanding and unsuccessful Ss were defensive and rigidly moralistic. The low-demanding and successful were composed and unafraid. The low-demanding and unsuccessful were inclined to be depressed, despondent, and even without hope. These associations seem reasonable, but there remains the question of which is cause and which is effect, if causal relationships are involved.

Role of previous experience   It is important to investigate the relation of insight to past experience because of its theoretical significance, among other reasons. Some psychologists with associati̇..nal bias have been too ready to dismiss insight as being completely accounted for on the basis of previous learning, by which they probably mean a direct dependence upon learned associations that are revived in replicated recall in the insight situation (McGeoch & Irion, 1952). In holding such a view, there seems to be a self-blinding to the new elements involved in an insight.

Birch (1945a) did a transfer experiment in which six young chimpanzees were first tested to determine whether they could use a hoe to bring in food from a distance. Two of the apes succeeded. All were given training in the act of hauling in things by using plain sticks and were then retested on the hoe problem. All of them succeeded very quickly on the second hoe test. The conclusion that practice with plain sticks transferred to the use of the hoe seems to be justified. But even more significant is the fact that two apes could develop insight into the use of the hoe without the training with sticks. The associationist's answer would be that the two apes had had other prior incidental experiences to account for their early insights in the hoe problem, but it is highly unlikely that they had had raking experiences with a hoe. They may have had other experiences that transferred to success in the hoe problem on its first presentation, but that would be transfer recall, not replicative recall.

Several studies have been concerned with the way in which additional given information pertaining to a problem may help in solving it. With graduate students, Maier (1930) first taught separately three principles that would be needed in solving a complex problem that involved all three. In five different groups of Ss he presented the complex problem, giving different numbers of hints in different groups. Only 9 of the 84 Ss got the correct solution, and 8 of these were in the group receiving the most hints. Thus, experience of the kind that Maier gave may not be sufficient to bring about solutions. Something more was necessary, as in the form of hints that helped Ss to use the previously given information. Maier (1940) thought that the "something else" is what he called "direction." A little further thinking would have brought him to the conclusion that what was needed was the formation of a new product of information, an integration of the given principles into a system.

Weaver and Madden (1949), who took up the study of Maier's hypothesis of direction, found difficulty with the concept, because all Ss, regardless of what information is given them, seem to have some direction. They concluded that "directions" involve strategies, which point toward the formation of structures (systems) to which the goal idea is a contributor. In the process, we can say that perceptual and conceptual changes (transformations) occur.

That scattered items of information can have their bearings upon successful insights is suggested by some results of Judson, Cofer, and Gelfand (1956). Students who had previously memorized lists of words some of which pertained to the Maier string problem, e.g., ROPE, SWING, PENDULUM, were more likely to reach the pendulum solution to the problem than Ss who had not memorized such a list.

Saugstad and Raaheim (1957) used a more complex concrete problem, which offered possibilities of more varied amounts of helpful information. The additional information was in the form of some short lists of unusual uses for the objects that were needed in solving the problem. Briefly, the problem was to move some steel balls from a glass to a cylinder, both at some distance from S. Objects available for use included a nail, pliers, newspapers, rubber bands, and string. The expected correct solution involved (1) making a hook out of the nail, using the pliers; (2) making a "fishing line" from the hook and string; (3) hooking the frame on which the glass of balls rested; (4) pulling the frame within reach; (5) rolling newspaper into a tube, holding it in place with rubber bands; and (6) rolling the balls through the tube into the cylinder.

The subjects were 149 high-school students who had had a course in physics. The kind of information given about the objects to be used was a list of five alternative uses for each object (three for the rubber bands), one of the uses being adaptable to solving the problem. Five experimental groups were given different amounts of information, some for one object and some for two. A control group had none of this kind of information. The results were that for the groups receiving information about two objects, 90 percent solved the problem; for the groups receiving information about one object, from 25 to 57 percent solved the problem (least for the tube uses, most for the hook uses); and of the control group, only 19 percent succeeded. There had been no matching of groups on problem-solving ability of any kind.

In a similar experiment with sixth-grade children (Saugstad and Raaheim, 1959), it was found that the younger subjects were less able to make use of the given information and that memory for it seemed less stable in that they showed more solutions when the delay of the test was fifteen minutes than when it was thirty minutes.

Role of motivation in insight   There is little information regarding degree of motivation as a condition of probability of insight. Birch (1945b) reported one such study with six young chimpanzees as subjects. These young apes solved a number of string problems differing in the degree of insight needed, six different degrees of food deprivation being involved, including deprivation for two, six, twelve, twenty-four, thirty-six, and forty-eight hours. Results, although based upon a small sample, were rather consistent. With two, thirty-six, and forty-eight hours without food, the success in problem solving was no better than chance. The best scores were obtained with six and twenty-four hours of deprivation. The condition of twelve hours of deprivation should not be considered because it was largely occupied with a period of sleep, no meal actually having been missed. At the shorter intervals of deprivation, there was such lack of interest in food that S was easily distracted from his task. At thirty-six and forty-eight hours S had such a strong hunger drive that he paid too much attention to the goal and not enough to methods of arriving at the goal. Being frustrated to the point of screaming and tantrums, he was in poor mental condition for problem solving.

A moderate degree of hunger drive was therefore optimal for these apes. This tells us very little about the relationship between motivation and insight in human individuals where the motivation is more intrinsic to the task, but it is likely that there, also, motivation can be too strong as well as too weak for best results. Creative producers attest to the need for strong effort followed by relaxation as being favorable for inspirations.

In addition to the problem of the relation of degree of motivation to insights, there is the problem, as yet unmentioned and unexplored, of how the specific nature of the motivation may affect the shaping of solutions, producing possible transformations during the state of incubation and at other times.

The role of flexibility   In earlier chapters, three different kinds of flexibility in thinking were pointed out, each with its distinct place in the structure-of-intellect model. One is flexibility with respect to classes, the readiness to shift from class to class; a second has to do with transformations in divergent-production activities; and the third type pertains to redefinitions or transformations in connection with convergent production.

Flexibility of classes   A factor first interpreted as spontaneous flexibility later became known as divergent production of semantic classes. The essence of the factor is the ready shifting from class to class in searching for information. It was demonstrated by Frick et al. (1959) that tests of tendency to perseverate within a class have strong negative load-ings on this factor, where tests like Brick Uses (shift score) and Alternate Uses, which forces the examinee to go from class to class, have strong positive loadings. More recently, tests requiring E to classify the same set of items of information in different ways have also measured the factor, justifying its place in the SI model. The factor is not the same as Spearman's factor of perseveration (in reverse), for he regarded his P factor as being com-pletely general, like g. It is now recognized that the same kind of spontaneous-flexibility factors pertain to figural and symbolic information, with parallel kinds of tests serving to demonstrate those factors.

It is likely that other writers have been coming close to the same conception as the idea of flexibility with classes. For example, in his book on teaching how to think cre-atively, W. J. J. Gordon (1961) stressed the importance of tackling a problem at a high level of abstraction. This could very well mean that the thinker's search model (a class idea) is very broad. Such a mental set should widen the scope of the search among stored information, thus increasing the probability of finding something useful. Narrowing the scanning operation within a limited class at the beginning might exclude the very informa-tion that is wanted.

Arnold (1962b) gave an example of this approach to a problem. He considered the problem of thinking of an entirely new type of printing device. In order to ensure a broad consideration of the problem, he recommended that printing equipment be defined to include all devices for producing multiple copies of permanent visual records in readable form. This is an abstract definition of a common, concrete object. Four main attributes or dimensions are recognized: (1) carrier of information, (2) method of information transfer, (3) visual rendering, and (4) production of multiple copies. This delineation provides a broad search model.

Arnold goes on to recommend that differentiations be made along each of the four dimensions to form what is essentially a morphological model, like the SI model. Then, by combining each distinguished step in a dimension with all other possible steps on other dimensions, a whole systematic set of hypothetical devices is generated. The ordinary printing press is one such combination. Anne Roe (1952) may have been considering the same breadth-of-scanning habit when she concluded that the top scientists whom she had studied seemed to be generalizers. Generalizing works toward larger, more inclusive classes, within which one can go from one subsidiary class to another.

It is interesting that too much familiarity with an object can work against a broader, more abstract view. Arnold (1962a) cited an example of this. Employees of the AC Spark Plug Co. were found to have difficulty in listing the attributes of a spark plug, but they had little difficulty in listing the attributes of a bicycle. Listing attributes of an object means becoming abstract about it. On the other hand, employees who were making heavy machinery had little difficulty in listing attributes of a spark plug.

Thus, it is difficult to become abstract about familiar things. It is reported that Albert

Einstein made a practice of denying his understanding of the obvious, in order that he might obtain a new look at things. It has also been reported that when a group is engaged in generation of ideas to solve a problem, it is sometimes the tyro or amateur who comes up with the key to the adopted solution. Experts in the field sometimes develop what has been called a "disease" of hardening of the categories. Flexibility with respect to classifications is an important asset for the creative thinker.

Flexibility and divergent production of transformations   The conception of divergent production of transformations arose first in the form of a factor recognized as adaptive flexibility, the characteristic test for which is Match Problems (see Chapter 6). It was later recognized that the factor first identified as originality is an adaptive flexibility in dealing with semantic information and that both factors pertain to transformations. Because the Match Problems items involve considerable trial-and-error behavior, the first interpretation was that adaptive flexibility is a matter of changing strategy, a habit-breaking disposition. Tests involving a tendency to persist along the same line of attack were found to have negative loadings on factor DFT (adaptive flexibility), supporting that interpretation (Frick et al., 1959). But an alternative interpretation was later given, in line with the identification of this factor with transformations. The change of strategy entails changes in the meanings and roles of lines in the Match Problems figures and changes in meanings or interpretations in tests of originality. The tests of persistence can be regarded as measures of resistance to transformations.

The mention of persistence brings to mind the kind of rigidity that Luchins (1942) has investigated so extensively (Luchins & Luchins, 1959). The task involved in his famous Water Jar Test is to measure out a specified quantity of water, given two jars with specified capacities. The first five problems are solvable by the same formula, which it is presumed most examinees will discover and adopt as a stock kind of solution for the items after item 5. But the later items can also be solved by shorter formulas. Will E (if we assume he has gained insight into the stock solution) continue to use the same formula, or will he shift to simpler ones?

As was mentioned in Chapter 6, a group form of the Water Jar Test was analyzed along with tests of flexibility factors (Frick et al., 1959). The test had a loading of only .18 on factor DFT and a loading of $-.09$ on factor DMT (originality). It is therefore not a measure of either figural or semantic divergent production of transformations. Whether it will be found to be loaded on factor DST, when that factor has been demonstrated, remains to be seen. A large part of the test's true variance was accounted for by two factors not in any flexibility category, however, both of them dealing with semantic content. Although the problems in the Luchins test require operations with numbers, they are like arithmetic-reasoning tests in general, in which the conceptions of the problems and of the strategies for solving them may well be in terms of semantic content. The failure to find any kind of flexibility variance in the Water Jar Test indicates that the wide use of this test as a measure of rigidity is highly questionable.

Redefinition and functional fixedness   The redefinition factors are in the operation category of convergent production, the kind of product being transformation. Three such abilities have been demonstrated. Logically, a low degree of these abilities is identifiable with the phenomenon of functional fixedness, a rigidity in the use of objects or in the definition of information. Functional fixedness has been noted most particularly with solutions in the Maier string problem and similar problems, in which the subject has to desert the common use of an object, e.g., pliers, in order to employ the object in some unusual way: in the string problem, as a weight for a pendulum. Such rigidity is not the same as that proclaimed in connection with the Luchins Water Jar Test; in other words, it is not the same as the Einstellung effect, for Adamson and Taylor (1954) found only a small, insignificant correlation between scores for the Maier and Luchins tests.

A number of experimental studies have been done to determine under what conditions functional fixedness (FF) is increased or decreased. Such experiments give *S*s some prior tasks in which they employ in various ways the object that is to be redefined. For example, in the string problem, Birch and Rabinowitz (1951) used an electric switch and an electric relay, both of which were suitable for becoming the weight of the contrived pendulum and were available during the solution of the problem. Prior to giving the problem, the experimenters asked one group of *S*s to use the switch in constructing an electric circuit and another group to use the relay for a similar purpose. The hypothesis was that recent uses of objects in conventional ways would make redefinition more difficult in solving the string problem. It turned out that way. All 10 of the *S*s having experience with the relay chose the switch to make the pendulum; 7 of the 9 with the switch experience chose the relay to make the pendulum; a control group was evenly divided in uses of the two objects.

Flavell, Cooper, and Loiselle (1958) gave their *S*s prior experience in terms of *unusual* uses of objects, with the expectation that this would facilitate redefinition in solving the string problem. One group was given prior experience with the *usual* use of a switch, and four other groups were given experiences with *unusual* uses. In the string-problem test later, only 3 of 24 *S*s having had the usual use of the switch employed it. Of those having had differing amounts of unusual uses, in increasing order, 8, 9, 13, and 12 employed the switch in making the pendulum. It appears unnecessary for an individual to have had much experience with unusual uses to prepare him for other unusual uses.

Other experiments add confirmatory and varied information bearing on the same hypothesis. Maltzman, Brooks, Bogartz, and Summers (1958) found that experiences with unusual uses of a string, a screwdriver, and balsa wood were followed by less FF behavior in solving the string problem. Bond (1955) found that it is necessary only for *S* to *observe* unusual uses of an object to help prevent the FF type of behavior in solving the problem.

Adamson and Taylor (1954) tested the hypothesis that effects of training affecting the FF behavior would decrease with a lapse of time, as in normal forgetting. The time interval between training and the FF test was varied from one minute to one week. The training was in *usual* uses of switch and relay. After different time lapses, the percentages *not* employing the previously used object were: after one minute, 70; thirty minutes, 70; one hour, 65; one day, 53; and one week, 50. Thus, the FF effect due to training in habitual uses of objects can wear off almost completely in a day's time, since the 53 percent was close to the chance level.

D. M. Johnson (1962) has demonstrated another condition that affects FF behavior: the degree of embeddedness of the needed information. This should be a very fruitful hypothesis, because tests of the redefinition abilities characteristically present embedded objects: hidden figures or faces and hidden words. Johnson worked with hidden words; hence his *S*s were dealing with symbolic information. Three degrees of embeddedness were represented: (1) single words presented for *S* to judge them for pleasantness versus unpleasantness (no embedding); (2) words in phrases, also to be judged; and (3) words in sentences. The task following required *S* to build anagrams in which the previously exposed words could be useful. From condition 1 to condition 3, the *S*s did more poorly in using the preexposed words. In another experiment, words used in the exposed instructions could be useful in solving anagrams. *S*s apparently did not make any use of this potential information that was continuously exposed to them.

Youtz (1948) has demonstrated the operation of rigidity in problem solving with a somewhat different kind of experiment. Women students first solved a series of arithmetic-reasoning problems, all of which could be solved by using a certain principle. Three groups had 10, 20, and 40 such problems as exercises. Then all were given a new set of problems that were solvable by a different principle. In the exercises, improvement was continuous and regular; those with the most practice problems were solving the problems most rapidly by the termination of practice. In the later test problems, the more practice on the first kind of problem, the slower were the solutions, indicating some kind of inhibition or interference. This interference could have been in failure to give a new interpretation (redefinition) to the test problems or in failure to transform the problem-solving strategy. In either case, failure to discriminate between systems or failure to effect transformations was involved.

The role of implications   Thus far, we have seen that various SI operations and products enter into problem solving in various ways. The role of units is ubiquitous. Classes play their roles in recall of information, and they have a unique function in connection with one of the kinds of flexibility versus rigidity. Systems seem to be the culminating goals for much of creative production, and strategies in problem solving are also in the category of systems. Transformations were given a special role in connection with incubation, and they are basic to two kinds of flexibility, adaptive flexibility and redefinition.

Wallas's stage of verification in creative production evidently involves both elaboration and evaluation. Although elaboration, which is basically a matter of implications, is more characteristic of later phases of problem solving after a skeletonlike system has been generated, it can occur at any place along the way. For whenever there is an inference, there is an implication. An illustrative problem, borrowed from Helson and Helson (1946), is very pertinent. It was offered by them as an example of productive thinking in the area of symbolic information to supplement Wertheimer's many illustrations (1945) in the figural or concrete area of information.

The problem statement was: 100 people attend a movie theater, men for 30 cents each, women for 20 cents each, and children for 1 cent. The money received for tickets one afternoon was $10. How many men, women, and children attended the theater on that afternoon?

In approaching the problem algebraically, two simultaneous equations each involving three unknowns were set up, for x women, y men, and z children:

$$x + \quad y + z = \quad 100 \tag{1}$$
$$20x + 30y + z = 1{,}000 \tag{2}$$

Setting up the equations may be regarded as the convergent production of symbolic systems, each a set of relations. The difficulty in solving these equations is that there are three unknowns and only two equations. The first tactic is to follow the usual treatment of simultaneous equations. With foresight (cognition of symbolic implications) it can be seen that one unknown can thus be eliminated, but it is still unknown. Since the *z*s have the same coefficient, a subtraction yields the equation

$$19x + 29y = 900 \tag{3}$$

There is now the task of solving for two unknowns, but with only one equation.

The next tactic is to look for properties of the elements in this equation that might be utilized. It was noted that 900 is a multiple of both 9 and 10 (cognition of symbolic classes) and that 19 and 29 can be subdivided into the same two values (more class cognition), leading to the breakdown (a symbolic transformation) in the next equation:

$$10x + 9x + 20y + 9y = 900$$

With regrouping (further transformation),

$$10(x + 2y) + 9(x + y) = 900 \qquad (4)$$

The Helsons then made some further useful inferences (implications). It was noted that two of the terms in equation (4) are multiples of 10; therefore the third term must also be a multiple of 10. This is the term $9(x + y)$. Since 9 is not a multiple of 10, $x + y$ must be a multiple of 10 (another implication). In other words the number of men plus the number of women must be a multiple of 10. Another implication is that $x + 2y$ must be a multiple of 9, making the first term of (4) a multiple of 90, which is true of the other two terms.

This information, convergently produced and therefore logically sound, makes possible the next tactic, which is to introduce two new variables, p and q, in writing the equations

$$x + 2y = \ 9q$$
$$x + \ \ y = 10p \qquad (5)$$

By solving for x and y,

$$x = 20p - \ 9q$$
$$y = \ \ 9q - 10p \qquad (6)$$

Substituting equations (5) in equation (4), we have

$$90p + 90q = 900$$

and from this, the information that

$$p + q = 10$$

One could now test various combinations of integers, each summing to 10, to see which combinations give nonnegative values for x and y. The Helsons short-circuited this procedure by using inequalities, finding that $p = 4$ and $q = 6$. From these values x is found to be 26 (women), y to be 14 (men), and z to be 60 (children), which satisfy the original equations.

The point illustrated here is that, besides the cognitive insights involving classes and relations and in addition to the transformations produced, there are other insights involving implications. These implications are in the form of deductions leading to additional information implied by the statement of the problem and also in the form of implied tactics to use next. Sometimes the tactics are recalled from the memory storage, based upon learned mathematical operations, but sometimes they have to be invented to fit the particular situation.

The role of evaluation   Evaluation is another aspect of Wallas's stage of verification, with the implication that it occurs near the end of the total creative process. From the flow of events pictured in Figure 14.1, we have quite a different picture, of evaluation all along the way, indicating a perpetual system of checks and balances. The difference lies in the fact that "evaluation," popularly conceived, is a broader concept than evaluation in the context of SI theory. There is undoubtedly positive correlation between the two conceptions, perhaps including the idea of relatively lower levels of SI evaluation early in the creative process and of higher levels near the end.

Suspended judgment   One of the main features of Alex F. Osborn's brainstorming method (1963) is its intentional suspension of evaluation during the idea-generating sessions of group thinking on a problem. One experiment designed to test for the benefits of this condition in creative production was reported by Meadow, Parnes, and Reese (1959). One group of subjects generated ideas with suspended judgment and another without. Additional steps were taken to use reinforcement, in the form of penalties for low-quality ideas. The problems called for thinking of unusual uses for a wire coat hanger and for a broom. In scoring the performances of the two groups, all responses were weighted for quality, applying the criteria of uniqueness and usefulness. The group with suspended judgment (with negative reinforcement for failure) produced an average of 7.9 high-quality ideas and the other group only 3.9. The two conditions were alternated in the two problems. The group having the suspended-judgment condition first did better under the other condition when it came second.

Suspension of judgment is not always an advantage where numbers of high-quality responses are concerned. Christensen et al. (1957) gave the Plot Titles test to some groups of adults without any mention of cleverness and in comparable groups with the explicit instruction to list clever responses. It was hypothesized that under the second type of instruction the examinee would impose some degree of censorship or evaluation, reducing his output. The result was rather decisive. Under the instruction to be clever, the total quantity of responses decreased but the total number of clever-rated responses increased, as did the average degree of rated cleverness.

There can be no doubt about the last two conclusions. But of the first conclusion, regarding total quantity, there can be some doubt. Under the instruction to be clever, we do not know how many titles E generated but discarded, not taking the trouble to write them down. There may have been some of this behavior under the other instructions, but it was probably not so common. We cannot say that there was a condition of complete suspension of judgment in the case of the instructions without mention of cleverness, but the difference would be in that direction. A group especially instructed to let itself go and record all possible responses would be needed to round out the experiment.

The results of the last-mentioned experiment were supported by similar results from the work of Weisskopf-Joelson and Eliseo (1961). They had groups brainstorming new names for a cigar, a deodorant, and an automobile, half of them with instructions to be critical and half of them not. The noncritical groups gave responses of higher quantity, but the critical groups gave a higher proportion of high-quality responses. This tendency may develop with age of the individual, for Torrance (1962a) found that instructions to give "clever, unusual, and original" responses tended to increase quantity of production at the fourth-grade level but to decrease it slightly above that grade.

Reactions to criticism   A number of studies have dealt with two kinds of criticism, constructive versus destructive, applied by self versus applied by others, with adults and with children. In one of them, Torrance (1965) instructed one group of graduate students to read previous-research reports with a constructive attitude and another group to read the same reports with a critical, faultfinding attitude. After these readings, the students were asked to list new ideas for research suggested by their readings. The number of high-quality ideas produced by the constructive-reading group exceeded that produced by the critical-reading group.

In another study, three groups of students were given three different instructions to apply in their reading: (1) to retain ideas they read about, (2) to evaluate them, and (3) to improve upon them (Torrance et al., 1960). They were later given four types of examinations: cognitive (multiple-choice items), memory (completion items), evaluative, and creative (new applications). The creative-set group had the highest mean on the creative items, the evaluative-set group had the highest mean on the evaluative items, and the memory-set group had the highest mean on the cognitive and memory items. These results highlight the fact that the kind of preparation has a bearing upon the score made in examinations with different kinds of items. In general, many students have learned to prepare for the kinds of examination they expect, and such slants in preparation determine what kind of mental exercise they derive from that effort.

Hyman (1964) has made a preliminary report of a systematic experiment on two kinds of criticism combined with self-criticism and with criticism of others. The subjects (students) were to offer solutions to the problem of how to improve education in spite of a shortage of teachers. There was an early attempt at solving the problem in which S listed his proposed solutions. The obtained solutions were criticized, some by the subject himself and some by other Ss. In either case, some Ss were to evaluate the solutions constructively, and some were to criticize them destructively. Then there was a second attempt with the problem to see what effect prior evaluative activity had had on later generation of solutions.

Several conclusions could be drawn. Ss who evaluated others' solutions constructively and their own destructively made the most changes in quantity and quality of solutions. Ss who evaluated others' solutions destructively and their own constructively were next best in the second attempt. Ss who made the same kind of evaluation of self and others, whether constructive or destructive, changed significantly but less than the others. Both were better than the control group. In terms of quality, the destructive-destructive group was the poorest of the four. The major finding, which was somewhat surprising, was that those who made both kinds of evaluation gained more from the evaluation experiences than those who made evaluations of the same kind when that kind was constructive. The hypothesis coming out of this conclusion is that there is more to learn by making both kinds of evaluation and that what is learned is probably in terms of ways of applying standards and criteria of judgment. In this way Ss gain more skill in discriminating good and poor solutions. A general comment was that one should be cautious in drawing blanket conclusions in the area of evaluation; there are likely to be interaction effects.

From extensive studies with evaluation exercises with schoolchildren, Torrance (1965) has a number of generalizations to offer. He has concluded that too frequent application of evaluation during practice sessions, regardless of type, tends to interfere with subsequent performance on similar tasks. Unevaluated or off-the-record practice tends to produce greater originality, more elaboration, and more sensitivity than does evaluated practice. One exception was at grade 6. When peer evaluation is constructive, it promotes more creative development than when it is critical, especially at grades 4 to 6. But even constructive suggestions can be worse than no evaluation at all, for they seem to call the children's attention to evaluation, as such, which works against suspended judgment. Thus, with children, also, there are interaction effects.

General conditions affecting creative production

As different phenomena in creative production have been discussed, for some of them special conditions affecting those phenomena have been mentioned, for example, in the case of insight and flexibility. Here we shall note some of the other conditions that have bearings on creative performance, conditions that lie mainly outside the individual himself.

Thinking in groups   Two of the most prominent special methods for giving individuals aid and training in creative thinking in solving problems are conducted in the form of group thinking. One is the brainstorming technique of Alex F. Osborn (1963), and the other is the syntectics method of W. J. J. Gordon (1961). Gordon maintains that group thinking is always superior to individual thinking. He claims that a group can condense into a few hours the production that might take one individual several months. Groups are said to encourage "irrational thinking," which is desirable during the idea-generating stages of problem solving. Groups encourage daring, invite competition, and broaden the scope of the search for ideas. All these claims have no more status than untested hypotheses, for the most part. Some of them have not passed without notice.

D. W. Taylor, F. C. Berry, and C. H. Block (1958) have provided some evidence against the superiority of the thinking of individuals in groups. They did not duplicate entirely the conditions of either the brainstorming or the syntectic procedures but studied the question of whether individuals are more productive when thinking in a group than when thinking in isolation, with suspended judgment as a condition in both cases. Subjects worked at problems calling for the generation of ideas in groups of four and by fours arbitrarily formed but with each subject working alone. The authors found that the sets of four working individually produced more unrepeated ideas than groups of four working together.

One of the claims for the brainstorming method is that interpersonal stimulation generates more ideas, one person's idea suggesting ideas to another person. Taylor et al. point out that in the process of interpersonal stimulation there is a danger that the group is kept going in more limited directions; one dominant person can channel the thinking of others, thus restricting the scope of exploration. Although the Taylor experiment does not provide a complete evaluation of the brainstorming method, it does throw doubt upon the value of group thinking per se.

The Taylor findings have been supported by similar results from a study by Dunnette, Campbell, and Jastad (1963). Using research scientists and advertising personnel as subjects, Dunnette et al. had them working in four-man teams and alone on four problems, with suspended judgment. Production of individuals was greater when they worked alone, in fact, 30 percent greater in terms of quantity, without reduction in quality. The authors found that group interaction actually appeared to inhibit the advertising personnel.

It is too early to draw a universal conclusion regarding the superiority of individual as compared with group thinking. There have been numerous studies of group problem solving, with varied results. Interaction effects are very likely, so that neither condition is universally better. Something may depend upon the kind of person and his preferences and also upon the kind of problem to be solved. It is said to be characteristic of highly creative persons that they are independent thinkers, with their own sets of values, and that they are less sociable than the average. Such traits would suggest that highly creative persons would not be likely to seek group-thinking activity, at least until the major insight has been achieved, when there may be some urge to communicate the new idea. Then the main need for idea generation has passed. A person of lesser creative talents might gain by group-thinking activity.

Homogeneous versus heterogeneous groups   If there is to be group problem solving, would it be better to compose the group of homogeneous or heterogeneous talents? Torrance (1961) has investigated this problem in the context of elementary-school education. Two kinds of groups were formed, either on the basis of IQ or on the basis of divergent-production scores.

In the production of ideas in connection with explaining the working of a scientific toy, Torrance found that homogeneous groups have several advantages. There were more signs of stress within the heterogeneous groups, as shown by behavior. The less creative child was more productive in homogeneous groups where he could compete on more equal terms. Members of homogeneous groups expressed more satisfaction with the exercise. The less able children in such groups also expressed more self-confidence and self-esteem. The more able child was more modest and self-effacing in homogeneous groups. The child with highest IQ in heterogeneous groups was expected to produce more ideas, and when he failed, he felt that he had let the group down.

Group restrictions   It has long been known that the individual who goes too far ahead of the pack suffers penalties imposed by his fellows. His new ideas are disparaged, and his sanity may even be questioned. There are efforts to see that his ideas are not implemented or adopted, and measures are sometimes taken to protect society from the dangerous person. Torrance (1962b) points out that parents and teachers of creative children often feel threatened by the expressions of those children. They do not know how to evaluate their work or how to answer their questions.

Torrance and his associates (Torrance, 1962b) were able to exhibit what happens to the more creative individuals within groups of elementary-school children. Each group was composed of five children, of whom one had scored high on divergent-production tests and the other four not. Each group was given a task to perform, the problem being to plan a demonstration of how a scientific toy works. The purpose was to see whether the high-divergent-production child would stand out in terms of suggesting ideas, how the other children would react to him, and how he would cope with their behavior.

There was clear evidence of the superiority of the high-DP members of the groups. Of the 25, 70 percent initiated more ideas than other members of the groups. The other children generally resented the most creative member, and only 25 percent of them were willing to recognize that his contributions were the most valuable. The typical group developed sanctions and methods for controlling the behavior of the most creative child. The sanctions and methods of control took the form of openly expressed hostility, criticism, ridicule, rejection, and ignoring. In the higher grades (5 and 6) there was use of organizational machinery, such as electing the creative child to an administrative position or making him a recorder or secretary, with paper work to do.

The creative children's counteractions are also interesting. Some of them were compliant, going along with the wishes of the group. Others showed counteraggression, indomitable persistence in spite of everything, ignoring of criticism, or clowning, the latter as if to direct attention away from their ideas and to gain group approval for a more acceptable exhibition. Others went off and worked by themselves, particularly in the lower grades. Some became apathetic and were silent and preoccupied. Some fluctuated in their performances from one strategy to another, in a trial-and-error attempt to make an adjustment to the situation. Still others forswore their intellectual leadership and offered minor aids to others.

These results delineate some of the problems of the creative person in society. The creative person who knows or senses that he is creative likes to express himself and to display his productions for others to see. He is somewhat self-assertive, which gives the appearance of aggressiveness. Being rebuffed, he is frustrated and shows counteraggression. Many writers have remarked on these qualities of recognized creative people. Torrance (1962b) reports that creative children show some awareness of this social treatment and that they exhibit that awareness in the stories they write.

Effects of competition   In noncreative psychological tasks, most individuals show greater performance under the motivating effects of competition, provided they feel that they can compete, and they extend themselves somewhat in order to do comparatively well. The same principle has been found to hold in tasks requiring creative thinking. Torrance (1962b) reports one experiment in which the task, for elementary-school children, was to suggest improvements for a toy stuffed dog. In one group of children an award was promised for the best performance in the class. The performance of this group in the task was compared with that of another group that had had previous practice in the same kind of task, the toy being a fire truck. There was a fairly consistent tendency for the competitive group to surpass the practiced group, in terms of scores for different divergent-production aspects. Exceptions were that the competitive group was better in fluency scores in grades 4 to 6 only and better in flexibility scores in grades 2 and 4 only.

Self-imposed restrictions   Some of the inhibitors of creative production have their sources in the social group, but the individual, influenced by group mores, applies them to himself to his disadvantage. One of these is the inculcation of sex roles. The developing boy is expected to become a he-man, excluding all things that are sissy or feminine. If the boy takes these pressures seriously or if he cannot swim against the current, he closes avenues toward creative occupations. The girl is pressured to become compliant and dependent. She must not show independent thinking or consider going into the more masculine occupations. One apparent outcome is what Torrance (1962b) calls the "fourth-grade slump," a marked drop in scores in divergent production. Recovery from this setback takes two or three years, and some children never recover. It is at about the fourth grade that the child is struck heavily with the forces that attempt to socialize him, including the adoption of sex roles.

Outstandingly creative adults seem to have escaped to some extent the pressure toward adopting sex roles, for the typical creative male scores as more feminine and the typical creative female scores as more masculine on masculinity-femininity scales, such as those provided by the Minnesota Multiphasic Personal Inventory (MMPI) and the Strong Vocational Interest Blank. As Torrance (1962b) points out, to be creative, boys must be sensitive, a feminine characteristic. To be creative, a girl must be independent, a masculine characteristic. Torrance reports observed instances in which boys and girls have forsworn their creative potentialities in order to maintain their expected sex roles. It can also be said that had many highly creative persons taken their sex roles more seriously, they probably would have gone into less creative professions.

Other pressures also help to dampen creative development. The child is faced with norms: height norms, weight norms, IQ norms, age-grade norms, and aptitude-achievement norms. Too much attention to norms arouses fears of being different, which is too readily interpreted as being abnormal. There is often a general pressuring of schoolchildren toward mediocrity. Every child is expected to become "well-rounded" and "well-adjusted," where adjustment probably means conformity to someone's ideal personality pattern, a pattern that would minimize individuality and independence of thought and values.

Another deterrent to creative ways is fear of alienation from others. The life of the highly creative person can be a lonely one. He is not understood by his parents, his teachers, and his peers. Estrangement from others is often the price to be paid. Another condition that detracts from creative development is lack of encouragement, even lack of opportunity, to engage in self-initiated activities. The creative child must not get too far ahead; instead, he is handed routine assignments, which to him may be dull.

Even adult scientists, of all people, are not immune to social inhibitions, many of which they impose upon themselves. We are reminded by Barber (1961) of how scientists often resist new ideas for various reasons. Older scientists resist the ideas of younger scientists. High-ranking scientists resist the ideas of low-ranking scientists. Rival schools of thought resist one another. Members of an area of specialization look with suspicion upon ideas of outsiders. Some scientists resist ideas in conflict with their religious convictions. Nor are scientists alone in being subjected to such restrictions and inhibitions. There are schools of thought, and there is defensiveness concerning home-produced ideas in almost any field.

Types of environments   The individual's living and working environments have something to do with his creative output. Torrance and his associates (Torrance et al., 1960) made a comparative study of urban versus small-town versus rural children on divergent-production tasks. One task was to write a story about "The Flying Monkey." The investigators' interest was in whether the child would let the monkey keep his unusual mode of locomotion or whether he would insist that the monkey return to more conventional methods.

The study, which involved "several thousand children" in two states, showed that the proportions of the children who would tolerate the unconventional flying monkey differed markedly. The urban percentage was smallest, being 38; the medium-sized–town percentage was 68; and the rural percentage was 74. Klausmeier and Wiersma (1964) have verified the difference between large- and small-city children by finding that in 7 of 10 divergent-production tests the small-city children had higher means. In 4 convergent-production tests there were no significant differences. The large-city atmosphere, although the mecca for the more creative people, is apparently not a good breeding ground from which the creative individuals of the future are to come. The city child may have many more models to inspire him, but he is apparently overly restricted in his development.

Family environment   Several investigators agree with Rossman's finding (1931) regarding recognized inventors, that creative scientists and engineers are likely to come from middle-class families. This may reflect the need for above-average IQ as a very important condition (but not a sufficient condition, as pointed out in Chapter 6) for creative potential (Knapp & Goodrich, 1952; Repucci, 1962; Roe, 1952). A few writers mention birth order as having some bearing, at least that creative scientists are likely to be among the firstborn children or among the first in the family (Repucci, 1962; Roe, 1952; Weisberg & Springer, 1961). The eldest child, if given responsibility for looking after the younger ones in the family and perhaps other responsibilities, could consequently develop more readily the habits of self-initiated thinking and independence of thinking.

Roe (1952) makes a great deal of the relatively high incidence of loss of a parent in the cases of her outstanding scientists. She suggests that this event leads to lack of personal closeness and to independence of acting and thinking. Parental loss was more common for natural scientists than for social scientists. Parents of social scientists (anthropologists and psychologists) were relatively more aware of social status, which might have turned the attention of the children to social phenomena. The social scientists, as children, also had difficult relationships with parents, which may have called attention to interpersonal behavior as something to be observed and reflected about.

There is general agreement that the home life of creative scientists and of some other professional groups has been less happy than average. MacKinnon (1960) reports this fact, for example. The male child often found it impossible to identify himself with his father. This circumstance may have lowered the boy's masculinity, a condition favorable for creative tendencies. Weisberg and Springer (1961) agree, in general. Through tests and interviews, they elicited the information that the family of the more creative child is not a close one. The marriage is likely to be poorly adjusted, with much dissension in the home. Little emphasis is placed on the child's adopting parental values, and little concern is paid to the child's regressions, two conditions that would seem to contribute to development along creative lines.

Goertzel and Goertzel (1962), who made studies of the biographies of eminent and presumably mostly creative people, found that there was a high incidence of troubled homes and wretched childhoods in their lives. Handicaps were common, and so were parents one or both of whom were uncommon in some way. Many of the eminent people suffered childhood experiences that are commonly found in the lives of those who later become delinquents, neurotics, and psychotics, reminding one of the old saying that the same fire that melts butter also hardens steel. The direction in which the difficult circumstances send the child, toward eminence or toward maladjustment, must depend upon other conditions, in the child or in his environment. Of course, some go in both directions, but certainly not all.

The working environments of adults also offer favorable and unfavorable aspects for creative performance. There is not space here to consider all the possibilities in this connection. Considerable attention has been given in this industrial society to the environmental factors that affect the creative scientist. For a comprehensive view of this area of interest the reader is referred to McPherson (1964). Studies thus far have considered the effects of organizational structure, management policies, types of supervision, time schedules, and so on upon the output of scientists under these various conditions. There is little to be gained from these directions concerning immediate conditions and the ways in which they affect certain aspects of problem-solving performance.

Religious background   Some attention has been given to the religious background of the growing child and the adult that he becomes in relation to creative performance. Lehman and Witty (1931) found that of 303 starred scientists in *American Men of Science* for 1927 who gave information regarding church affiliation, these distinguished scientists came in undue proportions from Protestant faiths and more particularly from liberal church groups. Only 3 of the 303 reported membership in the Catholic Church. Knapp and Goodrich (1952) have found confirming evidence on these points.

Training in creative thinking

Training possibilities   From numerous investigations on the question concerning training aimed at the improvement of creative potential we have considerable reason for guarded optimism. The writer shares the view of Bartlett (1958), who regards thinking abilities as intellectual skills that are trainable, by analogy to psychomotor skills. The intellectual skills are generalized as well as specific, and many of the generalized skills are in the form of intellectual factor abilities, each one unique. They have been developed largely by informal practice, and they should be improvable by virtue of formal practice. This does not mean that heredity plays no role in the development of intellectual abilities; it no doubt sets limits to development for individuals. The role of heredity will be treated in the next chapter.

We gain some supporting impressions from those who have studied highly creative people. Agnew (1922b), who studied composers, reported that they testify to the fact that they gain control over their auditory imagery through practice. One composer (Cowell,

1926), who has provided some personal biographical information, told of some of the steps by which he acquired controlled auditory imagery. As a child, he practiced hearing over and over musical selections that he had heard. After this self-training, new compositions began to flash through his awareness, but they could not be controlled. "With super-human effort," he reported, he gained control of such spontaneous imagery.

Rossman (1931) believes that an inventor with high aptitudes for invention will invent, no matter what or how much formal education he may have. But Rossman goes on to say that even high aptitude can be made more effective with training of the right kind. The last two statements raise the issue of whether training actually increases aptitude or whether it enables the person to make better use of the aptitude he has. There is no doubt that much of the learning of the creative person is in terms of specific information that he can utilize. But there are numerous experiments that seem to show gains in terms of generalized aptitude, as we shall see in what follows.

General training in school   A number of studies have been concerned with effects of special attention to development of creative abilities and attitudes in regular school courses. The variables have been teacher attitudes and teaching methods. The usual experimental design is a simple one. Pretests in divergent-production abilities are given, with designed treatment applied to an experimental group and not to a control group; then posttests of the same abilities are given. All such experiments, of course, suffer from lack of full control of conditions, but the results can be suggestive.

In one experiment of this type Torrance et al. (1960) taught 10 teachers some principles of how to teach creatively. The five principles were: (1) treat pupils' questions with respect, (2) treat imaginative ideas with respect, (3) show pupils that their ideas have value, (4) permit pupils to do some things "for practice" without threat of evaluation, and (5) tie evaluation in with cause and consequences. The teachers tried to teach in such a manner for four weeks. A control group taught for four weeks under their normal conditions. The tests showed superior gains for the experimental group of pupils in scores for originality and elaboration in four of the six grades, superiority in fluency in three, and superiority in flexibility in two. It was an incidental observation that about one-third of the teachers failed to understand the principles correctly. Such teachers tend to be authoritarian, defensive, dominated by time schedules, insensitive to their pupils' intellectual and emotional needs, preoccupied with disciplinary problems, and unwilling to give much of themselves.

On a more limited scale, Rusch, Denny, and Ives (1965) compared an experimental group taught creatively for the school year and a control group that was taught in the regular manner. Two teachers and two classes of sixth-grade students were in each group. Seven divergent-production tests were given at the beginning and end of the school year. The experimental group gained significantly more on five of the seven tests; in none was the control-group gain superior.

Cartledge and Krauser (1963) found that special training procedures could be effective in the first grade. The experimental Ss had five twenty-minute sessions on thinking of how they could improve toys. They gained significantly more than control Ss in scores for fluency, flexibility, and originality from the Torrance tests. Ss having motivation for quantity of output gained about the same as those having motivation for quality of output.

Since there are traditional associations between creativity and art, teachers of art have not been slow to propose that art instruction can play a key role in teaching for creative development. Two studies have been designed to test this hypothesis. C. Owens (1962) reports a study with experimental and control groups in the sixth and seventh grades.

Only posttests were given, however, and there was some question as to whether the two groups had been matched. The general impression is that the experimental group did significantly better in art tests scored for divergent-production performances and in non-art DP tests. Some transfer to performance was indicated in two semantic tests (Object Synthesis and creative writing) but not in a third test in social studies. The last named appears to involve factor CMI (conceptual foresight), however, not a divergent-production ability.

McFee (1964) has reported the findings from a major study with special training in an art course. The training included the solving of design problems and instruction on principles of perceptual organization, spatial relationships in three-dimensional space, and the nature of creative thinking. In connection with the last named, lectures were given by professionally creative people. The subjects were in the ninth grade and in the highest tenth for academic aptitude. Pretests and posttests, including tests of divergent production and of flexibility in convergent production, were given to the experimental group (volunteers) and to a control group.

Significant differences in score changes were found in favor of the experimental group in 7 of 10 DP tests, only 1 of the 7 being figural (Match Problems). The 3 DP tests without significant changes were 2 for factor DMU (ideational fluency) and 1 for DMS (expressional fluency). The training obviously went well beyond the field of art. The question of transfer beyond creative performance in art that can be obtained when training is restricted to art is still an open one.

Training in special courses on creativity   In connection with courses especially designed to teach creative thinking, pretests and posttests almost always show that trained Ss gain significantly more in most DP tests but definitely more in tests of originality (factor DMT) than in fluency (DMU), in which there is sometimes no gain (Gerry, DeVeau, & Chorness, 1957; Meadow & Parnes, 1959; Nicholson, 1959; Parnes, 1962; Parnes & Meadow, 1959). Inferences that might be drawn from the latter result are that ideational fluency is a personal quality that is little influenced by training, or that the kind of training is not suited to development of gains in fluency, or that the courses put emphasis upon high-quality ideas. Tests of ideational fluency put emphasis upon quantity, regardless of quality. The courses in question have varied in length from a few weeks to a whole semester. The special methods used have varied, but Osborn's brainstorming method has probably prevailed.

More detailed conclusions have been drawn. Parnes (1962) reported that the benefits of training apply to those who were initially high or low in DP tests, to those with high or low IQ (IQ was never actually low, only relatively so in students usually of college caliber), and to older (twenty-three to fifty-one years of age) as well as to younger Ss (seventeen to twenty-two). Parnes and Meadow (1960) have demonstrated that the training effects are somewhat persistent, since they could be found in testing students who had completed the course eight months to four years before.

There is also evidence of transfer effects. Inventory scores show changes in the direction of greater "dominance" (confidence, self-reliance, and the like) as well as in self-control (Meadow & Parnes, 1959; Parnes, 1962). These changes may be interpreted as very broad transfer effects. Performance in using the suggestion box in an industry also indicates transfer. At the AC Spark Plug Co. plants, Simberg and Shannon (1959) gave a ten-week training course to employees who had had very high records in feeding the suggestion box and also to some who had had very low records of this kind. For the year following the training, both experimental groups showed gains in total number of suggestions offered, number accepted, and amount of monetary reward. There were increases in both quantity and quality of ideas offered. The initially high-suggestion group kept its lead through training. This fact suggests that individuals performing at higher levels of creative output are not necessarily performing at their peak possibilities under normal conditions.

Some special methods of training   It is worthwhile to give attention to some of the special techniques that have been developed for the purpose of making individuals perform more creatively. Space does not permit full description of any method, but each method can be characterized and its relation to psychological principles pointed out. Few methods have been subjected to experimental testing. Although some of the methods have been designed for group thinking, they can be applied in principle to individual problem solving. Most of them concentrate on ways of idea generating, and they provide steps to facilitate the scanning process in the retrieval of stored information.

Osborn (1963) recommends a "checklist" procedure, a question-asking technique, which ensures a wide coverage of information. Every question calls for a transformation of some kind, which may be a change in a unit of information or in a system. In view of the importance of transformations in producing novel effects, such questioning, if well directed, should be effective.

Another method, which encourages divergent production as well as transformations, is Crawford's "attribute-listing" method (1954). In describing an object or a situation and applying this method, one thinks of specifications, limitations, needs, and so on. An example taken from Arnold (1962a) pertains to thoughts about an ordinary screwdriver. The attributes of a screwdriver are:

It has a round steel shank.
It has a wooden handle riveted to the shank.
It has a wedge-shaped end to enter a screw head.
It is manually operated.
Torque is applied to achieve a twisting movement.
Pressure is exerted to keep the end in the slot.

Now if one wished to improve upon a typical screwdriver, having such a list of attributes, one could change one attribute at a time. Osborn's checklist method could be applied at this point. One could change the handle from wood to plastic, which is a better insulator and is more durable. The last comments are evaluative. The shank could be changed from round to hexagonal, so that it could be turned with a wrench or more readily by pliers. Such changes have already been made, but they came after the screwdriver had been in a standard form for many years.

A comprehensive and systematic way of combining checklist and attribute listing is found in the method known as "morphological analysis," a logical approach named and used extensively by the astronomer Zwicky (1957) and advocated by Allen (1962). Suppose we wish to think of some new mode of human transportation, to use another example from Arnold (1962a). The problem is first analyzed in terms of fundamental dimensions or parameters of transportation. There is the type of carrier or support to the human being: cart, chair, sling, or bed. There is the medium of support for the carrier: hard surface, water, oil, air, rollers, or rails. There is the source of power: animal, man, internal-combustion engine, steam, electricity, compressed air, magnetic field, or atomic power. Having identified the major dimensions and the various categories pertinent to them, one can then combine those categories in all possible ways, obtaining numerous potential ways of transportation, each unique. Some will be feasible and useful; some not.

The reader has already probably recognized that the structure-of-intellect model comes in this methodological category. The preceding chapters testify to the utility of the method for leading to new intellectual abilities and to the fruitfulness of the concepts pertaining to the model for psychological theory.

Not the least important aspect of training for creative thinking is the imparting of information about the nature of the psychological events involved. The training experiment conducted by McFee (1964) mentioned earlier involved such an aspect. In a training course for administrative personnel employed by the United States government, Forehand and Libby (1962) found that exercises in thinking alone were not significantly effective in terms of innovative behavior later but that exercises combined with instruction about the nature of creative thinking were effective in that regard.

Upton and Samson (1963) have prepared a book of thinking exercises, following Upton's hypothesis that the best preparation in learning how to write in college-freshman English is instruction and exercise in the use of language. Many of the exercises look like psychological tests. They emphasize all the operations except memory, and they bring out differences between kinds of information (content) and kinds of products. The authors' claim is that a course including the use of the exercises contributed to a substantial gain in average IQ of the students. In a similar course, with groups matched for IQ, Brunelle (1964) has reported not only a significant gain in IQ (8.6 points for the experimental group, 2.6 points for the control group) but also a significant gain in a composite of divergent-production tests (10.6 versus 0.5 score points). It would appear that general training in the basic psychological use of information can contribute to intellectual development.

Associative training for originality   In the investigation of abilities thought to be relevant to creative thinking, Wilson et al. (1954) hypothesized that three kinds of tests would measure originality. One kind was constructed on the principle that clever responses would indicate that trait, one used the principle that ability to give remotely associated responses would be indicative, and a third scored responses with weights inversely proportional to their popularity (frequency) in a population. One test was Quick Responses, in which free-association word responses were obtained to stimulus words. Each response was scored inversely as its frequency in the group of examinees tested. In this case, infrequent responses were likely to be also remotely associated responses; thus the test satisfied two of the three principles. The Quick Responses did not stand up well in a subsequent analysis (Kettner et al., 1959a) as a measure of originality, however, and has not been used for that purpose since, for there are a number of much stronger tests, although less objectively scored.

Maltzman and his associates performed a series of experiments in which they hoped to teach subjects (college students) to be more original by giving them training in producing unusual and remote responses in word-association tasks. The major hypothesis was that giving uncommon responses is a habit that can be strengthened by the usual procedures of operant learning, in other words, by practice with reinforcement (Maltzman, Simon, Raskin, & Licht, 1960).

There have been a number of variations of the experimental conditions, but the typical experiment used a simple word-association task. Experimental and control groups have an initial test consisting of 25 stimulus words, scored with weights for unusualness. The experimental group then has further applications of the same list. The instruction each time is that S is not to repeat any response he has given previously, and he is rewarded for complying. A final test with 25 new stimulus words is given. Sometimes the Unusual

Uses test has been given in order to investigate possible transfer effects. Any gain in this test for the experimental group as compared with the control group would be indicative of transfer of some kind. But since Unusual Uses shares its common-factor variance with both factor DMT (originality) and factor DMC (spontaneous flexibility), with the latter leading, any conclusion as to which ability has been affected would be precluded. Either or both might be affected by the practice in the uncommon-word-association task.

As a consequence of the training in giving uncommon word associations, the experimental group usually shows gain in this respect in the final association test and sometimes also in the Unusual Uses test. Other conditions of training are effective, including rewarding Ss for giving uncommon responses during the training series (Maltzman, Bogartz, & Berger, 1958) and presenting pairs of remotely associated words, with S to select one of them. Giving S items from the Unusual Uses test, with S instructed to give a different response each time, also showed transfer effects in performance on the word-association test.

The larger the number of training trials in word association, the greater was the improvement. Ss having 5 and 10 trials improved more than those having 1 trial, but even the 1-trial group improved somewhat. Retention of training effects was found to persist at least forty-eight hours after training, with more gain shown after one hour than after forty-eight hours. There were also some persisting transfer effects. Hyman (1960) found that the Maltzman technique of training for originality transferred to creative performance in problem solving other than in Unusual Uses.

In attempting to account for the improvement in originality in his experiments on the basis of associational theory, Maltzman (1960) makes two assumptions, both of which are very questionable. One of his difficulties is the fact that the reinforcements are not applied to *specific* responses but to *classes* of responses. He first assumes that every associative response is associated with every other associative response. This assumption is made to account for the fact that S can give remotely associated responses. This is an example of insisting upon replicative recall only, whereas the concept of transfer recall is needed. The second assumption is that associations are stronger between uncommon responses than they are between common and uncommon responses.

In Maltzman's originality training, uncommon associations are reinforced. When no reward is specifically given, S's satisfaction in fulfilling the instruction, which he is strongly motivated to do, is the reinforcing agent. The reinforcement spreads or is transferred to other uncommon responses by virtue of Maltzman's second assumption; uncommon responses are more strongly associated with the reinforced responses than are common responses. A resistance is built up against giving common responses, which also transfers to other common responses.

An alternative hypothesis is that Maltzman's originality training is a case of learning how to learn, a theory that he rejects (1960). If one is willing to admit that Ss recognize uncommon responses as one class and common responses as another, the differential reinforcement of *classes* would provide a very simple explanation. When Ss are virtually instructed to give uncommon responses, they can hardly avoid being aware of classes of responses. The transfer of reinforcement would then readily occur through class membership.

Hyman (1960) offers another alternative. The training forces S to give more *difficult* responses and thus raises his standards as to quality of response. Perhaps the class information is in terms of difficulty rather than of remote association. Perhaps S is aware of both difficulty and remoteness as class properties.

Computer simulation of thinking

It was not long after the coming of the high-speed electronic computers that computer-wise psychologists and others initiated attempts to accomplish with computer operations some of the intellectual activities that human brains perform. Computers were designed to carry out the routine processing of information needed in solving problems, particularly those put in mathematical form. To what extent could they be harnessed to solve other types of problems? And could anything be learned about the nature of human problem solving by knowing how computers solve problems? These are some of the major questions to which answers have been sought.

The essential nature of computers   As Newell, Shaw, and Simon (1958a) point out, the basic features of a computer are few. It must contain a memory store of information that can be utilized when needed. It must be designed to perform certain basic operations. The information must be in symbolic form so that it is conveniently and economically coded. And the computer must have a program that instructs it in what operations to perform and in what sequence. There can be a change of program, depending upon the kind of problem to be solved. There must be a set of rules by which the processes can be combined in a program.

Parallels in structure-of-intellect theory   Many parallels between the workings of a computer, what it does and how, and the behavior of a human organism are rather obvious. Both emphasize information and kinds of operations. Even the kinds of operation and the kinds of information are parallel in many respects. Symbolic information is the much-preferred food of the computer. The computer is learning to handle figural information to some extent, but it is having much more difficulty with semantic information, and has not as yet tackled behavioral information, as far as the writer knows. Any information that can be translated into symbolic form so that it can be coded can be handled by computers. It may be that new symbolic systems will be generally needed; in fact, new languages of types that can be communicated to a computer are being developed.

If semantic information dealt only with denotative aspects of meaning, it would not present so much difficulty; its rich connotative contexts cause the trouble. Perhaps even this problem can be largely mastered. When we remember that human communication of semantic information has to go through symbols produced by the speaker or writer and then through the receiver's symbolic rendition before it gets translated to his semantic encoding, the task does not seem so formidable.

Christensen (1963) points out how the five SI kinds of operations and also the various kinds of products apply in computer operations and how some of the aptitude factors can be aligned with certain special computer events. Processes of receiving and sorting information are the computer's operation of cognition. Memory storage is of course obviously parallel, although the manner of storage may be quite different in computer and man. Retrieval of information is parallel with both divergent and convergent production. Computers are programmed to apply algorithms, which are ironclad sequences of operations that can be applied in solving mathematical problems and problems of logic. This is the analogue of convergent production. Where such programs are not possible, heuristics are applied. Heuristics are general rules or strategies that circumvent much trial-and-error activity. One such rule would be to start with the known answer (as in proving a theorem) and work backward. Another example would be to break a problem into subproblems. A number of examples were mentioned, in the form of strategies, in connection with the attainment of concepts, in Chapter 12. Almost any strategy that has somewhat general application can be regarded as a heuristic. We may say that the use of heuristics means indulging in divergent production. Heuristics impose some restraints upon the computer, whereas algorithms impose full restraints. Evaluation enters the computer's repertoire of basic operations in terms of matching information and of accepting or rejecting the matches in terms of criteria. Other parallels will be seen as we proceed in this section.

What computers can simulate   To those who are not well acquainted with computers and their operations, some of the things they do are rather remarkable. A certain computer known as the Logical Theorizer (LT) can produce proofs for theorems in symbolic logic (Newell et al., 1958a). Given the axioms of symbolic logic and a few previously proved theorems as stored information, the LT solved 38 of 52 problems given to it, half the proofs being solved in less than one minute each. The LT could also solve problems in chess, even playing with an opponent (Newell, Shaw, & Simon, 1958b). It could show creative production in the form of musical composition and the designing of electric motors. Computers have also been used to balance assembly lines and to prove theorems in geometry.

In terms of imitating certain psychological events, a computer shows the phenomenon of sets, as in being ready to respond to a certain stimulus in a certain way. It has shown insights, in the form of sudden grasping of a structure (system), observed when it was told to print out results of steps along the way in problem solving where trial-and-error activity was needed (Newell et al., 1958a). As with human problem solvers, the trial and error need not be blind, if the computer is programmed to follow rules that yield short-cuts. It can be taught to choose alternatives wisely.

A computer engages in divergent production, as when generating members of a set, an activity that essentially defines an ideational-fluency test. It can be programmed to form concepts (to educe relations and systems), as in solving items in the Thurstone Letter Series test (Simon & Kotovsky, 1963). Sample items are:

A B A B A B A B——   A T B A T B A T B A T——   Q X A P X B Q X A——

The next letter in the series is to be supplied. Such a test has been found to measure factors CSR (cognition of symbolic relations) and CSS (cognition of symbolic systems), more of the latter than of the former. It is interesting to know that items of this test that were difficult for the computer were also difficult for human examinees. What both human examinee and computer must have in memory storage to handle these items is information about alphabetical sequences and the kinds of systems that can be formed from them.

There are computers that learn to reproduce speech sounds and computers that learn to read (Simon & Newell, 1962). Others are being designed to translate languages, but this is very much in the experimental stage; the semantic problems, for one thing, present an important hurdle. Idiomatic expressions and nuances of meaning are other difficulties. To return to the psychological laboratory, Simon and Feigenbaum (1964) developed programs for memorizing syllables in lists and in paired associates. The computer was made sensitive to degree of similarity of items. Familiarity was varied by making different numbers of exposures of items, and meaningfulness was varied in terms of number of associations, to give the computer a more lifelike problem. Predictions were made as to the rate of learning as a function of the three variables. The results were similar to those found with human memorizers.

An evaluation of computer-simulation research   Probably the greatest benefit for psychology, and it is very significant, to be found in the kinds of computer research that have been mentioned in this section is the point of view that it encourages. That point of view may best be described as *informational-operational*. The operational aspect takes the form of developing operational models for describing events in significant form and sequence. The model in Figure 14.1 is an example, in general form. The programmer who lays out the sequence of operations by which a computer is to accomplish a certain psychological outcome is compelled to give the problem and its requirements for solution a detailed scrutiny so that no essential detail is omitted. He can test his program to see whether it works. His program is his theory of how a certain problem can be solved; his testing of the program is his experiment. The psychologist would do well to attempt such careful and detailed observation of problem solving of a certain kind. The result may be in terms of much more predictable outcomes.

The informational aspect of the point of view is that emphasized by the writer. The substance with which we should deal in psychology is information. We have had operational descriptions of behavior, but they have usually been in terms of stimulus-response sequences. This approach has been fruitful for some purposes in some areas of behavior, but it has fallen flat when it comes to the more important intellectual processes of problem solving and processes incident to it. It may be that the informational categories provided by the psychoepistemology of the structure-of-intellect theory can be improved, but they would seem to provide at least a good start.

Advantages and limitations   Writers on the advantages and limitations of computer research on psychological problems (Feldman, 1962; Hovland, 1960; Reitman, 1964) are fairly well agreed that the computer approach fosters theory development of a very useful and testable kind. Experiments testing those theories are much better controlled than similar experiments using human subjects would be. Such experiments are efficient, and conclusions can be clear-cut.

There are difficulties in translating the theories and conclusions to the description of human behavior, however. One is the greatly detailed account that needs to be given of a theory, in terms of a program. Reitman (1964) cites one program that contained 100 pages of steps plus 25 pages of supplementary information. It may be that principles that would solve this communication problem will evolve.

Another difficulty is that many problems are capable of solution by different routes. The route that the programmer conceives and works out may be a common one in human thinking, but it could be an uncommon one. There is also the difference between computer and human brain, in that the computer has only its limited set of memory items whereas the human brain has a lifetime of retained items of information. The human organism also has the problem of survival, which the computer does not have; it has motivations and emotions that can make contributions to the problem-solving process. Again, common principles may be developed to bridge the gap better, and more human characteristics may be worked into the computer operations and programs so as to make the simulations more realistic.

Summary

The many similarities between the phenomena known as problem solving and creative production make it possible and desirable to treat them essentially as one topic. Similarities are indicated both by the traditional steps proposed for them and by the intellectual abilities involved, which are numerous in both instances. An operational model was presented for a general conception of problem solving, incorporating structure-of-intellect concepts and information-processing ideas.

Besides the well-known more directly utilitarian motives involved in thinking, it is necessary to recognize some special sources of motivation of a more intrinsic nature. As elsewhere in the discussion of theory of intellectual operations, the role of information takes a leading place, with emphases upon systems and transformations. For example, a transformation hypothesis was proposed to account for what happens during the state known as incubation and also during moments of insight or intuition, explaining what is popularly known as "inspiration."

Three kinds of flexibility, definable in terms of categories of intellectual factors, emphasize classes as well as transformations. Classes also play an important role in terms of fluency of production of ideas by way of transfer recall. Many insights also come in the form of cognizing and producing implications, which are the kind of product featured in moments of elaboration of information. Evaluation is a persistent operation, but fluency of production is facilitated by the injection of moments of suspended judgment. Constructive and destructive criticism have differential effects, depending upon other conditions.

Specific and general conditions that affect thinking at many points were discussed. Among the more general conditions are those pertaining to thinking in groups and the restrictions upon thinking arising from group living. Studies of effects of training, devoted mostly to the development of creative potential and performance, give promise of much to be gained from this direction.

Computer simulation of problem solving and of other psychological events was considered and found to have desirable stimulating effects upon theory and research in psychology. The question of whether computers think can only be answered after one defines *thinking*.

IV Determiners of intelligence

15 Physical basis of intelligence

In the next four chapters we shall consider the various conditions, endogenous and exogenous, that are possible contributors to the level of intellectual functioning of individuals. Briefly, these will be grouped under the headings of physical mechanisms, environmental influences, and the age of the individual during development and decline.

The physical bases naturally include the contributions of heredity, in connection with which we shall look into the mechanics of heredity and how it contributes to development of the individual. The brain is the unquestioned seat of intellectual operations. We shall consider much of the new information about principles of brain function and how anatomical and functional aspects are related to intelligence. More specifically, we shall try to see whether there are things in the brain and its functions that are associated with categories of abilities and even with particular abilities as conceived in the structure-of-intellect theory. Some attention will appropriately be given to electrical and chemical aspects of brain functioning in relation to intellectual facets and to effects of certain drugs.

Heredity

Nowhere has the "explosion" of scientific information during the past score of years been more impressive than in the area of biological and biochemical knowledge with regard to heredity. Even a brief review of the highlights of that information to which we can give space here is enough to show how far scientists have gone since the days when Mendel made his discoveries of the unitary nature of hereditary transmission, in his study of primroses. While modern physicists have been examining in detail the internal nature of the atom and its nucleus, biologists and chemists have been studying in detail the inside of the gene, as well as other components of the living cell. Some of the things that they have found have had suggestive impacts upon theory of certain psychological functions, such as learning and memory, as we shall see.

The mechanism of heredity   It is well known that the carriers of human heredity are in the form of chromosomes within the nucleus of each germ cell. Half of each of the 48 chromosomes comes from the father and half from the mother, each chromosome being made up of the unit carriers, the genes. It is now known that the basic chemical is deoxyribonucleic acid (DNA), whose molecule is exceedingly complex and relatively large. It has been estimated that the DNA molecule is about 20 angstroms thick (an angstrom is one-hundred-millionth of a centimeter), and some of the DNA molecules may be 30,000 angstrom units in length (Crick, 1954). Each molecule has a backbone structure, with side groups of submolecules, a very long chain with alternate sugar and phosphate groups, in fact, two such chains welded together and wound in a helix form, like a winding staircase (see Figure 15.1). There may be as many as 10,000 turns in a single DNA molecule (Crick, 1954).

The DNA molecule contains as many as 3,000 constituent molecules of 5-carbon sugar, represented by clear pentagons in Figure 15.1, to each of which is attached a protein base. There are four kinds of such bases, of which two are purines known as adenine

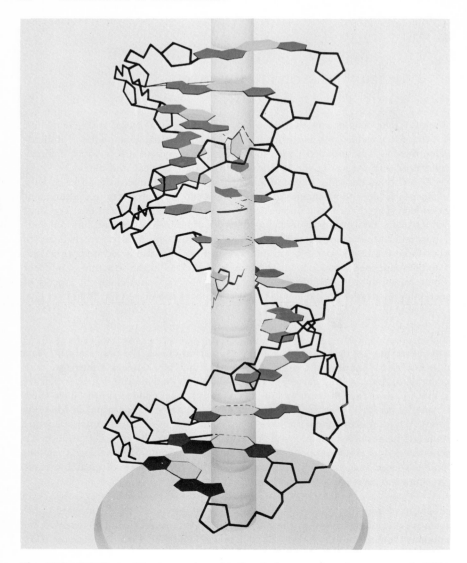

Fig. 15.1   A helix model representing a biochemical conception of a segment of a DNA molecule, carrier of hereditary determination of body development. (*From Crick, 1954. Copyright © 1954 by Scientific American, Inc. All rights reserved.*)

and guanine and two are pyrimidines known as thymine and cytosine, the first pair being larger than the second. Two such submolecules, one of the large ones and one of the small ones, hook together two sugar molecules, one in each strand of the helix. Such a subsystem is shown in Figure 15.2. In Figure 15.1 the subsystems are shown as dark hexagonal plates.

It is the four bases that furnish a four-letter alphabet for carrying the information that is transmitted in heredity and in cell division. "Words" are produced by various combinations of these four letters. Beadle (1948) speculates that the first living organism must have been like a gene, capable of replicating itself exactly. In sexual reproduction, splitting occurs so that the sperm carries one half of a molecule and the egg carries the other half that come together to form the new segment and the new DNA molecule.

The hereditary cryptogram, with its four-letter alphabet, carries the instructions for all further cell growth and cell division. It is the role of each gene to see to the manufacture of its own unique enzyme, made to its own pattern that is stored within the gene (Jukes, 1963). The enzymes, being catalyzers, play crucial roles in physical development, producing the specialized cells that we find in the fully developed individual. Even a four-letter alphabet, because of the enormous possibilities for various combinations, can carry all the detailed information required. It is said (Crick, 1954) that there is enough DNA in a single cell to encode the information in about ten thousand large textbooks.

The number of genes in the human chromosomes is unknown. It is estimated (Dobzhansky, 1950) that there are between 5,000 and 12,000 genes in the most studied animal, genetically, *Drosophila*. Dobzhansky suggests that even if the human cell contained only 1,000 genes, each with 2 conditions, the possible number of combinations would be $2^{1,000}$. Sexual reproduction makes possible a vastly greater chance of variety by recombining genes in different patterns.

To illustrate what the lack of an enzyme can do with respect to intellectual development, the instance of phenylketonuria may be mentioned. In cases of mental deficiency of this rare type, phenylpyruvic acid is found in the urine; the individual cannot oxidize that acid. He did not receive among his genes the plan for developing the mechanism that would do so. The disposition is inherited as a recessive trait.

Heredity and evolution   Since the physical basis for intellectual functioning came about through the general processes of evolution, it is of interest to consider the possibilities for further development from this direction. Without human intervention in the form of application of eugenic measures, the outlook has been painted as rather dark, if we accept some of the conclusions that have been current. In discussing human evolution, Simpson (1964) reiterates the biologists' prevailing belief that the DNA material is not changed

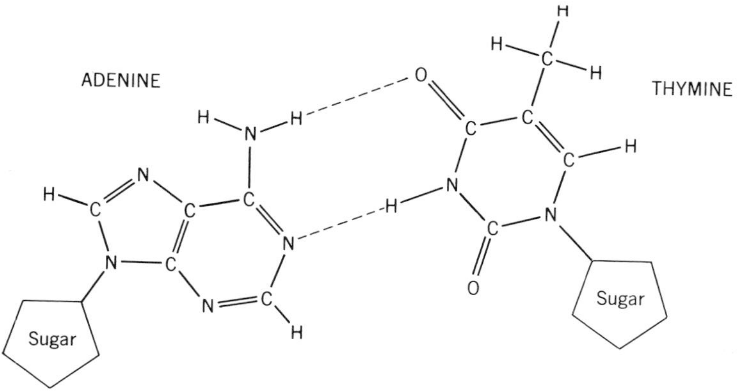

Fig. 15.2   A more detailed illustration of linkage of pairs of bases within a DNA molecule. (*After Crick, 1954.*)

by what the individual does. Insofar as life experiences of the individual are concerned, DNA is rigidly impervious to change; it represents the ultimate in conservatism, which, from the long-range point of view, is probably a wise policy.

Although the DNA transmits its message to the cytoplasm and it would seem that there is only a one-way communication, Simpson also says that there is a sense in which communication can go in the opposite direction: there is provision for feedback information to DNA. Not that we may expect changes in DNA as a consequence in the individual, but, in the long run, we may expect changes in DNA in the population. The ultimate criterion for evaluation of any inherited characteristic is survival. Any source of effective change in DNA must be exogenous, never endogenous; so the doctrine goes. Cosmic rays are said to be the major source of mutations or changes in gene structure. Dobzhansky (1950) has estimated that the frequency of any specific change due to a mutation would be about 1 in 1 billion in a certain kind of bacteria, about 1 in 100,000 to 1 million in corn or in *Drosophila* in one generation, and 1 in 2,500 to 100,000 for human sex cells in one generation (twenty-five years).

In human affairs, the great majority of mutations are disadvantageous. This suggests that man has so many good traits that it is unlikely that any mutation can be an improvement with respect to survival. A mutation can be advantageous if it improves the probability of survival. Apparently no credence is given to the idea that some improvements may merely make living better, as a kind of luxury. A need for change that improves chances of survival is likely to occur when there is some marked change in the environment. Let us suppose, with Dobzhansky (1950), that there are 1 billion bacteria of the variety *Escherichia coli,* a harmless inhabitant of the colon, and that they are subjected to treatment with an antibiotic. All except a few, perhaps all but 1, would be killed. The survivor or survivors have a mutation that makes it possible to live in the presence of the antibiotic. From that source would come new colonies of the bacteria to replace the old. Thus is evolution supposed to occur, according to present biological information and inferences therefrom.

Growth of specialized cells   Let us come back to the individual. How does the genetic code for any individual get translated into bones, muscles, viscera, and nervous system? Studies in embryology have yielded considerable information about how this takes place, how the nuclear material, which is identical in every cell, guides the development of cytoplasm that is somewhat different in every cell and markedly different in the various tissues.

One of the secrets is that DNA has a flock of messengers that it can and does send into the cytoplasm. One of the important messengers is a similar chemical known as ribonucleic acid, or RNA. Other, less direct messengers are the enzymes. The structure of the messengers duplicates that in the DNA molecules, and with the aid of the cytoplasm they determine the cell's development. It is appropriate to say "with the aid of the cytoplasm," because the latter does have much to do with directing development as well as with carrying it out.

The fertilized human egg does not contain a homunculus, a little man that can be observed, but in addition to the blueprints that are in the nucleus, there is a kind of differentiation within the cytoplasm. Even before fertilization, the egg is observed to be fairly well mapped out in terms of general body structure. The nucleus is near the upper pole of the egg, with RNA in abundance around it, tapering off in quantity from that point. There is a radial symmetry, which is to give way later to a bilateral symmetry (Fischberg & Blackler, 1961). When the fertilized egg divides, the nucleus is identical in the progeny but the cytoplasm differs. It is the interaction of differing cytoplasm with the nucleus that brings about development in special directions. The cytoplasm of each cell calls upon the genes selectively. Some writers (Gray, 1957; Waddington, 1953) speak of an organizer, which has overall, general supervision of development, and suborganizers, which oversee the special developments in different kinds of tissue and different organs. It is as if the cytoplasm, which furnishes the organizers, determine what organs should be produced and the genes determine the details of construction. We shall find parallels to general development later when we come to neurological theories of learning.

Some evidence on heredity and intelligence   We shall avoid any lengthy debate on the perennial issue of nature versus nurture in the development of intelligence, staying within a limited treatment of the subject. Heredity's case will be considered here; the case for certain environmental influences will be examined in the chapter to follow. We shall also consider here the eugenic question of differential birthrate.

Similarities in IQ among offspring   We shall consider first the traditional question of the relation of heredity to composite measures of intelligence, in terms of mental age, IQ, or equivalent values. Later we shall consider relations of heredity to abilities such as are represented in the SI model. In either case, one of the most fruitful approaches has been through intercorrelations between siblings and between children and their parents as compared with correlations between unrelated individuals, with special attention to one-egg, or identical, twins. Such studies have been beset with the difficulty that environmental sources of determination have been necessarily confounded with hereditary sources, from which conditions the resulting picture must be considerably blurred. It is probably necessary to remind the reader that the evidence from correlational methods pertains to individual differences or variances and that any results must be interpreted in the light of the nature of the population studied. Any conclusions we may be able to suggest must be understood as applying to individual differences.

One-egg twins have been of special interest, because nature gives them identical genes and if heredity determines intellectual status completely, two such twins should test as much alike as the same person would if we could give him the same test twice without any aftereffects due to the first testing experience. The test of the hypothesis that heredity is the sole determiner would be to compare the correlation between one-egg twins with retest reliability coefficients for subjects of similar age, culture, and education. A great deal of interest has been given to the similarity of one-egg twins reared together as compared with the similarity of one-egg twins reared apart. It is assumed that those reared together have very similar environments whereas those reared apart have differing environments. A difference in the correlations for two such conditions would indicate the contribution of differences in environment. A number of studies have been of this type.

Table 15.1 summarizes the correlational results from 56 studies, involving 113 groups of paired subjects, twins and others. Reference was just made to the correlation between one-egg twins reared together versus that of such twins reared apart; so let us examine the first two rows of Table 15.1. There were 15 instances of correlations of one-egg twins reared together and 4 instances of such twins reared apart. In the former case, the median correlation was .88, with a range of .76 to .95. The correlation of such twins who were reared apart ranged from .62 to .85, with a median r of .75. In the difference between .88 and .75 lies information regarding the differences between the same homes, the same schools, and other similarities in environment and different homes, different schools, and other divergences in environmental stimulation and opportunity.

Comparisons can be made more meaningfully between coefficients of determination, or the *r*s squared, which are also given in Table 15.1. A coefficient of determination tells us the proportion of variance in the one variable that is accounted for by variance in the other. We can say that the one-egg twins have 77 percent of their variances in common when reared together and 56 percent in common when reared apart. There is a difference of 21 percentage points that can be attributed to the differences in environments for the two kinds of groups.

Assuming that the reliability of the kind of test used was .95 in each case, correcting the coefficients of determination for unreliability of measurement gives corrected coefficients of .86 and .62, with a difference of 24 percentage points.

We do not know just how great the differences in environmental conditions were when pairs were separated; they might have been very small in some cases and the average difference not at all large. More extreme differences in pairs of environments of separated twins might enlarge the differences in coefficients of determination. As a matter of fact, we cannot assume that when children are reared together, environmental conditions are the same. The lack of similarity in this respect might be indicated by the difference between .95 (the assumed reliability of the IQ test) and .77, the coefficient of determination for one-egg twins reared together. The difference is .18, or 18 percentage points.

The comparison of correlations between one-egg twins and correlations between two-egg twins is of interest. When both kinds of twins are reared together, it is sometimes assumed that environmental differences for pairs are the same (except where similar appearances of identical twins may encourage an increasing similarity of home and school treatments). Differences in correlation would then be attributable to differences in similarity of heredity for one-egg versus two-egg twins. In Table 15.1 there are two groups of two-egg twins, one group of like sex and one of unlike sex, both presumably under the condition of "reared together." In either case the median correlation is .53, and the coefficient of determination is .28. Comparing this value of .28 with that of .77 for one-egg twins reared together, we see a difference of .49. Ordinary siblings reared together

Table 15.1   Summary of correlational information concerning children with various degrees of relationship, when reared together and apart and when measured by means of intelligence measurements, mostly IQ tests *

Kind of pairing	Number of groups	Range of correlation coefficients	Median r	Coefficient of determination
One-egg twins, reared together	15	.76–.95	.88	.77
One-egg twins, reared apart	4	.62–.85	.75	.56
Like-sex twins, from two eggs	11	.44–.87	.53	.28
Unlike-sex twins	10	.38–.66	.53	.28
Siblings, reared together	39	.30–.77	.49	.24
Siblings, reared apart	3	.34–.49	.46	.21
Parent-child, parent-reared	13	.22–.80	.52	.27
Foster parent with child	4	.18–.39	.19	.04
Unrelated, reared together	7	−.17–.31	.16	.03
Unrelated, reared apart	7	−.04–.27	.09	.01

* From data provided by L. Erlenmeyer-Kimling, enlarged from data published by Erlenmeyer-Kimling and Jarvik (1963).

come close to the two-egg twins in similarity, with a difference of .04, which can be attributed to the fact that twins have more similarity in opportunity than do other siblings, who may be a few years apart. The numbers of groups involved might lend significance to even such a small difference.

Other comparisons of these kinds can be made in Table 15.1, but because of the confounding of the determiners of nature and nurture and other conditions short of well-controlled experiments, mentioned earlier, such comparisons are merely suggestive. A good experiment would see that identical environments were actually identical in every significant respect and that different environments were actually different in all significant respects. The amount and kind of difference in environmental features would be regulated in accordance with the experimenter's hypotheses. Such conditions are almost impossible to achieve with human subjects.

Before leaving this particular topic, we should consider a special point. Although Burt's data (1958) were probably included among those summarized in Table 15.1, they should be given special notice. The correlations tend to run a little higher than the medians for the same kinds of groups; for example, a few of the coefficients of correlation were: for identical twins reared together, .92; identical twins reared apart, .84; other twins reared together, .53; siblings reared together, .49; and siblings reared apart, .46. From this information, using an analysis-of-variance procedure, Burt estimated that 23 percent of the variance in scores could be attributed to environment and 77 percent to heredity. After certain adjustments had been made in the assessments of intelligence, the percentages became 12 and 88, respectively. It must be remembered that these percentages pertain to Burt's particular groups, with the use of particular tests and his particular statistical operations, as he readily recognizes. The generality of the conclusion is therefore open to question.

The general conclusion to be drawn from all such information, to which there is considerable agreement, is that both heredity and environment contribute conditions determining the general intellectual status of individuals, as measured by intelligence tests. Both heredity and environment, to the extent that the latter is stable during the formative years, establish upper limits for development. Rarely does any individual reach either limit. The status that he achieves will be below the limit determined by either heredity or environment, whichever is lower. No statement can readily be made regarding lower limits.

Special abilities and heredity   It is well agreed that generally the hereditary basis of intelligence cannot be confined to one gene. The finding of many different intellectual abilities in terms of factors definitely calls for a multiple-gene contribution of heredity to intelligence. Problems of biological inheritance of the conditions for intellectual status should now be cast in terms of the intellectual factors, and studies along these lines are already appearing.

As far back as thirty years ago, Luria (1936) was raising the question of differential hereditary determination of different memory abilities. His tests were for visual-memory ability and for paired-associates memory involving picture-word combinations, both when the connections were direct (logical) and when they were indirect (no logical implication). Comparing similarities of identical and fraternal twins, in very small groups, he concluded that there was evidence of hereditary contribution to status in all three memory-test performances at the preschool level (ages five to seven), but only for visual memory at school ages (eleven to thirteen).

Vandenberg (no date) recently studied the Thurstone PMA test scores of identical and fraternal pairs of twins, trying out a new method that emphasized similarities of profiles. He correlated intertwin differences in pairs of PMA scores, comparing similarly derived correlations for the two kinds of twins. From this information he concluded that there was evidence of hereditary determination in the case of scores for Number, Space, Verbal, and Word Fluency but not for Reasoning and Memory.

T. G. Thurstone and H. H. Strandskov (1953) approached the problem of inheritance in connection with certain special abilities by a different method. In each test, they obtained the difference between scores made by each pair of twins, some identical and some fraternal, with about fifty in each group (ages not given). Frequency distributions of the absolute differences on scaled scores were obtained; the distributions were dichotomized at the same score point; and from the 2×2 contingency table resulting, chi squares were computed. Of the 53 tests used, some were intellectual, some perceptual, and some psychomotor.

Of the intellectual tests that measure recognized factors, 6 had chi squares significant at the .05 or .01 level, with more numerous large differences in scores appearing for the fraternal twins. From the PMA list, significant chi squares were found for Space, Verbal, Word Fluency, and Memory. Differences between the two kinds of twins were not significant for the Number and Reasoning tests. There are two inversions as compared with Vandenberg's findings, just cited, with respect to Memory and Number. Since number-computation skill is so heavily practiced, it would not be surprising to find that heredity has little to do with status in it, even in a population where all have indulged in this practice.

Another factor in which Thurstone and Strandskov found indications of hereditary involvement is CFU-V, the cognition of visual-figural units, represented by two tests, Street Gestalt Completion and Mutilated Words, for both of which chi squares were significant. A factor whose test did not show a significant chi square was a Gottschaldt-figures test, which usually measures factor NFT, convergent production of figural transformations. One might have expected this ability to have a hereditary basis, since there is no clear place for its exercise in the natural course of learning. Perhaps such practice, like most perceptual learning, has just not been observed.

Stafford has done the most refined work with respect to inheritance in connection with special abilities, extending his interest to sex-linked traits. In a study with fathers and mothers and their teen-age sons and daughters (Stafford, 1961), he investigated the possible sex linkage for visual-spatial ability. His test was the Identical Blocks Test, in which the examinee is to tell whether two pictured cubes could be the same, considering interrelations of markings on their faces.

As is usual, Stafford found a sex difference in means of the spatial-orientation test. In the 18-item test, the fathers' and mothers' scores averaged 10.2 and 6.3, respectively, and boys' and girls' scores averaged 11.9 and 9.6, respectively. The correlations for the various pairings were as follows:

Father-mother	.03
Father-son	.02
Father-daughter	.31
Mother-son	.31
Mother-daughter	.14

Stafford estimated that these correlations are about what should be expected if the hypothesis of sex linkage is correct and the "gene frequencies" are 20 percent. The theoretical phi coefficients he estimated on this basis were .00, .00, .41, .41, and .17, respectively. When allowance is made for probable unreliability of the short test, the agreements are remarkable. Stafford's hypothesis that visual-spatial ability (factor CFS-V in the structure-of-intellect model) is inherited as a recessive gene in the X chromosome was well supported.

Differential birthrate   Some years ago, Raymond B. Cattell (1940) sounded the alarm to the effect that because parents of lower IQ tended to have larger families and those of higher IQ tended to have small numbers of offspring, the genetic effect of differential birthrate would in time be a systematic lowering of IQ in the general population. The correlation he found between size of family and IQ was −.30, and he cited other correlations in the negative .20s. Cattell also cited evidence for a drop of 4.4 IQ points in the United States and a decline of 3.0 points in Britain, the rate being 1.0 to 1.5 IQ points per decade.

Burt (1946) seconded the alarm, citing indirect evidence that the population IQ in England was declining by 1.3 to 2.5 points per generation. From retesting in certain communities, however, he found an actual decline of only 0.9 IQ point in the twenty-year period from 1919 to 1939. Allowing for some possible mitigating circumstances, such as migration, he estimated that the change might go as high as 1.5 points.

S. Smith (1942) had already reported that in Honolulu children aged ten to fifteen had been tested in 1924 and other children in the same age range in 1938. With no material change in population due to migration to account for it, the average change was a gain of 20 points in IQ. The change was greater in nonverbal than in verbal tests; so better acquaintance with English could not be the reason.

Cattell (1950) tested his own hypothesis by examining ten-year-olds in the same city in England in 1936 and in 1949, finding an average gain of 1.28; not a loss, as he had predicted. In a study in Scotland, Thomson et al. (1953) reported results of testing eleven-year-olds by the tens of thousands. The mean change in IQ was a gain of 2.3 points in fifteen years.

The only known study of this kind with adults was done by Tuddenham (1948). He selected 768 men in military service in the United States in World War II so as to be representative of all servicemen, and he administered to them a form of the Army Alpha Examination of World War I fame.

The mean score in that test during World War I was 62, from very large and presumably representative samples. The mean score obtained by the sample of World War II men was 104. A score of 62 fell at the 22d centile of World War II men, and a score of 104 fell at the 83d centile of World War I men. The gain was a full standard deviation. Of all the conditions that Tuddenham considered that might account for the increase in IQ status, the strongest contender, logically, seems to be the higher level of education of men in 1942–1945 as compared with men in 1917–1918. The means in years of formal education were approximately ten for World War II men versus eight for World War I men.

When Tuddenham selected from the files of data on World War I a sample of men with an average educational level of ten years, the mean Alpha score was 85. He speculates that in addition to the number of additional *years* of education typical in the later group of men there had been an improvement in *quality* of education, in terms of better schools, better teachers, and longer school terms. Other incidental information given was the correlation of .63 between Alpha score and amount of education in the World War I setting and .75 in the World War II setting. The correlation between the Alpha score and the Army General Classification Test score, of World War II, was .90.

Penrose (1954) injected a word of caution regarding Cattell's hypothesis and suggested some genetic principles that would also work against decline for hereditary reasons. His estimates of correlation between family size and IQ were as low as —.10, which is about the same as the correlation between physical height and size of family. Yet there has been a progressive increase in height over the years, perhaps due to improved economic conditions for the masses of people. Longevity is another trait that, for hereditary reasons, should be expected to decline, but the opposite trend is the case.

One genetic feature that works against decline is assortive mating, the tendency for like to marry like, with respect to IQ as well as other characteristics. But a more probable explanatory circumstance is that adults with the very lowest IQs tend not to marry and to have families; many of them are in institutions. Adults with the lowest grades of intelligence are therefore unreproductive. Individuals of the highest IQs continue to arise from matings of parents of moderate intelligence, which helps to keep up the numbers at the higher levels of IQ.

The gains that some investigators, such as Tuddenham, have found in successive generations could perhaps be accounted for in some part by evolutionary processes after all. S. C. Reed (1965) has pointed out the commission of a sampling error that has occurred in studies of correlation between IQs and size of family. He presents data showing that people of different IQ levels in the parent *generation* do not reproduce at the differential rates indicated by the negative correlation, if the childless members who were potential parents are taken into account. Without the childless members included, he found a typical correlation of —.30. With those members included, the reproduction rates at different IQ levels are as indicated in Table 15.2. Whereas the overall rate is 2.26 offspring per family, above an IQ of 115 the rates for IQ categories are 2.49 and 2.98; below an IQ of 86 the rates are 2.30 and 2.09. In such a situation there is room for natural selection to yield a progressive improvement in the genes that determine intellectual status. Reed points out that as our society becomes more technical, with a greater premium on intelligence, the differential in favor of higher IQs should increase.

General features of the human brain

In considering the ways in which intellectual functioning is dependent upon the brain and its physiological functions, we shall pay most attention to changing conceptions of the human brain during recent years. There are some misconceptions to be cleared away, misconceptions that have beset the paths of brain investigators and also psychologists who

Table 15.2   Reproductive rate of adults at different IQ levels when those who are childless are included *

IQ	Number of siblings in parent generation	Mean number of offspring
131 and above	48	2.98
116–130	376	2.49
101–115	1,122	2.20
86–100	1,010	2.22
71–85	283	2.30
70 and below	106	2.09
Total	2,945	2.26

* From a table prepared by S. C. Reed (1965).

have theorized about the subject. There have been some important discoveries by new methods and techniques, so that some things look quite different than they did even twenty years ago. Some of those changes will be brought out and their significance for psychology considered.

Some earlier misconceptions   In considering former misconceptions about the brain and its functioning, we shall not go back as far as Gall and Spurzheim and their discredited conclusions. But some of the misconceptions do have historical roots of long standing, and not without some foundation in empirical fact.

Functions of the forebrain   In deciding concerning the major excuse for the forebrain, for many years we have been misled by phylogenetic information. Because the chief contrast between the human brain and those of lower animals is the size of the forebrain, particularly the cerebral cortex, relative to the size of the brainstem and because the chief difference between man and lower animals psychologically is in intellectual level, it was natural to assume that the development of the forebrain and its cortex as seen in the animal scale is the secret of intelligence and of intellectual functioning. One of the frequent surprising findings in recent times is the fact that large portions of the cerebral cortex can be removed or injured without appreciable loss in IQ tests.

This is true of adults, but when similar cortical losses are sustained by infants or young children, the latter do not develop normally with respect to performance on intelligence tests. Hebb (1949) has consequently suggested that there are two kinds of intelligence, inherited and environmental. The latter is measured by traditional intelligence tests; the former not. Hebb defined the latter in terms of accumulated knowledge and skills, which require a functioning cerebral cortex to acquire but do not require so much cortex to retain. He conceives of the inherited kind of intelligence as being in the area of problem solving. In terms of SI theory, Hebb's environmental intelligence may be at least partially identified with cognitive abilities, for they, too, are very dependent upon the amount of stored information. His inherited intelligence may be at least partially identified with the producton abilities, divergent and convergent, which are essential to problem solving.

Another reaction to the general finding of little dependence of traditionally measured intelligence upon the cerebral cortex is that of Halstead (1947). He blamed this situation upon the limitations of intelligence tests. He hypothesized that what is largely missed in measurement with IQ tests is what he calls "biological intelligence." Performing a factor analysis, Halstead found a factor that did seem to be significantly affected by cortical injuries in adults. If his tests for that factor were compared with those for SI factors, it would appear that what he was measuring most is a composite of factors CSC (cognition of symbolic classes) and CSS (cognition of symbolic systems), two abilities that *are* probably missed entirely by ordinary IQ tests.

The conclusion to which all this leads is, first, that the trouble with traditional IQ tests in connection with the brain is that they define an intelligence that is far too restricted. When all kinds of intellectual abilities have been recognized, it is not necessary to posit a biological intelligence or to make a crude distinction between inherited and environmental intelligence. The methodological solution is obvious. One should use tests that measure known factors, and one must know that they do so even when applied to brain-injured individuals. It will then very likely be found that some abilities are affected by brain insults and others are not and that the location of the damage may have definite bearings upon which abilities are affected most.

The "misconception" under discussion here is in the context of the traditional limited view of intelligence, but it goes further, because it is being found that subcortical organs have much more to do with intelligent behavior than was formerly supposed. It was formerly supposed that the cerebrum is the seat of consciousness. But Penfield (1958) has pointed out that large portions of the cerebral cortex can be removed without loss of consciousness. A lower center known as the reticular formation has been found to have much more to do with whether or not a person is conscious. There will be a discussion of this particular organ later.

It was formerly supposed that the cerebral cortex is the main organ for integration of behavior. Why should it not be, for almost every afferent inlet sends excitations into it and it initiates fibers that connect eventually with all effector systems? But it has been found again and again that even cortical activities appear to need subcortical sources of integration, a point that will receive further notice later. Penfield (1958) concluded that integration between the two hemispheres of the forebrain is, indeed, a cortical affair but that integration between parts of the same hemisphere is a subcortical affair.

Milner (1954) has reported that connections between visual projection areas and the temporal lobe are through subcortical elements, not through the great "silent," "association" areas of the parietal lobe. Penfield and Roberts (1959) have said that connections between three speech centers in the cortex are through the thalamus, for removal of cortex between those centers has no observable effect, while severing connections with the thalamus does have effects. Tumors in the thalamus may result in aphasia. Thus, some of our cherished notions of the superior status of the cerebral cortex and of its areas formerly identified as associative or integrative must be drastically revised.

Pathway theory of nervous conduction   With the advent of Watson's behaviorism, the reflex arc became the basic model for all conceptions of nervous functioning in behavior. Between the stimulating energy in the receptor and the instigating activity of efferent nerve fibers at muscles and glands, between stimulus and response, there are to be found well-established conduction pathways in chains of neurons, afferent, central, and efferent. Such pathways were easily conceived to be true also for activity involving the cerebral cortex. Pavlov gave considerable support for this idea with his neurological theory of cortical activity in classical conditioning.

The brain was conceived as a passive receiver of stimulation, at the mercy of the individual's environmental forces. The central neural organs were conceived by analogy to a telephone exchange, whose only responsibility is to make and to maintain connections. The picture did not remain as simple as that, as we all know, but in principle the conception has been much as described. To complete the picture, it should be said that the formation of pathways from receptor to effector was believed to be by way of conditioning, classical and operant, with breaking down of resistances at synapses to complete the new pathways in learning.

Voices have been raised against this crude picture, and as new neurological information has come to light, they have become bolder and more convincing. Lashley was one of the earliest, when in 1929 he reported that cutting the cortex this way and that, presumably cutting pathways between visual and motor centers, did not eliminate memory for visually controlled maze habits. The amount of cortex removed from functioning was important, but its location was not.

A bit later, Lashley (1941) retreated somewhat from an extreme view of equipotentiality, a principle meaning that almost any part of the cerebral cortex could take care of almost any function. He suggested that segregated functioning of the cortex might more reasonably be correlated with unitary ways of psychological functioning such as are found by factor analysis.

Lashley (1951) later presented evidence against a strictly pathway conception of nervous functioning, evidence of a different kind from human subjects. He demonstrated that a skilled musician can make as many as 16 strokes per second, which is much too fast for the operation of successive S-R cycles; it would be impossible for that many innervations to be initiated separately in succession. He found that the experienced musician reads arpeggios as units and ripples them off also as units. Lashley's inference was that responses issue as organized systems, as in ordinary speech, when we initiate a remark by intending to express an idea and the organized speech pattern rolls out.

Hebb (1949) has rejected the idea of linear pathways through the brain centers, between afferent and efferent nerves, but holds to the idea of synaptic control of the direction of nervous impulses. He does accept the possibility of conditions other than synaptic resistance as the determiners of direction of impulses, such as timing of activities that could affect each central neuron, and the conditions of other neurons that might be involved.

Pribram (1960) has pointed out that even a simple spinal reflex does not fit the textbook picture of a functioning reflex arc. The reflex is demonstrably affected by both central excitatory and inhibitory activities. In general, even receptor activity is under some control from the cerebral cortex. About one-third of the efferent fibers in the spinal cord are said to serve such a function, contrary to previous notions. It is now known that efferent fibers leave the sensory projection areas of the cerebral cortex and that afferent fibers go to the cerebral motor centers. The effect of efferent impulses upon sense organs has been demonstrated by Hernandez-Peon, Scheerer, and Jouvet (1956). If action currents are recorded from the auditory nervous input from a cat's ears when a visual stimulus in the form of mice in a beaker, or olfactory and visual stimuli in the form of a fish, are applied, the auditory action currents are very much reduced. Thus, sensory input is regulated from the brain centers. Those centers are not merely victims of input from the environment. The organism is active prior to such stimulation and regulates to some extent the input from its receptors.

Pribram (1961) has also added the information that during classical conditioning, when nervous activity is electrically recorded, it is possible to trace the transmission of impulses from subcortical centers to cortical centers but not to trace impulses from there across to cortical motor centers. Either the method failed to detect such cortical connections, or Pavlov and many others have been wrong about the formation of new cortical connections during conditioning. Jasper (1961) also reported that after a human subject has been conditioned to withdraw an arm when a stimulus is applied to that arm, he will also withdraw the other arm if a like stimulus is applied to it. From all this we see that the nervous centers have active regulating functions rather than passive connecting functions.

Some special features of the brain

Before we consider relations of intellectual processes to the brain, it is important to have some further information about that organ. We shall give attention to only the more pertinent aspects of brain activities. We shall take a brief look at some of the subcortical and cortical parts and their operations and how they work together and also at features of the conduction of impulses within the brain.

The reticular formation   In the days when the concept of "attention" was acceptable in psychology, it was generally believed that this phenomenon, too, is a cortical affair. With the discovery of the reticular formation and its functions, attention has come back into psychology, although under different and more operationally descriptive terminology, such as *vigilance* and *filtering,* and it is now attributed to the reticular formation.

The reticular formation is variously described as being more or less inclusive by different writers. J. D. French (1957) describes it as being about the size of a man's little finger, located in the central part of the brainstem. Wooldridge (1963) states that it extends from the spinal cord to the thalamus and hypothalamus. Samuels (1959) extends it even farther, mentioning division into two functional systems, one the brainstem reticular formation, about which most writers speak, at the level of the medulla, pons, midbrain, subthalamus, and hypothalamus; and the other system the thalamic reticular formation, which consists of diffusely projecting thalamic nuclei.

It is the brainstem reticular formation (RF) that probably has the most to do with wakefulness, vigilance, and filtering. One of the RF's chief functions is to arouse and alert the cortex to incoming excitations. It does this through nonspecific fibers, which appear to convey no other information except that something of significance is coming. Without being sustained by this activity, the organism becomes drowsy and goes to sleep. When the RF is removed from monkeys, they go into a sustained coma. In view of these facts, the RF can properly be called the instigator of consciousness. The RF receives input from all sensory receptors, which makes possible integrating and regulating activity with regard to input. It is regarded by some writers as a "traffic-control" center (J. D. French, 1957), for besides serving its filtering function for input, it regulates and coordinates output to the motor organs.

Besides alerting the cortex as a whole, the RF provides selective alerting to certain areas at different times (Magoun, 1958). In an inattentive brain, input is diffuse and widespread. With attention to any one sense or even to any one part or aspect of input from the same receiving organ, there is a corresponding differential in the input. Spong, Haider, and Lindsley (1965) have shown by means of electrical recordings that while S is undergoing a vigilance task, electrical activity is increased in either visual or auditory centers when his attention is given to flashes of light or to clicks, respectively, the stimulus strengths remaining constant.

Patterned inputs from the sense organs seem to follow different pathways from those whose function is to alert the cortex or its parts. During normal sleep, patterned excitations may reach the cortex, but because there is no supporting alerting from the RF, there is no awareness. Such input, as we know, may be the instigator of dreams. It is probably correct to say that dreams come under the category of conscious experience, and apparently without alerting activation from the RF, although it is possible that there is a minimal degree of such activation, sufficient to sustain the dream consciousness. Without this qualification, it would not be correct to say that the RF is the basic center for consciousness. The patterned representation of information that is a function of the cerebral cortex is, after all, *its* contribution to what is called consciousness. But the way is open for a great deal of unnoticed information, as has been indicated in earlier chapters. The filtering operation in the problem-solving model of the preceding chapter can now be traced to its major brain center, the reticular formation.

Although the RF is in an excellent location to serve integrative functions, with all ascending and descending tracts passing through or near it, it must not be assumed that all kinds of integration are cared for by this center. As Fessard (1961) points out, there are other places involved in integrating sensory input, for example, the caudate nucleus. Side connections from both ascending and descending fibers are provided by lateral branches along the way at different levels, so that many other loci for integrative activity are possible. The direct integrating of the two hemispheres was mentioned earlier.

The hypothalamic centers   Centers in the hypothalamus have primarily motivational functions, without being the only centers involved in the motivational aspects of behavior. It is now well known that within the hypothalamus are centers concerned with maintaining homeostatic conditions with respect to temperature and water and food intake, as well as centers pertaining to sex, fear, and anger. Such centers are important to the initiation and sustaining of problem-solving activities and hence are important to the occasioning of exercise of intellectual functions. They are also very relevant to reinforcement in learning.

Through the work of Olds and others (Olds & Milner, 1954), there have been located a number of "reward" centers (or pleasure centers, by inference), which if stimulated directly by weak electric currents, are very reinforcing. When conditions are arranged so that by performing a certain act the animal closes the circuit that stimulates one of his reward centers directly, he is reinforced to repeat the act and to keep repeating it for some time. According to Bishop, Elder, and Heath (1963), such centers have been located in rats, goldfish, guinea pigs, dolphins, cats, dogs, goats, and monkeys and in the brain of a thirty-five-year-old schizophrenic.

These centers have been found in several locations, not only in the hypothalamus but also in the caudate nucleus, septal area, and amygdala, as well as in the mid-hypothalamus, posterior hypothalamus, and the boundary of the hypothalamus tegmentum. Stimuli that are too strong, however, may lead to aversive actions; there is punishment rather than reward. The connections of these centers to the reticular formation provide for the effects of motivating activity upon attention. Connections to the frontal lobes and underlying tissues suggest ways in which reinforcement effects in learning may take place.

While we are on the subject of motivation, something should be said about the operation of the feedback principle in this connection. The hypothalamus, among other parts of the brain, has a running account of organic conditions, through negative feedback mechanisms. The expression "negative feedback" implies need for corrective action. If the body temperature drops, a sensitive center in the hypothalamus sets in motion measures to step up body temperature. If this change goes too far, measures are set in motion to cool the body, as in a home that has automatic control of both heating and cooling devices. Thus are maintained homeostatic conditions, with primitive evaluative activities, in which certain centers match input information with desired status and act to change matters if the matches are not sufficiently close. The desired or adopted optimal condition can change under unusual circumstances, as when a person moves to a cold or a hot climate, thus changing his "adaptation level," as Helson (1964) calls such conditions.

Regulation by virtue of feedback information can be quite elaborate and precise, as Wooldridge (1963) points out. The cerebellum has long been known as a regulator of bodily movements. Wooldridge suggests that the cerebellum, receiving feedback information from widespread sensory sources, is sensitive to the center of gravity of the body and, like the stabilizer of the flight of a guided missile, in effect solves numerous mathematical equations in the process of issuing appropriate corrective orders.

Some features of cerebral functions   We shall be concerned more with psychological correlates of cerebral activity in the next section. Here we are dealing with some of the general facts of anatomy and physiology, giving special attention to the nature of nerve impulses and the operations of nerve cells. The electroencephalogram (EEG) will come in for consideration.

The cerebrum and its cells   The normal human adult cerebrum weighs about 3.5 pounds. Its much-folded gray cortex covering is said to be from ⅛ inch thick (Feindel,

1960) to 0.1 inch thick (Eccles, 1958) and to have an area of 400 square inches. It contains 10 to 12 billion nerve cells or neurons (according to different estimates), each so small that 200 placed contiguously in a row would extend as far as the diameter of a dime. Each of these neurons has several hundred inlets (dendrites) and outlets (axons), connecting up with numerous other cells. Each cell requires more than one other cell to excite it; hence a linear functioning chain is out of the question. But through the liberal number of connections a cell makes, it has been estimated that it could excite 8 billion other cells in 0.004 second (Feindel, 1960). The human brain is often compared with a computer, with the neurons corresponding to the electronic tubes or to the transistors in miniaturized computers. On this basis, it is estimated that a computer having as many units as a brain would be as large as a huge grain elevator, even with the best miniaturization.

While the young adult starts with the proverbial 12 billion neurons in his cerebral cortex, it has been found that he does not grow any more of them but loses many of what he has. Unexcited neurons undergo degenerative changes (B. D. Burns, 1958). Under normal conditions, the number of cortical nerve cells decreases by about 30 percent between the ages of twenty and eighty, and the brain shrinks in size by about 10 percent. At this rate, on the average, 100,000 cortical neurons are lost per day of adult life. It would seem that one way of stemming such a loss would be to ensure the exercise of those cells.

The limbic system   One subcortical mechanism that has received a great deal of attention in recent years from Pribram (1960) and others is the limbic system, an important part of which is the amygdala. This system encircles the thalamus and hypothalamus and, according to Weiskrantz (1964), has to do with affective evaluation. That is, it functions in classifying things as pleasant or unpleasant, in discriminating between things that are good to eat and things that are not, and in distinguishing between what to fear and what not, among other affairs. We shall find mention of these organs in connection with learning, for they appear to have some connection with reinforcement. Goddard (1964) states that the amygdala is a general regulator of drives, particularly fear. It is rich in connections with the cerebral cortex, the hypothalamus, and the reticular formation; hence it presumably has something to offer in connection with filtering processes.

Purpose of the cerebral cortex   Why do we have a cerebral cortex? The finding that the lower brain centers are capable of doing so much more than was formerly believed possible leaves us with the necessity to reassess the cerebral cortex's excuse for being. What can it do that the lower centers cannot do? Pribram (1961) has concluded that an important function of the cortex is to abstract the common properties of things, at least in its posterior areas. Although there are many variations in appearances of objects, we learn to identify them in spite of change and in spite of distracting information. This suggests the formation of class ideas or concepts.

The functioning of the cerebral cortex is by no means confined to the formation and use of classes, nor does Pribram believe that this is so. But a similar conclusion comes from Goldstein and Scheerer (1941), who found so often that cortical damage, particularly of the frontal lobes, was associated with loss of what they called the "abstract attitude," which in terms of abilities could be described as cognition of classes and perhaps as production of classes.

From an informational point of view, it may be offered as a general principle that the cerebral cortex provides an enormously increased refinement in information processing, beyond that possible by virtue of the lower centers. From the way in which fibers to and from lower centers fan out to the cortex, there are numerous correspondences to be expected in functioning between the two. The sensory projection areas, such as the visual, striate area, have detailed and systematic correspondences with the sensory surfaces, and the spreading of the cortex allows a kind of magnification of representations that could not occur with lower-center functioning alone. Finer distinctions are thus possible, and more elaborate systems can be formed. If there is duplication of effort between cortex and lower centers, it is part of the general policy of redundancy of mechanisms that is found to apply generally in the brain.

Cortical neurons and their operations   It is worth our while to see how neurons transmit information, especially because this provides a much richer basis of physiological fact on which to hang physiological theories of psychological events. Transmission from cell to cell is of unique importance because of its historical relevance for theories of learning.

Nature of the cortical nerve cell   The most distinctive thing about nerve cells generally is their projecting fibers that come into contact with fibers from other nerve cells at synapses. It looks as if their obvious function is that of transmission or communication, but there is much more treelike branching of dendrites than would seem to be needed for transmission purposes only. Bushton (1961) suggests that the nerve fiber is essentially a dilute salt solution with the very high resistance of 25 megohms per millimeter. Excitations are helped along by boosters at every millimeter, between nodes that can be seen under a microscope.

In its resting state, a neuron is electrically positive, with potassium ions on the inside 20 times as numerous as on the outside of its surface membrane and with sodium ions on the outside 10 times as numerous as on the inside, giving the cell a potential of 70 or more millivolts (Humphrey & Coxon, 1963). When the cell is excited by another cell or cells (it is said that it takes more than one other cell to do this), the excitation reduces the potential by the membrane surface's becoming more open to allow ions to pass through. The wave of excitation of this sort sweeps along the cell, with a pulse that lasts only a small fraction of a second. Many discharges may occur per second. The cell may also be subject to the action upon it of inhibitory cells, which increases potential rather than reducing it. With several excitatory and several inhibitory cells acting on it, the neuron responds to the algebraic summation of these two kinds of influence.

At any instant of time, a cell is either discharging or it is not. This on-off alternative has suggested another analogy to a digital computer, whose elements are also on or off at any moment. The combinations of on-off conditions provide the coding that transmits information. Thus, one view is that the coding of information in the brain is in terms of patterns of on-off firing and resting nerve cells. The transmission of the photographs of Mars that were taken by a camera in Mariner IV as it flew by that planet was a matter of one point at a time, each in its own shade of gray, which was coded in terms of sequences of 1s and 0s. It takes only 6 on-off elements to provide for 64 shades of gray, since 2 to the power 6 is 64, all the possible combinations of 6 digits, each of which is 1 or 0.[1] Such a line of thinking makes more reasonable the possibility of a collection of cortical neurons' providing sufficient coding to account for complex mental structures like the products of information.

Conduction at synapses   The way in which an excitation gets across a gap between neurons has been an intriguing problem of long standing. The reduction-of-resistance

[1] See Chapter 10 for further information on this point.

theory of learning has made the question important to the psychologist concerned with learning. It is now believed, and observations well support the belief, that a certain chemical is the bridger of the gap. When the cell is excited, its axon produces a chemical called acetylcholine (abbreviated as Ach), which has the chemical formula $CH_3 \cdot CO \cdot O \cdot CH_2 \cdot N(CH_3)_3 \cdot OH$ (Humphrey & Coxon, 1963). Having served its transmission purpose, this chemical is destroyed at the synapse. It is also found that two other chemicals, adrenaline and noradrenaline, or epinephrine and norepinephrine, have inhibitory effects. These chemicals are now receiving much attention in connection with psychological functioning.

Other possible modes of conduction   Although the picture of cortical neurons and their operations as briefly described is the most common one, there have been suggestions of ways other than through synapses in which one cell can affect another. One active fiber has been known to affect a neighboring fiber directly, but the effect is only a fraction of that through synapses (B. D. Burns, 1958). Nothing is said about possible induction effects, the fact that an activated neuron could generate an electromagnetic field that might affect other cells. Those who hold to field theory must assume something of this sort. If one neuron cannot produce much of an electromagnetic aura, a number acting together might do so.

After failing to find localized pathways in the cortex of a rat to account for learned habits, Lashley (1929) became partial to field theory, which has also been the view favored by gestalt psychologists. Lashley suggested that it is the *pattern* of excitation that is important, not that certain particular cells are involved. For example, when we turn our eyes, even slightly, in looking at a letter, different retinal and cortical cells are excited, but we still recognize the same letter in spite of the change of locus of activity in the brain. The analogy suggested by Lashley is that of an advertising sign composed of a bank of lights, with letters made by a certain combination or pattern of lights on, the pattern moving along the bank. The pattern is invariant, but the particular elements turned on are not.

It is probable that most theorists today would agree with Hebb (1949), who considers it adequate to find the basis for each cognitive invariance in some one location in the cortex outside the sensory projection center. Some kind of multiple-transmission theory is held rather than a field theory. A compromise might be that a field is set up by means of the multiple-transmission activity.

Some nonconductive possibilities   There are occasional suggestions that conduction is not the only function of nerve cells. Of course, it is believed that they also have retentive functions, which are not attributable to continuing activity as in the original experience. But the prevailing doctrine is that retention is in terms of semipermanent changes at the synapses. An alternative idea, as we shall see shortly, is that retention is in terms of changed molecules within the cell body. Humphrey and Coxon (1963) have suggested that a cell might even contribute to thinking without acting as a conductor. If retention is in terms of an altered structure within the cell body, of course, the fact that thinking depends upon stored memory, as was emphasized in the preceding chapter, would make their suggestion reasonable. Then there are glial cells, more numerous by far than the neurons and surrounding them, that may have psychological functions as yet unknown.

The electroencephalogram (EEG)   The typical electroencephalogram is a written record of fluctuations of electrical potential, obtained from electrodes attached to the scalp, with locations over various cortical centers. Various types of fluctuations have been identified and variously interpreted. It is generally believed that the record indicates brain activity, although some doubts have been expressed occasionally about this belief.

From the normal adult brain that is in the resting state, with eyes closed, the record is a sinusoidal rhythmic curve, with about 10 cycles per second, varying from 8 to 13 cycles in different individuals. This is the famous alpha rhythm, which is believed to be initiated and controlled in lower brain centers. Hebb (1949) cites Adrian as believing that the alpha rhythms come from synchronized discharges of neurons, but Wooldridge (1963) asserts that they cannot be attributed to the firing of neurons. Such conflicting views only reflect the fact that there are still many unknowns with respect to the meaning of the EEG.

Walter (1954), who has investigated the phenomena of brain waves rather extensively, reports that the rhythms differ in different parts of the cortex, being most marked in the occipital lobes. There are also great individual differences, in that one person in five shows no alpha rhythms at all and that in one person in five they continue when S opens his eyes. With most individuals, opening the eyes, with visual attention, is almost certain to break up the alpha rhythms, giving what are called beta waves, of much higher frequency. The beta waves are said to be composites of a number of different rhythms. Walter (1954) ventures to say that one component of the beta waves may be associated with attempts to visualize, another may be linked with verbal expression, and still another with visual recall. Patterns in the beta waves differ depending upon the ways in which individuals attempt to solve problems, says Walter.

The resting-state rhythms undergo changes with the age of the individual. Lindsley (1940) found that they show up first in the human infant during the first few months, with a rate of 3 to 4 per second in the occipital area. By the end of the first year, says Walter (1954), the rate has increased to 5 or 6 per second, rhythms which he calls theta waves. Faster rhythms occur at ages seven to eight, but the mature alpha rate is not achieved until ages thirteen to fourteen. Walter makes the interesting comment that a regressing adult reverts to theta and even delta (slower than theta) rhythms.

The EEG recordings are of interest to us here for the prospect that they offer for general psychological theory and for possible relationships to intelligence. One could be sure that it would not take long after the alpha rhythm became known before someone asked about its relation to intelligence and investigated the problem. Probably the first to do so was Kreezer (1940), who, with 50 mongolian subjects with mental ages ranging from 1.5 to 7.5, correlated the alpha index with mental age and found the coefficient to be .35. The alpha index is the percentage of the time during the recording in which alpha waves prevail. The measure of alpha amplitudes correlated .31 with mental age, and the alpha rate correlated .21. With 46 undifferentiated familial mentally deficient subjects, the correlation with alpha frequency was .32, the correlations with the other two indices being not significant.

With normal children, Lindsley (1940) found a correlation of only .02 with the alpha index. Theoretically, there are bases for predicting both positive and negative correlations. The fact that the alpha rate increases with age should lead to the prediction of a positive correlation with that value. If the percentage of time alpha is present indicates lack of attention and if attention is an aspect of intelligence, as Binet believed, the correlation with the alpha index should be negative. There is little basis for prediction of the correlation with amplitude, except as amplitude might be related to rate or to index.

In considering a number of studies relating EEG to intelligence, Vogel and Broverman (1964) conclude that alpha rate is correlated with intelligence but only in special populations, including the mentally deficient, young children, geriatric cases, and the brain-injured. The correlations with young children would probably be dependent upon the range of ages involved. Because of the natural maturing in both respects, the greater the range, the stronger the correlation should be.

The same authors state that no correlation of alpha rate with intelligence occurs in normal adults, and they offer the hypothesis that it should correlate with some component abilities and not with others. Mundy-Castle (1958) and Mundy-Castle and Nelson (1960), however, have reported significant positive correlations between alpha rate for adults and scores from the WAIS: .42 for the verbal IQ, .40 for the nonverbal IQ, and .51 for the total IQ. Five of the subscales also correlated significantly, but one of them, Picture Completion, had a negative correlation, —.43. It should be noted that one of these authors' samples had a mean IQ of 75 and included 15 mental defectives and 17 border-line cases. Studies with the EEG in relation to IQ and to intellectual functioning still have a long way to go.

Intellectual functions and the brain

In reviewing the relations of various intellectual functions to the brain, it would be desirable in a psychological presentation to organize the information along psychological lines. In accordance with earlier organizations, it would be consistent, for example, to follow structure-of-intellect categories throughout, taking up in turn the categories of operation, content, and product. Unfortunately, brain investigations have not proceeded along such lines, but the information issuing from the findings of such investigations can, nevertheless, be partially organized along those lines in a rough sort of way.

After some of the problems of brain-function investigations, from which inferences regarding psychological phenomena are to be drawn, have been considered, it will be convenient to group the information first under the headings of figural functions and semantic functions and then to give special attention to memory for any kind of information. It will be necessary to depart from psychological categorization, finally, in treating the category of frontal-lobe functions as a special case, the reasons for which brain investigators will readily understand.

Some problems of brain-function investigations   The dominant interest in brain functions, where intellectual matters are concerned, has been on localization of cortical areas that are associated with psychological events, for there has been much historical precedent, dating back to Gall and Spurzheim and to Flourens, Munk, Broca, and others. Having found definite brain parts from anatomical studies, it is most natural to ask what each part does. Very general consensus seems to have developed with respect to the primary sensory and motor centers, which have been mapped in some detail.

As to functions of the remaining parts of the cortex there is still much debate. Hebb (1949) pessimistically concludes that only the localizations of speech functions have been achieved. Jasper (1961) warns that if we do find cortical localizations, we may be dealing with something reflected by relative segregations of function of the lower centers that project their fibers onto the cerebral cortex. Stanley and Jaynes (1949) and also Zangwill (1963–64) may have found one of the reasons why the search for centers in the cortex has been less than successful when they suggest that the localization of functions is subject to individual differences. The fact of vicarious functioning, one part taking on new functions when another part has been lost, lends some logical basis for this idea, in that it suggests how flexible the brain tissue can be. Orbach (1959) makes the pertinent suggestion that we talk about "focalization" rather than "localization." The latter expression suggests compartmentalization that we know cannot exist; the multiplicity of interconnections makes this impossible. But certain "links in the chain" may well be more crucial than others in the performances of certain psychological processes.

Difficulty with methods   The methods that have been available are far from perfect. The oldest and yet widely used method, for what values it has to offer, is based upon brain injuries. Investigators have felt free to operate upon the brains of lower animals, making controlled excisions as desired in order to test certain hypotheses. They can also sacrifice the subject to see what parts of the brain were put out of use. But extrapolating inferences derived from such observations to human behavior is with some risk, and many of the distinctly human operations cannot thus be brought into consideration.

Not being able to apply such controls to human subjects, investigators can take brain-injured cases as they come, with brain insults in varied locations, patterns, and extents, and try to make the most of what the natural course of events has given them. Only post-mortem examination would show the extent and location of the full damage, and this perhaps years after the psychological examination. Clinical observations of some cases are sometimes dramatic, but exact replication is almost impossible.

Some of the psychological consequences of brain damage are transient, and some are due to secondary reasons. Behavior changes are often subtle, and no psychological tests of the right kind may be available. The lack of sensitivity of standard IQ tests for detecting deficits has been noted, as has the need for special tests, such as those representing factors, and for tests not now represented in IQ scales. Halstead (1951) makes further pertinent observations when he asks whether the tests used are adequate at all ranges of ability and whether a repeated testing measures the same ability as the first testing did. These are technical difficulties that need to be examined more closely.

Electrical methods have served better. Stimulation of points on the cortex has given most of the refined information about localization within the sensory and motor areas. But outside those areas, Jasper (1961) reports that stimulation yields some unpredictable results. Stimulation at one point may inhibit or disrupt speech; at another point it sets off a chain of integrated activity. With improvements, electrical stimulation at well-selected points and the recording of potentials in a similar way, in subcortical as well as cortical tissue, promises to be a most fruitful approach.

Assessing deficit with special tests   Consequent to the disillusionment with the use of IQ tests, more attention is being given to the use of tests of special abilities. The fact that many clinical symptoms come close to describing factors of intelligence suggests that this should be a promising approach. For example, Goldstein (1948) reported a patient who could count but could not say whether 7 is larger than 4. One might infer that the patient's numerical-facility ability was intact but that he had sustained a loss in ability CSR, the cognition of symbolic relations, which would include awareness of the serial order of numbers. Such a surprising combination of ability and lack of ability could thus be more meaningfully described.

Howson (1948) reported that his brain-injured sample was especially deficient in producing varied classifications of blocks with different objects pictured on their faces. His patients could classify the blocks in one way, which indicated that factor CMC, cognition of semantic classes (if it is assumed that the things classified were meaningful), was intact but that the patients had lost ground in factor DMC, the divergent production of semantic classes. If the things sorted were geometric figures, we should need to substitute F for M in referring by code to the two abilities.

Teuber (1956) has reported somewhat consistent losses in scores on a Gottschaldt-figures test in brain-injured cases, with little relation to cortical locations of the damage. One distinctive thing about this test is its measurement of factor NFT, the convergent production of figural transformations, at least in the normal adult population. This finding might suggest the hypothesis that transformations, as a product of information, have no localization in the cortex, but one would need to test this hypothesis systematically by applying other transformation tests, varying the content and operation aspects of the tests. As further instances of symptoms are discussed, their possible relations to intellectual abilities will be pointed out.

Figural functions

The right and left hemispheres   There is much accumulating evidence that in the great majority of people the right cerebral hemisphere is associated with figural abilities or functions and the left hemisphere, which ordinarily contains the bases for speech functions, is devoted largely to semantic abilities and functions. Much of the evidence will be cited.

Halstead (1947) stated that the correlation just mentioned depends upon the handedness of individuals; the right-handed, with left hemisphere dominant, have the speech centers in the left hemisphere. Penfield and Roberts (1959) comment that when the left hemisphere is injured in childhood, the right hemisphere may take over the speech functions. The latter case would be expected to provide an exception to the principle.

Milner (1954) concluded that right-temporal-lobe disorders are associated with defects in visual organization, as shown, for example, in performance on the Porteus Maze Test, which is very likely a measure of factor CFI (cognition of figural implications). Some tactual defects were also reported, but nothing is known as yet about tactual-intellectual abilities. Milner also concluded that left-temporal-lobe damage is associated with aphasia and other language disorders. One discordant result was that with right-temporal-lobe damage there was lower performance on the Wechsler Picture Arrangement test, a kind of test that measures factor NMS, convergent production of systems, the story produced in that test being a *semantic* system.

Reitan (1958) reported that Ss with right-hemisphere damage had losses in spatial orientation, which is a common name for factor CFS-V (cognition of visual-figural systems). Shure and Halstead (1958) reported more loss in verbal-logical tests in cases of left-hemisphere damage. K. B. Fitzhugh, L. C. Fitzhugh, and R. M. Reitan (1962) found verbal-test scores lowered for Ss with left-hemisphere lesions and performance (mostly figural) scores lowered with right-hemisphere lesions. Both differences were significant for recently acquired damage, but only the verbal impairment was significantly apparent for the chronic left-hemisphere cases. For cases with diffuse cortical damage, there was no difference in regard to loss of verbal versus figural abilities.

H. B. C. Reed and R. M. Reitan (1963) compared patients with right-side motor disorders with those having left-side motor disorders, assuming that the former had left-brain damage and the latter had right-brain damage. Right-side motor disorders went with inferiority in verbal tests, and left-side motor disorders went with losses in spatial and temporal tests, in accordance with the general principle.

With a still different approach, Matthews and Reitan (1964) obtained average profiles on the Wechsler tests for a number of different groups of brain-damaged cases, the groups being composed of those with right-hemisphere damage (R), those with left-hemisphere damage (L), and those with nonlateralized injury (N). They intercorrelated the profile for each group with that for every other group. The median of correlations for RR group combinations was .80, and for LL combinations .67. Other combinations of groups had the following median correlations of profiles: RL, .04; RN, .58; LN, .45; and NN, .64. It is clear that there were characteristic profiles for R cases and L cases and no similarity in profiles between the R and L groups. We need to know the nature of those characteristic profiles in order to say much more than that.

Matthews et al. (1962) applied factor analysis to the profiles of the Wechsler-Bellevue test scores, intercorrelating pairs of groups and finding two factors. Factor I applied to groups with lower performance-test scores, and factor II applied to groups with lower verbal-test scores. The right-hemisphere–injury cases had relatively high loadings on factor I and the left-hemisphere–injury groups on factor II, in line with most of the evidence contrasting right- and left-hemisphere functioning, i.e., figural versus verbal.

Zangwill (1964) concluded that defects in abstractions regarding visual objects are associated with right-hemisphere damage and that verbal defects are associated with left-temporal-lobe damage. He further cited evidence for the importance of the left-anterior temporal area for verbal memory and also for the affiliation of defects in spatial judgments with right-hemisphere injury (Zangwill, 1963–64). Right-side temporal lesions were found to be more important for picture interpretation and for nonverbal auditory perception. The last-mentioned defect might have been in factor CFU-A (cognition of auditory-figural units). One discordant note on the right-left distinction comes from Graham and Kendall (1960), who did not find that a visual-memory test was done more poorly by Ss with right-hemisphere damage.

Some striking clinical evidence has been brought out by Gazzaniga (1965), who studied several patients who had had the connections between right and left hemispheres separated surgically. Some marked differences in function appeared when tests affecting each hemisphere separately were applied. The left hemisphere functioned essentially normally with respect to language, but it had definitely poorer ability in executing drawings involving spatial relations. The right hemisphere was unable to communicate either orally or in writing. In nonverbal activities, the right hemisphere performed fairly well. When stimulation of the right hemisphere aroused emotion, this was shown also in the speech of the left hemisphere, without verbal understanding of what had caused the emotion, showing that there was some lower-center connection between the two hemispheres insofar as emotions were concerned but that there was apparently little translation between figural and semantic areas of information. We may infer that such translation ordinarily depends upon an intact corpus callosum.

Figural cognition; agnosia There is general agreement that cognition of perceived (figural) objects and events requires the involvement of something more than the primary sensory projection centers. Most is known about this problem in connection with vision. It was formerly believed that cortical areas adjacent to the visual, striate area are involved in the recognition of visual objects, but recent investigators have thrown considerable doubt on this conclusion (Lashley, 1948; Semmes, 1953). On the other hand, there is much evidence to support the rear portion of the temporal lobe as the main secondary visual center (Klüver, 1951; Semmes, 1953; Weiskrantz, 1964). Removal of the temporal areas of monkeys produced visual agnosias, a lack of recognition of visual objects, which can be interpreted as a loss in ability CFU-V.

It is not so certain that the same temporal region is a secondary center for somesthetic perception (Semmes, 1953). Weinstein (1964) has concluded that impairment in the right hemisphere in the parietotemporal area entails loss of tactual discrimination of three-dimensional sizes and discrimination of form. Some psychological impairments not associated exclusively with either hemisphere include discrimination of roughness, pattern, texture, and form in learning tactual patterns and in complex visual or tactual problem solving. In the latter instance we do not know how much the problems might involve semantic information; such information would presumably not be involved in the simpler discriminations of tactual information.

It is difficult to decide just how much visual perception is provided by activity in the striate area. Wooldridge (1963) reported that in the frog even the retina does a great deal toward providing meaningful discriminations. The eye of the frog is said to transmit four kinds of information simultaneously, analogously to a color-television set. It has a mechanism for detecting high contrasts; a moving-edge detector, in response to moving boundaries; a net-dimming detector, responding to sudden dimming produced by a spreading shadow; and a net-convexity detector, which responds to small dark objects entering the visual field. The cat's retina is said not to have these kinds of discrimination, those functions having been taken over by its visual cortex. Presumably the same is true of man's visual apparatus.

It is often reported that destruction of the striate areas means complete blindness. Teuber (1959) reports scotoma, or localized blindness, as a consequence of injuries to the brain in those areas, but he also observed that there was often much recovery shortly after the lesion had occurred. Symptoms included impairment of movement perception, of dark adaptation, and of tachistoscopic vision. Weiskrantz (1964) states that loss of the projection centers alone is not very damaging to either vision or hearing. On the other hand, Pribram (1960) expressed the opinion that even the recognition of stimuli (which could be interpreted as units of visual information), which means the cognition of constancies in objects, appears to depend upon the visual projection area. Although objects could thus be identified and presumably classified by virtue of striate activity, the formation of relationships (which could be interpreted as other products of visual information) depends upon what he calls the posterior intrinsic area, including the parietal lobe and posterior temporal lobe.

In Hebb's theory of visual perception, the elements of visual objects, such as lines and angles, are attributable to the striate area, but anything more than that, including appreciation of the identity of complete objects, depends upon prestriate and temporal areas. Semmes et al. (Semmes, 1953; Semmes, Weinstein, Ghent, & Teuber, 1955) seem to be of the opinion that the temporal area is necessary for recognition of visual objects but that visual-spatial orientation is a function of the parietal lobe.

Types of agnosia   In the history of neurological studies, a number of types of agnosia that very readily suggest cognitive abilities of the structure of intellect have been proposed. It would not be necessary for any localized injury or ablation to cause a defect limited to any one intellectual factor, and there are few uncomplicated cases. But when clinical observers find replications of symptoms that seem to line up with recognized unique abilities, we should give some attention to those symptoms.

Critchley (1953) reported two forms of visual agnosia, attributed to Lissaur's work, one of which Lissaur called apperceptive and the other associational. The former pertains to distortions of visual objects and the latter to recognition of familiar objects. The two kinds could be distinguished by means of drawing tests. With apperceptive agnosia, the individual cannot reproduce figures that he sees; with associational agnosia, he cannot recognize objects that he may have copied. The former type may represent a visual-perceptual factor not yet demonstrated, or it may represent factor CFS-V, while the latter is more clearly a matter of CFU-V.

Teitelbaum was credited with making even finer distinctions in the way of symptoms that apparently can occur separately (Critchley, 1953). There are a pictorial agnosia, an object agnosia, and a color agnosia; the second of these seems to suggest CFU-V, but the other two may represent perceptual abilities or they may arouse suspicions of functional disorders.

Mention of a spatial agnosia suggests factor CFS-V, and a body agnosia suggests CFS-K. A temporal agnosia could be either a perceptual factor or CMS (cognition of semantic systems), depending upon the more precise nature of the defect. The spatial agnosia involves disorientation and lack of appreciation of relationships between objects in space. Errors in location of two or more objects are common. There is difficulty in avoiding objects and in counting them, either by touching or by looking. The individual has difficulty in finding the right line in reading. S may report that objects are seen clearly but that his visual field is jumbled. He has lost ability to read time or to set the hands of a clock, to read maps, to do jigsaw puzzles or form boards, and to construct things in accordance with blueprints.

Of special interest is a disorder called "prosopagnosia" by Bodamer (Critchley, 1953), an inability to recognize faces, which might be a symptom of CFU-V. But a special form of the same agnosia involves ability to recognize facial expressions, which would suggest factor CBU, the cognition of behavioral units.

Inability to learn to read is primarily a cognitive type of disorder and should be classed with the agnosias rather than with the aphasias as is sometimes done. As Penfield and Roberts (1959) say, aphasia is not a defect of understanding, which is cognition; it is a disorder of *production* of information, a matter of encoding rather than decoding. The fact that dyslexia and alexia often occur with aphasias in the same person and the fact that both pertain to speech have been responsible for putting these disorders with the aphasias.

Dyslexia is defined by Critchley (1953) as an inability to recognize printed symbols. It is not clear whether this means inability to recognize single letters or letter combinations (words), or both. There have been reports of individuals who could copy letters, which may mean that ability CFU-V is intact, but who could not recognize even the most familiar words, which would mean a defect in ability CSU-V. Since Critchley defines alexia as word blindness, with little other agnosia, dyslexia must cover both letter and word blindness. He states that alexia may accompany lesions all the way from the occipital to the frontal lobes, but often alexia is found combined with aphasias; so we are not sure how much of the damage would be sufficient for alexia without aphasia.

In addition to dyslexia, there is a reading agnosia, in which it is word meanings that cannot be recognized. Presumably the individual can copy words and can say that he has seen them before. The defect suggests factor CMU, or verbal comprehension. Various degrees of alexia and even dyslexia may occur with reading agnosia. But at this point we must raise the question whether it is merely lack of an adequate fund of semantic units that is to blame. If there is reading agnosia in spite of a good vocabulary, we cannot attribute that disorder to low status on CMU. This would mean that the disorder is in the form of poor connections between visual word symbol and semantic unit. Such a connection should be interpreted as an implication of semantic units from visual-symbolic units.

A number of the visual-agnosia disorders have their parallels in the form of auditory agnosias. Goldstein (1948) reported three forms of auditory agnosia that parallel those just mentioned in connection with vision. One form is designated as "pure word deafness," an inability to recognize that certain sounds are language symbols. This would be a defect in factor CFU-A, cognition of auditory-figural units. In "auditory aphasia proper," Goldstein says, the sounds are recognized as being language symbols but the symbols, as such, are not discriminated to give recognition of words. This would be a defect in CSU-A and is parallel to the defect of not recognizing a word on a printed page as a familiar letter combination. What Goldstein calls "transcortical sensory aphasia" is described as inability to know what a word means when the person hears the familiar verbal symbol. This might suggest a defect in factor CMU, but as the question was discussed in connection with reading agnosia, it evidently happens in spite of adequate vocabulary. In this case it appears to be a weakness in auditory symbols implying semantic units.

Semantic functions; aphasias   Aphasias, like agnosias, offer symptoms that are very suggestive of intellectual factors. Although some writers express doubts about the relation of aphasias to intelligence, the knowledge of new intellectual abilities found by factor analysis definitely ties the aphasias to intelligence when the latter is appropriately conceived.

History of the aphasias   In view of doubts expressed in recent years regarding the distinctions that were formerly made within the category of aphasia, it is pertinent to review some of the history of those distinctions. Undoubtedly one of the most important steps in the history of neurology was Broca's discovery in 1861 of the cortical area that bears his name, in the posterior part of the third frontal convolution in the left hemisphere. Wernicke's discovery in 1874 of a second speech center in the first and second temporal convolutions of the left hemisphere also ranks high. It gave rise to the distinction between the sensory and motor aphasias, the former being classed with the agnosias above. Charles K. Mills was reported (Penfield & Roberts, 1959) as finding a special "naming center" in the 1890s, in the rear left temporal lobe. The only really recent addition (1958) to such knowledge was Penfield's identification of a "superior speech center," high in the central fissure, in the motor center of the dominant hemisphere.

Varieties of aphasia   Penfield and Roberts (1959), then, recognize three speech centers: the one in the temporal lobe (for visual agnosia), the superior center, and Broca's area. The connections between them are through the thalamus, not directly through intervening areas of the cerebral cortex. Habitually the centers function together, and damage to one is likely to be reflected to some extent in the others, but symptoms attributable to one and not to others indicate some independence of symptoms of the others.

In aphasia without agnosia, understanding (cognition) is not affected, nor is semantic memory, for with recovery from aphasia the person's memory store for concepts is found to be essentially intact. Neither is thinking apparently affected, although Goldstein (1948) has found that those who habitually think in terms of verbal concepts may show defects in thinking along with their aphasia.

Aphasias are troubles with verbal expression. One of the clearest symptoms is inability to think of a particular word, although the individual knows very well what he wants to say. Sometimes the person has this difficulty when the word he wishes to say represents an abstract idea, whereas he has no trouble with naming objects. The naming of abstractions is precisely the definition now given to factor NMU, the convergent production of semantic units. It is also well described as a word-finding ability. We do not yet know whether the task of naming objects will be found to be loaded on the same factor. We do know that NMU pertains to naming abstractions.

Elmgren (1958) points out some interesting parallels between some other historical categories of aphasia and factors of intellect. A jargonaphasia, identified by Pierre Marie, is a disorder in which the individual is able to produce a flow of words without understanding what they mean; it is sometimes found in mentally deficient individuals. It is tempting to associate this disorder with a high status on word fluency or factor DSU, the divergent production of symbolic units, where meaning is of no importance. A nominal aphasia, attributed to Head, may involve either the naming ability, NMU, or the ideational-fluency factor, DMU. A syntactical aphasia, also attributed to Head, a difficulty in producing connected discourse, sounds like factor DMS, or expressional fluency. With the emphasis upon grammatical or syntactical organization of sentences, however, it might be more in the order of DSS, the divergent production of symbolic systems rather than semantic systems.

Aphasia as a single dimension   Some of the most recent studies on varieties of aphasia have served to muddy the waters considerably. Schuell and Jenkins (1959) started with the hypothesis that there is essentially one dimension involved in aphasia, a general language ability, and that various symptoms indicate low levels on that dimension rather than kinds of defect or else are not very relevant indices of defect. These workers attempted to develop a Guttman scale, on the mistaken assumption that if such a scale were achieved, it would represent a single dimension. Even though a high degree of reproducibility in the Guttman sense can be achieved, the variable underlying the items (symptoms) may be representative of a multidimensional domain.

Schuell et al. (1962) later reported a factor analysis of symptoms for which they used a heterogeneous population of aphasic patients. The five factors that they reported had a little resemblance to known intellectual dimensions; for example, there were a factor that they called "visual discrimination," which bears some resemblance to factor CFU-V, and a factor of "visual-spatial behavior," which bears some resemblance to factor CFS-V, both of which have been identified as visual-figural cognitive abilities in preceding discussions and are associated with agnosias, not aphasias. A third factor was called "recognition of stimulus equivalence," which seems to be a composite of EFU (evaluation of figural units) and NMU, for it had some naming tests on it. The other two factors were a composite language ability and a composite motor-speech ability, not reduced to their more meaningful components. In a reanalysis (Schuell & Jenkins, 1962), the factors were much the same, except that the equivalence factor seemed more like ESU than EFU.

Meanwhile, Lyle V. Jones and J. M. Wepman (1961) were approaching the problem of dimensions of symptomatology in the aphasias with a quite different kind of test. Their tests were constructed on the basis of an associative or pathway theory, with the belief that the abilities, or defects, to be found in the domain of aphasic symptoms are concerned with connecting various sensory inputs with different motor outputs. The tests therefore require examinees to perform tasks of responding by speaking or writing, when the input is either oral or written. Several tests of each kind of connection were constructed, which means that for any one kind of input-output connection, the tests look like alternate forms of the same test. The outcome was quite predictable: Jones and Wepman found essentially input-output factors which may be regarded as artifacts due to method. Schuell et al. (1962) did not find that kind of factor. What needs to be done is to analyze symptoms of speech disorders along with marker tests for structure-of-intellect factors, including the factors hypothesized earlier in connection with various kinds of symptoms. It can be predicted that the latter kind of factors will be found to go a long way in accounting for symptoms of both agnosia and aphasia.

Memory and learning   One of the major concerns in the subject of the neurology of memory has naturally been with regard to the brain structures most responsible for storage of information. Some major issues have involved the matter of pathway versus field theory, the role of synapses, and the question whether emphasis should beat the cellular level or the molecular level in development of theory. We shall examine these matters briefly.

Learning to perceive   Quite commonly cited are Hebb's neurological theory of how we learn to perceive, at least visually, with the presumption that what happens for vision also holds by analogy for other sense modalities. His theory rests on the two concepts of "cell assemblies" and "phase sequences."

Cell assemblies are relatively closed systems composed of collections of cortical neurons that underlie perceptual elements, such as a line or an angle. As the learner fixates each part of a visual object, certain patterns of neurons in the striate area are excited together, as is a pattern in some area outside the visual projection center. In inspecting an object, the eye does not always fixate on the same point; thus in the striate-area activity the same cells do not always enter the pattern, but in the secondary visual center the same neurons in a pattern are excited together, thus forming a kind of constancy, underlying a figural concept. The varied inputs from the projection area become unified through a short period of reverberation that lasts beyond the time of each fixation, for a matter of perhaps half a second. Certain neurons get the habit of exciting other neurons within the closed system by virtue of the swelling or growth of knobs at the appropriate synapses. Supporting the idea of reverberation and the swelling of synaptic knobs are observed facts.

For the perception of objects as wholes, for example, a triangle, Hebb hypothesizes that more complex systems of neurons, called phase sequences, are developed. Eye movements play an important role in this kind of development also. Having developed cell assemblies for the elements of the figure, the individual learns to tie them together by much the same basic operations as those by which he learned to perceive the elements. As his eyes rove from one element to another, the cell assemblies underlying those elements persist in activity and the overlapping activities become welded together. What was learned about elements transfers to the learning of wholes.

The supporting evidence for Hebb's theory comes from the way in which mature human individuals, born blind but gaining their vision, go through steps in learning to perceive visual objects; also from the way in which rats who are exposed to elementary visual stimulation early in life, versus those who are not, later more readily learn to discriminate visual objects. The facts lend support to the theory but do not exclude other possible theories.

Localization of stored memories   The question of where in the brain memory storage occurs involves several special questions. Is storage in the same tissue that was active when the experience or the learning occurred, or does the storage occur elsewhere? Is storage in nervous tissue or in nonnervous tissue, or in both? Is storage in the cerebral cortex or in lower centers, or in both? If storage is in the cortex, are there special places for different kinds of things remembered? Are the mechanisms involved in learning and fixating memories the same as those that retain them? On all these questions there are quite varied opinions because there are few compelling facts. Are there different locations for storage of long-term memories than there are for short-term memories, not to mention intermediate-term memories?

Cortical role in memory   We start with somewhat negative notes. B. D. Burns (1958) points out that large portions of the cortex can be removed without loss of memory, exceptions being in parietotemporal regions. He also states that excision of any particular part of the cortex has never been found to be associated with the loss of any particular memory. The whole motor and premotor cortex of monkeys can be removed without loss of skilled movements, which suggests subcortical bases for retention for the latter.

Russell (1959) expressed the belief that memory is stored at all levels of the nervous system, even in the spinal cord, except for the motor tracts. Gerard (1963) expressed the conclusion that early in learning the whole cerebral cortex is involved, but with practice the physical basis for the ability contracts, becoming narrowly circumscribed. If this were true, it would not be surprising to find that particular memories could be eliminated with the surgical knife. Gerard cites evidence from electrical recordings in support of the principle, however, and it may be that the circumscribed nervous elements are nevertheless rather widespread as to location.

Galambos (1961) concluded that in some mammals conditioned reflexes (CR) can be lost by ablation of the cortex but that the same CR can be relearned. He takes this to mean that in learning a CR the cortex is the preferred organ but that it is not essential. He also reported the observation that certain simple discrimination habits can be more readily learned without the cortex, but not complex ones.

In support of the role played by the cortex in learning, Wooldridge (1963) cites the experiments of Sperry (1961) on the transfer of learning from one hemisphere to another. In the Sperry experiments, the animal is taught to make a certain discrimination, with visual or tactual input, conditions being so arranged that only one hemisphere is involved. The corpus callosum that connects the two hemispheres, point for point, is then severed, and the subject is tested for the retention of the skill in the presumably nonexercised hemisphere. He performs successfully, which leads to the inference that while he was learning the discrimination with activity in the one hemisphere, a "carbon copy" of the memory trace was being laid down in the other hemisphere. With the two hemispheres cut apart before training, the animal could be trained for contradictory habits in the two. Sperry was able also to locate the basis for the learned discriminations in the cortex near the projection areas concerned. Habits involving coordinations of inputs from tactual and visual sources, however, involve the brainstem, for cutting the cortex between the projection centers after learning did not interfere with such a coordination. The evidence from these sources favors the conclusion that memories are retained in neural elements where the activity occurred in learning. Konorski (1961) supports this view in finding that recent memory for auditory information is lost with ablation of temporal areas adjacent to the auditory projection centers in both hemispheres.

Storage of veridical memories Penfield (1955) announced the startling discovery that with electrical stimulation in the temporal lobe of a human brain, a whole sequence of memories from life experiences could be revived with hallucinatory strength and character. This could be done in only certain individuals, but the revival was complete and presumably exactly as the person had experienced it. Such memories cannot be voluntarily recalled. There is no evidence for deciding whether the location of this storage is in the temporal lobes, the hippocampal regions underneath them, or some connected cortical region. Penfield's conclusion, however, was that a full running account of our experiences is stored somewhere and that the key that unlocks it must be applied in the temporal lobe.

In summarizing this section, we may give the following answers to the questions asked at the beginning. As to place of storage of memory traces, we may say that the cerebral cortex is definitely involved but that no one trace is restricted to a limited position; storage probably has a relatively widespread basis. Storage may also involve lower brain centers, perhaps, as Russell (1959) states, even the spinal cord. In the cortex, memory storage is evidently not a function of the primary sensory or motor centers; they appear to have only input and output functions, respectively. There is some support for the idea that traces are stored where the activity was initially and that areas near the sensory projection centers are significant for storage of at least figural information associated with those centers. Questions of the locus of learning and of temporary storage remain to be discussed.

Roles of the amygdala and hippocampus   A number of investigators and writers agree that the limbic system, particularly the amygdala and the hippocampus, have something significant to do with learning and with committing information to the permanent memory store. Just what those organs have to do with memory storage, however, is not definitely known. Much evidence may be cited: Pribram (1961) stated that the hippocampus seems essential for conditioning. Kimble and Pribram (1963) found evidence that bilateral hippocampal lesions interfere with learning a sequence of responses, in other words, a behavioral system, but that they do not interfere with learning simple discriminations. Wooldridge (1963) states that loss of amygdaloid-hippocampal areas means loss of long-term memory. He offers the hypothesis that organs under the temporal cortex are necessary for transforming intermediate-term memory into long-term memory, when the former is defined in terms of a few minutes' duration. He finds it significant that these organs are immediately under the points at which Penfield can arouse complete recall of experiences.

On the other hand, Zangwill (1963–64) finds that bilateral loss in the hippocampal system is associated with loss of memory for recent events. Nauta (1964) suggests that the hippocampal formation and the limbic system are not the place where storage occurs but that they may act as a kind of a valve, determining what information gets into permanent storage. There is an impression, from common observation, and there is much experimental evidence as well, that we remember things that we intend to remember and that there is some tendency to remember them for about as long as we intend to remember them. There must be some mechanism that makes such distinctions and determines what shall be remembered for longer periods of time.

Gerard (1961) states that the amygdala exerts an inverse influence on fixation of memory traces; other parts of the limbic system must have the reverse effect, in view of all the evidence cited. This implies that the limbic system does have a kind of yes-no decision prerogative with respect to what is stored. Gerard also finds that the hypothalamus and the recticular formation are involved. Glickman (1961) attributes the fixation of memory traces to the hippocampus and amygdala and suggests that they may act through the reticular formation, which, in turn, alerts the cerebral cortex. The alerting step may furnish additional excitatory energy to help fix the memory trace. Thus, the limbic system together with the hypothalamus, acting through the reticular formation, may be the neural basis for reinforcement in learning and consequent fixation of the trace.

Fixation of the memory trace   Ever since the discovery of the phenomenon of retroactive inhibition, announced about seventy years ago by Müller and Pilzecker (1900), there have been numerous efforts to determine its causes, with the expectation that very much could be learned about retention in general if those causes could be found. Müller and Pilzecker held to a perseveration hypothesis, to the effect that following the stimulation of the brain tissues involved in the learning, a perseverating activity that naturally goes on is instrumental in fixing the memory trace. Anything that interferes with this perseveration can damage the fixation of the trace, causing forgetting.

In spite of the fact that modern experimental studies have demonstrated that interfering information, whose input (interpolated learning, IL) follows that of the original learning (OL), can account for at least some loss of retention in terms of confusions of information, there has been no proof that perseverative action is not a natural event and is not needed for fixation. Support for the perseveration hypothesis has been provided by certain experiments, those by Duncan (1949) being most often cited. Duncan taught rats a conditioned avoidance response; then, after selected time intervals following completion of practice, he gave the brains of different groups electric shocks sufficient to produce convulsions, with the assumption that this should be sufficiently violent to break up any natural perseverations. For increasing intervals up to one hour after practice, he found losses in retention of the conditioned response with decreasing amounts of forgetting. Attempts to show that Duncan's type of results can be attributed to other causes, such as anxiety or conflict, have apparently not been sufficient to call for adoption of an alternative to the perseveration hypothesis (Glickman, 1961).

The well-known phenomenon of retrograde amnesia, in which a brain injury causes forgetting for most recent events preceding the insult, with decreasing loss for earlier events, also supports the perseverative hypothesis. The application of electroconvulsive-shock treatment to psychotic patients provides evidence of a similar nature.

Drastic drops in oxygen supply, to a level equivalent to that found at an altitude of 30,000 feet, which permits only a very low cortical activity, are also effective in interfering with fixation of memory traces. Reducing the body temperature of a human subject to 15°, as during heart surgery, thereby reducing brain activity to a low level, apparently does not produce forgetting (Humphrey & Coxon, 1963). With hamsters, Gerard (1963) reduced body temperature to 5°, at which they hibernated, with almost no brain activity. After an hour or two the hamsters were warmed and then given electroconvulsive shocks. This treatment seemed effective in producing loss of memory for maze running. It appeared that the cooling merely suspended the perseverative process, which could have been revived on warming, with interruption by the shocks. Animals cooled and tested after recovery that was not followed by shocks were found to have had no loss of memory.

The recent conception of the perseveration process is that it occurs in reverberating circuits. There are observations to the effect that cells do continue to be active and more sensitive immediately after they have been excited. Fessard (1961) suggests that an alternative to a pulsating, ghostlike hangover would be a persistent tetanoid condition in a set of cells. Feindel (1960) has suggested a means by which a cell may reexcite itself. Some cortical cells, he says, have axons that connect up with the cell's own dendrites, giving them samplings of their own outputs and possibly serving to keep a circular activity going.

Another possibility, in view of discussion in the previous section, is that something in the limbic system, with its connections with hypothalamus and reticular formation, contributes to keeping certain patterns of excitations active, thus deepening or extending traces, or both. The last statement is made in recognition of the traditional view that repeated excitation deepens impressions. Also to be considered is that the perseverating activity might serve to bring additional neurons into the pattern or might duplicate the pattern in other cells. Sperry demonstrated how learning produces "carbon copies" in the opposite hemisphere; it is possible that there is a mechanism whereby carbon copies can be made within the same hemisphere. This would produce a redundancy of stored information, but that is precisely what we may have, particularly in overlearning.

Molecular theories of retention   It is a minimal step in the theory of retention of memory traces to say that neurons are changed; this much is obvious. The significant aspect of any neurological theory of learning and memory is to specify the nature of that change.

The most striking new answer to the question of how information is coded and recorded in memory storage puts the finger first on the nucleic acids, DNA and RNA, which were discussed under the topic of heredity earlier in this chapter. It was indicated there how the DNA molecule can code and transmit from one generation to the next the instructions for the construction of a new organism. By a process of decoding, the new organism develops according to plans laid down in the pattern of bases along the DNA molecule. DNA molecules, or DNA-like molecules, have been found to exist outside the nucleus, in other words, to be apparently free to serve purposes other than carrying hereditary information. But, as Gaito (1963) has pointed out, the DNA molecule is known to be very stable, presumably not subject to ready changes, such as would be required in learning.

The RNA molecule, which is patterned after the DNA molecule of the individual and which is said to serve as a "messenger" from the nucleus to the cytoplasm and to control the development of proteins, is suspected of being less stable, yet of being so constructed as to carry a multitude of coded information. Could it be the memory molecule? Hydén (1959) has usually been given credit for suggesting that RNA may play a key role in personal memory, as DNA serves the role for family and racial memory.

Considerable indirect evidence can be cited in favor of the idea, much of it having been assembled by Gaito (1963) and Landauer (1964). RNA is found in unusual quantities in the gray matter of the brain. Its quantity increases and decreases with the age of the person, in parallel with the waxing and waning of his memory powers (but also in parallel with changes in other powers). The production of RNA molecules in cells is proportional to the amount of activity of those cells; concentration increases with stimulation, and also changes in base ratio. Injection of RNA into presenile patients was accompanied by improvement in memory.

When planaria have been trained to contract as a conditioned response to a light stimulus paired with shock, evidence that RNA molecules may have carried the memory trace has been elicited in various ways (Jacobson, 1963). When one of the planaria is cut in two, head and tail being separated, each regenerates another tail or head end and the regenerated animals show some savings in conditioning. When the worms were regenerated in ribonuclease, an inhibitor of RNA development, the regenerated heads showed savings, the regenerated tails not. Cannibal worms that had eaten trained worms showed some savings.

The evidence has not all been in favor of the theory. Bennett and Calvin (1964) report complete failure in attempts to teach planaria habits of any kind. Hartry, Keith-Lee, and Morton (1964) found that it is necessary only to expose planaria to light and to shock, then to feed them to other planaria, to find that the cannibals learn the light-shock conditioning more rapidly. As a matter of fact, it was necessary only to feed and handle the planaria that were to become cannibal food in order to give the cannibals an advantage in conditioning. In the latter instances, it may be that the extra stimulation given the planaria that were to become food instigated a greater production of RNA, which served as an available supply for the cannibal members of the species.

There is evidence, such as that with flatworms, from animals higher in the phylogenetic scale—rats. Rats injected intraperitoneally with RNA daily for fifty-three days learned an avoidance CR to a buzzer in an average of about ten trials, as compared with a control group that learned in an average of about twenty-five trials. Similar results were obtained after treatment lasting one month and also one or two weeks, but not just three days (L. Cook, A. B. Davidson, D. J. Davis, H. Green, & E. J. Fellows, 1963). Rats receiving intracisternal injections from brain substance obtained from trained rats, over a period of seven days, performed better than rats receiving injections from untrained rats or than rats with no such treatment. Babich, Jacobson, and Bubash (1965) found that hamsters that were trained to run to a food cup in response to a click signal furnished brain RNA that apparently facilitated learning of the same habit in rats, in a cross-species transfer. But Luttges, Johnson, Buck, Holland, and McGaugh (1966) failed to find that when there was injection of nucleic-acid material from trained mice to untrained mice, there was any transfer of memory, even with the experiment varied in many ways.

It is difficult to see why the animals receiving such injections do not treat the RNA molecules as foreign proteins and attempt to destroy them. It is also possible that the injections contain other chemical substances that have facilitating effects, apart from the supplying of coding material. As Briggs and Kitto (1962) point out, even a changed RNA molecule produced by learning in an organism's brain might be treated as a foreign substance and be attacked and eliminated. The individual's RNA structure is determined by its DNA structure, and its structures are compatible with its defense systems. The upshot of the conflicting evidence is that the individual's RNA may well have something to do with his learning and memory, but we do not yet know just what its contribution is.

There have been other ideas as to what kinds of molecules may be the coded holder of memory traces and also suggestions as to how RNA may play its role. There are large and complex molecules other than RNA that might serve the purpose of recording information. Halstead (1951, p. 269) commented that learning leaves ". . . transformation of proteins from random to oriented, organized configurations. . . ." Briggs and Kitto (1962) believe that enzyme changes within the neuron are the most likely carriers of memories. Enzymes can differ from one cell to another, in kind as well as in quantity. The amount of an enzyme produced in a cell depends upon a substrate. Repeated stimulation of a cell increases activity of the substrate in producing enzymes. The sensitivity of the cell depends upon the amount of enzyme available. Enzyme production is dependent upon RNA, which, in this view, has an indirect and general relation to the formation of memory traces and is not the actual carrier of information.

Such a view is consistent with the report of Gerard (1953) that nerve fibers swell on the passage of impulses and that the swelling persists at least for hours, if not for days or even years. They also show changes in potential, which could be the perseverating condition in place of reverberating discharges. Humphrey and Coxon (1963) are of the opinion that the increase in enzymes occurs in the knobs at the synapses, thus combining a molecular theory with a synapse theory.

But Landauer (1964) has a somewhat different conception of how enzymes operate in memory. Enzymes serve not to reduce resistance at synapses but rather to make the nerve cell more selectively sensitive. He suggests that when neurons are excited, RNA molecules enter them from surrounding glial cells. This alters the neurons' synthesis of proteins in accordance with what is going on in the central nervous system at the moment. Each cell becomes more sensitive to certain patterns or frequencies of excitation, thus being tuned to unique patterns of excitation.

There is some evidence that the chemical basis for very recent memories is different from that for longer-term memories. There is a hypothesis that for the first minutes after learning there are reversible molecular changes, following which self-replicating biosynthetic processes are needed (Barondes & Cohen, 1966). The evidence is that injection of puromycin dihydrochloride into the temporal regions of mice does not seem to interfere with learning an avoidance response or with normal retention for as long as fifteen minutes, but longer retentions become progressively worse with later injections. Injections of saline solutions in control mice did not have such effects, nor did the injection of puromycin into the frontal lobes have such effects. Again, the temporal lobes appear to have some critical role in determining long-term memories. But the actual storage could be elsewhere.

One source of hesitation in accepting memory recording in terms of molecular structure has been that it is difficult to see how excitations entering the brain centers in terms of patterns of pathways get translated into molecular changes, on the one hand, and how molecular structures get translated into activity in efferent pathways in leaving the center, on the other. Such difficulties should not be used as arguments against a theory; there are possibilities that they could be overcome. The concept of tuning, with possible electrical-induction activities, might help to solve the problem. There should be encouragement from knowing that coded information in the genes is translated into differentiated body structure. A theory that envisages memory storage in terms of conditions for patterns of on-off combinations among conducting neurons does not encounter so much difficulty with the translation problem, hence probably has more popular appeal.

There appears to be a superabundance of alternative conditions and processes in connection with neuron activity that could contribute to the operations of memory storage. What is needed now is information that would help to make some decisions among them. Possibly some feature of neuron activity or structure that is important has still been overlooked. All that can be said at present is that the search is warming up and that prospects of finding relevant information have improved.

Frontal-lobe functions   Although the frontal lobes are often popularly believed to be the main seat of intelligence, no doubt because of man's apparently superior development there, investigators of brain functions are quick to tell us that this is not so. They point out that other cortical areas have had as much superior development and that it has been much easier to demonstrate associations between intellectual functions and the parietal and temporal regions. They also point out that large parts of the frontal lobes can be removed without much apparent effect upon intellectual functioning. There are more observable effects in terms of other personality traits.

More detailed assessments of intellectual functioning associated with damaged frontal lobes, however, reveal deficits on which there is some agreement. Shure and Halstead (1958) find that with frontal-lobe damage there is some loss in abstracting ability, which can be interpreted as concept formation, a loss also found by Teuber (1959). Somewhat frequent mentions of loss of judgment suggest involvement of the frontal lobes with the operation of evaluation (Halstead, 1951; Wooldridge, 1963). Pribram (1961) has insisted that the brain has a mechanism for matching information and for accepting or rejecting matches, which is a fair description of evaluation. More specifically, Teuber (1950) found a deficiency in figure-matching ability, which appears to describe factor EFU, the evaluation of figural units. Pribram (1960) mentions that what he calls the anterior intrinsic area, of which the frontal lobes are an important part, is concerned with judging whether our actions fulfill our intentions. This would seem to describe the factor hypothesized by the structure-of-intellect model as EBS, the evaluation of behavioral systems. Loss of aesthetic sensitivity is sometimes mentioned (Halstead, 1951). This, also, might represent an evaluative ability, although no evaluative abilities involving aesthetic criteria have as yet been demonstrated. Clinical observations sometimes indicate deficiency with respect to judging conduct, which is also logically within the evaluation category.

Other kinds of symptoms associated with frontal-lobe damage appear to be concerned with the product of systems. There are relatively frequent mentions of loss of organizing ability or of complex planning (Halstead, 1951; Pribram, 1960; Wooldridge, 1963) and of dealing with complexity in general (Rosvold & Mishkin, 1950). In both human and simian individuals, there is difficulty in carrying out sequences of actions as formerly (Pribram, 1960; Stanley & Jaynes, 1949). Sequences of actions can be regarded as behavioral systems. The learning of sequences of actions is also hampered by damage to the frontal lobes (Stanley & Jaynes, 1949). Under the same circumstances, there have been reports of difficulty of lower animals with delayed-reaction tasks (Stanley & Jaynes, 1949). Konorski (1961) regards the ability to perform in the delayed-reaction task as a matter of memory for spatial arrangements, which would be SI factor MFS-V, another systems ability.

Two other defects found associated with the frontal lobes also suggest SI factors. There have been reports of deficiency in maze tests of the Porteus type (Porteus & Peters, 1947; Zangwill, 1964). By analysis it has been found that tests of this kind measure a factor of perceptual foresight, or CFI (the cognition of figural implications) in SI designation. Zangwill (1964) cited evidence to the effect that there is some loss in ability to shift classes in making classifications. This would seem to be SI factor DFC or DMC, depending upon whether the information classified was figural or semantic.

It would appear, then, that the frontal lobes are rather rich in prospects for identification with certain intellectual functions, when special tests are used to assess those functions. The most likely SI operation to be associated with the frontal lobes appears to be evaluation. The most likely product to be involved seems to be that of systems, with some possibility, also, of implications and with the product of classes a possible third case. No kind of content appears to be distinctive in connection with those lobes, unless it should be behavioral, of the self-information type.

Chemical conditions

In the survey of what is known concerning the relations of certain chemical conditions to intellectual development and functioning, several distinctions are conveniently made. The chemical condition in question may be endogenous, a natural state of the individual; or it may be exogenous, something imposed upon the nervous system from without the individual, such as food, drugs, injections, or accidental ingestion. The endogenous drugs may be natural components of the brain, or they may be brought to the brain by way of the bloodstream, as in the form of hormones. Most of the studies of the relation of chemicals to brain functioning, as usual, have emphasized general consequences, such as changes in IQ-test performance. More recently there has been some interest in whether special abilities are related to or affected by certain chemicals differentially. There is also the difference between temporary and continued application of the chemical and between temporary and lasting effects.

Effects of endogenous chemicals

Oxygen supply; anoxia   A universally needed chemical element in brain functioning is oxygen. Much interest has naturally been centered in that substance. A good supply of oxygen is essential for brain functioning and is said to be more important for the cerebral cortex than for other parts (Carmichael, 1940). Deprivation of oxygen may leave permanent defects, even when limited to a period of eight to ten minutes. This has become an increasingly important consideration because of medical success in returning individuals to life after heart stoppage. Chronic anemia in childhood is said to have permanent damaging effects (Carmichael, 1940), and mental symptoms accompany pernicious anemia in adults (Shock, 1939).

Experiments with human subjects in decompression chambers and at high altitudes have not always shown much lowering of intellectual functioning (Phillips, Griswold, & Pace, 1963; Shock, 1939), because individuals can compensate by exerting extra effort. In the second case, they can also become adjusted to higher altitudes. Shock reported some deficit in memory, attention, and judgment, however, as well as in scores from the Army Alpha Examination given under oxygen equivalent to an altitude of 20,000 feet. Thirty subjects lost from 1 to 54 points in the latter test.

Anoxia at the time of birth has unfavorable effects, and an even greater effect has been found in rats when anoxia is applied before birth. F. K. Graham, C. B. Ernhart, D. Thurston, and M. Craft (1962) reported that children with anoxia at birth, as compared with those without that experience, were significantly lower in Stanford-Binet IQ when tested at the age of three. The most marked loss was found in a special Concepts test, more than in a Vocabulary test.

B. W. Meier, M. E. Bunch, C. Y. Nolan, and C. H. Scheidler (1960) applied controlled reduction in oxygen to prenatal rats at different times preceding birth, as well as to both rats and cats immediately after birth. Under the latter condition, thirty minutes of anoxia gave no effects later in learning or retention of a complex maze habit. Sixty minutes of anoxia, however, did have later effects in maze performance but not in learning simple discriminations. Anoxia with cats immediately following birth affected adversely later learning in a puzzle box and retention of a learned symbolic solution. There was no damage to learning simple discriminations, but stereotyped kinds of behavior were observed and the discriminated stimuli had to be kept in close proximity to each other.

Rats that had had two hours of anoxia (equivalent to an altitude of 30,000 feet) before birth were later significantly inferior in learning and retention of a maze habit. Simple discrimination learning was poorer, and there was slightly less transfer of learning. The greatest amount of defect occurred when the anoxia preceded birth by ten days. The least defect came with anoxia treatment fourteen to seventeen days before birth.

In a follow-up study of children who had suffered different degrees of anoxia at the time of birth, Corah, James, Painter, Stern, and Thurston (1965) found that intellectual differences that appeared at the age of three years had diminished by the age of seven. As compared with a control group, the anoxic children were slightly deficient in the WISC Vocabulary test, and observations led to the conclusion that they were deficient in the area of social competence.

Thyroxine; the basic metabolic rate   Because of the long-known fact that deficiency of thyroid secretion in the infant, if not corrected, entails severe mental deficiency, there has been interest in the possible relation between availability of thyroid secretion and intelligence within the normal range. Hinton (1936; 1939) reported some amazingly strong correlations between Stanford-Binet IQ and a measure of basal metabolic rate (BMR) given three times to each of 200 children in ages six to fifteen. For the total group, the correlation was .71. When fractionated by age groups, the samples gave correlations near .80 for the youngest groups, which dropped systematically to about .55 in the oldest groups, with an unusual drop at age twelve. The relationships were reported to be linear, with no sex differences.

Others have found much less indication of a strong positive relation between BMR and IQ with adults. With 78 women students, Dispensa (1938) found a correlation between BMR and scores from the Thurstone Intelligence Test to be .28. Gaskill and Fritz

(1946) found the correlation with an academic-aptitude test to be close to zero for either men or women, in a sample of 613. From a different approach, Hudson and Politzer (1959) found no significant correlation between level of iodine-bound protein and intelligence-test scores in an illiterate African population.

From all these findings, it would appear that if there is a substantial correlation between intelligence-test scores and BMR, it is very much confined to children. It is curious, however, that the striking results found by Hinton seem not to have been replicated or followed up, as such positive-looking results should be.

Effects of drugs

Alcohol and caffeine   In the treatment of these two drugs, it is not the intention to survey all the pertinent literature. The lasting effects of continued, excessive use of alcohol are well known. The recent studies bearing upon temporary effects are of interest because factor tests of intellectual abilities have been used.

Frankenhaeuser, Myrsten, and Järpe (1962) used four tests with subjects under the influence of alcohol, finding significant losses in two of them, Multiplication and Block Counting, with respect to both speed and accuracy. The tests can be identified with factors MSI plus NSI (numerical facility) and CFS-V plus CFT (spatial orientation and spatial visualization), respectively. Two tests showing no significant differences were Opposites and Letter Groups, which are ordinarily measures of NMR (convergent production of semantic relations) and CSC (cognition of symbolic classes), respectively. Not enough different factors were represented to permit drawing conclusions of a categorical nature.

Nash (1962) used a variety of tests involving divergent production and other associative activities. Mild doses of alcohol (equivalent to the alcohol found in two martinis) had little effect on performances, except a tendency to facilitate associative processes slightly. Larger doses (equivalent to four martinis) impaired performances of different kinds: discriminating rapidly, attaching meaning to visual objects, and immediate memory. In part, it was suspected that these losses depended upon poorer visual acuity and faulty focusing of the eyes. Some lack of expected impairment was suspected as being a function of attitudes. Although the doses of alcohol, as well as the placebo, were disguised, the subject could observe his own symptoms and perhaps also his loss in performances and could put forth enough effort to compensate for it.

The dose of caffeine was equivalent to that in two cups of coffee. A marked effect was increased spontaneity of association, as seen in better performance in tests of free association, ideational fluency, and word fluency. The subject rarely seemed at a loss for words, which might indicate increased status in factor NMU, convergent production of semantic units. Immediate memory for auditory information was enhanced, addition was facilitated, and input information was generally more readily organized and remembered.

It was suspected that attitude might have made some contribution to these differences in performance, in that, noting his own enhanced mental alertness, S was more confident and more active. In summing up the effects of the two chemical conditions, Nash concluded that caffeine tended to "mobilize intellectual resources," whereas larger doses of alcohol tended to immobilize them. Another generalization would be that caffeine markedly facilitates recall or retrieval of information from memory storage.

Glutamic acid   Because glutamic acid is one of the amino acids and because there is some possibility that it may have a role in the production of acetylcholine, the chemical link between neurons (Hughes & Zubek, 1956), there has been some interest in its relation to intelligence. Hughes and Zubek (1956; 1957) found that it did appear to improve the maze-learning performance of rats when administered daily from the twenty-fifth to the fortieth days of life, with tests one and three months later in the case of maze-dull rats but not in the case of maze-bright rats (the rats being from two strains). Their hypothesis was that dull rats are deficient in glutamic acid but bright rats are not; hence improvement can be brought about by dosage with that chemical in the former but not in the latter. A later experiment did not bear out the improvement in the case of dull rats, however (Hughes, Cooper, & Zubek, 1957).

Astin and Ross (1960) reviewed 33 studies dealing with glutamic-acid treatment of mentally deficient human subjects, finding that in 14 studies that did not use a control group, there were increases in performance. But in 19 studies that used control groups, 13 of them gave negative results. The conclusion was that it is doubtful whether glutamic acid has any specific effect upon intelligence conceived as a composite.

Lysergic acid diethylamide   Lysergic acid (LSD) is in the category of the hallucinogenic drugs, along with mescal buttons and peyote. One of the most consistent symptoms while the individual is under its influence is that of visual hallucinations. Experiments on performances with tests of intellectual abilities have been done with subjects under the influence of the drug.

With the Wechsler-Bellevue scale as the task for young adults and with doses of 50 to 200 micrograms, E. Levine, H. A. Abramson, M. R. Kaufman, and S. Markham (1955) found that the IQs of their subjects ranged from 89 to 136, with a mean of 111.8, to be compared with predrug scores for the same group of 100 to 136, with a mean of 122.9; they had sustained a mean loss of 11 points. There were significant mean losses on all tests in the scale except Digit Span and Object Assembly. The conclusion was that the loss was due not to anxiety but to poorer concentration, distractibility, disturbances of conceptual abilities, and difficulty with shifting set. One would like to know to what extent visual hallucinations during test taking may have interfered with the tasks. From these results there is no indication that primarily visual tasks were affected more than others.

Fortunately, other studies have employed quite a number of special tests, with doses of LSD of 0, 50, and 100 micrograms in different groups. Jarvik, Abramson, and Hirsch (1955) used a number of memory tests, of which three presented apparently semantic information through the auditory channel and five presented what appears to be visual-figural information through the visual channel. There were significant losses under LSD administration for all five of the visual tests and for only one of the tests with semantic information presented auditorily. In tests of addition and subtraction there were significant losses under LSD (Jarvik, Abramson, Hirsch, and Ewald, 1955), the input being visual, as usual. In two spatial-orientation tests, Thurstone's Hands test (factor CFS-K) and the Minnesota Paper Form Board test (probably factor CFT), there were losses under LSD, significantly in one case of the larger dose. A hypothesis of interferences from visual hallucinations would seem to have some support.

Morphine and amphetamine   Evans and Smith (1964) attempted to determine whether morphine and amphetamine, or a mixture of the two, would have differential effects upon special tests of different factors, including tests of cognition, divergent production, and evaluation. As compared with a placebo group, the one having morphine showed significant improvement in tests involving evaluation and implications—Perceptual Speed (EFU), Logical Reasoning (EMI), and the Apparatus Test (CMI). The investigators offered the hypothesis that this improvement came about in these tests because morphine decreased distractions, which was especially helpful in tasks requiring fine distinctions. Amphetamine enhanced performance on the Apparatus Test (CMI), Spatial Orientation (CFS-V), and Consequences (DMT). No differences were found under either drug for Ideational Fluency (DMU), Expressional Fluency (DMS), Associational Fluency (DMR), Alternate Uses (DMC), Anagrams (CSU), or General Reasoning (CMS). Most of the unaffected tests were in the divergent-production area, having to do with fluency and flexibility. This is of interest because such abilities are believed to make special contributions to creative potential. Only one of five such tests was done better under amphetamine and none under morphine. As far as these results go, one should not expect these two drugs to facilitate creative production.

Vitamin B complex   It is known that B vitamins have some role in keeping nerve cells in good working condition. Guetzkow and Brozek (1946) kept some subjects on a restricted intake of vitamin B complex for a period of 161 days, then on an almost total reduction for 23 days. They used some Thurstone PMA tests to assess possible changes in intellectual performance. During partial reduction of intake, no significant loss was found. During total reduction of intake there were significant losses in the tests Flags and Multiplication. Biochemical, physiological, and motivational assessments showed much greater effects of lowered intake. Partial restoration of thiamine alone for 10 days brought about some improvement in test performances. The study of effects of vitamins upon intellectual performances has hardly been touched.

Summary

An important physical basis for the intellectual status of the individual is found in the genetic material that directs the development of his nervous system in great detail. Studies of similarity of IQs of identical twins, fraternal twins, and other siblings have demonstrated that both heredity and environmental conditions contribute to variances among individuals with respect to general intellectual level. Studies of the problem of heredity and the IQ have been giving way to more refined investigations in terms of intellectual factors.

A number of previously popular views, some of them scientifically based, regarding the paramount role of the cerebrum and particularly of the cortex and of the forebrain in intellectual functioning, have had to give way in the light of new evidence that lower brain centers have a great deal to contribute. The reticular formation of the brainstem is now credited with being the foundation of consciousness and of attention. The hypothalamus furnishes the mechanisms of motivation that play a dominant role in reinforcement in learning, with reward and punishment centers. The limbic system, a subcortical organ, appears to play a role, also, in reinforcement. The cerebral cortex seems to serve mainly as a refined representational organ, whose activities are largely integrated by lower centers, the thalamus and reticular formation.

The Pavlovian-Watsonian conception of reflex pathways through the cerebrum now appears more ridiculous than ever, as it is found that that center actually regulates input as well as output and that functioning pathways connecting afferent and efferent fibers cannot be demonstrated in the cerebrum.

A major parallel between brain functioning and categories of the structure of intellect is that usually the right hemisphere underlies the processing of figural information and the left hemisphere underlies verbal (and hence probably semantic) information. No indications are apparent as to bases for symbolic and behavioral information, except that the frontal lobes seem to be involved in connection with behavioral information arising from the individual himself.

Within the hemispheres, there appear to be certain locations that are relatively more important for cognitive versus production abilities and for distinctions between products, particularly units, classes, and systems. There are some remarkable parallels between certain factors of intelligence and certain classical symptoms, particularly in types of agnosias and aphasias.

Problems of the physical basis for learning and memory storage have been enlivened by many new discoveries with regard to neuron composition and functioning. Molecular theories of information storage are becoming strong rivals for synaptic theories. Efforts to show that the RNA (ribonucleic-acid) molecule is the recorder of retained information have not succeeded, but they have produced very strong evidence that RNA has an important role in fixing and retaining memories. Ideas that seem to be gaining favor conceive of the change in learning to be in the nature of sensitizing or tuning neurons to make them responsive to patterns of excitation.

In the past, traditional intelligence tests have not been very sensitive to intellectual defects brought on by damage to the frontal lobes, but, according to preliminary results, applications of new kinds of factor tests are likely to reveal a great many significant relationships.

Certain chemical conditions of the brain have been investigated in connection with intellectual functioning, but results are as yet very limited. A number of chemical substances, such as oxygen and thyroxine, have been shown to be necessary for normal intelligence; some, such as alcohol, can be detrimental; but few offer much promise of beneficial results. Caffeine provides temporary benefits in activities involving recall of information, but glutamic acid has not demonstrated its value for any permanent benefits in human subjects.

16 Environmental and other conditions

The preceding chapter considered the hereditary and neurological and other conditions of a physical nature that may have bearings upon the development of intelligence of individuals. This chapter will treat other possible determiners of intellectual status, most of which come under the heterogeneous category of environmental conditions.

Among the environmental determiners, the global variable of socioeconomic level has most often been singled out for attention. Closer examination of that variable reveals more special conditions that in general have depressing or inhibiting effects upon development. They can be identified as environmental deprivations. Examination also reveals conditions that are favorable or facilitating for development. The latter can be identified as environmental enrichments. Among the latter, education stands out above all the rest.

Other, more incidental conditions include sex difference, circumstances of birth, race, bilingualism, and motivation. We shall find that great difficulties exist in reaching firm answers about any of the major conditions, because of their essential confoundings and because of the complexity of variables.

Socioeconomic status

Variables included   The global index of socioeconomic level has usually given greatest weight to the parent's occupation. A graded ranking of occupations, in terms of prestige, education required, income, and value to society, yields scales with quantification, such as those of Sims (1952) and Warner, Meeker, and Eells (1949), with the professions in the top category and the unskilled-labor occupations in the lowest. The major interest has been concerned with the child's intellectual status as a function of such a scale.

In attempting to understand the impact of any such socioeconomic level upon the developing child, it is more meaningful and operational to break down the global variables, both independent and dependent. Breakdown of the intelligence variable has been the major concern of this volume. Breakdown of the socioeconomic variable, likewise, should yield less ambiguous conclusions, more closely pinpointing sources of determination so that we can do something more knowingly about them.

Among the subvariables sometimes given attention are educational level of the parents, family income, value of the home, and other home assessments. Cultural advantages of the home, such as a home library, a tool shop, radio and television programs of favorable kinds, and so on, could be evaluated as special variables. Attitudes and beliefs prevailing in the home should not be overlooked. Is the parental attitude toward education and culture favorable, unfavorable, or one of ignoring and neglect? What are the prevailing child-rearing philosophies and practices in the family? H. E. Jones (1954) reported a correlation of .32 between children's IQs and number of hours spent with the child, for example. What are the family values? Few of these variables are given weight in the global index.

Then there are neighborhood features to be considered: the kind of school and quality of teaching; the proximity to a community library and other cultural media; the kinds of playmates; and many other circumstances, some of which are incident to socioeconomic level and some not. As an example of how special variables can be meaningful,

Jones (1954) also reported a correlation of .16 between IQ and the number of playmates in the home, thus possibly detecting a minor but a real contributor to intellectual development.

Difficulties in investigation   Besides the composite index of socioeconomic level and its ambiguities, there are other difficulties that beset the investigator's path in the study of environmental determiners of intellectual development. Some of these difficulties pertain to sampling problems, some to the nature of tests and the manner in which they are given, and some to statistical pitfalls that are overlooked by the unwary investigator.

Sampling problems   Sampling problems are not unique to environmental studies, by any means, but there are unusual sampling conditions in the context of such studies. In longitudinal studies, and all those that involve retesting of subjects after they have been subjected to some recognized treatment come in this category, only available children can be utilized. This usually entails obtaining parental consent, and there are differences between the kinds of parents who will and who will not consent. These differences may vary with socioeconomic level or with other independent variables. Parents must also be cooperative, in the way of bringing children for examination when needed and of supplying dependable information about the home and about the child. Do cooperative parents affect intellectual development differently from uncooperative parents? There are inevitably some dropout cases from the investigation. Which kinds drop out? [1]

Nature of the tests   It is most improper, paraphrasing Gertrude Stein, to say that an IQ test is an IQ test is an IQ test, as earlier chapters should have well demonstrated. Studies of environmental influence naturally involve children and adolescents of all ages. It is impossible to give the same test at all ages, keeping the factorial composition uniform. The infant and preschool tests measure abilities mostly other than those measured by the more common scales. Stott and Ball (1963) have recently provided considerable evidence on this point. Even without this knowledge, the point has been reiterated in the literature, without much apparent effect. Even standard scales like the Stanford-Binet change in factorial composition from one age level to another, with greater differences between the early and the late years (Lyle V. Jones, 1949; see Meeker, 1965, for a procedure for hypothesizing factorial composition of test items).

Figure 16.1, which was adapted from a similar figure by Bayley (1949), shows how well tests given for obtaining IQ evaluations at different age levels correlate with similar evaluations at other ages. During the first year, the California First-Year Intelligence Scale was administered. The correlations for the administration of that scale at two months and eleven months are represented in Figure 16.1. In years two through five, the California Preschool Scale was administered. Correlations for the scores from that scale at the ages of two and four are represented in the figure. At each year for years six through twelve, some form of the Stanford-Binet was given. Correlations for administration at years six and eight are shown. In year thirteen and also in year fifteen, the Terman-McNemar test was given. A form of the Stanford-Binet was given in years fourteen and seventeen. In years sixteen and eighteen, the Wechsler-Bellevue scale was administered.

In Figure 16.1, the correlation coefficients are plotted as points. The writer has provided smoothed curves to show what appear to be the general trends. There are in places a few systematic departures of data from the curves, but the overall system among the

[1] Bayley (1965) has discussed in greater detail the problems besetting longitudinal studies of intellectual growth.

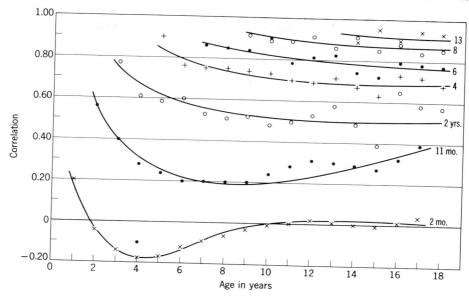

Fig. 16.1 Curves representing trends in the sizes of correlations between IQ-test scores obtained at one age with scores obtained at various other ages, where the test or its content changes from one age level to another. (*Adapted by permission from Bayley, 1949.*)

curves dominates the picture. It is clear that even the same scale, the California First-Year scale, given at two months and eleven months, does not show either the same pattern of correlations or the same level. Although correlating positively with the eleven-month results, the two-month administration otherwise correlated slightly negatively with other tests during the first years and zero thereafter. Not until the age of six do the correlations from testing at the age correlate at the level of about .80. The generally slow declines for the curves at ages six, eight, and thirteen reveal in part the general principle that the farther apart in time two forms of even the same test are correlated, the lower the correlation.

H. E. Jones (1954) has cited changes in kinds of standardization samples with age and changes in variability of scores with age. L. S. Hollingworth (1940) pointed out that preschool tests have been standardized on superior groups, which would tend to give IQs that are underestimated for the general run of children at those ages. When the same children are tested later, on other scales, they would thus appear to have gained in IQ. Any other systematic changes in standardizing samples with age would contribute to changes in measured IQs in longitudinal studies. There is also the constant error introduced by retesting, which, on the average, entails a gain of 2 to 4 IQ points, depending upon the length of time interval. A matched control group is needed but too often is not used.

Testing conditions Conditions of tester and testee also need consideration. Young children are often either shy or negativistic, conditions either of which would possibly make them look less intelligent in terms of IQ than is justified. They could easily show increased IQs later if they overcame their shyness or negativism. Furthermore, such traits may go systematically with certain cultural and economic backgrounds, thus biasing comparisons. Other children may be tested under unfavorable emotional conditions, as following the death of a parent or just before placement in a foster home. The examination itself may be anxiety-inducing for some children and not for others, and this difference may be related to certain independent variables.

Examiners of children are supposed to be trained and experienced, but according to H. E. Jones (1954) "personal equations" are still involved. Some examiners are lenient and some strict in deciding whether items are passed. The examiner may know to which group children belong and cannot help being biased by this information. The examiner may be affected by a halo impression, which may be determined by the appearance of the child or the way in which he impresses the examiner by apparent brilliance or dullness on certain items. Most of these and other sources of bias, of course, are not confined to investigations of socioeconomic level but operate in studies of other determiners of intellectual development.

The statistical regression effect   In testing a group and retesting after some particular treatment, it is quite commonly reported that those of initially high IQ tend to decline in IQ points whereas those of initially low IQ tend to gain in IQ points. This phenomenon can be accounted for in whole or in part by the Galton principle of regression toward the mean. The lower the correlation between test and retest scores, the larger is the purely statistical regression effect. Very often the tests have been of the preschool and even the infant type and the final tests not, or there has been some notable change of factorial content between pretest and posttest assessments that has kept the correlation from being high. There are ways of making allowance for the statistical regression, such as analysis of covariance, but almost no investigator has taken the trouble to make such a modification or has even been concerned about it.

Some general conclusions   In considering results from the many studies in connection with variations in IQ associated with socioeconomic variables, then, each study must be evaluated in the light of the difficulties that have just been briefly surveyed.

Parental occupation and IQ   Before coming to a conclusion about the effect of family environment upon the child's IQ from relating socioeconomic variables to the child's IQ, we must remember that the independent variable is confounded with hereditary determination. There is a substantial correlation between the parent's occupational level and his hereditary status with respect to IQ. In a mobile society, where movement from class to class is fairly easy and is effected largely on the basis of ability, the same hereditary determiners help to determine both the parent's occupation and the child's IQ.

The relation of a parent's IQ to his occupational level has been demonstrated by Fryer (1922) from Army Alpha scores of servicemen in World War I and by Harrell and Harrell (1945) and Stewart (1947) with the Army General Classification Test (AGCT) in World War II. Although there is considerable overlapping of score distributions, the mean scores increase progressively as we go from unskilled-labor groups up to professional groups. The parent who furnishes the child with a favorable hereditary basis for development of intelligence also furnishes him with favorable environmental conditions, and the two sources of determination are confounded.

For the relationship of IQs of children to occupational level of the father, McNemar's results (1942) are probably representative. At four age levels, the youngest being 2 to 2.5 years and the oldest 15 to 18, the mean IQ of children of fathers in the professions and that of children of fathers in unskilled occupations were 20 points apart, the former being about 115 and the latter about 95. The reason that the means were not equidistant from

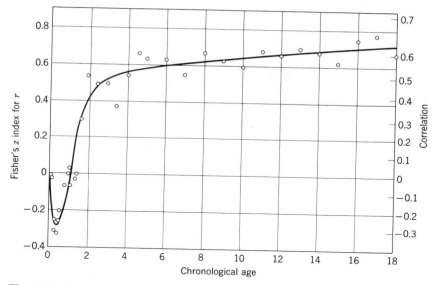

Fig. 16.2 Correlations of IQs with amount of education of parents as a function of the ages at which the tests are given. (*From data presented by Bayley, 1954. Reproduced by permission.*)

the general population mean of 100 is that there are fewer professional fathers and they and their children are farther out in the tail of the distribution on their side of the scale.

When the index of family status was in the form of a rating of the home (Leahy, 1935), the correlation of this index with IQ of children was about .40, for children in the age range three to eighteen. Below the age of three, the correlation drops because of change in what is measured by the tests.

Similar relationships between occupation of father and IQ of child have been found in other countries, e.g., England (R. B. Cattell, 1934–35; Foulds & Raven, 1948); Sweden (Carlsson, 1955); Scotland, in the 1947 national survey (Thomson et al., 1953); France, with children aged six to twelve (Heuyer et al., 1950); and Poland (Pieter, 1939). In Russia, in contrast to results in the United States with the California First-Year scale, the correlation was reported to be .44 between IQ and father's salary (Dubnoff, 1938).

Correlation with parent education The most complete information that we have concerning correlation of children's IQs and the amount of formal education of their parents comes from Bayley (1954). Her data are represented by the illustration in Figure 16.2. To a large extent, the relationship is a picture of the relations of different tests to parental education. Since there is undoubtedly a high correlation between parent education and parent IQ, as well as the correlation of about .50 between parent and child IQ, we could almost forecast the curve in Figure 16.2 from the information in Figure 16.1. From the age of five, after which the nature of the test content becomes more stabilized, there is almost a linear increase of child IQ as a function of parental education.

Correlations with tests of special abilities When the assessment of intellectual status of children has been in terms of special tests, such as tests for mechanical aptitudes or clerical aptitude and the Thurstone PMA tests, similar relationships to parental occupation are found, but the strength of relationship differs from one kind of test to another. Positive relationships were found for ten-year-olds in the Goodenough Draw-a-Man IQ, Paper Form Board, Porteus Maze mental age, and Minnesota Mechanical Assembly (Havighurst & Janke, 1944).

The six PMA tests given to thirteen-year-old children (Havighurst & Breese, 1947) correlated with ratings of parents on the Warner scale to the extent of .42 for Verbal Comprehension, .32 for Number, .30 for Word Fluency, .25 for Space, .23 for Reasoning, and .21 for Memory. On the whole, correlations of test status of children with parental socioeconomic status are higher for academic-aptitude types of tests and lower for nonverbal abilities.

Urban versus rural populations   Differences in IQs of urban and rural populations have been investigated as a special comparison, still very much within the area of effects of socioeconomic conditions. IQs of farm owners and farmhands have been relatively low among those in the lists of occupations examined in the armed services in the two World Wars. It is not known how representative those groups were, for with some emphasis upon exemptions of farmers from the draft, probably the laborers rather than farm owners more often found themselves in the armed services, and this would tend to give appreciable underestimates.

But score differences from urban versus rural homes have been in the same direction. According to data presented by McNemar (1942), the differences in IQ means were about 5 points at the 2 to 5.5 age level, 11 at the 6 to 14 age level, and 12 at the 15 to 18 age level. The smaller difference at ages 2 to 5.5 is undoubtedly attributable to the less academic type of test content. Urban-rural differences in IQ have been reported from France, Germany, and Italy (Klineberg, 1931), with less difference in England (Anastasi, 1958).

Differences between urban and rural children are smaller for nonverbal than for verbal tests. For example, rural children are not so inferior in the Knox Cube and Form Board tests and actually have been found superior in the Mare and Foal test, a jigsaw-puzzle type of test featuring farm information (H. E. Jones, H. S. Conrad, & M. B. Blanchard, 1932). Urban children have an advantage in items that involve specific information about things more often encountered in city life, e.g., coins and streetcars. Shimberg (1929) found that by selecting items in which rural children excel, she could produce a test in which rural children have a higher mean total score. Standard tests have been constructed by people who live and work in an urban culture. Insofar as this favors items that emphasize generalized intellectual skills, there can be little charge of unfairness to rural children. Insofar as it emphasizes specific information that is not relevant to those generalized skills, the test can be unfair to rural children, and such biases should be avoided.

There are many reasons why the rural setting has not offered so much opportunity for intellectual development as the urban milieu; it is not necessary to mention details. The cultural gap has been narrowing, however, as channels of communication have increased and as rural educational opportunities have improved. The question of culture-fair tests will receive more attention in a later part of this chapter.

Environmental deprivations

Still concerned with cultural problems, we shall next focus on some of the environmental conditions that on the whole have inhibiting effects upon mental development and then, in the next section, emphasize those environmental features that facilitate development. In each case we shall consider reasons for effects, negative or positive.

Sensory deprivations in animals and men   In the preceding chapter it was mentioned that stimulated brain cells increase in size as they become more ready to function as a consequence of learning and unstimulated cells are more likely to die. As a general principle, the implication seems obvious: brains must be exercised in order to keep them alive and in condition to function, and they must be programmed by exercise so that they may function in skilled ways. There is much evidence to bear out this generalization. There have been experiments with rats, dogs, and monkeys, as well as with human children.

Animals with poverty of stimulation   The first experiment to be mentioned applied deprivation of stimulation to rats selected from the "bright" and "dull" strains of rats, bred from ancestors who had originally been selected on the basis of performance on the Hebb-Williams maze test (Cooper & Zubek, 1958). The deprivation treatment consisted of keeping the subjects from the twenty-fifth to the sixty-fifth day in cages in which they could see only the gray walls of the cage and of the room. They were then tested on the Hebb-Williams maze and their scores compared with those from normal control groups from the same strains.

The maze-bright deprived group made significantly more errors as compared with its control group (170 versus 117), and the maze-dull deprived group made insignificantly more errors (170 versus 164). Even the bright rats seem to have needed visual experiences (as under the control conditions) by which to learn perceptual and other habits that facilitated maze learning. Control rats of the dull strain apparently did not learn enough by virtue of normal experience to help them a great deal in maze learning, nor did they do more poorly than the bright rats as a result of sensory deprivation.

In an experiment with dogs (Scotch terriers), W. R. Thompson and R. Melzack (1956) kept an experimental group in plain cages with solid walls. The dogs saw no other dogs or human individuals. The treatment lasted from birth to the end of ten months. Upon release, the experimental dogs showed a number of personality differences: they were active, playful, and immature-acting. Put in a larger room, they continued to explore for some time, whereas the control dogs soon became bored and stopped exploring. The interpretation given by the investigators was that the control (undeprived) dogs learned the new environment more quickly. Apparently the author did not give thought to the possibility that the difference might have been primarily a motivational one. In tests involving a number of mazes, the experimental dogs made 50 percent more errors than the controls. A general conclusion was that animals need stimulation in general in order to develop normally.

In another experiment (Melzack & Thompson, 1956), three groups of dogs were given three levels of opportunity for learning social reactions with other dogs and with humans, one of normal opportunity and two with degrees of deprivation. In dominance tests later and in reactions to a bold man versus a friendly man versus a timid man, the deprived Ss showed more inappropriate behavior, indicating retardation in the area of social intelligence.

Harlow and Harlow (1962) reared monkeys, each in a separate cage, depriving them of contacts with mothers and with peer monkeys. At ages five to eight months, much abnormal behavior was observed in these experimental monkeys. Deprivation of experience with peers seems to be more damaging than deprivation of experience with mothers. A conclusion was that there is a period from the third to the sixth month during which social deprivation is most serious for producing social retardation. The authors point out that this period is analogous to the period of twelve to twenty-four months for the human child.

Children with stimulus deprivation   There is very little evidence about effects of sensory deficits with young children. There are few, if any, investigators who would have the courage or heartlessness to try such experiments. Dennis (1941) reported an instance in which two infants were reared for fifteen months with minimum stimulation from parents. Results were recorded mainly in terms of motor and emotional development. Dennis reported that practically all responses normally found during the first year developed in these children without apparent assistance from others. Learning did seem to play roles in this development, with the child taking some initiative and having some opportunity to learn. There was no report of any later intellectual effects.

Hard-of-hearing children are partially deprived of sound stimuli, which might lead us to expect some degree of intellectual retardation. Pintner and Lev (1939) administered verbal and nonverbal tests to such children in grades 5 to 8. The children did show a little retardation, more in verbal tests (mean IQ was 93, as compared with 101 for other children) than in nonverbal tests (mean IQ was 99, as compared with 102). As a consequence, the authors recommended nonverbal tests for the hard-of-hearing children. But of course that would mean that they would be measured for a different kind of intelligence than children measured by verbal tests.

Underprivileged homes   There have been reports of studies in which children came from homes with mentally deficient parents and with other inadequacies with respect to conditions for mental development. Speer (1940b) correlated the IQs of children obtained at the time of arrival at a placement agency with the length of time the children had lived with feebleminded mothers. He reported that the correlation was negative, whereas in the case of mentally normal mothers such a correlation was zero. The longer the time the children lived with their feebleminded mothers, the lower their IQs on arrival at the agency.

Skeels (1940) reported on about four hundred children one to eighteen years of age who were tested as they came to an orphanage from underprivileged homes. It was found that IQs tended to decline systematically with age, in the range from two to twelve years, the means declining from 93 to 82. Comparing older and younger siblings, where differences in age were more than three years, he found that the older siblings had a significantly lower mean IQ.

Institutional life   Two kinds of institutions, foundling homes and orphanages, have figured prominently in studies of child development. Because infants and children in such places lack frequent contacts with mothers and because their care is more impersonal, sometimes with little personal attention, it has been expected that such children should show some effects in the form of retarded intellectual development. This is not to say that the educational opportunities are necessarily inferior, but during infancy and preschool years the opportunities for learning may be severely restricted as compared with those of children reared in their own homes with mothers.

Environments with and without mothers   Spitz (1949) compared two groups of infants, one that had more normal contacts with their mothers in a "nursery" and the other composed of infants who had been reared in a foundling home with overworked nurses, one nurse to 8 to 12 infants. At the age of two to three months, the developmental quotients (DQ) averaged 95 for the infants who were mothered and 130 for those in the foundling home. At ages of eight to ten months, the DQs averaged 110 for the mothered infants and 72 for the others. At two years of age the foundling children were reported as not having learned to walk or talk or to feed themselves and were described as being "emotionally starved" and "human wrecks," in spite of the fact that their physical wants had been well cared for.

The study of Spitz has been severely criticized on several bases (Pinneau, 1955), but it has been replicated, in a sense, by Dennis and others, with confirming results in some respects. In a Lebanese foundling home and a well-baby clinic, Dennis and Najarian (1957) obtained the use of institutionalized infants on the one hand and mothered infants on the other. In the foundling home, the infants were kept in swaddling to the age of two months and for much of the time then to the age of four months. During years one to three they played in groups of 20, with few toys available. During years three to four they spent much of their time sitting at tables, and at four they were in kindergarten.

At the age of two to three months there was no significant difference on the Cattell infant scale. During the interval from three to twelve months, the DQ means were 63 for the foundling children and 102 for the clinic children. At ages 4.5 to 6, mean IQs were about the same, suggesting that the earlier retardation was not permanent. There was a change of test content, however, which calls for caution in drawing this conclusion. The IQ was based upon three figural tests, Knox Cube, Draw-a-Man test, and Porteus Maze test. Nothing can be said about effects upon *verbal*-intellectual development.

Orphanage life   In two instances, children of preschool ages were said to lose in IQ even in a short span of time of residence in orphanages, with a mean loss of 16.2 points in one case (Wellman, 1940) and 1.0 point in the other (Wellman & Pegram, 1944). Because of the changing content of tests in those years, such changes are difficult to evaluate.

Goldfarb (1943) compared children remaining in orphanages for the first three years with those adopted immediately after birth. Hereditary backgrounds were said to be similar. In terms of percentage showing defective speech, 80 percent of the orphanage children and only 15 percent of those who had gone into foster homes were in this category. This is understandable, since much personal attention is needed for correcting faulty speech development. In terms of mental retardation, 37.5 percent of the orphanage residents and 7.5 percent of those in foster homes were so classified. Goldfarb concluded that there were no signs that such defects were due to emotional retardation. Rather, he attributed them to lack of stimulation.

In another study, Goldfarb (1947) compared at the time of adolescence two groups of foster children, of which one had spent the period of infancy in an institution and the other not. One notable difference was that the group that had spent its infancy in an orphanage approached problems more concretely and the other group more abstractly. From the fact that the two groups had shown a similar difference when tested earlier, he concluded that subsequent experiences had done nothing to correct matters.

After reviewing a great many studies involving deprivation of one kind or another, Yarrow (1961) reached some generalizations that are worth noting. Intellectual impairment is not appreciable if the deprivation is restricted to the first three months of life. We may hypothesize that the infant may necessarily have a normal amount of stimulation during that period and that such stimulation is about all his nervous system is prepared to handle. Most intellectual impairment, says Yarrow, is observed if the deprivation comes between the ages of three and twelve months. It may be hypothesized that it is normally during this time that the infant is developing in his brain what Hebb (1949) calls the cell assemblies and phase sequences that are basic to all further intellectual development. Yarrow concludes that social stimulation in the period from six to eight months seems important for development of good social discriminations, in other words, for cognitive abilities concerned with behavioral information, an important base for social intelligence. Deprivation before six months does not seem to be very detrimental to personality development in general.

Intellectual impairment may arise consequent to deprivation during later childhood and even during adolescent years, as shown by the fact that the more years the deprivation applies, the greater the deficit. Unfavorable environmental conditions appear to have diminishing potency, however, as the child grows older. Some general principles relating environmental effects to age will be discussed after considering favorable environmental conditions.

Environmental enrichments

It has just been shown that a number of environmental conditions can be unfavorable to intellectual development. Is there also the possibility that favorable conditions over and above the normal can effect improvements in intellectual status? The evidence on this question comes from much the same kinds of sources: enriched stimulation and conditions in an institution or in a home that encourage learning.

Stimulation and encouragement   If lower animals that have been deprived of sensory stimulation early in life show later deficits in intellectual performance, is it possible that an overabundance of stimulation provides supernormal performance? The experiment of Cooper and Zubek (1958), cited before, also provided rats between the ages of twenty-five and sixty-five days with something more than normal views of cage and objects in the room; outside the cage were modernistic designs exposed to their view, and inside the cage were objects that could be manipulated. Two groups of rats from the "bright" and "dull" strains, matched with controls from the same sources, were compared on a maze test. The maze-bright exposed rats made fewer errors than the bright controls, but insignificantly so, the numbers being 111 versus 117. The dull exposed rats, however, made significantly fewer errors, the numbers being 120 versus 164. Thus, the extra stimulation appeared to help the dull-strain rats considerably and the bright-strain rats possibly not at all. The authors state, however, that the test's ceiling might have been too low to let the bright exposed group show what it could really do. An alternative hypothesis is that the bright-strain rats were sufficiently stimulated by an ordinary environment for full development.

With extra stimulation of a less specific nature, S. Levine (1960) has found that either handling very young rats or giving them mild electric shocks each day promotes general physical and behavioral development as compared with the development of rats that have not been touched. The effects are brought about when the treatment is applied during days 2 to 5 after birth but not when applied later. In discussing the effects of similar handling of young rats, Bovard (1958) hypothesized that the treatment instigates permanent changes in the balance of hypothalamic activity, an increased output of growth hormones and a decreased activity of the adrenal system.

With human subjects, there are a few reports about acceleration in mental functioning under the condition of extra stimulation. Fowler (1962) states that there have been many cases of children's learning to read by the age of four if given special instruction. He emphasizes the fact that maturation is not the only way in which development can occur and that experiments on early inception of learning have not had observable ill effects upon the personalities of children of average or below-average intelligence.

One of the common pressures that is sometimes applied to the child is the mother's attitude, her concern for rapid development, which can be exhibited in various ways. Moss and Kagan (1958) studied the possible effects of this particular kind of pressure by developing an acceleration index, a measure of the mother's concern for rate of development. A rating was obtained incident to assessment of the home status during the child's first three years and correlated with the child's IQ. The correlation was significantly positive (.41) for the boys, at the age of three but not at the age of six, and was not significant at either age level for the girls. The correlations between the acceleration index and the mother's IQ and educational level were not considered to be enough to account for the one significant correlation, those correlations being in the range .21 to .28.

In the Berkeley growth study, attention was given to attitude and treatment by the mother in relation to IQ of the child. Boys who had loving mothers during the first three years tended to make lower scores in the infant tests but to make higher scores in later years, even through their eighteenth years. The difference in direction of the relationship can be accounted for on the basis of changes in what the tests measure. The IQs of girls do not seem to be much affected by mother attitudes, except that "intrusiveness" of mothers correlated slightly negatively with IQs of daughters during the school years of the latter (Bayley, 1965).

Superior institutional environment   Some orphanage situations have been regarded as having better-than-normal conditions for intellectual development, at least for children of school age. Reymert and Hinton (1940) checked the possibility that children coming from inferior homes to an orphanage that provided a good school might be improved with respect to IQs as they continued in that environment. One hundred children entered the institution at ages varying from three to fourteen years. They were tested at the time of entrance and also each year following, for the next four years. All children considered, there were no significant gains in IQ even after four years, but children entering at the age of six or below did show significant gains. The latter fact would suggest that one or both of two variables were responsible: the length of time the child had remained in the inferior home and the age at which the child entered the institution. It may be that the age at which favorable environmental conditions can produce results is below six. There was no control group, however; so it cannot be said that all the difference for the younger *S*s was due to the school experience.

Kephart (1940) reported a much more positive finding with a smaller sample of 50 high-grade mentally deficient and borderline subjects with an average IQ of 68. The children entered the institution at ages from four to fifteen. In their own homes they had shown losses in IQ with increasing age, but during an average of 4.4 years in the institution they showed a mean gain of 10 points, with a range of 2 to 22, except for one, who showed a loss. Some of the gains may be attributed to retesting and perhaps some to change of test content. When these contingencies are allowed for, some genuine gain could be left.

Skeels (1940) reported some interesting results from an institutional "experiment" of putting very young children under the care of superior caretakers. There were 13 children under the age of three (the mean was 19.4 months), with a mean IQ of about 64, who were placed in an orphanage ward with brighter older girls. Another group of 12 with a mean IQ of about 88 was left in the ward with other young children. After two years, the mean of the first group had gained 27.5 points in IQ, whereas the mean of the second group had declined 16.1 points. The gain in the first group could be attributed to some extent to regression and perhaps to change in test content, and the loss in the second group could be attributed partly to regression.

Fortunately, further light on the matter has been provided by Skeels (1965), in a study following up all 25 cases after an interval of twenty-one years. Some of the particular findings appear very striking. Of the 13 experimental children (in the more favorable institutional environment), 11 had later been placed in foster homes, whereas the 12 children in the control group remained in their unstimulating environment for numbers of years. As adults, the two groups were very different with respect to education, marriage, and economic status.

In the experimental group the average amount of formal education completed was twelve years. Some members had had one or more years of college, and one boy had received a B.A. degree. In the control group, the mean educational status was at the third grade. Members of the experimental group were self-supporting, with occupations ranging into the professional level. Fifty percent of the control group were unemployed, and of those employed only one was not in the unskilled category.

Except for the reservation that we do not know to what extent tests given at an average age of nineteen months may have missed most of the intellectual potential, the results look very good for the beneficial effects of stimulating environments.

Foster children in superior homes   As a group, foster children have been given special attention in research on problems of nurture, research that can be placed under the heading of effects of superior environments. The environments are typically superior because adopting agencies attempt to find good homes for their children and because average or more economically able homes are likely to apply for adoptees. Another circumstance that should be remembered is that the more intelligent orphans will be placed for adoption or will tend to be selected by foster parents. This kind of selection has been facilitated since the advent of the mental test in the adoption situation. Thus, when it is generally found that foster children have a mean IQ slightly higher than that of the general population, this may be due in part to the fact that those children have had superior advantages from living in those homes, but it can also be attributed in part to these other variables. The main question to be answered in this section is whether the superior home and community environments tend to raise the IQs of foster children.

Evidence from correlations   Decisions concerning the influence of home and parental dispositions upon the child's IQ can be reached from the indirect evidence of correlations of the foster child's IQ with the parent's IQ or with some rating of the home, of IQs of unrelated children, and of those of foster and real children in the same home. In interpreting all such correlations, we must bear in mind that there is confounding with differential placement, that is, some tendency to send children of different apparent levels of intelligence into homes of similar levels. When there has been a check on this point, it is found that there is some correlation between the child's IQ and foster-parent status at the time of placement. There are also some small correlations between real and foster parents in regard to IQ and education.

Much of the correlational information comes from Freeman, Holzinger, and Mitchell (1928), Leahy (1935), Snygg (1938), and Skodak and Skeels (1949). The correlation of foster-father and foster-child IQs has been estimated twice, at .19 and .37. The corresponding estimates for correlations with foster mother have been .24, .28, .27, and .13. None of these have been very impressive, but we must remember that by virtue of the selection of adoptive homes, some restriction of range is involved. In Leahy's study, the standard deviation for Otis scores of adoptive parents was 12.5, compared with a standard deviation of 15.4 for a group of other parents matched for mean score and in other respects. The typical correlation between parent and own-child IQs has been about .50. All we can say is that there is greater similarity of parent-child IQs for real children than for foster children, and if all known biases in the figures are considered, the similarity for real children seems to be much greater. Correlations between foster-child's IQ and cultural rating of the home have been higher (Freeman et al., 1928), being .48 for all children included and .52 for children who were adopted below the age of two years.

From Table 15.1 we see that from seven estimates the correlation between IQs of children reared in the same "home" (including orphanages as well as foster homes) ranged from —.17 to .31, with a median of .16. Freeman et al. (1928) gave a figure of .37, which is about the same as for the correlation between IQs of foster and own children living in the same home. This is to be compared with an estimate of .50 as the typical correlation for siblings reared by their own parents.

Changes of IQs of foster children   The fact that the parental IQs and educational levels of the *real* parents of adopted children have been quite low in comparison with those of foster parents has focused interest upon possible changes in children's IQs consequent to living in foster homes. Groups of real mothers of children who became adopted have been reported to be heavily populated with mentally deficient and borderline cases (Skodak & Skeels, 1945; Speer, 1940b), with home conditions to match. Fathers of illegitimate children, the category to which large numbers of the experimental children have belonged, have not always been known, and none has been tested for these studies, but they have been described as being typically in the skilled-labor level economically. Educational levels of both real mothers and real fathers have been relatively low. Adoptions have usually been made before the age of two years.

Under these circumstances, the tested IQs of foster children who have spent some few years in their adopted homes are rather impressive, being of the order of 105 to 115 (Skeels & Harms, 1948; Skodak & Skeels, 1945, 1949). Other reports indicate much more modest gains. For example, Freeman et al. (1928) tested 74 children before and after residence averaging four years in foster homes, finding means of 91.2 and 93.7, respectively. In the better homes, the changes averaged 5 points in IQ, and in the poorer homes there was no average change. It should be said that adoptions were made at ages of four years and higher. The children who were younger at adoption gained more than those older at adoption.

Skeels (1940) reported a mean change in IQ of about 6 points for 65 children adopted between the ages of 2.5 and 5 years, the younger children gaining more than older ones. Hildreth (1940) reported on 54 foster children in homes of professional parents. They attended good private schools with the parents' own children. Where children had been adopted before the age of two, later medians of IQs were found to be 120 for the own children and 102 for the foster children. Thus, the same superior homes and schools did not bring the foster children up to the level of the parents' own children.

Skeels (1965) has indicated that the foster children whose real mothers were judged to be mentally retarded have been followed up after intervals of sixteen and twenty-one years. The preliminary information from this source for cases already approached presents a picture of socioeconomic status in line with that of the general population; the children of the next generation show a normal range of intelligence-test performance.

Not knowing that the foster children with whom the Skeels studies started were themselves feebleminded, we cannot justifiably conclude that good homes and schools, such as those of twenty to twenty-five years ago, generally make feebleminded children into normal children or better. There is little doubt that when a child remains in a psychologically impoverished home and school environment, his IQ is likely to drop systematically. When a young child of subnormal IQ is adopted into a family with high IQ and high educational level, he is likely to show some gain. The sooner he starts in such a home, the greater the gain. It is not known what such favorable home and educational conditions can do for the child whose heredity should place him at about average IQ or for a child destined for a better-than-average IQ under average circumstances. Such research has not been done. Neither is it known just what a superior home and high-level parents do, precisely, to facilitate intellectual development. We should find out more about what parents and schools could do to bring out the best development of which the child is capable. This brings the spotlight around to education.

Education and intellectual development

There can be no doubt concerning the fact of a high correlation between amount of education and intelligence, as measured by intelligence tests, in a population of adult individuals. This comes about in two major ways. Those of higher potential seek and obtain education or have educational opportunities come their way. And those who take advantage of education are prepared to do better in intelligence tests. It has been somewhat disconcerting to those who conceive of an inherited potential that they would like to believe is measured by intelligence tests to find the relationship to be so high between education and test performance. But when we remember that traditional intelligence tests overwhelmingly emphasize cognitive abilities and that cognitive abilities indicate essentially how much information we possess, the very strong relationship should occasion no surprise. Among the best single indicators of verbal-intellectual status are vocabulary and general-information tests, two aspects of ability very obviously developed by education.

General evidence on the relationship   Although proof of relationship is not needed, there are some subsidiary questions that need attention: the strength of the relationship under different conditions and the way in which different aspects of intelligence are affected by different kinds of educational policy and practice. We are a long way from answering questions of the latter category.

Effects of educational deprivation   The canalboat children of England have often been cited as evidence for the effects of impoverished environment. Since lack of education appears to be a key variable in their environmental complex, this case may be cited for evidence regarding that variable. According to H. Gordon (1923), the canalboat children attended school on the average about 5 percent of the school year, and the parents were illiterate. The mean Stanford-Binet IQ for a sample of 76 children was 70, and there was a marked decline of IQ with age. At ages four to six, the mean IQ was about 90; in the age range twelve to twenty-two it was 60. The correlation between IQ and age in the sample was —.76.

In a sample of gypsy children in England, Gordon (1923) found that school attendance was a little better but averaged only 35 percent of the school year. The correlation between IQ and amount of school attendance was .37. The mean IQ for a sample of 82 gypsy children was 74.5, and the correlation between IQ and age was —.43.

Comparable studies in the United States were done in the mountain regions of eastern Kentucky and Tennessee some thirty years ago (Ascher, 1935; Chapanis & Williams, 1945; Hirsch, 1928; Sherman & Key, 1932; Wheeler, 1932). Generally, they found definitely lower-than-normal average IQ, more so in verbal than in nonverbal tests, with declining IQ as a function of age. For example, Sherman and Key found mean IQs of 84, 70, and 53 for age groups six to eight, eight to ten, and ten to twelve, respectively, in the Pintner-Cunningham verbal test. They also found mean IQs from 80 down to 49 in the Goodenough Draw-a-Man test in the age range from six to sixteen and mean IQs from 89 down to 73 in the Pintner-Paterson scale.

Wheeler (1942) returned ten years after he had tested 1,147 children in 1930 for the testing of new children in the same grades. In the interim there had been many improvements in terms of better roads and better transportation to schools, a higher average daily attendance, and better-trained teachers, in addition to economic improvements for the families. In 1930 the mean IQ had been 82 and 78 in two tests (Dearborn and Illinois scales); in 1940 the mean IQ was 93. It is tempting to give increased and improved education most of the credit for the change in intellectual development.

Amount and kind of education   Although there have been many studies that indicate a relationship between the *amount* of education and IQ, few have held other variables constant while varying education alone. A study that is better in this respect was reported by Husén (1951). Husén tested 722 boys while they were in the third grade in Swedish schools. Ten years later the boys were retested, and by that time various amounts of education had been achieved by individuals in the group. Two groups were formed: those who had gone to the junior secondary school without achieving a certificate and those who had matriculated in grades 12 and 13. The former showed a mean gain of 2.1 points in IQ and the latter 11.0 points. Presumably, most of the difference could be attributed to differences in amount of formal education; there could be no control of amounts of informal education.

Two studies tested the hypothesis that exceptionally good educational practices would contribute to accelerated development. In a demonstration school, Lamson (1938) tested the six successive classes in the fourth grade, comparing their IQs with those they had achieved in grades 1, 2, and 3, in different groups. The resulting gains proved to be near zero, with a range from −1.5 to +1.5. It is possible that there were gains in certain abilities that were not measured by the tests that were used (see later paragraphs).

In three private schools that were considered to be exceptionally good, large numbers of students were retested after residence of at least 2.5 years. The mean differences were 1.4, 0.6, and 6.2. If the students were of superior ability to begin with, perhaps little gain could be expected from the supposedly enriched educational treatment, a principle that seemed to apply in studies cited earlier with regard to enriched environments in terms of stimulation. If the gain in the third school is assumed to have been genuine, it would be important to find out what that school did that the other two did not do in possible ways of stimulating accelerated development.

Also to be considered is the mean gain of 5.2 points in the IQs of children attending the University of Iowa elementary school as compared with a mean gain of 1.2 points of children attending other elementary schools (Wellman, 1940). Both groups had attended the university's nursery school previously. The mean IQ was initially well above average for both groups.

Enhancement of special abilities   In studies such as those just cited, where the IQ scales were composites of tests of different abilities, it is possible that gains in certain abilities were canceled by losses in others. Hartson (1936) has provided evidence to this effect. Men and women tested as freshmen and again as seniors in a composite test (Ohio State Psychological Examination) that emphasized verbal and numerical aspects showed little overall gain, but it was found that a gain in the verbal aspect had been offset by a loss in the numerical aspect of the test. Students who had taken English and a foreign language and no mathematics gained more in the verbal tests, and students who had taken mathematics gained more in the numerical tests.

On a much grander scale, Brolyer, Thorndike, and Woodyard (1927) gave about thirteen thousand high-school students in New York some psychological tests involving a variety of parts, at the beginning of the school year and at the end. In the meantime, various curricula were followed by different groups of students. The main objective of the study was to determine which curriculum would yield the greatest gain in IQ. Greater positive effects upon IQ were found for students taking sciences, languages, mathematics, business arithmetic, and bookkeeping. The least gains were found for students taking dramatic arts and domestic science. But the most significant finding, from the point of view of factors of intelligence, is that academic, commercial, and shop types of curricula seemed to promote development relatively more in verbal, numerical, and spatial-visualization components of the intelligence test, respectively.

The several experiments on special types of training and effects upon enhancement of status in different factors cited in Chapters 12 and 14 have direct bearings upon the problem of special educational effects.

Nursery-school education   Promoters of nursery-school education at one time found it desirable to show that the institution was good for children. One of the benefits to be expected would be general improvement in intellectual development that would show up in terms of increases in IQ. Among the first investigations in this area were the University of Iowa studies that stirred up considerable controversy.

The Iowa studies of nursery-school effects   In summarizing several studies involving 652 children, Wellman (1940) reported that starting with a mean IQ of 116, the overall mean gain was 6.6 IQ points. The children were tested in the fall of each year and again in the spring. For children attending two years, the two yearly mean gains were 7.0 and 3.8. For those attending three years, the gains were 7.7, 4.3, and 1.7. There was some tendency for those of higher IQs initially to gain less and those with lower initial IQs to gain more. This principle was also indicated in the results of Starkweather and Roberts (1940), but Goodenough and Maurer (1940) found that if the amount of statistical regression to be expected from imperfect correlations between initial and final tests is taken into account, the principle is entirely accounted for.

Other Iowa studies pertained to nursery-school instruction within orphanages. Two groups of children were matched for IQ, age, sex, and length of residence. One group attended nursery school for a maximum of 400 days. The nursery-school group gained with a mean change of 0.5 IQ point. In comparison with the change in the control group, however, this figure represents a relative positive gain, for the control group lost 16.2 IQ points on the average. In another orphanage study (Wellman & Pegram, 1944), children who attended nursery school more than 50 percent of the total of 572 days showed a mean gain of 8.4 IQ points, while a control group showed a mean loss of 1.0 point.

Investigators at other places have not replicated the Wellman results. They have found either no change in mean IQ or small positive changes that were statistically insignificant (Dewey Anderson, 1940; Bird, 1940; Frandsen & Barlow, 1940; H. E. Jones & A. P. Jorgensen, 1940; Lamson, 1940; Page, 1940; Starkweather & Roberts, 1940). Most of these investigators used control groups. Whereas Wellman and Pegram (1944) mention a positive correlation between gain in IQ and length of time in attendance at nursery school, there are two other reports of zero correlation (Jones & Jorgensen, 1940; Wellman, 1940) and one report of a slight negative correlation (Page, 1940).

Where it can be convincingly demonstrated that significant gains in IQ are associated with nursery-school attendance, there should be an effort to see why it does occur in contrast to other places where it does not occur. If some children gain and some not after allowance has been made for any regression effect, the reasons should be sought. Another very important consideration is whether the kinds of tests that have been used to assess possible gain have been appropriate. One should not expect appreciable gains in verbal tests when most of the instruction has dealt with figural experiences. Many real gains would be missed if the kind of assessment were inappropriate. Those who are responsible for designing nursery-school curricula should also take a second look to see whether sufficient opportunities have been provided for building up semantic and even symbolic abilities that will be important in later years. In addition, too little attention has been given to possible benefits of nursery-school experience upon assessed achievement in later years. Such benefits might also be missed by IQ tests.

Some other conditions

Sex differences   The sex of the child can logically be a contributor to his intellectual status in two major ways. It is possible that there is some sex linkage in the genes that helps to determine status in certain abilities, an example of which was mentioned in the preceding chapter. The other way is through a culture's attitudes and beliefs in connection with sex roles. It is common to accept certain kinds of ability to be natural and appropriate for the growing male and others for the growing female. Occupational traditions have much to do with these differentiations.

Differences in IQ   In comparing the two sexes with respect to IQs obtained from standard intelligence scales, we become more aware than usually of the ambiguity involved in composite scores. Sometimes there is a difference in favor of the females, sometimes in favor of the males, and in either direction the differences can be statistically significant, provided the samples are sufficiently large. It depends somewhat upon the age levels at which the comparison is made. With young children the difference usually favors the girls; with adolescents and above the difference more often favors the males.

It depends much upon the composition of the scale that is used. There are quite a few sex differences on special kinds of tests, some favoring the males, some the females. If a composite score is heavily weighted with component tests in which the differences favor one of the sexes, the total score will also be likely to favor that sex. When Wechsler (1958) states that the average IQ is higher for males on his WAIS scale, it is to be expected because males tend to do better on five tests, Information, Comprehension, Arithmetic, Picture Completion, and Block Design, whereas females do better on only three, Similarities, Vocabulary, and Digit Symbol. A vocabulary test could probably be slanted in favor of either sex, depending upon its selection of items.

Variability in IQ   There has been a common opinion that in the distribution of intelligence along its continuum the male is more variable than the female. By one approach to the evidence this is true; by another there appears to be no differences in variability. In a sample of 5,000 children for each sex in grades 3 to 8, Rigg (1940) found that on the National Intelligence Test the two standard deviations were exactly the same. By this approach others usually obtain similar results. In four vocabulary tests, with 2,000 children involved, Dunsdon and Roberts (1957) found no sex difference in variability for children in ages five to eight, but they found that boys were increasingly more variable in ages nine to thirteen, after which there was some decrease again.

It is when extremes of the distributions are compared that the sex differences become observable. L. S. Hollingworth (1922) reported that in institutions and in special classes for the mentally deficient, the ratio of boys to girls was typically 54 to 46. She commented that some of this difference could be attributed to the fact that more mentally deficient girls escape notice and can be kept at home, but it could not be ascertained to what extent this circumstance accounted for the difference.

At the other extreme, the Terman gifted group (IQs 140 and above) contained more boys than girls, and this was more true at the high-school level than at the elementary level. Terman and Oden (1940) suggested that this difference indicates that girls tend to lose in IQ just before or early in adolescence. Such a systematic change would also account for the shifting from a difference in IQ in favor of girls in early childhood to a difference in favor of boys in adolescence, provided the test content would permit it. The sex difference at the extremes, combined with equal standard deviations, means that the frequency distributions for the two sexes are different, that for the males being relatively more leptokurtic.

Differences in factor tests   Some inferences concerning probable sex superiorities can be made from the use of tests that are known to be relatively unique for some of the intellectual abilities and of other tests for which we can guess what the strongest factor component should be. We can observe only the differences in scores on such tests: we have to make inferences regarding sex differences in the factors. There is some risk in this exercise, in that a change of population may change the factor composition of the test somewhat, and there are after all some contributions to the variances of the total score other than that from the dominant factor. Even so, the ambiguity is much less than that with composite scores.

Table 16.1   Intellectual factors in which there are evidences for sex differences *

Males higher		Females higher	
Factor symbol	Examples of tests	Factor symbol	Examples of tests
CFU	Street Gestalt Completion	CSC	PMA Reasoning
CFS-V	G-Z Spatial Orientation	CMR	Opposites; Verbal Analogies
CFT	G-Z Spatial Visualization	CMT	Wechsler Similarities
CFI	Porteus Maze	MFU-V	Memory for Figures
CMS	Arithmetic Reasoning	MSI	Digit Symbol
DFT	Match Problems	MMU	Memory for Words
NFT	Gottschaldt Figures	DSU	Word Fluency
		DMU	Ideational Fluency
		DMS	Expressional Fluency
		ESU	Symbol Identities

* For other known factors where sexes have been compared there is conflicting evidence, evidence for probable equality, or no evidence.

A survey of all available information about sex differences in factor tests has resulted in the conclusions represented in Table 16.1. Most of the sources are quite scattered; some of the information comes from a factor analysis in which the writer was involved (Guilford, Merrifield, & Cox, 1961). No factor has been included in the table if there are conflicting indications as to the direction of the sex difference or if the differences are negligible. More attention has been paid to verification than to statistical significance of the differences. A list of factors in which the two sexes appear to be about equal is not given, because such information is somewhat indecisive; we cannot demonstrate the truth of the null hypothesis.

There are certain trends to be seen in Table 16.1, some of which have already been pointed out by writers, e.g., Anastasi (1958). One generalization is that males tend to excel in figural abilities. Of the 7 factors listed for male superiority, 6 are for figural abilities, whereas only 1 of the 10 listed for female superiority is figural. Of the 10 in the list for females, 5 are for semantic abilities and 4 are for symbolic abilities. The common recognition of female superiority in verbal tests and male superiority in nonverbal tests (if they are figural) is well borne out. Recalling that figural abilities tend to go with right-hemisphere functioning and semantic abilities with left-hemisphere functioning, as discussed in the preceding chapter, one might predict that the right hemisphere is relatively better developed in males and the left hemisphere in females.

We might consider some other generalizations and see whether there is any supporting evidence whatever in Table 16.1. Anastasi (1958) states that females excel in memory abilities; there are three memory factors in their list and none in the males' list. Females are said to excel in number work and in clerical-aptitude tests (involving the checking of letter sets, number sets, and names, for identity with other sets). This statement implies the two factors, numerical facility and ESU (evaluation of symbolic units). Anastasi wrongly attributes the clerical matching ability to factor EFU, perceptual speed, which is the parallel ability in the figural column in the structure-of-intellect model. Females are said to be more fluent, and we find three factors in their list to support this idea: DSU (word fluency), DMU (ideational fluency), and DMS (expressional fluency). Such a difference goes consistently with females' history of earlier language development and with greater exemption from language disorders.

Males are often found to excel in spatial abilities, and we find them ahead in tests for factors CFS-V (spatial orientation) and CFT (spatial visualization). One might hypothesize that the male superiority could come about because boys are more active and, getting about more, have more experience with space. But if this were correct, it would seem that the sex difference should appear before the age of five. Gesell, Halverson, Thomson, Ilg, Castner, Ames, and Amatruda (1940) reported no evidence of male superiority during the first five years. L. L. Thurstone (1948) concluded that the space factor is differentiated by the ages of three to four, but this tells us nothing about any sex difference at that age level. Stafford (1961) has provided some evidence that spatial ability is a sex-linked characteristic, as discussed in Chapter 15.

Males are found to excel in tests of mechanical aptitude. Besides the mechanical-knowledge aspect of such tests, spatial visualization is known to play an important role in most of them. Factor CFT is represented in the males' list in Table 16.1. Anastasi (1958) cites a male superiority in arithmetical reasoning, in which CMS is a leading component, with some contribution from CFT. It could be the latter component that in part accounts for the male superiority. But such a test is also strongly weighted with numerical facility, in which females are superior. This difference should offset that due to CFT. A male superiority in a score for arithmetical reasoning, then, is most likely attributable to CMS.

There is just a trace of support for another interesting generalization. Sweeney (1953) concluded that in problem solving males are superior where there must be changes in direction or method. This seems to describe the product of transformations. Transformation is the kind of product in 3 of the 7 factors in the list of males. Witkin, Lewis, Hertzman, Machover, Meissner, and Wapner (1954) have reported a consistent sex difference favoring males in seeing hidden figures, which indicates male superiority in factor NFT. When Kostik (1954) reported that males are more able to make transfers of learned information and methods to meet new situations, he may also have been talking about transformation abilities. This matter should be followed up.

In general there are still a great many tests of structure-of-intellect abilities that need to be given to the two sexes in order to make more substantial tests of the generalizations that have been suggested and possibly to find others.

Relation to attitudes   Although it has often been suggested that some of the sex differences in aptitude may be accounted for in terms of interests and attitudes, there has been little clear evidence on this point. Milton (1959) tested the hypothesis that men tend to score higher in problem solving because the tests contain content more appropriate for men. Using two 10-item tests, the problems in one designed to appeal to men and those in the other designed to appeal to women, he found that with masculine content the means were 5.7 and 3.3 for men and women, respectively, a highly significant difference. For the test with feminine content, males were insignificantly superior, with means of 5.0 and 3.8. The male superiority that is often found in problem-solving tests was apparently not lost with problems of feminine content, but this could have been an effect of the tradition of more masculine problems in such tests, hence of more benefit from practice.

Torrance (1963) presents evidence that a change of attitude in a year's time can be quite effective. The test was in the form of a task for children in grades 4, 5, and 6, in which a toy is presented to a small group, with the problem of demonstrating ideas about how the toy works and of explaining suggested principles. When the test was first given to a sample of children, there were sex differences in favor of the boys, with means of 6.2 and 3.1 for boys and girls, respectively, for the number of ideas demonstrated and means of 4.6 and 1.8, respectively, for the number of principles explained. Girls generally indicated less enjoyment of the task and thought it less appropriate for girls. Another such test given to the same children a year later yielded scores of 4.5 and 4.3, respectively, for the number of ideas demonstrated and 2.3 and 2.1, respectively, for the number of principles explained. At that time the girls rated their degree of enjoyment as high as did the boys. The change in sex difference was attributed to changed attitudes on the part of the girls.

Motivation in test taking   The discussion of interests and attitudes in connection with sex differences leads us to the more general question of the role of motivation of whatever kind in test performance. When we administer aptitude tests, we ordinarily exhort examinees to do their best, and this stimulus, together with a general cultural encouragement to do well if not to excel in what they do, is depended upon to a large extent to help ensure relatively high and uniform levels of effort. Examinees from other cultures sometimes show disadvantages because motivation is not sufficiently aroused or not sufficiently pointed toward making a good score, particularly in speed tests. Even within our own culture, we do not know to what extent different levels of motivation prevail during testing and what effect these differences may have upon scores.

Effect of reasons for taking tests   There have been reports of a few experiments that compared means and other statistics describing test scores when the tests were taken for purposes of assignment of individuals versus when they were taken for experimental purposes and the examinees knew this. Burt and Williams (1962) reported that children who took examinations for promotion versus for experimental purposes showed differences of 3 to 5 points in means in favor of the promotional situation. Variances and reliabilities of the scores were also reported to be increased slightly under the more serious condition. Children with and without monetary rewards showed less difference. Students taking examinations to obtain teacher's certificates or diplomas versus taking them for experimental purposes showed a mean difference of 5.8 points in favor of the competitive situation. Similar results were found for students taking an examination for honors versus for experimental reasons.

The application of incidental incentives does not seem to have much effect. Tiber and Kennedy (1964) tested middle-class and lower-class white children in grades 2 and 3, as well as lower-class Negro children, with and without certain incentive conditions: praise after each item, verbal reproof, candy reward, and no particular incentive. There were no significant differences in means between different groups and no interaction between incentive and social class in spite of rather large samples. The authors concluded that score differences that are ordinarily found between such groups cannot be attributed to differences in motivation. Such a conclusion generalizes to other incentives and motives at some risk.

Self-rated interest and effort   With high-school seniors who were taking an eight-hour battery of tests for a factor analysis, two self-rating devices were used in order to obtain some possible information regarding differences in motivational level and the possible effects upon test scores (Hoepfner et al., 1964). After each test had been completed, the examinee gave his rating as to how well he liked that test. A summation of all these ratings was used as an index of motivation. After completing the tests in each booklet, which took about an hour of his time, the examinee rated the degree of effort he had given to the tests in the booklet. A composite score was obtained from these ratings.

The composite rating for degree of liking was correlated with each of 47 aptitude tests, with a range from −.01 to +.30 and a mean of about .18. Of the 47 correlation coefficients, 27 were significant at the .01 level. The index based upon ratings of effort gave a distribution of correlations essentially between +.15 and −.15, indicating no relationship. The veracity of the ratings of effort, of course, can be questioned.

Another index of general drive for achievement was obtained from the departure of each student's grade-achievement index from his general academic-aptitude index; this was an overachievement-underachievement index. This measure designed for motivational level correlated essentially zero with all test-score variables. Except for the ratings for liking of tests, these indices intended to measure motivation indicated no bearing of such variables upon test scores. It is possible that if ratings of liking for particular tests rather than an overall rating were correlated with those same tests, some of the correlations with that kind of index would have been higher. But such correlations might merely mean that examinees liked tests that they found easy and could do well.

Compensatory basis of abilities   According to Adler's general theory, abilities are developed in an attempt to overcome weaknesses that are more or less recognized by the individual. A weakness in hearing should predispose efforts toward music, and a weakness in vision should predispose efforts toward the development of aptitude for painting. When subjected to experimental testing, the principle has not been found to work. Atwell (1939) did not find the theory to apply in connection with weakness in color vision in relation to art aptitude as measured by tests. Where the correlation should be negative, it turned out to be slightly positive. Adler was quoted as saying that 70 percent of art students have ocular anomalies.

Farnsworth (1941) verified the Atwell findings in connection with art aptitude and also demonstrated similar results relative to hearing weaknesses and musical status. Again, the correlations were low-positive, not negative. It is questionable whether any of the other psychoanalytic theories about development of abilities of different kinds, which find the secret in motivational bases, will be found to be any better supported when rigorous studies have been made. As has too often happened, far-reaching generalizations have been made on the basis of observations of limited numbers of atypical clinical cases.

Racial differences   The efforts to demonstrate differences among races in intellectual status have been beset with many difficulties and personal biases. It is difficult to say where the boundaries should be drawn among the races. It is difficult to obtain representative samples and to know that they are representative. The best that can be done is to select at random from among more restricted cultural subgroups, whose typicality for the race in question can readily be doubted. Then there is the question of what tests should be used. Tests are developed within the context of a particular race and a particular culture within that race. We have already noted that subgroups within broad cultural groups may show significant differences in various ways. The problems of this kind are only magnified when different races are to be compared.

That there are differences in means of test scores among racial groups, no one can deny. The meanings of these differences are not easy to determine. It can be stated as a general principle, from all that we have considered with respect to conditions and their effects upon test scores, that differences among means reflect differences in needs and opportunities for the development of various kinds of abilities within the culture in which the individuals have their existence.

In comparing two racial groups on the basis of scores from a particular test, it would be important to know that the test measures the same ability or abilities in both groups. If it does not, the use of the scores would be like comparing weight for one group with basal metabolic rate for another. There have been only a few studies comparing factor structures for the same tests in different cultural and racial groups. They have shown more similarities than differences, but there have been some notable differences. These studies have been mentioned in Chapter 2.

"Culture-fair" tests   In an effort to achieve tests by which different racial and cultural groups might be compared, some tests labeled as "culture-fair" and even "culture-free" have been devised. The culture-free goal is almost impossible to achieve; the culture-fair goal leads to misplaced effort and misleading consequences. When tests are sought toward achievement of either of these goals, tests in which members from different cultures make essentially equal mean scores, it is found that the tests are likely to have figural content, which limits testing to a small segment of intelligence (one-fourth, at the most, according to the SI categories). The notion that such tests measure *intelligence* is a vain hope, for within the same culture the correlations between scores from such tests and scores from verbal tests will be found to be near zero if appropriate experimental controls have been applied in the selection of samples. In ruling out verbal tests, probably the socially

most important aspects of intelligence have been lost. In the selection of personnel for jobs, the claim is often made that intelligence tests are "unfair" to certain cultural groups. If the job demands abilities in which a particular cultural group happens to be low, the employer would be unwise to make selection on the basis of some other test that measures abilities in which that cultural group does better but which are irrelevant for selection purposes.

A well-known scale of tests, the Davis-Eells Test of General Intelligence or Problem-Solving Ability, was designed by selecting items in which members of low socioeconomic status would be as likely to succeed as those of middle-class status, at the same age, in order to avoid the "middle-class bias." The result was a scale that does not correlate as high with other intelligence scales as is common, because by the kind of selection of items that was made the authors washed out some of the very kind of discrimination that is needed for measurement of intellectual abilities commonly represented in IQ scales. Nor was their goal of a culture-free test achieved, for scores from this scale still show some relation to socioeconomic level (Angelino & Shedd, 1955; Geist, 1954; Haggard, 1954; Rosenblum, Keller, & Paponia, 1955). The statistical reason is a kind of regression effect. There was selection only for items that did not favor the middle class in samples of subjects for item analysis, and there was a slippage back toward class discrimination in other samples.

In spite of the figural nature of the Cattell Culture Fair Intelligence Test, Anastasi and Cordova (1953) found that Puerto Rican children in New York City fell considerably below average on the test norms. They offered several hypotheses to account for this result. One was the low socioeconomic status of these children (but this is not supposed to matter in culture-free tests). One was the bilingualism of the group (but this should not, and ordinarily does not, affect nonverbal tests). One was the lack of sophistication with tests, for which no evidence was given; nor was evidence given for the fourth hypothesis of lack of emotional adjustment. Some other explanation is needed.

The condition of bilingualism was just mentioned in connection with the Puerto Rican children. This condition has come in for considerable study, probably because it is noticeably bothersome in the early school years. The studies that have been made, or at least those with reports available to this writer, pertain almost entirely to English-speaking schools for children whose native language is something other than English.

There is almost uniform agreement that the bilingual child is handicapped and that this shows in terms of his IQ in standard IQ tests, much more in verbal than in nonverbal tests (G. B. Johnson, Jr., 1953; W. R. Jones & W. A. C. Stewart, 1951; Kittell, 1959; M. E. Smith, 1949). The handicap seems to disappear by the time the individual reaches high school and college (Darcy, 1963). The child is usually below average in his own language as well as in English.

It must not be assumed that all cases of bilingual status are alike or that the variable of bilingualism is the only determiner of the lower IQ. Cultural and socioeconomic conditions may accompany the language condition. Another consideration is the age of the child when he begins the second language.

Nor are all the effects detrimental. There have been instances in which bilingual children are found to have higher IQs. In a recent study in six French schools in Montreal (Peal & Lambert, 1962), it was found that the English-speaking French children at the age of ten scored higher than those who had spoken only French, in both verbal and non-verbal tests, and they appeared to be more flexible. It was suggested that acquaintance with two cultures was an advantage for these bilinguals. Also helpful was their favorable attitude toward the English-speaking community.

Conditions connected with birth

Birth injury   In the preceding chapter, the effect of anoxia at the time of birth was mentioned as an unfavorable condition for development of intelligence. We are concerned here with structural damage to the brain as a condition affecting development. Doll (1940) stated that the most common consequence of such injuries is in the form of motor defects and that only about one-third of affected individuals are mentally deficient as a consequence, with all degrees of retardation. Of the feebleminded population, about 10 percent can be attributed to brain lesions acquired at the time of birth. The effects are permanent but nonprogressive. Some individuals with birth injuries have been known to be intellectually superior.

Premature birth   Children of premature birth who have lived have not been found to be handicapped with respect to intellectual development. In a group of 205 cases, Knehr and Sobol (1949) found only 5 were mentally deficient, which is considered a normal rate. For 99 who were assessed with a group test, the mean IQ was 98.2. For 26 who were tested with the Stanford-Binet, the mean IQ was 102.7. It was quite a normal-appearing group as far as these indications are concerned.

Month or season of birth   Quite a bit of attention has been given to the relation of IQ to the time of year at which the individual was born, and many conflicting results have been obtained. In summarizing many studies, H. E. Jones (1954) concluded that the most favorable time at which to be born has been late spring or early summer. This has been found true for both Northern and Southern Hemispheres (Pintner & Forlano, 1943). For high-IQ children in the Northern Hemisphere, the period from February to April has been even better. Goodenough (1941) found that parents of higher socioeconomic levels tend to have more births during the spring months and fewer in the winter months, which might account for some of the statistics. The net conclusion is that month or season of birth probably has little or no effect upon IQ of the individual. If the spring months are best, the differential birthrate may help to account for it; otherwise the fact that the infant receives more sunshine can be a reasonable hypothesis.

Summary

Of all the variables in the environment that have been investigated in connection with development of intelligence, that called socioeconomic level has received most attention. It is a very complex composite, of course, and needs to be broken down into better-defined variables in order to achieve less ambiguous conclusions. Numerous difficulties beset the path of the investigator in this field of study.

It is much easier to demonstrate the inhibiting effects of environmental deprivations than it is the beneficial effects of environmental enrichments in the development of intellectual status in both man and lower animals.

Among the inhibiting conditions are deficiency of stimulation of the young during infancy, lack of attention and of intelligent models, and poor educational opportunities. The major facilitating conditions are opposite to those just mentioned. We have yet to become aware of and to invent the best procedures for promoting optimal intellectual development.

Sex differences are most meaningfully described in terms of factors of ability, in connection with which some general principles are emerging. Differences are very small in the great majority of instances.

Sound deductions regarding racial differences are virtually impossible to infer from tests as now constituted. The search for culture-free or completely culture-fair tests is a futile and misleading objective.

17 Intellectual development

Of all the variables considered in relation to intelligence, that of age has continued to hold the greatest interest; the waxing and waning of intellectual status with age have far-reaching ramifications and consequences in our society. This chapter deals with growth of intelligence, and the one following deals with decline. Only ontological development will be under consideration, for in this volume we have been concerned only with human intelligence.

Efforts in the investigation of genetic aspects of intellectual functioning have fairly well divided themselves along two lines, quantitative and qualitative. The first line of research asks questions of "how much" ability exists under certain conditions, and the psychological aptitude test has been the major weapon. The second line of research delves into the ways in which intellectual functioning changes as later and higher manifestations come into being. Piaget and his associates have been outstanding contributors of qualitative investigations. Psychologists in the major child-welfare centers in the United States have been the followers mainly of the first approach.

In the meantime, there has developed a third major approach that combines features of both qualitative and quantitative interests, namely, the application of factor analysis to genetic problems of intelligence. We shall see some of the fruits of the three lines of investigation in what follows. We shall treat the first and third approaches together under the heading of "psychometric."

Psychometric descriptions

The structure of intelligence in childhood   We are going to be concerned early with the growth curves that represent intellectual development, but before taking a look at curves such as have been developed, we first ask about application of the structure of intellect to the developing child, in keeping with the main theme of this volume. From earlier chapters, primarily Chapters 4 through 8, we saw that quite a number of factors of intelligence that are differentiated for adults and that give rise to the model also apply to children at various ages. The evidence of extensive differentiations for younger children is very sketchy and generally lacking. In addition to the question of whether the same model applies to children or how far down the age scale it applies, there is also the genetic question of how that structure comes about and, if it does not apply during childhood, whether there is a structure of a different kind.

The Garrett hypothesis   This line of thought naturally brings us to the Garrett hypothesis, formally presented about twenty years ago (Garrett, 1946). This hypothesis can be very simply stated. It is to the effect that the abilities that are found by factor analysis come about by differentiation from a single, general intellectual ability that prevails in infancy and early childhood.

The Garret hypothesis would seem to go best with a hierarchical model of the intellectual factors, with successions of differentiations, first into broader abilities and later into narrower abilities. There would be some logical difficulties in associating the hypothesis with the structure-of-intellect theory, especially in saying where the differentiation would begin and what the order of events would be after that.

Kinds of evidence on the Garrett hypothesis   The writer is aware of at least 27 published papers that bear upon the Garrett hypothesis, most of them reporting studies designed to test it, which attests to the fruitfulness of that suggestion for instigating research. Several kinds of evidence have been sought in these various studies, all derived from intercorrelations of tests and factor analyses in most cases. If the hypothesis were true, there should be a systematic decrease in the average size of intercorrelations of tests with increasing age. In the infant and young child correlations of zero should be absent; in the adult they should be somewhat common.

A major difficulty with this criterion has been that of ensuring that tests of the same kind are comparable for adults and young children, also for adolescents. Numerous forms of tests that can be given to adults are completely out of the question as tests for young children and infants. Another weakness of the method is that the size of correlations depends upon the reliability of tests; the lower their reliabilities, the lower their intercorrelations. Comparisons should take reliability into account, which means correcting intercorrelations for attenuation, and this in turn means having good estimates of reliability.

Another implication of the hypothesis is that the correlations among factors themselves should decrease with age. The customary way of estimating correlations among factors has been the use of cosines of angles between pairs of primary (factor) vectors. The difficulty comes in the location of the factor vectors when they are rotated obliquely. The writer has never been able to accept such estimates, for too much depends upon the particular combination of tests one happens to analyze in the same battery and upon how well the tests have achieved experimental control of the measurement of their factors (Guilford & Zimmerman, 1963).

Other evidence is dependent upon the appearance of a *g* factor and its relative prominence in factor analysis. There should be a very strong *g* in analyses with young children, which, in the same or comparable batteries of tests, should decrease in absolute as well as relative weight in the tests with increasing age. If the first centroid factor or the first principal component were taken to represent *g*, then the proportion of variance accounted for by that first-extracted factor should tell us the relative importance of that factor. The *g* test of the hypothesis has been impossible to apply in most studies, because they do not find a *g* factor. Those who insist upon having a *g* factor obtain one, and then there is some arbitrariness as to where to locate its axis. Location has a bearing upon the factor's relative weight or importance in the particular analysis.

One of the most commonly used criteria for decision has been the number of group factors that appear to be involved in the intercorrelations of a battery of tests. The number should increase with age. But the number of common factors to extract has been one of the factor analysts' most debated issues. At best, there is some uncertainty as to how many factors to extract, which makes this criterion somewhat doubtful. Some investigators have solved this problem by extracting the same percentage of variance in all age groups. If one uses the number-of-factors criterion, the least that should be done to remove some of the doubt is to equate the proportions of variance extracted.

One or two sources of errors, errors that have rendered some of the studies bearing on the Garrett hypothesis less useful, should be pointed out. One condition has been the search for the differentiation of factors in different age groups in all of which all the adult factors have probably already appeared. Reference to the early chapters will show that very commonly subjects of fourteen or older show the same factors as adults. The search for undifferentiated abilities will have to include younger, probably much younger, samples.

Another condition that has probably affected some studies is the lack of control for age within each tested age sample. Where a range of ages is involved in a sample, hardly any test correlates as low as zero with any other because of the fact that all test variables are related to age. Even a range of one year might well bring in the age source of covariance at the lower age levels. Let us say that the three ages chosen are three to four, seven to eight, and eleven to twelve. One could predict the highest intercorrelations of the same tests at age three to four and the lowest age at eleven to twelve because of the decreasing rate of development during childhood. The results would look like support for the Garrett hypothesis but would be due entirely or in part to an artifact. The obvious remedy would be to partial out age if it had any appreciable correlations with tests within any age group.

Another weakness that hindsight permits us to see, in the light of known intellectual factors at the adult levels, concerns the choice of tests to go into the battery. If there is to be a factor analysis, of course, the usual care in sampling and in control of conditions as mentioned in Chapter 3 should be observed. Tests of the same factor naturally tend to intercorrelate higher and tests of different factors to intercorrelate lower. A further implication from the Garrett hypothesis is that tests of the same factor should intercorrelate higher for older subjects, as the factor becomes better differentiated. Tests of two different factors should intercorrelate lower as age increases and as the factor vectors pull apart. With tests of both factors in the battery, the one change (higher correlations within factors) as a function of age would offset the other (lower correlations between factors) to some extent. The best solution to this problem would be to use the most nearly univocal test for each factor. But most batteries in studies of the Garrett hypothesis have included unknown mixtures of tests: one test for each of some factors, two or more for each of others. Also, some investigators have mixed in psychomotor tests, which should have no bearing whatever on the hypothesis.

Evidence for the Garrett hypothesis In presenting evidence bearing on the hypothesis here, some arbitrary evaluations were made on the basis of the various weaknesses that have just been pointed out, with a separation of studies into "strong" and "weak" categories, both for results favoring the hypothesis and for those not favoring the hypothesis. On the whole, 11 of the 27 studies seem to yield results that are favorable, and of these 11 studies, 5 are regarded as strong; 16 studies yield evidence not favoring the hypothesis, 9 of them being regarded as strong. A few have evidence pointing in both directions. Only a few studies will be singled out for mention.

One of the "strong" reports with favorable support is from the originator of the hypothesis (Garrett, Bryan, & Perl, 1935). The investigators used seven memory tests and four nonmemory tests. From the description of the tests, probably each represents one factor, except for two tests that may represent two factors each. One test is a psychomotor test and is therefore irrelevant. The subjects were in three groups, with ages nine (to ten), twelve (to thirteen), and fifteen (to sixteen). The means of correlations in the three groups were .29, .26, and .14, respectively, in an order that could be said to support the hypothesis, but differences were very small. The authors remarked that the memory tests had increasing means of scores from age nine to age twelve, leveling off in the interval from twelve to fifteen. This suggests that there was some possible confounding with chronological age for correlations within the two younger groups. The authors also reported that when correlations were corrected for attenuation, the rs came in the same rank order. With four factors extracted for each of the three groups, the proportions of variance accounted for by the first-extracted factor in each case were .31, .24, and .19, an order that also supported the hypothesis, but these differences were small. It should, however, be pointed out that this criterion and the one based upon averages of intercorrelations are not independent; higher intercorrelations give rise to higher first-factor loadings.

Using the intercorrelation criterion, L. L. and T. G. Thurstone (1954) correlated four of the PMA test variables in grade 1 and grade 10 and also in a group with grades 7 to 11 combined. The four factors CMU, numerical facility, EFU, and CFS-V were represented in common for those different age levels. The average intercorrelations were .64, .22, and .27, respectively, indicating a marked drop from the first grade to high school.

Reichard (1944) had followed the same route, with samples at ages nine, twelve, and fifteen. In going from age nine to age twelve, the mean r rose; so the evidence is ambiguous.

Evidence against the Garrett hypothesis   Some of the results that do not favor the hypothesis are in flat contradiction to some of the results that do favor it. Chen and Chow (1948) reported that, with the use of 10 selected tests in samples of ages seven to thirteen and thirteen to nineteen and of college freshmen, the factor structure became *simpler* with age. A g factor was extracted in all three analyses, with three, two, and one additional group factor, respectively, in the three age-group results. Age had been partialed out of the intercorrelations.

O'Neil (1962) used the Wechsler WAIS and WISC tests with six groups from 7.5 to 50 years of age. Comparing the angles of separation of the two rotated factors, he found that the factor structure remained constant over the range of ages studied.

Sumita and Tchitani (1958) gave a battery of 17 tests, including some psychomotor tests, and extracted a g factor and group factors. They reported that the proportion of variance for the g factor remained fairly constant with age, which is against the hypothesis, and that the proportions for the group factors increased with age, which favors the hypothesis. The authors concluded that since the importance of g did not decrease, the source of the group factors in development is something other than g.

In a bifactor analysis, which included g and group factors, Curtis (1949) found the importance of g *increased* in going from age nine to age twelve. The hypothesis calls for a decrease. With the same kind of analysis, Swineford (1949) found no evidence either for a decrease in importance of the g factor or for an increase in the importance of group factors.

Some of the best evidence against the hypothesis is the finding of differential abilities in very young children without signs of a g factor. Very early in multiple-factor–analytic studies, with a sample of children ranging from three to six years of age, T. L. Kelley (1928) found factors identifiable as verbal, memory, and two spatial abilities. There was a general factor, but because he was aware of the age range of three years at such low age levels, Kelley interpreted it not as g but as a composite of age and other sources of heterogeneity. In subjects aged thirty-six to forty-two months, Hurst (1960) found signs of three factors, one for seeing relations, perceptual speed, and a space ability.

At the mental ages of two, four, and six in both normal and mentally deficient populations, with tests designed to check the hypothesis that such factors could be differentiated at those ages, separations of the following factors were found: perceptual speed, verbal, and figural reasoning of some kind (Meyers et al., 1964; Meyers, Orpet, Atwell, & Dingman, 1962). The number of factors extracted to account for 99 percent of the variance were seven, six, and six for ages two, four, and six, respectively, in the normal groups and seven, eight, and seven in the mentally deficient groups. The authors found no evidence of decreasing factor intercorrelation as a function of age. There was no evidence of greater differentiation in normals than in mentally deficient subjects.

McCartin and Meyers (1966) tested the hypothesis that six structure-of-intellect abilities could be demonstrated as differentiated with six-year-old children, aged seventy to seventy-five months, with a mean IQ of 105 on the WAIS. The list included two cognitive abilities (CMU and CMS), two divergent-production abilities (DMU and DMS), and two convergent-production abilities (NMU and NMS). The separation of such parallel abilities, each differing from its parallel by only one of the parameters of the SI model, was an exacting task. The six abilities were successfully demonstrated as distinct. Two others were found but were not easy to interpret. One may have been CMR, the cognition of semantic relations.

The greatest wealth of intellectual factors in infant and preschool children has been derived from analyses by Stott and Ball (1963). They analyzed a number of batteries of items from several infant and preschool scales: Cattell Infant Intelligence Scale, California First-Year Intelligence Scale, Gesell Developmental Schedules, Merrill-Palmer Scale of Mental Tests, and Stanford-Binet Form L. Altogether, 31 factors were identified as intellectual and 5 as psychomotor. An effort was made to align the intellectual abilities with SI categories. There was a risk in this attempt, as the authors were ready to admit. But if we accept their identifications as correct, the 31 factors represented all five of the operation categories, all four of the content categories, and five of the six product categories. Missing only is the category of classes, which is also badly slighted in test scales for older children. The important consideration here is the surprisingly large amount of differentiation found, of whatever nature. The investigators found no g factor, which is not to say that one could not be produced if they had so desired.

Alternative hypotheses   The balance in the evidence seems to be rather decisively against the Garrett hypothesis. When age and other irrelevant ability-related variables are controlled experimentally and when there is no insistence on a g factor, no g factor is found, even down to the first year. There is therefore no need for assuming a general ability from which differentiation can proceed in development.

The intellectual factors that we find from later childhood to adult levels evidently have various sources. The important remaining question is how extensively the SI model does apply at early age levels. This is not going to be easy to determine, because of the difficulty of producing tests appropriate for the factors at those age levels and the uncertainty as to whether the factors found there are morphologically the same as those found for adolescents and adults.

Because of the very prominent role of kinds of information, in terms of categories of content and categories of products, in the nature of intellectual factors, the child's experiences must have a great deal to do with the development of abilities along various lines, in interaction with the natural steps in maturation of the brain in increasing readiness for entertaining information and for learning ways of coping with information. It is clear that visual-symbolic information does not come within the child's sphere of experiences until he reacts to letter combinations as units. He becomes acquainted with auditory-symbolic information in the ages before two years, by which time certain sounds take on reference properties.

Perhaps the child's first kind of experience is in the form of behavioral information, information with regard to his own states of hunger, thirst, and discomfort. Very early, as soon as he uses his eyes and his ears begin to function, his acquaintance with figural information, visual and auditory, begins. His transactions with things in his immediate environment go on day after day, in perceptual and cognitive learning. Most of his earliest learning deals with figural information. Probably he has possession of many semantic products of information before he attaches verbal labels to them, as he learns some abstracted concepts from the constancies in his experience. The sources of information differ; hence there is a natural categorizing of them without his awareness of the categories as such. The environment more or less categorizes the kinds of content for him.

As for the categories of operation, the brain is apparently predesigned to perform in the five major ways, and it may also be predesigned to handle information in the form of the different kinds of products. But the child's environment is probably mostly responsible for the kinds of products as well as for the kinds of content, for as was proposed in an earlier chapter, the contents-times-products interaction represents an epistemology, a set of systematic, natural classifications of information (see Chapter 10). Intelligence develops by virtue of interactions between these categories as they impinge upon the child and the five hereditarily determined operations.

In his development, the child learns how to bring together the three aspects as represented by the three parameters of the structure of intellect in the various combinations, each combination being unique. How well any particular combination develops depends upon how much and how effectively he exercises that combination, and these circumstances depend upon what his environment offers to him and the needs he has for coping with those offerings. Individuals differ with respect to how much they have exercised each kind of combination, by necessity or by incidental involvement.

The child exercises in terms of particular actions, which are the building materials from which a generalized skill develops. Transfers occur by virtue of similarities of activities pertaining to each ability, as distinct from other abilities. An ability then grows by virtue of forming a generalized habit or skill. There will be periods in childhood when the lines between such habits may not be clearly and sharply drawn. If by a certain age level a skill of a certain type has not developed sufficiently in many children in the population, enough to produce appreciable individual differences, factor analysis would not detect that kind of ability; there must be sufficient stable variance with respect to a certain kind of ability if that ability is to come out as a factor.

An inference from this theory of aptitude-factor development would be that there is increasing clarity of the factors with more experience. Evidence in support of this deduction is provided by Mitchell (1956). Mitchell analyzed the same battery of tests in two populations, one of high and one of low socioeconomic status, the subjects being at ages eleven to twelve. There were two tests for each of five of Thurstone's primary mental abilities, plus a few other tests. Essentially the same factors were identified in the two groups, but the factor structure was clearer in the higher group, with generally higher common-factor loadings.

Growth curves   Curves of growth of human beings with respect to certain specified characteristics provide the best simple, generalized pictures of how such characteristics change as functions of age. This is true of intellectual functions, whether the measurement is in terms of some standard global variable or in terms of more uniquely defined traits. But we cannot interpret growth curves of intelligence properly and avoid certain wrong inferences from them unless we take into account some of the problems and difficulties that affect the needed measurements.

Difficulties in deriving growth curves   Some of the difficulties and sources of error in assessing the intelligence of individuals in longitudinal studies were mentioned in the preceding chapter, and they will not be repeated here. Some of those difficulties pertain to sampling problems, and others pertain to tests and testing operations. Wherever longitudinal data are employed for the purpose of deriving growth curves, the same difficulties apply. Another variable, however, that of retesting with the same test, or with different forms of the same test, or with different scales, becomes even more important in this connection. Little has been done to make allowances for constant errors arising from these sources.

It has been more common to derive growth curves by cross-sectional sampling, using different individuals at different ages. The longitudinal approach loses its appeal when there is the prospect of waiting many years to complete the study. Cross-sectional methods also present sampling problems. It is impossible to obtain samples, at different age levels, of individuals who have lived under uniform cultural conditions. Some individuals who might otherwise be included drop out along the way, by death, by migration, or by commitment to institutions. Over the years there are systematic trends in economic conditions, medical and health conditions, educational opportunities, availability of informal sources of education such as television, and international tensions and strife.

There are a number of measurement problems, problems of scaling. In order to make a growth curve tell us accurately about rate of growth at different ages, we should have a scale of equal units. That is, a certain increment in ability at one age level should be equivalent to the same increment in ability at the other age levels. We cannot depend upon a mental-age scale to achieve this for us; a gain of one year at the age of fifteen is not the same as a gain of one year at the age of five. Raw-score scales for group tests give us numbers, but we cannot be sure that an increment of one more item correct at the level of 75 score points is the same as an increment of one more item correct at the level of 50 or at the level of 15 score points. Many published growth curves are based upon particular test scales, but as far as we know, the shapes of the curves are, in fact, peculiarities of those test scales.

In view of this principle, there might well be as many different shapes of growth curves as there are different tests. This is not to say that growth curves should not differ where different intellectual abilities are concerned, but a test scale is a function of a particular test, and the continuum of intellectual ability is something else. We want to learn about rates of growth on this continuum from evidence provided by the test in terms of scores. We should probably have to transform the test-score scale in order to achieve our goal. Thurstone offered one solution to the problem by applying his method of absolute scaling.

It should be emphasized, again, as it was in connection with the longitudinal studies, that the tests given at different ages should be equivalent in factorial content, whether the aim is a univocal score for one factor or a composite, representing a weighted summation of factor components. This is an exacting requirement that has possibly never been met. The same kind of test may not measure the same factor or factors at different ages. Another problem is that the same kind of test might be challenging at one age and even insulting at another; it might be interesting to one age group and tedious to another. All these considerations should lead to some reservations in the use and interpretation of growth curves.

Curves for general intellectual status   We begin, as usual, with data of the more traditional type, obtained from a total score from which an IQ would ordinarily be obtained. We are not talking about gains in IQ, for IQ is an index of *rate* of development, not of level or status. The measure of status or level should be some function of mental age or of the number of score points in a group test.

In any case, the typical growth curve is one with negative acceleration, in which the averages for age groups cease to gain further at various ages in the late teens. An example is derived from the use of the Otis test by Miles and Miles (1932) at ages seven to ninety-four. The correlation between chronological age and total score in the age range from seven to seventeen was .80, which is unusually high. The maximum average score was obtained at the seventeen- to eighteen-year level, after which there was a slight decline to the age of fifty, with a correlation of −.28 within the range of ages twenty to fifty.

The age at which a test's maximum score is reached differs from one test to another; some curves top out before seventeen and others in the twenties. If we are not sure that the test's "ceiling" is high enough to measure higher ability levels, we cannot be sure that the ability or abilities, as such, have reached the maximum for the average person.

The fact that the average reaches a maximum level at a certain age does not mean that all members of the population stop growing at that age. Some probably keep on developing while others decline, and a balance is reflected in the means. It is an important fact, generally hidden by averages, that each person's growth curve has its own peculiarities. Although his development is generally on the upgrade, he shows periods of little change and periods of rapid change (Bayley, 1949), as shown by longitudinal data. There are also different rates of growth in different intellectual abilities, as we shall see shortly.

Because it is based upon Thurstone's absolute-scaling procedure, the writer prefers the growth curve presented by Thurstone and Ackerson (1929).[1] It was derived from data from 4,208 children and adolescents who had been given the Stanford-Binet tests at ages three through seventeen. Thurstone located an absolute-zero point by following a rational principle. After absolute scaling, which theoretically gave equal units for all age levels, he found that the variability of scores around the mean was a linear function of age, with a positive relationship.[2] He reasoned that the absolute zero should be at an age at which variability would be zero. By extrapolating beyond the given data, he found that the absolute zero came before birth, a finding which can be defended on other logical grounds. Although the kind of intelligence composite that can be measured above the age of three cannot be measured before birth, naturally, and even after birth for some time, hereditary sources have made some contribution to intellectual development in the way of preparation of the brain mechanisms.

Figure 17.1 shows the Thurstone curve. Instead of a trend that has negative acceleration throughout, this curve starts out with positive acceleration, going into negative acceleration after an inflection point that comes somewhere between the ages of nine and twelve. The curve is asymptotic to a mental-maturity–index value of zero and also to a maximal value of maturity, or the young-adult level. The upper asymptote appears definitely not to be closely approached at the age of seventeen.

Curves for different abilities   The clearest example of the rates of growth with respect to structure-of-intellect abilities also comes from Thurstone, who derived a curve for each of seven of his primary mental abilities. His PMA tests were administered to

[1] Berglund (1965) has also used the Thurstone scaling method effectively in connection with growth curves over the age range of nine to sixteen.
[2] Applying absolute scaling to scores derived from the Berkeley mental-growth study, Bayley (1965) has confirmed the systematic increase in variability with age and has found a growth curve very similar to that in Figure 17.1.

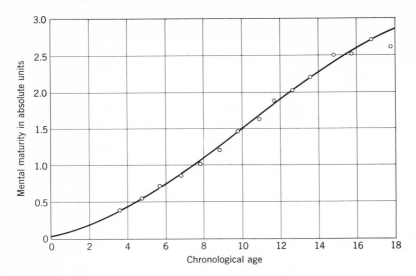

Fig. 17.1   Growth curve representing gains in intellectual status as measured by a typical IQ test, with absolute scaling of scores and estimation of an absolute zero, which came before birth. (*From Thurstone & Ackerson, 1929.*)

large numbers of individuals in the Chicago schools in ages five through seventeen. His absolute scaling was also applied in order to achieve appropriate scales. As in the case of his growth curve for the Stanford-Binet scale, each of the curves for a different ability proved to be S-shaped, starting somewhere above absolute zero at the time of birth and approaching the adult level as an asymptote. The zero point on the ability scale turned out to be 5 to 6 standard deviations below the mean for the group of subjects at any age level. By fitting the data for each test to a Gompertz curve, he was able to extrapolate the growth curves to the time of birth at the one extreme and to the age of nineteen at the other.

By rescaling all seven curves so that the upper asymptote had a value of 1.0, for the young-adult mean level, it was possible to compare the seven curves, which have been reproduced in Figures 17.2 and 17.3. By comparing the curves on the basis of the age at which the average child reaches 80 percent of maturity, the following approximate ages were estimated:

P—perceptual speed (EFU)	12
S—space (CFS-V)	14
R—reasoning (CSS)	14
M—memory (SI factor not certain)	16
N—numerical facility	16
V—verbal comprehension (CMU)	18
W—word fluency (DSU)	later than 20

It is likely that there are individual differences in growth curves for each of these abilities.

Development of speech   For information concerning the development of speech in the young child, we turn to the laboratories of child development. For speech in the infant, much of the information comes from O. C. Irwin (1949). In terms of SI concepts, early speech development is a matter of acquisition of auditory-figural units of information, the elements of which are 44 phonemes, the distinguishable speech sounds. It is also a matter of acquisition of semantic units, some of which are probably in the child's possession before he employs the auditory units as symbols or signs.

Even during the first few days after birth, the infant utters as many as 5 of the 12 vowel phonemes and 3 of the consonant sounds. The sound of *a* in *fat* accounts for about 90 percent of his utterances. There follows a period of practice of the elements of speech, some in combinations, with almost endless repetitions, in what is called the "babbling" stage. The phenomenon of compulsive repetition mentioned earlier also applies to speech activity. Up to the age of 2.5 years, the rate of development of use of phonemes can be described by the equation $N = 7.53A^{.47}$, which is a negatively accelerated function. In

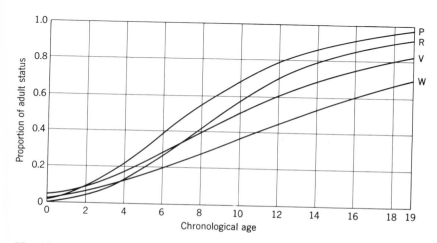

Fig. 17.2 Growth curves derived from scores on four of the Thurstone PMA tests, scaled to a value of unity at the mature level for each ability. (*After Thurstone, 1955. Reproduced by permission.*)

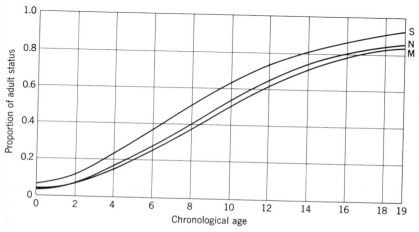

Fig. 17.3 Growth curves for Thurstone's other three PMA abilities.

other words, the number of phonemes used N is approximately proportional to the square root of age A. The frequency with which any phoneme is used, however, increases with positive acceleration during the same period. Boys gain more rapidly than girls in this respect, and children from professional families gain more rapidly than those from laborers' families.

After about a year of babbling, something like meaningful words begin to appear on a background of babbling. Development proceeds with transformations to achieve better approximations, with some aid from elders who supply the models. The roles of feedback information and evaluative operations are obvious. The early growth of vocabulary proceeds somewhat as follows:

Months of age	Number of words
10	1
12	3
18	20
21	100 or more
24	250 or more

The positive acceleration at this stage is obvious. By the age of three years the child may be quite a conversationalist.

With regard to the formation of sentences, which in adults appears to be largely a matter of producing semantic systems, Irwin concluded that the first genuine sentence appears at about the age of fifteen months. The first sentences are one-word affairs, which may indicate that what the child is producing is actually a semantic unit, a telescoped sentence idea. At the age of two years, the average sentence length is only 1.7; at five years the average is 4.6 words. Nouns and verbs are used first, followed by adjectives and connectives. According to some results on the same problem, McCarthy (1954) stated that the length of written sentences averages in later years as follows:

Age in years	Words in sentences
8	10
18	20
Adult	21

Development of vocabulary A number of studies have been made of the relation of size of vocabulary to age. Such studies are of interest because of the relevance of vocabulary tests to the measurement of factor CMU. It must not be assumed that size of vocabulary or score on a vocabulary test is perfectly correlated with status on factor CMU, nor is the regression necessarily linear.

Different vocabulary tests give somewhat different impressions of the kind of relation of vocabulary size to age. When we put data from different sources together, it appears that the curve has positive acceleration in the years up to about twelve to fourteen, with negative acceleration after that age (Markey, 1928). M. K. Smith (1941) estimated that children in grade 1 know about 16,000 basic words, on the average, and 23,700 as the total number of words, including derivatives. It appeared that students in grade 12 know an average of 47,000 basic words and 80,300 total words. The test was the English Recognition Vocabulary Test, by Seashore and Eckerson (1940), administered in three small towns.

Growth in creative potential   There is no good evidence regarding the rates of growth of other SI abilities such as Thurstone has provided in Figures 17.2 and 17.3. But there is one special area of abilities to which considerable attention has been given in recent years, namely, abilities relevant for creative potential, among which are the divergent-production abilities. The evidence available on this area shows some interesting peculiarities.

Torrance (1962b) has reported some of the evidence in the form of growth curves based upon raw scores from his Ask and Guess test. This test has not been analyzed, but it would appear to be relevant to measurement of ideational fluency and originality, two important semantic divergent-production abilities, DMU and DMT.

A number of observers had previously reported that children in grades 1 to 3 seem to be more imaginative and generally creative than those in the grades immediately following. Torrance's results show increases in scores for both boys and girls during those three years; then comes what he calls the "fourth-grade slump," a decided drop in mean scores. Torrance also reports that there is less self-initiated writing on the part of children at that stage, where such activity has been encouraged, and that less interest is shown in producing new songs. There are a less marked setback again at grade 7 and a leveling off after grade 10, which appears to continue in fairly uniform status at the graduate-school level.

Not all children show the fourth-grade slump; some continue to gain in scores. Some others who do show it seem never to recover. The average, however, does show general recovery and continued gain except at grade 7. The most likely hypothesis for the fourth-grade slump is that the socializing forces of conventions are heavily encountered by the child at that age. Boys and girls must begin to give more attention to proper sex roles, and peer opinion becomes more important. The minor setback at the seventh grade comes at the time of change to the junior high school, when the child perhaps feels less secure and is more cautious generally about his behavior, lest he attract unfavorable attention from his seniors in that institution.

We need information concerning trends with age for other kinds of tests in the area of divergent-production abilities, as well as in the area of transformation abilities, before deciding about the whole of creative potential as a function of age. Other tests may show features such as are found with the Ask and Guess test, but Yamamoto (1962) has pointed out that in this particular test he has found that children tend to go to a different kind of questioning at the fourth-grade level. Through the third grade, children tend to ask "why" questions, a kind that drops to a lower frequency level thereafter. There is a rise in the frequency of "what" questions, with a maximum frequency at grades 5 and 6. It may be that "what" questions are not so potentially numerous as "why" questions and that the drop in total number at grade 4 is due to the latter type's going out of favor.

There is some indication that the Ask and Guess test does not offer sufficient ceiling to permit measurement of creative potential beyond high-school ages. Trembly (1964a) obtained scores from thousands of individuals fifteen years of age and older, using a test like Consequences (mentioned in Chapter 6). A total score from that kind of test should also measure factors DMU and DMT. The trend of scores in relation to age is a rapid rise from the age of fifteen, reaching a maximum at the age of thirty for men and twenty-eight for women. The topping out at these ages is interesting because it agrees so well with findings with regard to the ages at which recognized creative people produce their most outstanding creations.

The most creative years   The information concerning relations of adult creative production to age has come from studies of biographies of distinguished persons. For many years, H. C. Lehman (1953) collected data on the ages of creative people in various fields when they produced their most outstanding works. The results show that in most fields the productions recognized as being of highest quality for different individuals came most often in the early thirties. The optimal years for some of the fields were as follows:

Chemists	26–30
Mathematicians	30–40
Musicians	30–40
Philosophers	35–39

In another place, Lehman (1960) gives the years of best production of chemists as being thirty to thirty-five. This information pertained to 57 chemists, mentioned in 19 histories. H. E. Jones (1959) cites evidence from Adams to the effect that the years of peak quality for social scientists are in the late forties.

Even within the same general field, such as writing, the years for highest quality depend upon specializations within that field. Lehman and Heidler (1949) have provided the following approximate peak years for different kinds of writers: [1]

Elegies (40 superior elegies by 25 poets)	30
Odes (50 superior odes by 19 poets)	28
Satiric poems (80 poems by 40 poets)	33
Sonnets (29 sonnets by 19 poets)	30
Lyric poems (113 poems by 41 poets)	27
Narrative poetry (61 poems by 27 poets)	28
Tragedies and comedies (113 products, 82 authors)	35
Novels (161 novels by 47 authors)	45
Novels (400 lesser novels, 128 authors)	35
Prose selections (274 products, 102 authors)	42
Hymns (290 hymns by 163 authors)	35
Hymns (245 hymns by 152 women)	35

The same authors comment that many superior products are accomplished after the age of sixty-five.

In general, *quality* of production comes to a maximum during the decade from thirty to forty and then declines. *Quantity* of production, however, remains at a rather uniform level from thirty to seventy, for those who live that long (see Figure 17.4). Dennis (1954; 1958) has found reasons to discount some of Lehman's findings but does not present any data calling for drastic revisions. He agrees with Lehman on the uniform quantity of production of physical scientists and mathematicians for the ages thirty to eighty, with individuals in their eighties producing more publications than in their twenties (Dennis, 1956).

Figure 17.4 does not show many productions of highest quality at twenty or below, but Lehman (1949) has given examples, citing 96 individuals who produced outstanding innovations, though perhaps not their best, at the age of twenty and before. Some examples are:

Aristotle investigated acceleration of falling bodies at nineteen.
Francis Bacon started rebellion against orthodoxy in science at fourteen.
Sir William Crookes published his first paper on selenocyanides at nineteen.
Leonhard Euler began working on synchronism of vibrations at seventeen.

[1] Presented with the permission of the *American Journal of Psychology*.

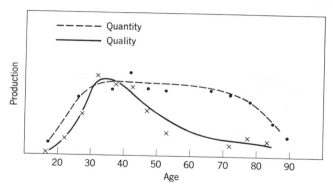

Fig. 17.4 Generalized curves representing the quality (best personal production) and quantity of creative output as functions of age from twenty to ninety. (*From various data of Lehman, 1953.*)

Hermann von Helmholtz demonstrated the connection between nerve cells and nerves when receiving his medical degree at twenty-one.

Antoine Laurent Lavoisier received a gold medal for offering the best method of street lighting at twenty-one.

According to Rossman (1935), inventors begin production of inventions at ages earlier than the first creative productions appear in other creative groups. Of 710 inventors whom he studied, 61 percent made their first inventions before the age of 25, the mean age being 21.3. He reported the most active ages to be between 25 and 29. He gave no information as to the ages at which inventions of the highest quality were produced.

In attempting to account for the fact that the peak of quality of creative productions comes a little later than creative potential apparently reaches its maximum for most groups, it is suggested that there must often be an accumulation of considerable information, frequently of a very specialized nature, before an individual is ready to present his best output. The information that an inventor or a poet needs can be gathered in shorter time; hence he can show an earlier start in creative production. The prose writer and the philosopher, however, must provide a broader base of experiences that takes more time; hence their better works come later.

If a creative producer should learn to improve by producing, however, we might expect to find the best output to come later than it ordinarily does. Lehman (1953) has offered 16 hypotheses as to why the creator does not maintain at least the same high level that he reaches relatively early in his career. Of course, many of the average person's abilities, even those more directly concerned with creative potential, show declines. It may be that the added acquisition of information and the mastery of skills of invention do not compensate for those natural declines.

We know of many circumstances of life that may contribute to the decline in quality. Some creators, receiving recognition of a highly gratifying sort, may rest on their laurels, but others should be stimulated to replicate the experience with a new production. Some scientists who win recognition are kept busy, following their masterpieces, working out some of the consequences of their discoveries. They may be given positions of an administrative nature, or they may be kept busy making speeches about their work. Lack of recognition, in other cases, and even destructive criticism may be discouraging, with negative reinforcement; hence no attempts of equal magnitude are later forthcoming. Another possibility is that later productions are undervalued in comparison with the earlier ones. The early productions came when the adaptation level was lower; the first distinguished production raised the adaptation level, which is a new base for evaluation of later output. It may be, also, that the judges of rank order of a creator's work take into account his age at the time the production occurred. An incidental circumstance may have biased Lehman's age estimates slightly upward. The creator's great idea may have been generated a year or so before it became known through publication.

Qualitative descriptions

For most of the qualitative descriptions of the development of certain aspects of intelligence in the human child, we are deeply indebted to Piaget. His concepts and findings and the findings of others inspired by him dominate this section. We shall consider his general theory of development, his stages and transitions, and some of the experimental work by others who have tested his hypotheses. As the story develops, we shall attempt to relate things to structure-of-intellect theory.

General theory of development   As indicated in Chapter 2, Piaget mapped the whole area of human intelligence in terms of content (observed data), function (principles of activity), and structure (knowledge). His attention has been given almost exclusively to structure, reflecting his strong interest in epistemology. In terms of structure-of-intellect terminology, he has ignored intellectual operations as such almost entirely, but by implication he has devoted considerable attention to cognition. Although giving primary attention to information, he shows no overt recognition of the four kinds of content. Yet the distinction between figural and semantic categories plays some role in his concrete versus formal "operations." It may be said that his greatest interest has been in the different products of information, of which classes and relations (under the heading of "seriation") have been given the most explicit attention. Systems come in for attention under the heading of what he calls "groupings." Implications and transformations receive implicit treatment.

Aside from Piaget's exceptional attention to the products of classes and relations, his interest has been in the development of some of the more culturally prominent *particular* conceptions of space, time, quantity, conservation, number, and the like, concepts that have played important roles in science. Although he believes that heredity determines the development of organs, their limitations being determined in advance, without environmental stimulation and interaction between organism and environment, there is no intellectual development.

Development is in the form of accretions of information, and only through a study of the growth of information can we understand the development of intelligence. The acquisition of information is through two supplementary functions of assimilation and accommodation, which are fundamental biological concepts. Assimilation is a taking in of information as imposed upon the organism by its environment; accommodation is rearrangement or adjustment of already existing informational structures as needed in the light of new assimilations. In a general sense, accommodations are transformations, in SI terminology, as discussed in Chapter 14.

Schemas   The infant begins life with a few inherited *schemas,* such as sucking, looking, listening, waving arms and legs, and grasping. A schema is a sensorimotor structure, a *class* of action sequences. In SI terminology, it could be regarded as a behavioral system. These schemas do not come into complete form until they have been stimulated into action, and they are modified by action in various directions, incorporating new sensory and motor variations. That is why a schema is defined as a class of actions. Each schema is also a cognitive structure, in other words, a product of information.

Inherent in the infant's makeup is a kind of repetition compulsion. Having exercised a schema, the infant does the act over and over again, as if practicing it. The exercise is with variations because the environmental situation changes, so that during normal practice modifications (transformations) occur. The sucking schema involves handling the bottle in different ways and substituting the thumb or a blanket for the nipple. Thus, there develops a concept, with certain constant and essential aspects (denotative meaning) and variable aspects (connotative meaning). It would not be out of place to conclude that a semantic unit is being formed, but Piaget probably would not go that far. He is insistent, however, that motor activity plays a very important role in development of mental structures and is even the foundation for thinking in later formal stages.

Equilibration Another general principle, also borrowed from biology, is equilibration. Development takes the direction of achieving new states of equilibrium. Equilibrium is perpetually being upset by new stimulation, with new assimilation. Accommodations then occur to bring about a new steady state, a condition of equilibrium. This concept has only a most general application, and unless we have better descriptions of what constitutes states of equilibrium and some principles in this connection, the concept is not very helpful.

Periods and stages of development

Periods of development Piaget (1964) has marked off intellectual development into periods and stages of child life. The first period, from birth to the age of two, is characterized as one of sensorimotor intelligence. Starting with the very few inherited reflex-type schemas, the infant develops more complex sensorimotor habits as needed in getting along in his limited environment. The period from two to eleven years is characterized as one of development of concrete operations, looking forward to later formal operations. Within this period are recognized six major stages, each with substages.

Before actual operations (dealing in terms of classes and relations) occur, the young child first experiences the beginnings of representational information. We might say he is stockpiling units of information. A little later, perhaps in ages four to six, he shows some intuitions, which are suggestive of the product of implications. In ages seven to eleven, concrete operations appear. The child can form workable classes of things and operate with relations, as in ranking objects for size. The period of development of formal operations is assigned to years eleven to fifteen, during which the child's thinking shows signs of formal logic. He thinks in terms of representations of things, freed from space-time existence, much of his information being put into propositional form as needed in logic. This is the average-adult level, which many individuals do not achieve.

Stages during infancy As examples of how much detailed mapping has been made of developments during a period, let us take the first two years, the period of sensorimotor intelligence. For this period, Piaget's chief source of information was found in the behavior of his own babies, Lucien, Jacqueline, and Laurent.

Stage 1: 0 to one month. *Exercising the inherited schemas.* During the first month Piaget observed a transition from a passive to an active use of the schemas and some conditionings of the responses to new stimuli. In addition to fixating a light, the infant would follow it with his eyes and show interest in it.

Stage 2: one to four months. *Primary circular reactions.* Modifications in the original schemas appear, and a variety of stimuli may initiate them. Coordinations develop between schemas. Things seen are reached for; things heard are looked at; things touching the hand are looked at. Discriminations, e.g., between things to suck and not to suck, develop. There is considerable hand watching.

Stage 3: four to eight months. *Secondary circular reactions.* There appear some signs of intentional movements and anticipations of effects. These reactions indicate that the infant has implications. The infant will attempt to prolong something he sees. He shows interest in things beyond his body and may try to make them move. He discriminates between strange and familiar things. Things that hold his attention are neither completely strange nor completely familiar. He has some conception of the permanence of objects, for if an object falls to the floor, he looks for it. Space conceptions develop. He watches his hand go from one object to another and to his mouth. He reaches for some things and not for others, which indicates some depth perception. He has the first realization that he can be a cause of movement of objects by making certain movements of his own. There is some beginning of imitation, which may be instigated because the parent imitates him.

Stage 4: eight to twelve months. *Coordination of learned schemas.* The infant acquires further discriminations of means and ends, of making a certain movement to achieve a certain goal. If an obstacle is put in his way, he learns to go around it, to push it, or to thrust it aside. He can observe that a thing outside himself can cause something to happen, which shows a discrimination between self and the world, the dawning of a conception of reality and a departure from extreme egocentrism. He learns to expect one event to follow another: a good example of his having implications.

Stage 5: twelve to eighteen months. *Tertiary circular reactions.* The infant shows interest in novelty for its own sake, varying his own movements and watching those movements. He shows a more active and intentional experimentation and a growing conception of reality.

Stage 6: eighteen to twenty-four months. *Representations of schemas.* Language is developing during these months, which facilitates considerably the formation of semantic conceptions, that is to say, verbalized representations of things. Mastery of delayed-reaction problems is clearly shown. Being given some indication of the location of a hidden object, the infant searches for it. Spatial orientation is extended to a much larger framework, for when he is some little distance from home, he can point in the direction of it. Imitations can be delayed, showing development of memory for actions and events. The infant is also likely to recognize that he has memory.

Growth of class concepts   According to Inhelder and Piaget (1964), something like classification occurs before the child begins to talk. This fact indicates to them that language is not essential for the act of classification. A new object that the infant encounters is often tried out by rocking, by rattling, or by rubbing, as if to see whether it belongs to the class with other objects that are "for rocking," "for rattling," or "for rubbing." This activity is reminiscent of the inclination of older subjects to define things in terms of use.

But Inhelder and Piaget do not take such behavior as indicating appreciation of class concepts. The first step toward classifying behavior is observed in a form that they call the production of "graphic collections," graphic because the collections are of concrete objects. The child needs to perceive such collections. If a child below the age of five is given a set of flat objects differing in shape and in color and is told to put together the things that are alike, he probably fails. With those who can do anything at all in response to the task, several primitive partial successes can be observed. The child may produce what Inhelder and Piaget call "small partial alignments," by which they mean that S lays out a few of the objects in a row, but he does not stick to any one criterion and he has no apparent grasp of the set as a whole. Another child produces larger collections but still shifts his criterion of grouping. Still another S may see ways of improving his system as he goes along, with more coherent results. But the result is likely to be an organized system, not a class. One child produced the outline of a motor bus, for example. Some such collections are geometric in form. The interpretation of this behavior is that the child does not distinguish between similarity and belonging. If he does understand the difference, he loses sight of his original goal and adopts a new one. He finds a construction goal easier to achieve than a classifying goal.

At the next higher stage, the children produce what are called "nongraphic collections." Objects are assigned entirely on the basis of similarity, but there is no apparent conception of inclusion. All objects are classified, with a preference on the part of S for a small number of classes. There is no conception of hierarchy, that the classes formed are members of a larger class or that two small classes can be added to produce a larger class. In terms of symbolic operations, the child has to learn that class A and class A' are included in a larger class B, so that $A + A' = B$. To reach this stage, S must learn the meanings of *all* and *some*.

When shown a collection of flowers, some of which are tulips, the child is asked, "Are there more flowers than tulips?" Children often answer "No" to this question. What they are apparently doing is comparing class A with class A', not A with B. What the child has to learn is that three classes are involved. There is class A and all the other objects, which form class A'; and there is class B, which is made up of A and A'. It is difficult for him to see that an object can belong to more than one class or have more than one attribute simultaneously. This might be interpreted as low status with respect to factor DMC, divergent production of classes. Inhelder and Piaget (1964) state that the average child does not achieve the conception of class inclusion and class addition until the ages of seven to eight.

Experiments on learning inclusion   Those who have done systematic experiments on this point find that the feature of inclusion and addition appears or can be learned somewhat earlier than believed by Piaget. Elkind (1961d) asked children, 25 in each age group from five through eight, the question: "Are there more boys [girls] or more children in your class?" Three levels of response were distinguished: (I) more boys [girls] than children, (II) recognition that classes are involved, and (III) more children than boys [girls]. The percentages of the subjects giving responses of type III were 48, 56, 76, and 92 for ages five, six, seven, and eight, respectively. Thus, about half the Ss in the range from five to six could master the problem. Elkind's conclusion was that the child does not fail so much in forming classes or in comparing classes for size as he does in applying operations in combination.

Kohnstamm (1963) approached the problem as a matter of *teaching* the child to perform the operations. He used a set of 25 statements such as: "In the whole world are there more animals or cows?" The statements were read to each child individually, immediate feedback of whether he was right or wrong being given to him. Of 20 five-year-old subjects, 6 developed insight. Insight was shown by the fact that all answers thereafter were correct. A second exercise for the children was a presentation of such questions in connection with pictures, with feedback information also given. Of the 20, 8 developed insight. The third task was with blocks in two colors in a set. This time, 18 of the 20 Ss gave correct answers. Kohnstamm concluded that a half hour of instruction is sufficient to develop the concept of greater quantity in the more inclusive class and that transferable insight develops. The concrete logical operation can be developed by training two years before Piaget thought it appeared. Kohnstamm's subjects were found to remember the insight two weeks later, and some who were tested remembered it six months later.

Development of quantitative relations   Inhelder and Piaget (1964) report that something like seriation or ordering behavior occurs rather early, as when a child stacks boxes in order of size, without any conception of "larger than" or of "size" being involved. The fact that he achieves this schema, however, prepares the child for later development of those concepts. Ideas of seriation are reported to develop parallel to ideas of inclusion of classes and to come into being as a concrete operation at about ages seven to eight, with no apparent connection between the two. The latter observation is interesting in view of the finding of distinct abilities for dealing with classes versus relations by factor analysis.

Piaget has recognized three stages in learning to rank-order a series of sticks as to length. At about age four, the child can put in rank order three or four sticks, not more. At about five, he is able to rank a larger number, but if told to alternate some additional sticks within the series, he fails. He has not yet abstracted a continuum of length. At six to seven he is able to insert the additional sticks in alternate positions. Thus, he can discriminate sticks for length long before he abstracts a concept of length. We might say that he has a figural conception but not a semantic one.

Experiments on ranking   In testing Piaget's hypotheses systematically, Elkind (1964) used material varying in number of dimensions: sticks, slats, and blocks. Three groups of children at ages four to six were given a discrimination test (pick out the largest and smallest in each set), a ranking test, and an alternating test with one-week intervals between them. In general, Elkind confirmed three stages of development. At stage 1, the child can select pairs of objects differing in size, but he does not combine relations to obtain a series. Shown a "stairway" composed of a series of objects, he takes it as a whole. As soon as the stairway has been destroyed, it no longer exists for him; he cannot reconstruct it. His main difficulty, says Elkind, is in coordinating relations.

At stage 2, S seems to possess some conception of a series that enables him to rank the objects. He does not yet have the adult conception of a continuum with many possible steps; hence he fails to insert the second set of objects. He can use them to produce a new series alongside the first. He apparently thinks of the first series he has made as a completed product. At stage 3 he can insert the new objects properly, and this appears to be possible because he connects one relation with another meaningfully. He is essentially ready to operate with the relation $A > B$ and $B > C$, to give the inference $A > C$. No particular test of this operation, which would be the convergent production of an implication, seems to have been made.

Elkind thus found that this inferential type of response commonly occurs before the ages of seven to eight. In another replication of Piaget's type of study, Braine (1959) concluded that the inferential response could be elicited two to three years in advance of Piaget's standard age. He agreed that when the response is acquired, it comes as something emergent, evidently as an insight.

Investigators other than Piaget have commonly found that his estimates of the ages at which certain informational products are achieved have a positive bias. In fairness to Piaget, it should be said that he was interested in the times at which such events came about in the natural course of events, whereas others, either intentionally or unintentionally, may have injected some training features into their experiments.

There is a quite common impression, also, that the age standards need to be more flexible than those stated by Piaget. Further evidence for this generalization has recently been provided by Wolman and Barker (1965). They proposed that the child's shift from giving definitions of objects in terms of use to definitions of higher types, i.e., in terms of class membership or in terms of synonyms, should be evidence of the transition to Piaget's formal-operational level. Examining children in ages four through twelve, they found no very limited age range at which the change occurs but, instead, a gradual shifting in probability of giving the higher types of definition. The percentages of "use" definitions were 78 at age four, 63 at age six, and 25 at age twelve: surely a gradual transition for a population. There may have been more abrupt changes for individuals, but if so, they come at rather widely different ages. It is unlikely, however, that an individual changes suddenly and thereafter avoids use definitions.

Development of conceptions of quantity   One of the important steps toward adult conceptions and ways of thinking is the achievement of the idea of conservation of quantity. A typical Piaget demonstration (1952) of this concept is to show the child two beakers of identical size and shape partly filled with liquid. The contents of one of them are then poured into another beaker that is taller and narrower or shorter and wider than the others, and the child is asked to say whether the new beaker contains more, less, or the same as the original beaker.

Younger children are likely to say that the amount is greater or less than before, depending upon whether they use the height or the width of the new beaker as the criterion. Children do not ordinarily see that the quantity of liquid is the same in spite of change of shape until the ages of eleven to twelve. To realize that the quantity remains constant means there is some conception of reciprocity. It also means that quantity has been abstracted from the concrete object. The concept of conservation of substance is achieved by children at ages seven to eight, according to Piaget, and the concept of conservation of weight at ages nine to ten.

Elkind (1961b) checked these age standards by applying conservation tests to 25 children at each age from kindergarten through the sixth grade. In general, he found that the proportion of conservation responses increased continuously as a function of age. The proportions for substance conservation ranged from .19 to .92, showing no particular age at which the insight came abruptly. The order of difficulty for the variables was substance (easiest), weight (not far behind substance), and volume. Even at age eleven, only 25 percent of the volume responses were correct. The median ages (ages at which about 50 percent of the Ss gave correct answers) were six for substance (52 percent), seven for weight (51 percent), and something above eleven for volume. Piaget's standard for accepting an age criterion was 75 percent. On that basis, his standard age for substance was eight, and for weight it was nine. Even so, his age standards are higher than those of Elkind.

Development of number concepts   It is generally agreed that a child can learn to count without having much conception of the nature of numbers. He may learn counting as a trick or skill by imitating an elder. The child's interest may be in the counting activity, not in the product of the activity, the numbers themselves. To know numbers, as numbers, there must be a recognition of the constancy of meaning of each number, of its universality, and of its membership in a number system. There is usually no concept of cardinal numbers up to the age of four or five; a concept such as the average adult possesses comes after the age of seven.

Piaget (1952) used a number of types of tests for probing into the kind of understanding a child has of numbers. He saw that the child's development of number ideas is akin to the child's conceptions of quantity, and he saw that ideas of quantity involve conservation of weight or volume. One type of experiment substituted marbles for liquid in the beakers and other containers, with questions of "how many" rather than "how much."

Another type of experiment asked the child to match numbers of eggs with numbers of eggcups, or flowers with holders, on a one-to-one basis. In still another type of experiment, after the child had counted out a certain number of objects, like beads, they would be arranged in different shapes and spacings. The younger children were likely to say that there were more beads when they were spread out than when they extended over less space: a confounding of number with space.

As in the learning of conceptions of mass and volume, there comes a realization that there must be compensations for height and width of containers or for spacings and that the number of objects can remain the same in spite of spatial arrangements. But at first, even though there is a realization of need for allowances, the child may not know what to do about the matter.

Experiments on number conceptions   It is sometimes supposed that the development of class ideas and ideas of quantitative relations (seriation) is helpful in learning the concept of number, for numbers are an ordered class. This may be injecting too much logic into what the child knows or does, however. Dodwell (1962) tested this hypothesis by giving tests for conceptions of numbers and understanding of classes in a group of children aged five to eight. He found that although the two developments proceeded simultaneously, there seemed to be little correspondence between them. Correlations between scores for the two kinds of development were generally low and insignificant. He suggested that longitudinal studies are needed in order to obtain a better indication of possible interdependencies.

The kind of class learning that children usually encounter is for either figural or semantic information, not for symbolic information. The number system is a symbolic system, and we know that symbolic abilities are relatively independent of both figural and semantic abilities. It is probably too much to expect that a child's knowledge of semantic classes and relations would readily transfer to the understanding of numbers as members of an ordered class.

Repeating a number of Piaget's tests, Estes (1956) found many points of disagreement with respect to Piaget's conclusions. Piaget found that although a child could count objects correctly when placed in a line, he could not do so if they were arranged in a heap. Estes found that the child could do the one if he could do the other. The successes at different ages were: at age four, 7 of 14; at five, 17 of 20; and at six, 18 of 18. Piaget found that children under seven thought that when spacing was farther apart, the number of objects was greater. Estes found the majority of children below seven realized the conservation of number in spite of different spacing, with the following proportions correct: at age four, 12 of 14; at five, 18 of 20; and at six, 18 of 18. When comparing marbles in a taller column with those in a lower, wider column in beakers after having previously counted them, Estes's children judged them to be of the same number in 10 of 14 cases at age four, 15 of 20 cases at age five, and 18 of 18 cases at age six. Again there is the systematic difference at age levels for performing the same tasks successfully.

Whether the hiatus can be attributed to differences in culture or in experimental conditions or to other circumstances is hard to say. One significant difference in conditions might be that Piaget held to a higher standard for comprehension of cardinal number because of his appreciation of the logical principles involved. The conception of number is something that is not either present or absent; there is a scale of understandings, with small insights to be achieved along the way. One should not attribute to the child who has achieved the idea of cardinal number all the logical ramifications that would be true of the philosopher or mathematician or even true of the average adult.

Conceptions of space   In considering the development of the child's conceptions of space, it is important to keep in mind the distinction between his figural and his semantic conceptions. This distinction has been only implicit in connection with most investigations. There is also a distinction to be observed between shapes and locations. The discussion to follow will be restricted to locations or orientations.

The infant's first commerce with space is in terms of his movements among objects that surround him, with tactual and visual monitoring of his movements and his contacts with objects. It is natural that in his egocentric existence his own body becomes his frame of reference. Objects are perceived in relation to that frame of reference. Gradually, the infant learns that objects can have relations to one another in space and also that there are other frames of reference than his own. For example, he learns that other individuals have directions of right and left that do not coincide with his own. He can thus shift frames of reference, and from this standpoint he can make an abstraction regarding space as a concept.

Stages in space learning   Piaget is said to have recognized four stages in mastering conceptions of space (Rivoire, 1962): topological space, affine and projective concepts, and finally a Euclidean type of reference system. E. Meyer (1940) derived somewhat different descriptions after studies with young children. To the age of about 2.5, the child behaves as if he moved in a "practical" space, with appreciation of the relations of objects to himself but not of objects to one another. Between the ages of 3 and 4, he moves into a "subjective" or "empirical" space. He is still his own frame of reference, but he is more adaptable and more readily modifies his dealings with space, using particular space constructs in new situations. After the age of 4, he moves into an "objective" space. Activity with objects becomes relatively less important and observation of them relatively more important. Things are recognized as having a separate existence and their own interrelationships in space. The child recognizes himself as one object among other objects; he seems to have achieved a *general* reference frame.

Rivoire (1962) reports that the achievement in Euclidean reference systems may come at any age from 4 to 14. As a sign that the child has achieved the general reference frame, Elkind (1961a) took the child's success in seeing that the middle of three objects is both to the right and to the left of two other objects. He found that 50 percent of the children at 8 years of age and 75 percent of those at 9.5 had achieved this status.

Relations to space factors   Since two factor abilities dealing with the cognition of spatial orientation were mentioned in Chapter 4, it is of interest to see what relations there may be between the genetic pictures of spatial cognition and the generalized skills for dealing with space. The abilities in question were considered to be exclusively in the figural category. One is factor CFS-V, and the other is factor CFS-K. Any abstract conceptions of space are in the semantic category of information, probably as special systems, along with other semantic systems. Imagined spatial arrangements, however, would again be in the figural category, as in memory for locations and arrangements that are visualized (in static form; with any changes introduced, transformations would be involved).

The two figural factors have been conceived as visual and kinesthetic, respectively. The question arises as to whether there is also an auditory-space ability. The CFS-A factor already found pertains to such systems as melodies and rhythms, neither of which has anything to do with spatial locations or orientation. An inference might be that auditory space involves a second CFS-A factor, which is not likely. It is probable that sound localizations are within the visual reference frame. This hypothesis implies that there should be substantial positive correlation between accuracy of auditory localization and performance on tests of visual-spatial orientation. This problem needs investigation.

The two spatial-aptitude factors, being figural, could well develop before the Euclidean conception arrives, for the latter is semantic. Development with respect to figural-space cognition is probably gradual, allowing for moments of insight along the way. If definite ages are recognized as times at which certain specified improvements appear, it is because the criteria for those increments are based upon certain kinds of tasks. As we know, different kinds of tests, within limits, can be loaded with the same factor; there can be different tests for indicating the growth of the same factor. Disagreements among investigators as to the ages at which children arrive at certain stages may well be due to the fact that they use tests of different factors as criteria.

Where a test is not a single-item affair, with only two scores, 1 and 0, there are likely to be ranges of scores at any age at which the test is suitable for measurement. A test is suitable for measurement when not all pass all items or when none fail all of them. Individual differences in spatial-cognition tests and evidence for factor CFS-V have been indicated by the seventh year (Emmett, 1949) and even by the age of two (Stott & Ball, 1963). As indicated before, the Euclidean conception is a particular semantic construct; thus it appears not to be a factor of intelligence.

Social cognition   Just as there has been a neglect of definitive work on the concept of social intelligence and social cognition, so there has been little investigation of development along these lines. Piaget has appeared to take it more or less for granted that if a child develops certain forms of figural or semantic information, he is also capable of having the same forms with behavioral information (Flavell, 1963).

An exception to the general neglect of development of behavioral cognition is a study by Burns and Cavey (1957), under the heading of "empathic ability." Children in the age range from 3 to 6.5 were shown pictures of a child frowning at a birthday party and of a child smiling in the presence of a doctor with a hypodermic needle and were asked to comment. A score of 1 point each was given if the examinee described the feeling of the child as shown and no point if he described his own feeling in such a situation. Children older than five were more likely to obtain scores of 1 and 2 points. It is not clear whether something more than behavioral cognition was involved; probably so.

Formal operations   The period of the child's life from the age of about seven to eight until the age of eleven to twelve has been considered by Piaget as that of concrete operations. During this period, the child can deal with classes and with relations as long as he has the objects present for perception. This does not mean that he is limited to figural information. He fairly obviously has semantic conceptions, but they are more or less stimulus-bound; much depends upon sensory input. On arriving at the stage in which he can perform formal operations, the child no longer depends upon perceived data; he becomes freed from the here and now and deals also with timeless and spaceless information.

Such differences entail other contrasts. No longer dependent upon what is actually present, the child can think of the possible or potential, and he is ready to try to re-form reality. In addition to being able to think about data, he can think about propositions; his thinking is largely propositional. He was able to form propositions before, but now he can interrelate them. Previously he probably developed ideas of negation, but now he also has ideas of reciprocity, of how one cause acting upon a thing can nullify another cause. He thinks in terms of variables and of multiple determination of events. He is ready to act like a quasi scientist, applying some of the principles of scientific experimentation to his problems and taking the hypothetico-deductive approach. This means that a puzzling phenomenon touches off a number of hypotheses. Piaget emphasizes the fact that the child typically runs through *all* logical possibilities, a generalization that can be doubted. Generating abstract hypotheses is usually a matter of abilities CMI, DMI, and NMI, the cognition and the production of implications. This aspect of development, therefore, can be conceived as a spurt in growth of implicational abilities of cognition and production, probably also of evaluation, for the child can test his hypotheses or implications logically.

In Chapter 10 it was pointed out that cases of implication can be treated as predictions in a correlational model, where two propositions are concerned and where either of them can be true or false, in the relating of two variables. The four basic combinations, repeated here, are:

1. $p \cdot q$
2. $p \cdot \bar{q}$
3. $\bar{p} \cdot q$
4. $\bar{p} \cdot \bar{q}$

which were also represented in terms of a 2×2 contingency table in Figure 10.8.

At the formal level of development, Piaget recognizes the combinations of these combinations in 16 ways, giving a group what he calls a "lattice." In application to any problem, the 16 alternative combinations provide many possibilities for describing the situation. In 1 case among the 16, none of the 4 basic combinations apply, and in another all 4 apply. There are 4 alternative combinations in which any 2 of the basic combinations apply and 4 alternatives in which any combination of 3 of them applies. Some of these higher-order combinations were mentioned in Chapter 10.

There is no implication that the thinking adolescent is aware of these 16 combinations and applies them systematically in every problem-solving situation. Piaget's point is that they are principles of thinking operations and that one can often see them represented in the individual's thinking when he talks aloud as he tries to solve a problem, each hypothesis implying one of the combinations. Such representations are best seen in the response to a scientific problem, as when the adolescent is asked to discover the Archimedes principle or to discover the concept of specific gravity, when he can observe objects of different kinds of material and different sizes float or sink when placed on water. In time he can develop the conception of "everything else being equal" and of how to hold constant certain variables while varying another possible causal factor.

The adolescent also exhibits what Piaget calls a "four group," or INRC group, which includes four kinds of transformations that apply to propositions:

I—identity (leaves any proposition unchanged)
N—negation (an inverse of the proposition)

R—reciprocal (relations between disjunction and incompatibility; conjunction and conjoint negation)

C—correlate (relations between disjunction and conjunction; incompatibility and conjoint negation)

Acquisition of the INRC group is said to be necessary for dealing with proportionality and analogies. As with the higher-order combinations of propositions, these operations imply an increasing ability for dealing with complexity, which should mean higher status in such SI factors as CMS and CSS, involving cognition of systems.

Errors in reasoning   In spite of the fact that Piaget can find so much isomorphism between the thinking of adolescents and the principles of logic, it should be remembered that logic was invented to tell us how to think if we want valid conclusions, not to describe human thinking in a general way and hence to provide a theoretical model for it. There is some risk of reading too much logic into ordinary thinking, and there is also the need for asking why it is that individuals so often come to wrong conclusions.

Henle (1962) raised the latter question and has done some studies of the matter, attempting to determine the conditions under which faulty conclusions are drawn. Observations of the instances of incorrect conclusions led to principles regarding several common sources of error. One source is the failure on the part of the subject to distinguish between a logically valid conclusion and one that he believes to be true as a generalization. In other instances, S ignores premises. In still others, S restates a premise for himself, altering its meaning, or he misinterprets the premise. This can readily happen when some ambiguity arises from the way in which the premise is stated. One special distortion of the premise is taking it to mean "all" when it says "some." For example, the following argument is cited:

Youth is a time of rapid growth.
Some youths do not get enough vitamins.
Some vitamin deficiency is dangerous to health.
Therefore the health of many youngsters is endangered by inadequate diet.

Consideration of Henle's findings suggests that the trouble is often connected with the premises and not with the process of deduction. In other words, the trouble is with cognition rather than production. The trouble may not be with evaluation, either, for S may be comparing his conclusion with faulty premises and a check is apparently achieved. The information brought into consideration by S is incomplete or ambiguous or is distorted in some way. The conclusion reached may be logically sound in view of the information that actually determines it. Even a computer cannot give correct answers if it is fed the wrong data.

Another important determiner of invalid conclusions has been known as the *atmosphere effect,* proposed by Woodworth and Sells and demonstrated by Sells (1936). By this term is meant that one or both of the premises given to S arouse a general "halo," such as an affirmative versus negative flavor, or of universality versus restriction, to mention two such global impressions. An invalid conclusion is likely to be consistent with such general impressions. That is, an affirmative atmosphere predisposes S to accept affirmative conclusions even when they are wrong. Such effects are less likely to appear when the propositions are stated regarding meaningful information than when they are purely symbolic.

George A. Miller (1951) adds another suggestion of a determiner of invalid conclusions, in the form of language habits. In habits of speaking, certain words follow other words with higher degrees of probability, thus introducing restraints upon what we say and consequently on what we think when we are thinking in terms of propositions. As an example of how a statement can suggest a faulty inference, Miller gives the example of the proposition "If some A are not B," which sometimes easily leads to the inference "then some B are not A," which does not necessarily follow. If we made a parallel meaningful statement, "If some dogs are not collies," the subject would be likely to avoid the inference "then some collies are not dogs," which he knows from experience to be false.

Although Piaget is evidently correct in saying that intellectual development in the individual is in the direction of operations as in formal logic, it is obvious that this goal is not generally reached at the time of adolescence or even in the average adult. Only in the case of logicians, mathematicians, scientists, and other individuals in some occupations, such as the legal profession, do we find a close approach to thinking consistently restricted to logically valid conclusions. It is best that for descriptive purposes we emphasize a psychologic, in which latitudes for logical errors are applied as a realistic policy. The search for principles of behavior in connection with the various products of information should be rewarding in this connection. An awareness of the distinctions between the operations of cognition, production, and evaluation should be of considerable help in designing experiments in this area of problems.

Summary

Quantitative descriptions of intellectual development have been investigated by those of psychometric inclinations, and the results have been in terms of growth curves. Qualitative aspects have been emphasized by those with genetic interests, mainly by Piaget and his associates, and the results have been in terms of stages and age norms for passing special tests, the passing of which is expected to indicate level of development in certain respects.

Most quantitative growth studies have been in terms of composite scores from standard IQ tests. With those scores accepted at face value, the growth curves have had negative acceleration, leveling off in the late teens. Not accepting such scores as providing a good metric and applying his methods of absolute scaling, L. L. Thurstone has found an S-shaped function, which starts slightly above absolute zero at birth and approaches the adult level, which is closely approximated shortly after the age of twenty as a limit. In longitudinal studies, individuals show departures from curves based upon averages. Thurstone has found similar S-shaped curves for primary mental abilities.

In studies of development, the Garrett hypothesis has played a prominent role. From numerous studies bearing upon this hypothesis, the impression is that the special abilities found by factor analysis do not come about by differentiation from a single unitary ability like Spearman's g. The best evidence against the Garrett hypothesis is the finding that numerous intellectual-aptitude factors are differentiated in early childhood, some even by the end of the first year, and that there is no need for a g factor.

A hypothesis alternative to Garrett's is that each intellectual factor has its own unique origin and that all of them come about through the interaction of hereditary dispositions and environmental sources of information. It is suggested that heredity provides the basis for the five kinds of operations of the structure of intellect. The environment provides input that is more or less preclassified along the lines of the 24 categories of the psycho-epistemology included in the SI model. The interactions of contents with products and of these with operations provide unique classes of mental activities, each class representing a special ability.

Development as investigated by Piaget has emphasized three categories of abilities, those pertaining to units (semantic concepts), classes, and relations, with more incidental references to systems, implications, and transformations. He thus implicitly recognizes products of information and believes that examination of what information (knowledge) is in the possession of the individual at different ages is the best approach to the study of mental development. Special attention is given to development of one of the SI factors, spatial orientation (CFS-V). Special semantic concepts to which Piaget gives considerable attention are all, some, quantity, conservation, and number. To a large extent, then, his efforts have been directed to vocabulary development.

With a conviction that the principles of logic can become a good theoretical foundation for the psychology of thinking, Piaget has devoted considerable effort to demonstrating the isomorphism between logic and thinking operations. The best evidence is found in children who have reached the level he describes as that of formal operations. At this level the child or adolescent is in fair possession of abstract conceptions which permit him to approach problems somewhat in the manner of a theoretical scientist.

18 Intellectual decline

As in the preceding chapter, we are concerned with intellectual abilities in relation to age, but here we are concentrating on the ages at which typical individuals reach their primes and the ages beyond which they lose in measured abilities. The rates of decline with age and for different abilities have both social and theoretical interest. We shall look into some of the conditions that are known to have some bearing upon rate of decline and shall be on the lookout for general principles of decline. Before we consider the known facts and theories about decline, however, it will be necessary to pay some attention to methods of investigation, for the results cannot be properly interpreted and evaluated without considering how they came about.

Research methods

As in the investigation of growth of abilities, there are two major strategies, cross-sectional and longitudinal. Neither approach is fully satisfactory, and both have weaknesses that need to be kept in mind. As before, some of the difficulties pertain to sampling problems and changing environmental conditions, and others pertain to tests and testing conditions. Since very much of the research has involved scores from separate tests, whether they have been designed as measures of intellectual-aptitude factors or not, it is important to consider the factorial nature of tests used with the aged and middle-aged groups. Factor structures for elderly populations is of some theoretical interest.

Sampling problems   Many of the same sampling problems are encountered whether the cross-sectional or the longitudinal approach is taken. Certain conditions that are related to measured abilities change systematically with age. Conditions such as education, its quantity, its quality, its kind, and the time since formal education of any consequence has ceased, income and what opportunities money can purchase, and occupation constitute the major potential environmental determiners of what individuals can do on tests. They contribute to individuals not only different supplies of information for memory storage but also exercise in skills for handling that information, skills that are also represented in memory storage preparatory to test performance. The time elapsing since rehearsal is also unusually relevant and generally is not controlled. Ideally, one should want stratified-random sampling, as in a Gallup poll, with control of all pertinent variables. Only one such study has been reported (R. L. Thorndike & G. H. Gallup, 1944).

There is also the problem of selective survival. It has been found with the use of twin subjects past the age of sixty that the twins who died during a nine-year interval following the first testing had averaged significantly lower than their twin mates in five Wechsler tests, Digit Symbol, Substitution, Block Design, Similarities, and Vocabulary (Jarvik, Feingold, Kallman, & Falek, 1962). They were not lower on other tests. If the same kinds of differences apply to groups tested in younger years, the variable of longevity is potentially even more widely relevant. Surviving populations are apparently not like nonsurviving populations in every intellectual ability. It is obvious that we can never know what some individuals who did not survive might have done on tests had they lived. Nor can we select for testing at earlier ages only those who are destined to survive to the age of eighty or whatever year applies to the oldest group used in a study.

Of the various possible confounding variables, Schaie (1959) found that the most relevant ones were family income, education, and occupation, which were most closely related to test scores after the age of fifty. But when Schaie obtained a multiple-regression equation predicting test scores from those three demographic variables and adjusted the scores, taking into account these predictions, he found that the age differences in PMA scores remained much the same as before adjustment.

Although the correlations between these variables and test scores may be negligible, as in Schaie's study, it is well to know whether they are high enough to be of some consequence in particular studies. As an example of such correlations, Bilash and Zubek (1960) found coefficients ranging from .20 to .42 between amount of education and test scores, with age partialed out. For a large sample ranging from twenty-five to sixty-four years of age, Birren and Morrison (1961) found that the correlations between the 11 WAIS tests and age ranged from −.02 to −.46, with a mean of −.21. With education held constant, the range was +.22 to −.38, with a mean of −.07. A greater effect of education might well have been apparent if the age range had been extended to eighty. On the whole, because of the positive correlations between education and test scores (Birren and Morrison report WAIS correlations of .40 to .66 with a mean of .51, with age not partialed out) and the negative correlation between education and age (−.29, from the same source), the effect would have been to show slightly more decline in scores as functions of age than would have occurred with education controlled.

Besides the possible application of analysis-of-covariance procedures, as Schaie (1959) suggests, if samples are sufficiently large, groups could be fractionated according to educational level, as Pacaud (1955) did with 4,000 French railway employees. With two levels for education, she did find the same rates of decline in test scores in the two groups. But she had the assurance that educational level had been controlled. With other kinds of tests that are more strongly related to education, the result might have been different. Later in the chapter some instances of effects of occupation will be mentioned.

In the study of growth, institutional life has appeared to be of substantial importance in some instances, depending upon the kind of environment provided. The same may be true of studies of the elderly. If stimulation of the brain is a significant contributor to development, it may also be important for maintaining intellectual status already achieved. Residence for a number of years in Veterans Administration hospitals and in rest homes for aged should be taken into account. If continued stimulation of the brain is needed to keep the intellectual level from declining, the elderly who "just vegetate" must surely lose intellectually.

At the higher ages, particularly past sixty, one also has to consider the possibility of degenerative diseases, such as arteriosclerosis, that might be contributing to decline. Usually investigators have been careful to distinguish between normally aging subjects and others with organic degeneration. Even the condition of general physical health should be considered, for Birren, Botwinick, Weiss, and Morrison (1963) have demonstrated some significant differences in mean scores of elderly subjects with good versus poor physical health.

Tests and test conditions   Both Wechsler (1958) and H. E. Jones (1959) have raised some pertinent questions concerning appropriateness of tests for older individuals. Since testing as a social institution has been increasing in its application in the general population, younger persons are more experienced and more familiar with tests of different kinds than the elderly. There is no question of the general benefits from having had such experiences. The variable of test-wiseness should contribute to more apparent decline in cross-sectional studies.

In longitudinal studies, the effects of taking the same test or a different form of the same test on repeated occasions are contaminating biases. As we shall see later, longitudinal studies, with retesting after one to thirty years, are likely to yield increases in means of scores, whereas comparing age groups in cross-sectional studies is likely to show decreases with aging in almost all tests. How much of this can be attributed to retesting is hard to say. Some of this kind of result may be incidental to the fact that in longitudinal studies investigators have happened to use tests heavily weighted with verbal content, emphasizing factor CMU, in which increases are common even in cross-sectional studies. But the aged show increases in scores in other kinds of tests also, as Kamin (1957) has found. Two groups with mean ages of about seventy-two were tested four times with Thurstone's PMA test. The gains in scores were attributed not to specific memory of items but to more general skills in test taking. Such effects of practice tend to wear off with time, as in normal forgetting, and if there are several years between testings, such effects should not be so important in comparing results related to age.

Another question often raised pertains to motivation. Many of the tests were designed to appeal to children and young adults. How well will they also appeal to older adults and to the elderly, particularly if some of the latter happen to be teachers and university faculty members, as in two studies (Garfield & Blek, 1952; Sward, 1945)? Mature individuals are differentiated with regard to occupations, also, differing from school populations in this respect. Tests that appeal to a mechanic may not appeal to an artist or to a businessman.

There is also the problem of motivation for competing in tests, regardless of their contents. Defensive middle-aged and elderly individuals will not volunteer and will not compete. Those who are not sure of themselves and who have pride will not enter into studies voluntarily. Subjects who enter without volunteering will come to the testing with different degrees of cooperation. This condition is better controlled in individual testing, but group testing is the expedient way and therefore tempting to use. Older subjects, less sure of themselves, are less likely to guess, which may be a handicap in multiple-choice tests. Kamin (1957) found that a little extra inducement, in the form of offering a prize for the most improvement shown in taking the PMA tests a fourth time, was followed by marked increases in scores in some of his aged subjects. Some Ss who had not gained in the second and third administrations gained suddenly. The most improvement was apparent in the Word Fluency test, a highly speeded test. Even under normal conditions, such a test may reflect some variance in a motivational variable.

Speed as a test condition It is well recognized that with advancing age there is a general slowing down in almost all respects. This tendency is obvious in the natural ways of doing things, and it shows up in tests that demand rapid work in order to achieve a good score. Particularly since Lorge (1936) emphasized the problem, investigators of age in relation to abilities have given it considerable attention.

Lorge demonstrated the principle with minimal evidence. He administered to subjects ranging in age from twenty to seventy three intelligence scales that varied with respect to degree of speeding: a form of the CAVD,[1] which allows unlimited time; the Army Alpha, which has moderate time limits for its parts; and the Otis twenty-minute test,

[1] A test title using initials for its components: Completions, Arithmetic, Vocabulary, and Directions.

which is highly speeded. The correlations of scores with age were $-.27$, $-.36$, and $-.48$ for the three tests, respectively. Lorge concluded that decline curves are somewhat exaggerated in the losses that they show for intelligence, in spite of the fact that the CAVD test correlated negatively with age to about the same degree as the Army Alpha. Tests of the Army Alpha type with respect to speeding have usually been employed in deriving decline curves. Lorge went much too far in concluding on the basis of his results that intellectual *power* probably does not decline with age, particularly when the CAVD test did show some negative correlation.

In order to gain a better idea of how much speed conditions for some tests bias the decline curves, some investigators have given the same tests, for example, the Wechsler tests, which are widely used in studies of aging, under normal time limits and with unlimited time. Dibner and Cummins (1961) gave the Wechsler tests in the two ways except for Digit Symbol, which would probably yield all perfect scores when given without a time limit. They found little gain for the unspeeded condition, with a mean gain of 2 points in IQ for the performance battery and a mean gain of 1 point for the total IQ.

Doppelt and Wallace (1955) gave five of the Wechsler tests to subjects of sixty and older with and without time limits. The "power" scores averaged 5 percent higher, but the means were never so much as 1 unit higher. With the PMA tests, Schaie et al. (1953) found little difference in the decline curves whether the regular or the untimed scores were used. It does not appear, then, that in two of the popular scales used in studies of normal aging the speed feature is much of a handicap to the elderly or biases the decline curves materially. This does not justify our generalizing the same conclusion to all kinds of tests, of which there are a great many not represented in these two scales, or generalizing to pathological populations.

There are some tasks in which speed has been shown to matter. For example, Chown and Heron (1965) cite an instance in which elderly subjects make better learning scores when they pace themselves in memorizing. This is not true of younger subjects. Systematic addition to exposure time for the elderly also gives them some advantage in learning. The elderly seem to need much redundancy of input, which the extra time allows them.

Botwinick, Brinley, and Robbin (1959) proposed a "modulation" hypothesis to the effect that the elderly are not so adaptable to speeds other than those that they prefer or that come naturally to them. Elderly subjects (mean age of seventy-two) could neither increase nor decrease their writing speeds as much as young subjects (mean age of twenty-two) could under instruction to do so. There are some who might cite these results as another indication of lowered flexibility, but the kind of flexibility would need to be specified; there are several kinds.

In the study just cited, the normal writing speed was slower for the elderly, the mean writing time for a certain task being fifteen seconds, as compared with eleven seconds for the young group. Birren (1955) questioned whether differences in writing speed might be a factor in a test such as addition. He obtained correlations between writing speed and scores in an addition test. The correlation between writing-speed scores and addition scores was highest if the addition problems each contained 2 digits, when relatively more of the working time was spent in writing, and dropped systematically as the number of digits per problem increased to 10, when the least writing was involved. Since this decrease in correlation was about the same for the elderly as for the young, Birren concluded that writing speed did not ". . . disproportionately impair the output of the elderly" in addition tests. He suggested the hypothesis that the slower adding speed of the elderly reflects a slowing of their perceptual processes.

There are other studies that bear upon speed and aging. The few examples given show that the speed variable needs to be investigated in connection with each kind of task, and the source of the slowing of the elderly needs to be pinpointed if we are to derive some really useful general principles on the role of speed.

Speed as a test control   On the general role of speed in aptitude tests, there are some theoretical points that should be mentioned. There are certain tests, like Digit Symbol, that would be pointless without time limits such that almost no one can complete all items, for errors could be zero and all scores maximal if liberal time were allowed. There are some abilities for which speed is an essential condition, for example, tests of fluency, in which speed of recall, or retrieval of information, is an essential aspect of the aptitude.

In other instances, time limitation is a condition that is needed in order to control the way in which the examinees work on the items. If given too much time, they can devise strategies that involve operations that change the nature of the test. It would then measure an ability or abilities for which it was not intended. Under the speed condition, the person who is high in the ability that the test is designed to measure, visualization, for example, can do the items successfully, thus emphasizing his visualizing function. Under liberal time, the person who is low in visualizing ability might reason out the answers and make a good score, which would be misleading as to what is measured. In other words, speed is often an important experimental control where other controls are less effective. In a vocabulary test, liberal time can be given because there is only one way a good score can be obtained: the examinee knows the meanings of the words. Determining the optimal timing for tests for the elderly, optimal in terms of measuring the intended ability, presents a technical problem of which there has been no apparent investigation.

Factor structure at different age levels   There are two important reasons for wanting to know about the factor structure of tests at different age levels among adults. One is the question of whether the aptitude factors, once developed in differentiated form, remain so throughout the ordinary life-span. There has been no prominent general hypothesis about this question as a counterpart to the Garrett hypothesis that applies at the lower end of the age scale. The other reason is a question of methodology. Investigators of decline in different abilities sometimes merely question whether a certain kind of test measures the same factor or factors at all age levels. It is important to know whether this is so if we are not to be led astray by decline curves, which might represent one factor through the age of fifty and another factor thereafter. One should not expect such sharp transitions as this statement implies, but there could be relative shifts in factor content as a function of age.

Evidence from factor analysis   There have been attempts to answer the question insofar as the 11 Wechsler tests are concerned. As the writer has stated earlier, the tests of the Wechsler scales are poor material for factor analysis if they are analyzed alone, for probably as many SI factors are represented as there are tests, perhaps more. The outcome has usually been a verbal factor, a performance factor, a weak memory factor, and sometimes as many as three additional factors. There is a general, or *g*, factor where that is demanded. The verbal and performance factors are, of course, composites, roughly representing the difference between certain combinations of semantic and figural abilities.

Analysis of the 11 Wechsler tests by themselves can do one thing: it can tell us whether there is general stability of intercorrelations at different age levels, and if there is, we may conclude that the verbal and performance scores represent rather stable composites. We can draw no conclusions regarding any more refined stabilities of factor assessment that the tests measure singly. One qualification should be stated, lest the impression be left that the two standard composites, verbal IQ and performance IQ, can be accepted as purely semantic and figural. There is a semantic-ability test within the performance group, Picture Arrangement, which should measure factor NMS, the convergent production of semantic systems. And there are symbolic tests, Memory Span and Digit Symbol, in both composites. These two are, indeed, memory tests, but they represent two symbolic-memory abilities. They might be scored as a third composite, leaving the other two less complex.

Where factors for the Wechsler tests are found at all testable age levels, interpretations of factors are much the same (Birren, 1952; Cohen, 1957; Green & Berkowitz, 1964; Riegel & Riegel, 1962). One finding that may be of some significance is the fact that fewer interpretable factors sometimes appear at the oldest levels. This trend was clearest in the study by Green and Berkowitz (1964). The trend suggests some simplification of factor structure for the oldest tested groups, usually above seventy, in a possible retreat from earlier differentiations.

Evidence from intercorrelations   Some of the intercorrelation data support this trend, but one study does not. Green and Berkowitz (1964) found that the averages of correlation coefficients increased with age, from .41 in the youngest group (under twenty-nine) to .51 in the oldest (over sixty-five). Kamin (1957), using the PMA tests with samples of only 25 each, found the following ranges of coefficients in three different groups:

Kind of group	Range of coefficients
Normal aged (mean age seventy-two)	.20–.56
Institutionalized aged (mean age seventy-two)	.13–.59
High-school level	−.35–.49

The discordant results were reported by Schaie et al. (1953), who used the PMA tests with subjects aged fifty-three to seventy-eight. The correlations ranged from .06 to .31, which were lower than those cited for young adults by Thurstone and others. The reliabilities were as high as are usually reported. The unusual range of ages should lead one to expect substantial correlations because of some declines with age common in most of these tests. The ranges of correlations reported by Kamin and Schaie et al. are promising for the possibility of separation of factors in the normal aged.

Intercorrelations for senile psychotics   When the population is diagnosed as senile, the intercorrelation picture is quite different. From such information and other sources, Dörken (1954) concluded that senile dementia is not merely a more rapid pace of aging such as is found in the normal aged. For the senile population he reported an average correlation of .63. Some data to which the writer has had access provide similar results.[1] With a sample of 360, five-sixths of whom were suffering from various degrees of senile dementia, the intercorrelations of 11 tests ranged from .44 to .81, most of them being above .60. When the total group had been divided into a higher and a lower subgroup on the basis of a rating for intellectual status derived independently of the tests but correlating highly with them, in each group the intercorrelations were factor-analyzed. Because of the generally high correlations, axes were rotated obliquely. For the higher group, the

[1] The writer is indebted to Oscar J. Kaplan for the use of these data.

average of the cosines between pairs of the six primary vectors was .58. For the lower group, the corresponding mean was .67. Seven factors were extracted in the latter case, two experimental variables having been added to the analyzed battery.

It is fairly clear that the factor structure is rather different for senile and normal adult populations. To cite a particular instance, the correlation between a vocabulary test and a number-skills test was .78 for the combined sample of 360. There would be no chance of separating a verbal from a number factor, as would be true in young adults and possibly in normal aged adults. Hallenbeck (1963) concurs in the belief that with brain damage the elderly do differently on tests than the normal elderly, for which he gives evidence. The general increase in intercorrelations can be attributed to organic deterioration that affects abilities in the same direction. There are other, less systematic changes, apparently, for Dörken (1954) concluded that for seniles tests correlate zero with age, whereas for normals they ordinarily correlate negatively. Only by analyzing the same battery of tests for SI factors in the senile, the normal elderly, and normal adult samples can we make good comparisons of factor structures. It may be that the senile population would show little more than a general factor, with few other systematic underlying variables of ability, depending upon the degree of deterioration.

Whatever increasing intercorrelation is found in the *normal* aged can be attributed to other possible causes, as well as to organic conditions that may affect different abilities similarly. For example, Welford (1958) has pointed out that the normal elderly have a remarkable capacity for organizing their behavior strategically so as to compensate for declining abilities. Such a capacity might affect scores in many different tests in similar ways and thus contribute to increments in correlations.

Decline in composite scores

Although decline curves from different tests are more strikingly different than are growth curves, thus calling for a more analytical approach to the study of decline, there has been some interest in decline as indicated by single scores from IQ tests. The Wechsler scale for adults has been the favored instrument for this kind of study. Somewhat different conclusions are reached from cross-sectional versus longitudinal approaches to the problem.

Decline shown by cross-sectional methods   Wechsler (1958) presents a decline curve for total score from his scales, based upon very large samples, as reproduced in Figure 18.1. The scale for ability is in terms of standard scores with the mean of zero at the highest point, which comes near the age of twenty-five. The decline after the age of thirty is almost linear to the age of seventy-five. It should be remembered that this curve represents performance in a particular composite of tests, on a certain kind of scale. Since the scale does not include all intellectual factors, it should not be regarded as representative of all intelligence.

Wechsler also provides decline curves for his verbal and performance scales separately. The former shows less rapid decline than the total scale, and the latter shows more rapid decline. These two curves are not shown here, because there is much more to be learned from information concerning declines in particular tests. Wechsler tests showing the most rapid declines are Digit Symbol, Picture Arrangement, and Block Design. The tests showing the least rapid declines are Information, Vocabulary, and Comprehension, all semantic tests, the first two dominated by factor CMU and the third by CMS and CMU.

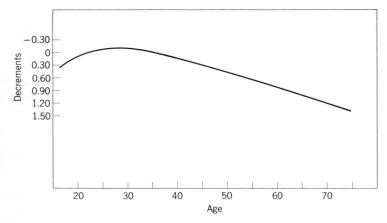

Fig. 18.1   Curve representing intellectual decline in terms of IQ-test scores. (*From Wechsler, 1958. Reproduced by permission.*)

The Wechsler deterioration quotient   Wechsler has taken advantage of the differential rates of decline of his separate tests to derive from combinations of them a score known as a deterioration quotient (DQ). This is a ratio derived from the "hold" tests, those showing little decline, and the "don't-hold" tests, those showing much decline. The hold combination includes Vocabulary, Information, Object Assembly, and Picture Completion. The don't-hold combination includes Digit Span, Similarities, Digit Symbol, and Block Design. The DQ is given by the formula

$$DQ = \frac{\text{hold} - \text{don't hold}}{\text{hold}}$$

where standardized composite scores are used.

The basic assumption is that normal aging is a manifestation of deterioration. The application of the DQ index, however, is designed to indicate deterioration attributable to pathological origins. This use involves a very serious risk. In an earlier discussion, evidence was cited for the fact that the effects of normal aging upon tests are not the same as the effects of senile dementia and that deterioration in dementia produces different and perhaps unpredictable effects in test performances. For example, in some individuals, verbal ability might be one that declines drastically (Inglis, 1958).

The greatest source of error of interpretation of the index, however, is that a ratio may simply indicate how strong the individual is in one set of factors relative to another set. The mean of the DQ values from a population is approximately zero at all ages above sixteen, and standard deviations are just about the same at all ages (Wechsler, 1958). This would mean that the DQ index should show many young deteriorated cases. Negative DQ values would also be difficult to interpret. What is the opposite of deterioration? The older person who shows strong deterioration according to Wechsler's DQ index might have had such a DQ score most of his life. This would be true if his profile of WAIS scores remained fairly constant over the years.

In terms of discrimination of senile from nonsenile aged subjects, the Wechsler DQ has done poorly. For example, Botwinick and Birren (1951) found that 31 senile patients were not significantly different from a control group of 50. Total IQ on the WAIS, however, discriminated the two groups significantly.

Longitudinal studies   Longitudinal studies of changes in general intellectual status of adults more often than not actually show gains in scores. The study with the longest delay interval was done by W. A. Owens, Jr. (1953). Owens retested in 1950 with the Army Alpha Examination 127 men who had had the same examination as college students in 1919, with an interval of thirty-one years. The average change in score was a gain equal to ½ standard deviation. This gain could be attributed entirely to gains in four verbal tests, in which the gains varied from 0.5 to 0.9 standard deviation. There was no significant loss in any test. Younger subjects tended to make greater gains, as did those who had attended college more than five years as compared with those who had attended less than four.

In evaluating these findings, there should be some reservation because of a sampling feature. The subjects retested were volunteers, and it may be questioned whether those who would not cooperate were among those gaining less or possibly losing. Because of the single long interval and because there was no testing at the time of graduation, we do not know when the observed gains occurred, whether during the years in college or in the interval after leaving college. We also do not know how much to attribute the gains to retesting, even after so long an interval.

Of the 127 in Owens's sample, 96 were retested again in 1961, eleven years after the first retesting (Schoenfeldt, Gillmer, Kelley, & Owens, 1963). By comparing means for three factors (verbal, number, and reasoning), it was found that the verbal mean had dropped slightly, the reasoning mean had held fairly constant, and the numerical mean, which had dropped slightly in the first retesting, had dropped more in the later interval.

Jarvik et al. (1962) tested many pairs of twins who were past sixty, then retested them after one year and also after nine years, with some of the Wechsler tests. There were increases in means of scores for the first retesting, which the authors attributed to improvement with experience in being tested. There were decreases between second and third testings in all tests except Digits Forward. It would be desirable to know whether the same subjects would have gained as much if they had been retested immediately after their first testing. Owing to a probable increasing incidence of poor physical health during the seventh decade, it would be important to know whether the average status in this respect was the same in the third testing as in the second.

An exception to the general rule appeared in a study by Berkowitz and Green (1963). Their subjects were inmates of a Veterans Administration hospital, with a mean age of 56.3 at the time of first testing and 65.0 at the time of second testing. Decrements were found in all the Wechsler tests after the interval, which averaged about nine years. The slight but significant declines in IQ were about the same for both verbal and performance scales. It is possible that the institutional life of these individuals contributed to the losses.

Decline in intellectual factors

An example of how decline curves for particular tests differ is shown in Figure 18.2 for four of the Wechsler tests. Such differences are found even when the tests are not univocal for intellectual factors. The Information test is essentially univocal for factor CMU (verbal comprehension), Block Design is for factor CFT (spatial visualization), and Digit Symbol appears to be for factor MSI (memory for symbolic implications) (P. C. Davis, 1956). The Arithmetic test, like arithmetical-reasoning tests in general, may have two leading factor components, CMS (general reasoning) and numerical facility. Its decline curve then represents two or three factors in combination, which means that its rate of decline may be a compromise or an average, one component declining at a more

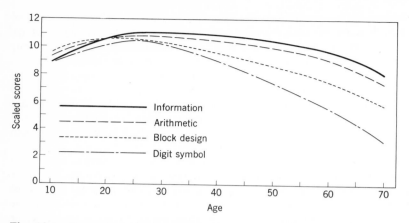

Fig. 18.2 Curves representing differential rates of decline in four Wechsler tests. (*From Wechsler, 1958. Reproduced by permission.*)

rapid rate than another. Again, we see the desirability of using univocal tests if we want unambiguous pictures of declining functions.

Tests of cognition   Enough special tests have been used in studies of decline to make it worth our while to attempt to see whether there are any systematic relations of decline to structure-of-intellect categories. The evidence is very spotty, at best. At least the categories will serve as a basis for organizing the discussion.

Welford (1958) has made the comment that the apparent weaknesses of the elderly in learning and retention may actually be due to weaknesses in cognition; new experiences are not sufficiently impressed upon the individual's nervous equipment because input has not been well developed. The fact that the elderly often show very good retention and recall for earlier experiences also indicates that insofar as retention itself is concerned, there is not general impairment. But since there are quite a number of cognitive abilities, it is necessary to consider whether all or just certain ones are impaired.

Vocabulary   Of all tests, those for CMU have shown the least decline with age. In a cross-sectional study, Trembly (1964b) has reported that with a 150-item multiple-choice vocabulary test, the performance curve continues to rise at a decelerated rate to the age of sixty. R. L. Thorndike and G. H. Gallup (1941) found no change from age twenty to age fifty, with an average loss of only 1 point (in a 20-item test) to the age of sixty-five, a loss equivalent to ten months of mental age. Garfield and Blek (1952) gave a certain vocabulary test to teachers in training (ages twenty to thirty), teachers, and retired teachers, one group with ages forty to fifty and the other sixty to seventy. The means of scores were approximately 31, 35, and 38, respectively, all differences being significant. Even in cross-sectional assessments, such as all these examples have been, vocabulary continues to grow slightly, particularly in populations in which words are an important commodity.

The conclusion is sometimes drawn that "verbal ability" remains high, but generalizations beyond one semantic ability to others is not justified. Within the category of semantic-cognition abilities, in which there are six, there is evidence for decline in only one or two other than CMU. The decline in CMS (general reasoning), which is the leading component of arithmetic-reasoning tests, is suggested by the curve in Figure 18.2. K. F. Riegel (1959) has demonstrated that a young group (mean age about nineteen) had a higher mean than an older group (above sixty-five) in a test that probably measures factor CMC. A sample item reads:

A GRANARY belongs with: field, stable, farm, barn, plough.

A recognition of classes must be a feature of such a test.

Some figural-cognition abilities   There are a few indications of declines in figural-cognition abilities. Welford (1964) states that in tests involving the viewing of objects under difficult conditions the elderly make more errors. This description fits tests of factor CFU-V, the cognition of visual-figural units. For factor CFS-V, Schaie (1958) has reported that in Thurstone's PMA Space test there is a linear decline after the age of thirty-three. Bilash and Zubek (1960) found that the curve for a test of Space Relations kept to a high level to the age of forty-five, after which there was a rapid decline. The test may have had some involvement with factor CFT (visualization). Wechsler (1958) reports that the test Block Design, another CFT test, is one of three in his battery with most rapid decline.

Some symbolic-cognition abilities   Information about decline in symbolic-cognition abilities is limited to two tests: King's Reasoning test, which has some items that should measure CSC and others that should measure CSS; and Thurstone's PMA Reasoning, which should measure CSS. The King test showed an almost continuous decline from twenty to seventy, with some arrest between twenty and forty-five (Bilash & Zubek, 1960). The Thurstone test showed a linear decline from twenty to sixty (Schaie, 1958).

Memory abilities   A survey of the scattered experimental and psychometric information regarding memory of different kinds reveals conflicting pictures. There are no reports of actual evidence to the effect that any memory abilities improve with age, beyond the youthful period, but in some respects there is decline and in some respects not. Most of the studies need to be replicated and extended to other areas of information, and further studies in depth are needed for particular varieties of memory.

Short-term memory   Discussions of what is called "short-term" memory in Chapter 13 adopted the view that it deals with a phenomenon lasting only a second or two after stimulation. The somewhat vivid persisting aftereffects of stimulation permit the individual to extend his capacity for input, his momentary capacity being very limited. By virtue of this overlapping of current experiences he is able to take in and perhaps to fixate more information than would otherwise be possible.

Experiments of the Broadbent type, in which digits are spoken into earphones in the two ears, three in one and three in the other, simultaneously or alternately in the two ears, have been applied to the elderly. It is found that the elderly do as well as younger subjects in reporting the set of three digits to be reported first but show relative defects in reporting the second set of three exposed digits (Welford, 1958; 1964). Although debate has continued over whether in younger subjects the loss of information is due to time delay or to interferences, with the elderly it looks as if interference were the key determiner. In previous chapters the view has been that interference can best be interpreted as confusion of information, which means loss of discrimination or loss of information. Thus, the increased intake capacity offered to younger subjects by virtue of short-term memory seems to be more or less withheld from the elderly. Any such possible gain in capacity is offset by interferences, very likely more than offset.

Memory for units and systems   There happens to be a little evidence regarding the memory for units and systems of information, figural, symbolic, and semantic. Memory-span tests, for series to be recited in the forward direction, should be at least in part measures of factor MSS. Gilbert (1941) reports only a moderate amount of decline. Cameron (1943) found that even seniles can remember three digits for several minutes but that interpolated spelling activity ruins recall for the digits. This episode of retro-active inhibition is obviously an interference effect, having its influence apparently beyond the short-term–memory interval. It is an interesting question to what extent the common use of telephone numbers, social security numbers, and the like in the United States culture has helped to keep memory-span ability from declining more than it otherwise would.

For a test of Design Memory, which should be a measure of factor MFU, Trembly (1964b) has reported a curve that reaches its maximum at the age of seventeen and starts its decline after about thirty. In the study of memory by H. E. Jones, H. S. Conrad, and A. Horn (1928), in which subjects answered questions about facts presented in a motion picture, a performance curve in relation to age was very similar to those for composite scores of intelligence, as in Figure 18.1. The kind of memory involved should have been largely for semantic units, that is, for factor MMU.

Memory for implications   The only memory-for-implications ability about which much is known is MSI. From at least two studies (P. C. Davis, 1956; de Mille, 1962) there is evidence that numerical-operations tests and the Wechsler Digit Symbol test both measure this ability to some extent. The former emphasize well-practiced implications of long standing in the case of adults, whereas the latter deals with very recently formed associations, so recent they can even be put in the category of short-term memory, as the examinee looks back and forth from code to items on which he is working.

With a numerical-operations test, Bilash and Zubek (1960) found that performance remained at about the same high level to the age of forty-five, then declined rapidly. Schaie (1958) reported from use of the PMA Number test a slight rise to about fifty, then a rapid decline. Wechsler (1958) reported the Digit Symbol test among the three with most rapid decline. His curve shows the decline starting somewhere between twenty-five and thirty years of age.

Birren, Allen, and Landau (1954) made a rather intensive study of performances on addition tests in ages from sixteen to ninety. There would be much risk in attributing their conclusions to factor MSI. Recent experience shows that an addition test has a relatively large specific component besides MSI variance (Tenopyr, 1966). Other findings (Petersen et al., 1963) show that numerical-operations tests are also loaded with NSI. Some of the features shown in Birren's experimental results could thus be possibly attrib-uted to factor NSI, a second common-factor component of numerical-operations tests, or to the specific component in an addition test.

Birren et al. were concerned with speed and accuracy as functions of age and of the numbers of additions per item, also with interactions between age and the other condition. They varied the items with respect to numbers of additions from 1 to 25 (2 to 26 digits). The measurements taken were average time per item and proportion of correct item sums. One thing that they found was that the time T required as a function of n (number of additions) could be expressed at any age level by the equation

$$T = Kn^m$$

where K and m are constants to be derived from the data and T and n have been defined. K and m were found to be related to age. K increased from about .88 in ages below fifty to 3.3 in ages above seventy, while m decreased from 1.26 below age thirty to about .98 above age seventy. When m equals 1.0, the time is in direct proportion to the number of additions per item. With m greater than 1.0, there is positive acceleration. A decrease in m, which changes very little with age, is more than offset by the increase in K, which increases with positive acceleration. The net effect is that the elderly take more time per addition as age increases.

The equation is given to demonstrate how searchingly performance on any test may be studied experimentally. In addition to this equation, the investigators derived an empirical equation for p (proportion of correct answers) as a function of n, and they found that parameters of this equation also changed systematically with age. A rational equation relating T, p, and n was developed. Analyzing the addition test logically into the components of perception of digits, addition of digits, carrying digits, and writing answers, they concluded that the elderly slow down in every respect but that decline in adding with age is largely a matter of weakness in organizing input information and relating it in relevant ways. This seems to describe cognitive defect rather than memory defect.

In general, paired-associates memorizing should be a matter of memory for implications, the second member of a pair being implied by the first member. Hulicka and Weiss (1965) have reported an experiment on the memorizing of figures paired with boys' names, with one group of subjects with mean age of thirty-eight and another with mean age of sixty-eight. The superiority of the younger group depended upon what kind of score was used, revealing some interesting age differences.

In runs of 15 trials for either group of subjects, the younger group made more correct responses, with scores of 92 versus 54. With equal exposure to material, then, the older Ss were decidedly poorer. In a recall test twenty minutes later, the means were approximately 8 versus 4, in favor of the younger group. When the two groups were compared on the basis of trials-to-criterion scores, the younger group also did better, with means of 14 versus 21. But recall scores after twenty minutes were the same (7.6 and 7.6). This could be attributed to the fact that the elderly had had more exposure to the items, 50 percent more, in fact.

Further comparisons were made by matching young and old who had had the same mastery scores and presumably equivalent exposures to the input information. After a twenty-minute delay the means were about the same (7.8 and 7.6). After one week another test showed the older group remembering more, with mean scores of 6.5 and 7.5. The general picture is that the elderly were handicapped in acquisition of new information but that once they had acquired it, their retention was as good as that of the younger group. A correlation of .92 between learning scores and retention scores indicates the high degree of dependence of the latter on the former.

Divergent-production abilities   In the preceding chapter much attention was given to the ages at which tested creative potential appeared to reach its maximum, and it was found that just past thirty seemed to be typical, in tests for ideational fluency and originality (Trembly, 1964a) and from the facts concerning the time for best creative output of distinguished people. With respect to decline, we have more analytical information.

Word fluency   Tests calling for the rapid listing of words that satisfy some letter requirement have been common successful measures of factor DSU. With the King test, Bilash and Zubek (1960) found that means tend to keep at a high level to the age of forty-five, then decline rapidly. With the Thurstone PMA test of Word Fluency, Schaie (1958) more or less confirmed this picture, with a curve showing a very slight rise to about age forty-three, then a decline at an increasing rate.

Birren (1955) has made a more searching study of the way in which the elderly react to this kind of test in comparison with young subjects. In each test, the examinees were told to write in two minutes as many words as they could beginning with a specified letter or letters. The initial letters were chosen so as to vary systematically the potential number of responses. The initial letters, with estimates of potential supply of such words, were *S,* 29,002; *C,* 22,909; *N,* 4,088; *Q,* 1,416; and *Gi* (no number given). An additional form of the test prescribed no initial letter or other restriction. There is an implied assumption that the potential supplies are the same for the elderly as for the young. This would depend very much upon each person's size of vocabulary. Since vocabulary declines little or none in relation to age, such an assumption is defensible.

One result was that the older subjects, whose ages ranged up to eighty-nine, gave fewer words in all test forms, regardless of potential supply. The elderly were relatively slower in the "easier" tasks, i.e., those with greater potential.

One interpretation of this result could be that with greater supply there is more interference in recall, as D. M. Johnson et al. (1951) have pointed out in connection with rapid successive recalls of items of a class of information from memory storage. The greater susceptibility of the elderly to interferences has been noted before, and it has been interpreted as confusion of information. The interference hypothesis is further supported by Birren's findings that the elderly gave fewer words relative to their writing speeds, which looks as if something related to recall were holding them back. They also gave more inappropriate responses, responses not fitting the prescribed class. This could also be attributed to confusion that cuts across classes, or it can be attributed to poor maintenance of set or to poor evaluation. Letting the inappropriate responses stand would suggest some role for evaluation.

Flexibility with respect to classes and transformations   Although the last-mentioned idea would seem to suggest that the elderly err by slipping into wrong classes, there are other indications that they have difficulty in going from one class to another. The circumstances are somewhat different, however. The context here is in terms of classification tests, in which the person must shift from class to class to make a good score; the shifts of class are not slips or errors.

Thaler (1956) found that in the Weigel test elderly subjects tended to sort the objects in fewer classes and that some of the *S*s were inclined to stick to the first classes they formed. This test should pertain to factor DFC, the divergent production of figural classes, or spontaneous flexibility with respect to figural classes. A result reported by Korchin and Basowitz (1956) may have similar significance. In a test in which successive pictures are shown, beginning with a cat, for example, and shifting gradually over into a dog, it takes the elderly longer to notice the shift. The change in cognition implies a shift in classification of the pictured object. The elderly also have relatively more trouble in seeing a greater change, as from a mouse to a car.

Some of the evidence we have with respect to decline curves for shifting of classes comes from Chown (1961). Five different tests for factor DMC, such as Brick Uses and Unusual Uses, were given to subjects of different ages. The five age curves were similar (thus giving replication with respect to rise and decline in the factor), rising slowly in the interval twenty to forty, remaining level from forty to fifty-five, and declining thereafter.

Other evidence comes from Bromley (1964), who gave tasks in the form of card sorting, and the Vygotsky and Shaw tests, in which S is to make successive classifications. Age brought systematic decrements in sorting output. The elderly showed relatively greater decrement in producing the more unusual classes, which suggests weakness in transformation ability, which should mean factor DFT. In fact, Bromley attributed the lower performance of the elderly to lack of transformation ability. But probably flexibility with respect to both classes and transformations was involved. Chown (1961) has reported a consistent rate of decline for a Match Problems test, a DFT test, with some acceleration.

Semantic fluency and originality   From Trembly (1964a) we have information regarding a performance curve on a test like Consequences, which was described in Chapter 6. The examinees write an essay in response to the kind of question that begins: "What would happen if . . . ?" The score used by Trembly is the number of words written in the given time. It had been determined that a count of the number of words correlates very high with qualitative scores that require judgment. Summing obvious and remote consequences should give a measure of both DMU and DMT (ideational fluency and originality), with DMU dominant, because it is the writer's experience that the variance in scores for obvious consequences is about double that in scores for remote consequences.

Trembly's decline curves for both sexes show a maximum performance level being reached at about the age of thirty and a moderate rate of decline coming in by the age of thirty-five. By the age of sixty the mean score is equivalent to that obtained at about the age of eighteen, which is not nearly so great a decline as is found in many other abilities. As pointed out in the preceding chapter, the maximal score near the thirtieth year agrees very well with the Lehman findings that creatively productive people are most likely to create their most valued products in the early thirties or shortly thereafter, this event depending upon the accumulation of information, sometimes of a specialized kind.

Convergent-production abilities

Convergent-production abilities, being less well known, have been much less investigated in connection with age. Garfield and Blek (1952) happened to give what is essentially a measure of factor NSR, the convergent production of symbolic relations, when they administered the Abstraction test of the Shipley-Hartford scale to teachers and teachers in training, in age groups in their twenties, forties, and sixties. The corresponding means were 31.6, 28.3, and 29.2. Only one of these differences was significant, and the declines were obviously small.

One of K. F. Riegel's tests (1959) given to old and young groups was a multiple-choice Antonyms test, and another was a multiple-choice Analogies test. Both should be expected to measure factors CMR and NMR, the latter if the examinee does much producing of related information before inspecting the alternative answers. The young group (mean age about nineteen) was significantly superior to the older group (above sixty-five) in both these tests.

There is indication of decline in tests of two other factors in the convergent-production category. Chown (1961) reported a very gradual decline from age twenty to age fifty in Hidden Figures, a measure of factor NFT (convergent production of figural transformations), then a rapidly increasing decline. Here is indication of decline in one kind of flexibility, of which there are a number of varieties. The other test that can be mentioned is Picture Arrangement, a measure of factor NMS (convergent production of systems), which Wechsler lists among his three tests showing most rapid declines.

Evaluation abilities   There is some evidence of decline in a test called Perceptual Ability, a combination of King's tests that should measure factors EFU and ESU, both pertaining to evaluation of units, one figural and the other symbolic (Bilash & Zubek, 1960). It was reported that there were a slow decline to age forty-five and a more rapid one thereafter. Because the two factors are involved in the same test, it is difficult to decide how each factor's age curve would look if its test were scored alone. Since the two factors are parallel and contiguous in the SI model, the two curves might well be similar.

Friend and Zubek (1958) produced an age curve for the Watson-Glaser Critical Thinking Appraisal test. Although composed of several parts with somewhat different kinds of items, this test is most like a syllogism test, which is strongest for factor EMI (evaluation of semantic implications), with a secondary loading for factor EMR, a parallel relations ability. The curve was at its maximum in the twenties and into the thirties, after which there was a gradual decline. Even at seventy and older, 9 percent of the examinees scored above the mean at maximal ages. Estimation of part scores showed that the elderly tended to give more extreme T and F responses and fewer moderate ones (probably true and probably false), a result that was taken to mean some loss of flexibility. The elderly also tended to make relatively lower scores on items with personal reference as compared with those on impersonal items, which was taken to mean some loss in objectivity.

Welford (1964) made some comments about other apparent weaknesses in the area of evaluation. Older subjects seem to take more liberties in changing premises and in expanding upon their opinions. They sometimes have difficulty in selecting relevant items of information. And they show some loss of sensitivity to incompatibility of statements as well as permitting personal views to help determine conclusions.

In a different kind of test, but of a kind that has shown some loading on factor EMI and also on EMR (Nihira et al., 1964), K. F. Riegel (1959) has found that a younger group did better than an elderly one. A sample item reads:

A GRANARY always has: grain, elevator, cellar, mice, entrance.

The decision is to be made among alternative implications.

Decline in flexibility   It is often observed that the elderly have lost in flexibility in various ways. Flexibility is not a single trait; so we should not expect individuals to be equally flexible or inflexible in every respect. Two kinds of flexibility in which declines have been demonstrated, flexibility in shifting from one class to another and flexibility in the sense of being ready to produce transformations, were mentioned earlier. Declines in these respects have been found in the production of classes and transformations. There are other indications of lowered flexibility.

Birren (1955) has reported that the elderly find it relatively more difficult to learn wherever there are conflicting associations and that learning to eliminate errors is likely to be more difficult than learning a new series of items. Entwisle (1959) has reported that in learning to drive a car the elderly are handicapped at first by conflicting earlier habits. Talland (1959) found that the elderly are disturbed by tasks that call for changes of set. As with other instances of weakness in coping with interferences mentioned earlier, these examples, also, may be confusions of information, which means that information is not sharply discriminated. Other instances may indicate a lack of readiness to produce transformations that are demanded by situations.

Complexity and systems   Welford (1958) has remarked that the elderly show no notable decline in ability to have insights but that they show defect in maintaining condi-

Lights

Code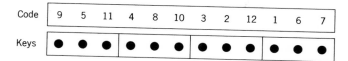

Keys

Fig. 18.3 Schematic diagram of arrangement of 12 stimuli and 12 response keys in a choice reaction-time experiment and the position of the code relating the two. (*From Kay, 1954. Reproduced by permission.*)

tions favorable for insight. Some insights depend upon keeping under consideration several items of information. Deficiency in this respect suggests low capacity for handling many items of information, whether this is a matter of short-term memory or is to be described by some other concept, such as the product of system. Other descriptions imply the latter interpretation.

Jerome (1962) observed that older individuals fail to understand methods that are described to them for dealing with tasks or reject methods that are demonstrated to them. Rejection under such circumstances may be due to lack of understanding, the subject having too much pride to admit that he does not understand. Methods are systems. Strategies are systems. Jerome also reports that the elderly lack clear analysis of the goal in problem solving, and they evidently lack good, clear search models, for their search behavior is often disorderly.

There are other indications that the elderly have much trouble because they cannot organize items of information into coherent wholes or systems. This phenomenon is also shown in reaction-time tasks. In a simple reaction-time task there is relatively little change in score in the ages between twenty and sixty (Welford, 1964), but there is pronounced decline when complexity is involved, as in discrimination reactions or choice reactions, when the number of alternatives increases.

A good example of reactions to a choice reaction-time task is found in Kay's experiment (1954). Twelve stimulus lights in a horizontal row (see Figure 18.3) were grouped by threes so as to be easily counted, number 1 being at the subject's left. The subject had a row of 12 response keys, but they were not related in direct correspondence with the stimulus lights. The stimulus lights were coded so that stimulus light 9 went with response key 1, stimulus light 5 with response key 2, and so on (see Figure 18.3). In the easiest arrangement, the code was provided for S's use directly above his response keys. In the next hardest arrangement the code was set midway between the lights and the keys, and in the hardest arrangement the code was laid next to the row of lights. The distance between lights and keys was 3 feet.

The results for the elderly and the younger groups were very systematic. Errors increased as an accelerated function of both age and difficulty, as represented in Figure 18.4. The main source of difficulty was the complexity of the system of light-key relationships.

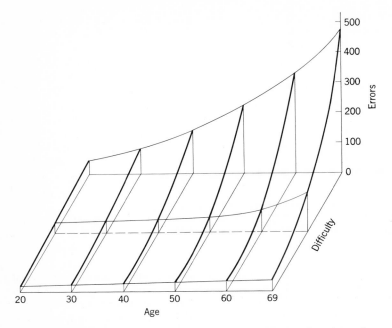

Fig. 18.4   Errors in a choice reaction-time experiment as functions of
age and difficulty level. (*From Kay, 1954. Reproduced by permission.*)

The oldest group made four times as many errors and took five times as long as the subjects below the age of twenty-five in the most difficult task. The age differential decreased
considerably for the simpler tasks. If we assume that sensory time and motor time remained fairly constant under all arrangements, the increasing time must be attributed to
central brain processes apart from the primary sensory and motor centers.

Clay (1954) has demonstrated the effects of complexity with age by means of another
type of task. Given counters with digits 1 to 4 on them, S was to enter them in the cells
of a small matrix so as to achieve given sums for the rows. The task was made more complex by varying the order of the matrix from 3×3 to 6×6. Elderly subjects showed
relatively more errors for the more complex tasks. They could often see that they had
made errors but did not seem to know what to do about them. This observation suggests
some strength in evaluation but weakness in divergent production.

In another kind of task, involving problem solving of an inductive type, S was to
discover which keys turned on which lights (Clay, 1957). From age twenty to age eighty,
time was an increasing function of age. After reaching a maximum, however, the average
time again dropped off as some of the subjects gave up the task. Ss gave up when they
became confused. The number of errors rose more sharply after the maximum time had
been reached. The more complex the task, the earlier the age of giving up. Clay's hypothesis was that S takes more time in order to handle the additional information with
which he must deal. But added time means more dependence upon short-term **memory**,
which has definite limits. Another interpretation is that the more complex problem requires the development of a more elaborate system, which is beyond the individual's
system-construction powers. Systematizing input, in any case, reduces the number of *items*

of information with which the individual has to deal and thus keeps the input within his capacity for handling it.

Some general conditions of decline

Considerably less attention has been given to the determiners of decline of intellectual abilities than to their growth, but as populations of the elderly increase, the problem of how to prolong mental fitness and to prevent senescence becomes more important. A knowledge of determiners is of first importance in this connection. Many of the same conditions that promote or retard intellectual development are naturally suspected of having some bearing on the maintenance of intellectual status and perhaps on retarding its decline. As in the last chapter, these conditions will be examined under the headings of heredity and the brain and of various environmental determiners.

Heredity and the brain   Not a great deal is known about the relation between heredity and mental decline. But since heredity helps to determine development, it also determines the status from which decline starts. The new problems would be concerned with rates of decline and with the possibility of senility before death.

Falek, Kallman, Lorge, and Karvik (1960) found that elderly one-egg twins show greater similarity of longevity than do two-egg twins. On the one hand, this might suggest that the same hereditary disposition that leads to longevity also provides for prolongation of better status in mental powers. On the other hand, this might have the indirect effect of providing opportunity for senility if the brain gave out before other organs. There is a little indication in favor of the first of these two contingencies. Jarvik et al. (1962) found that the survivors of pairs of twins had higher mean scores when tested past the age of sixty than did their mates who died. In both the studies mentioned in this paragraph, it was found that one-egg twins make more similar scores in tests than do two-egg twins. All that can be said is that at least some of the similarities of one-egg twins found during development appear to persist in old age.

Some of the brain conditions that affect development of intellectual status are known, as mentioned in Chapters 15 and 17. We need to consider whether any of them play any special roles during decline. One of the variables is the amount of brain tissue available. Many years ago, Pearl (1905) found a curve for decline in human-brain weight that looks very much like that for general intellectual decline, as in Figure 18.1. But other physical decline curves could probably be found to parallel either of them. If loss in brain weight is highly significant, how does it bring about loss of intellectual ability? In this connection, we are reminded of Lashley's classical finding that in rat-maze learning it does not matter where the cortical loss occurs but that it does matter how great the loss is.

The loss of human brain cells by death has been noted before. How does loss of brain cells affect functioning? Welford (1958) has theorized that loss of brain cells lowers "informational capacity." This is supposed to reduce the strength of communication signals, increasing the "random" brain activity or "noise." Or, the absolute amount of noise may remain constant, but with loss of cells the average noise per cell is greater. In either case, there is a decrease in signal-to-noise ratio, with danger of overloading circuits, causing momentary lapses of attention.

Such a theory is clearly derived from concepts in communication engineering, which is not a bad source of analogies where brain functioning is concerned. The reduced capacity for input of the elderly has seemed to be descriptive of a number of their weaknesses. There may be a reduced capacity for productive activities as well. But there seems to be another feature that is just as important, and that is the reduction in clarity of discriminations, which opens the way for interferences and confusions. Whatever condition of the brain that permits clear discriminations should be found to decline in natural aging.

After considering reduced speed of nerve conduction as a possible source of mental decline, Birren (1955) rejected that condition as being very important. He has considered the number of cells available for use in any operation and conditions of nerve fibers as possible determiners (Birren et al., 1954). Lowered oxygen supply is often mentioned as a suspected determiner of aging, for with anoxia brain cells die or their chemical composition changes (Bondareff, 1959). It has been observed that pigment accumulates in the brain cells, but just how this condition affects their functioning is not known. Possibly it affects the cells' replicating activity in the formation of proteins that are needed in mental functioning. Such a condition would make difficult the formation of phase sequences in Hebb's sense.

Environmental and other conditions

Decline at different levels of ability   Much interest has been expressed in the rates of decline and the ages of beginning of decline for individuals of different intellectual status. The variable of intellectual status should mean standard assessment of all individuals at some particular age, for example, at the time of young adulthood. A really satisfactory study of this problem would require a longitudinal investigation of a large sample of wide range of status over the years of adulthood to old age. No study of this kind has come near these specifications or is in any way comparable to the Berkeley growth study (Bayley, 1949). We shall have to be content at present with some piecemeal attempts, with groups followed over limited numbers of years.

There has been a more or less common hypothesis that the bright young people stay bright longer and the dull young people start to decline earlier. This principle should show up in the form of increasing dispersions of scores with advancing age. There are two cross-sectional studies that bear upon this hypothesis. H. E. Jones (1959) cited a study by Raven with his Progressive Matrices test, in which he compared scores at centiles 2, 50, 75, and 95 at ages five to sixty. The trend curves as functions of age did diverge, but more during the years before twenty than after that age. This finding was confirmed by Foulds (1949) with the same test and also with the Mill Hill Vocabulary Scale in a range of sixteen to sixty-five.

In Terman's gifted group, Bayley and Oden (1955) applied the Terman Concept Mastery Test at the average age of 41.5 to some of the individuals and to their spouses, all of whom had taken the same test at the average age of 29.5; in other words, retested them after an interval of twelve years. There was an average increase of about ½ standard deviation for both men and women and for all levels of ability within the sample, which had been selected during childhood with a minimum IQ of 140. There were some slight indications of a regression effect for the very highest individuals, but it was suspected that the test did not provide enough scope for these cases. There was no group with initially average IQ or with initially low IQ with which to compare the gifted group. The result for the gifted group might have been nothing more than the usual gain in retesting, particularly with a vocabulary type of test in which there is often gain as a function of age.

According to the general hypothesis, mentally deficient groups should show more than average decline in tests. Clare W. Thompson (1951) also tested the hypothesis that declines should begin earlier in the mentally deficient than in the intellectually normal. She reasoned that since the mentally defective tend to achieve their maximum scores at earlier ages and since their life-spans are shorter than those of normal individuals, they live a kind of telescoped existence. They should start a decline earlier in intellectual abilities.

Thompson compared a group of morons whose IQs were in the range 50 to 70 on the Stanford-Binet scale with a group of normals. In the interval of ages twenty to thirty, the mentally defective groups showed declines in all 10 of the performance tests (from the Wechsler scale and other sources), whereas the normals showed declines in only 4, in a cross-sectional study. The hypothesis of the earlier declines for the mentally deficient thus appeared to be supported. In two verbal tests, however, the mentally deficient did not show declines in their twenties; so the hypothesis was not supported for all kinds of abilities.

A study that gave results counter to the expected differential decline of the mentally deficient was reported by Bell and Zubek (1960). Four groups of mentally deficient subjects at mean ages of twenty, thirty, forty, and fifty were retested with the Wechsler scale after five years. The changes in IQ at the successive age levels were the following gains, respectively:

Total-scale IQ	9.1, 7.6, 5.7, 4.4
Verbal IQ	4.1, 4.2, 4.3, 4.4
Performance IQ	12.0, 9.3, 7.4, 1.7

It was pointed out that these trends are similar to those found in other longitudinal studies with normal groups, in contrast to the results of cross-sectional studies. The fact that the verbal tests held up better in the older groups is also consistent with other findings.

Possible reasons for the gains were considered. Practice effects were discounted in view of the low IQs of the subjects. The same administrator gave the tests in both instances. There was an improved environment that applied to some cases, in the form of moving to a better institution. It was admitted that there could have been some underestimates of IQ on the first testing. Even considering all these incidental possible determiners, the loss in IQs for the mentally deficient population expected from the hypothesis did not seem to apply. We have a long way yet to go to determine changes in intellectual level in all respects as functions of characteristic status.

Education   There is no doubt of the strong correlation between amount of formal education and *development* of intellectual abilities. Is there also a bearing of amount of education upon the rate of decline of abilities? To the extent that individuals maintain their rank orders from maturity to old age in tests of intellectual abilities, of course, we should expect the correlation between education and status in old age to remain strong. The relation to *rate* of decline is a different problem, and it is akin to the problem of the relation of rate of decline to mature status in the abilities, because of the confounding of education and intellectual status.

Education is becoming more and more hazy as a variable, as the institution of adult education and opportunities for informal education become more general. Definitive studies with the education variable must pay much attention to the content of the education and to its quality as well as its quantity. To the extent that individuals keep up with educational activities they should be exercising many of the intellectual functions, and exercise should contribute to keeping abilities at higher levels.

That highly educated persons are not exempt from some degree of decline is suggested by a study by Sward (1945). His subjects were university teachers, active and retired. One group were of ages twenty-five to thirty-five with a mean of thirty-one, and the others were of ages sixty to eighty with a mean of sixty-six. There was a matching on other variables. In seven of eight tests used, the younger group was significantly superior. The seven tests were Ingenuity, Problems, Symbol Digit, Number Series, Word Meanings, Analogies, Arithmetic Problems, and Artificial Language. On the Synonym-Antonym test the older group was significantly superior. It is unlikely that the difference on the last-mentioned test was due to CMU variance, since the difference was in the opposite direction to that on the Word Meanings test, which is more likely to measure CMU. On that test, however, the difference was significant only at the .05 level. Within the two groups, with their relatively short ranges of ages, the correlations of test scores with age were generally small but tended to be stronger (negatively) for the older group, indicating more rapid decline in that group. It was concluded that the elderly were more impaired with respect to rate of work than with respect to accuracy or quality.

Occupation   Individuals who engage in occupations that exercise intellectual functions should keep themselves at higher levels, depending upon the demands for those functions in their work and in their occupational milieu. Foulds (1949) had an opportunity to test this hypothesis in a limited way in his investigation with the Raven Progressive Matrices test and the Mill Hill Vocabulary Scale with two occupational groups, engineers and manufacturing employees who were concerned with photographic equipment. Subjects were in groups with ages sixteen to sixty-five. Foulds compared decline curves for the two kinds of personnel in the two tests, one of figural content and one of semantic content, the latter being more specifically for factor CMU. The Raven score is probably weighted with factors CFR and NFR.

For the engineers, the average Raven score was maximal between the ages of fifteen and twenty; for the factory workers, who presumably had inspectional and manipulative types of assignments, the maximal mean score came between twenty and twenty-five. After thirty the declines were similar for the two groups, but the factory workers kept a slight lead to the age of fifty-five. In the vocabulary test, engineers came to their highest average between forty and forty-five and the workers between thirty-five and forty. There were similar, slow declines after forty, with the engineers keeping a slight lead that narrowed to the age of sixty.

It is tempting to attribute the differentials in ages of maximal status and in retaining superiority during decline to the fact that engineers were of necessity keeping up development in acquiring new verbal concepts while the factory workers were practicing skills involving figural abilities. But it should be noted that declines set in for the two groups at about the same time in both tests and that their mean scores converged to about the same level at age sixty-five. It may be that both groups had developed as far as was needed rather early in their careers and that they had acquired specific skills that carried them through. The generalized skills could then lapse normally without undue handicap in their work.

That occupational experiences may have bearings upon keeping certain relevant aptitudes strong or even upon improving them is suggested by some limited data presented by Glanzer and Glaser (1959). Air Force Reserve pilots and commercial-airline pilots who had taken the Air Force classification battery during World War II were retested thirteen years later with four of the same tests. The later mean scores were significantly higher (at the .001 level) in all four tests. The tests, their known factor contents, and the first and second means were as follows:

Instrument Comprehension (CFS-V, spatial orientation): 34.8, 47.4
Mechanical Principles (CFT, visualization): 18.7, 25.4

Numerical Operations (numerical facility): 69.1, 83.1
Spatial Orientation (EFU, perceptual speed): 29.6, 32.9

All except Numerical Operations are known to have relevance for prediction of learning to fly an airplane. It is possible that the pilots' later work involved some computational exercise. Some of the gains may be the general increments such as are found in retesting, even after a period of years, in longitudinal studies. Control groups would be needed to determine how much could be attributed to the pilots' occupational experiences.

Gains in measures of factors consequent to educational experiences, as cited in Chapters 12 and 14, should lead us to expect benefits from occupational experiences that provide exercises in tasks in which the factors are relevant. There is no available experimental information of this kind for middle-aged and elderly populations.

Summary

Investigation of decline of intellectual status with age presents more numerous difficulties than the study of development, owing to the multitude of variations in life circumstances that interfere with experimental control. Cross-sectional and longitudinal studies have been made, but the two approaches tell somewhat divergent stories. Whereas the former show almost universal declines in test performances among older groups, the latter more often than not show gains, although longitudinal studies have not been numerous, especially in the later years of life.

There is evidence that the factorial structure pertaining to certain factors remains about the same in groups of individuals who are aging normally, with only a slight indication that some simplification of structure occurs later in life, as shown by slightly higher intercorrelations of tests. Decline in the case of senile dementia is qualitatively different from normal decline. For the senile population, intercorrelations of tests rise markedly, suggesting changes in factor structure.

Most of the research has been in terms of changes in scores from special tests rather than in a global score, for differential rates of decline are numerous and striking. Not enough of the range of structure-of-intellect factors has been explored in relation to adult ages to give rise to many general principles related to SI categories. Within any one operation category, decline curves based upon test scores are quite varied. Scores that measure factor CMU, verbal comprehension, have represented an outstanding exception, by showing continued gains even into the sixties and by showing late-starting declines. Other semantic-cognition abilities, however, show more typical declines.

Two kinds of SI abilities stand out with respect to defects in the elderly. One has to do with the formation and use of systems of information, which is manifest in tests involving complex operations. An alternative hypothesis is that the older person's capacity for information intake and perhaps, also, for handling information in productive thinking is more limited. In the case of input, this limitation may depend upon a weakness in short-term memory.

The other notable area of weakness is in the abilities involving flexibility, flexibility with respect to shifting between classes and with respect to transformations in information. A rather general weakness is susceptibility to interferences and inability to correct errors. Interferences go with lack of clear discriminations and, therefore, with loss of information.

Little is yet known about the causes of intellectual decline in the various respects. Heredity appears to have a bearing, but possibly largely because it has a bearing upon development. The most suspected brain condition in connection with decline is inadequate oxygen supply, as a consequence of which brain cells change chemically and may die. Exercise of brain cells by virtue of continued education, formal and informal, including that provided by occupational activity, may have halting effects, but this hypothesis needs much better experimental investigation.

V Reflections

19 Retrospect and prospect

There would not be a sense of completeness to this treatment of human intelligence without some efforts toward a general summary and some reflections as to general implications, implications regarding future investigations of the nature of intelligence and some of their possible consequences. Speculations are also called for concerning some of the social implications of what is now known about intelligence, particularly in connection with the operations of testing and of education, for which many new bases have been laid.

Preceding content

Glances over previous chapters and their summaries will show in capsule form what this volume has been about. Beginning in Chapter 1 and very much throughout, there has been a significant emphasis upon intellectual tests, for they provide the necessary empirical referents for meaningful conceptions that can be communicated. From the early varied tests of Galton, Binet, and others, through the single-score practice of Binet and Terman, to the multiple-aptitude view generated on the basis of factor analysis, we have a progressive development in conceptions and in practices of testing of intellectual status of individuals.

Orientation The first approach to orientation to the subject matter of this volume was through the history of intelligence tests. Nothing more need be said on this subject here. Of greater importance was the discussion of the most popular conception, that intelligence is the ability to learn and that learning is adaptation to new situations in new ways. In addition to the fact that the major concepts of this definition—learning and adaptation—have no unique empirical referents, there are no one unitary ability called intelligence and no unitary ability to learn. In both cases, multiple abilities and processes are involved. Learning to understand the component aspects of intelligence has helped very much to comprehend the operations of learning, as Chapter 12 attempted to point out.

A second contribution to orientation was made by consideration of three major approaches that have yielded information about the subject: experimental psychology; genetic studies; and multivariate theory and procedures, factor analysis, in particular. Of those concerned with intellectual development, only the work of Piaget and of others inspired by him has made much direct contribution to the understanding of the nature of intelligence. General experimental psychology, beginning with Binet and the Germans in this field, has made a much greater contribution to understanding intelligence than the intelligence testers have realized or used. In more recent times, the findings of factor analysis are of much more relevance and significance for psychological theory than experimental psychologists recognize. It is time that communication should improve among those who have adopted the three major approaches.

The third avenue to orientation was concerned with general theory of intelligence. Emphasis was placed on the importance of having a general theory for the sake of guiding research efforts into fruitful paths, for generating hypotheses to be investigated, which is a way of asking questions about nature, and for giving findings systematic significance. The preferred type of theory is cast in the form of models, especially those with logical and mathematical properties.

The dimensional model of factor analysis provides frames of reference both for describing individuals with respect to trait dimensions and for specifying tests in terms of underlying variables that have much claim to invariance and to psychological meaning. As for logical relationships among the factors of intelligence, whose number has been growing at an accelerated rate, two types of models have been proposed. One is the hierarchical type proposed by both Cyril Burt and Philip E. Vernon. Both their models rest very critically upon the reality of a g factor such as Spearman championed so vigorously. Unfortunately, the most telling evidence against a universal factor in tests of intellectual performance is the decisive number of zero correlations that have been found when tests have been sufficiently varied in kind and have been constructed with good experimental control and when other experimental controls have been exercised in testing operations.

The second type of model is known as morphological; it is a multidimensional matrix of the factors, or a cross classification. The structure-of-intellect model, with its three parameters—operation, content, and product—makes possible the unique definition of each intellectual ability in terms of one of five kinds of operation, combined with one of four kinds of content and with one of six kinds of product. Although each factor shares one or two properties in common with every other factor, something about the unique combinations makes them relatively independent in terms of individual differences in a population.

Intellectual factors and their tests   Five chapters were devoted to providing the evidence for some 81 unique intellectual abilities, occupying 77 of the cells of the SI model, the discrepancy in numbers being due to some cells' containing more than one factor—visual and auditory in four instances and a third kinesthetic factor in one instance. A fourth dimension of sensory modality, applying to the category of figural content and perhaps to some extent to the category of symbolic information, may have to be added to the model. Thus, the prospect is for more than the 120 abilities originally hypothesized when all become known. Whether the self-versus-other distinction will call for two full sets of behavioral abilities remains to be seen. The demonstration of abilities involving information about oneself would present some unusual experimental difficulties.

As most traditional tests of intellectual abilities have strongly emphasized cognitive abilities, that operational category of abilities has been most fully explored, with all 24 of the cells filled for abilities dealing with visual input. There are also 3 known cognitive abilities dealing with auditory input and 1 dealing with kinesthetic input, according to conclusions current when this was written. The next-best-explored operation category is divergent production, because of its apparent special relevance for creative potential; 16 such abilities have been demonstrated as factors. The memory category follows very closely, with 15 factors in 14 cells accounted for. The categories of convergent production and evaluation have been least explored, with 10 and 13 factors, respectively, believed to have been demonstrated. This situation is likely to be temporary, of course, for efforts are continuing toward demonstration of the remaining unknown abilities.

Structure-of-intellect categories   The structure-of-intellect theory entails 5 operation categories and 10 categories of information, 4 of the latter for content and 6 for products. Of the 5 operation categories, we may say that cognition is largely a matter of decoding information. This process depends very heavily upon a large supply of previously stored information, which is partially dependent upon memory abilities. In the general process of living, which very frequently presents problems to be solved, stored information must be retrieved for use. Retrieval depends upon a search or scanning operation. A broad search involves divergent production; a search restricted to one determined item of information involves convergent production. Judgments as to suitability of the retrieved information in meeting criteria inherent in the search model involve the operation of evaluation. Thus, the 5 kinds of operation are well discriminated in terms of language that commonly applies to the modern electronic computer.

With respect to the 10 information categories, it was proposed that the 24 subcategories, obtained from intersections of 4 content and 6 product categories, can serve as a basic psychoepistemology. It was also proposed that the 6 product categories can serve as the basis for a psychologic, for those categories have clear parallels in concepts of modern logic.

Considerable attention was given to the meaning of meaning. With Garner (1962), it was recognized that there is a figural kind of meaning that is nonsemantic and that is best conceived in the nature of structure. By application of the methods of information measurement, Garner has shown that it is possible to quantify degrees of structure, but this does not provide a means whereby one structure can be fully discriminated from another. For semantic meaning a new core-context theory was developed, with denotative aspects being the core and connotative aspects the context. This is not the same as the historical context theory of meaning proposed by Titchener, for his conception envisaged only figural information. In fact, he attempted to build a complete psychology in terms of sensory information only, which cannot be done. The nature of any meaning in terms of symbolic or behavioral information still has to be specified.

As to the product categories, steps have already been taken to specify the logical properties of units, classes, relations, and implications. The products of systems and transformations are not so readily described in logical concepts, except as certain complex models apply to them, those models being based upon the more elementary concepts. New logical forms may be needed to account for these products adequately.

Basic psychological theory   In four chapters, efforts were made to point out the potential contributions of SI concepts to traditional psychological problems in the areas of perception, learning, retention, recall, problem solving, and creative thinking. But first, let us review some of the special traditional concepts that seem to be accounted for.

The concept of "induction" seems more than adequately covered by the *cognition* of different kinds of products. If it is desired to retain the term *induction* at all, we can do better by recognizing different kinds of induction, for example, classificatory, relational, systemic, and implicational. The arrival at new class concepts, relations, principles, and cause-effect types of connections from integrative action on disparate inputs can be well described in terms of the formation of such kinds of products: classes, relations, systems, and implications.

The traditional concept of "deduction" can be well accounted for in terms of convergent production in connection with at least two kinds of products, relations and implications. One kind of deduced conclusion is the item of information that completes a tight analogy, and the other is the item of information that follows logically from given premises. If the term *deduction* is to be retained in the technical terminology, the distinction should be made between "relational" or "analogical" deduction and "implicational" deduction. If both induction and deduction are to be kept in the psychologist's vocabulary, for the first time they have empirical referents through associated factor tests.

The concept of "perception," as usually applied, pertains to input activities, including precognitive operations but overlapping with cognition as defined in this volume where figural units are involved (this is an arbitrary delimitation). The idea that there can be unconscious perceptual discriminations and even learning without awareness has not been sufficiently supported by experimental evidence. Like cognition in general, most perception requires considerable learning.

SI theory suggests a revolutionary way of looking at learning. It was proposed that the historical concept of association be largely replaced and extended in the form of the 6 products of information. Learning means development of new products of information or revisions (transformations) of old ones. The issue of one-trial versus gradual learning is regarded as somewhat spurious, since at some point in the continuum of complexity there must be increments of quantal nature and some quanta can be relatively large, as in observed cases of insight.

The learning of motor skills is conceived in the form of the acquisition of behavioral systems of the self-knowledge type. Connections developed between perceived or cognized products of information and motor patterns are facilitated by virtue of isomorphism between them. Intellectual and psychomotor abilities are known to play roles in tasks during learning, with systematic shifts in importance. There is also evidence that certain kinds of exercises contribute to increases in individual status on factors. Reinforcement in learning is in the nature of evaluation, using feedback information.

Information is not only learned in the form of products but is also retained in memory storage in the same form. But there is evidence that transformations can occur in stored information, from impacts provided by new input and under the influence of motivational stresses. Recall or retrieval of information from memory storage is the essential process in either divergent or convergent production. Principles of transfer recall, which plays such an important role in productive thinking, are seriously in need of investigation.

Genuine problem solving involves some degree of novelty, and since novelty is the *sine qua non* of creative production, problem solving involves creativity. The principles that account for the one process should also largely account for the other. An operational model built on SI concepts was developed to represent a generic picture of problem solving. The memory store makes itself felt all along the way. Evaluation, as a process of self-checking, also makes frequent contributions. Within a main linear trend, behavior also involves loops and, in the total operation, loops within loops.

Creative production, formerly attributed to that vague concept of "creative imagination," is now given considerable empirical foundation in SI theory. Although the psychologist's picture of creative production must be very largely inferential, since so much goes on behind the scenes, that picture is developing. The popular conceptions of "incubation," "inspiration," and "intuition," for example, are being replaced with empirically founded conceptions, such as the divergent-production category of functions and the functions involving transformations, in addition to other aspects of intellect. Some of the conditions that affect creative output are becoming known and were reviewed in Chapter 14.

Conditions of intelligence   There has been no end to interest in the roles of heredity and of brain properties as determiners of intellectual status of individuals and as physical correlates for intellectual functioning. The impact of the multidimensional conception of intelligence upon studies of these problems is just beginning to be felt, and the factorial picture offers considerable promise of fruitful attack on these problems. The nature of heredity calls for a trait approach, which the multivariate view of intelligence provides. The increasing emphasis upon information-transmission conceptions in connection with both heredity and brain functioning finds a nice parallel in the informational conceptions of mental functioning provided in SI theory. As pointed out in Chapter 15, the detailed parallels between intellectual factorial abilities and certain special symptoms appearing with organic brain damage are most striking. Studies of brain functions have become increasingly analytical; the study of psychological functions must keep pace with that trend.

Studies of effects of environmental conditions upon intellectual status of individuals have been beset with numerous difficulties, many of which stem from the ambiguity of inclusive variables both with respect to descriptions of environment and with respect to intellectual assessment. The lack of invariance of test content from one IQ scale to another and from one age level to another has added to the difficulties. But it is quite apparent that impoverished environments, those low in stimulation value with respect to learning, can be very damaging to intellectual development. It is not so clear that enriched environments provide advantages to individuals who are already normal or superior in mental status. It may be, however, that the appropriate analytical assessments required to detect such effects have not been applied. There are some small sex differences in intellectual status, which are meaningful in terms of SI categories, but such differences have been investigated in only limited areas of intellectual functioning. Effects of drugs and other chemical conditions have had only limited investigation, but with differential information about intellectual abilities a psychopharmacological approach should be fruitful.

Nowhere is the value of differential intellectual aptitudes more keenly felt than in the study of intellectual growth and decline, and much has already been done on genetic problems from a psychometric point of view by using measures of factor abilities. One general finding about development of abilities is that the former beliefs about the ages at which intellectual development reaches its adult maximum have had to be revised drastically upward. Whereas formerly it was believed that maturity is reached in the teens, with the use of tests of other kinds of abilities, such as those in the divergent-production category, it is now apparent that mature maxima may not be reached until the age of thirty and even beyond. While it has been recognized that individuals may show their own unique growth curves, with peculiarities that average out when data from individuals are combined, it is further known that growth curves also differ considerably among the different intellectual abilities.

Differentiated abilities have been demonstrated, even for young children, which fairly well disposes of the Garrett hypothesis. Environmental pressures appear to be the main source of development along the lines of factor abilities, for the environment presents information along the lines of the 24 epistemological categories of the SI model. The picture of intellectual development provided by Piaget is in accord with this view. On the one hand, he emphasizes that development is in terms of acquiring information. On the other hand, much of his description of details of development can be fitted into the scheme of SI concepts.

What was just said concerning curves of growth also applies, and even more strongly, to curves of intellectual decline. For the different abilities there are marked differences for the age of beginning of decline and for the rate of decline thereafter. There are distinct differences between normal decline of abilities with age and decline that takes place incident to deteriorative organic conditions. Indices that have been proposed for measurement of degree of mental deterioration are open to serious objections for a number of reasons.

Some of the more notable normal declines can be described as loss in abilities to deal with systems and with transformations, the former showing in the form of difficulty in handling input of information and the latter in terms of difficulty in revising methods, for example. It is questionable whether correlations among intellectual abilities tend to increase in normal aging, but organic conditions that can affect some or all abilities adversely definitely serve to increase such correlations.

As much as has already been learned in relating factors of intellectual ability to heredity, brain functioning, environmental conditions, and age, the findings have been very much limited to the half-dozen factors represented in Thurstone's PMA tests. There is a much-expanded situation in current times, calling for extensive and detailed investigation of the same problems in connection with numerous other abilities or functions.

Factor-analytic investigation of intelligence

What has gone before in this volume should be ample evidence of the fruitfulness of factor analysis in the major taxonomic project of answering the question of what the significant components of intelligence are. The path of research by this approach has not been a smooth one. Although the mathematical theory and the computational steps in a factor analysis have been clearly demarcated and can be rigorously carried out, the application of those procedures has presented many problems that have not often been solved satisfactorily. It has definitely not been safe simply to give n tests to N individuals and then to turn the score matrix over to a computer, abdicating all responsibility for the outcome.

Some problems in the factor-analytic approach   It is not necessary to repeat here what the writer has said so many times in other places regarding the importance of experimental conditions in conducting a factor analysis. Good experimental conditions pertain to controls of the population of individuals tested, the population of test variables analyzed together, and the nature of the test contents. The conditions of examinee sampling and test-variable sampling have been treated elsewhere (Guilford, 1952; Guilford & Zimmerman, 1963). Something more needs to be said about good tests for factor analysis.

Experience in the investigation of SI abilities has taught us that simple tests are definitely to be preferred to complex tests, each test being simple in its own unique way. Examination of the tests that are factorially most nearly unique for their respective factors —a vocabulary test for factor CMU, a word-fluency test for factor DSU, or a symbol-identities test for factor ESU—will show this to be the case. There is a natural tendency on the part of some investigators who realize the complex nature of intelligence to prefer complex tests. Complex tests defeat the purposes of factor analysis. When we want to achieve a test such that the individual differences in total scores reflect only one unique ability, it is necessary to write the test, its instructions and its item content, so as to minimize variance in all other abilities—a very exacting task. There should be no fear that any "essence" of intelligence is lost thereby. Where a factorially complex criterion, such as performance in a course in mathematics, is to be predicted, it is sufficient merely to combine measures of the relevant abilities in a weighted summative equation in order to predict the criterion, as has been shown, for example, by the writer and others (Guilford et al., 1965). The application of multiple-cutoff procedures in some situations should by no means be overlooked. Factor tests are much to be preferred both for multiple-regression and multiple-cutoff procedures.

In developing a test for some particular SI ability, it has been one major strategy of the Aptitudes Research Project to take advantage of the expected factor's three parameter properties, seeing to it that each property and no other for the same parameter are satisfied. A second major strategy has been to develop a new test by analogy to a test of a factor that differs in only one parametric property. For example a test of ESU is developed by analogy to a test of DSU or to one of CSU or NSU, changing only the operation to be emphasized.

Test instructions are designed to control the examinee's strategy in the right directions, but even then the examinee is likely to take the test and its items as problems to be mastered, and if he can, he apparently substitutes a preferred strategy of his own. It can be hypothesized that such substitutions of procedures are more likely to occur when the examinee happens to be weak with respect to the ability intended and by changing method is able to capitalize on some other ability in which he has greater strength. He can do this without specific, conscious knowledge of the abilities involved. He may, indeed, be aware of the fact that he is weak in dealing with symbols, as in memorizing nonsense material, and resorts to semantic aids. The translation among content areas may be somewhat common; we do not know how common. The substitution of products may also be common enough to help inject secondary variances from abilities the examiner did not intend to measure.

One measure of control that is probably effective, although there is no experimental evidence on this point, is to make the time limit for a test so short that an examinee who feels it desirable to make translations and substitutions is handicapped, for it takes longer to solve the items by such indirect routes. Before one finds fault with the speed condition that applies to a test, he should consider whether or not that condition may be necessary as an experimental control. The test constructor should, of course, consider whether some other form of test, with some control other than time limitation, can measure the factor as well and as univocally.

Some needs for further studies   Considering what has been accomplished in the exploration of intellectual abilities and the many predicted but undemonstrated abilities, we see that there is much to be done in the way of taxonomic discovery in order to fill out the picture of the SI model and its possible extensions. The area of cognitive abilities, as indicated by Table 4.1, seems to be completely mapped until we note the many possibilities of abilities dealing with auditory and kinesthetic information, not to mention tactual information. The importance of the auditory abilities in connection with speech and music cannot be overemphasized. The importance of potential kinesthetic-information processing should be very substantial in connection with physical education, athletics, sports, choreography, and physical therapy. The importance of possible tactual-intellectual abilities may be somewhat confined to the blind. Abilities involving auditory, kinesthetic, and tactual inputs may also be pertinent to the operation categories other than cognition.

Another content area with limited exploration is that of behavioral information. Nothing has been done as yet with respect to convergent production or evaluation abilities dealing with behavioral information. And nothing whatever has been done to determine whether self-initiated behavioral information calls for processing in terms of the various operation and product categories. The approach to such hypothesized abilities is a forbidding challenge, but if we are to understand behavior thoroughly in terms of information processing, such hypotheses will at least have to be tolerated.

The area of figural information, even when restricted to the visual modality, also needs considerable investigation. Figural-memory, figural–convergent-production, and figural-evaluation abilities are mostly undemonstrated. Such abilities already found lead us to expect the usual full sets of factors in these areas.

Among other needs are better, more univocal tests for some of the factors. There has been little difficulty in writing tests that distinguish content categories fairly well. There have been some bothersome shiftings and crossovers with respect to operation categories, particularly between parallel cognition and evaluation tests. There is probably most confusion with respect to product categories, in some places between units and systems and in other places between relations and implications. As more is learned about the performance of tests pertaining to these categories, however, some mistakes can apparently be avoided and future prospects for more univocal tests are good.

A more general problem that needs investigation but has not seemed so very important, compared with other problems, is the question of intercorrelations among the intellectual factors. Such correlations are evidently very much functions of the person population in question and also of the test population, so that any statements of universal factor intercorrelation are probably out of the question. The writer's inclination has been to regard the intellectual factors as logically orthogonal and to accept orthogonal reference frames as approximating any set of primary axes belonging to an oblique factor structure that would possibly yield better simple structure. The tests are projected on orthogonal reference axes in the same rank order as they would be on primary axes and, even better than that, with projections that are directly proportional. There is little point in seeking to learn about high-order factors when such factors rest upon information about intercorrelations of first-order factors, whose values are uncertain.

The future of intelligence testing

It is very difficult to forecast what the nature of intelligence testing will be, say, thirty years from now or even twenty years hence. It is possible, however, to gain a picture of what current and recent tests represent in terms of measurement of individuals on factor variables and to propose some general principles that seem justified on the basis of new knowledge about tests and what they do or do not measure.

Apart from scales like Wechsler's, there has been practically no change in the nature of IQ tests for the past fifty years. Apart from the institution of two scores in place of one, there has been no great change in academic-aptitude tests for the past forty-five years. There have been two noteworthy attempts to institute multivariate scoring along the lines of factors, in the Thurstone PMA battery and the General Aptitude Test Battery, both of which took advantage of what had become available in terms of enlightened theory and techniques. It appears, however, that such tests have not gained much acceptance in general use, in part probably because examiners have not learned how to utilize them. And this situation, in turn, may have occurred for lack of any general theory of intelligence as a whole.

Factorial composition of current IQ scales   We consider next the question of what SI abilities are represented in the two most popular IQ scales, the Stanford-Binet and the WAIS. In both cases, attempts have been made to hypothesize the dominant SI factors involved in each test of the scales, and in the case of the WAIS, we have one suitable analysis on which to depend (P. C. Davis, 1956).

The 1960 revision of the Stanford-Binet (Terman & Merrill, 1960) is called Form L-M. It contains 140 tests, from mental age II to the superior-adult level, including the alternative tests, making 7 tests at each level. The writer has hypothesized the apparent leading factor for each test, and Bonsall and Meeker (1964) have hypothesized one or more SI abilities for each test, calling also on their experience in administering the tests.

Since each SI ability is clearly and uniquely defined, the task of hypothesizing factors for tests is fairly easy, but experience with analyses shows that one can sometimes go wrong in making such predictions.

With regard to the operation categories, cognitive abilities are decidedly overrepresented, while divergent-production abilities are seriously underrepresented. The latter finding comes as no surprise. Comparisons with respect to content categories show that more than half the tests fall in the semantic area, with very few having symbolic content and none whatever having behavioral content. In terms of products, the most heavily represented are units, with relations not very far behind, but classes and transformations are underrepresented, classes seriously so. In view of the logical importance of classes in connection with concepts, it is surprising that tests involving the use of classes have been so uncommon, not only in the Stanford-Binet scale but elsewhere.

According to the writer's own count, considering only one strong factor per test in the Stanford-Binet scale L-M, 28 of the SI abilities are represented at some place in the scale but with uneven frequencies. The most frequently appearing factors are CMU (30 times) and CMS (14 times), with CFT, CMI, CFS, CMT, and NMI appearing from 6 to 9 times each. Distributions of these more frequent abilities are rather uneven over the year levels. Factor CMU seems to be represented as many as 5 times at age II-6 but not at all in four other age groups between III and X. Factor CMS seems not to be represented at all until age VII, only twice before age XIV, and from 1 to 3 times at each level from there on. Other abilities are represented only from time to time.

The fact that all abilities are related to chronological age and that their development is advancing on growth curves, if not fully abreast of one another, helps to provide much stability of measurement in spite of changes of test content from year to year. The fact that each individual is examined with tests ranging over more than one year also helps to broaden the sampling of factors. But in spite of these mitigating circumstances, the changes in test content should not be overlooked when mental-age and IQ assessments are used, particularly in research.

For the 11 tests in the WAIS, one can readily hypothesize as many as 11 of the SI factors to be represented, 8 of which are in the cognitive category, 2 in the memory category, and 1 in the convergent-production category. None is in the divergent-production category, and probably none touches upon evaluation. Six are semantic as to content, three are figural, and two symbolic, with none behavioral, unless Picture Arrangement involves some of that kind of information. Two symbolic factors, hence nonverbal, are represented among the tests scored for the verbal IQ, in the Arithmetic Reasoning and Memory Span tests, and one semantic (verbal) factor is represented in the tests scored for the performance IQ, in Picture Arrangement.

The Davis factor analysis (P. C. Davis, 1956) verified the presence of 5 of the 11 expected factors, the 6 others not being detectable because they were represented each by only one test in the analyzed battery, which included a number of marker tests for other factors. The 5 factors found by Davis were CFT (in Picture Completion, Object Assembly, and Block Design), CMU (in General Information, Comprehension, Similarities, and Vocabulary), CMS (in Arithmetic Reasoning, Comprehension, and Similarities), MSI (in Digit Symbol and Arithmetic Reasoning), and EFU (in Object Assembly and Block Design). The multiple appearance of most of these abilities in the WAIS tests is revealing of the tests' many redundancies. Instead of measuring the same ability a number of times, it might be better to devote some of the time to the measurement of additional abilities, thus gaining new information.

Some general principles for future tests   The nature of future testing of intellectual abilities will depend very much upon uses to be made of the test-score information. If a single composite measure is demanded or even if two scores are called for, the least that should be done is to determine empirically what the factorial components of that composite or those composites should be. Only in such a manner will a composite score become a known quantity and possess a degree of invariance of meaning. It will probably be found that an all-purpose composite score cannot be universally useful. Needless to say, if any composite is to have the same meaning at all ages and in different special groups and cultures, it will have to be demonstrated that the factorial composition of such a composite is fairly constant with any such changes of population.

Thurstone recommended the use of multiple scores and a profile for each individual. This is definitely the way in which to extract a maximum of information from test measurements, with each score strongly univocal. Such employment of scores cannot be effective unless the users of them are well aware of the psychological meaning of every ability and of its roles in areas of activity in which the scores are to be utilized. It would be desirable for those who guide developing intellects to be aware of all the kinds of intellectual resources. It would be well for every child to be tested in every relevant ability as soon as individual differences appear with respect to that ability and to have assessments repeated at appropriate intervals as long as this practice is useful. Much developmental research needs to be done to find out at what ages different abilities can first be measured, which ones are relevant for certain purposes, and what kinds of tests will measure the abilities best in each kind of population.

Tests used to determine academic aptitudes should be selected in view of explicit educational philosophy, which should point the way not only to useful course contents but to needs and opportunities for development of intellectual skills. The plural expression "academic aptitudes" is used in consistency with the multiple-aptitude nature of man. The problem of such aptitudes should be approached subject by subject and year by year, perhaps even teacher by teacher and method by method. Whatever the delimitation of educational aptitude, it will probably be found that a weighted pattern of factor abilities is involved, as for aircraft-pilot training, navigator training (Guilford, 1948), or learning in different courses of ninth-grade mathematics (Guilford et al., 1965).

The future of education

It is trite to say that since the advent of the space age, less than ten years ago, education has come in for reexamination from different directions. Are we doing all that we know we could do in the direction of education, and are we doing the right things? Can children be prepared better for school life, and can more adolescents be prepared to remain profitably in educational programs? Can anything be done to improve educational practices and techniques? It takes years to make an educated adult, and the explosion of information has not made this situation any easier. Can anything be done to facilitate the educational process, making it more efficient? It is increasingly recognized that education is the answer to many a difficult social problem, whether economic, political, governmental, or international. Will the problems of the world outrun the capacity to deal with them, capacity that should be acquired through education?

Because it deals with the central core of the educational process, which is the intellect of children and of older individuals, information from the structure-of-intellect theory should have much to offer toward the solutions of these important social problems. It has become realized more than ever that psychology of the past has had too little to offer to the teacher who wants to know about the nature of mental functioning of pupils and how to promote development of that functioning. The stimulus-response paradigm put education on a basis of exceeding simplicity but of a very low order of behavior. A theory of learning that puts it on the basis of forming S-R connections makes use of only one of the six products of information, namely, implications; mostly implications of a limited variety, namely, of S implying R. The other five kinds of products of information and even many kinds of implications have been very much ruled out of consideration.

An educator or a teacher cannot proceed very far working toward worthwhile goals without having a definite philosophy of education. Philosophy considers human values and establishes general goals for education. Until those goals are adopted, there can be little cogent planning in the form of curriculum, teaching operations, or examining procedures, three of the most important areas in which educational decisions must be made. In all these decisions, human intellectual development plays significant roles. Let us try to see where knowledge of the nature of intelligence fits into this picture. The history of educational philosophy has been very much the history of man's understanding of and his attitude toward human intelligence. There is no doubt that, in one way or another, some of the effort going into education has been directed at intellectual development, whatever the terminology or the views prevailing at the time.

The transfer problem   As is well known, ancient faculty psychology taught that broad powers of the mind can be strengthened by mental exercise or mental gymnastics, in the form of study of rhetoric, classical languages, or mathematics. Associational psychology had no use for faculties, since it was concerned with showing how items of information are stockpiled and become connected through sensory and reflective events. William James's classical experiment showing that practice in one kind of memorizing task did not facilitate development of ability to memorize in different tasks was another blow to faculty-theory thinking, for it threw serious doubt upon the reality of a unitary memory faculty and, by inference, doubt upon faculties in general. On the basis of present information, with knowledge that there are quite a number of relatively independent memory abilities, it is no wonder that James obtained the results that he did. It should be predicted that when a memory task involves one of the memory factors, practice with it should not affect status in another memory factor if that other factor is independent.

Another blow of a similar nature was dealt to the doctrine of formal discipline of faculty psychology by experiments of E. L. Thorndike and R. S. Woodworth (1901), performed some sixty years ago. They found that exercise in making one kind of psychophysical judgment with one kind of stimulus did not facilitate perceptual judgments of other sensory nature. Their generalized conclusion was that learning is quite specific, being limited to the kind of task exercised. Again, there is a real question of whether they were attempting to find transfer across boundaries of perceptual factors, which could be quite narrow in scope. They had selected an excellent area to support a case for specificity of learning.

Some years later, we saw that Thorndike carried out the general implications of this experiment by recommending the S-R–bond theory of learning. This took the form of exercising specific number combinations as isolated items of information, for example, precluding possibilities of insights about numbers that could be learned by inspecting multiplication tables and the like (in other words, the formation of relations and systems as well as implications). In fairness to Thorndike, we must not forget his principle of transfer in terms of identical elements. Many have interpreted his "identical elements" as S-R connections, but Thorndike came to a much broader conception that could not be confined to S-R bonds.

What we know about intellectual factors today forces us to reconsider the whole problem of formal discipline and specificity versus generality of learning. It is true that the conception of factors of intellect is similar in kind to the conception of faculties, the latter being conceived as powers and the former as abilities. But there are great differences in the scopes of the two kinds of mental unities and in the manner in which they have been derived. The old faculties had very little observational support and no univocal empirical referents; intellectual factors have both. Besides the ways in which the two kinds of concepts have been derived, there is growing evidence of intrafactor transfer, which could not be demonstrated for faculties. We are thus brought to a new and enlightened form of formal discipline.

Learning is neither so broad as faculties nor so narrow as to be completely specific. This is not to say that there is nothing specific about learning, for there is, as the experiments of Fleishman and others have demonstrated (see Chapter 12). Some specificity in learning is not contrary to factor theory, for there is room for a specific-component variable in individual differences in performance in any task. It is exercise with respect to the general or common-factor components that produce many of the transfer effects. Some specific components, each unique to its own task, presumably make no contribution to transfer in terms of increased generalized abilities.

But specific products of information can contribute to transfer in their own way because of their transposability. This is true because products belong to classes and enter into other forms of connection. The last conception comes close to Thorndike's general principle of transfer by way of identical elements, where *element* is broadly defined. The use of the same items of information in multiple connections was emphasized in relation to transfer recall, in Chapters 13 and 14.

The goal of intellectual growth   If we grant that one of the major objectives of education is to foster intellectual growth of individuals, the new information regarding the nature of intelligence should not only contribute to the philosophy of education by helping to refine that objective but also provide suggestions for implementing it. It is now better known what intellectual development means. In large part it means the strengthening of the intellectual abilities.

But some subsidiary issues are opened up. Should all children be educated so as to enhance all the abilities? In the extreme case, this would mean attempting to even up each child's status in all respects, as if one ideal were to produce a "well-rounded," balanced individual. The other side of the issue is that such a goal is impossible to achieve and is even undesirable and that we should discover early where a child's strong points are and capitalize upon them, for in these directions the individual is likely to make his greatest contributions to society. As usual, there is a middle ground. While seeing to it that no ability is allowed to remain below a minimum needed for ordinary living, we should also, in recognition of the specializing that prevails in the modern world, allow the individual to make the most of what he can do best and what gives him the greatest satisfaction.

Fostering intellectual development   If we conceive of the factorial functions as somewhat generalized, basic intellectual skills for dealing with information, it would seem that education should proceed along two lines. One of these would aim toward the development of the skills and the other toward the stockpiling of specific items of information. One of these approaches emphasizes the *possession* of information (cognition), and the other emphasizes the *use* of information (production). A third objective should be concerned with evaluation of information, or what is sometimes called "critical thinking." Retentive capacities depend very much upon achievements with respect to the other operation categories.

Development of the intellectual skills, as in acquiring any kind of skills, depends upon practice. The kinds of intellectual abilities indicate clearly the kinds of exercises that must be applied. Evidence cited in earlier chapters strongly suggests that exercise appropriate to each intellectual ability is likely to promote increase in that ability. We still have to determine how generally this principle applies and what the optimal kinds of exercises are. There is a little evidence (Forehand & Libby, 1962) that instruction concerning the nature of the abilities in question can be even more important than drill exercises aimed at those abilities. It might make a significant general contribution to intellectual development to inform all children, as soon as they are ready, concerning their kinds of intellectual resources.

Training the intellectual skills can be done either in the form of formal exercises, such as those designed and published by Myers and Torrance (1964) for schoolchildren, by Upton and Samson (1963) for college students, and by Parnes (1961b) for adults in general. But such training should not be restricted to formal exercises. There are numerous opportunities for emphasis upon cultivation of intellectual functions in regular courses, and such points of opportunity should be welcomed by the teacher who is concerned with the intellectual-development objective. Whereas much teaching effort is directed at the formation of concepts, which is weighted toward the cognition of semantic units, considerably more is needed in the exercise of the other products: classes, relations, systems, transformations, and implications. It is involvement with the latter that gives significance and meaning to units of information and that makes information useful.

The choice of curriculum should give attention to opportunities that different courses and subject matters have for development of the general skills as well as for their more immediate and special utilities. In determining whether any proposed subject has something unique to offer in the way of intellectual exercise or whether it will be redundant in that respect and whether the courses, collectively, provide sufficient extension and balance, the SI arrays of abilities should be of considerable help. Transfer benefits to be expected from each course can be decided in part in terms of the probable factors exercised.

Teaching methods and techniques can also be significantly guided on the basis of the SI abilities. The way in which a subject is taught may make all the difference in the world as to which abilities are favored. The unimaginative teacher who follows the easiest routes is not likely to arouse much intellectual exercise of any kind. The imaginative and challenging teacher sets the stage for productive-thinking exercises. Specific techniques of presentation of material to be learned can be suggested by the nature of the SI abilities and the tests designed to measure them.

The educational function of examining can be very important. Students prepare for the kinds of examinations they learn to expect in ways that are needed in order to do well in the examinations. Numerous studies have shown this statement to be true. The obvious implication is that if we want students to prepare for examinations in ways that exercise the more valuable intellectual abilities, examinations will have to be designed accordingly. The use of the answer-sheet examination has often put teacher convenience ahead of student needs. While, as testing experience shows, we can assess cognitive abilities (with the exception of those involving implications) with answer-sheet tests and while evaluative and memory abilities can be so tested to a large extent, it is virtually impossible to assess the more creative divergent-production and many of the convergent-production abilities in this manner. Thus, the exclusive use of answer-sheet tests does not encourage productive-thinking effort. In fact, it discourages it by rewarding other kinds of performance in an-swer-sheet tests. Even within the answer-sheet category of tests, attention should be given to forms that may encourage something more than the cognition and memory for units of information. It is alarming to contemplate what an exclusive use of answer-sheet tests could do to the intellectual character of a nation.

References

Adamson, R. E., & Taylor, D. W. Functional fixedness as related to elapsed time and set. *J. exp. Psychol.*, 1954, **47**, 122–126.

Adkins, D. C., & Lyerly, S. B. *Factor analysis of reasoning tests.* Chapel Hill, N.C.: Univer. of North Carolina, Dep. of Psychology, 1951.

Agnew, M. The auditory imagery of great composers. *Psychol. Monogr.*, 1922, **31**, 279–287. (a)

Agnew, M. A comparison of the auditory images of musicians, psychologists, and children. *Psychol. Monogr.*, 1922, **31**, 268–278. (b)

Allen, M. S. *Morphological creativity.* Englewood Cliffs, N.J.: Prentice-Hall, 1962.

Allport, F. H. *Theories of perception and the concept of structure.* New York: Wiley, 1955.

Anastasi, A. Further studies on the memory factor. *Arch. Psychol.*, N.Y., 1932, No. 142.

Anastasi, A. *Differential psychology: individual and group differences in behavior.* New York: Macmillan, 1958.

Anastasi, A., & Cordova, F. A. Some effects of bilingualism upon the intelligence test performance of Puerto Rican children in New York City. *J. educ. Psychol.*, 1953, **44**, 1–19.

Anastasi, A., & Levee, R. F. Intellectual defect and musical talent: a case report. *Amer. J. ment. Defic.*, 1959, **64**, 695–703.

Anderson, L. D. A longitudinal study of the effects of nursery-school training on successive intelligence-test ratings. In *Yearb. nat. Soc. Stud. Educ.*, 1940, 39, Part II. Pp. 3–10.

Andrews, D. P. Error-correcting perceptual mechanics. *Quart. J. exp. Psychol.*, 1964, **16**, 104–115.

Andrews, E. G. The development of imagination in the pre-school child. *Univer. Iowa Stud. Charact.*, 1930, 3 (4).

Andrews, T. G. A factorial analysis of responses to the comic as a study of personality. *J. gen. Psychol.*, 1943, **28**, 209–224.

Angelino, H., & Shedd, C. L. An initial report of a validation study of the Davis-Eells Test of General Intelligence or Problem-Solving Ability. *J. Psychol.*, 1955, **40**, 35–38.

Arnheim, R., Auden, W. H., Shapiro, K., & Stauffer, D. A. *Poets at work.* New York: Harcourt, Brace & World, 1948.

Arnold, J. E. Education for innovation. In S. J. Parnes & H. F. Harding (Eds.), *A source book for creative thinking.* New York: Scribner, 1962. Pp. 127–138. (a)

Arnold, J. E. Useful creative techniques. In S. J. Parnes & H. F. Harding (Eds.), *A source book for creative thinking.* New York: Scribner, 1962. Pp. 252–268. (b)

Asch, S. E. The process of free recall. In C. Scheerer (Ed.), *Cognition: theory, research, promise.* New York: Harper & Row, 1964. Pp. 79–88.

Asch, S. E., & Ebenholtz, S. M. The process of free recall: evidence for non-associative factors in acquisition and retention. *J. Psychol.*, 1962, **54**, 3–31.

Asch, S. E., & Lindner, M. A note on "strength of association." *J. Psychol.*, 1963, **55**, 199–209.

Ascher, E. J. The inadequacy of current intelligence tests for testing Kentucky mountain children. *J. genet. Psychol.*, 1935, **46**, 480–486.

Astin, A. W., & Ross, S. Glutamic acid and human intelligence. *Psychol. Bull.*, 1960, **57**, 429–434.

Atwell, S. Color vision in relation to artistic ability. *J. Psychol.*, 1939, **8**, 53–56.

Ausubel, D. P. A subsumption theory of meaningful verbal learning and retention. *J. gen. Psychol.*, 1962, **66**, 213–224.

Ausubel, D. P. The role of frequency in learning and retention: a cognitive structure interpretation. *J. gen. Psychol.*, 1965, **72**, 359–368.

Babich, F. R., Jacobson, A. L., & Bubash, S. Cross-species transfer of learning: effects of ribonucleic acid from hamsters on rat behavior. *Proc. nat. Acad. Sci.*, 1965, **54**, 1299–1302.

Baker, L. E. The pupillary response conditioned to subliminal auditory stimuli. *Psychol. Monogr.*, 1938, **50**, No. 3 (Whole No. 223).

Barber, B. Resistance by scientists to scientific discovery. *Science*, 1961, **134**, 596–602.

Barondes, S. H., & Cohen, H. D. Puromycin effects on successive phases of memory storage. *Science*, 1966, **151**, 594–595.

Barron, F. Complexity-simplicity as a personality dimension. *J. abnorm. soc. Psychol.*, 1953, **48**, 163–172.

Barron, F. The disposition toward originality. *J. abnorm. soc. Psychol.*, 1955, **51**, 478–485.

Barron, F. Originality in relation to personality and intellect. *J. Pers.*, 1957, **25**, 730–742.

Barron, F. The psychology of imagination. *Scient. Amer.*, September, 1958, **199**, 151–166.

Bartlett, F. C. *Remembering*. London: Cambridge, 1932.

Bartlett, F. C. *Thinking: an experimental and social study*. New York: Basic Books, 1958.

Basmajian, J. C. Control and training of individual motor units. *Science*, 1963, **141**, 440–441.

Bass, A. R., Hatton, G. I., McHale, T. J., & Stolurow, L. M. *Originality, intelligence, and performance on problem solving tasks: a pilot study of their relationship*. Urbana, Ill.: Univer. of Illinois, Training Research Laboratory, Tech. Rep. No. 2, 1962.

Bass, R. I. An analysis of the components of tests of semicircular canal function and of static and dynamic balance. *Res. Quart. Amer. Ass. Hlth phys. Educ.*, 1939, **10**, 33–52.

Bayley, N. The California First-Year Mental Scale. *Univer. Calif. Syllabus Ser.*, 1933, No. 243.

Bayley, N. Consistency and variability in the growth of intelligence from birth to eighteen years. *J. genet. Psychol.*, 1949, **75**, 165–196.

Bayley, N. Some increasing parent-child similarities during the growth of children. *J. educ. Psychol.*, 1954, **45**, 1–21.

Bayley, N. On the growth of intelligence. *Amer. Psychologist*, 1955, **10**, 805–818.

Bayley, N. Research in child development: a longitudinal perspective. *Merrill-Palmer Quart. Behav. Develpm.*, 1965, **11**, 183–208.

Bayley, N., & Oden, M. H. The maintenance of intellectual ability in gifted adults. *J. Geront.*, 1955, **10**, 91–107.

Beadle, G. W. The genes of men and molds. *Scient. Amer.*, September, 1948, **179**, 30–39.

Bechtoldt, H. P. Factorial investigation of the perceptual speed factor. *Amer. Psychologist*, 1947, **2**, 304–305.

Beittel, K. R. Creativity in the visual arts in higher education. In C. W. Taylor (Ed.), *Widening horizons in creativity*. New York: Wiley, 1964. Pp. 379–395.

Bell, A., & Zubek, J. P. The effect of age on the intellectual performance of mental defectives. *J. Geront.*, 1960, **15**, 285–295.

Bennett, E. L., & Calvin, M. Failure to train planarians reliably. *Neurosci. Res. Program Bull.*, 1964, **2** (4), 3–24.

Berger, R. M., Guilford, J. P., & Christensen, P. R. A factor-analytic study of planning. *Psychol. Monogr.*, 1957, **71**, No. 6 (Whole No. 435).

Berglund, G. W. *Mental growth*. Uppsala: Almquist and Wiksells, 1965.

Berkowitz, B., & Green, R. F. Changes in intellect with age: I. Longitudinal study of Wechsler-Bellevue scores. *J. genet. Psychol.*, 1963, **103**, 3–21.

Berkowitz, L. Leveling tendencies and the complexity-simplicity dimension. *J. Pers.*, 1957, **25**, 743–751.

Berlyne, D. E. Uncertainty and epistemic curiosity. *Brit. J. Psychol.*, 1962, **53**, 27–34.

Betke, J. E., & Lighthall, F. F. Detection and cognition without awareness. *Percept. mot. Skills*, 1963, **17**, 711–717.

Beveridge, W. J. E. *The art of scientific investigation*. New York: Norton, 1950.

Bilash, I., & Zubek, J. P. The effects of age on factorially "pure" mental abilities. *J. Geront.*, 1960, **15**, 175–182.

Binder, A. A statistical model for the process of visual recognition. *Psychol. Rev.*, 1955, **62**, 119–129.

Binet, A. *Les idées modernes sur les enfants*. Paris: Flammarion, 1909.

Binet, A., & Henri, V. La psychologie individuelle. *Année psychol.*, 1896, **2**, 411–465.

Binet, A., & Simon, Th. Méthodes nouvelles pour le diagnostic du niveau intellectuel des anormaux. *Année psychol.*, 1905, **11**, 191–244.

Birch, H. G. The relation of previous experience to insightful problem solving. *J. comp. physiol. Psychol.*, 1945, **38**, 367–383. (a)

Birch, H. G. The role of motivational factors in insightful problem solving. *J. comp. physiol. Psychol.*, 1945, **38**, 295–317. (b)

Birch, H. G., & Rabinowitz, H. S. The negative effect of previous experience on productive thinking. *J. exp. Psychol.*, 1951, **41**, 121–125.

Bird, G. E. The effect of nursery-school attendance upon mental growth of children. In *Yearb. nat. Soc. Stud. Educ.*, 1940, 39, Part II. Pp. 81–84.

Birren, J. E. A factorial analysis of the Wechsler-Bellevue scale given to an elderly population. *J. consult. Psychol.*, 1952, **16**, 399–405.

Birren, J. E. Age changes in speed of simple responses and reception and their significance for complex behavior. In *Old age in the modern world*. Report of the Third Congress of the International Association of Gerontology. Edinburgh: Livingstone, 1955. Pp. 235–247.

Birren, J. E. *The psychology of aging*. Englewood Cliffs, N.J.: Prentice-Hall, 1964.

Birren, J. E., Allen, W. R., & Landau, H. G. The relation of problem length in simple addition to time required, probability of success, and age. *J. Geront.*, 1954, **9**, 150–161.

Birren, J. E., Botwinick, J., Weiss, A. D., & Morrison, D. F. Interrelations of mental and perceptual tests given to healthy elderly men. In J. E. Birren, R. N. Butler, S. W. Greenhouse, L. Sokoloff, & M. R. Yarrow (Eds.), *Human aging*. U.S. Dep. of Health, Education, and Welfare, Publ. 986, 1963. Pp. 143–156.

Birren, J. E., & Morrison, D. F. Analysis of the WAIS subtests in relation to age and education. *J. Geront.*, 1961, **16**, 363–369.

Bishop, M. P., Elder, S. T., & Heath, R. G. Intracranial self-stimulation in man. *Science*, 1963, **140**, 394–396.

Blade, M. F., & Watson, W. S. Increase in spatial visualization test scores during engineering study. *Psychol. Monogr.*, 1955, **69**, No. 12 (Whole No. 397).

Blakey, R. I. A factor analysis of a non-verbal reasoning test. *Educ. psychol. Measmt*, 1941, **1**, 187–198.

Bloom, B. S. (Ed.) *Taxonomy of educational objectives. Handbook I: Cognitive domain*. New York: Longmans, 1956.

Bloom, R. S. Testing cognitive ability and achievement. In N. L. Gage (Ed.), *Handbook of research on teaching*. Chicago: Rand McNally, 1963.

Bond, N. A. An experimental study of transfer effects in human problem solving. Unpublished doctoral dissertation, Univer. of Southern California, 1955.

Bondareff, W. Morphology of the aging nervous system. In J. E. Birren (Ed.), *Handbook of aging and the individual: psychological and biological aspects*. Chicago: Univer. of Chicago Press, 1959. Pp. 136–172.

Bonsall, M. R., & Meeker, M. M. *Structure-of-intellect components in the Stanford-Binet Form L-M*. Experimental Draft No. 3. Los Angeles: Los Angeles County Schools, 1964.

Boring, E. G. Intelligence as the tests test it. *New Republic*, 1923, **34**, 35–37.

Boring, E. G. *A history of experimental psychology*. (2nd ed.) New York: Appleton-Century-Crofts, 1950.

Botwinick, J., & Birren, J. E. The measurement of intellectual decline in the senile psychoses. *J. consult. Psychol.*, 1951, **15**, 145–150.

Botwinick, J., Brinley, J. F., & Robbin, J. S. Modulation of speed of response with age. *J. genet. Psychol.*, 1959, **95**, 137–144.

Botzum, W. A. A factorial study of the reasoning and closure factors. *Psychometrika*, 1951, **16**, 361–386.

Bousfield, W. A. The occurrence of clustering in recall of randomly arranged associates. *J. gen. Psychol.*, 1953, **49**, 229–240.

Bousfield, W. A., & Barclay, W. D. The relationship between order and frequency of occurrences of restricted associated responses. *J. exp. Psychol.,* 1950, **40,** 643–647.

Bousfield, W. A., Cohen, B. H., & Whitmarsh, G. A. Associative clustering in the recall of words of different taxonomic frequencies of occurrence. *Psychol. Rep.,* 1958, **4,** 39–44.

Bousfield, W. A., & Sedgewick, C. H. W. An analysis of sequence of restricted associative responses. *J. gen. Psychol.,* 1944, **30,** 149–165.

Bovard, E. W. The effects of early handling on viability of the albino rat. *Psychol. Rev.,* 1958, **65,** 257–271.

Brain, W. R. Some reflections on genius. *Eugen. Rev.,* 1948, **40,** 12–20.

Braine, M. D. S. The ontogeny of certain logical operations: Piaget's formulation examined by nonverbal methods. *Psychol. Monogr.,* 1959, **73,** No. 5 (Whole No. 475).

Briggs, M. H., & Kitto, G. B. The molecular basis of memory and learning. *Psychol. Rev.,* 1962, **69,** 537–541.

Brittain, W. L., & Beittel, K. R. A study of some tests of creativity in relationship to performance in the visual arts. *Stud. Art Educ.,* 1961, **2,** 54–65.

Broadbent, D. E. Immediate memory and simultaneous stimuli. *Quart. J. exp. Psychol.,* 1957, **9,** 1–11. (a)

Broadbent, D. E. A mechanical model for human attention and immediate memory. *Psychol. Rev.,* 1957, **64,** 205–215. (b)

Broadbent, D. E. *Perception and communication.* London: Pergamon, 1958.

Broadbent, D. E. Short-term memory. *New Scientist,* 1962, **16,** 20–21.

Broadbent, D. E. Flow of information within the organism. *J. verb. Learn. verb. Behav.,* 1963, **2,** 34–39.

Brolyer, C. R., Thorndike, E. L., & Woodyard, E. A second study of mental discipline in high school subjects. *J. educ. Psychol.,* 1927, **18,** 377–404.

Bromley, D. B. Age and sex-differences in sequential categorization behavior. Unpublished paper, Univer. of Liverpool, Dep. of Psychology, 1964.

Brown, J. Short-term memory. *Brit. med. Bull.,* 1964, **20,** 8–11. (a)

Brown, J. Two tests of all-or-none learning and retention. *Quart. J. exp. Psychol.,* 1964, **16,** 123–133. (b)

Brown, S. W., Guilford, J. P., & Hoepfner, R. A factor analysis of semantic-memory abilities. *Rep. psychol. Lab. Univer. Southern Calif.,* 1966, No. 37.

Brunelle, E. A. Problem solving: intelligence and creativity. Unpublished paper, Orange State Coll., Fullerton, Calif., 1964.

Bruner, J. S. In going beyond the information given. In *Contemporary approaches to cognition.* Cambridge, Mass.: Harvard, 1957. Pp. 151–156.

Bruner, J. S., Goodnow, J. J., & Austin, G. A. *A study of thinking.* New York: Wiley, 1956.

Bruner, J. S., & Tagiuri, R. The perception of people. In G. Lindzey (Ed.), *Handbook of social psychology.* Reading, Mass.: Addison-Wesley, 1954. Pp. 634–654.

Brunswik, E. Scope and aspects of the cognitive problem. In *Contemporary approaches to cognition.* Cambridge, Mass.: Harvard, 1957. Pp. 5–31.

Burchard, E. M. L. The use of projective techniques in the analysis of creativity. *J. proj. Tech.,* 1952, **16,** 412–427.

Burkhart, R. C. *Spontaneous and deliberate ways of learning.* Scranton, Pa.: International Textbook, 1962.

Burns, B. D. *The mammalian cerebral cortex.* London: E. Arnold, 1958.

Burns, N., & Cavey, L. Age differences in empathic ability among children. *Canad. J. Psychol.,* 1957, **11,** 227–230.

Burt, C. *Annual Report of the London County Council's Psychologist,* 1915, 1917.

Burt, C. *Intelligence and fertility: the effects of the differential birth rate on inborn mental characteristics.* London: Hamilton, 1946.

Burt, C. The structure of the mind: a review of the results of factor analysis. *Brit. J. educ. Psychol.,* 1949, **19,** 100–111, 176–199.

Burt, C. The evidence for the concept of intelligence. *Brit. J. educ. Psychol.,* 1955, **25,** 158–177.

Burt, C. The inheritance of mental ability. *Amer. Psychologist,* 1958, **13,** 1–15.

Burt, C., & Williams, E. L. The influence of motivation on the results of intelligence tests. *Brit. J. stat. Psychol.,* 1962, **15,** 127–136.

Bushton, W. A. H. Peripheral coding in the nervous system. In W. A. Rosenblith (Ed.), *Sensory communication.* New York: Wiley, 1961. Pp. 169–181.

Calvin, A. D., & Dollenmayer, K. S. Subliminal perception: some negative results. *J. appl. Psychol.,* 1959, **43,** 187–188.

Cameron, D. E. Impairment of the retention phase of remembering. *Psychiat. Quart.,* 1943, **17,** 395–404.

Canisia, Sister M. Mathematical ability as related to reasoning and use of symbols. *Educ. psychol. Measmt,* 1962, **22,** 105–127.

Carlson, H. B., Fischer, R. P., & Young, P. T. Improvement in elementary psychology as related to intelligence. *Psychol. Bull.,* 1945, **42,** 27–34.

Carlsson, G. Social class, intelligence, and the verbal factor. *Acta Psychol.,* 1955, **11,** 269–278.

Carmichael, L. The physiological correlates of intelligence. In *Yearb. nat. Soc. Stud. Educ.,* 1940, 39, Part I. Pp. 93–106.

Carnap, R. *Introduction to semantics.* Cambridge, Mass.: Harvard, 1946.

Carnap, R. *The nature and application of inductive logic.* Chicago: Univer. of Chicago Press, 1951.

Carroll, J. B. A factor analysis of verbal abilities. *Psychometrika,* 1941, **6,** 279–307.

Carroll, J. B. *The study of language.* Cambridge, Mass.: Harvard, 1953.

Carroll, J. B. The prediction of success in intensive foreign language training. In R. Glaser (Ed.), *Training and education research.* Pittsburgh, Pa.: Univer. of Pittsburgh Press, 1962.

Cartledge, C. J., & Krauser, E. L. Training first-grade children in creative thinking under quantitative and qualitative motivation. *J. educ. Psychol.,* 1963, **54,** 295–299.

Cattell, J. McK. Mental tests and measurements. *Mind,* 1890, **15,** 373–380.

Cattell, P. *The measurement of intelligence of infants and young children.* New York: Psychological Corp., 1940.

Cattell, R. B. Occupational norms of intelligence and the standardization of an adult intelligence test. *Brit. J. Psychol.,* 1934–35, **25,** 1–28.

Cattell, R. B. Effects of human fertility trends upon the distribution of intelligence and culture. In *Yearb. nat. Soc. Stud. Educ.,* 1940, 39, Part I. Pp. 221–233.

Cattell, R. B. The fate of national intelligence: tests of a thirteen-year prediction. *Eugen. Rev.,* 1950, **42,** 136–148.

Cattell, R. B. *Factor analysis.* New York: Harper & Row, 1952.

Champion, J. M., & Turner, W. W. An experimental investigation of subliminal perception. *J. appl. Psychol.,* 1959, **43,** 382–384.

Chapanis, A., & Williams, W. C. Results of a mental survey with the Kuhlman-Anderson Intelligence Tests in Williamson County, Tennessee. *J. genet. Psychol.,* 1945, **67,** 27–55.

Chassell, L. M. Tests for originality. *J. educ. Psychol.,* 1916, **7,** 317–329.

Chen, T. L., and Chow, H. A factor study of a test battery at different educational levels. *J. genet. Psychol.,* 1948, **73,** 187–199.

Cherry, C. *On human communication.* New York: Wiley, 1957.

Chown, S. M. Age and the rigidities. *J. Geront.,* 1961, **16,** 353–362.

Chown, S. M., & Heron, A. Psychological aspects of aging in man. *Annu. Rev. Psychol.,* 1965, **17,** 417–450.

Christal, R. E. Factor analytic study of visual memory. *Psychol. Monogr.,* 1958, **72,** No. 13 (Whole No. 466).

Christensen, P. R. The function-sharing approach to research on joint man-machine intelligence. Santa Monica, Calif.: System Development Corp., 1963.

Christensen, P. R., & Guilford, J. P. *Ship Destination Test*. Beverly Hills, Calif.: Sheridan Psychological Services, 1955.

Christensen, P. R., & Guilford, J. P. An experimental study of verbal fluency factors. *Brit. J. stat. Psychol.*, 1963, **16**, 1–26.

Christensen, P. R., Guilford, J. P., & Wilson, R. C. Relations of creative responses to working time and instruction. *J. exp. Psychol.*, 1957, **53**, 82–88.

Churchill, R. D., Curtis, J. M., Coombs, C. H., & Harrell, T. W. Effect of engineer training on the Surface Development test. *Educ. psychol. Measmt*, 1942, **2**, 279–280.

Clay, H. M. Changes of performance with age on similar tasks of varying complexity. *Brit. J. Psychol.*, 1954, **45**, 7–13.

Clay, H. M. Age changes in problem-solving tasks. *Fourth Congress of the International Association of Gerontology*. Merano, Italy: Luglio, 1957.

Cohen, J. The factorial structure of the WAIS between early adulthood and old age. *J. consult. Psychol.*, 1957, **21**, 283–290.

Cook, J. O., & Brown, J. E. Familiarity and novelty of stimulus and response terms in paired-associate learning. *Psychol. Rep.*, 1963, **12**, 535–545.

Cook, L., Davidson, A. B., Davis, D. J., Green, H., & Fellows, E. J. Ribonucleic acid: effect on conditioned behavior in rats. *Science*, 1963, **141**, 268–269.

Cooper, R. M., & Zubek, J. P. Effects of enriched and restricted early environments on the learning ability of bright and dull rats. *Canad. J. Psychol.*, 1958, **12**, 159–164.

Corah, N. L., James, A. E., Painter, P., Stern, J. A., & Thurston, D. Effects of perinatal anoxia after seven years. *Psychol. Monogr.*, 1965, **79**, No. 3 (Whole No. 596).

Corter, H. M. Factor analysis of some reasoning tests. *Psychol. Monogr.*, 1952, **66**, No. 8 (Whole No. 340).

Cowell, H. The process of musical creation. *Amer. J. Psychol.*, 1926, **37**, 233–236.

Crawford, R. P. *Techniques of creative thinking*. Englewood Cliffs, N.J.: Hawthorn, 1954.

Crick, F. E. H. C. The structure of the hereditary material. *Scient. Amer.*, October, 1954, **191**, 54–61.

Critchley, M. *The parietal lobes*. London: E. Arnold, 1953.

Crossman, E. R. F. W. Information processes in human skill. *Brit. med. Bull.*, 1964, **20**, 32–37.

Crutchfield, R. S. Personal and situational factors in conformity to group pressure. Proceedings, XVth International Congress of Psychology. *Acta Psychol.*, 1959, **15**, 386–388.

Curtis, H. A. A study of the relative effects of age and of test difficulty upon factor patterns. *Genet. Psychol. Monogr.*, 1949, **40**, 99–148.

Darcy, N. T. Bilingualism and the measurement of intelligence: review of a decade of research. *J. genet. Psychol.*, 1963, **103**, 259–282.

Dattman, P. E., & Israel, H. E. The order of dominance among conceptual capacities: an experimental test of Heidbreder's hypothesis. *J. Psychol.*, 1951, **31**, 147–160.

Davis, D. R., & Sinha, D. The effect of one experience upon the recall of another. *Quart. J. exp. Psychol.*, 1950, **2**, 43–52. (a)

Davis, D. R., & Sinha, D. The influence of interpolated experience upon recognition. *Quart. J. exp. Psychol.*, 1950, **2**, 132–137. (b)

Davis, P. Discrimination without awareness in a psychophysical task. *Percept. mot. Skills*, 1964, **18**, 87–90.

Davis, P. C. A factor analysis of the Wechsler-Bellevue scale. *Educ. psychol. Measmt*, 1956, **16**, 127–146.

Dearborn, G. V. A study in imagination. *Amer. J. Psychol.*, 1898, **9**, 183–190.

Deese, J. On the structure of associative meaning. *Psychol. Rev.*, 1962, **69**, 161–175.

de Latil, P. *Thinking by machines*. (Tr. by Y. M. Golla.) Boston: Houghton Mifflin, 1957.

de Mille, R. Intellect after lobotomy in schizophrenia. *Psychol. Monogr.*, 1962, **76**, No. 16 (Whole No. 535).

Dennis, W. Infant development under conditions of restricted practice and of minimum social stimulation. *Genet. Psychol. Monogr.*, 1941, **23**, 143–189.

Dennis, W. Bibliographies of eminent scientists. *Sci. Monthly,* 1954, **19**, 180–183.

Dennis, W. Age and productivity among scientists. *Science,* 1956, **123**, 724–725.

Dennis, W. The age decrement in outstanding scientific contributions. *Amer. Psychologist,* 1958, **13**, 457–460.

Dennis, W., & Najarian, P. Infant development under environmental handicap. *Psychol. Monogr.,* 1957, **71**, No. 7 (Whole No. 436).

Deutsch, J. A. Higher nervous function: the physiological bases of memory. *Annu. Rev. Physiol.,* 1962, **24**, 259–286.

Dewey, J. *How we think.* Boston: Heath, 1910.

Dibner, A. S., & Cummins, J. F. Intellectual functioning in a group of normal octogenarians. *J. consult. Psychol.,* 1961, **25**, 137–141.

Dispensa, J. Relationship of the thyroid with intelligence and personality. *J. Psychol.,* 1938, **6**, 181–186.

Dixon, N. F. The effect of subliminal stimulation upon autonomic and verbal behavior. *J. abnorm. soc. Psychol.,* 1958, **57**, 29–36.

Dobzhansky, T. The genetic basis of evolution. *Scient. Amer.,* January, 1950, **182**, 32–41.

Dodwell, P. C. Relation between the understanding of the logic of classes and of cardinal number in children. *Canad. J. Psychol.,* 1962, **16**, 152–160.

Doll, E. A. Psychological consequences of cerebral birth lesions. In *Yearb. nat. Soc. Stud. Educ.,* 1940, 39, Part I. Pp. 119–122.

Doppelt, J., & Wallace, W. The performance of older people on Wechsler Adult Intelligence Scale. *Amer. Psychologist,* 1955, **8**, 338–339.

Dörken, H. Psychometric differences between senile dementia and normal senescent decline. *Canad. J. Psychol.,* 1954, **8**, 187–194.

Dubnoff, B. A comparative study of mental development in infancy. *J. genet. Psychol.,* 1938, **53**, 67–73.

Dudek, F. J. The dependence of factorial composition of aptitude tests upon differences among pilot trainees. I. The isolation of factors. *Educ. psychol. Measmt,* 1948, **8**, 613–634.

Dudek, F. J. The dependence of factorial composition of aptitude tests upon differences among pilot trainees. II. The factorial composition of tests and criterion variables. *Educ. psychol. Measmt,* 1949, **9**, 95–104.

Duncan, C. P. The retroactive effect of electroshock on learning. *J. comp. physiol. Psychol.,* 1949, **42**, 32–44.

Duncker, K. On problem solving. (Tr. by L. S. Lees.) *Psychol. Monogr.,* 1945, **58**, No. 5 (Whole No. 270).

Dunn, S. S. Pattern and process in mental measurement. *Austr. J. Psychol.,* 1962, **14**, 165–181.

Dunnette, M. D., Campbell, J. & Jastad, K. Effect of group participation on brainstorming effectiveness for two industrial samples. *J. appl. Psychol.,* 1963, **47**, 30–37.

Dunsdon, M. I., & Roberts, J. A. F. A study of the performance of 2,000 children on four vocabulary tests. II. Norms, with some observations on the relative variability of boys and girls. *Brit. J. stat. Psychol.,* 1957, **10**, 1–16.

Dvorak, B. J. The new USES General Aptitude Test Battery. *J. appl. Psychol.,* 1947, **31**, 372–376.

Eagle, M., Wolitzky, D. L., & Klein, G. S. Imagery: effect of a concealed figure in a stimulus. *Science,* 1966, **151**, 837–839.

Ebbinghaus, H. Ueber eine neue Methode zur Prüfung geistiger Fahigkeiten und ihre Anwendung bei Schulkindern. *Z. angew. Psychol.,* 1897, **13**, 401–459.

Eccles, J. C. The physiology of imagination. *Scient. Amer.,* September, 1958, **199**, 135–142.

Edwards, T. B. Measurement of some aspects of critical thinking. *J. exp. Educ.,* 1950, **18**, 263–278.

Eindhoven, J. E., & Vinacke, W. E. Creative process in painting. *J. gen. Psychol.,* 1952, **47**, 139–164.

El-Abd, H. A study of certain closure factors in relation to Guilford's structure of intellect. Unpublished doctoral dissertation, Univer. of London, 1963.

Elkind, D. Children's conceptions of right and left: Piaget replication study IV. *J. genet. Psychol.*, 1961, **99**, 269–276. (a)

Elkind, D. Children's discovery of the conservation of mass, weight, and volume: Piaget replication study II. *J. genet. Psychol.*, 1961, **98**, 219–227. (b)

Elkind, D. The development of quantitative thinking: a systematic replication of Piaget's studies. *J. genet. Psychol.*, 1961, **98**, 37–46. (c)

Elkind, D. The development of the additive composition of classes in the child: Piaget replication study III. *J. genet. Psychol.*, 1961, **99**, 51–57. (d)

Elkind, D. Discrimination, seriation, and numeration of size and dimensional differences in young children: Piaget replication study VI. *J. genet. Psychol.*, 1964, **104**, 275–296.

Elkind, D., Koegler, R. R., & Go, E. Effects of perceptual training at three age levels. *Science,* 1962, **137**, 755.

El Koussy, A. H. The visual perception of space. *Brit. J. Psychol., Monogr. Suppl.*, 1936, **7**, No. 20.

Elliott, J. M. Measuring creative abilities in public relations and in advertising work. In C. W. Taylor (Ed.), *Widening horizons in creativity.* New York: Wiley, 1964. Pp. 396–400.

Elmgren, J. *Some fundamental problems in psychological factor analysis.* Göteborg: Univer. of Göteborg, 1958.

Emmett, W. G. Evidence of a space factor at 11+ and earlier. *Brit. J. Psychol., stat. Sec.*, 1949, **2**, 3–16.

Engen, T., Levy, N., and Schlosberg, H. A new series of facial expressions. *Amer. Psychologist,* 1957, **12**, 164–166.

Entwisle, D. G. Aging: the effects of previous skill in training. *Occup. Psychol.*, 1959, **33**, 238–243.

Ericksen, C. W. Discrimination and learning without awareness: a methodological survey and evaluation. *Psychol. Rev.*, 1960, **67**, 279–300.

Erlenmeyer-Kimling, L., & Jarvik, L. F. Genetics and intelligence: a review. *Science,* 1963, **142**, 1477–1478.

Essman, W. B. Awareness of reinforcement in "earning without awareness." *Psychol. Rev.*, 1957, **3**, 399–400.

Estes, B. W. Some mathematical and logical concepts in children. *J. genet. Psychol.*, 1956, **88**, 219–222.

Evans, W. D., & Smith, R. P. Some effects of morphine and amphetamine on intellectual functions and mood. *Psychopharmacology,* 1964, **6**, 49–56.

Falek, A., Kallman, F. J., Lorge, I., & Jarvik, L. F. Longevity and intellectual variation in a senescent twin population. *J. Geront.*, 1960, **15**, 305–309.

Fantz, R. L. The origin of form perception. *Scient. Amer.*, May, 1961, **204**, 66–72.

Fantz, R. L. Pattern vision in newborn infants. *Science,* 1963, **140**, 296–297.

Farnsworth, P. R. Further data on the Adlerian theory. *J. gen. Psychol.*, 1941, **24**, 447–450.

Faubian, R. W., Cleveland, E. A., & Harrell, T. W. The influence of training on mechanical aptitude test scores. *Educ. psychol. Measmt,* 1942, **2**, 91–94.

Feifel, H. Qualitative differences in the vocabulary responses of normals and abnormals. *Genet. Psychol. Monogr.*, 1949, **39**, 151–204.

Feindel, W. The brain considered as a thinking machine. In W. Feindel (Ed.), *Memory, learning and language.* Toronto: Univer. of Toronto Press, 1960. Pp. 11–23.

Feldman, J. Computer simulation of cognitive processes. In H. Borko (Ed.), *Computer applications in the behavioral sciences.* Englewood Cliffs, N.J.: Prentice-Hall, 1962.

Ferguson, G. A. On learning and human ability. *Canad. J. Psychol.*, 1954, **8**, 95–112.

Ferguson, G. A. On transfer and the abilities of man. *Canad. J. Psychol.*, 1956, **10**, 121–131.

Fessard, A. The role of neuronal networks in sensory communication. In W. A. Rosenblith (Ed.), *Sensory communication.* New York: Wiley, 1961. Pp. 585–606.

Festinger, L. The relation between behavior and cognition. In *Contemporary approaches to cognition*. Cambridge, Mass.: Harvard, 1957. Pp. 127–150.

Fischberg, M., & Blackler, A. W. How cells specialize. *Scient. Amer.*, September, 1961, **205**, 124–128.

Fisichelli, V. R., & Welch, L. The ability of college art majors to recombine ideas in creative thinking. *J. appl. Psychol.*, 1947, **31**, 278–282.

Fitzhugh, K. B., Fitzhugh, L. C., & Reitan, R. M. Wechsler-Bellevue comparisons in groups with "chronic" and "current" lateralized diffuse brain lesions. *J. consult. Psychol.*, 1962, **26**, 306–310.

Flanagan, J. C. The definition and measurement of ingenuity. In C. W. Taylor and F. Barron (Eds.), *Scientific creativity: its recognition and development*. New York: Wiley, 1963. Pp. 89–98.

Flavell, J. H. *The developmental psychology of Jean Piaget*. Princeton, N.J.: Van Nostrand, 1963.

Flavell, J. H., Cooper, A., & Loiselle, R. H. Effect of the number of pre-utilization functions on functional fixedness in problem solving. *Psychol. Rep.*, 1958, **4**, 343–350.

Fleishman, E. A. Dimensional analysis of psychomotor abilities. *J. exp. Psychol.*, 1954, **48**, 437–454.

Fleishman, E. A. A comparative study of aptitude patterns in unskilled and skilled psychomotor performances. *J. appl. Psychol.*, 1957, **41**, 263–272.

Fleishman, E. A. Abilities at different stages of practice in rotary pursuit performance. *J. exp. Psychol.*, 1960, **60**, 162–171.

Fleishman, E. A., & Fruchter, B. Factor structure and predictability of successive stages of learning Morse code. *J. appl. Psychol.*, 1960, **44**, 97–101.

Fleishman, E. A., & Hempel, W. E., Jr. Changes in factor structure of a complex psychomotor test as a function of practice. *Psychometrika*, 1954, **19**, 239–252.

Fleishman, E. A., & Hempel, W. E., Jr. The relation between abilities and improvement with practice in a visual discrimination reaction task. *J. exp. Psychol.*, 1955, **49**, 301–312.

Fleishman, E. A., & Rich, S. Role of kinesthetic and visual-spatial abilities in perceptual-motor learning. *J. exp. Psychol.*, 1963, **66**, 6–11.

Fleishman, E. A., Roberts, M. M., & Friedman, M. P. A factor analysis of aptitude and proficiency measures in radiotelegraphy. *J. appl. Psychol.*, 1958, **42**, 129–137.

Floyd, R. L. Semantic satiation: replication and test of further implications. *Psychol. Rep.*, 1962, **11**, 274.

Forehand, G. A., & Libby, W. L., Jr. Effects of educational programs and perceived organizational climate upon changes in innovative administrative behavior. In *Innovative behavior*. Chicago: Univer. of Chicago, Center for Programs in Government Administration, 1962.

Forgus, R. H. Advantage of early over late perceptual experience in improving form discrimination. *Canad. J. Psychol.*, 1956, **10**, 147–156.

Foulds, G. A. Variations in the intellectual activities of adults. *Amer. J. Psychol.*, 1949, **62**, 238–246.

Foulds, G. A., & Raven, J. C. Normal changes in the mental abilities of adults as age advances. *J. ment. Sci.*, 1948, **94**, 133–142.

Fowler, W. Cognitive learning in infancy and early childhood. *Psychol. Bull.*, 1962, **59**, 116–152.

Frandsen, A., & Barlow, F. P. Influence of the nursery school on mental growth. In *Yearb. nat. Soc. Stud. Educ.*, 1940, 39, Part II. Pp. 143–148.

Frankenhaeuser, M., Myrsten, A. L., & Järpe, C. Effects of a moderate dose of alcohol on intellectual functions. *Psychopharmacology*, 1962, **3**, 344–351.

Freeman, F. N. The meaning of intelligence. In *Yearb. nat. Soc. Stud. Educ.*, 1940, 39, Part I. Pp. 11–20.

Freeman, F. N., Holzinger, K. J., & Mitchell, B. C. The influence of the environment on the intelligence, school achievement, and conduct of foster children. In *Yearb. nat. Soc. Stud. Educ.*, 1928, 27, Part I. Pp. 103–217.

French, J. D. The reticular formation. *Scient. Amer.*, May, 1957, **196**, 54–60.

French, J. W. The description of aptitude and achievement tests in terms of rotated factors. *Psychometr. Monogr.*, 1951, No. 5.

French, J. W. The relationship of problem-solving styles to the factor composition of tests. *Educ. psychol. Measmt,* 1965, **25**, 9–28.

Frick, J. W., Guilford, J. P., Christensen, P. R., & Merrifield, P. R. A factor-analytic study of flexibility in thinking. *Educ. psychol. Measmt,* 1959, **19**, 469–496.

Friend, C. M., & Zubek, J. P. The effects of age on critical thinking ability. *J. Geront.*, 1958, **13**, 407–413.

Fruchter, B. The nature of verbal fluency. *Educ. psychol. Measmt,* 1948, **8**, 33–47.

Fruchter, B. *An introduction to factor analysis.* Princeton, N.J.: Van Nostrand, 1954.

Fryer, D. Occupational-intelligence standards. *Sch. & Soc.*, 1922, **16**, 273–277.

Fuhrer, M. J., & Ericksen, C. W. The unconscious perception of the meaningful verbal stimuli. *J. abnorm. soc. Psychol.*, 1960, **61**, 432–439.

Furth, H. G. Research with the deaf: implications for language and cognition. *Psychol Bull.*, 1964, **62**, 145–164.

Gabriel, R. F. The influence of order information and stimulus display time on short-term retention. Unpublished doctoral dissertation, Univer. of Southern California, 1963.

Gagné, R. M., & Paradise, N. E. Abilities and learning sets in knowledge acquisition. *Psychol. Monogr.*, 1961, **75**, No. 14 (Whole No. 518).

Gaito, J. DNA and RNA as memory molecules. *Psychol. Rev.*, 1963, **70**, 471–480.

Gaito, J. Stages of perception, unconscious processes, and information extraction. *J. gen. Psychol.*, 1965, **70**, 183–197.

Galambos, R. Changing concepts of the learning mechanism. In J. F. Delafresnaye (Ed.), *Brain mechanisms and learning.* Springfield, Ill.: Charles C Thomas, 1961. Pp. 231–242.

Galton, F. *Hereditary genius: an inquiry into its laws and consequences.* New York: Macmillan, 1869.

Gardner, R. W., & Lohrenz, L. J. Leveling-sharpening and serial reproduction of a story. *Bull. Menninger Clin.*, 1960, **24**, 295–304.

Gardner, R. W., & Long, R. I. Cognitive controls as determinants of learning and remembering. *Psychologia,* 1960, **3**, 165–171.

Gardner, R. W., & Long, R. I. Control, defence and centration effect: a study of scanning behavior. *Brit. J. Psychol.*, 1962, **53**, 129–140.

Garfield, S. L., & Blek, L. Age, vocabulary level, and mental impairment. *J. consult. Psychol.*, 1952, **16**, 395–398.

Garner, W. R. *Uncertainty and structure as psychological concepts.* New York: Wiley, 1962.

Garnett, J. C. M. General ability, cleverness, and purpose. *Brit. J. Psychol.*, 1919, **9**, 345–365.

Garrett, H. E. A developmental theory of intelligence. *Amer. Psychologist,* 1946, **1**, 372–378.

Garrett, H. E., Bryan, A. I., & Perl, R. E. The age factor in mental organization. *Arch. Psychol., N.Y.,* 1935, No. 176.

Garskof, B. E., & Houston, J. P. Measurement of verbal relatedness: an idiographic approach. *Psychol. Rev.*, 1963, **70**, 277–288.

Garskof, B. E., & Houston, J. P. Relation between judged meaning similarity, associative probability, and associative overlap. *Psychol. Rep.,* 1965, **16**, 220–222.

Gaskill, H. V., & Fritz, M. F. Basal metabolic rate and the college freshman psychological test. *J. gen. Psychol.*, 1946, **34**, 29–45.

Gazzaniga, M. S. Psychological properties of the disconnected hemispheres in man. *Science,* 1965, **150**, 372.

Geist, H. Evaluation of culture-free intelligence. *Calif. J. Educ.,* 1954, **5**, 209–214.

Gerard, R. W. What is memory? *Scient. Amer.*, September, 1953, **189**, 118–126.

Gerard, R. W. The fixation of experience. In J. F. Delafresnaye (Ed.), *Brain mechanisms and learning.* Springfield, Ill.: Charles C Thomas, 1961. Pp. 21–32.

Gerard, R. W. Symposium: theoretical-experimental approaches to memory. The material basis of memory. *J. verb. Learn. verb. Behav.,* 1963, **2,** 22–33.

Gerry, R., DeVeau, L., & Chorness, M. H. A review of some recent research in the field of creativity and the examination of an experimental creativity workshop. Lackland Air Force Base, Training Analysis and Development Division, 1957.

Gershon, A., Guilford, J. P., & Merrifield, P. R. Figural and symbolic divergent-production abilities in adolescent and adult populations. *Rep. psychol. Lab. Univer. Southern Calif.,* 1963, No. 29.

Gesell, A., Halverson, H. M., Thomson, H., Ilg, F. L., Castner, B. M., Ames, L. B., & Amatruda, C. S. *The first five years of life, the preschool years.* New York: Harper & Row, 1940.

Gesell, A., & Staff. *Gesell developmental schedules.* New York: Psychological Corp., 1949.

Getzels, J. W., & Jackson, P. W. *Creativity and intelligence.* New York: Wiley, 1961.

Ghiselli, E. E., & Brown, C. W. Validity of aptitude tests for predicting trainability of workers. *Personnel Psychol.,* 1951, **4,** 243–260.

Gibson, E. J. Learning to read. *Science,* 1965, **148,** 1066–1072.

Gibson, E. J., Walk, R. D., Pick, H. L., Jr., & Tighe, T. J. The effect of prolonged exposure to visual patterns on learning to discriminate similar and different patterns. *J. comp. physiol. Psychol.,* 1958, **51,** 584–587.

Gilbert, J. G. Memory loss in senescence. *J. abnorm. soc. Psychol.,* 1941, **36,** 73–86.

Glanzer, M., & Glazer, R. Cross-sectional and longitudinal results in a study of age-related changes. *Educ. psychol. Measmt,* 1959, **19,** 89–101.

Glaze, J. A. The association value of nonsense syllables. *J. genet. Psychol.,* 1928, **35,** 255–269.

Glickman, S. E. Perseverative neural processes and the consolidation of the memory trace. *Psychol. Bull.,* 1961, **58,** 218–233.

Goddard, G. V. Functions of the amygdala. *Psychol. Bull.,* 1964, **62,** 89–110.

Goertzel, V. H., & Goertzel, M. G. *Cradles of eminence.* Boston: Little, Brown, 1962.

Golann, S. E. The creativity motive. *J. Pers.,* 1962, **30,** 588–600.

Goldfarb, W. Infant rearing and problem behavior. *Amer. J. Orthopsychiat.,* 1943, **13,** 249–265.

Goldfarb, W. Variations in adolescent adjustment of institutionally reared children. *Amer. J. Orthopsychiat.,* 1947, **17,** 449–457.

Goldstein, K. *Language and language disturbances.* New York: Grune & Stratton, 1948.

Goldstein, K., & Scheerer, M. Abstract and concrete behavior: an experimental study with special tests. *Psychol. Monogr.,* 1941, **53,** No. 2 (Whole No. 239).

Goldstein, K., & Scheerer, M. Tests of abstract and concrete thinking. In A. Weider (Ed.), *Contributions toward medical psychology.* Vol. 2. New York: Ronald Press, 1953, pp. 702–730.

Gomulicki, B. R. Individual differences in recall. *J. Pers.,* 1956, **24,** 387–400.

Gomulicki, B. R. The development and present status of the trace theory of memory. *Brit. J. Psychol., Monogr. Suppl.,* 1963, No. 29.

Goodenough, F. L. Some special problems of nature-nurture research. In *Yearb. nat. Soc. Stud. Educ.,* 1940, 39, Part I. Pp. 367–384.

Goodenough, F. L. Month of birth as related to socioeconomic status of parents. *J. genet. Psychol.,* 1941, **59,** 65–76.

Goodenough, F. L., & Maurer, K. M. The relative potency of the nursery school and the statistical laboratory in boosting the IQ. *J. educ. Psychol.,* 1940, **31,** 541–549.

Gordon, H. *Mental and scholastic tests among retarded children.* London: Bd Educ. Pamphlet No. 44, 1923.

Gordon, W. J. J. *Synectics.* New York: Harper & Row, 1961.

Goss, A. E. Acquisition and use of conceptual schemes. In C. N. Cofer (Ed.), *Verbal learning and verbal behavior.* New York: McGraw-Hill, 1961. Pp. 42–67.

Gottschaldt, K. Über den Einfluss der Erfahrung auf die Wahrnehmung von Figuren. *Psychol. Forsch.,* 1926, **8,** 261–317.

Graham, C. Differential marking of two vocabulary tests. *Psychol. Rep.*, 1963, 12, 421–422.

Graham, F. K., Ernhart, C. B., Thurston, D., & Craft, M. Development three years after perinatal anoxia and other potentially damaging newborn experiences. *Psychol. Monogr.*, 1962, 76, No. 3 (Whole No. 522).

Graham, F. K., & Kendall, B. S. Memory-for-Designs Test: revised general manual. *Percept. mot. Skills*, 1960, 11, 147–188.

Gray, G. W. "The organizer." *Scient. Amer.*, November, 1957, 197, 79–88.

Green, R. F., & Berkowitz, B. Changes in intellect with age: II. Factorial analysis of Wechsler-Bellevue scores. *J. genet. Psychol.*, 1964, 104, 3–18.

Green, R. F., Guilford, J. P., Christensen, P. R., & Comrey, A. L. A factor-analytic study of reasoning abilities. *Psychometrika*, 1953, 18, 135–160.

Griffin, D. P. Movement responses and creativity. *J. consult. Psychol.*, 1958, 22, 134–136.

Griswold, F. H. *Creative power, the phenomena of inspiration; an inquiry into the practical methods used by men of genius in developing original ideas.* New York: McKay, 1939.

Guetzkow, H., & Brozek, J. Intellectual functions with restricted intakes of B-complex vitamins. *Amer. J. Psychol.*, 1946, 59, 358–381.

Guilford, J. P. A note on the discovery of a G factor by means of Thurstone's centroid method of analysis. *Psychometrika*, 1941, 6, 205–208.

Guilford, J. P. Factor analysis in a test-development program. *Psychol. Rev.*, 1948, 55, 79–94.

Guilford, J. P. Creativity. *Amer. Psychologist*, 1950, 14, 469–479.

Guilford, J. P. When not to factor analyze. *Psychol. Bull.*, 1952, 49, 26–37.

Guilford, J. P. *Psychometric methods.* (2nd ed.) New York: McGraw-Hill, 1954.

Guilford, J. P. Les dimensions de l'intellect. In H. Laugier (Ed.), *L'analyse factorielle et ses applications.* Paris: Centre National de la Recherche Scientifique, 1956. Pp. 53–74. (a)

Guilford, J. P. The structure of intellect. *Psychol. Bull.*, 1956, 53, 267–293. (b)

Guilford, J. P. Creative abilities in the arts. *Psychol. Rev.*, 1957, 64, 110–118.

Guilford, J. P. New frontiers of testing in the discovery and development of human talent. In *Seventh Annual Western Regional Conference on Testing Problems.* Los Angeles: Educational Testing Service, 1958. Pp. 20–32. (a)

Guilford, J. P. A system of the psychomotor abilities. *Amer. J. Psychol.*, 1958, 71, 164–174. (b)

Guilford, J. P. *Personality.* New York: McGraw-Hill, 1959. (a)

Guilford, J. P. Three faces of intellect. *Amer. Psychologist*, 1959, 14, 469–479. (b)

Guilford, J. P. Basic conceptual problems in the psychology of thinking. In E. Harms (Ed.), Fundamentals of Psychology: the psychology of thinking. *Ann. N.Y. Acad. Sci.*, 1960, 91, 6–21.

Guilford, J. P. Factorial angles to psychology. *Psychol. Rev.*, 1961, 68, 1–20.

Guilford, J. P. An informational view of mind. *J. psychol. Res.*, 1962, 6, 1–10.

Guilford, J. P. An informational theory of creative thinking. *USAF Instructors' J.*, 1963, 1, 28–33.

Guilford, J. P. Intelligence, creativity, and learning. In R. W. Russell (Ed.), *Frontiers in psychology.* Chicago: Scott, Foresman, 1964. Pp. 125–147. (a)

Guilford, J. P. Zero intercorrelations among tests of intellectual abilities. *Psychol. Bull.*, 1964, 61, 401–404. (b)

Guilford, J. P. *Fundamental statistics in psychology and education.* (4th ed.) New York: McGraw-Hill, 1965. (a)

Guilford, J. P. Motivation in an informational psychology. In D. Levine (Ed.), *Nebraska symposium on motivation, 1965.* Lincoln, Nebr.: Univer. of Nebraska Press, 1965. Pp. 313–332. (b)

Guilford, J. P. Basic problems in teaching for creativity. In C. W. Taylor & F. E. Williams, (Eds.), *Instructional media and creativity.* New York: Wiley, 1966. Pp. 71–103.

Guilford, J. P., Christensen, P. R., Frick, J. W., & Merrifield, P. R. Factors of interest in thinking. *J. gen. Psychol.*, 1961, 65, 39–56.

Guilford, J. P., Fruchter, B., & Zimmerman, W. S. Factor analysis of the Army Air Forces Sheppard Field battery of experimental aptitude tests. *Psychometrika,* 1952, **17**, 45–68.

Guilford, J. P., Green, R. F., Christensen, P. R., Hertzka, A. F., & Kettner, N. W. A factor-analytic study of Navy reasoning tests with the Air Force Aircrew Classification Battery. *Educ. psychol. Measmt,* 1954, **14**, 301–325.

Guilford, J. P., & Hoepfner R. Sixteen divergent-production abilities at the ninth-grade level. *Multiv. Behav. Res.,* 1966, **1**, 43–64.

Guilford, J. P., Hoepfner, R., & Petersen, H. Predicting achievement in ninth-grade mathematics from measures of intellectual-aptitude factors. *Educ. psychol. Measmt,* 1965, **25**, 659–682.

Guilford, J. P., & Lacey, J. I. (Eds.) *Printed classification tests: Army Air Forces Aviation Psychology Research Program Reports.* Rep. No. 5. Washington, D.C.: GPO, 1947.

Guilford, J. P., Merrifield, P. R., Christensen, P. R., & Frick, J. W. Some new symbolic factors of cognition and convergent production. *Educ. psychol. Measmt,* 1961, **21**, 515–541.

Guilford, J. P., Merrifield, P. R., & Cox, A. B. Creative thinking in children at the junior high school levels. *Rep. psychol. Lab. Univer. Southern Calif.,* 1961, No. 26.

Guilford, J. P., & Zimmerman, W. S. *The Guilford-Zimmerman Aptitude Survey.* Beverly Hills, Calif.: Sheridan Psychological Services, 1948.

Guilford, J. P., & Zimmerman, W. S. Some variable-sampling problems in the rotation of axes in factor analysis. *Psychol. Bull.,* 1963, **60**, 289–301.

Guthrie, E. R., & Horton, G. P. *Cats in a puzzle box.* New York: Holt, 1946.

Guthrie, G. M. Structure of abilities in a non-Western culture. *J. educ. Psychol.,* 1963, **54**, 94–103.

Guttman, L. The structure of interrelations among intelligence tests. In C. W. Harris (Ed.), *Invitational conference on testing problems.* Princeton, N.J.: Educational Testing Service, 1965. Pp. 25–36.

Hadamard, J. S. *An essay on the psychology of invention in the mathematical field.* Princeton, N.J.: Princeton, 1945.

Haggard, E. A. Social-status and intelligence: an experimental study of certain cultural determinants of measured intelligence. *Genet. Psychol. Monogr.,* 1954, **49**, 141–186.

Hallenbeck, C. E. Evidence for a multiple process view of mental deterioration. Paper read at Midwest. Psychol. Ass. convention, 1963.

Halstead, W. C. *Brain and intelligence.* Chicago: Univer. of Chicago Press, 1947.

Halstead, W. C. Biological intelligence. *J. Pers.,* 1951, **20**, 118–120.

Hanfmann, E. Tests of abstract and concrete thinking. B. Concept Formation Test. In A. Weider (Ed.), *Contributions toward medical psychology.* Vol. II. New York: Ronald Press, 1953. Pp. 731–749.

Hargreaves, H. L. The 'faculty' of imagination. An inquiry concerning the existence of a general 'faculty' or group factor of imagination. *Brit. J. Psychol. Monogr.,* 1927, Suppl. No. 10.

Harlow, H. F. The formation of learning sets. *Psychol. Rev.,* 1949, **56**, 51–56.

Harlow, H. F. The evolution of learning. In A. Roe and G. G. Simpson (Eds.), *Behavior and evolution.* New Haven, Conn.: Yale, 1958.

Harlow, H. F., & Harlow, M. K. Social deprivation in monkeys. *Scient. Amer.,* November, 1962, **207**, 136–146.

Harman, H. H. *Modern factor analysis.* Chicago: Univer. of Chicago Press, 1960.

Harrell, T. W., & Harrell, M. S. Army General Classification Test scores for civilian occupations. *Educ. psychol. Measmt,* 1945, **5**, 229–240.

Hartry, A. L., Keith-Lee, P., & Morton, W. W. D. Planaria: memory transfer through cannibalism reexamined. *Science,* 1964, **146**, 274–275.

Hartson, L. D. Does college training influence test intelligence? *J. educ. Psychol.,* 1936, **27**, 481–491.

Harvey, H. Cognitive changes in brain-injured children: a preliminary survey. Unpublished doctoral dissertation, Univer. of Southern California, 1950.

Havelka, J. Problem-seeking behavior in rats. *Canad. J. Psychol.*, 1956, **10**, 91–97.

Havighurst, R. J., & Breese, F. H. Relation between ability and social status in a Midwestern community. III. Primary mental abilities. *J. educ. Psychol.*, 1947, **38**, 241–247.

Havighurst, R. J., & Janke, L. L. Relation between ability and social status in a Midwestern community. I. Ten-year-old children. *J. educ. Psychol.*, 1944, **35**, 357–368.

Haynes, J. R., & Sells, S. B. Assessment of organic brain damage by psychological tests. *Psychol. Bull.*, 1963, **60**, 316–325.

Hebb, D. O. *The organization of behavior.* New York: Wiley, 1949.

Heese, K. W. A general factor in improvement with practice. *Psychometrika*, 1942, **7**, 213–223.

Heidbreder, E. An experimental study of thinking. *Arch. Psychol., N.Y.*, 1924, No. 73.

Heidbreder, E. Toward a dynamic psychology of cognition. *Psychol. Rev.*, 1945, **52**, 1–22.

Heinonen, V. A factor analytic study of transfer of training. *Scand. J. Psychol.*, 1962, **3**, 177–188.

Helson, H. *Adaptation level theory.* New York: Harper & Row, 1964.

Helson, H., & Helson, H. B. Some common features of concrete and abstract thinking. *Amer. J. Psychol.*, 1946, **59**, 458–472.

Helson, R. M., & Cover, A. Specificity-generality of classificatory categories as a variable in recall. *Percept. mot. Skills*, 1956, **6**, 233–236.

Henle, M. On the relation between logic and thinking. *Psychol. Rev.*, 1962, **69**, 366–378.

Henry, S. Children's audiograms in relation to reading attainment. *J. genet. Psychol.*, 1947, **71**, 3–48.

Hernandez-Peon, R., Scheerer, H., & Jouvet, M. Modification of electrical activity in cochlear nucleus during "attention" in unanesthetized cats. *Science*, 1956, **123**, 331–332.

Hertzka, A. F., Guilford, J. P., Christensen, P. R., & Berger, R. M. A factor-analytic study of evaluative abilities. *Educ. psychol. Measmt*, 1954, **14**, 581–597.

Heuyer, G., et al. Le niveau intellectuel des enfants d'âge scolaire. *Inst. nat. d'études démographiques: travaux et documents*, 1950, Cahier 13.

Hildreth, G. Adopted children in a private school. In *Yearb. nat. Soc. Stud. Educ.*, 1940, 39, Part II. Pp. 179–184.

Hilgard, E. R. *Theories of learning.* (2nd ed.) New York: Appleton-Century-Crofts, 1956.

Hills, J. R. Factor-analyzed abilities and success in college mathematics. *Educ. psychol. Measmt*, 1957, **17**, 615–622.

Hinton, R. T., Jr. The role of the basal metabolic rate in the intelligence of ninety grade-school children. *J. educ. Psychol.*, 1936, **27**, 546–550.

Hinton, R. T., Jr. A further study of the role of the basal metabolic rate in the intelligence of children. *J. educ. Psychol.*, 1939, **30**, 309–314.

Hirsch, N. D. M. An experimental study of East Kentucky mountaineers. *Genet. Psychol. Monogr.*, 1928, **3**, 183–244.

Hobson, J. R. Sex differences in primary mental abilities. *J. educ. Psychol.*, 1947, **41**, 126–132.

Hochberg, J. E. Effects of the gestalt revolution: the Cornell symposium on perception. *Psychol. Rev.*, 1957, **54**, 73–84.

Hoepfner, R., Guilford, J. P., & Merrifield, P. R. A factor analysis of the symbolic-evaluation abilities. *Rep. psychol. Lab. Univer. Southern Calif.*, 1964, No. 33.

Hollingworth, L. S. Differential action upon the sexes of forces which tend to segregate the feebleminded. *J. abnorm. Psychol.*, 1922, **17**, 35–37.

Hollingworth, L. S. *Special talents and defects: their significance for education.* New York: Macmillan, 1923.

Hollingworth, L. S. The significance of deviates. In *Yearb. nat. Soc. Stud. Educ.*, 1940, 39, Part I. Pp. 43–66.

Holmes, J. A. Factors underlying major reading disabilities at the college level. *Genet. Psychol. Monogr.*, 1954, **49**, 3–95.

Holt, R. R. Imagery: the return of the ostracized. *Amer. Psychologist*, 1964, **19**, 254–264.

Houston, J. P., & Mednick, S. A. Creativity and the need for novelty. *J. abnorm. soc. Psychol.,* 1963, **66,** 137–144.

Hovland, C. I. Computer simulation in thinking. *Amer. Psychologist,* 1960, **15,** 687–693.

Howson, J. D. Intellectual impairment associated with brain-injured patients as revealed in the Shaw test of abstract thought. *Canad. J. Psychol.,* 1948, **2,** 125–133.

Hudson, W., & Politzer, W. M. The relationship between general ability level and serum protein-bound iodine value in a sample of tribesmen from Portuguese East Africa. *J. nat. Inst. Personnel Res.,* 1959, **7,** 203.

Hughes, K. R., Cooper, R. M., & Zubek, J. P. Effect of glutamic acid on the learning ability of bright and dull rats: III. Effect of varying doses. *Canad. J. Psychol.,* 1957, **11,** 253–255.

Hughes, K. R., & Zubek, J. P. Effect of glutamic acid on the learning ability of bright and dull rats: I. Administration during infancy. *Canad. J. Psychol.,* 1956, **10,** 132–138.

Hughes, K. R., & Zubek, J. P. Effect of glutamic acid on the learning ability of bright and dull rats: II. Duration of the effect. *Canad. J. Psychol.,* 1957, **11,** 182–184.

Hulicka, I. M., & Weiss, R. E. Age differences in retention as a function of learning. *J. consult. Psychol.,* 1965, **29,** 125–129.

Hulin, W. S., & Katz, D. The Frois-Wittman pictures of facial expression. *J. exp. Psychol.,* 1935, **18,** 482–498.

Hull, C. L. Quantitative aspects of the evolution of concepts. *Psychol. Monogr.,* 1920, **28,** No. 1 (Whole No. 123).

Hull, C. L. The conflicting psychologies of learning—a way out. *Psychol. Rev.,* 1935, **42,** 491–516.

Humphrey, G., & Coxon, R. V. *The chemistry of thinking.* Springfield, Ill.: Charles C Thomas, 1963.

Humphreys, L. G. The organization of human abilities. *Amer. Psychologist,* 1962, **17,** 475–483.

Hunt, E. B. *Concept learning: an information-processing problem.* New York: Wiley, 1962.

Hunt, E. B. Simulation and analytical models of memory. *J. verb. Learn. verb. Behav.,* 1963, **2,** 49–59.

Hunt, J. McV. *Intelligence and experience.* New York: Ronald, 1961.

Hunt, J. McV. Intrinsic motivation and its role in psychological development. In D. Levine (Ed.), *Nebraska symposium on motivation, 1965.* Lincoln, Nebr.: Univer. of Nebraska Press, 1965. Pp. 189–282.

Hurst, J. G. A factor analysis of the Merrill-Palmer with reference to theory and test construction. *Educ. psychol. Measmt,* 1960, **20,** 519–532.

Husband, R. W. Intercorrelations among learning abilities: I. *J. genet. Psychol.,* 1939, **55,** 353–364.

Husband, R. W. Intercorrelations among learning abilities: III. The effect of length of tests. *J. genet. Psychol.,* 1941, **58,** 427–430. (a)

Husband, R. W. Intercorrelations among learning abilities: IV. Effects of age and spread of intelligence upon relationships. *J. genet. Psychol.,* 1941, **58,** 431–434. (b)

Husén, T. The influence of schooling upon IQ. *Theoria,* 1951, **17,** 61–88.

Hydén, H. Biochemical changes in glial cells and nerve cells at varying activity. In *Proceedings of the Fourth International Congress on Biochemistry.* London: Pergamon, 1959.

Hyman, R. *Some experiments in creativity.* New York: General Electric Co., 1960.

Hyman, R. On prior information and creativity. *Psychol. Rep.,* 1961, **9,** 151–161.

Hyman, R. Knowledge and creativity. In C. W. Taylor (Ed.), *Widening horizons in creativity.* New York: Wiley, 1964.

Inglis, J. Psychological investigations of cognitive deficit in elderly psychiatric patients. *Psychol. Bull.,* 1958, **55,** 197–214.

Inhelder, B., & Piaget, J. *The growth of logical thinking from childhood to adolescence.* (Tr. by A. Parsons & S. Milgram.) New York: Basic Books, 1958.

Inhelder, B., & Piaget, J. *The early growth of logic in the child.* (Tr. by E. A. Lunzer & D. Papert.) New York: Harper & Row, 1964.

Irwin, O. C. Infant speech. *Scient. Amer.,* September, 1949, **181**, 22–24.

Jacobsen, T. L., & Asher, J. J. Validity of the concept constancy measure of creative problem solving. *J. gen. Psychol.,* 1963, **68**, 9–19.

Jacobson, A. L. Learning in flatworms and annelids. *Psychol. Bull.,* 1963, **60**, 74–94.

Jarvik, M. E., Abramson, H. A., & Hirsch, M. W. Lysergic acid diethylamide (LSD-25): VI. Effect upon recall and recognition of various stimuli. *J. Psychol.,* 1955, **39**, 443–454.

Jarvik, M. E., Abramson, H. A., Hirsch, M. W., & Ewald, A. T. Lysergic acid diethylamide (LSD-25): VIII. Effect on arithmetic test performance. *J. Psychol.,* 1955, **39**, 465–473.

Jarvik, M. E., Feingold, L., Kallman, F. J., & Falek, A. Intellectual changes in aged twins. *J. Geront.,* 1962, **17**, 289–294.

Jasper, H. H. Implications for the neurological studies. In D. E. Sheer (Ed.), *Electrical stimulation of the brain.* Austin, Tex.: Univer. of Texas Press, 1961. Pp. 557–562.

Jenkins, H. M., & Ward, W. C. Judgment of contingency between responses and outcomes. *Psychol. Monogr.,* 1965, **79**, No. 1 (Whole No. 594).

Jenkins, J. J., & Palermo, D. S. A note on scoring word association tests. *J. verb. Learn. verb. Behav.,* 1964, **3**, 158–160.

Jensen, A. R., & Rohwer, W. D., Jr. What is learned in serial learning? *J. verb. Learn. verb. Behav.,* 1965, **4**, 62–72.

Jerome, E. A. Decay of heuristic processes in the aged. In C. Tibbits and W. Donahue (Eds.), *Aging around the world.* New York: Columbia, 1962. Pp. 808–823.

Johnson, D. M. *The psychology of thought and judgment.* New York: Harper & Row, 1955.

Johnson, D. M. Problem-solving processes. *Amer. Psychologist,* 1962, **17**, 327. (Abstract)

Johnson, D. M., Johnson, R. C., & Mark, A. L. A mathematical analysis of verbal fluency. *J. gen. Psychol.,* 1951, **44**, 121–128.

Johnson, E. S. An information-processing model of one kind of problem solving. *Psychol. Monogr.,* 1964, **78**, No. 4 (Whole No. 581).

Johnson, G. B., Jr. Bilingualism as measured by a reaction-time technique and the relationship between a language and a non-language intelligence quotient. *J. genet. Psychol.,* 1953, **82**, 3–9.

Johnson, H. M. Definition and uses of the concept "isomorphism." *Percept. mot. Skills,* 1959, **9**, 12–14.

Jones, A., Manis, M., & Weiner, B. Learning as a function of subliminal reinforcements. *Psychol. Rep.,* 1963, **12**, 387–398.

Jones, C. A. Some relationships between creative writing and creative drawing of sixth grade children. Unpublished doctoral dissertation, Pennsylvania State Univer., 1960.

Jones, F. N. A factor analysis of visibility data. *Amer. J. Psychol.,* 1948, **61**, 361–369.

Jones, F. N. A second factor analysis of visibility data. *Amer. J. Psychol.,* 1950, **63**, 206–213.

Jones, H. E. (Comment.) In *Yearb. nat. Soc. Stud. Educ.,* 1940, 39, Part I. Pp. 454–456.

Jones, H. E. The environment and mental development. In L. Carmichael (Ed.), *Manual of child psychology.* New York: Wiley, 1954. Pp. 631–696.

Jones, H. E. Intelligence and problem-solving. In J. E. Birren (Ed.), *Handbook of aging and the individual: psychological and biological aspects.* Chicago: Univer. of Chicago Press, 1959. Pp. 700–738.

Jones, H. E., Conrad, H. S., & Blanchard, M. B. Environmental handicap in mental test performance. *Univer. California Publ. Psychol.,* 1932, No. 3, 63–99.

Jones, H. E., Conrad, H. S., & Horn, A. Psychological studies of motion pictures: Il. Observation and recall as a function of age. *Univer. Calif. Publ. Psychol.,* 1928, **3**, 225–243.

Jones, H. E., & Jorgensen, A. P. Mental growth as related to nursery-school attendance. In *Yearb. nat. Soc. Stud. Educ.,* 1940, 39, Part II. Pp. 207–222.

Jones, L. V. A factor analysis of the Stanford-Binet at four age levels. *Psychometrika,* 1949, **14**, 299–331.

Jones, L. V., & Wepman, J. M. Dimensions of language performance in aphasia. *J. Speech Hear. Res.,* 1961, 4, 220–232.

Jones, M. B. Practice as a process of simplification. *Psychol. Rev.,* 1962, **69**, 274–294.

Jones, W. R., & Stewart, W. A. C. Bilingualism and verbal intelligence. *Brit. J. Psychol., stat. Sec.,* 1951, **4,** 3–8.

Judson, A. J., Cofer, C. N., & Gelfand, S. Reasoning as an associative process: II. "Direction" in problem solving as a function of prior reinforcement of relevant responses. *Psychol. Rep.,* 1956, **2,** 501–507.

Jukes, T. H. The genetic code. *Amer. Scientist,* 1963, **51,** 227–245.

Kamin, L. J. Differential changes in mental abilities in old age. *J. Geront.,* 1957, **12,** 66–70.

Karlin, J. E. Music ability. *Psychometrika,* 1941, **6,** 61–65.

Karlin, J. E. A factorial study of auditory function. *Psychometrika,* 1942, **7,** 251–279.

Karp, S. A. Field dependence and overcoming embeddedness. *J. consult. Psychol.,* 1963, **27,** 294–302.

Katona, G. *Organizing and memorizing.* New York: Columbia, 1940.

Kay, H. The effects of position in a display upon problem solving. *Quart. J. exp. Psychol.,* 1954, **5,** 155–169.

Kelley, H. P. Memory abilities: a factor analysis. *Psychometr. Monogr.,* 1964, No. 11.

Kelley, T. L. *Crossroads in the mind of man: a study of differentiable mental abilities.* Stanford, Calif.: Stanford, 1928.

Kephart, N. C. Influencing the rate of mental growth in retarded children through environmental stimulation. In *Yearb. nat. Soc. Stud. Educ.,* 1940, 39, Part II. Pp. 223–230.

Kettner, N. W., Guilford, J. P., & Christensen, P. R. A factor-analytical study of the factor called general reasoning. *Educ. psychol. Measmt,* 1956, **16,** 438–453.

Kettner, N. W., Guilford, J. P., & Christensen, P. R. A factor-analytic study across the domains of reasoning, creativity, and evaluation. *Psychol. Monogr.,* 1959, **73,** No. 9 (Whole No. 479). (a)

Kettner, N. W., Guilford, J. P., & Christensen, P. R. The relation of certain thinking factors to training criteria in the U.S. Coast Guard Academy. *Educ. psychol. Measmt,* 1959, **19,** 381–394. (b)

Kimble, D. P., & Pribram, K. H. Hippocampectomy and behavior sequences. *Science,* 1963, **139,** 824–825.

Kincaid, C. E. The determination and description of various creative attributes of children. *Stud. Art Educ.,* 1961, **2,** 45–53.

Kintsch, W. All-or-none learning and the role of repetition in paired-associate learning. *Science,* 1963, **140,** 310–312.

Kittell, J. E. Bilingualism and language–non-language intelligence. *J. educ. Res.,* 1959, **52,** 263–268.

Klausmeier, H. J., & Wiersma, W. Relationship of sex, grade level, and locale to performance of high IQ students on divergent thinking tests. *J. educ. Psychol.,* 1964, **55,** 114–119.

Klein, G. S., Gardner, R. W., & Schlesinger, H. J. Tolerance for unrealistic experience: a study of the generality of a cognitive control. *Brit. J. Psychol.,* 1962, **53,** 41–55.

Klineberg, O. A study of psychological differences between "racial" and national groups in Europe. *Arch. Psychol., N.Y.,* 1931, No. 132.

Klüver, H. Functional differences between the occipital and temporal lobes. In L. A. Jeffers (Ed.), *Cerebral mechanisms in behavior: the Hixon symposium.* New York: Wiley, 1951.

Knapp, R. H., & Goodrich, H. B. *Origins of American scientists.* Chicago: Univer. of Chicago Press, 1952.

Knehr, C. A., & Sobol, A. Mental ability of prematurely born children at early school age. *J. Psychol.,* 1949, **27,** 355–361.

Kogan, N., & Wallach, M. A. *Risk taking: a study in cognition and personality.* New York: Holt, 1964.

Köhler, W. *The mentality of apes.* (Tr. by E. Winter.) New York: Harcourt, Brace & World, 1925.

Köhler, W. On the nature of association. *Proc. Amer. phil. Soc.,* 1941, **84,** 489–502.

Kohnstamm, G. A. An evaluation of part of Piaget's theory. *Acta Psychol.,* 1963, **21,** 313–356.

Konorski, J. The physiological approach to the problem of recent memory. In J. F. Dela-fresnaye (Ed.), *Brain mechanisms and learning.* Springfield, Ill.: Charles C Thomas, 1961. Pp. 115–130.

Korchin, S. J., & Basowitz, H. The judgment of ambiguous stimuli as an index of cognitive functioning in aging. *J. Pers.,* 1956, **25**, 81–95.

Korzbyski, A. What I believe. In *Manhood and humanity.* (2nd ed.) Lakeville, Conn.: International Non-Aristotelian Library Publishing Co., 1950.

Kostik, M. M. A study of transfer: sex differences in the reasoning process. *J. educ. Psychol.,* 1954, **45**, 449–458.

Kreezer, G. The relation of intelligence level and the electroencephalogram. In *Yearb. nat. Soc. Stud. Educ.,* 1940, 39, Part I. Pp. 130–133.

Kreezer, G., & Dallenbach, K. M. Learning the relation of opposition. *Amer. J. Psychol.,* 1929, **41**, 432–441.

Kristofferson, A. B. Word recognition, meaningfulness, and familiarity. *Percept. mot. Skills,* 1957, **7**, 219–220.

Krumboltz, J. D., & Christal, R. E. The short-term practice effects in tests of spatial aptitude. *Personnel Guid. J.,* 1960, **38**, 385–391.

Kuhlmann, F. A revision of the Binet-Simon system for measuring the intelligence of children. *J. Psycho-asthenics, Monogr. Suppl.,* 1912, **1**, 1–41.

Kuhlmann, F. *Tests of mental development.* Minneapolis, Minn.: Educational Testing Bureau, 1939.

Lamson, E. E. To what extent are intelligence quotients increased by children who participate in a rich vital school curriculum? *J. educ. Psychol.,* 1938, **29**, 67–70.

Landauer, T. K. Two hypotheses concerning the biochemical basis of memory. *Psychol. Rev.,* 1964, **71**, 167–179.

Lashley, K. S. *Brain mechanisms and intelligence.* Chicago: Univer. of Chicago Press, 1929.

Lashley, K. S. Coalescence of neurology and psychology. *Proc. Amer. phil. Soc.,* 1941, **84**, 461–470.

Lashley, K. S. The mechanism of vision: XVIII. Effects of destroying the visual "associative areas" of the monkey. *Genet. Psychol. Monogr.,* 1948, **37**, 107–166.

Lashley, K. S. The problem of serial order in behavior. In L. A. Jeffers (Ed.), *Cerebral mechanisms in behavior: the Hixon symposium.* New York: Wiley, 1951.

Lauritzen, E. S. Semantic divergent thinking factors among elementary school children. Unpublished doctoral dissertation, Univer. of California at Los Angeles, 1963.

Lawrence, D. H., & De Rivera, J. Evidence for relational discrimination. *J. comp. physiol. Psychol.,* 1954, **47**, 465–471.

Lazarus, R. S., & McCleary, R. A. Autonomic discrimination without awareness: a study in subception. *Psychol. Rev.,* 1951, **58**, 113–122.

Leahy, A. M. Nature-nurture and intelligence. *Genet. Psychol. Monogr.,* 1935, **17**, 236–308.

Leavitt, E. E. The water-jars Einstellung test as a measure of rigidity. *Psychol. Bull.,* 1956, **53**, 347–370.

Lehman, H. C. Young thinkers and great achievements. *J. genet. Psychol.,* 1949, **74**, 245–271.

Lehman, H. C. *Age and achievement.* Princeton, N.J.: Princeton, 1953.

Lehman, H. C. The age decrement in outstanding scientific creativity. *Amer. Psychologist,* 1960, **15**, 128–134.

Lehman, H. C., & Heidler, J. B. Chronological age vs. quality of literary output. *Amer. J. Psychol.,* 1949, **62**, 75–89.

Lehman, H. C., & Witty, P. A. Scientific eminence and church membership. *Sci. Monthly,* 1931, **34**, 544–549.

Levine, E., Abramson, H. A., Kaufman, M. R., & Markham, S. Lysergic acid diethylamide (LSD-25): XVI. The effect on intellectual functioning as measured by the Wechsler-Bellevue scale. *J. Psychol.,* 1955, **40**, 385–395.

Levine, S. Stimulation in infancy. *Scient. Amer.,* May, 1960, **202**, 80–86.

Licht, M. The measurement of one aspect of personality. *J. Psychol.,* 1947, **24**, 83–87.

Lindsley, D. B. The ontogenetic development of brain potentials in human subjects. In *Yearb. nat. Soc. Stud. Educ.,* 1940, 39, Part I. Pp. 127–130.

Lorge, I. The influence of the test upon the nature of mental decline as a function of age. *J. educ. Psychol.,* 1936, **27**, 100–110.

Luchins, A. S. Mechanization in problem-solving behavior. *Psychol. Monogr.,* 1942, **54**, No. 6 (Whole No. 248).

Luchins, A. S., & Luchins, E. H. *Rigidity of behavior: a variational approach to the effect of Einstellung.* Eugene, Ore.: Univer. Oregon, 1959.

Luria, A. R. The development of mental functions in twins. *Char. & Pers.,* 1936, **5**, 35–47.

Luttges, M., Johnson, T., Buck, C., Holland, J., & McGaugh, J. An examination of the "transfer of learning" by nucleic acid. *Science,* 1966, **151**, 834–837.

McCarthy, D. Language development in children. In L. Carmichael (Ed.), *Manual of child psychology.* (2nd ed.) New York: Wiley, 1954. Pp. 492–630.

McCartin, Sister Rose Amata, & Meyers, C. E. An exploration of six semantic factors at first grade. *Multiv. Behav. Res.,* 1966, **1**, 74–94.

McCleary, R. A., & Lazarus, R. S. Autonomic discrimination without awareness: an interim report. *J. Pers.,* 1949, **18**, 171–179.

McCloy, C. H., & Young, N. D. *Tests and measurements in health and physical education.* (3rd ed.) New York: Appleton-Century-Crofts, 1954.

McFee, J. K. Creative problem-solving abilities of academically superior adolescents: a preliminary report. Tempe, Ariz.: Arizona State Univer., 1964.

McGeoch, J. A., & Irion, A. L. *The psychology of human learning.* New York: McKay, 1952.

McKellar, P. *Imagination and thinking.* New York: Basic Books, 1957.

MacKinnon, D. W. The highly effective individual. *Teach. Coll. Rec.,* 1960, **61**, 367–378.

MacKinnon, D. W. Fostering creativity in students of engineering. *J. Engng Educ.,* 1961, **52**, 129–142.

McNemar, Q. *The revision of the Stanford-Binet Scale.* Boston: Houghton Mifflin, 1942.

McPherson, J. H. Environment and training for creativity. In C. W. Taylor (Ed.), *Creativity: progress and potential.* New York: McGraw-Hill, 1964. Pp. 130–153.

Magoun, H. W. *The waking brain.* Springfield, Ill.: Charles C Thomas, 1958.

Maier, N. R. F. Reasoning in humans. Part I. On direction. *J. comp. physiol. Psychol.,* 1930, **10**, 115–143.

Maier, N. R. F. Reasoning in humans: the solution of a problem and its appearance in consciousness. *J. comp. physiol. Psychol.,* 1931, **11**, 181–194.

Maier, N. R. F. The behavior mechanisms concerned with problem solving. *Psychol. Rev.,* 1940, **47**, 43–58.

Maltzman, I. On the training of originality. *Psychol. Rev.,* 1960, **67**, 229–242.

Maltzman, I., Belloni, M., & Fishbein, M. Experimental studies of associative variables in originality. *Psychol. Monogr.,* 1964, **78**, No. 3 (Whole No. 580).

Maltzman, I., Bogartz, W., & Berger, L. A procedure for increasing word association originality and its transfer-effects. *J. exp. Psychol.,* 1958, **56**, 392–398.

Maltzman, I., Brooks, L. O., Bogartz, W., & Summers, S. S. The facilitation of problem-solving by prior exposure to uncommon responses. *J. exp. Psychol.,* 1958, **56**, 399–406.

Maltzman, I., Simon, S., Raskin, D., & Licht, L. Experimental studies in the training of originality. *Psychol. Monogr.,* 1960, **74**, No. 6 (Whole No. 493).

Mandler, G. From association to structure. *Psychol. Rev.,* 1962, **69**, 415–427.

Markey, J. F. *The symbolic process.* New York: Harcourt, Brace & World, 1928.

Marks, A., Guilford, J. P., & Merrifield, P. R. A study of military leadership in relation to selected intellectual factors. *Rep. psychol. Lab. Univ. Southern Calif.,* 1959, No. 21.

Marshall, G. R., & Cofer, C. N. Associative indices as measures of word relatedness: a summary and comparison of ten methods. *J. verb. Learn. verb. Behav.,* 1963, **1**, 408–421.

Massarik, F., & Weschler, I. R. Empathy revisited: the process of understanding people. *Calif. Mgmt Rev.,* 1959, **1,** 36–46.

Matin, L., & Adkins, D. C. A second-order factor analysis of reasoning abilities. *Psychometrika,* 1954, **19,** 71–78.

Matthews, C. G., Guertin, W. H., & Reitan, R. M. Wechsler-Bellevue subtest rank orders in divers diagnostic groups. *Psychol. Rep.,* 1962, **11,** 3–9.

Matthews, C. G., & Reitan, R. M. Correlates of Wechsler-Bellevue rank orders of subtest means in lateralized and non-lateralized brain-damaged groups. *Percept. mot. Skills,* 1964, **19,** 391–399.

Meadow, A., & Parnes, S. J. Evaluation of training in creative problem-solving. *J. appl. Psychol.,* 1959, **43,** 189–194.

Meadow, A., Parnes, S. J., & Reese, H. Influence of brainstorming instructions and problem sequence on a creative-problem-solving test. *J. appl. Psychol.,* 1959, **43,** 413–416.

Mednick, S. A. The associative basis of the creative process. *Psychol. Rev.,* 1962, **69,** 220–232.

Mednick, S. A., & Mednick, T. An associative interpretation of the creative process. In C. W. Taylor (Ed.), *Widening horizons in creativity.* New York: Wiley, 1964.

Meeker, M. A procedure for relating Stanford-Binet behavior samplings to Guilford's structure of intellect. *J. Sch. Psychol.,* 1965, **3,** 26–36.

Meier, B. W., Bunch, M. E., Nolan, C. Y., & Scheidler, C. H. Anoxia, behavioral development, and learning ability: a comparative-experimental approach. *Psychol. Monogr.,* 1960, **74,** No. 1 (Whole No. 488).

Meier, N. C. Factors in artistic aptitude: a final summary of a ten-year study of special ability. *Psychol. Monogr.,* 1939, **51,** No. 231.

Melametsä, L. The influence of training on the level of test performance and the factor structure of intelligence tests. *Scand. J. Psychol.,* 1965, **6,** 19–25.

Melton, A. W. Implications of short-term memory for a general theory of memory. *J. verb. Learn. verb. Behav.,* 1963, **2,** 1–21.

Melzack, R., & Thompson, W. R. Effects of early experience on social behavior. *Canad. J. Psychol.,* 1956, **10,** 82–90.

Merrifield, P. R., Gardner, S. F., & Cox, A. B. Aptitudes and personality measures related to creativity in seventh-grade children. *Rep. psychol. Lab. Univer. Southern Calif.,* 1964, No. 28.

Merrifield, P. R., Guilford, J. P., Christensen, P. R., & Frick, J. W. Interrelationships between certain abilities and certain traits of motivation and temperament. *J. gen. Psychol.,* 1961, **65,** 57–74.

Merrifield, P. R., Guilford, J. P., Christensen, P. R., & Frick, J. W. The role of intellectual factors in problem solving. *Psychol. Monogr.,* 1962, **76,** No. 10 (Whole No. 529).

Merrifield, P. R., Guilford, J. P., & Gershon, A. The differentiation of divergent-production abilities at the sixth-grade level. *Rep. psychol. Lab. Univer. Southern Calif.,* 1963, No. 27.

Meyer, E. Comprehension of spatial relations in preschool children. *J. genet. Psychol.,* 1940, **57,** 119–151.

Meyer, G. Temporal organization and the initial reproductive tendency. *J. Psychol.,* 1939, **7,** 269–282.

Meyer, W. J. The stability of patterns of primary mental abilities among junior high and senior high school students. *Educ. psychol. Measmt,* 1960, **20,** 795–800.

Meyers, C. E., Dingman, H. F., Orpet, R. E., Sitkei, E. G., & Watts, C. A. Four ability-factor hypotheses at three preliterate levels in normal and retarded children. *Monogr. Soc. Res. Child Develpm.,* 1964, **29,** No. 5.

Meyers, C. E., Orpet, R. E., Atwell, A. A., & Dingman, H. F. Primary abilities at mental age six. *Monogr. Soc. Res. Child Develpm.,* 1962, **27,** Whole No. 82.

Michael, W. B. Factor analysis of tests and criteria: a comparative study of two AAF pilot populations. *Psychol. Monogr.,* 1949, **63,** No. 3 (Whole No. 298).

Michael, W. B., Guilford, J. P., Fruchter, B., & Zimmerman, W. S. The description of spatial-visualization abilities. *Educ. psychol. Measmt,* 1957, **17,** 185–199.

Michael, W. B., Zimmerman, W. S., & Guilford, J. P. An investigation of the nature of the spatial relations and visualization factors in two high school samples. *Educ. psychol. Measmt,* 1951, **11,** 561–577.

Miles, C. C., & Miles, W. R. The correlation of intelligence scores and chronological age from early to late maturity. *Amer. J. Psychol.,* 1932, **44,** 44–78.

Miller, G. A. Speech and language. In S. S. Stevens (Ed.), *Handbook of experimental psychology.* New York: Wiley, 1951. Pp. 789–810.

Miller, G. A. What is information measurement? *Amer. Psychologist,* 1953, **8,** 3–11.

Miller, G. A. The magical number seven, plus or minus two: some limits to our capacity for processing information. *Psychol. Rev.,* 1956, **63,** 81–97.

Miller, G. A., Galanter, E., & Pribram, K. H. *Plans and the structure of behavior.* New York: Holt, 1960.

Miller, G. A., & Selfridge, J. A. Verbal context and the recall of meaningful material. *Amer. J. Psychol.,* 1950, **63,** 176–185.

Miller, J. G. Toward a general theory for the behavioral sciences. *Amer. Psychologist,* 1955, **10,** 513–531.

Miller, W. H., Ratliff, F., & Hartline, H. K. How cells receive stimuli. *Scient. Amer.,* September, 1961, **205,** 222–228.

Milner, B. Intellectual functions of temporal lobes. *Psychol. Bull.,* 1954, **51,** 42–62.

Milton, G. A. Sex differences in problem solving as a function of role appropriateness of the problem content. *Psychol. Rep.,* 1959, **5,** 705–708.

Mitchell, J. C., Jr. A comparison of the factorial structure of cognitive functions for a high and low status group. *J. educ. Psychol.,* 1956, **47,** 397–414.

Mooney, C. M. A factorial study of closure. *Canad. J. Psychol.,* 1954, **8,** 51–60.

Moran, L. J. Vocabulary knowledge and usage among normal and schizophrenic subjects. *Psychol. Monogr.,* 1953, **67,** No. 20 (Whole No. 370).

Moray, N. Broadbent's filter theory: postulate H and the problem of switching time. *Quart. J. exp. Psychol.,* 1960, **12,** 214–220.

Moss, H. A., & Kagan, J. Maternal influences on early IQ scores. *Psychol. Rep.,* 1958, **4,** 655–661.

Moursey, E. M. The hierarchical organization of cognitive levels. *Brit. J. Psychol., stat. Sec.,* 1952, **5,** 151–170.

Muenzinger, K. F., Koerner, L., & Ivey, E. Variability of a habitual movement in guinea pigs. *J. comp. Psychol.,* 1929, **9,** 425–436.

Müller, G. E., & Pilzecker, A. Experimentelle Beiträge zur Lehre vom Gedächtniss. *Z. Psychol.,* 1900, Ergbd No. 1.

Mundy-Castle, A. C. Electrophysiological correlates of intelligence. *J. Pers.,* 1958, **26,** 184–199.

Mundy-Castle, A. C., & Nelson, G. K. Intelligence, personality and brain rhythms in a socially isolated community. *Nature,* 1960, **185,** 484–485.

Münsterberg, H. Zur individualpsychologie. *Zbl. Nervenheilk. Psychiat.,* 1891, **14,** 196–198.

Murphy, G., & Hochberg, J. Perceptual development: some tentative hypotheses. *Psychol.* C Thomas, 1962.

Myers, R. E., & Torrance, E. P. *Invitations to thinking and doing.* Boston: Ginn, 1964.

Nash, H. *Alcohol and caffeine: a study of their psychological effects.* Springfield, Ill.: Charles C Thomas, 1962.

Nauta, W. J. H. Some brain structures and functions related to memory. *Neurosci. Res. Program Bull.,* 1964, **2,** 1–35.

Newell, A., Shaw, J. C., & Simon, H. A. Elements of a theory of problem solving. *Psychol. Rev.,* 1958, **65,** 151–166. (a)

Newell, A., Shaw, J. C., & Simon, H. A. *The processes of creative thinking.* Santa Monica, Calif.: RAND Corp., 1958. (b)

Nicholson, P. J. An experimental investigation of the effects of training upon creativity. Unpublished doctoral dissertation, Univer. of Houston, 1959.

Nihira, K., Guilford, J. P., Hoepfner, R., & Merrifield, P. R. A factor analysis of the semantic-evaluation abilities. *Rep. psychol. Lab. Univer. Southern Calif.,* 1964, No. 32.

Noble, C. E. An analysis of meaning. *Psychol. Rev.,* 1952, **59,** 421–430.

Noble, C. E. The meaning-familiarity relationship. *Psychol. Rev.,* 1953, **60,** 89–98.

Noble, C. E. Psychology and the logic of similarity. *J. gen. Psychol.,* 1957, **57,** 23–41.

Noble, C. E. Verbal learning and individual differences. In C. N. Cofer (Ed.), *Verbal learning and verbal behavior.* New York: McGraw-Hill, 1961. Pp. 132–146.

Nyssen, R., & Crahay, S. Étude des capacités de définition et d'évocation des mots en fonction de l'âge. *Acta Psychol.,* 1960, **17,** 1–22.

Oehrn, A. Experimentelle studien zur individualpsychologie. *Psychol. Arbeiten,* 1895, **1,** 95–152.

Ogden, C. K., & Richards, I. A. *The meaning of meaning.* New York: Harcourt, Brace & World, 1930.

Olds, J., & Milner, P. Positive reinforcement produced by electrical stimulation of septal area and other regions of rat brain. *J. comp. physiol. Psychol.,* 1954, **47,** 419–427.

Oléron, P. *Les composantes de l'intelligence.* Paris: Presses Universitaires de France, 1957.

Oliver, J. A., & Ferguson, G. A. A factorial study of a test of rigidity. *Canad. J. Psychol.,* 1951, **5,** 49–59.

O'Neil, W. M. The stability of the main pattern of abilities with changing age. *Austr. J. Psychol.,* 1962, **14,** 1–8.

Orbach, J. "Functions" of striate cortex and the problem of mass action. *Psychol. Bull,* 1959, **56,** 271–292.

Ornstein, L. Computer learning and the scientific method: a proposed solution to the information theoretical problem of meaning. *J. Mt. Sinai Hospital* (N.Y.), 1965, **32,** 437–494.

Orpet, R. E., & Meyers, C. E. A study of eight structure-of-intellect hypotheses in six-year-old children. Report, NIMH Grant No. MH08666-01, Univer. Southern California, 1965.

Osborn, A. F. *Applied imagination.* (Rev. ed.) New York: Scribner, 1963.

Osgood, C. E. A behavioristic analysis of perception and language as cognitive phenomena. In *Contemporary approaches to cognition.* Cambridge, Mass.: Harvard, 1957. Pp. 75–121.

Osgood, C. E., Suci, G. J., & Tannenbaum, P. H. *The measurement of meaning.* Urbana, Ill.: Univer. of Illinois Press, 1957.

O'Sullivan, M., Guilford, J. P., & de Mille, R. Measurement of social intelligence. *Rep. psychol. Lab. Univer. Southern Calif.,* 1965, No. 34.

Owens, C. An investigation of creative potential at the junior high level. *Stud. Art Educ.,* 1962, **3,** 16–33.

Owens, W. A., Jr. Age and mental abilities: a longitudinal study. *Genet. Psychol. Monogr.,* 1953, **48,** 3–54.

Pacaud, S. Experimental research on the aging of psychological functions. In *Old age in the modern world.* Report of the Third Congress of the International Association of Gerontology. Edinburgh: Livingstone, 1955. P. 279.

Page, J. D. The effect of nursery school attendance upon subsequent IQ. *J. Psychol.,* 1940, **10,** 221–230.

Parker, J. F., Jr., & Fleishman, E. A. Use of analytical information concerning task requirements to increase the effectiveness of skill training. *J. appl. Psychol.,* 1961, **45,** 295–302.

Parnes, S. J. Effects of extended effort in creative problem solving. *J. educ. Psychol.,* 1961, **52,** 117–122. (a)

Parnes, S. J. *Student workbook for creative problem-solving courses and institutes.* Buffalo, N.Y.: Univer. of Buffalo, 1961. (b)

Parnes, S. J. Can creativity be increased? In S. J. Parnes & H. F. Harding (Eds.), *A source book for creative thinking.* New York: Scribner, 1962. Pp. 185–192.

Parnes, S. J., & Meadow, A. Effects of brainstorming instructions on creative problem-solving by trained and untrained subjects. *J. educ. Psychol.,* 1959, **50,** 171–176.

Parnes, S. J., & Meadow, A. Evaluation of persistence of effects produced by a creative problem-solving course. *Psychol. Rep.,* 1960, **7,** 357–361.

Patrick, C. Creative thought in poets. *Arch. Psychol., N.Y.,* 1935, **26,** 1–74.

Patrick, C. Creative thought in artists. *J. Psychol.,* 1937, **5,** 35–73.

Patrick, C. Scientific thought. *J. Psychol.,* 1938, 5, 55–83.

Patrick, C. Whole and part relationship in creative thought. *Amer. J. Psychol.,* 1941, **54,** 128–131.

Peak, H. Psychological structure and psychological activity. *Psychol. Rev.,* 1958, **65,** 325–347.

Peal, E., & Lambert, W. E., The relation of bilingualism to intelligence. *Psychol. Monogr.,* 1962, **76,** No. 27 (Whole No. 546).

Pearl, R. Variations and correlation in brain weight. *Biometrics,* 1905, **4,** 13–104.

Penfield, W. The permanent record of the stream of consciousness. *Acta Psychol.,* 1955, **11,** 47–69.

Penfield, W. Some mechanisms of consciousness discovered during the electrical stimulation of the brain. *Proc. nat. Acad. Sci.,* 1958, **44,** 51–66.

Penfield, W., & Roberts, L. *Speech and brain-mechanisms.* Princeton, N.J.: Princeton, 1959.

Penrose, L. S. *The biology of mental defect.* (Rev. ed.) London: Sidgwick & Jackson, 1954.

Petersen, H., Guilford, J. P., Hoepfner, R., & Merrifield, P. R. Determination of "structure-of-intellect" abilities involved in ninth-grade algebra and general mathematics. *Rep. psychol. Lab. Univer. Southern Calif.,* 1963, No. 31.

Peterson, J. *Early conceptions and tests of intelligence.* New York: Harcourt, Brace & World, 1925.

Phillips, L. W., Griswold, R. L., & Pace, N. Cognitive changes at high altitude. *Psychol. Rep.,* 1963, **13,** 423–430.

Piaget, J. *The psychology of intelligence.* New York: Harcourt, Brace & World, 1950.

Piaget, J. *The child's conception of number.* London: Routledge, 1952.

Piaget, J. *Logic and psychology.* (Tr. by W. Mays & T. Whitehead.) Manchester: Manchester Univer. Press, 1953.

Piaget, J. *Origins of intelligence.* New York: International Universities Press, 1964.

Piers, E. V., Daniels, J. M., & Quackenbush, J. F. The identification of creativity in adolescents. *J. educ. Psychol.,* 1950, **51,** 346–351.

Pieter, J. (Intelligence quotient and environment.) *Kwart. Psychol.,* 1939, **11,** 265–322.

Pinneau, S. R. The infantile disorders of hospitalization and anaclitic depression. *Psychol. Bull.,* 1955, **52,** 429–452.

Pintner, R., & Forlano, G. Season of birth and mental differences. *Psychol. Bull.,* 1943, **40,** 25–35.

Pintner, R., & Lev, J. The intelligence of the hard of hearing school child. *J. genet. Psychol.,* 1939, **55,** 31–48.

Poincaré, H. *The foundations of science.* New York: Science Press, 1913.

Porteus, S. D. Porteus Maze Test development. *Percept. mot. Skills,* 1956, **6,** 135–142.

Porteus, S. D. Maze test reactions after chlorpromazine. *J. consult. Psychol.,* 1957, **21,** 15–21.

Porteus, S. D., & Peters, H. N. Maze test validation and psychosurgery. *Genet. psychol. Monogr.,* 1947, **36,** 3–86.

Postman, L. Does interference theory predict too much forgetting? *J. verb. Learn. verb. Behav.,* 1963, **2,** 40–48.

Postman, L., & Riley, D. A. A critique of Köhler's theory of association. *Psychol. Rev.,* 1957, **64,** 61–72.

Pribram, K. H. A review of theory in physiological psychology. *Annu. Rev. Psychol.,* 1960, **11,** 1–40.

Pribram, K. H. Implication for systematic studies of behavior. In D. E. Sheer (Ed.), *Electrical stimulation of the brain.* Austin, Tex.: Univer. of Texas Press, 1961. Pp. 561–574.

Rapaport, D., Gill, M., & Schafer, R. *Diagnostic psychological testing.* Vol. 1. Chicago: Year Book Publishers, 1945.

Razik, T. A. An investigation of creative thinking among college students. Unpublished doctoral dissertation, Ohio State Univer., 1963.

Reed, H. B. C., Jr., & Reitan, R. M. Intelligence test performances of brain damaged subjects with lateralized motor deficits. *J. consult. Psychol.*, 1963, **27**, 102–106.

Reed, S. C. The evolution of human intelligence. *Amer. Scientist*, 1965, **53**, 317–326.

Reichard, S. Mental organization and age level. *Arch. Psychol., N.Y.*, 1944, No. 295.

Reitan, R. M. Validity of the Trail Making Test as an indicator of brain damage. *Percept. mot. Skills*, 1958, **8**, 273–276.

Reitman, W. R. Information-processing models in psychology. *Science*, 1964, **144**, 1192–1198.

Repucci, L. C. Biographical differences between hi and lo creative subjects. Unpublished paper. Midland, Mich.: Dow Chemical Co., 1962.

Restle, F. Significance of all-or-none learning. *Psychol. Bull.*, 1965, **64**, 313–325.

Revesz, G., and Berkeley, G. *Psychology and the art of the blind.* New York: Longmans, 1950.

Reymert, M. L., & Hinton, R. T., Jr. The effect of a change to a relatively superior environment upon the IQs of one hundred children. In *Yearb. nat. Soc. Stud. Educ.*, 1940, **39**, Part II. Pp. 255–268.

Reynierse, J. H., & Brach, A. M. Semantic satiation and generalization. *Psychol. Rep.*, 1963, **13**, 790.

Riegel, K. F. A study of verbal achievements of older persons. *J. Geront.*, 1959, **14**, 453–456.

Riegel, R. M., & Riegel, K. F. A comparison and reinterpretation of factor structures of the W-B, the WAIS, and the HAWIE on aged persons. *J. consult. Psychol.*, 1962, **26**, 31–37.

Riesen, A. H. Arrested vision. *Scient. Amer.*, July, 1950, **183**, 16–19.

Rigg, M. C. The relative variability in intelligence of boys and girls. *J. genet. Psychol.*, 1940, **56**, 211–214.

Rimland, B. *Infantile autism.* New York: Appleton-Century-Crofts, 1964.

Rimoldi, H. J. A. The central intellective factor. *Psychometrika*, 1951, **16**, 75–101.

Ripple, R. E., & May, F. B. Caution in comparing creativity and IQ. *Psychol. Rep.*, 1962, **10**, 229–230.

Rivoire, J. L. Development of reference systems in children. *Percept. mot. Skills*, 1962, **15**, 554.

Rock, I. Repetition and learning. *Scient. Amer.*, August, 1958, **194**, 68–70.

Rock, I., & Ceraso, J. Toward a cognitive theory of associative learning. In C. Scheerer (Ed.), *Cognition: theory, research, promise.* New York: Harper & Row, 1964. Pp. 110–146.

Roe, A. Artists and their work. *J. Pers.*, 1946, **15**, 1–40.

Roe, A. *The making of a scientist.* New York: Dodd, Mead, 1952.

Roff, M. A factorial study of tests in the perceptual area. *Psychometr. Monogr.*, 1952, No. 8.

Rogers, C. A. The structure of verbal fluency. *Brit. J. Psychol.*, 1953, **44**, 368–380.

Rogers, C. A. The orectic relations of mathematically derived fluency scores. *J. gen. Psychol.*, 1956, **55**, 85–102.

Rogers, C. R. Toward a theory of creativity. In S. J. Parnes & H. F. Harding (Eds.), *A source book for creative thinking.* New York: Scribner, 1962. Pp. 64–72.

Rosenblum, S., Keller, J. E., & Paponia, N. Davis-Eells ("culture-fair") test performance of lower-class retarded children. *J. consult. Psychol.*, 1955, **19**, 51–54.

Rossman, J. *The psychology of the inventor.* Washington, D.C.: Inventors Publishing Co., 1931.

Rossman, J. A study of the childhood, education, and age of 710 inventors. *J. Patent Office Soc.*, 1935, **17**, 411–421.

Rosvold, H. E., & Mishkin, M. Evaluation of the effects of prefrontal lobotomy on intelligence. *Canad. J. Psychol.*, 1950, **4**, 122–126.

Rusch, R. R., Denny, D. A., & Ives, S. Fostering creativity in sixth grade. *Element. Sch. J.*, 1965, **65**, 262–268.

Russell, W. R. *Brain, memory, learning.* Fair Lawn, N.J.: Oxford, 1959.

Rust, R. M. Some correlates of the movement response. *J. Pers.*, 1948, **4**, 369–401.

Samuels, I. Reticular mechanisms and behavior. *Psychol. Bull.*, 1959, **56**, 1–25.

Sándor, B. The functioning of memory and the methods of mathematical prodigies. *Charact. & Pers.*, 1932, **1**, 70–74.

Sarason, S. B., & Gladwin, T. Psychological cultural problems in mental subnormality: a review of research. *Genet. Psychol. Monogr.*, 1958, **57**, 3–289.

Saugstad, P., & Raaheim, K. Problem-solving and availability of functions. *Acta Psychol.*, 1957, **13**, 263–278.

Saugstad, P., & Raaheim, K. Problem-solving and availability of functions. *Acta Psychol.*, 1959, **16**, 45–58.

Schaeffer, R. W. Learning without running in a Y-maze. *Psychol. Rec.*, 1964, **14**, 95–99.

Schaie, K. W. Occupational level and the primary mental abilities. *J. educ. Psychol.*, 1958, **49**, 299–303.

Schaie, K. W. Cross-sectional methods in the study of psychological aspects of aging. *J. Geront.*, 1959, **14**, 208–215.

Schaie, K. W., Rosenthal, F., & Perlman, R. M. Differential mental deterioration of factorially "pure" functions in later maturity. *J. Geront.*, 1953, **8**, 191–196.

Scheerer, M., Rothmann, E., & Goldstein, K. A case of "idiot savant"; an experimental study of personality organization. *Psychol. Monogr.*, 1945, **58**, No. 4 (Whole No. 269).

Schoenfeldt, L., Gillmer, R., Kelley, P., & Owens, W. A. Some longitudinal evidence regarding the validity of indices for intellectual deterioration. Paper read at Midwest. Psychol. Ass., 1963.

Schooley, M., & Hartmann, G. W. Role of insight in the learning of logical relations. *Amer. J. Psychol.*, 1937, **49**, 287–292.

Schuell, H., & Jenkins, J. J. The nature of language deficits in aphasia. *Psychol. Rev.*, 1959, **66**, 45–67.

Schuell, H., Jenkins, J. J., & Carroll, J. B. A factor analysis of the Minnesota Test for Differential Diagnosis of Aphasia *J. Speech Hear. Res.*, 1962, **5**, 349–369.

Schwartz, F., & Lippman, F. Cognitive and associative structures in recall. *Psychol. Rep.*, 1962, **11**, 91–101.

Searle, L. V. The organization of hereditary maze-brightness and maze-dullness. *Genet. Psychol. Monogr.*, 1949, **39**, 281–325.

Seashore, R. H., & Eckerson. L. D. The measurement of individual differences in general English vocabularies. *J. educ. Psychol.*, 1940, **31**, 14–38.

Seguin, E. *Idiocy: its treatment by the physiological method.* New York: Teachers Coll., 1907.

Sells, S. B. The atmosphere effect: an experimental study of reasoning. *Arch. Psychol., N.Y.*, 1936, No. 200.

Selz, O. *Die Gesetze der produktiven und reproduktiven Geistestätigkeit.* Bonn: Cohen, 1924.

Selz, O. Die Umgestaltung der Grundanschauungen vom intellektuellen Geschehen. *Kantstudien*, 1927, **32**, 273–280.

Semmes, J. Agnosias in animals and man. *Psychol. Rev.*, 1953, **60**, 140–147.

Semmes, J., Weinstein, S., Ghent, L., & Teuber, H. L. Spatial orientation in man after cerebral injury: I. Analysis by locus of lesion. *J. Psychol.*, 1955, **39**, 227–244.

Sharp, S. E. Individual psychology: a study in psychological method. *Amer. J. Psychol.*, 1898–99, **10**, 329–391.

Shaw, D. C. A study of the relationships between Thurstone primary mental abilities and high school achievement. *J. educ. Psychol.*, 1949, **40**, 239–249.

Shepard, R. N., Hovland, C. I., & Jenkins, H. M. Learning and memorization of classifications. *Psychol. Monogr.*, 1961, **75**, No. 13 (Whole No. 517).

Sherman, M. *Intelligence and its derivation.* New York: Ronald, 1945.

Sherman, M., & Key, C. B. The intelligence of isolated mountain children. *Child Developm.*, 1932, **3**, 279–290.

Shimberg, M. E. An investigation into the validity of norms with special reference to urban and rural groups. *Arch. Psychol., N.Y.*, 1929, No. 104.

Shipley, W. C. A self-administering scale for measuring intellectual impairment and deterioration. *J. Psychol.*, 1940, **9**, 371–377.

Shock, N. W. Some psychophysiological relations. *Psychol. Bull.*, 1939, **36**, 447–476.

Shure, G. H., & Halstead, W. C. Cerebral localization of intellectul processes. *Psychol.
Monogr.*, 1958, **72**, No. 12 (Whole No. 465).

Silverstein, A. B., & Mohan, P. J. A factor-analytic approach to object-sorting behavior. *J.
consult. Psychol.*, 1965, **29**, 89.

Simberg, A. L., & Shannon, T. E. The effect of AC creativity training on the AC suggestion
program. AC Personnel Res. Rep. No. 27. Flint, Mich.: AC Spark Plug, 1959.

Simon, H. A., & Feigenbaum, E. A. An information-processing theory of some effects of similarity, familiarization and meaningfulness in verbal learning. *J. verb. Learn. verb. Behav.*,
1964, **3**, 385–396.

Simon, H. A., & Kotovsky, K. Human acquisition of concepts for sequential patterns. *Psychol. Rev.*, 1963, **70**, 534–546.

Simon, H. A., & Newell, A. Computer simulation of human thinking and problem solving. In
W. Kessen and C. Kuhlman (Eds.), Thought in the young child. *Monogr. Soc. Res. Child
Develpm.*, 1962, **27**, Whole No. 83, 137–155.

Simpson, G. G. Organisms and molecules in evolution. *Science,* 1964, **146**, 1535–1538.

Sims, V. M. *Sims SCI Occupational Rating Scale: manual of directions.* New York: Harcourt, Brace & World, 1952.

Skeels, H. M. Some Iowa studies of the mental growth of children in relation to differentials
of the environment: a summary. In *Yearb. nat. Soc. Stud. Educ.,* 1940, 39, Part II. Pp.
281–308.

Skeels, H. M. Effects of adoption of children from institutions. *Children,* 1965, **12**, 33–34.

Skeels, H. M., & Harms, I. Children with inferior social histories: their mental development
in adoptive homes. *J. genet. Psychol.*, 1948, **72**, 283–294.

Skodak, M., & Skeels, H. M. A follow-up study of children in adoptive homes. *J. genet.
Psychol.*, 1945, **66**, 21–58.

Skodak, M., & Skeels, H. M. A final follow-up study of one hundred adopted children. *J.
genet. Psychol.*, 1949, **75**, 85–125.

Slack, C. W. Feedback theory and the reflex arc theory. *Psychol. Rev.*, 1955, **52**, 263–267.

Slamencka, N. J. An inquiry into the doctrine of remote associations. *Psychol. Rev.*, 1964,
71, 61–76.

Smedslund, J. The concept of correlation in adults. *Scand. J. Psychol.*, 1963, **4**, 165–173.

Smith, A., & Kinder, E. F. Changes in psychological test performance of brain-operated
schizophrenics after 8 years. *Science,* 1959, **129**, 149–150.

Smith, G. M. Group factors in mental tests similar in material and in structure. *Arch. Psychol., N.Y.*, 1933, No. 156.

Smith, K. U. *Delayed sensory feedback and behavior.* Philadelphia: Saunders, 1962.

Smith, M. E. Measurement of vocabularies of young bilingual children in both of the languages used. *J. genet. Psychol.*, 1949, **74**, 305–310.

Smith, M. K. Measurement of the size of general English vocabulary through the elementary
grades and high school. *Genet. psychol. Monogr.*, 1941, **24**, 311–345.

Smith, S. Language and non-verbal test performance of racial groups in Honolulu before and
after a fourteen year interval. *J. genet. Psychol.*, 1942, **36**, 51–93.

Snygg, D. The relation between the intelligence of mothers and their children living in foster
homes. *J. genet. Psychol.*, 1938, **52**, 401–406.

Snygg, D. The need for a phenomenological system of psychology. In A. E. Kuenzli (Ed.),
The phenomenological problem. New York: Harper & Row, 1959.

Solley, C. M., & Long, J. Perceptual learning versus response set learning. *Percept. mot.
Skills,* 1958, **8**, 235–240.

Solley, C. M., & Murphy, G. *Development of the perceptual world.* New York: Basic Books,
1960.

Solley, C. M., & Santon, J. F. Perceptual learning with partial verbal reinforcement. *Percept. mot. Skills*, 1958, **8**, 183–193.

Spearman, C. *The abilities of man.* New York: Macmillan, 1927.

Speer, G. S. The intelligence of foster children. *J. genet. Psychol.*, 1940, **57**, 49–55. (a)

Speer, G. S. The mental development of children of feebleminded and normal mothers. In *Yearb. nat. Soc. Stud. Educ.*, 1940, 39, Part II. Pp. 309–314. (b)

Spence, K. W. The basis of solution by chimpanzees of the intermediate size problem. *J. exp. Psychol.*, 1942, **31**, 257–271.

Spencer, H. *The principles of psychology.* (3rd ed.) New York: Appleton, 1895.

Sperling, G. The information available in brief visual presentations. *Psychol. Monogr.*, 1960, **74**, No. 11 (Whole No. 498).

Sperry, R. W. Cerebral organization and behavior. *Science,* 1961, **133**, 1749–1757.

Spiker, C. C., & McCandless, B. R. The concept of intelligence and the philosophy of science. *Psychol. Rev.*, 1954, **61**, 255–266.

Spitz, R. A. The role of ecological factors in emotional development in infancy. *Child Developm.*, 1949, **20**, 145–155.

Spong, P., Haider, M., & Lindsley, D. B. Selective attentiveness and cortical evoked responses to visual and auditory stimuli. *Science,* 1965, **148**, 395–397.

Staats, A. W., & Staats, C. K. The meaning of *m:* correlated but separate. *Psychol. Rev.*, 1959, **66**, 136–144.

Stafford, R. E. Sex differences in spatial visualization as evidence of sex-linked inheritance. *Percept. mot. Skills,* 1961, **13**, 428.

Stafford, R. E. An investigation of similarities in parent-child test scores for evidence of hereditary components. *Res. Bull.* (RB-63-11), Princeton, N.J.: Educational Testing Service, 1963.

Stanley, W. C., & Jaynes, J. The function of the frontal cortex. *Psychol. Rev.*, 1949, **56**, 18–32.

Starkweather, E., & Roberts, K. E. IQ changes occurring during nursery-school attendance at the Merrill-Palmer School. In *Yearb. nat. Soc. Stud. Educ.*, 1940, 39, Part II. Pp. 315–335.

Stewart, N. A.G.C.T. scores of Army personnel grouped by occupation. *Occupations,* 1947, **26**, 5–41.

Storms, L. H. Apparent backward associations: a situational effect. *J. exp. Psychol.*, 1958, **55**, 390–395.

Storms, L. H. Further evidence of the generality of the priming effect in verbal associations. *Psychol. Rev.*, 1961, **9**, 391.

Stott, L. H., & Ball, R. S. *Evaluation of infant and preschool mental tests.* Detroit, Mich.: Merrill-Palmer, 1963.

Stutsman, R. *Mental measurement of pre-school children.* New York: Harcourt, Brace & World, 1931.

Sumita, K., & Tchitani, T. A factor analytic study of the differentiation of intellectual abilities. *Tohoku Psychol. Folia,* 1958, **16**, 51–82.

Sward, K. Age and mental ability of superior men. *Amer. J. Psychol.*, 1945, **59**, 443–479.

Sweeney, E. J. Sex differences in problem solving. Stanford Univer., Dep. of Psychology, Tech. Rep. No. 1, 1953.

Swineford, F. General, verbal, and spatial bi-factors after 3 years. *J. educ. Psychol.*, 1949, **40**, 353–360.

Taft, R. Some characteristics of good judges of others. *Brit. J. Psychol.*, 1956, **47**, 19–29.

Talland, G. A. Age and the effect of anticipatory set on accuracy of perception. *J. Geront.*, 1959, **14**, 202–207.

Tanimoto, T. T. Non-linear model for a computer assisted medical diagnostic procedure. *Trans. N.Y. Acad. Sci.,* Ser. 2, 1961, 576.

Taylor, C. W. A factorial study of fluency in writing. *Psychometrika,* 1947, **12**, 239–262.

Taylor, C. W., Smith, W. R., & Ghiselin, B. The creative and other contributions of one sample of research scientists. In C. W. Taylor and F. Barron (Eds.), *Scientific creativity: its recognition and development*. New York: Wiley, 1963.

Taylor, D. W., Berry, F. C., & Block, C. H. Does group participation when using brainstorming facilitate or inhibit creative thinking? *Admin. Sci. Quart.*, 1958, **3**, 23–47.

Taylor, F. W. R. The discrimination of subliminal visual stimuli. *Canad. J. Psychol.*, 1953, **7**, 12–20.

Tenopyr, M. A factor-analytic study of symbolic-memory abilities. Unpublished doctoral dissertation, Univer. of Southern California, 1966.

Tenopyr, M., Guilford, J. P., & Hoepfner, R. A factor analysis of symbolic-memory abilities. *Rep. psychol. Lab. Univer. Southern Calif.*, 1966, No. 38.

Terman, L. M. Genius and stupidity: a study of some of the intellectual processes of seven "brighter" and seven "stupid" boys. *Pedag. Sem.*, 1906, **13**, 307–373.

Terman, L. M., & Merrill, M. A. *Measuring intelligence*. Boston: Houghton Mifflin, 1937.

Terman, L. M., & Merrill, M. A. *Stanford-Binet Intelligence Scale: manual for the third revision*, Form L–M. Boston: Houghton Mifflin, 1960.

Terman, L. M., & Oden, M. Status of the California gifted group at the end of sixteen years. In *Yearb. nat. Soc. Stud. Educ.*, 1940, 39, Part I. Pp. 67–89.

Teuber, H. L. Neuropsychology. In R. E. Harris (Ed.), *Recent advances in diagnostic psychological testing*. Springfield, Ill.: Charles C Thomas, 1950. Pp. 30–52.

Teuber, H. L. Ability to discover hidden figures after cerebral lesions. *A.M.A. Arch. Neurol. Psychiat.*, 1956, **76**, 360–379.

Teuber, H. L. Some alterations in behavior after cerebral lesions in man. In *Evolution of nervous control*. Washington, D.C.: American Association for the Advancement of Science, 1959. Pp. 157–194.

Thaler, M. Relationships among Wechsler, Weigl, Rorschach, EEG findings and abstract-concrete behavior in a group of normal aged subjects. *J. Geront.*, 1956, **11**, 404–409.

Thomas, E. D. Qualitative aspects of vocabulary in an institutionalized senile population. Unpublished master's thesis, San Diego State Coll., 1964.

Thompson, C. W. Decline in limit of performance among adult morons. *Amer. J. Psychol.*, 1951, **64**, 203–215.

Thompson, G. G., & Witryol, S. L. The relationship between intelligence and motor learning ability, as measured by a high relief finger maze. *J. Psychol.*, 1946, **22**, 237–246.

Thompson, W. R., & Melzack, R. Early environment. *Scient. Amer.*, January, 1956, **194**, 38–42.

Thomson, G. H., et al. *Social implications of the 1947 mental survey*. London: Univer. of London Press, 1953.

Thorndike, E. L. Intelligence and its uses. *Harper's Mag.*, 1920, **140**, 227–235.

Thorndike, E. L. *Human learning*. New York: Appleton-Century-Crofts, 1931.

Thorndike, E. L., et al. *The measurement of intelligence*. New York: Teachers Coll., 1927.

Thorndike, E. L., & Woodworth, R. S. The influence of improvement in one mental function upon the efficiency of other functions. *Psychol. Rev.*, 1901, **8**, 247–261; 384–396; 553–564.

Thorndike, R. L. Factor analysis of social and abstract intelligence. *J. educ. Psychol.*, 1936, **27**, 231–233.

Thorndike, R. L., & Gallup, G. H. Verbal intelligence of the American adult. *J. gen. Psychol.*, 1944, **30**, 75–85.

Thurstone, L. L. The learning function. *J. gen. Psychol.*, 1930, **3**, 469–491.

Thurstone, L. L. Primary mental abilities. *Psychometr. Monogr.*, 1938, No. 1. (a)

Thurstone, L. L. The perceptual factor. *Psychometrika*, 1938, **3**, 1–17. (b)

Thurstone, L. L. A factor analysis study of perception. *Psychometr. Monogr.*, 1944, No. 4.

Thurstone, L. L. Psychological implications of factor analysis. *Amer. Psychologist*, 1948, **3**, 402–408.

Thurstone, L. L. *The differential growth of mental abilities.* Chapel Hill, N.C.: Univer. of North Carolina, Psychometric Laboratory, 1955.

Thurstone, L. L., & Ackerson, L. The mental growth curve for the Binet tests. *J. educ. Psychol.,* 1929, **20,** 569–583.

Thurstone, L. L., & Thurstone, T. G. Factorial studies of intelligence. *Psychometr. Monogr.,* 1941, No. 2.

Thurstone, L. L., & Thurstone, T. G. *SRA Primary Mental Abilities technical supplement.* Chicago: Science Research, 1954.

Thurstone, T. G., & Strandskov, H. H. *A psychological study of twins: 1. Distributions of absolute twin differences for identical and fraternal twins.* Chapel Hill, N.C.: Univer. of North Carolina, Psychometric Laboratory, 1953, No. 4.

Tiber, N., & Kennedy, W. A. The effects of incentives on the intelligence test performance of different social groups. *J. consult. Psychol.,* 1964, **28,** 187.

Tilton, J. W. Intelligence test scores as indicative of ability to learn. *Educ. psychol. Measmt,* 1949, **9,** 291–296.

Titchener, E. B. *A beginner's psychology.* New York: Macmillan, 1915.

Tolman, E. C. *Purposive behavior in animals and man.* New York: Appleton-Century-Crofts, 1932.

Tolman, E. C. Cognitive maps in rats and men. *Psychol. Rev.,* 1948, **55,** 189–208.

Tolman, E. C. There is more than one kind of learning. *Psychol. Rev.,* 1949, **56,** 144–155.

Torrance, E. P. Can grouping control social stress in creative activities? *Element. Sch. J.,* 1961, **62,** 139–145.

Torrance, E. P. Developing creative thinking through school experiences. In S. J. Parnes & H. F. Harding (Eds.), *A source book for creative thinking.* New York: Scribner, 1962. Pp. 31–47. (a)

Torrance, E. P. *Guiding creative talent.* Englewood Cliffs, N.J.: Prentice-Hall, 1962. (b)

Torrance, E. P. Changing reactions of preadolescent girls to tasks requiring creative scientific thinking. *J. genet. Psychol.,* 1963, **102,** 217–223. (a)

Torrance, E. P. Explorations in creative thinking in the early school years: a progress report. In C. W. Taylor & F. Barron (Eds.), *Scientific creativity: its recognition and development.* New York: Wiley, 1963. Pp. 173–183. (b)

Torrance, E. P. *Rewarding creative behavior.* Englewood Cliffs, N.J.: Prentice-Hall, 1965.

Torrance, E. P., et al. *Rewarding creative thinking.* Minneapolis, Minn.: Univer. of Minnesota, 1960.

Treisman, A. M. Selective attention in man. *Brit. med. Bull.,* 1964, **20,** 12–16.

Trembly, D. Age and sex differences in creative thinking potential. *Amer. Psychologist,* 1964, **19,** 516. (Abstract) (a)

Trembly, D. Age-curve differences between natural and acquired individual characteristics. *Amer. Psychologist,* 1964, **19,** 546. (Abstract) (b)

Tryon, R. C. The genetics of learning ability in rats—a preliminary report. *Univer. Calif. Publ. Psychol,* 1929, **4,** 71–89.

Tuddenham, R. D. Soldier intelligence in World Wars I and II. *Amer. Psychologist,* 1948, **3,** 54–56.

Tyler, L. E. The stability of patterns of primary mental abilities among grade school children. *Educ. psychol. Measmt,* 1958, **18,** 769–774.

Underwood, B. J. Interference and forgetting. *Psychol. Rev.,* 1957, **64,** 49–60.

Underwood, B. J. Ten years of massed practice on distributed practice. *Psychol. Rev.,* 1961, **68,** 229–247.

Underwood, B. J., & Schulz, R. W. *Meaningfulness and verbal learning.* Philadelphia: Lippincott, 1960.

Upton, A., & Samson, R. W. *Creative analysis.* New York: Dutton, 1963.

Vandenberg, S. G. Innate abilities, one or many? A new method and some results. Research Report from Louisville Twin Study. Louisville, Ky.: Univer. of Louisville, no date.

Vandenberg, S. G. The primary mental abilities of Chinese students: a comparative study of the stability of factor structure. *Ann. N.Y. Acad. Sci.,* 1959, **79,** 257–304.

Vandenberg, S. G. The hereditary abilities study: hereditary components in a psychological test battery. *Amer. J. hum. Genet.,* 1962, **14,** 220–237.

Van Steenberg, N. J. Factors in the learning behavior of the albino rat. *Psychometrika,* 1939, **4,** 179–200.

Vernon, P. E. The structure of human abilities. New York: Wiley, 1950.

Viaud, G. *Intelligence: its evolution and forms.* New York: Harper & Row, 1960.

Vinacke, W. E. The investigation of concept formation. *Psychol. Bull.,* 1951, **48,** 1–31.

Vinacke, W. E. *The psychology of thinking.* New York: McGraw-Hill, 1952.

Vogel, W., & Broverman, D. M. Relationship between EEG and test intelligence. *Psychol. Bull.,* 1964, **62,** 132–144.

Voor, J. H. Subliminal perception and subception. *J. Psychol.,* 1956, **41,** 437–458.

Vygotsky, L. S. *Thought and language.* New York: Wiley, 1962.

Waddington, C. H. How do cells differentiate? *Scient. Amer.,* September, 1953, **187,** 108–116.

Wallace, H. R. Creative thinking: a factor in sales productivity. *Voc. Guid. Quart.,* 1961, **9,** 223–226.

Wallas, G. *The art of thought.* London: Watts, 1926; 1945.

Walter, W. G. The electrical activity of the brain. *Scient. Amer.,* June, 1954, **190,** 54–63.

War Manpower Commission, Division of Occupational Analysis. Factor analysis of occupational aptitude tests. *Educ. psychol. Measmt,* 1945, 5, 147–155.

Ward, W. C., & Jenkins, H. M. The display of information and the judgment of contingency. *Canad. J. Psychol.,* 1965, **19,** 231–241.

Warner, W. L., Meeker, M., & Eells, K. *Social class in America: a manual of procedure for the measurement of social status.* Chicago: Science Research, 1949.

Waugh, N. C., & Norman, D. A. Primary memory. *Psychol. Rev.,* 1965, **72,** 89–104.

Weaver, H. E., & Madden, E. H. "Direction" in problem solving. *J. Psychol.,* 1949, **27,** 331–345.

Wechsler, D. *The measurement and appraisal of adult intelligence.* (4th ed.) Baltimore: Williams & Wilkins, 1958.

Wedeck, J. The relationship between personality and psychological ability. *Brit. J. Psychol.,* 1947, **37,** 133–151.

Weiner, B. Effect of motivation on the availability and retrieval of memory traces. *Psychol. Bull.,* 1966, **65,** 24–37.

Weinstein, S. Deficits concomitant with aphasia or lesions of either cerebral hemisphere. *Cortex,* 1964, **1,** 154–169.

Weisberg, P. S., & Springer, K. J. Environmental factors influencing creative function in gifted children. Cincinnati, Ohio: Univer. of Cincinnati, 1961. (Mimeographed)

Weiskrantz, L. Neurological studies and animal behavior. *Brit. med. Bull.,* 1964, **20,** 49–53.

Weisskopf-Joelson, E., & Eliseo, T. S. An experimental study of the effectiveness of brainstorming. *J. appl. Psychol.,* 1961, **45,** 45–49.

Welch, L. Recombination of ideas in creative thinking. *J. appl. Psychol.,* 1946, **30,** 638–643.

Welford, A. T. *Aging and human skill.* London: Oxford, 1958.

Welford, A. T. Experimental psychology in the study of aging. *Brit. med. Bull.,* 1964, **20,** 65–69.

Wellman, B. L. Iowa studies of the effects of schooling. In *Yearb. nat. Soc. Stud. Educ.,* 1940, 39, Part II. Pp. 377–399.

Wellman, B. L., & Pegram, E. L. Binet IQ changes of orphanage children: a re-analysis. *J. genet. Psychol.,* 1944, **64,** 239–263.

Werkmeister, W. H. *The basis and structure of knowledge.* New York: Harper & Row, 1948.

Wertheimer, M. *Productive thinking.* New York: Harper & Row, 1945.

Westcott, M. R. On the measurement of intuitive leaps. *Psychol. Rep.,* 1961, **9,** 267–274.

Westcott, M. R. Empirical studies of intuition. In C. W. Taylor (Ed.), *Widening horizons in creativity*. New York: Wiley, 1964. Pp. 34–53.

Wheeler, L. R. The intelligence of East Tennessee children. *J. educ. Psychol.*, 1932, **23**, 351–370.

Wheeler, L. R. A comparative study of the intelligence of East Tennessee mountain children. *J. educ. Psychol.*, 1942, **33**, 321–334.

White, R. W. Motivation reconsidered: the concept of competence. *Psychol. Rev.*, 1961, **66**, 297–333.

Whorf, B. L. *Language, thought, reality*. New York: Wiley, 1956.

Wilson, R. C., Guilford, J. P., Christensen, P. R., & Lewis, D. J. A factor-analytic study of creative-thinking abilities. *Psychometrika*, 1954, **19**, 297–311.

Wissler, C. The correlation of mental and physical tests. *Psychol. Rev., Monogr. Suppl.*, 1901, **3**, No. 16.

Witkin, H. A. Origins of cognitive style. In C. Scheerer (Ed.), *Cognition: theory, research, promise*. New York: Harper & Row, 1964. Pp. 172–205.

Witkin, H. A., Dyk, R. B., Faterson, H. F., Goodenough, D. R., and Karp, S. A. *Psychological differentiation: studies of mental development*. New York: Wiley, 1962.

Witkin, H. A., Lewis, H. B., Hertzman, M., Machover, K., Meissner, P. B., & Wapner, S. *Personality through perception*. New York: Harper & Row, 1954.

Wohlwill, J. F. Developmental studies of perception. *Psychol. Bull.*, 1960, **57**, 249–288.

Wolman, R. N., & Barker, E. N. A developmental study of word definitions. *J. genet. Psychol.*, 1965, **107**, 159–166.

Woodrow, H. The relation between abilities and improvement with practice. *J. educ. Psychol.*, 1938, **29**, 215–230.

Woodrow, H. The application of factor-analysis to problems of practice. *J. gen. Psychol.*, 1939, **21**, 457–460. (a)

Woodrow, H. The common factors in fifty-two mental tests. *Psychometrika*, 1939, **4**, 99–108. (b)

Woodrow, H. Factors in improvement with practice. *J. Psychol.*, 1939, **7**, 55–70. (c)

Woodrow, H. The relation of verbal ability to improvement with practice in verbal tests. *J. educ. Psychol.*, 1939, **30**, 179–186. (d)

Woodworth, R. S. *Experimental psychology*. New York: Holt, 1938.

Wooldridge, D. E. *The machinery of the brain*. New York: McGraw-Hill, 1963.

Wulf, F. Über die Veränderung von Vorstellung (Gedächtniss und Gestalt). *Psychol. Forsch.*, 1922, **1**, 333–373.

Yamamoto, K. Development of ability to ask questions under specific testing conditions. *J. genet. Psychol.*, 1962, **101**, 83–90.

Yamamoto, K. Evaluation of some creativity measures in a high school with peer nominations as criteria. *J. Psychol.*, 1964, **58**, 285–293.

Yarrow, L. J. Maternal deprivation: toward an empirical and conceptual reevaluation. *Psychol. Bull.*, 1961, **58**, 459–490.

Yerkes, R. M. (Ed.) *Memoirs of the National Academy of Sciences*, No. 15. Washington, D.C.: GPO, 1921.

Yerkes, R. M., Bridges, J. W., & Hardwick, R. S. *A point scale for measuring mental ability*. Baltimore: Warwick and York, 1915.

Yntema, D. B., & Trask, F. P. Recall as a search process. *J. verb. Learn. verb. Behav.*, 1963, **2**, 65–74.

Youtz, R. P. The relation between number of confirmations of one hypothesis and the speed of accepting a new and incompatible hypothesis. *Amer. Psychologist*, 1948, **3**, 248–249.

Zaccaria, M. A., Chorness, M. H., Gerry, R., & Borg, W. R. *Student evaluation and grading; prediction of creative ability*. Lackland Air Force Base, Training Analysis and Development Division, 1956.

Zachert, V., & Friedman, G. The stability of the factorial pattern of aircrew classification tests in four analyses. *Psychometrika*, 1953, **18**, 219–224.

Zangwill, O. L. The cerebral localization of psychological function. *Advancement Sci.,* 1963–64, 1–10.

Zangwill, O. L. Neurological studies of human behavior. *Brit. med. Bull.,* 1964, **20,** 43–48.

Zimmerman, W. S. A note on the recognition and interpretation of composite factors. *Psychol. Bull.,* 1953, **50,** 387–389. (a)

Zimmerman, W. S. A revised orthogonal solution for Thurstone's original primary mental abilities test battery. *Psychometrika,* 1953, **18,** 77–93. (b)

Zuckerman, C. B., & Rock, I. A reappraisal of the roles of past experiences and innate organizing processes in visual perception. *Psychol. Bull.,* 1957, **54,** 269–296.

Zwicky, F. *Morphological analysis.* Berlin: Springer, 1957.

Name index

Name index

Name index

Subject index

Date Due
